U•X•L Encyclopedia of

Native American Tribes

THIRD EDITION

U•X•L Encyclopedia of
Native American Tribes

THIRD EDITION

VOLUME 1

NORTHEAST

SUBARCTIC

Laurie J. Edwards, Editor

U·X·L
A part of Gale, Cengage Learning

GALE
CENGAGE Learning·

Detroit • New York • San Francisco • New Haven, Conn • Waterville, Maine • London

GALE
CENGAGE Learning·

U•X•L Encyclopedia of Native American Tribes, 3rd Edition

Laurie J. Edwards

Project Editors: Shelly Dickey, Terri Schell

Rights Acquisition and Management: Leitha Etheridge-Sims

Composition: Evi Abou-El-Seoud

Manufacturing: Wendy Blurton

Imaging: John Watkins

Product Design: Kristine Julien

For product information and technology assistance, contact us at
Gale Customer Support, 1-800-877-4253.
For permission to use material from this text or product,
submit all requests online at **www.cengage.com/permissions.**
Further permissions questions can be emailed to
permission request@cengage.com

Cover photographs reproduced by permission of Dreamcatchers, ©Francis Vachon/Alamy; Thatched Hut, Cahokia IL, ©Joseph Sohm/The Image Works.

While every effort has been made to ensure the reliability of the information presented in this publication, Gale, a part of Cengage Learning, does not guarantee the accuracy of the data contained herein. Gale accepts no payment for listing; and inclusion in the publication of any organization, agency, institution, publication, service, or individual does not imply endorsement of the editors or publisher. Errors brought to the attention of the publisher and verified to the satisfaction of the publisher will be corrected in future editions.

LIBRARY OF CONGRESS CATALOGING-IN-PUBLICATION DATA

U•X•L Encyclopedia of Native American Tribes / Laurie J. Edwards ; Shelly Dickey, Terri Schell, project editors. -- 3rd ed.
    5 v. . cm.
    Includes bibliographical references and index.
    ISBN 978-1-4144-9092-2 (set) -- ISBN 978-1-4144-9093-9 (v. 1) -- ISBN 978-1-4144-9094-6 (v.2) -- ISBN 978-1-4144-9095-3 (v.3) -- ISBN 978-1-4144-9096-0 (v. 4) -- ISBN 978-1-4144-9097-7 (v. 5),
    1. Indians of North America--Encyclopedias, Juvenile. 2. Indians of North America--Encyclopedias. I. Edwards, Laurie J. II. Dickey, Shelly. III. Schell, Terri, 1968-

E76.2.U85 2012
970.004'97003--dc23   2011048142

Gale
27500 Drake Rd.
Farmington Hills, MI, 48331-3535

978-1-4144-9092-2 (set)   1-4144-9092-5 (set)
978-1-4144-9093-9 (v. 1)   1-4144-9093-3 (v. 1)
978-1-4144-9094-6 (v. 2)   1-4144-9094-1 (v. 2)
978-1-4144-9095-3 (v. 3)   1-4144-9095-X (v. 3)
978-1-4144-9096-0 (v. 4)   1-4144-9096-8 (v. 4)
978-1-4144-9097-7 (v. 5)   1-4144-9097-6 (v. 5)

This title is also available as an e-book.
ISBN 13: 978-1-4144-9098-4 ISBN 10: 1-4144-9098-4
Contact your Gale, a part of Cengage Learning, sales representative for ordering information.

Printed in U.S.A.
1 2 3 4 5 6 7 16 15 14 13 12

Contents

Tribes Alphabetically

First numeral signifies volume number. The numeral after the colon signifies page number. For example, 3:871 means Volume 3, page 871.

Reader's Guide

Long before the Vikings, Spaniards, and Portuguese made land-fall on North American shores, the continent already had a rich history of human settlement. The *U•X•L Encyclopedia of Native American Tribes, 3rd Edition* opens up for students the array of tribal ways in the United States and Canada past and present. Included in these volumes, readers will find the stories of:

- the well-known nineteenth century Lakota hunting the buffalo on the Great Plains
- the contemporary Inuit of the Arctic, who in 1999 won their battle for Nunavut, a vast, self-governing territory in Canada
- the Haida of the Pacific Northwest, whose totem poles have become a familiar adornment of the landscape
- the Anasazi in the Southwest, who were building spectacular cities long before Europeans arrived
- the Mohawk men in the Northeast who made such a name for themselves as ironworkers on skyscrapers and bridges that they have long been in demand for such projects as the Golden Gate Bridge
- the Yahi of California, who became extinct when their last member, Ishi, died in 1916.

The *U•X•L Encyclopedia of Native American Tribes, 3rd Edition* presents 106 tribes, confederacies, and Native American groups. Among the tribes included are large and well-known nations, smaller communities with their own fascinating stories, and prehistoric peoples. The tribes are grouped in the ten major geographical/cultural areas of North America in which tribes shared environmental and cultural connections. The ten sections, each beginning with an introductory essay on the geographical area and the shared history and culture within it, are arranged in the volumes as follows:

- Volume 1: Northeast and Subarctic
- Volume 2: Southeast and Great Plains
- Volume 3: Southwest
- Volume 4: California and Plateau
- Volume 5: Great Basin, Pacific Northwest, and Arctic

The *U•X•L Encyclopedia of Native American Tribes, 3rd Edition* provides the history of each of the tribes featured and a fascinating look at their ways of life: how families lived in centuries past and today, what people ate and wore, what their homes were like, how they worshiped, celebrated, governed themselves, and much more. A student can learn in depth about one tribe or compare aspects of many tribes. Each detailed entry is presented in consistent rubrics that allow for easy access and comparison, as follows:

- History
- Religion
- Language
- Government
- Economy
- Daily Life
- Arts
- Customs
- Current Tribal Issues
- Notable People

Each entry begins with vital data on the tribe: name, location, population, language family, origins and group affiliations. A locator map follows, showing the traditional homelands and contemporary communities of the group; regional and migration maps throughout aid in locating the many groups at different times in history. Brief timelines in each entry chronicle important dates of the tribe's history, while an overall timeline at the beginning of all the volumes outlines key events in history pertinent to all Native Americans. Other sidebars present recipes, oral literature or stories, language keys, and background material on the tribe. Color photographs and illustrations, further reading sections, a thorough subject index, and a glossary are special features that make the volumes easy, fun, and informative to use.

A note on terminology

Throughout the *U•X•L Encyclopedia of Native American Tribes, 3rd Edition* various terms are used for Native North Americans, such as *Indian*, *American Indian*, *Native*, and *aboriginal*. The Native peoples of the Americas have the unfortunate distinction of having been given the wrong name by the Europeans who first arrived on the continent, mistakenly thinking they had arrived in India. The search for a single name, however, has never been entirely successful. The best way to characterize Native North Americans is by recognizing their specific tribal or community identities. In compiling this book, every effort has been made to keep Native tribal and community identities distinct, but by necessity, inclusive terminology is often used. We do not wish to offend anyone, but rather than favor one term for Native North American people, the editors have used a variety of terminology, trying always to use the most appropriate term in the particular context.

Europeans also had a hand in giving names to tribes, often misunderstanding their languages and the relations between different Native communities. Most tribes have their own names for themselves, and many have succeeded in gaining public acceptance of traditional names. The Inuit, for example, objected to the name Eskimo, which means "eaters of raw meat," and in time their name for themselves was accepted. In the interest of clarity the editors of this book have used the currently accepted terms, while acknowledging the traditional ones or the outmoded ones at the beginning of each entry.

The term *tribe* is not accepted by all Native groups. The people living in North America before the Europeans arrived had many different ways of organizing themselves politically and relating to other groups around them—from complex confederacies and powerful unified nations to isolated villages with little need for political structure. Groups divided, absorbed each other, intermarried, allied, and dissolved. The epidemics and wars that came with non-Native expansion into North America created a demographic catastrophe to many Native groups and greatly affected tribal affiliations. Although in modern times there are actual rules about what comprise a tribe (federal requirements for recognition of tribes are specific, complicated, and often difficult to fulfill), the hundreds of groups living in the Americas in early times did not have any one way of categorizing themselves. Thus, some Native American peoples today find the word *tribe* misleading. In a study of Native peoples, it can also be an elusive defining term. But in facing the challenges of maintaining traditions and heritage in modern times, tribal or community identity is acutely important to many Native Americans. Tremendous efforts have been undertaken to preserve native languages, oral traditions, religions, ceremonies, and traditional arts and economies—the things that, put together, make a tribe a cultural and political unit.

Comments and suggestions

In this third edition of the *U•X•L Encyclopedia of Native American Tribes* we have presented in-depth information on 106 of the hundreds of tribes of North America. While every attempt was made to include a wide representation of groups, many historically important and interesting tribes are not covered in these volumes. We welcome your suggestions for tribes to be featured in future editions, as well as any other comments you may have on this set. Please write: Editors, *U•X•L Encyclopedia of Native American Tribes, 3rd Edition,* U•X•L 27500 Drake Road, Farmington Hills, Michigan 48331-3535; call toll-free 1-800-877-4253; or fax 248-699-8097; or send e-mail via http://www.gale.com.

Words to Know

Aboriginal: Native, or relating to the first or earliest group living in a particular area.

Activism: Taking action for or against a controversial issue; political and social activists may organize or take part in protest demonstrations, rallies, petitioning the government, sit-ins, civil disobedience, and many other forms of activities that draw attention to an issue and/or challenge the authorities to make a change.

Adobe: A brick or other building material made from sun-dried mud, a mixture of clay, sand, and sometimes ashes, rocks, or straw.

Alaska Native Claims Settlement Act (ANCSA): An act of Congress passed in 1971 that gave Alaska Natives 44 million acres of land and $962.5 million. In exchange, Alaska Natives gave up all claim to other lands in Alaska. The ANCSA also resulted in the formation of 12 regional corporations in Alaska in charge of Native communities' economic development and land use.

Allotment: The practice of dividing and distributing land into individual lots. In 1887 the U.S. Congress passed the General Allotment Act (also known as the Dawes Act), which divided Indian reservations into privately owned parcels (pieces) of land. Under allotment, tribes could no longer own their own lands in common (as a group) in the traditional ways. Instead the head of a family received a lot, generally 160 acres. Land not alloted was sold to non-Natives.

American Indian Movement (AIM): An activist movement founded in 1966 to aggressively press for Indian rights. The movement was formed to improve federal, state, and local social services to Native Americans in urban neighborhoods. AIM sought the reorganization of the Bureau of Indian Affairs to make it more responsive to Native American needs and fought for the return of Indian lands illegally taken from them.

Anthropology: The study of human beings in terms of their populations, culture, social relations, ethnic characteristics, customs, and adaptation to their environment.

Archaeology: The study of the remains of past human life, such as fossil relics, artifacts, and monuments, in order to understand earlier human cultures.

Arctic: Relating to the area surrounding the North Pole.

Assimilate: To absorb, or to be absorbed, into the dominant society (those in power, or in the majority). U.S. assimilation policies were directed at causing Native Americans to become like European-Americans in terms of jobs and economics, religion, customs, language, education, family life, and dress.

Band: A small, loosely organized social group composed of several families. In Canada, the word band originally referred to a social unit of nomadic (those who moved from place to place) hunting peoples, but now refers to a community of Indians registered with the government.

Boarding school: A live-in school.

Breechcloth: A garment with front and back flaps that hangs from the waist. Breechcloths were one of the most common articles of clothing worn by many Native American men and sometimes women in pre-European/American settlement times.

Bureau of Indian Affairs (BIA): The U.S. government agency that oversees tribal lands, education, and other aspects of Indian life.

Census: A count of the population.

Ceremony: A special act or set of acts (such as a wedding or a funeral) performed by members of a group on important occasions, usually organized according to the group's traditions and beliefs.

Clan: A group of related house groups and families that trace back to a common ancestor or a common symbol or totem, usually an animal such as the bear or the turtle. The clan forms the basic social and political unit for many Indian societies.

Colonialism: A state or nation's control over a foreign territory.

Colonize: To establish a group of people from a mother country or state in a foreign territory; the colonists set up a community that remains tied to the mother county.

Confederacy: A group of people, states, or nations joined together for mutual support or for a special purpose.

Convert: To cause a person or group to change their beliefs or practices. A convert (noun) is a person who has been converted to a new belief or practice.

Coup: A feat of bravery, especially the touching of an enemy's body during battle without causing or receiving injury. To "count coup" is to count the number of such feats of bravery.

Cradleboard: A board or frame on which an infant was bound or wrapped by some Native American peoples. It was used as a portable carrier or for carrying an infant on the back.

Creation stories: Sacred myths or stories that explain how Earth and its beings were created.

Culture: The set of beliefs, social habits, and ways of surviving in the environment that are held by a particular social group.

Dentalium: Dentalia (plural) are the tooth-like shells that some tribes used as money. The shells were rubbed smooth and strung like beads on strands of animal skin.

Depletion: Decreasing the amount of something; depletion of resources such as animals or minerals through overuse reduces essential elements from the environment.

Dialect: A local variety of a particular language, with unique differences in words, grammar, and pronunciation.

Economy: The way a group obtains, produces, and distributes the goods it needs; the overall system by which it supports itself and accumulates its wealth.

Ecosystem: The overall way that a community and its surrounding environment function together in nature.

Epidemic: The rapid spread of a disease so that many people in an area have it at the same time.

Ethnic group: A group of people who are classed according to certain aspects of their common background, usually by tribal, racial, national, cultural, and language origins.

Extended family: A family group that includes close relatives such as mother, father, and children, plus grandparents, aunts, and uncles, and cousins.

Fast: To go without food.

Federally recognized tribes: Tribes with which the U.S. government maintains official relations as established by treaty, executive order, or act of Congress.

Fetish: An object believed to have magical or spiritual power.

First Nations: One of Canada's terms for its Indian nations.

Five Civilized Tribes: A name given to the Cherokee, Choctaw, Chickasaw, Creek, and Seminole during the mid-1800s. The tribes were given this name by non-Natives because they had democratic constitutional governments, a high literacy rate (many people who could read and write), and ran effective schools.

Formal education: Structured learning that takes place in a school or college under the supervision of trained teachers.

Ghost Dance: A revitalization (renewal or rebirth) movement that arose in the 1870s after many tribes moved to reservations and were being encouraged to give up their traditional beliefs. Many Native Americans hoped that, if they performed it earnestly, the Ghost Dance would bring back traditional Native lifestyles and values, and that the buffalo and Indian ancestors would return to the Earth as in the days before the white settlers.

Great Basin: An elevated region in the western United States in which all water drains toward the center. The Great Basin covers part of Nevada, California, Colorado, Utah, Oregon, and Wyoming.

Guardian spirit: A sacred power, usually embodied in an animal such as a hawk, deer, or turtle, that reveals itself to an individual, offering help throughout the person's lifetime in important matters such as hunting or healing the sick.

Haudenosaunee: The name of the people often called Iroquois or Five Nations. It means "People of the Longhouse."

Head flattening: A practice in which a baby was placed in a cradle, and a padded board was tied to its forehead to mold the head into a desired shape. Sometimes the effect of flattening the back of the head was achieved by binding the infant tightly to a cradleboard.

Immunity: Resistance to disease; the ability to be exposed to a disease with less chance of getting it, and less severe effects if infected.

Indian Territory: An area in present-day Kansas and Oklahoma where the U.S. government once planned to move all Indians, and, eventually, to allow them to run their own province or state. In 1880 nearly one-third of all U.S. Indians lived there, but with the formation of the state of Oklahoma in 1906, the promise of an Indian state dissolved.

Indigenous: Native, or first, in a specific area. Native Americans are often referred to as indigenous peoples of North America.

Intermarriage: Marriage between people of different groups, as between a Native American and a non-Native, or between people from two different tribes.

Kachina: A group of spirits celebrated by the Pueblo Indians; the word also refers to dolls made in the image of kachina spirits.

Kiva: Among the Pueblo, a circular (sometimes rectangular) underground room used for religious ceremonies.

Lacrosse: A game of Native American origin in which players use a long stick with a webbed pouch at the end for catching and throwing a ball.

Language family: A group of languages that are different from one another but are related. These languages share similar words, sounds, or word structures. The languages are alike either because they have borrowed words from each other or because they originally came from the same parent language.

Legend: A story or folktale that tells about people or events in the past.

Life expectancy: The average number of years a person may expect to live.

Linguistics: The study of human speech and language.

Literacy: The state of being able to read and write.

Loincloth: See "Breechcloth".

Longhouse: A large, long building in which several families live together; usually found among Northwest Coast and Iroquois peoples.

Long Walk of the Navajo: The enforced 300-mile walk of the Navajo people in 1864, when they were being removed from their homelands to the Bosque Redondo Reservation in New Mexico.

Manifest Destiny: A belief held by many Americans in the nineteenth century that the destiny of the United States was to expand its territory and extend its political, social, and economic influences throughout North America.

Matrilineal: Tracing family relations through the mother; in a matrilineal society, names and inheritances are passed down through the mother's side of the family.

Medicine bundle: A pouch in which were kept sacred objects believed to have powers that would protect and aid an individual, a clan or family, or a community.

Midewiwin Society: The Medicine Lodge Religion, whose main purpose was to prolong life. The society taught morality, proper conduct, and a knowledge of plants and herbs for healing.

Migration: Movement from one place to another. The migrations of Native peoples were often done by the group, with whole nations moving from one area to another.

Mission: An organized effort by a religious group to spread its beliefs to other parts of the world; mission refers either to the project of spreading a belief system or to the building(s)—such as a church—in which this takes place.

Missionary: Someone sent to a foreign land to convert its people to a particular religion.

Mission school: A school established by missionaries to teach people religious beliefs as well as other subjects.

Moiety: One of the two parts that a tribe or community divided into based on kinship.

Myth: A story passed down through generations, often involving supernatural beings. Myths often express religious beliefs or the values of people. They may attempt to explain how the Earth and its beings were created, or why things are. They are not always meant to be taken as factual.

Natural resources: The sources of supplies provided by the environment for survival and enrichment, such as animals to be hunted, land for farming, minerals, and timber.

Neophyte: Beginner; often used to mean a new convert to a religion.

Nomadic: Traveling and relocating often, usually in search of food and other resources or a better climate.

Nunavut: A new territory in Canada as of April 1, 1999, with the status of a province and a Inuit majority. It is a huge area, covering most of Canada north of the treeline. Nunavut means "Our Land" in Inukitut (the Inuit language).

Oral literature: Oral traditions that are written down after enjoying a long life in spoken form among a people.

Oral traditions: History, mythology, folklore, and other foundations of a culture that have been passed by spoken word, often in the form of stories, from generation to generation within a culture group.

Parent language: A language that is the common structure of two or more languages that came into being at a later time.

Parfleche: A case or a pouch made from tanned animal hide.

Patrilineal: Tracing family relations through the father; in a patrilineal society, names and inheritances are passed down through the father's side of the family.

Per capita income: The average personal income per person.

Petroglyph: A carving or engraving on rock; a common form of ancient art.

Peyote: A substance obtained from cactus that some Indian groups used as part of their religious practice. After eating the substance, which stimulates the nervous system, a person may go into a trance state and see visions. The Peyote Religion features the use of this substance.

Pictograph: A simple picture representing a historical event.

Policy: The overall plan or course of action issued by the government, establishing how it will handle certain situations or people and what its goals are.

Post-European contact: Relating to the time and state of Native Americans and their lands after the Europeans arrived. Depending on the part of the country in which they lived, Native groups experienced contact at differing times in the history of white expansion into the West.

Potlatch: A feast or ceremony, commonly held among Northwest Coast groups; also called a "giveaway." During a potlatch goods are given to guests to show the host's generosity and wealth. Potlatches are used to celebrate major life events such as birth, death, or marriage.

Powwow: A celebration at which the main activity is traditional singing and dancing. In modern times, the singers and dancers at powwows came from many different tribes.

Province: A district or division of a country (like a state in the United States).

Raiding: Entering into another tribe or community's territory, usually by stealth or force, and stealing their livestock and supplies.

Ranchería: Spanish term for a small farm.

Ratify: To approve or confirm. In the United States, the U.S. Senate ratified treaties with the Indians.

Red Power: A term used to describe the Native American activism movement of the 1960s, in which people from many tribes came together to protest the injustices of American policies toward Native Americans.

Removal Act: An act passed by the U.S. Congress in 1830 that directed all Indians to be moved to Indian Territory, west of the Mississippi River.

Removal Period: The time, mostly between 1830 and 1860, when most Indians of the eastern United States were forced to leave their homelands and relocate west of the Mississippi River.

Repatriation: To return something to its place of origin. A law passed in the 1990s says that all bones and grave goods (items that are buried with a body) should be returned to the descendants. Many Native American tribes have used that law to claim bones and other objects belonging to their ancestors. Museums and archaeological digs must return these items to the tribes.

Reservation: Land set aside by the U.S. government for the use of a group or groups of Indians.

Reserve: In Canada, lands set aside for specific Indian bands. Reserve means in Canada approximately what reservation means in the United States.

Revitalization: The feeling or movement in which something seems to come back to life after having been quiet or inactive for a period of time.

Ritual: A formal act that is performed in basically the same way each time; rituals are often performed as part of a ceremony.

Rural: Having to do with the country; opposite of urban.

Sachem: The chief of a confederation of tribes.

Shaman: A priest or medicine person in many Native American groups who understands and works with supernatural matters. Shamans traditionally performed in rituals and were expected to cure the sick, see the future, and obtain supernatural help with hunting and other economic activities.

Smallpox: A very contagious disease that spread across North America and killed many thousands of Indians. Survivors had skin that was badly scarred.

Sovereign: Self-governing or independent. A sovereign nation makes its own laws and rules.

Sun Dance: A renewal and purification ceremony performed by many Plains Indians such as the Sioux and Cheyenne. A striking aspect of the ceremony was the personal sacrifice made by some men. They undertook self-torture in order to gain a vision that might provide spiritual insight beneficial to the community.

Sweat lodge: An airtight hut containing hot stones that were sprinkled with water to make them steam. A person remained inside until he or she was perspiring. The person then usually rushed out and plunged into a cold stream. This treatment was used before a ceremony or for the healing of physical or spiritual ailments. Sweat lodge is also the name of a sacred Native American ceremony involving the building of the lodge and the pouring of water on stones, usually by a medicine person, accompanied by praying and singing. The ceremony has many purposes, including spiritual cleansing and healing.

Taboo: A forbidden object or action. Many Indians believe that the sacred order of the world must be maintained if one is to avoid illness or other misfortunes. This is accomplished, in part, by observing a large assortment of taboos.

Termination: The policy of the U.S. government during the 1950s and 1960s to end the relationships set up by treaties with Indian nations.

Toloache: A substance obtained from a plant called jimsonweed. When consumed, the drug causes a person to go into a trance and see visions. It is used in some religious ceremonies.

Totem: An object that serves as an emblem or represents a family or clan, usually in the form of an animal, bird, fish, plant, or other natural object. A totem pole is a pillar built in front of the homes of Natives in the Northwest. It is painted and carved with a series of totems that show the family background and either mythical or historical events.

Trail of Tears: A series of forced marches of Native Americans of the Southeast in the 1830s, causing the deaths of thousands. The marches were the result of the U.S. government's removal policy, which ordered Native Americans to be moved to Indian Territory.

Treaty: An agreement between two parties or two nations, signed by both, usually defining the benefits to both parties that will result from one side giving up title to a territory of land.

Tribe: A group of Natives who share a name, language, culture, and ancestors; in Canada, called a band.

Tribelet: A community within an organization of communities in which one main settlement was surrounded by a few minor outlying settlements.

Trickster: A common culture hero in Indian myth and legend. tricksters generally have supernatural powers that can be used to do good or harm, and stories about them take into account the different forces of the universe, such as good and evil or night and day. The Trickster takes different forms among various groups; for example, Coyote in the Southwest; Ikhtomi Spider in the High Plains, and Jay or Wolverine in Canada.

Trust: A relationship between two parties (or groups) in which one is responsible for acting in the other's best interests. The U.S. government has a trust relationship with tribal nations. Many tribes do not own their lands outright; according to treaty, the government owns the land "in trust" and tribes are given the use of it.

Unemployment rate: The percentage of the population that is looking for work but unable to find any. (People who have quit looking for work are not included in unemployment rates.)

Urban: Having to do with cities and towns; the opposite of rural.

Values: The ideals that a community of people shares.

Vision quest: A sacred ceremony in which a person (often a teenage boy) goes off alone and fasts, living without food or water for a period of days. During that time he hopes to learn about his spiritual side and to have a vision of a guardian spirit who will give him help and strength throughout his life.

Wampum: Small cylinder-shaped beads cut from shells. Long strings of wampum were used for many different purposes. Indians believed that the exchange of wampum and other goods established a friendship, not just a profit-making relationship.

Wampum belt: A broad woven belt of wampum used to record history, treaties among the tribes, or treaties with colonists or governments.

Weir: A barricade used to funnel fish toward people who wait to catch them.

Timeline

25,000–11,000 BCE Groups of hunters cross from Asia to Alaska on the Bering Sea Land Bridge, which was formed when lands now under the waters of the Bering Strait were exposed for periods of time, according to scientists.

1400 BCE Along the lower Mississippi, people of the Poverty Point culture are constructing large burial mounds and living in planned communities.

500 BCE The Adena people build villages with burial mounds in the Midwest.

100 BCE Hopewell societies construct massive earthen mounds for burying their dead and possibly other religious purposes.

100 BCE–400 CE In the Early Basketmaker period, the Anasazi use baskets as containers and cooking pots; they live in caves.

1 CE: Small, permanent villages of the Hohokam tradition emerge in the southwest.

400–700 In the Modified Basketmaker period, Anasazi communities emerge in the Four Corners region of the Southwest. They learn to make pottery in which they can boil beans. They live in underground pits and begin to use bows and arrows. The Anasazi eventually design communities in large multi-roomed apartment buildings, some with more than 1,200 rooms.

700 CE The Mississippian culture begins.

700–1050 The Developmental Pueblo period begins. The Anasazi move into pueblo-type homes above the ground and develop irrigation methods. A great cultural center is established at Chaco Canyon. Anasazi influence spreads to other areas of the Southwest.

800–950 The early Pecos build pit houses.

900 The Mississippian mound-building groups form complex political and social systems, and participate in long-distance trade and an elaborate and widespread religion.

984 The Vikings under Erik the Red first encounter the Inuit of Greenland.

1000–1350 The Iroquois Confederacy is formed among the Mohawk, Oneida, Onondaga, Cayuga, and Seneca nations. The Five Nations of the Haudenosaunee are, from this time, governed by chiefs from the 49 families who were present at the origin of the confederation.

1040 Pueblos (towns) are flourishing in New Mexico's Chaco Canyon. The pueblos are connected by an extensive road system that stretches many miles across the desert.

1050–1300 In the Classic Pueblo period, Pueblo architecture reaches its height with the building of fabulous cliff dwellings; Acoma Pueblo is a well-established city.

1200 The great city of Cahokia in the Mississippi River Valley flourishes.

1250 Zuñi Pueblo is an important trading center for Native peoples from California, Mexico, and the American Southwest.

1300–1700 During the Regressive Pueblo period, the Anasazi influence declines. The people leave their northern homelands, heading south to mix with other cultures.

1350 Moundville, in present-day Alabama, one of the largest ceremonial centers of the Mound Builders, thrives. With twenty great mounds and a village, it is probably the center of a chiefdom that includes several other related communities.

1400s Two tribes unite to start the Wendat Confederacy.

1494 Christopher Columbus begins the enslavement of American Indians, capturing over 500 Taino of San Salvador and sending them to Spain to be sold.

1503 French explorer Jacques Cartier begins trading with Native Americans along the East Coast.

1524 The Abenaki and Narragansett, among other Eastern tribes, encounter the expedition of Giovanni da Verrazano.

1533 Spaniards led by Nuño de Guzmán enter Yaqui territory.

1534 French explorer Jacques Cartier meets the Micmac on the Gaspé Peninsula, beginning a long association between the French and the Micmac.

1539–43 The Spanish treasure hunter Hernando de Soto becomes the first European to make contact with Mississippian cultures; De Soto and Spaniard Francisco Coronado traverse the Southeast and Southwest, bringing with them disease epidemics that kill thousands of Native Americans.

1540 Hernando de Alarcón first encounters the Yuman.

1570 The Spanish attempt to establish a mission in Powhatan territory, but are driven away or killed by the Natives.

1576 British explorer Martin Frobisher first comes into contact with the central Inuit of northern Canada.

1579 Sir Francis Drake encounters the Coast Miwok.

1590 The Micmac force Iroquoian-speaking Natives to leave the Gaspé Peninsula; as a result, the Micmac dominate the fur trade with the French.

1591 Spanish colonization of Pueblo land begins.

1598 Juan de Oñate sets up a Spanish colony and builds San Geronimo Mission at Taos Pueblo. He brings 7000 head of livestock, among them horses.

1602 Spanish explorer Sebastián Vizcaíno encounters the Ohlone.

1607 The British colonists of the Virginia Company arrive in Powhatan territory.

1609 The fur trade begins when British explorer Henry Hudson, sailing for the Netherlands, opens trade in New Netherland (present-day New York) with several Northeast tribes, including the Delaware.

1615 Ottawa meet Samuel de Champlain at Georgian Bay.

1621 Chief Massasoit allies with Pilgrims.

1622 Frenchman Étienne Brûlé encounters the Ojibway at present-day Sault Sainte Marie.

1634–37 An army of Puritans, Pilgrims, Mohican, and Narragansett attacks and sets fire to the Pequot fort, killing as many as 700 Pequot men, women, and children; Massacre at Mystic ends Pequot War and nearly destroys the tribe.

1648–51 The Iroquois, having exhausted the fur supply in their area, attack other tribes in order to get a new supply. The Beaver Wars begin, and many Northeast tribes are forced to move west toward the Great Lakes area.

mid-1600s The Miami encounter Europeans and provide scouts to guide Father Jacques Marquette and Louis Joliet to the Mississippi River.

1651 Colonists establish first Indian reservation near Richmond, Virginia, for what is left of the Powhatans.

1675–76 The Great Swamp Fight during King Philip's War nearly wipes out the tribe and the loss of life and land ends a way of life for New England tribes.

1680 The Hopi, Jemez, Acoma, and other Pueblo groups force the Spanish out of New Mexico in the Pueblo Revolt.

1682 Robert de la Salle's expedition descends the Mississippi River into Natchez territory.

1687 Father Eusebio Francisco Kino begins missionary work among the Tohono O'odham and establishes the first of twenty-eight missions in Yuman territory.

1692 The Spanish begin their reconquest of Pueblo land; Pecos make peace with Spaniards, in spite of protests from some tribe members.

1700 Pierre-Charles le Sueur encounters the Sioux.

1709 John Lawson discovers and writes about the "Hatteras Indians."

1729 French governor Sieur d' Etchéparre demands Natchez land for a plantation; Natchez revolt begins.

1731 The French destroy the Natchez, the last Mississippian culture. Most survivors are sold into slavery in the Caribbean.

1741 Danish-born Russian explorer Vitus Bering sees buildings on Kayak Island that likely belong to the Chugach; he is the first European to reach the Inuit of Alaska.

1760–63 The Delaware Prophet tells Native Americans in the Northeast that they must drive Europeans out of North America and return to the customs of their ancestors. His message influences Ottawa leader Pontiac, who uses it to unite many tribes against the British.

1761 The Potawatomi switch allegiance from the French to the British; they later help the British by attacking American settlers during the American Revolution.

1763 By the Treaty of Paris, France gives Great Britain the Canadian Maritime provinces, including Micmac territory.

1763 England issues the Proclamation of 1763, which assigns all lands west of the Appalachian Mountains to Native Americans, while colonists are allowed to settle all land to the east. The document respects the aboriginal land rights of Native Americans. It is not popular with colonists who want to move onto Indian lands and becomes one of the conflicts between England and the colonies leading to the American Revolution.

1769 The Spanish build their first mission in California. There will be 23 Spanish missions in California, which are used to convert Native Californians to Christianity, but also reduces them to slave labor.

1769–83 Samuel Hearne and Alexander Mackenzie are the first European explorers to penetrate Alaskan Athabascan territory, looking for furs and a route to the Pacific Ocean. Russian fur traders are not far behind.

c. 1770 Horses, brought to the continent by the Spanish in the sixteenth century, spread onto the Great Plains and lead to the development of a new High Plains Culture.

1776 Most Mohawk tribes side with the British during the Revolutionary War under the leadership of Thayendanégea, also known as Joseph Brant.

1778 The Delaware sign the first formal treaty with the United States, guaranteeing their land and allowing them to be the fourteenth state; the treaty is never ratified.

1778 The treaty-making period begins when the first of 370 treaties between Indian nations and the U.S. government is signed.

1786 The first federal Indian reservations are established.

1789 The Spanish establish a post at Nootka Sound on Vancouver Island, the first permanent European establishment in the territory of the Pacific Northwest Coast tribes; Spain and Great Britain vie for control of the area during the Nootka Sound Controversy.

1791 In the greatest Native American defeat of the U.S. Army, the Miami win against General Arthur St. Clair.

1792 Explorer George Vancouver enters Puget Sound; Robert Gray, John Boit and George Vancouver are the first to mention the Chinook.

1805 The Lewis and Clark expedition ecounter the Flathead, Nez Percé, Yakama, Shoshone, Umatilla, Siletz, and are the first to reach Chinook territory by land.

1811 Shawnee settlement of Prophet's Town is destroyed in the Battle of Tippecanoe.

1813 Chief Tecumseh is killed fighting the Americans at Battle of the Thames in the War of 1812.

1816 Violence erupts during a Métis protest over the Pemmican Proclamation of 1814, and twenty-one Hudson's Bay Company employees are killed.

1817 The First Seminole War occurs when soldiers from neighboring states invade Seminole lands in Florida looking for runaway slaves.

1821 Sequoyah's method for writing the Cherokee language is officially approved by tribal leaders.

1827 The Cherokee adopt a written constitution.

1830 The removal period begins when the U.S. Congress passes the Indian Removal Act. Over the course of the next thirty years many tribes from the Northeast and Southeast are removed to Indian Territory in present-day Oklahoma and Kansas, often forcibly and at great expense in human lives.

1831 Some Seneca and Cayuga move to Indian Territory (now Oklahoma) as part of the U.S. government's plan to move Native Americans westward. Other Iroquois groups stand firm until the government's policy is overturned in 1842.

1832 The U.S. government attempts relocation of the Seminole to Indian Territory in Oklahoma, leading to the Second Seminole War.

1838 The Cherokee leave their homeland on a forced journey known as the Trail of Tears.

1846–48 Mexican-American War is fought; San Juan lands become part of U.S. territory.

1847 Another Pueblo rebellion leads to the assassination of the American territorial governor. In retaliation U.S. troops destroy the mission at Taos Pueblo, killing 150 Taos Indians.

1848 Mexico gives northern Arizona and northern New Mexico lands to the United States. Warfare between the Apache people and the U.S. Army begins.

1850 New Mexico is declared a U.S. territory.

1851 Gold Rush begins at Gold Bluff, prompting settlers to take over Native American lands. As emigration of Europeans to the West increases, eleven Plains tribes sign the Treaty of Fort Laramie, which promises annual payments to the tribes for their land.

1851 Early reservations are created in California to protect the Native population from the violence of U.S. citizens. These reservations are inadequate and serve only a small portion of the Native Californians, while others endure continued violence and hardship.

1854 The Treaty of Medicine Creek is signed, and the Nisqually give up much of their land; the treaty also gives Puyallup lands to the U.S. government and the tribe is sent to a reservation.

1858 Prospectors flood into Washoe lands after the Comstock lode is discovered.

1859 American surveyors map out a reservation on the Gila River for the Pima and Maricopa Indians. It includes fields, but no water.

1861 Cochise is arrested on a false charge, and the Apache Wars begin.

1864 At least 130 Southern Arapaho and Cheyenne—many of them women and children—are killed by U.S. Army troops during the Sand Creek Massacre.

1864 The devastating Long Walk, a forced removal from their homelands, leads the Navajo to a harsh exile at Bosque Redondo.

1867 The United States buys Alaska from Russia for $7.2 million.

1870 The First Ghost Dance Movement begins when Wodzibwob, a Paiute, learns in a vision that a great earthquake will swallow the Earth, and that all Indians will be spared or resurrected within three days of the disaster, returning their world to its state before the Europeans arrived.

1870–90 The Peyote Religion spreads throughout the Great Plains. Peyote (obtained from a cactus plant) brings on a dreamlike feeling that followers believe brings them closer to the spirit world. Tribes develop their own ceremonies, songs, and symbolism, and vow to be trustworthy, honorable, and community-oriented and to follow the Peyote Road.

1871 British Columbia becomes part of Canada; reserve land is set aside for the Nuu-chah-nulth.

1874–75 The Comanche make their last stand; Quanah Parker and his followers are the last to surrender and be placed on a reservation.

1875 The U.S. Army forces the Yavapai and Apache to march to the San Carlos Apache Reservation; 115 die along the way.

1876 The Northern Cheyenne join with the Sioux in defeating General George Custer at the Battle of Little Bighorn.

1876 The Indian Act in Canada establishes an Indian reserve system, in which reserves were governed by voluntary elected band councils. The Act does not recognize Canadian Indians' right to self-government. With the passage of the act, Canadian peoples in Canada are divided into three groups: status Indian, treaty Indian, and non-status Indian. The categories affect the benefits and rights Indians are given by the government.

1877 During the Nez Percé War, Chief Joseph and his people try fleeing to Canada, but are captured by U.S. Army troops.

1879 The Ute kill thirteen U.S. soldiers and ten Indian agency officials, including Nathan Meeker, in a conflict that becomes known as the "Meeker Massacre."

1880s The buffalo on the Great Plains are slaughtered until there are almost none left. Without adequate supplies of buffalo for food, the Plains Indians cannot survive. Many move to reservations.

1884 The Canadian government bans potlatches. The elaborate gift-giving ceremonies have long been a vital part of Pacific Northwest Indian culture.

1886 The final surrender of Geronimo's band marks the end of Apache military resistance to American settlement.

1887 The General Allotment Act (also known as the Dawes Act), is passed by Congress. The act calls for the allotment (parceling out) of tribal lands. Tribes are no longer to own their lands in common in the traditional way. Instead the land is to be assigned to individuals. The head of a family receives 160 acres, and other family members get smaller pieces of land. All Indian lands that are not alloted are sold to settlers.

1888 Ranchers and amateur archaeologists Richard Wetherill and Charlie Mason discover ancient cliff dwellings of the Pueblo people.

1889 The Oklahoma Land Runs open Indian Territory to non-Natives. (Indian Territory had been set aside solely for Indian use.) At noon on April 22, an estimated 50,000 people line up at the boundaries of Indian Territory. They claim two million acres of land. By nightfall, tent cities, banks, and stores are doing business there.

1890 The Second Ghost Dance movement is initiated by Wovoka, a Paiute. It includes many Paiute traditions. In some versions the dance is performed in order to help bring back to Earth many dead ancestors and exterminated game. Ghost Dance practitioners hope the rituals in the movement will restore Indians to their formal state, before the arrival of the non-Native settlers.

1896 Discovery of gold brings hordes of miners and settlers to Alaska.

1897 Oil is discovered beneath Osage land.

1907 With the creation of the state of Oklahoma, the government abolishes the Cherokee tribal government and school system, and the dream of a Native American commonwealth dissolves.

1912 The Alaska Native Brotherhood is formed to promote civil rights issues, such as the right to vote, access to public education, and civil rights in public places. The organization also fights court battles to win land rights.

1916 Ishi, the last Yahi, dies of tuberculosis.

1920 The Canadian government amends the Indian Act to allow for compulsory, or forced, enfranchisement, the process by which Indians have to give up their tribal loyalties to become Canadian citizens. Only 250 Indians had voluntarily become enfranchised between 1857 and 1920.

1924 Congress passes legislation conferring U.S. citizenship on all American Indians. This act does not take away rights that Native Americans had by treaty or the Constitution.

1928 Lewis Meriam is hired to investigate the status of Indian economies, health, and education, and the federal administration of Indian affairs. His report describes the terrible conditions under which Indians are forced to live, listing problems with health care, education, poverty, malnutrition, and land ownership.

1934 U.S. Congress passes the Indian Reorganization Act (IRA), which ends allotment policies and restores some land to Native Americans. The IRA encourages tribes to govern themselves and set up tribal economic corporations, but with the government overseeing their decisions. The IRA also provides more funding to the reservations. Many tribes form tribal governments and adopt constitutions.

1940 Newly opened Grand Coulee Dam floods Spokane land and stops the salmon from running.

1941–45 Navajo Code Talkers send and receive secret messages in their Native language, making a major contribution to the U.S. war effort during World War II.

1942 As hostilities leading to World War II grow, the Iroquois exercise their powers as an independent nation to declare war on Germany, Italy, and Japan.

1946 The Indian Lands Commission (ICC) is created to decide land claims filed by Indian nations. Many tribes expect the ICC to return lost lands, but the ICC chooses to award money instead, and at the value of the land at the time it was lost.

1951 A new Indian Act in Canada reduces the power of the Indian Affairs Office, makes it easier for Indians to gain the right to vote, and helps Indian children enter public schools. It also removes the ban on potlatch and Sun Dance ceremonies.

1954–62 The U.S. Congress carries out its termination policy. At the same time laws are passed giving states and local governments control over tribal members, taking away the tribes' authority to govern themselves. Under the policy of termination, Native Americans lose their special privileges and are treated the same as other U.S. citizens. The tribes that are terminated face extreme poverty and the threat of loss of their community and traditions. By 1961 the government begins rethinking this policy because of the damage it is causing.

1955 The Indian Health Service (IHS) assumes responsibility for Native American health care. The IHS operates hospitals, health centers, health stations, clinics, and community service centers.

1958 Alaska becomes a state; 104 million acres of Native land are taken.

1960 The queen of England approves a law giving status Indians the right to vote in Canada.

1964 The Great Alaska Earthquake and tsunami destroys several Alutiiq villages.

1965 Under the new U.S. government policy, the Self-Determination policy, federal aid to reservations is given directly to Indian tribes and not funneled through the Bureau of Indian Affairs.

1968 Three Ojibway—Dennis Banks, George Mitchell, and Clyde Bellecourt—found the American Indian Movement (AIM) in Minneapolis, Minnesota, to raise public awareness about treaties the federal and state governments violated.

1969 Eighty-nine Native Americans land on Alcatraz Island, a former penitentiary in San Francisco Bay in California. The group calling itself "Indians of All Tribes," claims possession of the island under an 1868 treaty that gave Indians the right to unused federal property on Indian land. Indians of All Tribes occupies the island for 19 months while negotiating with federal officials. They do not win their claim to the island but draw public attention to their cause.

1971 Quebec government unveils plans for the James Bay I hydroelectric project. Cree and Inuit protest the action in Quebec courts.

1971 The Alaska Native Claims Settlement Act (ANCSA) is signed into law. With the act, Alaska Natives give up any claim to nine-tenths of Alaska. In return they are given $962 million and clear title to 44 million acres of land.

1972 Five hundred Native Americans arrive in Washington, D.C., on a march called the Trail of Broken Treaties to protest the government's policies toward Native Americans. The protestors occupy the Bureau of Indian Affairs building for a week, causing considerable damage. They present the government with a list of reforms, but the administration rejects their demands.

1973 After a dispute over Oglala Sioux (Lakota) tribal chair Robert Wilson and his strong-arm tactics at Pine Ridge Reservation, AIM leaders are called in. Wilson's supporters and local authorities arm themselves against protestors, who are also armed, and a ten-week siege begins in which hundreds of federal marshals and Federal Bureau of Investigation (FBI) agents surround the Indian protestors. Two Native American men are shot and killed.

1974 After strong protests and "fish-ins" bring attention to the restrictions on Native American fishing rights in the Pacific Northwest, the U.S. Supreme Court restores Native fishing rights in the case *Department of Game of Washington v. Puyallup Tribe et al.*

1978 U.S. Congress passes legislation called the Tribally Controlled Community College Assistance Act, providing support for tribal colleges, schools of higher education designed to help Native American students achieve academic success and eventually transfer to four-year colleges and universities. Tribal colleges also work with tribal elders and cultural leaders to record languages, oral traditions, and arts in an effort to preserve cultural traditions.

1978 The American Indian Religious Freedom Act is signed. Its stated purpose is to "protect and preserve for American Indians their inherent right of freedom to believe, express, and exercise their traditional religions."

1978 The Bureau of Indian Affairs publishes regulations for the new Federal Acknowledgement Program. This program is responsible for producing a set of "procedures for establishing that an American Indian group exists as an Indian tribe." Many tribes will later discover that these requirements are complicated and difficult to establish.

1982 Canada constitutionally recognizes aboriginal peoples in its new Constitution and Charter of Rights and Freedoms. The Constitution officially divides Canada's aboriginal nations into three designations: the Indian, the Inuit, and the Métis peoples. Native groups feel that the new Constitution does not adequately protect their rights, nor does it give them the right to govern themselves.

1988 The Federal Indian Gambling Regulatory Act of 1988 allows any tribe recognized by the U.S. government to engage in gambling activities. With proceeds from gaming casinos, some tribes pay for health care, support of the elderly and sick, housing, and other improvements, while other tribes buy back homelands, establish scholarship funds, and create new jobs.

1990 Two important acts are passed by U.S. Congress. The Native American Languages Act is designed to preserve, protect, and promote the practice and development of Indian languages. The Graves Protection and Repatriation Act provides for the protection of American Indian grave sites and the repatriation (return) of Indian remains and cultural artifacts to tribes.

1992 Canadians vote against a new Constitution (the Charlotte-town Accord) that contains provisions for aboriginal self-government.

1995 The Iroquois request that all sacred masks and remains of their dead be returned to the tribe; the Smithsonian Institution is the first museum to comply with this request.

1999 A new territory called Nunavut enters the federation of Canada. Nunavut is comprised of vast areas taken from the Northwest Territories and is populated by an Inuit majority. The largest Native land claim in Canadian history, Nunavut is one-fifth of the landmass of Canada, or the size of the combined states of Alaska and Texas. Meaning "Our Land" in the Inukitut (Inuit) language, Nunavut will be primarily governed by the Inuit.

2003 The first official Comanche dictionary is published, compiled entirely by the Comanche people.

2004 Southern Cheyenne Peace Chief W. Richard West Jr. becomes director of the newly opened National Museum of the American Indian in Washington, D.C.

2006 The United Nations censures the United States for reclaiming 60 million acres (90%) of Western Shoshone lands. The federal government uses parts of the land for military testing, open-pit gold mining and nuclear waste disposal. The Shoshone, who have used it for cattle grazing since the Treaty of Ruby Valley in 1863, have repeatedly had their livestock confiscated and fines imposed.

2011 The government gives the Fort Sill Apache 30 acres for a reservation in Deming, New Mexico.

2011 Tacoma Power gives the Skokomish 1,000 acres of land and $11 million.

Makah
Skokomish Duwamish
Puyallup Lake Spokane
Nisqually Umatilla Salish Blackfoot
Chinook Colville Flathead
Siletz Yakama Nakota
Nez Perc é
Yurok Crow Lakota
Chilula Modoc Northern Paiute Northern Cheyenne
Hupa Pit River Shoshone Arikara
Cahto Maidu Western Eastern Arapaho
Pomo Shoshone Shoshone
Washoe Pawnee
Miwok Kawaiisu
Costanoan Yahi and Yana
Southern Paiute Ute Southern Cheyenne
Chumash San Carlos
Anasazi Pueblo Kiowa
Hopi Navajo Jemez Jicarilla
Cahuilla Mohave Apache San Juan Taos Kio
Luiseño Apa
Yuman White Mountain Zuñi Acoma
Tohono O'odham Yaqui Pecos Comanche
Pima
Chiricahua

PACIFIC
OCEAN

N

California
Great Basin
Great Plains
Northeast
Pacific Northwest
Plateau
Southeast
Southwest

Abenaki

Mohawk

Iroquois

Narraganset

Menominee

Pequot

Sauk

Wampanoag

Fox

Wyandot

Dakota

Delaware

Potawatomi

Hopewell

Miami

Powhatan

Shawnee

Missouri

Mississippian
(Mound Builders)

Osage

Lumbee

Cherokee

Quapaw

Chickasaw

Caddo

Creek

Choctaw

Natchez

Seminole

ATLANTIC

OCEAN

Gulf of Mexico

0	100	200 mi
0	100	200 km

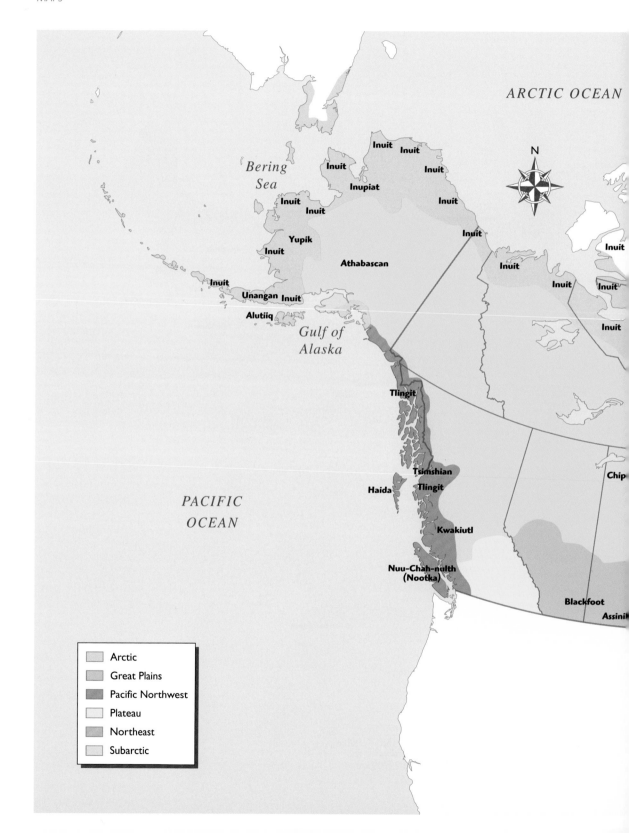

ARCTIC OCEAN

Bering
Sea

Inuit

Inuit   Inuit

Inuit   Inuit

Inupiat   Inuit

Inuit   Inuit   Inuit

Yupik   Inuit   Inuit

Inuit   Athabascan   Inuit   Inuit   Inuit

Inuit   Inuit   Inuit

Unangan Inuit

Alutiiq   Inuit

Gulf of
Alaska

Tlingit

Tsimshian

PACIFIC   Haida   Tlingit

OCEAN   Chip

Kwakiutl

Nuu–Chah–nulth
(Nootka)

Blackfoot

Assini

	Arctic
	Great Plains
	Pacific Northwest
	Plateau
	Northeast
	Subarctic

Baffin
Bay

Inuit
uit
Inuit
Inuit
Inuit
Inuit
Inuit
Inuit
Inuit

Labrador
Sea

Inuit
Inuit
Inuit
Inuit
Inuit
Inuit

Hudson
Bay

Innu

Cree

Micmac

ATLANTIC
OCEAN

étis

Ojibwa
Algonkin

Ottawa

Huron

Wyandotte

0	250	500 mi
0	250	500 km

Northeast

Northeast

The American Indian cultures of northeastern North America, also known as the Woodland Indians, inhabited a region that was rich in natural resources. This large region, which includes territory from the Atlantic coast to the Great Lakes, was characterized by extensive forests and numerous river systems and bodies of water. The environment supported a wide variety of mammals and fish that provided a valuable source of food for Native peoples. The forests contained large numbers of white-tailed deer, moose, and elk. In some areas of the Northeast woodland, bison and caribou also served as primary food sources. In addition, many bears and beaver, smaller mammals, and migrating waterfowl provided ready foodstuffs for Native peoples. The rivers and lakes of the region teemed with fish and clams.

Although farming was limited in the extreme northern reaches of the area, agriculture was, for the most part, quite productive. A variety of naturally occurring foodstuffs were also available. Wild rice was common to the region and was an important food because it could be stored for long periods of time. The resources that were a part of the ecology of the region helped sustain large populations of Native groups, such as the Iroquois, Ojibway, Delaware, Wampanoag, Ottawa, Huron, and many others, over an extensive territory in the period before Europeans arrived.

Tribal autonomy

Although the great many tribes that inhabited the Northeast shared a similar environment, they were extremely diverse in cultural patterns. The tribes had differences in languages, housing forms, ceremonial life, and kinship patterns, as well as in other areas of tribal life.

The one thing all of these tribal groups shared was a strong emphasis on tribal autonomy—the ability to govern their own affairs. Some of the tribes of the Northeast did confederate (join an alliance) over time for mutual purposes, such as the six tribes that formed the Iroquois Confederacy, but

A map of contemporary Native American communities in the Northeast region. MAP BY XNR PRODUCTIONS. CENGAGE LEARNING, GALE. REPRODUCED BY PERMISSION OF GALE, A PART OF CENGAGE LEARNING.

the vast majority of the Northeast groups maintained a high degree of independence. Their primary allegiance was to family and then to related families living within the village. There was little centralized government, and tribes were not easily persuaded to join others for unified political action.

Religion

The Native peoples of the Northeast, like other indigenous peoples, were very religious. Spiritual perceptions dictated their life patterns. All the Northeast tribal groups prayed and fasted before they hunted or gathered plants for food. They marked the changes of the seasons and the harvest with elaborate ceremonies that sought the favor of the spirits of the earth and sky. Devoted in their beliefs, they acknowledged life as a gift from the creator. Rituals and ceremonies were held to ensure the well-being of the community and the continuity of life.

Native peoples of the Northeast celebrated life. They had adequate food to provide for good health, the tools they needed to farm and hunt, and traditions that promoted social well-being. They made nets and spears for fishing, and they trapped animals with snares and deadfalls (traps with heavy weights that fell on the animals). They used fire as a tool to clear the lands for agriculture or to make openings for foraging mammals. With an intimate knowledge of local medicinal plants, they were able to treat a range of illnesses. They had a history of storytelling to make sense of their surroundings and to educate their children. Music and performance were vital parts of their ceremonial life and also an informal means of social expression.

Life for the Natives of the Northeast was hard work, though. The people toiled at farming with no horses or oxen to aid them. There does not seem to be an extensive history of wars of conquest during the period before European contact, but struggles between newcomers to the area and original tribes sometimes caused entire groups to move to another area. At the time of European contact, however, the clans in the respective villages prospered, and relations between them appear to have been relatively peaceful. This changed dramatically when the Europeans arrived.

Post-European contact period

Early contact brings catastrophic epidemics The world changed rapidly for Native peoples in the Northeast in the post-contact period. As Europeans explored and forged relations with Northeastern Indian tribes, diseases were unleashed that were new to the region: smallpox, measles, mumps, scarlet fever, and others. With no natural resistance to the new diseases, large numbers of Native peoples died. Introducing a disease into a population that has no immunity (ability to fight off disease) is called a virgin soil epidemic (VSE). It is not uncommon to lose 85 to 90 percent of a population over a century during the course of a VSE and to experience a decreasing birth rate at the same time.

The consequences of these VSEs for Native peoples of the region were catastrophic. Native communities lost hunters, shamans (pronounced *SHAH-munz* or *SHAY-munz*), and other specialists from their ranks. Traditional plant remedies had little impact on the new diseases, which came one after the other. The people struggled to understand what was happening. Many fled their homes, thereby spreading the diseases to neighboring tribes. The new diseases were clearly responsible for devastating

Native populations and paving the way for colonial experiments in the Northeast. Most of the Native peoples that inhabited these lands died, leaving their cleared lands and ancestral homes to a few survivors, who had to contend with an expanding European population.

Trade with the Europeans

Although many of the early British colonists in the Northeast were refugees from religious persecution in England, they also had strong economic motivations for colonizing the region. Most of the successful early British colonies were founded by joint stock companies. These companies clearly expected a return on their investments in the New World. Land was a much sought-after commodity because it was difficult to obtain within the rigid class structure and inheritance systems of Europe. To complicate matters, European nations established rival colonial empires in the New World. Wars of conquest between these powers soon came to involve the region's Native peoples as British, Dutch, and French colonies competed with each other for Native American allies and trade.

Additionally, Native peoples introduced commodities that quickly became very important in the world economy. As an example, trading and cultivating tobacco helped the Jamestown Colony prosper. (Jamestown was the first permanent British colony, settled in 1607 in southeast Virginia.) Tobacco was native to the Americas but soon became popular and profitable around the world. The fur trade also became an important part of European and Northeastern Native relations. Native hunters provided the furs to colonial traders in return for their goods, beginning cycles of trade that lasted into the nineteenth century.

New trade relations introduced Native peoples to an array of manufactured goods. Native peoples were happy to trade furs for metal pots, knives, and blankets. The problem, though, was in establishing the worth of the goods in the market. In other words, how many furs is a blanket worth? Native traders did not initially have access to that information, whereas European traders had purchased the blanket and knew what the furs would bring on the European market. The situation—ripe for exploiting Native trappers and their families—was the root of deteriorating relations between Native peoples and their new neighbors.

The introduction of alcohol into these trade relations compounded an already complex situation. Alcohol was a new commodity to Native peoples of the Northeast. They had not had hundreds of years to develop social behaviors around the consumption of alcohol as Europeans had done, and they tended to overindulge. It became a standard practice of European traders to use alcohol to loosen up their Native clients. This caused increased hostilities between the groups.

What evolved over time was a Native dependency on European trade goods. Native hunters spent more time trapping furs for the trade than engaging in more traditional ways of providing for themselves. The profits of these trade relations strengthened colonial governments and outposts. Once these centers of growing economic activity became strong enough, the Europeans there sought—and sometimes demanded—more land.

The trade between Northeastern peoples and colonial governments also promoted intertribal rivalries. After the Dutch were eliminated from trade in the Northeast, most of the tribes of the region split their trade allegiances between the British and the French. Both of these European nations profited from the trade and worked to keep their Native allies faithful. Northeastern Indians were often sought as allies in military

A Lanai Lanape family wears black-and-white wampum in an illustration from the 1650s. © NORTH WIND PICTURE ARCHIVES

U•X•L Encyclopedia of Native American Tribes, 3rd Edition

campaigns, which created bitter intertribal conflicts in the region. In trade and military interactions with the Europeans, however, Northeastern tribes actively adapted to situations as they evolved. The tribes attempted to make decisions that would prolong their way of life and guarantee a continuing quality of life to their relations and children.

Native American treaties

Treaties are agreements between two parties, signed by both, usually defining the benefits to each party that will result from one side giving up title to a territory. The treaties between European nations and Native groups favored the Europeans, who were attempting to build colonial empires and therefore wanting more land. Treaties that ceded (gave up) Native American lands to European nations or colonial governments were legal documents and, as such, were recognized in courts. Those same courts generally did not recognize the rights of Native peoples, only that the Natives had deeded lands to European powers. Signing treaties with Native Americans provided legal protection of land claims for colonial governments while providing little or no protection to Native American signatories (signers). Although Native peoples entered into these agreements and signed them, many questions have been raised about their legality, such as whether or not the individuals who signed the treaties had the power to do so.

Giving up tribal lands decreased the range and scope of the Native people's natural resources. Access to these resources was the basis of life for Native peoples in the Northeast. As colonial governments became stronger, tribes in the region came under increased pressures. With their traditional territories rapidly dwindling, they were forced to share their limited resources with other tribes who had been forced into the same space.

The history of the Northeastern tribes' encounter with Europeans is one of sickness, diminishing resources, and eventually, hostility. These same cycles were played out decade after decade in the colonial period as different powers arose. As a result of the French and Indian War (1754–63; a war fought in North America between England and France involving some Native Americans as allies of the French), France lost all of its colonial interests in North America. Shortly thereafter, the American colonists won their independence from Great Britain in the American Revolution (1775–83). After 1783 the U.S. federal government simply built upon British precedents in Native American affairs. Under the provisions of the Federal Proclamation of 1783, only an authorized representative of the federal government could enter into a treaty for or acquire Native American lands. This was an almost direct restatement of the British Royal Proclamation of 1763. Both of these acts created a virtual monopoly (exclusive rights) in the acquisition and resale of Native American lands. The sale of Native lands, acquired via treaty, proved to be an important source of funds to run governments and pay for military services. Under the burden of these policies, tribes of the region continued to adapt to changing national politics and goals as they sought to maintain their cultural identity and a degree of control over their future.

One of the major problems for tribal groups in the post-Revolutionary period was that they were suddenly faced with initiating political relations with a government that had not existed a few years earlier. American policies toward Native peoples were extremely high-handed and focused on one purpose: to facilitate the orderly transfer of their lands to American interests. Northeastern tribal groups were faced with difficult decisions as they worked to maintain tribal sovereignty (self-government) and lands. Treaty after treaty diminished their land base.

The Northeastern tribal groups during this period of time had little choice but to change and accommodate—often the only way to preserve some semblance of tribal autonomy and community. The U.S. Congress had decided that it had absolute power over Native affairs, and it was not reluctant to use that power. Those tribes that were able to attain reservations (what was not ceded as a part of a treaty was reserved for Native use; hence the common usage of the term "reservation") worked hard to keep their resource base and adapt to local economies. During the nineteenth century, Northeastern Indians found work in agriculture, the timber industries, ship building, commercial fishing, and mines. They did whatever was necessary to survive. It was a difficult period, but Native peoples clung to their heritage and what they believed was their birthright: the land. Many of the tribes lost their reservation base during the nineteenth century. Some of the tribes were affected by the passage of the Indian Removal Act (1830), and segments of their communities were moved to Indian Territory (present-day Oklahoma).

Assimilation

In the nineteenth century, Native peoples were viewed as standing in the way of progress. Conventional wisdom held that their lands were better used by farmers who would make the land profitable. Additionally, mainstream society viewed them as inferior and as needing instruction in the correct way to live. The federal government embarked on a large-scale program of assimilation—that is, they wanted Native peoples to behave like mainstream society and give up their ancestral ways. The federal government funded schools that had, as their sole purpose, the assimilation of Native children. Missionaries and churches were also funded to help remake the Native population. These efforts proved to be an extreme hardship for Native children and parents. The schools were usually boarding schools; parents and children were separated for long periods of time. Many of the children became sick in these institutions. Corporal (physical) punishment was used regularly, and some students also suffered sexual abuse. These schools, with their harsh environments, were often the only educational choices available.

The changes the Native peoples witnessed in their own territory were stark and long-lasting. The ecology of the region was irreversibly altered. The rise of industrialization changed the patterns of work and family life. New occupations supplanted traditional lifestyles; formal education replaced traditional systems that valued other forms of knowledge. In spite of all of these changes, tribal governments persisted and continued to assert the natural rights of indigenous peoples. Throughout the nineteenth and into the twenty-first century, tribal governments have continued to advocate for their rights.

Over time, many Americans have recognized the folly of past conceptions of Native peoples and the prejudice of policies that stripped them of their lands and resources. Many people have also realized the hypocrisy of attempting to destroy Native cultures while proclaiming democratic principles. This awareness helped foster reform and self-determination: Native peoples deciding what their future should be and working to actualize it. The struggle has been long and difficult for Native peoples of the Northeast. They were the first to be colonized and, in some cases, the first to resist the yoke of colonial oppression.

The struggle to preserve a heritage

The efforts of Northeastern Indian tribes to preserve their tribal lands and unique heritage spans more than four centuries and is an amazing testament to the human spirit and cultural survival. Great changes have taken place, and yet tribal governments have persisted and overcome many obstacles. The history of the Northeast Indians is a story of how a weakened group of indigenous peoples fought to maintain ancestral lands and natural rights and triumphed in the end. However, not all endings are happy. Some tribal groups perished as a result of the onslaught of the new American culture and economy. Others continue to struggle to be recognized and assert their rights. Those tribes that have survived are truly remarkable in their ability to adapt and find a middle ground between two cultures.

Many questions arise regarding the Northeastern tribes. What could have been done differently? Is it right to force another culture to abandon age-old traditions and ways of understanding the world? Is one world-view truly superior to another? Is there anything to be learned from these experiences that might aid society in the future? Is it possible to reestablish an ecological balance similar to what Native peoples fostered at one time? Answering these questions and others will not change the past for Native peoples, but it might change the future for untold generations.

BOOKS

Adil, Janeen R. *The Northeast Indians: Daily Life in the 1500s.* Mankato, MN: Capstone Press, 2006.

Ballantine, Betty, and Ian Ballantine, eds. *The Native Americans: An Illustrated History.* Atlanta: Turner Publishing, 1993.

Bragdon, Kathleen J. *The Columbia Guide to American Indians of the Northeast.* New York: Columbia University Press, 2005.

Brooks, Lisa. *The Common Pot: The Recovery of Native Space in the Northeast.* Minneapolis: University of Minnesota Press, 2008.

Champagne, Duane, ed. *The Native North American Almanac.* Detroit: Gale, 1994.

Ditchfield, Christin. *Northeast Indians.* Chicago: Heinemann Library, 2012.

Doherty, Craig A. *Northeast Indians.* Broomall, PA: Chelsea House Publications, March 2008.

Hyde, George E. *Indians of the Woodlands: From Prehistoric Times to 1725.* Norman: University of Oklahoma Press, 1962.

Johnson, Michael, and Jonathan Smith. *Indian Tribes of the New England Frontier.* Oxford: Osprey Publishing, 2006.

Johnson, Michael. *Native Tribes of the Northeast.* Milwaukee, WI: World Almanac Library, 2004.

Josephy, Alvin M., Jr. *500 Nations: An Illustrated History of North American Indians.* New York: Knopf, 1994.

King, David C. *First People.* New York: DK Children, 2008.

Kuiper, Kathleen. *American Indians of the Northeast and Southeast.* New York: Rosen Educational Services, 2012.

Lenik, Edward J. *Making Pictures in Stone: American Indian Rock Art of the Northeast.* Tuscaloosa: University of Alabama Press, 2009.

Peyer, Bernd C. *The Tutor'd Mind: Indian Missionary-Writers in Antebellum America. Native Americans of the Northeast.* Amherst: University of Massachusetts Press, 1997.

Sita, Lisa. *Indians of the Northeast: Traditions, History, Legends, and Life.* Milwaukee, WI: Gareth Stevens, 2000.

Taylor, Alan. *The Divided Ground: Indians, Settlers, and the Northern Borderland of the American Revolution.* New York: Alfred A. Knopf, 2006.

Terrell, John Upton. *American Indian Almanac.* New York: World Publishing, 1971.

Wyss, Hilary E. *Writing Indians: Literacy, Christianity, and Native Community in Early America.* Native Americans of the Northeast. Amherst: University of Massachusetts Press, 2003.

Abenaki

Name

The name Abenaki (pronounced *ah-buh-NAH-key*) means "people of the dawnlands." The Abenaki people call themselves *Alnombak,* meaning "the people." The Abenaki (also called "Abanaki" or "Abnaki") were part of the Wabanaki Confederacy of five Algonquian-speaking tribes that existed from the mid-1600s to the mid-1800s.

Location

The group known as Abenaki was actually a union of many tribes. They were divided into eastern and western branches. The eastern Abenaki resided in Maine, east of the White Mountains of New Hampshire, and in the Canadian provinces of New Brunswick and Nova Scotia. The traditional territory of the western Abenaki groups included most of Vermont and New Hampshire, as well as the northern part of Massachusetts. In the early 2000s, there were Abenaki reservations in Maine and additional ones in Canada. Other groups of Abenaki people who do not have reservations are spread across northern New England and throughout Quebec and New Brunswick, Canada.

Population

In 1524, there were about 40,000 Abenaki (10,000 western Abenaki and 30,000 eastern Abenaki). In the 1990 U.S. Census, 1,549 people identified themselves as Abenaki. By 2000, that total rose to 2,544, and 6,012 people claimed some Abenaki heritage. In 1991, Canadian Abenaki numbered 945; by 2006, they numbered 2,164.

Language family

Algonquian.

Origins and group affiliations

Some historians believe that the ancestors of the tribes making up the Abenaki confederacy first arrived in North America about three thousand

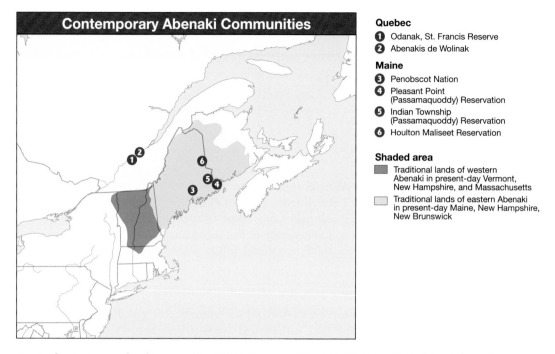

Contemporary Abenaki Communities

Quebec
1. Odanak, St. Francis Reserve
2. Abenakis de Wolinak

Maine
3. Penobscot Nation
4. Pleasant Point (Passamaquoddy) Reservation
5. Indian Township (Passamaquoddy) Reservation
6. Houlton Maliseet Reservation

Shaded area
- Traditional lands of western Abenaki in present-day Vermont, New Hampshire, and Massachusetts
- Traditional lands of eastern Abenaki in present-day Maine, New Hampshire, New Brunswick

A map of contemporary Abenaki communities. MAP BY XNR PRODUCTIONS. CENGAGE LEARNING, GALE. REPRODUCED BY PERMISSION OF GALE, A PART OF CENGAGE LEARNING.

years ago. The eastern Abenaki, the larger of the two branches, included the Penobscot, the Passamaquoddy, Maliseet, Androscoggin, Kennebec, Ossipee, and Pigwacket tribes. The western Abenaki tribes included the Sokoki, Cowasuck, and Missiquoi.

For thousands of years, the Abenaki people lived tranquil lives, hunting and fishing in the forests, ocean, lakes, and rivers of present-day Maine. Then Europeans came, and from the 1600s through the 1800s, the lives of Abenaki groups were terribly affected by war, starvation, and disease. Some tribal groups were forced to abandon their villages in New England and regroup in Canada during times of armed conflict. While the Native Americans were away from their New England territory, settlers took over the land. The Canadian Abenaki managed to maintain peace and retain many of their customs and traditions. The Abenaki who remained in their homelands in the United States also tried to live quietly and avoid trouble with European settlers, but they were not always able to do so.

HISTORY

Mythical city lures Europeans

During the early 1500s, people in Europe heard rumors of a wealthy city called "Norumbega," which was said to be located in northern Maine. Although Norumbega never existed, tales about the mythical city lured explorers to the area. One of the earliest was a French expedition led by the Italian explorer Giovanni da Verrazano (c. 1485–c. 1528) in 1524. Though suspicious of the foreigners, many of the Abenaki tribes engaged in fur trade with Europeans, especially the French and the British. In return, they received knives, iron axes, fishhooks, brass for making arrowheads, and cloth.

In 1604, the French explorer Samuel de Champlain (c. 1567–1635) visited many Abenaki villages while on a mission to trade furs and establish a French fort on the St. Croix River in present-day Maine. The British tried to establish a colony on Abenaki land in 1607, but, partly because of hostile encounters with the tribes, the settlement lasted less than a year.

Important Dates

1524: The Abenaki encounter the expedition of Giovanni da Verrazano.

1689–1763: The Abenaki are caught up in wars between European nations.

1805: The British government sets aside land near St. Francis, Quebec, to accommodate the flood of Abenaki moving there from the United States.

1980: President Jimmy Carter signs a bill granting the Passamaquoddy and Penobscot $81 million to make up for the loss of their homelands.

1982: The Vermont Abenaki apply for recognition by the U.S. government. Ten years later, the Supreme Court rule against them. The fight continues into the mid-2000s.

2006: The Vermont Abenaki are recognized by the state.

Abenaki relations with the French

For the next fifty years, the British and the French fought several wars for control of the Abenaki homeland, even though it belonged to the Native peoples of the area. All this tension led the Abenaki tribes to fight among themselves, and their competition for trade with the French only compounded the problems. The French traded mostly with the Penobscot, who became the most powerful of the Abenaki tribes.

The Abenaki had no true friends among the European nations, but their relationship with the French was much better than with the British colonists. The French won them over by providing guns and promising protection from their longtime enemies, the Iroquois (see entry), who conducted raids on Abenaki villages throughout the 1600s.

The Abenaki Confederacy and the Great Council Fire

The Abenaki (also known as Wabanaki) Confederacy was composed of a group of Algonquian-speaking tribes who banded together in the mid-1600s for common defense against the Iroquois confederacy. The Iroquois had overtrapped furs in their own homelands and began attacking nearby tribes to gain new hunting territories. The Iroquois alliance with the British further fueled the hostilities with the Abenaki, who were pro-French. At the time, England and France were bitter enemies, and both countries sought to dominate the unsettled territory.

Conflicts between the tribes of the Abenaki Confederacy and the Iroquois Confederacy were settled through a peace pact called the Great Council of Fire, made in 1749. Despite the differences between Abenaki and Iroquois tribes, the Great Council endured for more than twenty-five years. When the American Revolution began in 1775, some Abenaki groups supported the American colonists in their fight for independence from Britain. However, other Abenaki and Iroquois tribes, including the Passamaquoddy (Abenaki), sided with the British and withdrew from the Great Council of Fire. By 1862, the Abenaki Confederacy ceased to exist.

The British and the Iroquois

The British were unsuccessful in their attempts to befriend the Abenaki. Between 1616 and 1619, deadly epidemics (uncontrolled outbreaks of disease) swept through Native territories, killing many Abenaki. The French convinced the tribes that the British were solely responsible for the devastation. The British continued to depend on the friendship and support of the Iroquois tribe instead.

During the 1660s, a civil war took place in England. Many people fled from there to the New World and began to settle on Abenaki lands. After a time of peace, King Philip's War erupted in 1675 when a group of southern New England tribes led by the brilliant Wampanoag (see entry) leader Metacomet (King Philip; 1639–1676) attacked British settlements on the natives' homelands. By the time this tragic war was over, the colonists had nearly exterminated the Wampanoag, Nipmuck, and Narragansett (see entry) tribes. King Philip's death in July 1676 ended Native military action in southern New England. The Abenaki resented the growing alliance between the British and the Iroquois and feared the large number of British settlers who had begun to take over their land. Most Abenaki groups, however, remained neutral (did not take sides) throughout the conflict.

The French and Indian War begins

Between 1689 and 1763, the tribes in the Northeast became caught up in a struggle between England and France over who would dominate North America. These conflicts are referred to collectively as the French and Indian War (1754–63). This period consisted of occasional outbreaks of hostility followed by periods of quiet. The conflict also spread to Europe with the Seven Years War (1756–63), a war fought by Great Britain (allied with Prussia and Hanover) against France (supported by Austria, Sweden, Saxony, Russia and Spain).

King William's War King William's War (1689–97) was the first of the French and Indian War conflicts. Most Abenaki groups, with the exception of the Penobscot, joined French troops in attacking British towns in eastern New York, New Hampshire, and Maine. The British responded with raids of their own. Many Abenaki soon retreated to northern New England and Canada, where their French allies were based. England and France signed a peace treaty in 1697, but the Abenaki continued to fight, upset that more and more British colonists were taking over their territory. In 1699, the Abenaki, worn out from fighting, signed an agreement to stay neutral in any future conflicts between England and France.

Queen Anne's War The peace between the British and the French did not last long. Queen Anne's War broke out in 1702 as hostilities once again reached a fever pitch. Although many Abenaki stuck to the terms of their neutrality agreement, others joined the French in attacks on several British towns in present-day Maine.

The most famous raid of the war took place in February 1704 in Deerfield, Massachusetts. A large force of Abenaki and French carried out a sneak attack on the British at daybreak, killing more than fifty people, capturing more than one hundred, and burning a good part of the town to the ground. The Abenaki then withdrew back up the frozen Connecticut River, out of reach of the British, taking their captives with them. Even though they were successful, the greatly outnumbered Abenaki warriors suffered losses they could not afford. Weakened, the Abenaki traded more and more of their land to the French in exchange for safety in Canada. The pursuing British often encountered empty Abenaki villages as they marched northward.

Dummer's War In the treaty that ended Queen Anne's War in 1713, the French gave the territory of Acadia (in present-day Nova Scotia) to England. Acadia was largely made up of Abenaki land. The Abenaki felt angry and betrayed by the French, and many French people who lived in Acadia agreed with them.

Supported by several French priests, the Abenaki decided to defend their land, and in 1722, Dummer's War broke out. The great Abenaki warrior Grey Lock gained fame for his raids on the British, who were never able to capture him. The conflict was bloody, and the Abenaki eventually met with defeat in 1727.

King George's War Native peoples in the Northeast experienced relative peace from 1727 to 1744. Years of fighting and outbreaks of smallpox had greatly lessened their population. Furthermore, the intermingling of the Abenaki people with other tribes through ongoing association and intermarriage was changing the identity, culture, and lifestyle of these once fiercely independent groups. Peace ended for the tribes with the outbreak of King George's War in 1744. Some Abenaki tribes once again joined the French in attacking the British because they wanted to stop the British settlers who were now pushing their way up the Connecticut River valley. The Native American raids, which ended in 1748, succeeded in temporarily forcing the settlers to retreat southward.

In 1749, the Penobscot, one of the largest Abenaki tribes, left the confederacy in the hopes of making a separate peace with England and France. The tribe's plan to remain neutral could not last, however. England drew the Penobscot into battle by offering them very high prices for the scalps they could collect from Britain's enemies.

In 1759, the Abenaki were dealt a serious blow when British Major Robert Rogers (1731–1795)—nicknamed Wobi Madanondo ("White Devil") by the Abenaki—led a group of soldiers against the Abenaki village of St. Francis, Quebec, and burned it to the ground. The British defeated the French army and took full possession of Quebec and all of Canada. Following the French and Indian War, all French rule in the northeastern part of the North American continent ended. With the loss of their French allies, the Abenaki were forced to deal with their longtime enemies—the British—alone. Meanwhile, British colonists swarmed into Abenaki territory in New England in great numbers.

American Revolution splits Abenaki

More than seventy years of war, starvation, and disease greatly reduced the Abenaki's population and power. They had not seen the end of hardship, however. They endured further warfare and bloodshed when they were drawn into the American Revolution (1775–83; the American colonists' fight for independence from England).

The various Abenaki bands did not agree on which side to support in the revolution. Many of the St. Francis (Quebec) Abenaki supported the British, whereas a majority of the Penobscot, Passamaquoddy, Maliseet, and Micmac (see entry) bands of Abenaki fought with the freedom-seeking colonists under the command of General George Washington

(1732–1799). The colonists promised the Abenaki land in exchange for their support. For the most part, though, those promises would be broken by the victorious new nation.

Abenaki migrate north

In the newly formed United States, American-owned lumber companies took over Abenaki lands for their own profit. The United States and Canada further divided Abenaki lands when they drew boundary lines through them. The Abenaki's dealings with various state governments were largely unsuccessful. For example, on five separate occasions during the 1800s, the state of Vermont denied the Abenaki land.

At the beginning of the nineteenth century, some Abenaki continued to migrate north into Canada, a process that had been going on for a hundred years. The population of St. Francis, Quebec, swelled as Abenaki moved there to escape from the ever-growing number of American settlers. In 1805, the British government set aside land near St. Francis to accommodate the flood of Abenaki settlers. (Canada remained under British rule until 1867.)

U.S. Abenaki try to fit in

The Abenaki who stayed in the United States tried to survive by adopting American ways and speaking British. The Abenaki lifestyle was decimated as loggers destroyed their hunting, fishing, and trapping grounds. No longer able to support themselves by traditional means, many Abenaki began making and selling baskets and other crafts to survive. In time, though, the Abenaki tribes began a long fight with state and federal governments to preserve their lands and culture. Among themselves they continued to practice their ancient rituals and customs.

In New England, the Passamaquoddy and the Penobscot survived in their original homeland largely because the pressure from settlers was less severe in the north, but they barely maintained themselves on small

A Penobscot woman displays her Gala Day clothing in an 1884 portrait. Her tribe is among several that make up the Abenaki people.
THE LIBRARY OF CONGRESS

A Penobscot man poses for a portrait dressed in Gala Day apparel in 1884. The Penobscot are among several different groups that are part of the Abenaki tribe. THE LIBRARY OF CONGRESS

parcels of their old land. In 1786, they refused to sign a treaty with Massachusetts, but in 1794, they gave up more than a million acres to the state. By 1820, the Abenaki owned only a few thousand acres, and by 1850, they had been confined to two separate villages. Some, in fact, were forced out of villages in Vermont by the settlers and fled to live with relatives in Canada.

Abenaki in the early twentieth century

In 1929, a period of severe economic slowdown occurred in the United States. The Great Depression (1929–41), as it was called, put millions of Americans out of work. The late 1920s and the 1930s, however, were relatively good years for the Abenaki in the United States. They benefited from programs initiated by President Franklin D. Roosevelt (1882–1945; served 1933–45), who called the Native American the "forgotten man." Roosevelt's programs provided food and jobs for people like the Abenaki who were suffering hardships. Throughout Roosevelt's administration, government policies regarding the tribes changed, and emphasis was placed on maintaining and preserving indigenous (native) culture.

This forward-thinking trend did not necessarily extend to state government, however. Concerned about the number of Vermont men rejected by the draft during World War I (1914–18; a war in which Great Britain, France, the United States, and their allies defeated Germany, Austria-Hungary, and their allies), the state began a program to get rid of "undesirables"—people they felt did not benefit society. Many of these people were sterilized so they could not have children or confined to mental hospitals or prisons. One of the groups targeted was the Abenaki. To protect themselves, many Abenaki hid their Native American roots.

Some Abenaki were part of a sizeable group of Native Americans who fought in World War II (1939–45; a war in which Great Britain, France, the United States, and their allies defeated Germany, Italy, and Japan). After the war, Native soldiers were greatly disappointed to return

Abenaki Tribes: The Penobscot, Passamaquoddy, and Maliseet

The Penobscot and the Passamaquoddy were the largest of the tribes that made up the Abenaki Confederacy. They were the only ones who managed to remain on their homelands throughout the tremendous upheavals faced by all the Abenaki peoples. In the 1400s, about 10,000 Penobscot lived on the Atlantic Coast. When the United States was established, the lands of the Penobscot became part of the state of Massachusetts. The state quickly whittled away much of the Penobscot homeland. The state of Maine was eventually carved out of the Massachusetts region, and the Penobscot lost more land and the right to self-government. Most of the people left the reservation in disgust. By the mid-2000s, only about 2,040 Penobscot remained. Penobscot territory is made up of a 149,000-acre (60,300-hectare) reservation, which includes 146 islands in Maine's Penobscot River. The village of Old Town is the main population center.

The Passamaquoddy and Maliseet together numbered about 1,000 in the early seventeenth century. The Passamaquoddy lived along the coast of Maine and in New Brunswick, Canada. As of 2000, there were about 2,700 Passamaquoddy. They have two reservations: one in Maine at Pleasant Point on the Passamaquoddy Bay and another, Indian Township, located 50 miles (80 kilometers) inland.

Historians often link the Passamaquoddy with the Maliseet, a nearby tribe who spoke the same language. The Maliseet inhabited a large area north and west of the land of the Passamaquoddy, in Maine, New Brunswick, and Quebec, Canada. Most of the Maliseet fled to Canada after the wars of the seventeenth and eighteenth century. In the 1990s, most of the 885 Maliseet people resided in New Brunswick or Quebec, although there was one reservation for the tribe in Houlton, Maine, and other small groups of Maliseet were scattered throughout the United States. By 2000, the Maliseet population had risen to 972 in the United States and to 712 in Canada.

home and find that U.S. government policy had returned to one of assimilation (incorporating or blending Native Americans into mainstream white society).

Abenaki fight for rights

During the 1950s, American Abenaki voiced their dissatisfaction with federal and state government policies that had taken away most of their land, stripped them of their fishing rights, and virtually destroyed their economy. Then in the 1960s—with the civil rights movement (the fight for equal rights for people of all races) in full swing—the Abenaki, along with other Native groups, began to demand a full restoration of their rights as a tribe. They engaged in acts of civil disobedience (making their point by publicly disobeying certain laws) and used other forms of protest as part of a movement to reassert the power of Native peoples.

These efforts paid off for two Abenaki tribes. In 1972, the Penobscot joined the Passamaquoddy in a court battle over 200-year-old treaties they had made with the state of Maine and the U.S. government. The tribes claimed that the treaties were illegal and that nearly 12.5 million acres, or two-thirds of the state of Maine, had been wrongfully taken from them. They sought both money and federal recognition through the court system. In 1980, the court awarded the Penobscot and Passamaquoddy a total of $81 million from the federal government. Most of the money was put into a fund that permitted the tribes to buy 300,000 acres of their former land. The tribes also gained the federal recognition needed to obtain health and education benefits, as well the right to hunt and fish in their homeland.

Vermont Abenaki, however, continued to struggle with the issue of tribal recognition. During the 1970s and 1980s, the St. Francis/Sokoki band of the Abenaki Nation of Missisquoi reestablished cultural gatherings and began holding powwows in the 1990s to introduce others to their culture. They submitted an application to the Bureau of Indian Affairs (BIA) in 1982, which was denied in 2005. They remained determined to gain federal recognition for their tribe, so they reapplied. In 2006, the state of Vermont granted state recognition to four Abenaki bands; the legislation also allows other bands to petition for recognition in the future. This legislation meant that the Abenaki would be eligible for federal programs and social services. They were also granted the right to market their crafts as Native American products.

Canadian Abenaki in modern times

In 1979, the Grand Conseil (Council) of the Waban-Aki Nation was founded and included the Abenakis on the two Canadian reserves—Odanak and Wolinak. In 1999, this council helped form the Aboriginal Commission of Economic Development of Quebec and Labrador. The goal of this organization is to assist communities in these two provinces with economic and business development. The council also researched early land claims to request compensation for and/or to buy back some of the land that originally belonged to the Abenaki. Additionally, the Grand Conseil negotiated for fishing and hunting rights for the tribe.

Canadian Abenaki took steps to keep their culture alive by starting a cultural center, establishing a corporation to provide job opportunities and shops for Native products, and opening a tribal museum. Schools are teaching Abenaki history and language so the Abenaki culture will be passed on to the next generation.

RELIGION

The Abenaki were a deeply religious people. They believed that the earth had always existed and called it their "Grandmother." They also believed that a being called "The Owner" had created people, animals, and all natural things, such as rocks and trees, and that each natural thing had an individual spirit. Their hero, Gluscabi, who created himself, could make life good or bad for the people. For example, he might bring them tobacco or affect the weather to their advantage.

The spiritual leaders of the Abenaki were healers called shamans (pronounced *SHAH-munz* or *SHAY-munz*). Shamans enlisted the aid of the spirits to heal the sick and solve problems. (See "Healing practices.")

During the sixteenth and seventeenth centuries, French Catholic missionaries arrived, seeking to convert the Abenaki to Christianity. At first, the tribes feared and shunned the priests as witches, but the missionaries finally gained the trust of many Abenaki by learning their language and assisting with their health-care needs. Protestant missionaries met with much less success in their conversion attempts. In time, Roman Catholic churches and cemeteries became important parts of many Abenaki villages.

In recent years, some Abenaki have returned to their original beliefs and to their code of ethics, which includes self-respect and respect for

The Coming of Gluscabi

This Abenaki creation story describes how Gluscabi came to be.

After Tabaldak had finished making human beings, he dusted his hands off and some of that dust sprinkled on the Earth.

From that dust Gluscabi formed himself. He sat up from the Earth and said, "Here I am." So it is that some of the Abenaki people call Gluscabi by another name, *Odzihozo*, which means, "the man who made himself from something." He was not as powerful as Tabaldak, The Owner, but like his grandchildren, the human beings, he had the power to change things, sometimes for the worse.

When Gluscabi sat up from the Earth, The Owner was astonished. "How did it happen now that you came to be?" he said.

Then Gluscabi said, "Well, it is because I formed myself from this dust left over from the first humans that you made."

"You are very wonderful," The Owner told him.

"Let us roam around now," said The Owner. So they left that place and went uphill to the top of a mountain. There they gazed about, open-eyed, so far around they could see. They could see the lakes, the rivers, the trees, how all the land lay, the Earth.

Then The Owner said, "Behold here how wonderful is my work. By the wish of my mind I created all this existing world, oceans, rivers, lakes." And he and Gluscabi gazed open-eyed.

SOURCE: Caduto, Michael J., and Joseph Bruchac. *Native American Stories*. Golden, CO: Fulcrum Publishing, 1991.

Abenaki Words

The biggest difficulty in understanding the Abenaki language is that there is not always a literal translation for a given word. For example lists the word for clock as *babizookwazik,* which is translated as "that thing that ticks." Because Native Americans and Western Europeans had a very different concept of what time is and how it is measured, such a word could take on a confusing and complicated meaning.

Some other Abenaki words include:

ndakinna	"our land"
bitawbagok (the tribal name for Lake Champlain)	"the lake between"
kuai	"hello"
adio	"good-bye"
wliwnini	"thank you"

all creation. Central to these beliefs is a standard of conduct that includes love, compassion, forgiveness, and harmony. As in times past, elders—those possessing wisdom—give sacred instruction.

LANGUAGE

The Abenaki language is part of the Algonquian language family. The eastern and western Abenaki people spoke different dialects (varieties) of the language. The best known of the many eastern dialects was the Penobscot, which is still spoken. Many Abenaki place names remain in use in the New England area. For example, *Connecticut* means "the long river," and *Katahdin* (as in Mt. Katahdin, Maine) means "principal mountain." The dialect of the western Abenaki continues to be spoken as a second language by some of the people.

During the nineteenth century, Abenaki children were punished in American schools for speaking their traditional language; as a result, it has almost become extinct. In the 1980s and 1990s, the U.S. Abenaki tribes made great efforts to save their language, and since then, it has been taught in some Vermont schools. Canada, too, has initiated programs to ensure that the Abenaki language and culture are passed down to the younger generations.

GOVERNMENT

For the most part, at the time the Europeans arrived in the Northeast, the various Abenaki groups operated by consensus rather than using a central governing authority. Family bands were the usual means of organizations, and issues such as whether or not to go to war were decided by all the adult members of a tribe, often under the loose leadership of a well-respected person called a sachem (pronounced *SAY-chem*), or chief. A sachem not only directed the war efforts but also represented the people in meetings with other tribes or with different

Abenaki bands. Even after the formation of the Abenaki Confederacy in 1670, though, French military officers complained that Abenaki leaders had a hard time controlling their warriors. This perception probably arose from a misunderstanding of Abenaki beliefs regarding individuality and consensus.

In the mid-2000s, many Canadian Abenaki lived on reserves (the word Canadians use for reservations). Their leader was called *sagama*. Each band had its own government and operated like a small country, but the people were also Canadian citizens and had to obey those laws as well. In the United States, chiefs governed their tribes and had authority over internal tribal matters, but their leadership was subject to most American laws.

ECONOMY

The Abenaki economy was based originally on hunting, fishing, and gathering. After Europeans arrived, trade became more important. Wealthy Europeans who lived in drafty houses and castles were willing to pay large sums of money for furs to keep themselves warm in winter. The Abenaki and other tribes supplied European traders, especially the French, with a large number of the desired pelts. By the mid-1660s, however, the fur trade had fallen off because of overhunting. The British then allowed the Abenaki to buy European goods on credit, using their land for collateral (meaning the whites would have the right to take Native land if the Native Americans did not repay the loans on time). After a while, though, the British refused to be repaid in animal skins and only accepted Abenaki land.

By the late 1990s, the surviving Abenaki tribes such as the Penobscot and the Passamaquoddy were supporting themselves through a variety of business ventures. Several organizations were instrumental in helping other Abenaki tribes, who had not received federal recognition, to become self-sufficient. The Abenaki Self-Help Association, Inc. (ASHAI) was formed in Vermont in the 1970s to request state and federal funds to assist the tribe. In 2000, the Abenaki Microenterprise Project began providing low-income households with training and advice on self-employment. In 2010, the group received a $78,120 federal grant to help with its efforts. Other community efforts in Vermont in the early 2000s included a Tribal Trading Post, with Native products for sale, and an Abenaki Tribal Museum.

Abenaki Population: 2000 Census

The Abenaki tribe as a whole has never been federally recognized. This means that the U.S. government does not maintain official relations with the tribe. However, three Abenaki groups in the state of Maine—the Penobscot, the Passamaquoddy, and the Maliseet—have achieved federal recognition. Maliseet people also live on reserves located in New Brunswick and Quebec. Other people who claim Abenaki ancestry lost their lands but continue to live throughout New England.

DAILY LIFE

Families

Typical Abenaki lived with extended families that were made up of a father, a mother, their children, grandparents, aunts, uncles, and cousins. Several related families lived together in the same large house, but each had its own living space and fire. Family members shared food and possessions, and children repaid their older relatives by taking care of them in their later years. In the summer, family groups lived in separate hunting territories that were inherited through the fathers. Abenaki villages rarely contained more than one hundred people.

Abenaki childrearing practices differed greatly from those of the Europeans. In fact, early European settlers sometimes criticized Abenaki children as spoiled and said they ran wild. The Abenaki have always believed in nonviolence in childrearing, so they do not punish their children. Instead, they use storytelling to discipline them. Good habits and ethics are woven into most traditional tales. If a child misbehaves or acts foolishly, parents use a story to teach them a lesson.

Buildings

Most Abenaki structures were made of birchbark. The basic family dwelling for the western Abenaki was the longhouse, in which several families lived together. In the winter, when food became scarce, families sometimes moved into cone-shaped wigwams covered with elm-bark mats that resembled the tepees of the Great Plains tribes. Wigwams were not as sturdy as longhouses, but they could be moved easily when a family was out tracking game.

Eastern Abenaki people built either dome-shaped houses or square houses with roofs shaped like pyramids. Many villages also had dome-shaped sweat lodges where purification ceremonies took place.

Clothing and adornment

The Abenaki made most of their clothing from tanned deerskin or elk skin. In warm weather, men wore breechcloths (flaps of material suspended from the waist and covered the front and back) along with sashes that were wrapped around the waist and knotted. Women wore wraparound knee-length skirts. Both men and women sometimes added leggings, buckskin sleeves, and moccasins as the weather got cooler.

In the cold winter months, the Abenaki wore many of the same types of garments but made them from heavier materials such as moose hide; men often put on moose hide vests. Winter wear for both men and women included robes made from beaver pelts, fur hoods, and moccasins insulated with rabbit fur. A poncholike piece of skin with a hole or slit cut for the head provided extra warmth.

Both men and women wore their hair long, and women sometimes wore braids. The people wore decorated belts, necklaces, and pendants made from shells or slate. Many men hung sheathed knives from their necks.

Food

The Abenaki obtained most of their food by hunting and fishing along the streams and rivers of their tribal lands. In the spring, they fished from the shore or from canoes for smelt, salmon, sturgeon, shad, alewives, and eels. Their fishing tools included nets, three-pronged spears, and weirs (fencelike enclosures used to trap fish). At night, fishing took place by torchlight.

During the summer months, coastal groups harvested the ocean for fish, shellfish, and sea mammals. In the fall, the Abenaki used bows and arrows to hunt both large and small game. Inland Abenaki fished on frozen ponds during the winter. By wearing snowshoes made from wood and leather, the people could continue hunting moose, deer, bear, beaver, and otter throughout the cold weather. The Abenaki found a use for nearly every portion of a slain animal. They smoked leftover fish over a fire for later use and froze extra meat in wooden containers.

Crops such as corn, beans, squash, and tobacco (mostly used for ceremonies) were grown near the rivers. After the men cleared land near the village, the women planted crops there. In areas where the soil was less rich, the Abenaki used fish as fertilizer. Women also picked various greens and gathered food such as beechnuts, butternuts, hickory nuts, and berries to eat raw or bake into breads. Every February, the western Abenaki collected maple sap, which they boiled to make syrup.

Education

Abenaki children were often taught by their grandparents, aunts, or uncles. They learned tasks considered appropriate for their gender. Boys learned the skills of hunting and warfare and began practicing with a bow and arrow at a very young age. By age twelve, they were permitted to go hunting with the men of the family. Girls learned to weave baskets, grow crops, gather foods, sew clothing, and tend to smaller children.

In the late twentieth century, the Abenaki of Vermont began an Indian Education Program, a scholarship fund, a women's support group, and a children's dance company to educate their children in both the old and new ways.

Healing practices

Healers, or shamans, took care of the religious and medical needs in an Abenaki village. Most shamans were male. They used a variety of methods to cure the sick, including sweating and treatment with herbs, laxatives, teas, and salves (sticky substances applied to wounds or sores). European colonists learned about the use of plant medicines from the shamans; the use of these age-old treatments continues today.

If the use of herbs proved unsuccessful, shamans called upon special magical remedies to treat illness. They might attempt to blow or dance an illness away, sometimes placing the patient on a surface covered with magical signs. If it became obvious that an afflicted person was near death, villagers brought the event about more quickly by letting the patient starve, a practice they considered kind.

ARTS

Birchbark boxes and baskets

The Abenaki were known for the objects they fashioned out of the bark of white birch trees that grew in their region. They divided birchbark into flexible, waterproof sheets and shaped it into baskets, boxes, and canoes. Besides being useful, many of the objects were works of art. The Abenaki used sharp utensils to scrape the surface of birch boxes and expose the inner bark, producing contrasting patterns of dark and light woods. They also created beautiful baskets by weaving strips of ash wood together or by twisting or braiding sweetgrass. Such baskets are still sold throughout Maine and Quebec.

CUSTOMS

Games and festivities

Games played an important role in Abenaki culture. Boys began to race when they were small, and archery was considered an important part of a boy's development into adulthood. Handball and lacrosse (a game played with a ball and netted sticks) were among the most popular games. The feats of ballplayers were central to many Abenaki stories, including one that tells of a fantastic game in which the players had lights of many colors on their heads and wore belts made of rainbows.

The Abenaki liked to sing and tell stories while carrying out their daily chores. They also enjoyed riddles and word games. Dancing and singing were featured at most major social events, including marriages, the coming of visitors, funerals, and the first corn harvest.

At the end of the 1990s, the Abenaki of Odanak, Quebec, began holding an annual summer festival that revolved around storytelling, music, traditional foods, and political and social discussions. They hoped that sharing some of their customs and seasonal festivals with the public would promote greater cultural understanding. Other Abenaki tribes in Canada and the United States hold powwows to introduce others to their dances and culture.

War and hunting rituals

When conflicts broke out with other peoples, the Abenaki war chief stood up with a red club in his hands and asked for volunteers to unite for the fight. Other men known for their leadership skills also stood up and asked warriors to join them in forming battle groups of ten. Then the men feasted and danced well into the night. Before beginning a battle, they painted their faces red and drew pictures of past battle victories on their bodies.

Puberty

Around the time of puberty, an Abenaki boy embarked on a vision quest, a long period of fasting (going without food and water) in the woods, during which the young man waited alone for the appearance of the guardian spirit who was to guide him through life. Males were considered adults by the age of fifteen.

A girl's first menstrual period signaled the arrival of womanhood and her readiness for marriage. Menstruating women were isolated from others in a special wigwam and were not allowed to participate in their usual tasks because menstrual blood was considered powerful, even dangerous. Some girls also undertook vision quests.

Marriage

When a young man wanted to marry, he sent a representative to visit his intended bride with gifts to entice her into the marriage. If she refused the gifts, it meant that she rejected the proposal. If she and her parents agreed, the couple began a trial period of living together, although they were supervised by chaperones and were not yet allowed to engage in sexual relations.

Marriages became official when the groom's family accepted gifts offered by the bride's family and a wedding celebration was held. For western Abenaki, it was customary for couples to live with the man's family after marriage; if the bride's family was wealthier, though, the couple would go to live with them. Eastern Abenaki newlyweds usually resided with the bride's family. Some chiefs of the eastern Abenaki were permitted to have several wives.

Funerals

Abenaki dressed the bodies of the deceased in their finest clothing, wrapped them in birchbark, and tied them with a cord. They buried them quickly so their spirits would not linger over the corpses and the village. Graves contained food for the deceased person's journey to the other world, as well as weapons, tools, and personal items to use in the afterlife.

In the winter, the Abenaki placed the remains of the dead on a high platform until the earth thawed in the spring and the corpse could be buried. If a man died during a hunting trip, his body was left above ground, and the first person to find the body in the spring buried it.

A widow wore a hood on her head and did not participate in social events for one year after the death of her husband. After the death of a child, a grieving mother would usually cut off her hair and blacken her face. Relatives brought presents to the parents to help ease their pain; in return, the parents sometimes held a feast.

CURRENT TRIBAL ISSUES

In the 1980s, the Abenaki Indians of Vermont began a court battle for the right to hunt, fish, and travel on their traditional lands. In 1992, the Vermont Supreme Court ruled that all such Abenaki rights had ended. The Vermont band fought on, however, and in 2006, the General Assembly of Vermont recognized the tribal status of the Abenaki people, establishing an official relationship between the state and the Abenaki of Vermont. As a result, Vermont created a commission on Abenaki affairs to work out matters of concern to both the tribe and the state and to aid the tribe in its efforts to achieve recognition by the U.S. government. When the federal government recognizes a group of Native Americans as an Indian tribe, special services such as health care and educational opportunities become available to them, and they usually are granted the right to use their homeland for hunting and fishing purposes. In 2010, Vermont passed a law that set up a process for state recognition of tribes. In 2011, two bands—the Elnu Abenaki and the Nulhegan band of the Coosuk Abenaki Nation—became the first Abenaki tribes to gain Vermont recognition.

Another question the Abenaki face, as do other Native tribes, is whether the tribal government is sovereign (self-ruling) on Native land or whether the tribe must submit to federal laws. The Abenaki believe that, as a separate nation, they should make their own decisions. As of 2007, the U.S. government recognized their right to make tribal decisions but it insisted on overall authority in other matters. Two examples of ongoing areas of conflict include the rights of labor unions to organize in tribal casinos and the ability of Native Americans to cross the Canada/United States border freely. Natives do not want unions, nor do they feel they must abide by the federal government's minimum wage policy. They also insist that, because their reservation straddles the United States and Canada, they should be free to travel back and forth between the two countries at will.

Some Maine tribes were also concerned about pollution from outside sources upsetting the balance of their tribal waters and killing the wildlife. In 2004, several organizations joined together to create the Penobscot River Restoration Project. This group received federal funds in 2007 that enabled them to remove two dams and bypass a third one. They have since been working on restoring free-flowing water and improving river ecology for more than 500 miles (800 kilometers).

In 2011, the leaders of the Wabanaki nation and the governor of Maine signed an agreement intended to help bring healing to children who suffered or are suffering trauma as a result of the foster care system. Several Wabanaki women, who experienced this abuse firsthand, were instrumental in bringing about this event. They hope that a Truth and Reconciliation Commission will help people heal the past and prevent future problems.

NOTABLE PEOPLE

Joseph E. Bruchac III, PhD (1942–), is an award-winning author and poet whose works reflect his Abenaki heritage. (He is also of Slovakian and British descent.) Bruchac's stories and poems emphasize the importance of spiritual balance and address environmental concerns as well. His books, which include many stories for children, have been widely published. The author also founded a much-praised multicultural literary magazine as well as Greenfield Review Press, which publishes many books by Native authors.

Penobscot Louis Francis Sockalexis (1871–1913) was the first Native American to play professional baseball. He was an outstanding hitter for the Cleveland Spiders, but his career was cut short by a serious alcohol problem. He later worked as an umpire, basket weaver, canoeist, woodsman, and ferryman on the Penobscot River. In 1915, the Cleveland team was renamed the Indians in his honor (although in the 1980s and 1990s, many Natives protested the use of Indian names in sports as demeaning).

Samoset (1590–1653) was a sachem who lived on an island off the coast of present-day Maine. He served as a mediator between the Pilgrims and indigenous (native) groups. Samoset helped to create the first peace treaty between the Europeans and the Wampanoag tribe. He also signed the first land deed in America, giving nearly 12,000 acres (4,900 hectares) of Native lands to whites.

BOOKS

Bourque, Bruce J., and Laureen A. LaBar. *Uncommon Threads: Wabanaki Textiles, Clothing, and Costume.* Augusta: Maine State Museum in association with University of Washington Press, 2009.

Hardy, Kerry. *Notes on a Lost Flute: A Field Guide to the Wabanaki.* Camden, ME: Down East, 2009.

Day, Gordon M. *Western Abenaki Dictionary: Abenaki-English*. Vol. 1. Gatineau, Quebec: Canadian Museum of Civilization, 1994.

Mundell, Kathleen. *North by Northeast: Wabanaki, Akwesasne Mohawk, and Tuscarora Traditional Arts*. Gardiner, ME: Tilbury House, Publishers, 2008.

Pawling, Micah A., ed. *Wabanaki Homeland and the New State of Maine: The 1820 Journal and Plans of Survey of Joseph Treat*. Amherst: University of Massachusetts Press, 2007.

Prins, Harald E.L., and Bunny McBride. *Asticou's Island Domain: Wabanaki Peoples at Mount Desert Island, 1500–2000*. Boston, MA: Northeast Region Ethnography Program, National Park Service, 2007.

Wiseman, Frederick Matthew. *The Voice of Dawn: An Autohistory of the Abenaki Nation*. Lebanon, NH: University Press of New England, 2001.

WEB SITES

Bélanger, Claude. "Quebec History: Abnaki, Abénaki, Abenaqui." *Quebec History Encyclopedia: Marianopolis College.* http://faculty.marianopolis. edu/c.belanger/quebechistory/encyclopedia/abenaki.htm (accessed on June 5, 2011).

Bruchac, Joe. "Storytelling." *Abenaki Nation.* http://www.abenakination.org/ stories.html (accessed on June 5, 2011).

"Exploring and Sharing the Wabanki History of Interior New England." *No-Do-Ba.* http://www.nedoba.org/ (accessed on June 5, 2011).

"New Hampshire's Native American Heritage." *New Hampshire State Council on the Arts.* http://www.nh.gov/folklife/learning/traditions_native_ameri-cans.htm (accessed on June 5, 2011).

Redish, Laura, and Orrin Lewis. "Native Languages of the Americas: Abnaki-Penobscot Language (Abénakis, Alnôbak)." *Native Languages of the Americas.* http://www.native-languages.org/abna.htm (accessed on May 9, 2011).

Delaware

Name

Delaware (pronounced *del-UH-wair*). The Delaware call themselves *Lenape* (pronounced *len-AH-pay)*), meaning "the people." They are also called Lenni Lenape (also spelled Lenápe or Lenapi), meaning "the true people." It was not until the 1600s that the tribe was first called the Delaware. That name came from the Europeans, who named the river running through Lenape territory after Thomas West, commonly known as Lord De La Warr (1577–1618), the English governor of Jamestown. Since that time, the Lenape have been called Delaware by the U.S. government, and most tribes eventually adopted that as their official name. To avoid confusion, the tribe will be referred to as the Delaware throughout this entry.

Location

Originally, the tribe lived along the Delaware River in the mid-Atlantic area, including New Jersey, Delaware, New York, and eastern Pennsylvania. It was constantly pushed west—first to Ohio, then to Indiana, Missouri, Kansas, and finally Oklahoma. Small groups also fled to Ontario, Canada. Several tribes who claim Delaware heritage, but have not yet received federal recognition, live in New Jersey, Pennsylvania, Kansas, and Wisconsin. Today, most Delaware can be found in Oklahoma and Ontario.

Population

In 1600, there may have been 11,000 to 20,000 Delaware. By the 1700s, that estimate had dropped to 4,000. In 1910, the U.S. Census (count of the population) recorded 2,000 Delaware people. The 2000 U.S. Census showed that 8,419 people identified themselves as Delaware only, whereas 17,707 claimed some Delaware heritage. Of those who said they were Delaware, only 2,384 lived in Oklahoma. Statistics from First Nations of Canada indicated a Delaware population of 2,250 in 2007. In 2010, the census counted 7,843 Delaware in the United States, with a total of 18,264 people claiming some Delaware ancestry.

Language family

Algonquian.

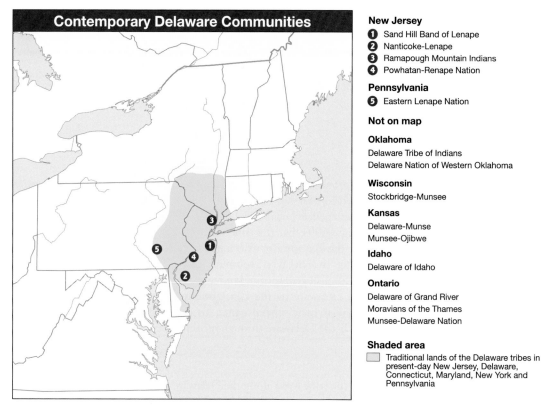

Contemporary Delaware Communities

New Jersey
1. Sand Hill Band of Lenape
2. Nanticoke-Lenape
3. Ramapough Mountain Indians
4. Powhatan-Renape Nation

Pennsylvania
5. Eastern Lenape Nation

Not on map

Oklahoma
Delaware Tribe of Indians
Delaware Nation of Western Oklahoma

Wisconsin
Stockbridge-Munsee

Kansas
Delaware-Munse
Munsee-Ojibwe

Idaho
Delaware of Idaho

Ontario
Delaware of Grand River
Moravians of the Thames
Munsee-Delaware Nation

Shaded area
Traditional lands of the Delaware tribes in present-day New Jersey, Delaware, Connecticut, Maryland, New York and Pennsylvania

A map of contemporary Delaware communities. MAP BY XNR PRODUCTIONS. CENGAGE LEARNING, GALE. REPRODUCED BY PERMISSION OF GALE, A PART OF CENGAGE LEARNING.

Origins and group affiliations

The three main traditional groupings of Lenape (Delaware) are Munsee, Unami, and Unalactigo. The tribe was also closely related to the Nanticoke. The Delaware traded with most New England tribes, especially the Wampanoag (see entry) and the Mahicans, but they fought with the Susquehannocks and the Iroquois Confederacy.

Long before Europeans reached the shores of America, the Delaware culture was thriving. Some say it has existed for fifteen thousand years. The people hunted, fished, and farmed the mid-Atlantic area, which they called *Lenapehaking* ("Lenape land"). A diplomatic and democratic tribe, they earned the nickname "the grandfathers" from other Algonquian tribes for their role in peacekeeping. At first they were hospitable to the white colonists, but they soon found themselves cheated out of land. The Delaware, who thought land should be shared by all, did not believe in the European concept of buying and selling land. By the mid-1800s, most Delaware, who had once lived freely in the territory from New York to Delaware, had been pushed from their homelands and, after several relocations, were forced onto reservations in Oklahoma.

HISTORY

Prior to European arrival

Lenapehaking stretched from the shores of the Atlantic coast to the inland rivers, and much of the land was thickly forested. Fish and game were plentiful. Villages dotted the area, ranging in size from small groups of thirty-five to large settlements of up to five thousand. Although each group had a chief, the Delaware believed in independence; thus they had no need for a central government.

Early fur trading

In 1609, explorer Henry Hudson (c. 1565–1611) claimed the Delaware's land for the Dutch. Soon, Dutch and Swedish colonists settled in the mid-Atlantic states. At first, relations were peaceful. The Delaware helped the colonists and learned from them. They traded beaver pelts for cooking pots, beads, guns, cloth, and alcohol. The desire for European goods, however, encouraged the Delaware to go against their traditions and overhunt and overtrap.

Trading also prompted tribal warfare. To gain a greater share of the trade, the Mohawks (see entry) attacked the Mahicans, and the Munsee (Delaware) came to their aid. Farther south, the Susquehannocks destroyed Delaware villages and forced the people across the Delaware River. After smallpox killed many members of the tribe, the Delaware could no longer resist, and the Susquehannocks demanded tribute for any furs the Delaware sold.

Important Dates

1609: Henry Hudson encounters the Lenape (Delaware).

1629: Lewes, Delaware, is the first recorded Delaware property sold to the Dutch.

1737: The Delaware are cheated of their land by the Walking Purchase.

1760s: The Delaware move to Ohio.

1778: The Delaware sign the first formal treaty with the United States, guaranteeing their land and allowing them to be the fourteenth state; the treaty is never ratified.

1781–82: Coshocton, a major Delaware settlement, is destroyed; the Moravian Delaware are massacred at Gnaddenhutten. Many flee to Indiana or Canada.

1783: Absentee Delaware move to Missouri.

1869: The Delaware are forced to move to Oklahoma.

1977: The western Delaware receive a small settlement for land claims and are given joint ownership of trust lands with the Caddo and Wichita.

1996: The Delaware Tribe of Oklahoma (Eastern Delaware) receives federal recognition.

2004: The Cherokee tribe wins a court case to overturn Delaware Tribe of Oklahoma's federal recognition.

2009: Bureau of Indian Affairs restores federal recognition to the Delaware tribe.

Dutch merchants trade goods with Native Americans on Manhattan Island in the 1600s. © NORTH WIND PICTURE ARCHIVES

Dutch settlers

In 1624, the Dutch bought Manhattan Island for $24 worth of trade goods. According to some sources, the Delaware sold it to them. The tribe claims that it was not involved in the sale; Manhattan Island was sold without its knowledge. The first actual record of a Dutch land purchase from the Delaware Indians was Lewes, Delaware, in 1629.

The Dutch government insisted on treating the Natives fairly and offering payment for any land they occupied. The Delaware, however, did not understand the European concept of purchasing land; to them, the earth could not be bought or sold any more than air could. They believed Europeans were offering gifts for sharing the land, which they were willing to do. Settlers and Native Americans lived in relative harmony for almost a decade, although many Europeans resented the Delaware for hunting and fishing on land they "owned."

Relations with the Dutch deteriorated in 1637, when Governor William Kieft (1597–1647) demanded taxes of corn, furs, and wampum (polished shells strung together as a belt or sash and used as money) from the Native Americans. The Delaware, who paid tribute only to make amends for wrongs they had done or for losing a war, did not understand this European order. They knew they had treated the colonists fairly, so they ignored the requests. In 1643, soldiers sent to collect the taxes killed 120 Delaware, including children and the elderly. The tribe's code of ethics demanded they avenge the deaths. Peaceful coexistence with the Europeans had ended.

Delaware losses

The next two decades were marked by wars, massacres, and diseases that decimated the Delaware tribe. Beginning with Kieft's War (1643–45), in which the Delaware and Dutch engaged in attacks and retaliation, the Delaware lost land and people. When a Native woman was shot for picking peaches on Dutch land, the Peach War (1655) ensued. A few years later, the Esopus Wars (1659–64) erupted over Dutch attempts to take over more land. At the same time, many Natives were dying from European diseases and intertribal warfare.

By this time, Swedish colonists had settled in the area. The Delaware shared their knowledge of fishing and farming with the Swedish, and from them learned to make splint baskets and to build log cabins. In 1664, when the British captured New Netherland and renamed it New York, English settlers moved onto Native lands as well. They signed treaties and paid for some of the properties, but they often took what they wanted without doing either.

Life in Pennsylvania

Eventually, the Delaware were forced from their lands into Pennsylvania, where they encountered William Penn (1644–1718), an English Quaker who had come to America seeking religious freedom. Penn treated them kindly. The peace treaty they both signed has often been termed the only treaty with the indigenous (native) peoples that has never been broken.

When William Penn died, his sons cheated the Delaware out of their land. Producing an unsigned document from 1686, Thomas Penn (1702–1775) insisted that the tribe honor it. According to this treaty, the Penns were entitled to whatever land a man could walk in one day.

Colonist William Penn signs a treaty to acquire land from the Delaware tribe in 1682. © NORTH WIND PICTURE ARCHIVES

The Delaware agreed, unaware that Penn had cleared a path through the woods and hired three runners. This 1737 Walking Purchase netted the Penns about 1,200 square miles (3,100 square kilometers) of land. When the Delaware sachem (chief) protested during a meeting with the Pennsylvania governor and the Iroquois, he not only received no support, but the Iroquois chief humiliated him by demanding that the Delaware leave the area.

By this time, the Munsee and Delaware had almost become two separate groups. With no land of their own, most of the Munsee were forced to move to western Pennsylvania. There they encountered Moravian missionaries who worked among the tribe. (The Moravians are Protestants belonging to a religious movement that originated in Moravia, part of present-day Czech Republic.) Many of the people converted to Christianity. Other members of the tribe joined the Mingo and Shawnee (see entry) in a move to eastern Ohio.

Troubles in Ohio

As the British and the Iroquois forced the tribe even farther west, the Delaware settled in eastern and northwestern Ohio along the rivers. There they again engaged in the fur trade. They tried to ally themselves with whatever European group was in power—first the French, then later the British. During the American Revolution (1775–1783; the American colonists' fight for independence from England), many Delaware remained neutral, especially the Moravians, who believed in living at peace.

In 1782, Pennsylvania soldiers, thinking the Moravian group was responsible for several raids, killed ninety-two people in the peaceful settlement of Gnadenhutten. Many of the survivors fled to Canada. A year later, the colonists won their independence and began their move into Delaware territory. Many Moravian Delaware migrated to Canada. They settled in Moraviantown, which would be burned down by the Americans in 1813.

The Delaware who remained in Ohio allied themselves with other tribes in the area. Following the Battle of Fallen Timbers (1794), after which the Delaware and their allies surrendered to the American general Anthony Wayne (1745–1796), the Delaware signed away most of their land in the Treaty of Greenville (1795) and moved to Indiana.

CHIEF OF THE DELAWARES.

A colored engraving depicts a chief from the Delaware tribe in the 1800s. © KEAN COLLECTION/STAFF/ARCHIVE PHOTOS/ GETTY IMAGES

Westward movements

When Indiana became a state in 1816, the citizens pressured the U.S. government to remove the tribes who were living there. Most of the Delaware moved to Missouri. A few Delaware remained in Sandusky, Ohio; another group, the Stockbridge, stayed in Indiana until 1834 and then moved to Wisconsin.

In Missouri, the Delaware faced raids by the Osage (see entry). As resources and hunting grounds became depleted, the government intervened to prevent war between the various groups. When a group of

Ohio Delaware joined them in 1829, the tribe moved to a reservation in Kansas. The land the government gave them was also owned by the Pawnee (see entry), so conflict arose between the two tribes as well as among the Plains Indians who hunted buffalo in the same territory.

About this time, the Kansas Delaware signed a treaty ceding (giving up) land that belonged to the Absentee Delaware who had moved to Texas. In 1854, the Absentee Delaware were moved onto a reservation with the Caddo (see entry), and in 1859, they were removed to Oklahoma, where they shared a reservation in Anadarko with the Caddo and Wichita (see entry). The Delaware were considered part of the Wichita band until federal recognition permitted them to operate as a separate, self-governing nation. This recognition also entitled them to government benefits and financial assistance.

Some Moravian Munsee migrated from Canada to Kansas. Although the Delaware assisted American explorers and served in the Union Army during the American Civil War (1861–65; a war between the Union [the North], which was opposed to slavery, and the Confederacy [the South], which was in favor of slavery), Kansas called for their removal in 1863. Most of the tribe agreed to relocate to Oklahoma; others joined the Ojibway (see entry) near Ottawa, Kansas.

Kansas Delaware join Cherokee

The Kansas Delaware now had no homeland, but they did have money from selling their property. In 1867, they signed an agreement with the Cherokee (see entry) to pay for Cherokee land in northern Oklahoma and become part of the Cherokee Nation. In 1904, though, the government ruled that the money the Delaware had paid only allowed them to use the land, not own it. In 1907, the U.S. government divided up the land, giving small parcels to each head of a household, and then sold the rest to settlers.

In 1979, the U.S. government ended the Delaware's legal status, saying the group was a part of the Cherokee Nation rather than a separate tribe. The Delaware challenged this decision, but it took until 1996 for the tribe to regain its federal recognition. The Cherokee Nation then challenged their claim, saying the Delaware had become part of its tribe when the Delaware moved onto the Oklahoma reservation and that a treaty gave the Cherokees the right to govern the Delaware. In 2004, the Cherokee won the case, and the Bureau of Indian Affairs withdrew the

Delaware's federal recognition, meaning that the tribe lost $7 million in government funding and is no longer recognized as a sovereign, or self-governing, nation (see "Current tribal issues").

RELIGION

The Delaware believe that the Creator made a huge turtle, big enough to carry the world. After the turtle surfaced and the mud on its back dried, a cedar tree grew from the dirt in the center of its back. Then man was created. Where the top of the tree bent and touched the earth, woman was created. These two people became the parents of all living beings. Because the turtle and the cedar tree had a part in creation, the tribe honored them as the Creator's helpers.

Some people believe that the *Wallam Olum* are the Delaware people's sacred writings. The *Wallam Olum* consisted of wooden sticks with pictographs on them. These sticks are sometimes called "Painted Tally," "Red Record," or "Red Score." The pictures tell Delaware history and creation stories, which seem to be genuine, and the Delaware did write on birchbark or wood at that time. Much controversy has surrounded the publication of the *Wallam Olum,* however. It was published in 1836 by a white man, Constantine Rafinesque (1783–1840), who claimed his friend, Dr. Ward, had received the sticks from the Delaware in Indiana. Many scholars debate whether Rafinesque's story was true, and the sticks have since disappeared, so there is no way to examine them to find out.

During the sixteenth and seventeenth centuries, missionaries arrived to preach to the Delaware. Under their influence, many were baptized. Some truly converted to Christianity; others were only being polite to the newcomers or felt coerced. One of the main groups to work among the tribe was the Moravians. A large settlement of Delaware became Moravians; many of them were massacred in 1782. A chief in the 1800s, Neshapanacumin (also called Charles Journeycake; 1817–1894), whose mother interpreted for the Methodist missionaries, became a Christian preacher.

Although many Delaware accepted Christianity, several Native prophets warned them to return to their traditional religion. One of the most influential was Neolin, known as the Delaware Prophet. In the late 1700s, he traveled among the tribes in the Lake Erie area to preach the message he had received from the Great Spirit. He carried a deerskin map showing the land the people had lost to settlers, and he begged the tribes to give up white beliefs and customs, especially drinking alcohol.

Delaware Words

alëm	"dog"
kišux	"sun"
lënu	"man"
màxke	"red"
mpi	"water"
naxkohoman	"sings"
pëntamën	"hears"
wanishi	"thank you"
xkwe	"woman"

His message encouraged other tribes to unite with Ottawa chief Pontiac (c. 1720–1769), who had organized a Native American alliance to drive the British off Native lands.

LANGUAGE

The Algonquian language spoken by the Delaware had three dialects (varieties of a language): Munsee, Unami, and Unalactigo. Unami and Unalactigo were spoken in Pennsylvania, Delaware, and New Jersey at one time, but there are no fluent speakers left. Southern Delaware, or Nanticoke, has not been spoken since the mid-1800s. The Delaware want to revive their language, but because it is not still in use, language specialists are combining Unami with Munsee. Some Canadian elders still speak Munsee. This dialect is so different from the other two, though, that most Delawares could not understand it. Munsee is actually similar to Mahican.

GOVERNMENT

Clans were an important part of Delaware life; most longhouses in a village belonged to the same clan. Each clan had two leaders: the clan chief took charge of the community life, and the clan captain led the tribe in battle. Although women did not speak in public or become chiefs, they decided on the leaders. If they did not feel a chief was doing a good job, they could choose someone else to take his place.

When the Delaware lived in their original homelands, the clans operated independently. Not until they reached Ohio in the 1740s did they unify under a central government. There they formed a tribal council composed of three captains, one from each of the clans (Wolf, Turkey, and Turtle). The captains inherited their positions, but the tribe had to confirm the selection. Usually the head chief, or captain, of the tribal council came from the Turtle clan. The people chose their war captains based on their skill in battle.

In the early 2000s, an executive committee made tribal decisions. A president, vice president, secretary, treasurer, and two committee members served staggered four-year terms. In addition, the tribe had several government departments to deal with social services, taxes, transportation, the environment, and business.

ECONOMY

The Delaware were hunter-gatherers, but they also farmed. After the arrival of the Europeans, they engaged in the fur trade. Not believing that land should be bought or sold, the Delaware shared their homeland with early settlers. Within a short time, they lost most of their property and moved west. Since 1867, they have shared reservations with other tribes.

Today, some Delaware raise livestock and others farm. The tribe's main sources of income, though, come from tribal government, federal funding, and tourism. The Delaware Nation operates the Gold River Bingo and Casino in Anadarko, Oklahoma, as well as a museum. The National Hall of Fame for American Indians is located nearby along with camping and water sports for tourists.

The tribe has joined the Four Tribes Consortium of Oklahoma, a group that provides job training and opportunities, and the tribal government offers a vocational rehabilitation program. The Wichita (see entry) and Caddo tribes share land and a company with the Delaware to promote business development in the area. In spite of these efforts, many tribe members have difficulty finding work.

DAILY LIFE

Families

The Delaware have three main clans: Turkey, Wolf, and Turtle. Children take on their mother's clan. (A clan is a group of people related to one common ancestor.) In the past, all the women of a family lived together in the same longhouse. When a man married, he moved into his wife's longhouse. Children belonged to the mother; their father was not considered a close relative.

Buildings

The tribe built frames for their longhouses by bending saplings into an arched shape. They tied these together with poles running lengthwise. Then they covered the sides of their homes with bark and left the ends open as doors. Animal skins were hung over these doorways to close them.

Pleiades: Bunched Up Stars

Many people see stories in the stars. The Delaware look at the constellation we call the Big Dipper and see a bear. The Northern Crown is its head. The small cluster of stars nearby, Pleiades, is his den. This Delaware tale explains how that group of stars ended up together in the sky.

> Because so many people came to a group of holy men for assistance, the prophets changed themselves into seven stones. Still the people came, and they changed themselves into beautiful pine trees, though some appeared as cedars. [Cedars, to the Delaware, are holy trees.] But still the people came. At last the prophets changed themselves into seven stars that move around in the sky during the year. They became the Bunched Up Stars, Pleiades.

SOURCE: Miller, Dorcas S. *Stars of the First People*. Boulder, CO: Pruett Publishing Company, 1997.

Because the homes were so long, many families could live in them. Families who lived opposite each other had their own compartments for sleeping but shared a central fire, so a row of fires lined the center of the longhouse, and a smoke hole 1 foot wide (0.3 meters wide) ran the length of the roof. Longhouses could be more than 100 feet (30 meters) in length, but an average 60-foot-long (18-meters-long) dwelling housed about twenty people from seven or eight different families.

During times of war, the tribe constructed their longhouses on a hill and surrounded them with stockades (fences made of posts). Villages contained a sweathouse to purify the body and cure diseases. The most important building in each village was the Big House. Its roof symbolized the sky; the floor represented the earth. In the center, a post with a face carved into it represented the staff of the Great Manitou. Door openings faced east and west. The western door stood for the afterlife because it looked toward the setting sun. The opposite door opened toward the rising sun. Between the two doors, a path represented the life cycle from birth to death. This building was the site of the Big House ceremony (see "Festivals").

After 1763, some Delaware paid whites to build them log cabins; others had learned to do it themselves. By the 1850s, the majority of the Delaware houses in Kansas were log. The chief's house had a stone fireplace, a staircase, and board floors. Early cabins had only raised platforms for sleeping, but by the beginning of the 1900s, most had furniture.

Transportation

Throughout their history, the Delaware lived near water, and they gained a reputation for their boat-building abilities. They made dugout canoes by burning out the center of split tree trunks. These canoes were heavy, so the men also made smaller, lightweight kayaks or canoes from birch or elm bark. Women helped by sewing the bark. Birchbark canoes were easy to carry but capable of transporting heavy loads.

Clothing and adornment

Men wore breechcloths (apronlike pieces of fabric attached at the waist), whereas women wrapped pieces of deerskin around their waists. Both wore leather or snakeskin belts decorated with wampum. They wrapped long blankets around their shoulders or knotted them around their necks; these also served as bedding. In winter the blankets were made of fur. Some Delaware wore cloaks of turkey feathers. Leggings and snowshoes were useful in winter. Men wore bandolier bags that had a beaded strap that crossed their chests. (Bandolier bags are elaborately decorated shoulder bags.) Moccasins made of deer or moose skin had ankle flaps and were tied on with thongs.

Men wore headbands of snakeskin with a few feathers or a circle of feathers on their heads. Roaches (headpieces of dyed deer hair) were popular. Older men wore their hair long and loose, whereas warriors shaved their heads, except for a scalplock, which they sometimes greased to make it stand up straight. Men plucked out their chin hairs with a hinged mussel shell. Women braided their hair in back and sometimes tucked the plaits into a square pouch decorated with wampum. Both sexes used animal grease to keep warm, to avoid bug bites and sunburn, and to keep their hair in place.

Men had pierced ears and silver nose rings. Later, men and women used copper for armbands and ornaments. They decorated their clothing with shells, beads, and porcupine quills. Men and women often had animal tattoos. They painted their faces and bodies with white, red, or yellow clay, or black shale. Women used red on their eyelids, on the rims of their ears, and to make a circle on each cheek. Both sexes painted the parts in their hair.

Many Delaware eventually adopted European dress. Men wore cotton or linen shirts with their breechcloths and leggings. Women wore blouses with large circular yokes. They covered them with small, round, silver brooches. They also decorated their clothes with ribbon work and beading.

Food

Each fall, the tribe burned sites for farming and trails for hunting game. The Delaware used circles of fire or natural barriers like rivers to channel game into a narrow area that made hunting easier. Deer were their main source of meat. They supplemented that with bear, wolf, raccoon, weasel, otter, turkey, and pigeon. They later added moose to their diet. They boiled their meat or roasted it on sticks set next to the fire.

The Delaware used nets or weirs (small fences of sticks in a stream) to catch fish. Their diet also included shellfish, which they preserved by drying it in the sun. Roots, berries, greens, and nuts came from the wild. The tribe grew corn, beans, and squash.

They preserved corn by scraping it from the cob with a deer or buffalo jawbone and sun-drying it. They also roasted green ears and shelled the kernels. Dried corn could be ground into meal, boiled in water, or pounded and cooked with liquid to make mush. Most people ate cornmeal mush daily; sometimes they mixed it with beans or fish. To make bread, the women wrapped ground cornmeal batter in husks and baked it in the ashes of the fire. For sweets, they added berries to the food, or people sucked on cornstalks.

Education

A woman's brothers trained her children. Uncles were considered closer relatives than the children's father. A man took care of his sister's children, but not his own. Children learned from their elders. Boys were trained to hunt, and before guns were readily available, they were taught flint knapping to make arrowheads and knives out of stone. Girls learned to cook, decorate clothing with dyed porcupine quills, make pottery, and tend babies.

Young boys learned to fast (go without eating) and pray to the spirits of the earth and sky. These spirits gave them power. Girls also fasted. The Delaware believed a spirit came in a vision and gave each person a special song. To gain their spirit's help, children only needed to sing their songs.

Healing practices

Most Delaware healers were women, but a man sometimes became a medicine person after having a vision. Healers had an extensive knowledge of herbs. They selected only the best and healthiest bark, roots, and plants for cures. Because it received the morning sun, bark from the east side of the tree was deemed life-giving. Before harvesting herbs, the medicine person dug a hole on the east side of the plant, put tobacco in the ground, and said a prayer to appease the spirit of the plant.

Some healers used herbs and medicine to treat the sick. Other doctors used sweathouse rituals to cure illness. Before performing a cure, a healer might crush some herbs or leaves in running water. If the leaves sank, it meant the patient would die. If they floated, the patient would recover.

In the early 2000s, the Delaware received services at the Indian Health Service Hospital in Anadarko, which provided outpatient services, dental care, and community outreach programs.

ARTS

Some early Delaware crafts included stone- and bone-working, shell-tempered pottery, and porcupine quill embroidery. They also sewed cornhusk mats. After the Europeans arrived, they taught the Delaware to make splint baskets and silver jewelry. The people made silver buckles, pins, and hair combs. By the early 1900s, many of the crafts had died out. Some Canadian Munsees continued to do woodworking, basket weaving, and beadwork.

CUSTOMS

Birth and naming

Babies were born in a special hut away from the other houses. Mothers washed their newborns in cold water and then tied them to a cradleboard. The cradleboard hung on the mother's back, and a strap on her forehead helped support its weight. After a year, when the baby grew too large for the cradleboard, the mother carried the child in a sling made of animal skin or cloth. Each boy had a tattoo of his mother's clan on his chest.

Puberty

When a girl began menstruating, she stayed in a separate hut until she had her second menses. During her stay in the hut, she kept a blanket over her head and did not touch her hair or any food or dishes. She ate with a stick and drank from her hands. (All women followed these practices monthly.) Afterward, she donned a special headdress and wore wampum to show she was ready for marriage.

Marriage

Marriages might be prearranged. A man would give wampum to his future bride or her family, after which the couple had a yearlong engagement. Sometimes a wedding feast was held, but couples had no wedding ceremony. Most Delaware stayed with one partner, and adultery was cause for public shaming. Divorces were easy and occurred frequently; the partners only had to agree to it and walk away.

Festivals

The most important ceremony for the Delaware was Ga'mwin, meaning "Big House." Usually a male took charge and chose three male helpers, who selected three female helpers. They called the tribe together; following prayers, the leader told them his vision, and others could also tell theirs. After praying to Misinghalikun, the guardian of game, a hunting party set out to kill deer. The carcasses were hung in the Big House, or temple, and eaten during the feasting that followed each night of dancing, singing, and sharing visions. After nine days, the people relit the sacred fire. On the twelfth night, women who shared their visions received venison.

In the Grease-Drinking Festival, either a bear or a hog was killed. After it was eaten, the Delaware drank some of the grease and threw some in the fire. During Doll Dances, first the men and then the women danced around the fire singing special songs, carrying a doll dressed as a woman or a man on a stick.

The Delaware also celebrated corn planting and harvest with special celebrations. Most ceremonies were either feasts or a gathering where people shared their visions. Singing and dancing often played a part in most ceremonies. After the Christian influence, many of the rituals changed and became more sedate.

War etiquette

Men preferred fighting at night and liked to use deception to defeat their enemies. Before they began a battle, they isolated women and children on an island or in a swamp to prevent them from being taken as prisoners of war. Warriors painted their faces, and they wore red turkey feathers in their headbands or tied foxtails or wolves' tails upright on their heads.

The Delaware scalped those they killed in battle. When they captured other tribes, they either tortured and executed their prisoners or adopted them to replace slain relatives. If a Delaware warrior was tortured by another tribe, he would sing until he died.

Death rituals

Burial occurred a few days after death. The Delaware usually dug pit-graves and buried the body in a sitting position. They placed tools, food, and wampum beside the corpse before covering it with dirt and stones. A fence enclosed the grave; a post pictured the dead man's deeds.

Sometimes they used a cemetery; other times they chose an isolated place to bury the body. Every year the family visited the spot to tend it.

While in mourning, relatives painted their faces black. Husbands and wives mourned for a year. If her spouse died, a woman might show her grief by crawling around the grave every day while she wept. Women also burned their hair on the graves of children or war victims. No one mentioned the dead person's name again. A man who lost his wife paid her parents when he wanted to remarry.

The Delaware believed the souls of the dead went west or south, where hunting would be good. Although they believed in an afterlife, most Delaware (even those who converted to Christianity) did not believe in heaven and hell.

By the 1800s, many Delaware had adopted some European burial customs. They spent the night at a wake. (A wake is a watch over the body the night before burial.) The next morning, they fired guns to the east. They used coffins and placed a post to mark a man's grave and a cross to mark a woman's. A feast followed the burial. Four days after that (and for the next four years), they made a special meal for someone who was younger than the deceased but of the same gender.

CURRENT TRIBAL ISSUES

Along with many other smaller Delaware tribes, the Delaware Tribe of Indians in Bartlesville, Oklahoma, is engaged in a struggle for federal recognition. In 1996, it was federally recognized, but it lost this status in 2004 after losing a court case to the Cherokee. The Cherokee insisted that the Delaware had given up their identity and become members of the Cherokee Nation. Although the Delaware paid the Cherokee for land and asked to be a part of the nation more than one hundred years ago, the Delaware believe they have kept their own identity as a tribe. Loss of federal recognition meant they were no longer eligible for government benefits and funding, nor were they able to function as a separate nation. In 2008, the Delaware settled their differences with the Cherokee Nation. They then reorganized and reapplied for recognition. In July 2009, the Bureau of Indian Affairs restored the Delaware Nation's federal recognition.

The Delaware Nation has programs in place to help the tribe. They have an economic development program to improve roads, establish new businesses, build housing for seniors, write grants for additional funding, develop casinos, and provide assistance for entrepreneurs. They also work to protect their heritage by gathering remains and artifacts, teaching language and crafts classes, and maintaining the Delaware Nation Museum and Library. Ongoing health concerns include diabetes, lupus, and arthritis—diseases that affect many Native Americans.

NOTABLE PEOPLE

Tamanend, or Tammany (c. 1628–1698), a chief of the Delaware when they lived in the Delaware Valley, was known as a peacemaker. He signed a treaty with William Penn (see "History"). At a meeting of Delaware and the leaders of the Pennsylvania colony, he declared that his people and the colonists would "live in peace as long as the waters run in the rivers and creeks and as long as the stars and moon endure." His words are recorded on a statue of him that stands in Philadelphia.

Shingas, an eighteenth-century war leader in the Turkey clan, was called "king" by the Americans who dealt with him. He was known as a fierce fighter and led many raids against the colonists in Pennsylvania and Virginia. When his village was destroyed, he and his people moved west into Ohio. His brother, Tamaqua, counseled him to make peace. Called "The Beaver" or "King Beaver," Tamaqua soon gained greater power and influence than his brother.

Lewis Ketchum, late chief of the Delaware Tribe of Indians in Bartlesville, Oklahoma, began Red Man Pipe and Supply Company in 1977 with a small business loan. Over the years, he opened many stores and bought other companies to build a multimillion-dollar business. In the early 2000s, the Ketchum family set up scholarships in his honor at Oklahoma State University.

BOOKS

Adams, Richard C. *A Delaware Indian Legend and the Story of Their Troubles.* Whitefish, MT: Kessinger Publishing, LLC, 2006.

Bial, Raymond. *The Delaware.* New York: Benchmark Books, 2006.

Brown, James W., and Rita T. Kohn, ed. *Long Journey Home: Oral Histories of Contemporary Delaware Indians.* Bloomington: Indiana University Press, 2008.

Fur, Gunlög. *A Nation of Women: Gender and Colonial Encounters among the Delaware Indians.* Philadelphia: University of Pennsylvania Press, 2009.

Gibson, Karen Bush. *New Netherland: The Dutch Settle the Hudson Valley.* Elkton, IN: Mitchell Lane Publishers, 2006.

Gipson, Lawrence Henry. *The Moravian Indian Mission on White River: Diaries and Letters, May 5, 1799, to November 12, 1806.* Indianapolis: Indiana Historical Bureau, 1938.

Harper, Steven Craig. *Promised Land: Penn's Holy Experiment, the Walking Purchase, and the Dispossession of Delawares, 1600–1763.* Bethlehem, PA: Lehigh University Press, 2006.

Hearth, Amy Hill. *"Strong Medicine Speaks": A Native American Elder Has Her Say: An Oral History.* New York: Atria Books, 2008.

Kraft, Herbert C. *The Lenape-Delaware Indian Heritage, 10,000 BC to AD 2000.* Union, NJ: Lenapebooks, 2001.

Levine, Michelle. *The Delaware.* Minneapolis, MN: Lerner Publications, 2006.

McCutchen, David. *The Red Record: The Wallum Olum.* Garden City Park, NY: Avery Publishing Group, Inc., 1993.

Myers, Albert Cook, ed. *William Penn's Own Account of the Lenni Lenape or Delaware Indians.* Somerset, NJ: Middle Atlantic Press, 1970.

Obermeyer, Brice. *Delaware Tribe in a Cherokee Nation.* Lincoln: University of Nebraska Press, 2009.

Schutt, Amy C. *Peoples of the River Valleys: The Odyssey of the Delaware Indians.* Philadelphia: University of Pennsylvania Press, 2007.

Tantaquidgeon, Gladys. *Folk Medicine of the Delaware and Related Algonkian Indians.* Harrisburg, PA: The Pennsylvania Historical Museum Commission, 1977.

WEB SITES

"Delaware Indian Chiefs." *Access Genealogy.* http://www.accessgenealogy.com/native/tribes/delaware/delawarechiefs.htm (accessed on June 8, 2011).

DelawareIndian.com. http://www.delawareindian.com/ (accessed on June 2, 2011).

"Delaware Indian/Lenni Lenape." *Delaware Indians of Pennsylvania.* http://www.delawareindians.com/ (accessed on June 8, 2011).

"Delaware Indians." *Ohio Historical Society.* http://www.ohiohistorycentral.org/entry.php?rec=584 (accessed on June 2, 2011).

The Delaware Nation. http://www.delawarenation.com/ (accessed on June 2, 2011).

Delaware Tribe of Indians. http://www.delawaretribeofindians.nsn.us/ (accessed on June 2, 2011).

"Native American Varieties of Moccasins: Lenape." *NativeTech: Native American Technology and Art.* http://www.nativetech.org/clothing/moccasin/detail/lenape.html (accessed on June 2, 2011).

Redish, Laura, and Orrin Lewis. "Lenape Culture and History." *Native American Language Net: Preserving and Promoting Indigenous American Indian Languages.* http://www.native-languages.org/lenape_culture.htm (accessed on June 2, 2011).

Iroquois Confederacy (Haudenosaunee Nation)

For more information on an individual tribe within the Iroquois Confederacy, please see the Mohawk entry.

Name

Iroquois (pronounced *EAR-uh-kwoy*) Confederacy. The Iroquois call themselves *Haudenosaunee* (pronounced *hoo-dee-noh-SHAW-nee*), meaning "people of the longhouse," or as they prefer to translate it, "they made the house." To the confederacy, this means that all nations are uniting as one. The nations that were members of the Iroquois Confederacy, now known as the Haudenosaunee Confederacy, thought of themselves as forming a longhouse (the typical Iroquois dwelling), with the different tribes at important corners of the jointly run central building. Another name the Six Nations call themselves is *Ongwehonweh,* meaning "original people" or "first people."

Location

Most of the nations of the Iroquois Confederacy originally lived in western-central New York, with the exception of the Tuscarora, who came from North Carolina. The various nations now have reservations in New York and Wisconsin, and reserves in Ontario, Canada, but some make their homes off reservation in different areas of the country. Bands also can be found in Oklahoma and near Montreal, Quebec, Canada, along the St. Lawrence River.

Population

There were 5,500 Iroquois in the seventeenth century. In the 1990 U.S. Census, 52,557 people said they were members of Iroquois tribes, making the Iroquois the country's seventh-largest Native group. In 1995, U.S. and Canadian census figures reported 74,518 Iroquois in the two countries. The 2000 census showed that 45,212 people identified themselves as Iroquois only, whereas 80,822 claimed some Iroquois heritage. The population of registered Iroquois both on and off the Canadian reserves in 2007 was 32,637.

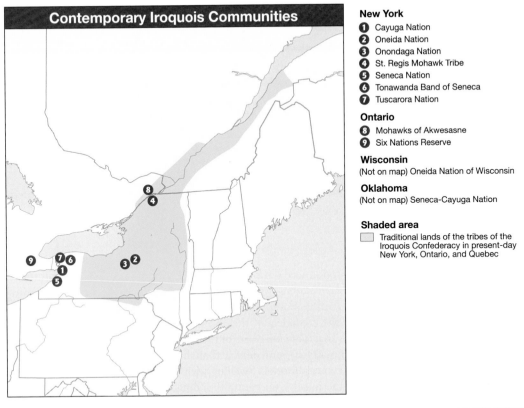

Contemporary Iroquois Communities

New York
1. Cayuga Nation
2. Oneida Nation
3. Onondaga Nation
4. St. Regis Mohawk Tribe
5. Seneca Nation
6. Tonawanda Band of Seneca
7. Tuscarora Nation

Ontario
8. Mohawks of Akwesasne
9. Six Nations Reserve

Wisconsin
(Not on map) Oneida Nation of Wisconsin

Oklahoma
(Not on map) Seneca-Cayuga Nation

Shaded area
Traditional lands of the tribes of the Iroquois Confederacy in present-day New York, Ontario, and Quebec

A map of contemporary Iroquois communities. MAP BY XNR PRODUCTIONS. CENGAGE LEARNING, GALE. REPRODUCED BY PERMISSION OF GALE, A PART OF CENGAGE LEARNING.

In 2010, the census counted 40,570 Iroquois in the United States, with a total of 81,002 people claiming some Iroquois heritage.

Language family

Iroquoian.

Origins and group affiliations

The six original tribes of the Iroquois Confederacy were the Cayuga, Mohawk, Oneida, Onondaga, Seneca, and Tuscarora. The Iroquois had many enemies, particularly during the fur-trapping era, as they drove other tribes from the region. The French allied with the Huron (see Wyandot entry), Ottawa (see entry), and other tribes against the Iroquois. In the 2000s, the confederacy expanded to form the Haudenosaunee League of Nations. The league includes the Delaware (see entry), Wyendot (Wyandot), and the Tutela nations.

The Iroquois Confederacy was an association of five (later six) tribes who lived in the northeastern woodlands at the time of their first contact with Europeans. Theirs was a sophisticated society of some 5,500 people when the explorers first encountered it at the beginning of the seventeenth century. The confederacy is said to be the only nation of Natives in the New World that was never conquered by the Europeans.

HISTORY

Legends of heroes

According to oral history, the Iroquois Confederacy formed sometime between the years 1350 and 1600. Accounts differ as to what people and events brought about the peaceful union of the great tribes of the Haudenosaunee.

One story indicates that the Mohawk, Onondaga, Seneca, Cayuga, and Oneida nations were engaged in near-constant warfare with one another and with neighboring tribes. This period, known as the "dark times," reached its lowest point during the reign of an Onondaga chief named Todadaho. People said that Chief Todadaho knew and saw everything, that his hair contained a tangle of snakes, and that he could kill with only a look. He was also reported to be a cannibal.

Into this warlike era entered a heroic figure that the Iroquois call the Peacemaker. Frustrated with the warring going on in his village, the Peacemaker journeyed far from home. He met Hiawatha (also called Aionwatha; of either the Mohawk or Onondaga tribes), and Hiawatha spoke to him about rules of life, good government, and peace. Impressed, the Peacemaker brought Hiawatha back to his own village to teach his people these rules. The two men travelled to other nations, and the Mohawk, Oneida, and Cayuga nations were soon united, persuaded by these messengers of peace. One day, they came upon the home of Todadaho.

Todadaho sees the light

According to one account, the Peacemaker watched through a hole in the roof as Todadaho prepared to cook his latest victim. Seeing the Peacemaker's face reflected in the cooking pot, Todadaho felt that, as a man with such a beautiful face, he no longer wanted to eat his victim. Going outside to dispose of the corpse, he met the Peacemaker. The stranger's words were so convincing that Todadaho became a loyal follower and

Important Dates

c. 1350–c. 1600: The Iroquois Confederacy is formed.

1799: Handsome Lake develops the New Religion.

1831: Some Seneca and Cayuga move to Indian Territory (now Oklahoma) as part of the U.S. government's plan to move Native Americans westward. Other Iroquois groups stand firm until the government's policy is overturned in 1842.

1924: Congress passes legislation conferring U.S. citizenship on all American Indians. The Iroquois reject citizenship.

1942: As hostilities leading to World War II grow, the Iroquois exercise their powers as an independent nation to declare war on Germany, Italy, and Japan.

1995: The Iroquois request that all sacred masks and remains of their dead be returned to the tribe; the Smithsonian Institution is the first museum to comply with this request.

2000s: The Haudenosaunee Confederacy expands to include the Wyendot (Wyandot), Delaware, and Tutela.

helped spread the message of peace. In another story, when Todadaho encountered the two messengers, his rage sprouted from his head in the form of serpents. The Peacemaker (or Hiawatha) asked the chief to join the confederacy and then reached forward and combed the serpents from his head. In both versions, the Onondaga chief agreed to join the union.

Ultimately, the Peacemaker and Hiawatha made peace among the five warring tribes and established the Iroquois Confederacy ruled by the Great Law. The five tribes shared a code of positive values and lived in mutual harmony. The Grand Council of Chiefs made up the governmental structure of the Iroquois Confederacy. The council included the Chief of the Chiefs and forty-nine other chiefs: nine chiefs from the Mohawk, fourteen from the Onondaga, ten from the Cayuga, nine from the Oneida, and eight from the Seneca. The Great Law also established rules for settling blood disputes, thus gradually resolving some generations-old cycles of feuding.

Europeans affect Iroquois way of life

When the first white explorers arrived in Iroquois territory in the early seventeenth century, they found a settled agricultural (farming) society. Members of the confederacy lived more or less peacefully among themselves but continued to carry out raids against other tribes. During these raids, the Iroquois saw the European goods that other tribes had acquired from French traders who had settled in Canada. European metal axes, knives, hoes, and kettles soon replaced traditional Iroquois implements of stone, bone, shell, and wood. The Iroquois also substituted European woven cloth for the animal skins they used for clothing.

The tribes raided by the Iroquois formed an alliance with French explorer Samuel de Champlain (c. 1567–1635) and attacked the Iroquois at Ticonderoga in 1609. In this way, the Iroquois were introduced to French body armor made of metal. (Iroquois armor was made of slatted wood.) The French fought with firearms, which were far more destructive than the traditional Iroquois weapons—bows and arrows, stone tomahawks, and wooden war clubs.

In response to these European influences, the Iroquois gradually changed their fighting style. Instead of brute power, they used stealth, surprise, and ambush. Their motives for fighting also changed. In the past, they had fought for prestige or revenge, or to obtain goods and captives. They now fought for economic advantage, seeking control over bountiful beaver-hunting grounds or for a stash of beaver skins to trade for European goods.

The European presence in their territory proved disastrous for the Iroquois tribes. Diseases brought to North America by Europeans—smallpox, measles, influenza (flu), lung infections, and even the common cold—took a heavy toll because the Native people had developed no immunity to these newly introduced diseases.

Sixth tribe joins Iroquois Confederacy

Early in the eighteenth century, the Tuscarora, an Iroquoian-speaking tribe living in North Carolina, moved into the territory occupied by the confederacy. They were fleeing from European settlers and traders, who had cheated them and taken their people as slaves. Although they came from far away, the Tuscarora found they spoke the same basic language as the other Iroquois. In 1722, the Tuscarora became the sixth nation of the Iroquois Confederacy.

The eighteenth century saw the Iroquois involved in two devastating wars. The French and Indian War (1754–63) pitted the French and some Native tribes against the British. The American Revolution (1775–83) was the American colonists' fight for independence from England. Members of the Iroquois Confederacy disagreed on which sides to support during these wars. Most favored the British, seeing them as a lesser threat than the colonists who coveted Iroquois lands. When the American Revolution ended in 1783, the victorious Americans punished any tribes who had sided with the British. Many Iroquois were driven from their homelands, and this badly disrupted the unity of the confederacy.

Cultures clash

Major changes in Iroquois culture took place in the 1800s. Alarmed that traditional Iroquois ways were giving way to European culture, many Iroquois turned to a religious movement called the New Religion (see "The New Religion"). It put new vitality into Iroquois culture, which was severely strained by white settlers pushing westward onto Native American lands.

To make way for settlers, the U.S. government began a program of assimilation, requiring tribes to give up their old ways and adopt American ways, including farming small plots of land rather than working the land in common. To further the goal of assimilation, members of the Quaker religion arrived to teach the Iroquois to read and write and to instruct them in modern farming methods. Men were encouraged to work on farms. Respected Seneca warrior Gaiantwaka (known as Cornplanter; 1750–1836), helped bring about the change to a farming lifestyle, as did his half-brother Ganiodayo (Handsome Lake; 1735–1815).

Throughout the nineteenth century, the Iroquois sold large amounts of land in exchange for goods. Shrinking land holdings made hunting increasingly difficult and left the men with little to do. Many men did not want to be seen doing the "women's work" of farming, but, encouraged by Quakers, an increasing number of Iroquois families left the longhouses and lived separately on small farms where the men could work in their fields unseen by their neighbors.

The Iroquois resist

In 1830, the U.S. Congress passed the Removal Act, which directed that all Native Americans should be moved to "Indian Territory" in present-day Kansas and Oklahoma. In 1831, some Seneca did move to Indian Territory, but a core group of the Iroquois people continued to resist efforts to assimilate them into American culture or remove them from their homelands. When the removal policy was overturned in 1842, ownership of some Seneca land was restored.

In 1924, Congress passed legislation granting U.S. citizenship to all American Indians; the Iroquois rejected such status. They remained a sovereign nation with the right to make their own decisions. They do not see themselves as another ethnic group within the United States or Canadian population. (In fact, federal law and more than four hundred treaties grant U.S. Indian tribes the power to act as independent nations.) The Iroquois have asserted their position in interesting ways. For example, when the United States declared war on Germany in World War I (1914–18; a war in which Great Britain, France, the United States, and their allies defeated Germany, Austria-Hungary, and their allies), the Iroquois

Confederacy issued its own independent declaration of war, claiming status as a separate nation in the war effort. In 1949, a delegation representing the Iroquois as a nation attended ground-breaking ceremonies for the United Nations building in New York City. Iroquois political leaders and athletes use Iroquois passports when they travel around the world.

Canada's Iroquois today

The Iroquois in Canada published a Declaration of Independence in 1970. They were responding to efforts by the Canadian government to force First Nations to become Canadian citizens, which would make them subject to Canadian laws and make their lands subject to taxes. The declaration stated in part:

> We, the Lords, Warriors, Principal Women and People, do hereby proclaim to the Dominion of Canada and to the Nations of the World, that we, the People of the Six Nations Iroquois Confederacy of the Great League of Peace … [are] politically sovereign and independent in our rights to administer over our domestic concerns.… We are obliged by conscience to declare and proclaim the right and responsibility of our authority for our lands, our laws and our people.

Canada's Minister of Indian Affairs rejected the Iroquois claim of sovereignty. He stated: "It is impossible to have a nation within a nation. Our nation is Canada and the Indian people of Canada are Canadians." The Iroquois disagree and feel, as the *Mohawk Nation News* declared when explaining why Canadian laws should not apply to the First Nations, that "Canadians don't let Americans apply their law in Canada. Why should they expect us to apply their laws … in our territory?" These opposing viewpoints continue to cause problems between the Iroquois people and the government of Canada.

Preservation of traditional values and artifacts

Much of the longstanding friction between the Iroquois and non-Natives has involved differing attitudes toward land. During one land dispute, the grave of Seneca Chief Cornplanter had to be moved to make way for a dam. His descendant, Harriett Pierce, commented: "The White man views land for its money value. We Indians have a spiritual tie with the earth, a reverence for it that Whites don't share and can hardly understand."

For decades, the Iroquois have worked to reclaim articles they consider sacred as well as the remains of dead ancestors held by museums.

In 1972, archaeologists were ordered to stop digging up Native burial sites in New York State. Tribal members were notified to arrange proper reburials for any remains unearthed accidentally. Wampum belts (embroidered belts made from strings of beads) held by the New York State Museum in Albany were removed from public display after Native Americans complained that they were being treated as curiosities, without proper respect being paid. The belts were finally returned to the Onondaga in 1989. Years of effort were rewarded in the early 1990s when the Smithsonian Institution in Washington, D.C., pledged to return human remains, objects buried with them, sacred objects, and other articles of importance to all the tribes. With the passage of the American Indian Museum Act (1989) and an amendment (1996), other museums have since followed the Smithsonian's lead and are now returning these items.

Traditional values are sustained on the various Iroquois reservations. People speak and teach their languages, perform their duties, and weave baskets. Material wealth is not characteristic of reservation life, but Tonawanda Seneca Chief Corbett Sundown, keeper of the Iroquois "spiritual fire," denies that the people are poor. He told *National Geographic* writer Arden Harvey: "We're rich people without any money, that's all. You say we ought to set up industries and factories. Well, we just don't want them. How're you going to grow potatoes and sweet corn on concrete? You call that progress? To me 'progress' is a dirty word." The Haudenosaunee have their own definitions of progress as they move through the first decades of the twenty-first century.

RELIGION

From ancient times, the Iroquois believed that a powerful spirit some called *Orenda* created everything that is good and useful, while the Evil Spirit made things that are poisonous.

French Jesuit missionaries converted many Iroquois to Catholicism in the seventeenth century. Quaker, Baptist, Methodist, and other church groups joined the effort to convert the Iroquois. An intense rivalry developed between the new Christian factions and those who clung to the old ways.

The New Religion

In 1799, the Iroquois way of life was eroding. They had lost their land, and living conditions on the reservations were poor. Problems developed with alcohol abuse, fighting, disintegration of family structure, and other hardships. At this time, a revival of the ancient Longhouse religion developed. It was led by a Seneca known as Handsome Lake (1735–1815). After many years of hard living, he fell gravely ill when he was about sixty-five years old. He expected to die, but instead he experienced a vision and recovered. Inspired, Handsome Lake began to spread the Good Word among his fellow Iroquois. His New Religion was a combination of ancient Native beliefs and Quakerism.

The New Religion called for abstaining from alcoholic beverages. (Europeans had introduced alcohol, which had become a problem for many tribes.) The New Religion also called for abandoning witchcraft. The fact that Handsome Lake's message had come in a dream made a profound impression on his followers, because the Iroquois believed that important information was revealed to people in dreams. Handsome Lake's religion showed the Iroquois how to retain their own culture while adapting to a world dominated by non-Natives.

The Code of Handsome Lake was published about 1850 and was revered throughout Iroquois nations in Canada and the United States. The Longhouse religion is practiced only by Iroquois nations. Today perhaps half of the Iroquois people are followers of the Code of Handsome Lake. Some practice only the Longhouse religion, while others maintain a simultaneous membership in a Christian church. Every other fall, members of the Six Nations come together for a traditional Longhouse religion ceremony.

LANGUAGE

The six Iroquoian dialects (varieties of a language) are similar enough to allow members of different tribes to talk easily with one another. In the Iroquois language, many terms describe characteristics of a single animal, but there is no general word for animal. There are also words for "good man," "good woman," or "good dog," but no word for "goodness."

The Iroquois language was written down in the twentieth century. Dictionaries and grammar texts have been developed for teaching the languages on the reservations.

GOVERNMENT

The Iroquois tribes were divided into clans (group of people related by a common ancestor), each with an animal name (Bear, Beaver, Turtle, and so on). In early times, the clan mother, who was usually the oldest woman in the group, led each clan. In consultation with the other women, the clan mother chose one or more men to serve as clan chiefs. The word that is actually used for *chief* in the original language means "caretaker of the peace." The chief was to serve as the "voice" of the clan. Each chief was appointed for life, but the clan mother and her advisors could remove him from office if he failed to carry out his duties. Handsome Lake and his followers revived this traditional system of chieftainship, and today it is present on the Onondaga, Tuscarora, and Tonawanda Seneca reservations in New York.

Under the Iroquois Confederacy, chiefs from the various tribes were chosen to act as tribal representatives at annual meetings of the Great Council. (This method of governing, as well as Iroquois ideas of political equality and freedom, separation of powers, and checks and balances between different parts of government, was used as a model by the founders of the United States when they were forming a government for the new nation.) All decisions of the confederacy were made by a unanimous vote of the chiefs, meaning they all had to vote the same way. If they did not reach unanimous decision, then they agreed to disagree, and the individual nations were free to act on their own.

When the Tuscarora Nation joined the confederacy at the invitation of the Oneida sometime after 1717, they were allowed no chiefs in the council, but the Oneida represented them in council. Thereafter, the Five Nations of the Iroquois Confederacy became known as the Six Nations.

In the 1800s, both the Mohawk and the Seneca living within the United States abandoned their traditional clan-based structure and established elective tribal governments. Other tribes eventually did the same, either abandoning their ancestral governments or modifying them to add elections. Traditionalists clung to the ancient structure, however, and hereditary chiefs continue to be appointed by clan matrons in some tribes. On some reservations, these two differing sets of governments exist simultaneously.

In the early 2000s, the Grand Council still met regularly at Onondaga to resolve disputes and make decisions concerning the Haudenosaunee Confederacy. In Canada, a Grand Council met at the Grand River Reserve, but both councils agreed that the central fire rested within the Onondaga Nation near Syracuse, New York. The people consider themselves one nation, although their land straddles the border between the United States and Canada. Both Grand Councils view themselves as independent of United States and Canadian control. The Haudenosaunee

Confederacy expanded their League of Nations to include the Wyendot (Wyandot), Delaware, and Tutela nations.

ECONOMY

Well before the Europeans came to America, the Iroquois were an agricultural people. They regarded the primary crops as sacred gifts from the Creator. Corn, beans, and squash were called the "Three Sisters": corn provided stalks for climbing bean vines, while squash plants controlled weeds by covering the soil. In addition to providing food, the corn plants were useful for making a variety of other goods, for personal use, or for trade with other tribes. After the Europeans came, the Iroquois traded furs, especially beaver, for European goods.

Beginning the 1930s, many men moved to New York to support their families. The Iroquois, especially the Mohawk, became famous as

Iroquois steel workers install rivets high atop a construction site in New York City in 1925. © BETTMANN/CORBIS

ironworkers in construction. They gained a reputation for walking steel girders high in the air and showing little fear of heights. Consequently, they participated in the construction of many of the country's skyscraper and bridge building projects, including such landmarks as the World Trade Center in New York City and the Golden Gate Bridge in San Francisco, California. This started a trend where Iroquois men lived and worked in large cities but travelled home regularly. For example, many Mohawk live in Brooklyn, New York, during the week, but return to their families on weekends. It also began the tradition of fathers passing their ironworking tools on to their sons (or sometimes daughters) in a ceremony.

About half of those living outside cities live on reservations. There, unemployment and underemployment (lack of high-paying jobs) are constant problems. A large number of people on the reservations work for the tribal governments, but many on the reservations who want to work are not able to find jobs.

DAILY LIFE

Families

The routines of Iroquois family life depended on the seasons. When the weather was right, for example, Iroquois men set out on hunting expeditions in bark canoes to provide meat and hides, while the women tended to the farming and other tasks associated with providing food. Women also had primary responsibility for child rearing. Young girls were responsible for caring for younger brothers and sisters or for their cousins if they had no siblings.

In Iroquois society, women owned the property and determined the kinship. For this reason, daughters were often considered more valuable than sons. After marriage, a man moved into his wife's longhouse, and the children became her children.

Buildings

Extended families (grandparents, their sons or daughters, and their children) of up to fifty people lived together in bark-covered, wood-framed longhouses that were 50 to 150 feet (15 to 45 meters) long. Longhouses were constructed with a small entrance hall at each end that could be used by all residents. Within the body of the house, a central corridor

8 feet (2 meters) wide separated two banks of compartments. A nuclear family (father, mother, and children) occupied each compartment.

Within the longhouse compartment, a raised wooden platform served as a bed by night and chair by day; some compartments included small bunks for children. An overhead shelf held personal belongings. Every 20 feet (6 meters) along the central corridor, a fire pit served the two families living on its opposite sides. Bark or hide doors at the ends of the buildings were attached at the top; these openings and the smoke holes in the roof 15 to 20 feet (4 to 6 meters) above each hearth provided the only ventilation.

Villages of three hundred to six hundred people were protected by a triple-walled stockade, consisting of wooden stakes 15 to 20 feet (4 to 6 meters) tall that were buried in the ground. About every fifteen years, the nearby supplies of wild game and firewood, as well as the soil, became depleted. During a period of two years or so, the men searched for and cleared another site for the village, which they then completely rebuilt. Although traditional longhouses are no longer built, buildings on Iroquois reservations set aside for religious activity are referred to as longhouses.

Clothing and adornment

The major item of traditional men's clothing was a breechcloth made of a strip of deerskin or fabric. It passed between the legs and was secured at the waist by a belt or sash. Decorated flaps hung in the front and back. The belt was a favorite article. Sometimes worn only around the waist, and sometimes also over the left shoulder, it was woven on a loom or by hand, and might be decorated with beadwork.

Both sexes wore fringed, sleeveless tunics, separate sleeves (connected to each other by thongs, but not connected to the tunic), leggings, moccasins, and a robe or blanket. Women adorned clothing with moose-hair embroidery featuring curved-line figures with coiled ends. Decorated pouches for carrying personal items completed the outfits.

By the end of the eighteenth century, cloth obtained from European traders replaced deerskin as the primary clothing material. Imported glass beads substituted for porcupine quills as decorative elements. In the mid-1800s, a sudden change occurred in the style of artwork used to decorate clothing with beads, quills, and embroidery. Rather than the traditional patterns of curving lines and scrolls, designs became images of plants and flowers, influenced by the floral style prominent among the seventeenth- and eighteenth-century French.

Food

Corn was the traditional staple of the Iroquois diet. People baked or boiled it, and they ate it on or off the cob. Unripe kernels were made into succotash, a type of stew combined with beans. The Iroquois processed some varieties of corn into a mixture called hominy by boiling the kernels in a weak lye solution of hardwood ashes and water. Bread, pudding, dumplings, and cooked cereal were made from cornmeal. Parched corn coffee was brewed by mixing roasted corn with boiling water.

Besides corn and the beans and squash they grew with it, the Iroquois people ate a wide variety of other plant foods. They gathered wild fruits, nuts, mushrooms, potatoes, and other roots to supplement their crops, and they dried berries for year-round use. Maple sap was used for sweetening, but salt was not commonly used.

The traditional diet featured many varieties of meat, such as deer, bear, beaver, rabbit, and squirrel. Birds, too, were plentiful. Partridge, quail, duck, and owl were boiled and then roasted. The cooking oil from the owl was used as medicine. Other meats included frog, fish, and eel. Iroquois enjoyed fresh meat during the hunting season, and they smoked or dried some to use in corn dishes during the rest of the year.

Education

Traditionally, mothers had primary responsibility for raising children and teaching them good behavior. Children learned informally by watching their family and clan elders. Girls learned practical skills by watching the women in the longhouse. Boys learned to hunt with miniature bows and arrows and blowguns when they were about six years old.

Children were not spanked, but they might be punished by splashing water in their faces. Difficult children might be frightened into better behavior by a visit from someone wearing the frightening mask of Longnose, a cannibal clown. Elders incorporated lessons about life and Iroquois history in the stories told around the fire.

Today, most children attend American or Canadian public and private schools. Some reservations operate their own Indian schools, where children (usually in the lower grades) can learn about the old ways as well as modern ways.

Healing practices

Traditional Iroquois rituals dealt with both physical and mental health issues. Medicine men or women were called shamans (pronounced *SHAH-munz* or *SHAY-munz*). They treated disorders caused by evil spirits, and they used herbs and natural ointments to cure physical ailments, including fevers, coughs, and snakebites. They also cleaned wounds and set broken bones.

Another type of healer, known as a conjurer, used chants to fight ailments caused by witchcraft. The conjurer might remove an affliction from the patient's body by blowing or sucking. Twice a year, groups of masked people called False Faces visited each house in the village, waving pine boughs and casting out sickness.

In Iroquois healing practices, the soul was the source of a person's physical and mental health, and dreams were considered the language of the soul. Everyone in the community felt a responsibility to help solve others' problems by reading their dreams, a process called dream guessing.

ARTS

The Iroquois have a rich ceremonial tradition involving music and dancing. From the time the Europeans arrived until 1945, missionaries and government officials discouraged dances and other traditional practices as they tried to get the tribes to adopt the ways of mainstream society. Nevertheless, the Iroquois preserved some of their traditional dances, both social and sacred. Sacred dances celebrate the creation of the world, while social dances are for amusement. The dancers are accompanied by the music of drums and turtle shell rattles, which are still made by Iroquois artisans. Flutes are used in sacred dances but not for social dancing.

The Iroquois are especially skilled at carving masks. Usually made of basswood, the masks are carved into the tree and then removed. The faces have bent or crooked noses and long, black or white horsehair. Before the Europeans introduced horses, the hair was made of buffalo hair or cornhusks. The use of masks, or "false faces," remains a part of Iroquois rituals. The masks, worn during festivals or healing ceremonies, symbolize spirit forces, and they are considered "living."

Because these masks are sacred, the Iroquois do not want anyone outside their culture to view them. Selling, purchasing, exhibiting, or even mimicking the masks is expressly forbidden. Since 1995 the tribes have been requesting that museums and collectors return any masks in their possession. They have asked that all photos and drawings of the masks be destroyed.

Storytelling was another prized ritual, a way of teaching moral values and tribal history. In the winter, Iroquois families would gather around the fire to hear stories told by people who had perfected the art.

CUSTOMS

Birth and naming

A hut located outside the village served as the birthing site. As the time of birth drew near, the expectant mother and a few other women withdrew to the hut and remained there until a few days after the birth. Until an infant could walk, the child spent its days attached to a wooden board called a cradleboard, which the mother hung from a tree branch while she worked in the fields.

The Iroquois tribes are organized into eight clans (groups of related families), and at birth, each person becomes a member of the clan of his or her mother. Members of a clan are considered blood relatives, regardless of whether they are members of the Mohawk, Seneca, or other Iroquois tribes.

Traditionally, babies were named at birth, but when the child reached puberty an adult name was given. Names referred to natural phenomena (such as the moon or thunder), landscape features, occupations, and social or ceremonial roles. Some examples of Iroquois names are Hanging Flower, In the Center of the Sky, He Carries News, and Mighty Speaker. The Iroquois never addressed a person by name during conversation. When speaking about a person, especially to a relative, they used a name only when that person could not otherwise be clearly identified using other words.

Puberty

Puberty marked the time of acceptance into adult membership in the society. When her first menstrual period began, a girl would retire to an isolated hut and stay there for as long as her period lasted. She was required to perform difficult tasks, such as chopping hardwood with a dull axe, and she was prohibited from eating certain foods.

A young man had a longer trial. When his voice began to change, he went to live in a secluded cabin in the forest for up to a year. An old man or woman took responsibility for overseeing his well-being. He ate sparingly and spent his time in physically demanding activities such as running, swimming, bathing in icy water, and scraping his shins with a stone. His quest was complete when he was visited by his spirit, which would remain with him during his adult life.

Marriage

In the Iroquois tradition, a man and woman wishing to marry would tell their parents, who then arranged a joint meeting of relatives to discuss the suitability of the two people for marriage to each other. If there were no objections, a day was chosen for the marriage feast. On the appointed day, the woman's relatives brought her to the groom's home for the festivities. Following the meal, elders from the groom's family spoke to the bride about wifely duties, and elders from the bride's family told the groom about husbandly responsibilities. Then the two began their new life together.

Divorce

In earlier times, when a woman was unfaithful to her husband she was punished by whipping, but the man who was her partner in the unfaithful act was not punished. If a married couple decided to separate, both of their families would be called to a council. The parties would state their reasons for wanting a divorce, and the elders would try to convince the couple to stay together. If those efforts failed, the marriage ended. In ancient times fathers kept their sons and mothers kept their daughters when a divorce occurred. By the early eighteenth century, however, mothers usually kept all of the children.

Festivals

Along with founding the Longhouse Religion, Handsome Lake revived the traditional Midwinter Ceremony, still considered by the Iroquois to be the most important of their ceremonies. Handsome Lake added four sacred rituals: The Feather Dance, Thanksgiving Dance, Rite of Personal Chant, and Bowl Game (also known as the Peach Stone Game).

The weeklong Midwinter Ceremony, a time of renewal and thanksgiving, is held in late January or early February during the new midwinter moon. To announce the beginning of the ceremony, medicine mask messengers appear at every house to stir the ashes of cold fires. At this time, names are announced for newborns or children taking on adult names. In former times, public confessions were part of the ceremony; those who admitted to failures pledged to reform.

In the spring, when the sap rose, it was time for the Thanks-to-the-Maple Festival. This one-day celebration included social dances and the ceremonial burning of tobacco at the base of a maple tree. In May or June, corn seeds saved from the previous year were blessed at the Corn Planting Ceremony. At this half-day observance, the Iroquois thanked the Creator and begged spirit forces for sufficient rain and moderate sun. Ripening strawberries in June signaled time for the Strawberry Festival. Dancers mimicked the motions of berry pickers. This one-day celebration was a time for giving thanks.

In August or early September, the corn was ready to eat. The Green Corn Festival, which involved ceremonies over four mornings, marked this event. When all the crops had been harvested and stored, but before the men left for the fall hunt, the tribe held the Harvest Festival. This one-day celebration took place in October.

War etiquette

A strict code of honor governed warfare among the tribes. When a tribe was attacked, it was bound by the code to attack in return. If the tribe did not do so, its members were labeled cowards. Deaths had to be avenged. Before departing for battle, the Iroquois held a war dance, a costumed event in which chiefs gave speeches about their past victories; the speeches excited a passion for revenge among the listeners. Then the warriors broke into a vigorous dance, featuring war cries by the chiefs and responses from the others. According to Lewis Morgan, who studied the Iroquois around 1850, "A well-conducted War dance is the highest entertainment known among the Iroquois."

Death rituals

When a person died, everyone who had names similar to the deceased gave them up until the period of mourning ended. Later, new people adopted into the clan were often given the name of the deceased person

An Iroquois woman brings sustenance to the body of a dead relative placed upon a burial platform. © MPI/STRINGER/ARCHIVE PHOTOS/GETTY IMAGES

whose place they took. The tribe held a wake the night following a death. (A wake is a watch over the body of a dead person before burial.) After a midnight meal, the best speakers of the village spoke about the deceased and about life and death in general.

The tribe then placed the body on a scaffold (a raised platform) for several days in case the person only appeared dead and might revive (which sometimes happened). Eventually, they buried the remains or housed the bones in or near the family lodge after the bones had been picked clean by animals. When the village relocated, the tribe placed all of the unburied skeletons in a common grave. By the end of the nineteenth century, the Iroquois conducted burials according to European customs.

CURRENT TRIBAL ISSUES

The Haudenosaunee are raising awareness of environmental issues. In 2009, the people came together to call attention to the pollution in Onondaga Lake in northern New York State during their third annual Roots of Peacemaking: Indigenous Values, Global Crisis festival. The league continues to voice its opinions on caring for the environment. In the years since, the various tribes have taken strong stands on respecting the earth. For example, they condemned hydrofracking, a gas drilling method that endangers the water sources in their traditional lands.

Another ongoing issue is land claims. The Onondaga have been trying to sue for land they say rightfully belongs to them according to early treaties. They believe that the territory from the Pennsylvania to the Canadian borders should be returned to them. Although their suit was denied by a federal judge, the nation intends to pursue the case until they feel justice has been done.

In an unusual, and unrelated, turn of events, plans were made in 2011 to transfer Murphy's Island (actually wild shoreline area rather than an island) along Onondaga Lake back to the Haudenosaunee. The area is sacred to their culture, because it is where the Peacemaker (see "Legends of heroes") traveled when he urged the tribes to bury their weapons and form the Iroquois Confederacy. That confederacy has now moved forward to become the Haudenosaunee Confederacy, whose League of Nations encompasses the Delaware, Wyendot (Wyandot), and Tutela.

NOTABLE PEOPLE

Oren Lyons (1930–) is an Onondaga chief who achieved recognition for his excellence in the traditional Iroquois sport of lacrosse as well as at boxing. (Lacrosse is a game of Native American origin played on a field by two teams of ten players each. Participants use a long-handled stick with a webbed pouch to get a ball into the opposing team's goal.) An artist, author, publisher, illustrator, and tribal faithkeeper, Lyons works on behalf of indigenous (native) people around the world. In 1992, he became the first indigenous leader to address the United Nations General Assembly.

Ely Samuel Parker (1828–1895; also known by the Seneca name Hasanoanda) was a tribal leader descended from such major Seneca figures as Handsome Lake, Cornplanter, and Red Jacket. A man of many and varied talents, he served as a valued military assistant to General Ulysses S. Grant (1822–1885) during the American Civil War (1861–65; a war between the Union [the North], which was opposed to slavery, and the Confederacy [the South], which was in favor of slavery) and helped prepare the terms of surrender that ended the war. He collaborated with anthropologist and author Lewis Henry Morgan on the first extensive study of Iroquois culture. After Grant was elected president of the United States in 1869, Parker was appointed Commissioner of Indian Affairs. He thus became the first Native American to head the office that controlled federal policies for the tribes.

John Napoleon Brinton Hewitt (1859–1937) was an influential Tuscaroran authority on American Indians. He brought it to the world's attention that the Iroquois Confederacy inspired the framers of the U.S. Constitution. He wrote many articles and preserved dozens of Native American legends that might otherwise have been lost.

Gary Dale Farmer (1953–) is a Cayuga actor, producer, and activist who has spoken out against negative portrayals of Native peoples in the media. He has lodged protests against casting non-Natives to play Natives in movies. Farmer has appeared in such films as *Friday the Thirteenth* (1980), *Police Academy* (1984), *The Dark Wind* (1992), *Dead Man* (1995), *Smoke Signals* (1998), and *A Thief of Time* (2004).

Roberta Hill Whiteman (1947–) is an Oneida poet and teacher known for her 1984 book, *Star Quilt.* The book contains her poem titled "In the Longhouse: Oneida Museum," which describes Oneida history and traditions. She has published several books of poetry.

BOOKS

Englar, Mary. *The Iroquois: The Six Nations Confederacy.* Mankato, MN: Capstone Press, 2006.

Graymont, Barbara. *The Iroquois.* New York: Chelsea House, 1988.

Harpster, Jack, and Ken Stalter. *Captive!: The Story of David Ogden and the Iroquois.* Santa Barbara, CA: Praeger, 2010.

Hauptman, Laurence M. *Seven Generations of Iroquois Leadership: The Six Nations since 1800.* Syracuse, NY: Syracuse University Press, 2008.

Johansen, Bruce E. *The Iroquois.* New York, NY: Chelsea House, 2010.

Keating, Neal B. *Iroquois Art, Power, and History.* Norman, OK: University of Oklahoma Press, 2012.

Parker, Arthur C. *Red Jacket: Last of the Seneca.* New York: McGraw-Hill, 1952.

Rhoades, Matthew L. *Long Knives and the Longhouse.* Madison: Fairleigh Dickinson University Press, 2010.

Shannon, Timothy J. *Iroquois Diplomacy on the Early American Frontier.* New York: Viking, 2008.

Sherrow, Victoria. *The Iroquois Indians.* New York: Chelsea House, 1992.

Smith, James Herbert. *Wah-Say-Lan: A Tale of the Iroquois in the American Revolution.* Concord, NH: Plaidswede, 2009.

Sneve, Victoria Driving Hawk. *The Iroquois.* New York: Holiday House, 1995.

Wilcox, Charlotte. *The Iroquois.* Minneapolis, MN: Lerner Publishing Company, 2007.

Wolfson, Evelyn. *The Iroquois: People of the Northeast.* Brookfield, CT: The Millbrook Press, 1992.

WEB SITES

Barry, Paul C. "Native America Nations and Languages: Haudenosaunee." *The Canku Ota—A Newsletter Celebrating Native America.* http://www.turtle-track.org/Links/NANations/CO_NANationLinks_HJ.htm (accessed on June 5, 2011).

"Haudenosaunee Guide for Educators." *National Museum of the American Indian.* http://www.nmai.si.edu/education/files/HaudenosauneeGuide.pdf (accessed June 8, 2011).

"The League of Nations." *The Haudenosaunee.* http://www.haudenosauneeconfederacy.ca/leagueofnations.html (accessed on June 2, 2011).

Redish, Laura, and Orrin Lewis. "Haudenosaunee (Iroquois) Indians." *Native Languages of the Americas.* http://www.bigorrin.org/iroquois_kids.htm (accessed on June 2, 2011).

Mohawk

Member of the Iroquois Confederacy. For more information on the Mohawk, please refer to the Iroquois Confederacy entry.

Name

Mohawk (pronounced *MO-hawk*). The Mohawk's name was given to them by the Algonquin people; it means "eaters of men" and refers to a Mohawk warrior's custom of eating the bodies of conquered warriors to ingest their strength. They call themselves *Kanien'Kehake,* which means "people of the flint" (the meaning is uncertain, but it may be related to making fire). The Mohawk were members of the Iroquois Confederacy (also known as the Six Nations) and thought of the confederacy as being like a longhouse (the typical Iroquois dwelling). The Mohawk guarded the lands in the eastern part of the confederacy and were known as "the keepers of the eastern door."

Location

The Mohawk formerly occupied areas along the St. Lawrence River in Canada and the Mohawk Valley in central New York State. In the early 2000s, they lived on reservations in central and upstate New York and Oklahoma and on several reserves (the Canadian term for reservations) in Canada.

Population

In 1755, there were an estimated 640 Mohawk. According to the U.S. Bureau of the Census, 17,106 people identified themselves as members of the Mohawk tribe in 1990. The 2000 census showed 14,322 Mohawk in the United States. An additional 39,200 Mohawk lived in Canada both on and off the reserves in 2007.

Language family

Iroquoian.

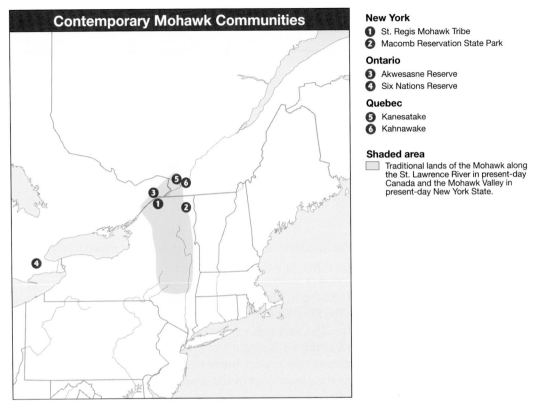

Contemporary Mohawk Communities

New York
1. St. Regis Mohawk Tribe
2. Macomb Reservation State Park

Ontario
3. Akwesasne Reserve
4. Six Nations Reserve

Quebec
5. Kanesatake
6. Kahnawake

Shaded area
Traditional lands of the Mohawk along the St. Lawrence River in present-day Canada and the Mohawk Valley in present-day New York State.

A map of contemporary Mohawk communities. MAP BY XNR PRODUCTIONS. CENGAGE LEARNING, GALE. REPRODUCED BY PERMISSION OF GALE, A PART OF CENGAGE LEARNING.

Origins and group affiliations

The Mohawk are one of the few Native American peoples who still live on the land where they originated in present-day New York State. They are one of the six nations that comprised the Iroquois Confederacy—the others are the Oneida, Onondaga, Cayuga, Seneca, and Tuscarora. The French allied with the Huron (see Wyandot entry), Ottawa (see entry), and other tribes against the Iroquois. In the 2000s, the Iroquois Confederacy expanded to form the Haudenosaunee League of Nations. The league includes the Delaware (see entry), the Wyendot (Wyandot; see entry), and the Tutela nations.

As part of the Iroquois Confederacy, the Mohawk had a constitution that the founders of the United States adopted for their new country. The Mohawk had a strong sense of justice and autonomy. The men were known as fierce fighters, easily recognized by the distinctive hairstyle that bears their name. In the twentieth century, Mohawk men gained a reputation as fearless when they worked as ironworkers on many of the country's skyscrapers and bridges. They walked steel girders high in the air with little fear of heights. The tribe is also known for being at the forefront of the modern Native rights movement, and they continue to defy efforts to weaken their traditional authority and rights.

HISTORY

Distinguished in peace and war

The legendary leader Hiawatha helped found the Iroquois Confederacy that brought five (later six) warring nations together under a peaceful, democratic government. Hiawatha, who probably lived during the fifteenth century, may have been a member of the Mohawk tribe, although some historians say he was Onondaga.

The Mohawk from New York often hunted wild game that was plentiful along the St. Lawrence River in Canada, long before their first encounter with French traders. After the French arrived in the region in the 1600s, some Mohawk established permanent settlements near them. They enjoyed a lively trading relationship, exchanging furs for European goods.

In the 1700s, Europeans arrived in Mohawk territory in present-day New York. There they found a large and thriving Mohawk community called Akwesasne (pronounced *ah-kwa-SAHS-nee*), which means "where the partridge drums." The name is based on an ancient Seneca legend. Christian missionaries established a mission, St. Regis, near Akwesasne in 1752.

When the American Revolution (1775–83; the American colonists' fight for independence from England) began, a bitter internal division arose among the members of the centuries-old Iroquois Confederacy. Many Iroquois, especially the Seneca and Onondaga, preferred the policy of neutrality. The Tuscarora and Oneida had a trade relationship with settlers and fought on the colonial side. A Mohawk leader named Thayendanégea convinced some of the Six Nations to take the British side in the war. The Mohawk at St. Regis supported the colonists.

Important Dates

1000–1450: Feuding among tribes over wild game and food resources ends with the founding of the Iroquois Confederacy by the Peacemaker and Hiawatha.

1776: Most Mohawk tribes side with the British during the Revolutionary War under the leadership of Thayendanégea, also known as Joseph Brant.

1989–90: Debates at Akwesasne Reservation about gambling on the reservation lead to violence.

1990: Attempts to build a golf course on sacred Mohawk land in Canada leads to violence.

2003: Wahta Mohawk in Canada receive about $9.7 million plus 8,300 acres to settle the Gibson Land Claim.

2000s: The Haudenosaunee Confederacy expands to include the Wyendot (Wyandot), Delaware, and Tutela.

The Iroquois League's Confederate Council, which required agreement among all six nations, could not arrive at a plan of action. Thus, individual nations, villages, and even families had to make their own decisions about alliance or neutrality. This division in the confederacy did not fully heal for centuries.

Thayendanégea (1742–1807)—also known as Joseph Brant because his mother married a man named Brant after Thayendanégea's father, a Mohawk chief, died—was both an officer in the British army and a Mohawk war chief. He led troops of Mohawk and British supporters in raids against farms and villages, destroying food supplies for the colonial armies. When the British were defeated, Brant retreated with a group of followers to Ontario, Canada. To reward him for his military services, the British gave him a retirement pension and a large tract of land along the Grand River in Ontario. Many

A Mohawk village stands along a riverbank in central New York around 1780. © NORTH WIND PICTURE ARCHIVES

Mohawk and other Iroquois followed him there, and the area eventually became the Six Nations Reserve.

Tribal lands under two governments

After the American Revolution, America became independent from Great Britain, but Canada did not. The Mohawk lands were now part of two different countries, a situation that continues to cause conflict among various local and national governing bodies (see "Government").

In 1796, thirteen years after Brant fled to Canada, New York State signed a treaty guaranteeing the Mohawk a 36-square-mile (93-square-kilometer) reservation that included the village of St. Regis and other assorted lands. It is called the Akwesasne Reserve on the Canadian side. (Land that is set aside for the use of a tribe is called a reservation; the Canadians call it a reserve.) The people refer to themselves as the Akwesasne Mohawk tribe.

The Mohawk people consider themselves one nation in spite of the boundary line drawn through their lands by the United States and Canada. This line has caused many problems, including what Canadian and American governments call "smuggling" of goods, such as cigarettes, from one side of the border to the other. The Mohawk believe that as a sovereign nation, they should not have to recognize the Canadian–U.S. border that runs through their territory. Stricter border laws in 2010 that required a passport upset many Native groups, the Mohawk included.

U.S. land claims issues

The state of New York purchased parts of the reservation without the required approval of the U.S. government and, at times, without proper Mohawk consent. This has led to numerous land claims; some still had not been resolved at the beginning of the twenty-first century. Also at issue between the Mohawk Nation and the federal government are land claims (demand for the return of lands the Mohawk claim were illegally taken from them). These claims have involved the Mohawk during the twentieth and early twenty-first centuries. The Mohawk have a history of being outspoken about their rights.

In 1953, Mohawk Chief Poking Fire sat outside the Vermont State House with about 200 Mohawk, demanding $1.2 million for the Vermont hunting grounds taken from them 154 years earlier. Four years later, a Mohawk named Standing Arrow led a group of Native Americans onto lands claimed by non-Natives on Schoharie Creek, near Amsterdam, New York. The Mohawk claimed that land under a 1784 treaty. They said that non-Indian claims to the land were illegal because the land was not bought from the Iroquois Confederacy but from only from one group of Iroquois. To press their point, Mohawk militants occupied a 612-acre (247-hectare) campsite for three years in the Adirondack Mountains, finally reaching an agreement with the state of New York in May 1977. The Mohawk were granted two sites totaling nearly 6,000 acres, located within Macomb State Park and near Altoona, New York.

In April 1980, the St. Regis Mohawk tribe in New York received more than 9,000 acres south of the reservation and $6 million in federal funds in an agreement with the federal government regarding lands the tribe claimed near the St. Lawrence Seaway.

Mohawk in Canada

Canadian Mohawk have been as assertive about their rights as American Mohawk. In 1899, two hundred Mohawk on the Akwesasne reserve drove off government police who were trying to force First Nations to

Mohawk supporters protest at the Canadian consulate in New York City against plans to expand a Quebec golf course onto a sacred Mohawk burial site in 1990. © AP IMAGES

hold elections. In December 1968, forty-five Mohawk from that same reserve protested a Canadian decision to charge them a duty (fee) on goods imported from the United States into Canada. They were arrested as they blocked the bridge connecting Cornwall, Ontario, to New York.

In the early 2000s, about 10,500 Mohawk lived in French-speaking Quebec, Canada. About 2,020 lived in and around the small village of Kanesataké (near the town of Oka), and about 8,000 lived on the Kahnawake Mohawk reserve, southwest of Montreal, Quebec's largest city. Relations between Mohawk residents and the citizens of Quebec have been uneasy for many years, and plans to enlarge a golf course onto a sacred Mohawk burial site at Oka led to violence in 1990. In protest, Kanesataké Mohawk set up barriers near the site. When Quebec police tried to dismantle the barriers, one officer was shot and killed. Police surrounded the Mohawk reserve. Meanwhile, members of the Mohawk Warrior Society at Kahnawake Reservation blocked access to a bridge linking Montreal suburbs to the city to show their support for the Mohawk at Oka. The action resulted in a seventy-eight-day standoff, with the police and the military on one side and the Mohawk Warriors of Kahnawake and Kanesataké on the other.

Quebecers gathered at the barricades and taunted the Mohawk; at one point a mob of 250 non-Natives stoned cars carrying about one hundred Mohawk women, children, and elders who were fleeing the reserve. The events at Oka were shown every night on television news shows, and the terrible state of relations between Native and non-Native Quebecers shocked many people. The government later purchased the piece of land in dispute, but the tension still lingers.

GOVERNMENT

In the early twenty-first century, Mohawk chiefs made up what is known as the Mohawk Nation Council of Chiefs (MNCC). They represented each of the traditional clans at Grand Council sessions of the Iroquois Confederacy. This ancient body, considered by its supporters to be the true governing body of the Mohawk people, oversees the community as a whole, in Canada and the United States.

Canada, the United States, and the state of New York believe that their agencies and governments should have a say in running the Mohawk Nation. As a result, eight government bodies claimed control over the small area of land at Akwesasne (or St. Regis) during the 1990s. The situation often led to conflicts. In 1990, for example, two people were killed when arguments arose over whether to allow gambling on tribal lands.

ECONOMY

When the French arrived in what is now Canada in the 1600s, they were mainly interested in furs. Mohawk men acted as scouts for the French, searching out the best hunting territory. Others acted as fur traders, canoe

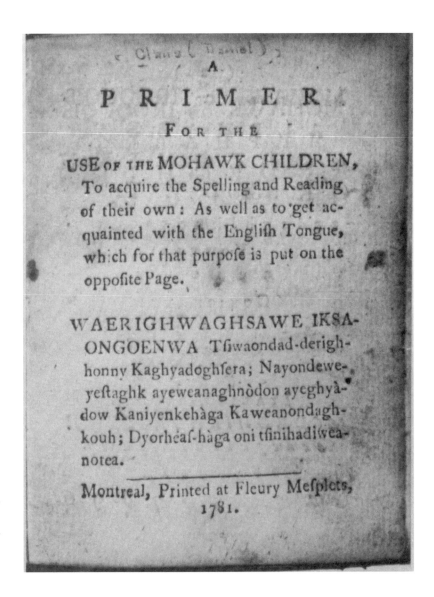

A Primer for the Use of Mohawk Children, written in 1781 by Daniel Clause, a German who studied the Mohawk people, was an attempt to teach Mohawk children the alphabet and to be able to read Christian doctrine in both the Mohawk language and English. LIBRARY OF CONGRESS PRINTS AND PHOTOGRAPHS

guides, and partners in battles with the British. Through trade with Europeans, Mohawk women became internationally famous for their woven sweetgrass baskets. In the 1800s, some Mohawk men found work in lumber camps, while others continued with their traditional occupations.

At the beginning of the twenty-first century, the Mohawk who remained on reservations were mainly employed in the service and tourist industries. The service industry includes a tribally owned shopping center and other businesses such as construction. The Mohawk, taking advantage of the growing interest of tourists in Native American life, opened arts and crafts galleries and allowed the public to attend and observe their celebrations.

As many other tribes have found, casinos create a steady source of income for the people. They opened slot machines in the 1970s; bingo proved especially popular, so they planned to expand these facilities and open new ones. By the mid-1990s, they were profiting from the casinos.

DAILY LIFE

Education

In the late 1800s and early 1900s, parents of Native children across the country were encouraged to send their children to government-run boarding schools, where students were not allowed to speak their Native language or follow their customs. Public schools were so unresponsive to the children's needs that by 1968, the Mohawk student dropout rate reached 80 percent. Mohawk parents demanded that authorities pay attention to how schools were failing their children. They became actively involved in education reform, and twenty years later the dropout rate had fallen to below 10 percent.

Because the boarding schools forced children to speak English, 1997 statistics showed that less than four thousand people of the total Iroquois population of seventy-six thousand could speak their Native language. Many tribes had fewer than thirty Native speakers. Most of those people were elderly. The Mohawk began the Mohawk Language Immersion Program in 1998. This ongoing summer program remains popular, and materials have been developed so students can practice speaking their Native language all year.

In 1985, the Akwesasne Mohawk Board of Education was formed on the reservation; today, it oversees several schools. Most students travel

Some Mohawk expressions	
shékon	"hello"
kwé kwé	"hello"
hén	"yes"
iáh	"no"
niáwen	"thank you"

off-reservation to attend high school. Some children attend the Akwesasne Freedom School in New York, which keeps traditional Mohawk culture and language alive for children from pre-kindergarten through eighth grade. In addition, the Mohawk Nation operates the Native North American Traveling College, founded in 1968. It travels throughout Canada and the United States to promote Mohawk/Iroquois culture and traditions. In 2000, the college changed its name to Ronathahon:ni Cultural Centre.

Clothing and adornment

Mohawk men were known far and wide by their distinctive haircut, known today as a "Mohawk." They shaved their heads on one or both sides, leaving a central strip of hair running from the forehead over the top of the head to the back of the neck. They smeared their hair and bodies with grease to protect themselves from insect bites. Men painted their faces blue to express health and well-being, black for war or mourning, and red to represent either life or violent death.

ARTS

The Mohawk talent for painting and wood carving can be seen in their elaborately carved and painted wooden cradleboards, which were used for carrying babies. Some of these survive today and are widely admired by art experts. They feature relief carvings of plants and animals. Some Mohawk women still carry on the tradition of weaving baskets from sweetgrass.

The Mohawk Nation at Akwesasne ventured into the broadcast arts when it became one of only about two dozen Native communities to own and operate a radio station. The station, plus a newspaper and a magazine called *Akwesasne Notes* published on the reservation, help keep the culture alive.

CURRENT TRIBAL ISSUES

The Mohawk continue to fight for their rights. Ongoing disputes with the government frequently escalate over self-government. Civil disobedience and protests have accompanied sales of property the Mohawk claim as part of their traditional territory. Disputes are not only with the Canadian or provincial governments. Several Mohawk communities are dealing with internal dissension among band members. These range from concerns about tribal chiefs involved in illegal activities or usurping (taking over without consent) power to disagreements over council decisions.

One of the ongoing concerns of the Mohawk is the issue of land claims (see "History"). The Haudenosaunee Confederacy Land Rights Statement stresses that the tribe is self-governing, so it should not be subject to Canadian laws. It asserts tribal rights to land that once belonged to them and explains the Native views on land. To deal with these and other concerns, several groups of Six Nations negotiators are studying and addressing these matters.

Because they feel strongly about caring for the earth, environmental issues are often a problem for the Mohawk. The Canadian Mohawk resisted plans for a golf course on their lands partly, they claimed, because the extensive use of fertilizers and pesticides on golf courses are ecological hazards. The Mohawk have been exposed to excessive air pollution, contaminated fish, and hazardous waste facilities that have damaged their health and their way of life. Both the Mohawk and government bodies are beginning to study and address these issues.

Haudenosaunee Confederacy Land Rights Statement

Land is envisioned as Sewatokwa'tshera't (the Dish with One Spoon); this means that we can all take from the land what we need to feed, house and care for our families, but we also must assure that the land remains healthy enough to provide for the coming generations. Land is meant to be shared among and by the people and with the other parts of the web of life. It is not for personal empire building....

In our worldview, land is a collective right. It is held in common, for the benefit of all. The land is actually a sacred trust, placed in our care, for the sake of the coming generations. We must protect the land. We must draw strength and healing from the land. If an individual, family or clan has the exclusive right to use and occupy land, they also have a stewardship responsibility to respect and join in the community's right to protect the land from abuse.

SOURCE: Selected text from the *Haudenosaunee Confederacy Land Rights Statement.* Full statement available online at: http://reclamation.kisikew.org/forum/viewtopic.php?f=12&t=3242 (accessed on June 7, 2011).

NOTABLE PEOPLE

Joseph Brant, also known as Thayendanégea ("He Places Two Bets"), was a Mohawk war chief and officer of the British army who led Native American troops into battle during the American Revolution. He negotiated with both Canadian and American governments for the land rights of his people. He is credited with having translated the Bible into the Mohawk language. Reflecting the Mohawk spirit and dignity, he told

King George III, "I bow to no man for I am considered a prince among my own people. But I will gladly shake your hand."

Jay Silverheels (1912–1980) is best known for his role as Tonto, the Native American partner of the Lone Ranger, in a popular television series of the 1950s. Silverheels, whose real name was Harold J. Smith, first came to this country as a member of Canada's national lacrosse team in 1938. (The Mohawk excel at lacrosse, a game of Native origin.) A short time later, he began acting in films. In 1950, he portrayed Geronimo in the movie *Broken Arrow,* hailed as the first film to portray Native Americans in a sympathetic light.

Kateri Tekakwitha (1656–1680) became the first Native American nun. Many miracles have been attributed to her, which led to her selection by the Catholic Church in 1980 as a candidate for sainthood.

BOOKS

Berleth, Richard. *Bloody Mohawk: The French and Indian War and American Revolution on New York's Frontier.* Hensonville, NY: Black Dome, 2009.

Crompton, Samuel Willard. *The Mohawk.* Edited by Paul C. Rosier. New York: Chelsea House Publishers, 2010.

Glenn, Charles L. *American Indian/First Nations Schooling: From the Colonial Period to the Present.* New York: Palgrave Macmillan, 2011.

Paponetti, Giovanna. *Kateri, Native American Saint: The Life and Miracles of Kateri Tekakwitha.* Santa Fe, NM: Clear Light Publishers, 2010.

Simpson, Leanne, and Kiera L. Ladner. *This Is an Honour Song: Twenty Years Since the Blockades.* Winnipeg, Manitoba: Arbeiter Ring, 2010.

Van den Bogaert, H. M. *Journey into Mohawk Country.* New York: First Second, 2006.

PERIODICALS

Bruchac, Joseph. "Otstango: A Mohawk Village in 1491," *National Geographic* 180, no. 4 (October 1991): 68–83.

Came, Barry. "A Time for Healing: Emotions Still Divide Oka and Kahnawake," *Macleans* 103, no. 46 (November 12, 1990): 26.

WEB SITES

"History of Ronathahon:ni Cultural Centre." *Ronathahon:ni Cultural Centre.* http://www.ronathahonni.com/index.cfm (accessed on June 7, 2011).

Kanatiiosh. "Kahniakehake (People of the Flint)." *Peace 4 Turtle Island.* http://www.peace4turtleisland.org/pages/mohawk.htm (accessed on June 7, 2011).

Kanatsiohareke Mohawk Community. http://www.mohawkcommunity.com/ (accessed on June 7, 2011).

Kanienkehaka Language Homepage http://www.kahonwes.com/language/kanienkehaka.html (accessed on June 7, 2011).

Mohawk Nation Council of Chiefs. http://www.mohawknation.org/ (accessed on June 7, 2011).

The Mohawk of the Bay of Quinte Research Department. "Tyendinaga Mohawk Territory," *Mohawk of the Bay of Quinte.* http://www.tyendinaga.net/history/ (accessed on May 15, 2011).

"The Mohawk Tribe." *Mohawk Nation.* http://www.mohawktribe.com/ (accessed on June 7, 2011).

Porter, Tom. "Mohawk (Haudenosaunee) Teaching." *FourDirectionsTeachings.com.* http://www.fourdirectionsteachings.com/transcripts/mohawk.html (accessed June 7, 2011).

Lumbee

Name

Lumbee (pronounced *LUM-bee*). The name came from the Lumber River, sometimes called the "Lumbee," which runs through the area of North Carolina where most members of the tribe live. Lumbee means "dark water" in Algonquian. Over the years, the government of North Carolina has called the tribe many different names, including Croatan (1885), Indians of Robeson County (1911), and Cherokee Indians of North Carolina (1913). In 1952, the tribe itself decided to change its name to Lumbee, which the state accepted as the official name the following year.

Location

There are conflicting theories as to where the Lumbee originated. Some believe they once lived on the islands off the North Carolina or Virginia coast and later moved inland to Robeson County, North Carolina, where most of them live today. Others believe the Lumbee have dwelt in their present location for thousands of years. The Lumbee population may have lived in parts of North Carolina, South Carolina, Virginia, and Maryland at one time. Baltimore, Maryland, and Bulloch County, Georgia, are home to some Lumbee in the early twenty-first century. The majority of the Lumbee, though, reside in North Carolina, and most are concentrated in four counties: Robeson, Hoke, Cumberland, and Scotland.

Population

The 1910 U.S. Census showed 6,317 Croatans—one of the early names for the Lumbee tribe—living in North Carolina. In 1960, researchers from the Smithsonian Institution identified 31,380 Lumbee in North and South Carolina. In the 2000 U.S. Census, 51,913 people said they were Lumbee, while 57,868 claimed some Lumbee heritage; by the 2010 census, the number of Lumbee reached 62,306, with a total 73,691 people who indicated some Lumbee ancestry.

Language family

Algonquian.

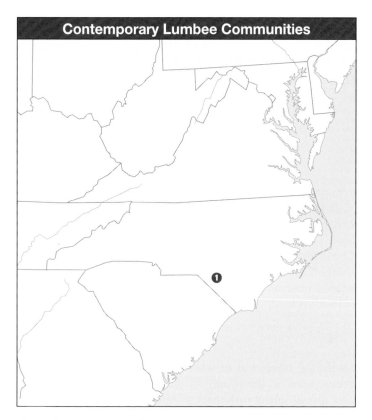

Contemporary Lumbee Communities

North Carolina
❶ Robeson County

A map of contemporary Lumbee communities. MAP BY XNR PRODUCTIONS. CENGAGE LEARNING, GALE. REPRODUCED BY PERMISSION OF GALE, A PART OF CENGAGE LEARNING.

Origins and group affiliations

Conflicting theories abound as to Lumbee origins. According to some sources, the Lumbee descended from the Cheraw and other Siouan-speaking tribes that lived in present-day Robeson County, North Carolina. Some have also connected them to the Cherokee and Tuscarora (see entries) tribes. Other historians believe that the Lumbee were Croatoan Indians who migrated from islands off the coast of North Carolina, where they had inter-married with white settlers from Roanoke. However, archaeological evidence also indicates an Indian presence in Robeson County dating back ten thousand years. Contemporary Lumbee have a tri-racial heritage, which includes Native American, European, and African American.

Archaeologists have established that Native Americans lived in present-day Robeson County, North Carolina, since 12,000 BCE. The Algonquian, Iroquoian, and Eastern Siouan Indians may have interacted and later joined with these tribes. By 1750, documents show that the people who call themselves the Lumbee existed as a tribe. Because the area where they lived was filled with swamps, white settlers had little interest in taking over their land. In the nineteenth century, escaped slaves joined the colony. Because the Lumbee are of mixed racial descent, they often face discrimination and have needed to fight for their rights throughout much of their history.

HISTORY

Lost Colony theory

In 1709, when English explorer John Lawson (1674–1711) traveled to the colony of Carolina, he was startled to discover that many of the "Hatteras Indians" living off the northeast coast of present-day North Carolina, had gray eyes. In his book, *History of Carolina,* he wrote that these people "either then lived on Roanoke Island, or much frequented it."

Governor John White and his men returned to the Roanoke Colony to find it abandoned without a trace except for the word "Croatoan" carved on a tree. © NORTH WIND PICTURE ARCHIVES

Important Dates

1709: John Lawson discovers and writes about the "Hatteras Indians."

1724: Cheraw community first seen along Lumbee River.

1835: North Carolina Constitution denies rights to people of color. Lumbee are classified as "mulattos" (having some African American heritage) and lose their rights.

1865–72: "Lowry Wars" begin. Henry Berry Lowry eludes capture.

1885: The Lumbee petition for and receive state recognition and funding for schools.

1952: Tribe votes to call themselves Lumbee.

1956: U.S. government recognizes Lumbee as a tribe, but denies them federal benefits.

1958: Tribe members break up a Ku Klux Klan gathering.

2001: The Lumbee elect first tribal council.

They were friendly toward the English and told him that some of their ancestors had been white, leading Lawson to speculate that they had descended from the settlers who had disappeared from the Roanoke Colony.

This colony, under the leadership of Sir Walter Raleigh (1554–1618), had been established in 1587. The governor of the colony, John White (c. 1540–c. 1593), returned to England for supplies. When he returned, he found the colony deserted. The only clues the colonists left behind were footprints, scattered possessions, and the word "Croatoan" carved on a tree. Croatoan, an island south of Roanoke, was the home of Natives who had been friendly to the colonists.

No trace of the colonists has ever been found, but many Lumbee have the last names of Roanoke settlers, and later European expeditions found groups of Natives who spoke English and had English customs and homes. Several historians believed this supported the theory that the Indians and whites had intermarried. Some Lumbee themselves also claimed to be descendants of both Native American and white ancestors.

Possible Cherokee or Tuscarora heritage

The Cherokee who lived in the mountains of western North Carolina had trails to the coast and to many of the rivers where the Croatan lived. Following the Tuscarora War (1711–13; a war between the British, Dutch, and German settlers and the Tuscarora Indians), the Cherokee, who fought with Colonel John Barnwell (1671–1724) against the Tuscarora, traveled through Robeson County. Some Cherokee may have stayed in the area and married Croatans. The government of North Carolina grouped the two tribes together in 1913, when it named the Croatans "the Cherokee Indians of North Carolina."

Some members of the Lumbee claim they were of Tuscarora descent. After the Tuscarora lost the war in 1713, they relocated to New York where they joined the Iroquois Confederacy (see entry). By the early 1800s, the

Tuscarora believed the migration was complete. It is possible, however, that some members of the tribe remained in North Carolina and intermarried with the Native Americans who lived in the area. In the 1970s, a small group of these Lumbee calling themselves the Eastern Carolina Indian Organization assembled to seek recognition as Tuscarora Indians.

Researchers investigate

In the 1930s, John R. Swanton, an anthropologist (a person who studies human origins) from the Smithsonian Institution, concluded the Lumbee had descended from Siouan tribes. He believed they may have been Saura (Cheraw) or Keyauwee. When the tribe prepared to submit a petition for federal recognition in 1987, Jack Campisi, an ethnohistorian (person who traces a culture's history), decided the Lumbee were Saura. Many Lumbee today accept this as their tribal affiliation.

Revised state constitution

In 1835, the state of North Carolina revised its constitution. People of color no longer had the same privileges and rights as whites. Because the Lumbee had intermarried, they were classified as "mulatto," or of mixed African American heritage. Since people of color had little status in the state at that time, the Lumbee suffered the same fate. They could not vote, join the army, or bear arms. The Lumbee fought for their rights, however. In 1853, the North Carolina Supreme Court upheld the law and convicted the Lumbee defendant Noel Locklear of illegally carrying a gun. Later, two other court cases challenged this law, and the Lumbee won the right to own guns.

Lowry War (1865–72)

During the American Civil War (1861–65; a war between the Union [the North], which was opposed to slavery, and the Confederacy [the South], which was in favor of slavery), Lumbee were conscripted, or forced into service, to help build Fort Fisher. A stronghold against the Union Army, it protected the port of Wilmington, North Carolina, from invasion. To avoid being taken, some Lumbee men hid out in the swamps. They were joined by runaway slaves and escaped war prisoners, and the period the Lumbee called "the starving times" began. To stay alive, they stole food and supplies. Although most Lumbee had originally supported the Confederacy, some ended up working for the Union and sabotaging Confederate efforts.

About the Croatan

In 1718, John Lawson wrote in his book, *History of North Carolina,* of the Croatan people:

> They naturally possess the righteous man's gift; they are patient under all afflictions, and have a great many other natural virtues....
>
> They are really better to us than we are to them; they always give us victuals [food] at their quarters, and take care we are armed against hunger and thirst; we do not so by them, (generally speaking) but let them walk by our doorway hungry, and do not often relieve them. We look upon them with scorn and disdain and think them little better than beasts in Humane shape, though if well examined, we shall find that, for all our religion and education, we possess more moral deformities and evils than [they] do, or are acquainted withal.

SOURCE: Butler, George E. *The Croatan Indians of Sampson County: Their Origin and Racial Status, A Plea for Separate Schools.* Durham, NC: The Seeman Printery, 1916, p. 37.

One of the most famous figures of this time period was Henry Berry Lowry (or Lowrie) (c: 1845–1872), a teen who saw his father and brother murdered by the Home Guard, the Confederate militia charged with guarding the home front during the Civil War (1861–65). To avenge their deaths, he and a gang (consisting mostly of his relations) stole guns, robbed plantations, and killed eighteen men who tried to capture them or those who had committed injustices against the tribe. The Lowry gang hid in the swamps and shared their spoils with the poor and hungry, especially those who lived in their hometown of Pembroke, often called "Scuffletown" by outsiders. In spite of a bounty of $12,000 offered for his death or capture, Henry was never caught; he disappeared in 1872. The Lumbee hail him as a Robin Hood type of hero and even today hold a yearly play, *Strike at the Wind,* in his honor.

Discrimination against the Lumbee

The North Carolina constitution was only one in a series of injustices the Lumbee faced. Because they had been classed as mulatto, their children could not attend school with whites. Public facilities like jails, hospitals, and rest homes kept them in separate areas. Until 1947, the government appointed a white mayor to oversee their town. When a movie theater opened in town in 1937, Native Americans and African Americans had to use different entrances than whites and could only sit in the balcony. Until 1950, Lumbee could not attend North Carolina colleges, except the Croatan Indian Normal School (see "Education"), nor could they attend graduate school until 1954.

The Lumbee also faced bigotry from some members of the public. In 1958, the Ku Klux Klan burned crosses at two Lumbee homes and organized a rally in Maxton, North Carolina. Accounts of the day vary, but the Lumbee planned to stop the rally. The Klan's loudspeaker

Two Lumbee men display a Ku Klux Klan banner that they confiscated in a raid on a Klan rally in Lumberton, North Carolina, in 1958. © MPI/ STRINGER/ARCHIVE PHOTOS/ GETTY IMAGES

was disabled, the lights were put out, shots were fired (although no one was injured), and Klan members fled. Newspapers across the country reported the incident.

The fight for rights continues

In 1972, the Lumbee organized to prevent Old Main, a building on the campus of the University of North Carolina at Pembroke, from being demolished to make room for new construction. Old Main was the last building still standing from the time when the school had been the Indian Normal School. The Lumbee were successful. The college decided to move the new building elsewhere and restore Old Main. The building now houses the American Indian Studies Department and the Native American Resource Center.

Another issue that received national publicity occurred in 1988. Two Lumbee men held nineteen people hostage in a local newspaper office to dramatize the need for an inquiry into discrimination and police misconduct. Although the men were arrested and convicted, they drew attention to ongoing problems in the community, and their action prompted an investigation.

A month later, Julian Pierce, a Lumbee attorney running for Superior Court judge, was murdered prior to the election. People still turned out to vote for him, and he beat the white candidate who had run against him. As a result, the voters (mostly minorities) petitioned the governor for a replacement for Pierce. A new position of Indian Superior Court judge was created, and Dexter Brooks (1943–2002) was appointed to fill it.

RELIGION

The first Native American church in Robeson County, Saddletree Meeting House, opened in 1792. By the end of the next century, most Lumbee were either Methodist or Baptist. In 1881, the Burnt Swamp Missionary Baptist Association began with three churches and expanded to eighteen by the early 1900s. Around this time, the Lumbee also formed an Indian Methodist Conference, so the tribe could make its own religious decisions.

In the early twenty-first century, most Lumbee attend Protestant churches, and all their ministers are Lumbee, some of whom broadcast on television. Religion is important to the Lumbee not only for spiritual reasons but also because it plays a vital part in the social life of the community. Family members sometimes attend different churches and form bonds and friendships with a wide variety of people who share their heritage and beliefs. Hymns also unite people from various denominations (see "Music").

LANGUAGE

The original language of the Lumbee, an Algonquian dialect known as Croatan or Pamlico, was lost over time. Intermarriage with Europeans, African Americans, and other Indian tribes eliminated much of the Lumbee culture. As the Lumbee added new races to their tribe, they adopted other customs and words. As a result, they speak a unique dialect of English.

Scholars who studied the language indicated that it bears many similarities to Scots-Irish, Welsh, and Old English languages. There are also traces of Outer Banks, Appalachian, and African American dialects in Lumbee speech. Some words and usages are found only in the Lumbee dialect.

Along with original and unusual words, the Lumbee also use some verbs in different ways. One verb is *be,* which has an *s* added to the end. It substitutes for the word "is": *She bes good. Be* is also used in place of the word "have": *He might be lost it.*

Although some people consider these Lumbee uses of verbs to be poor grammar, Walt Wolfram, a linguist (person who studies languages), disagrees. He sees Lumbee as a distinct dialect that the tribe developed in response to varied influences in their history and development. Ironically, one of the problems Lumbee had in receiving federal recognition (see "Current Tribal Issues") is that their present-day language is too similar to English.

Lumbee Words

Early Croatan

renepo	"woman"
bmishcosk	"red"
mpe	"water"
eembot	"one"
wopposhaumosh	"white"

Present-Day Lumbee

bog	"some chicken and rice"
chawed	"embarrassed"
cooter	"turtle"
ellick	"coffee"
juvember	"slingshot"
mommuck	"make a mess"
on the swamp	"in the neighborhood"

GOVERNMENT

Communities form the mainstay of Lumbee government. Each community is composed of family members who are related by marriage. The oldest adult is usually the head of the family. The elders in the group make decisions together. Because these small groups have always been self-governing, the Lumbee had no need for a central government.

During the 1900s, groups of men met and worked together in an organization called the Red Men's Lodge. They took charge of protecting the tribe from violence, conducting ceremonies, presiding over funerals, and keeping social order.

Created in 2001, the tribal government preserves the original concept of community organization. A chairperson heads the council and chooses a tribal administrator. The tribe votes to confirm this choice. These two positions form the executive branch of the government and are responsible for handling the budget and enforcing laws. The legislative branch

A Lumbee farmer in North Carolina tends to his land. ©

consists of twenty-one members who come from fourteen different districts. Five judges try cases in the Supreme Court.

ECONOMY

Agricultural economy

Early Lumbee were hunters and gatherers, but they became one of the first Native American tribes to use agriculture to provide the majority of their diet. They also raised livestock, particularly chickens and hogs. Because these animals came from Europe, many people believe this authenticates the Lumbee claims that some of their ancestors were from the Lost Colony of Roanoke (see "Lost Colony theory"). The Lumbee also used slave labor to assist with the farming.

By the nineteenth century, many Lumbee had begun raising cash crops, or crops grown mostly to be sold, such as cotton and tobacco. Men planted a portion of their farmland with vegetables for their families and the rest with crops that helped them earn a living. A small portion of farmland was set aside to grow food for the animals.

Branching out

Not all Lumbee farmed; many men traveled down the Lumber River to work in the logging industry. One popular job was rolling heavy logs to the river, tying them together, and then floating the log raft downstream to sell the logs in South Carolina.

Other men worked in the turpentine industry. The forests filled with pine trees around Robeson County provided plenty of turpentine, which the workers tapped and collected to sell. During the American Civil War (1861–65), advancing Union troops burned down many of the forests, leaving the men without jobs. Many Lumbee moved to Georgia, where pine forests were still abundant. Most missed their North Carolina homes and returned to Robeson County, but a small group of Lumbee remained in Georgia.

Today's economy

Today, many Lumbee students attend college, and the tribe's members are employed in many different professions. Several members have established profitable businesses. In 2002, the Lumbee Revitalization and Community Development Corporation formed to offer loans, financial and business assistance, and job development. The group also supervised the Office of Community Services (OCS) project, which provided construction jobs to low-income workers; the homes they built provided housing for low- to moderate-income families.

DAILY LIFE

Families

Family holds a special place in the Lumbee culture. Kinship is important, and it is not unusual to find several family groups living together or relatives taking care of each other's children. Even children who grow up and move away still consider Robeson County home.

Extended families, which include grandparents, parents, children, and other close relatives, form communities. Elder members of each family come together to discuss situations and make plans for the community. Lumbee call each network of families a "set," their name for a clan.

Buildings

By the early 1700s, when the first records are available for the tribe, the majority of the Lumbee lived in European-style houses. Most people constructed small, windowless cabins of logs or wood that had front porches held up by posts. Stone or brick fireplaces heated the houses.

Clothing and adornment

Little is known about early Lumbee clothing because the tribe adopted European dress early in their history. Engravings of the Croatan or Hatteras Indians show men in breechcloths (an apronlike piece of fabric attached at the waist). At that time, women may have worn knee-length skirts, but most Lumbee soon adopted European-style clothes.

Women wore their hair in Navajo fashion, with a bun at the top and bottom. Both men and women decorated their skin with tattoos. They may have worn beaded headbands with a feather in them. Some Lumbee wore feathered headdresses; the men who joined the Red Man Lodges (see "Government") in the 1930s and 1940s revived the custom of wearing war bonnets. Some pictures show women wearing these headdresses as well.

In more recent years, women made patchwork dresses in a distinctive design called the pine cone pattern. The dresses were traditional southern-style dresses with pine cone patchwork sewn on the apron bib and a matching shawl. With them, they often wore chinaberry necklaces (see "Arts"). In some places in the South, these necklaces were placed around babies' necks to ward off evil spirits.

Food

Like many other tribes, the Lumbee depended on hunting and gathering. They ate deer, turkey, and other small game along with any wild plants they gathered. They also relied on farming to fulfill many of their needs. Possibly as a result of the European influence, the Lumbee tilled fields and used slave labor to work their farms. Typical crops included corn, beans, and squash—the traditional Native diet—as well as tomatoes, cabbage, peas, okra, collard, turnips, and potatoes. Most Lumbee also raised chicken and hogs, animals brought to America by Europeans.

Education

Before the 1835 North Carolina constitution was adopted, Lumbee students went to school with whites. After the new laws were enacted, they were expected to attend African American schools. They refused to do this and petitioned for funds for their own schools. From 1885 (after they received some funds) until the 1970s, Lumbee attended tribal schools. The government also opened the Croatan Indian Normal School in 1887, a teacher training college where Native Americans learned to teach their own students. That school later became the University of North Carolina at Pembroke.

Not all counties received funds for schools, however, and some Lumbee had to maintain their own schools. In requesting funding for the Indians of Sampson County, George E. Butler, a lawyer and school superintendent, attempted to explain why the Lumbee deserved money for schools. He wrote that in 1912 a school census showed that every child in that county, both male and female, attended school, a very unusual record for the early 1900s. The Lumbee were determined to educate their

Lumbee girls on the Croatan Indian Normal School basketball team pose for a team portrait in 1928. LIBRARY OF CONGRESS

children and had been supporting local schools by private donations. In Dismal Township they operated a cotton farm and used the proceeds to pay for their children's schooling.

By the 1920s, the Lumbee had built more than thirty one-room schoolhouses and soon had 3,400 students enrolled. It was not until 1950, though, that Lumbee students could attend any North Carolina college other than the Croatan Indian Normal School.

Healing practices

The Lumbee used herbs to combat illness and promote healing. Many contemporary elders of the tribe have herbal knowledge that has been passed down through the generations. One of the most widely used traditional medicines was the dried sassafras root. Although modern

Desire for Education

In 1914, Indian agent O. M. McPherson reported to the government on the Croatan (Lumbee) Indians' interest in education:

> I might say here that in my judgment, the children of these Native Americans, as a rule, are exceedingly bright, quick to learn from books, as well as from example, and are very eager to obtain further educational advantages than are now open to them. If the reverse were true, there would be little encouragement to furnish them with higher institutions of learning when they were incapable of taking advantage of their present educational facilities or indifferent about obtaining a higher education; but I believe the more ambitious of their youth to be eager to attend higher institutions of learning than those now provided.

SOURCE: Butler, George E. *The Croatan Indians of Sampson County: Their Origin and Racial Status, A Plea for Separate Schools.* Durham, NC: The Seeman Printery, 1916, p. 37.

scientists say sassafras causes cancer, many Native American tribes used it as a tea to thin the blood. It also helped with kidney problems, rheumatism, arthritis, recovery from childbirth, high blood pressure, colds, flu, and bronchitis. Sassafras oil combined with cloves and other herbs relieved toothaches. It was sometimes used to flavor root beer.

In the early twenty-first century, the Lumbee tribe operates the Healing Lodge, which combines health outreach with ministry. To assist with social problems—including alcoholism, AIDS, suicide, domestic violence, and homelessness—the Healing Lodge conducts seminars and support groups and offers other services. In 2006, studies reported that Lumbee had a much higher rate of high blood pressure, diabetes, and heart disease than the general population. Doctors also noted that these problems were much more common in younger Lumbee women; they began working to determine both the cause and a cure.

ARTS

Arts and crafts

Lumbee crafts included basketry and wood carving. Although the tribe made reed and splint baskets, they also made unusual baskets from pine needles. They created utensils from gourds and decorated them with designs. Other traditional crafts included pottery, turtle shell rattles, and jewelry, especially necklaces made from chinaberries and pumpkin seeds. Women made chinaberry necklaces by boiling the berries to soften and remove the pulp from the seeds. Once they dried, the seeds turned white and could be dyed bright colors. Then they drilled a hole through each seed and strung them into necklaces.

The Lumbee are also known for their patchwork. One of their most famous designs is the pine cone pattern. This unusual pattern consists of overlapping layers of triangles pointing toward the center, giving the piece a three-dimensional look that resembles the end of a long-leaf pine cone.

In addition to keeping traditional crafts alive, many Lumbee artists earn their reputations in the fine arts field. Lloyd Oxendine opened the first gallery for contemporary Native American art in the United States in 1969. The American Indian Community House Gallery/Museum in New York City showcases art from Natives around the country. Oxendine himself is also a well-known artist. Another Lumbee artist with an international reputation is Gene Locklear (1949–; see "Notable people"). The Native American Resource Center at the University of North Carolina at Pembroke also houses an extensive collection of Lumbee art and music.

Music

Music plays an important role in the Lumbee lifestyle. Religious hymns and gospel music are part of a long-standing tradition uniting people of all denominations. Throughout the tribe's history, most denominations held singing conventions—gatherings of singers from all the churches in the area who met to sing religious music. In modern times, hymn sings are held frequently by various churches in the community and are open to everyone. Many people attend these to sing and enjoy the fellowship of others.

CUSTOMS

Early in their history, the Lumbee adopted many European customs and traditions. They followed the usual practices of white society in most of their rituals and rites. They did, however have a few customs that were uniquely their own.

Slaughter Day

A Lumbee tradition that brought family and friends together was a hog killing, or slaughter day. Everyone gathered and brought silverware, tables, and large pots. By 2:00 AM, the men had built huge fires and started boiling water. When the water was ready, they would butcher a dozen hogs, each weighing several hundred pounds. The men cut up the meat, and the women cleaned out the intestines for sausages.

The group shared a meal, then they stuffed the sausage casings (intestines) with meat and boiled the livers and mashed them with spices to make a pudding. Sometimes they added blood to the liver mixture to make blood pudding. Next, all the fat was melted to make lard. It had to be watched carefully and stirred with a green sweet bay stick, so the process was time consuming.

Other workers smoked hams over a fire. By the late nineteenth century, however, most families cured their meat with salt instead of smoking it. Curing the pork preserved it so it could be stored and eaten all year. In the days before grocery stores were common, this meat was an essential part of a family's diet. Hog killings continued to be held, but more for socializing than for necessity.

Woodsawing

Because community was important to the Lumbee, many activities were done as a group. A family would cut down as many trees as they needed for winter firewood, then they would invite relatives and friends for a woodsawing. All the men worked together to chop the trees into small logs for firewood. Meanwhile, the women prepared a feast for everyone to enjoy when the labor was over. Once chainsaws became common, neighbors no longer needed to gather to help with the sawing.

Community efforts

To clear farmland, men cut down trees and rolled them into a pile for burning. Logrolling required a team effort because many trees were huge. After the larger trunks and branches had been cleared, everyone, including women and children, worked together to dig up roots and stumps and move rocks.

When someone needed to build a house or a barn, the whole community pitched in to help. Men worked as a team to cut and lift the heavy logs into place. The owner finished the house later by building a roof from wood shingles.

Corn harvesting was another time the community worked together. Families invited friends and relatives over to help shuck corn. Many hands made the work go quickly. After all of these joint events, the family who had been helped hosted a feast for all the workers.

Festivals

School-Breaking Day was one of the largest festivals of the year. Both adults and children attended this celebration of the final day of the school year. Early in the day, the community assembled in the schoolyard bringing plenty of food to share. Music, dancing, and feasting lasted long into the evening.

Over the years, as people moved away from the area, some Lumbee decided to keep in touch with each other by holding a homecoming event each summer. Although it began in 1968 as small community gathering, it expanded over the years, and in the early 2000s, more than forty-five thousand people were known to attend the nine-day event. One of the highlights of the festival is the coronation ball for Mr. and Miss Lumbee. Younger contestants compete for Teen Miss, Junior Miss, and Little Miss. Sports, dinners, concerts, fireworks, a car show, and a parade all provide opportunities for fun. The play *Strike at the Wind* (see "Lowry War") rounds out the events.

To keep their Indian culture alive, the Lumbee began holding pow-wows, events at which traditional dances and culture are shared with the community. These have become a fall tradition.

CURRENT TRIBAL ISSUES

The Lumbee sought federal recognition for more than one hundred years. Not only did the Lumbee face opposition to their petition from those who questioned their identity as a unique tribe, but other tribes attempted to stop the process because they do not believe the Lumbee are a true Native American tribe. Nevertheless, the Lumbee pressed on with their petition since tribes receiving federal recognition are entitled to government services and other financial benefits. Recognized tribes also become sovereign (self-governing) nations. In the early 2000s, the Lumbee decided to bypass the Bureau of Indian Affairs and instead went directly to the U.S. Congress with their petition. To ensure that the bill had a better chance to pass, the tribal council voted to add an amendment prohibiting them from opening casinos. They agreed to forgo gaming to speed up the recognition process. After the bill had been introduced, internal dissension occurred among the tribe over the clause that prohibited gaming. In addition, questions about possible misuse of federal funds caused difficulties for the tribe and held up the pending bill.

Arlinda Locklear, attorney for the Lumbee Tribe of North Carolina, listens to testimony before a 2006 Senate Committee on Indian Affairs hearing to discuss Lumbee recognition. © AP IMAGES/ GERALD HERBERT

NOTABLE PEOPLE

Julian Pierce (1946–1988), a Lumbee attorney, was known for helping the poor. In 1978, he became the first director of Lumbee River Legal Services and was also instrumental in a school merger to provide all children with a quality education. He was murdered shortly before being elected a Superior Court judge. His death paved the way for Dexter Brooks, also a Lumbee, to be appointed to the court. Another Lumbee attorney, Arlinda Faye Locklear (1951–), was the first Native American woman to argue a case before the U.S. Supreme Court.

Gene Locklear (1949–) played major league baseball with the San Diego Padres and New York Yankees. In 1979, he left the world of professional sports to become an artist. He is one of the most well-known Lumbee artists, and his work hangs in museums across the United States as well as in the Smithsonian Institution and the White House.

Two successful Lumbee businessmen are Dennis Lowery, who began one of the nation's largest Indian-owned corporations in the 1970s, Continental Industrial Chemicals, Inc., and later expanded into other corporate ventures; and James Thomas, CEO of Thomas Properties Group, Inc., and a former owner of the Sacramento Kings professional basketball team. Other important Lumbee figures include Helen Maynor Scheirbeck (1935–2010), who worked for the National Museum of the American Indian and the Save the Children Federation and served in the U.S. Senate, where she was instrumental in developing the American Indian Civil Rights Act; Jana Mashonee (née Sampson), a pop singer who won multiple Nammys (Native American Music Awards) and was nominated for Grammy awards; and Brantley Blue, who served as Commissioner of the Indian Claims Commission.

BOOKS

Butler, George E. *The Croatan Indians of Sampson County: Their Origin and Racial Status, A Plea for Separate Schools.* Durham, NC: The Seeman Printery, 1916.

Dial, Adolph L., and David K. Eliades. *The Only Land I Know: A History of the Lumbee Indians.* Syracuse: Syracuse University Press, 1996.

Lowery, Malinda Maynor. *Lumbee Indians in the Jim Crow South: Race, Identity, and the Making of a Nation.* Chapel Hill: University of North Carolina Press, 2010.

Oakley, Christopher Arris. *Keeping the Circle: American Indian Identity in Eastern North Carolina, 1885–2004.* Lincoln: University of Nebraska Press, 2005.

School for Indians of Robeson County. Washington, DC: Government Printing Office, 1913.

Sider, Gerald. *Living Indian Histories: The Lumbee and Tuscarora People in North Carolina.* Chapel Hill: University of North Carolina Press, 2006.

PERIODICALS

Segrest, Mab. "Robeson County's 'Third World Ills.'" *Southern Changes* 10, no. 4 (1988): 14–16.

Shaffrey, Mary M. "Lumbee Get a Win, But Not without Stipulation." *Winston-Salem Journal,* April 26, 2007.

WEB SITES

"Hero: Henry Berry Lowrie." *University of North Carolina at Pembroke,* September 29, 2010. http://www.uncp.edu/nativemuseum/collections/hbl/index.htm (accessed on June 4, 2011).

"Lumbee History & Culture." *Lumbee Tribe of North Carolina.* http://www.lumbeetribe.com/History_Culture/History_Culture%20Index.html(accessed on June 4, 2011).

Redish, Laura, and Orrin Lewis. "Lumbee Language and the Lumbee Indian Culture (Croatan, Croatoans, Pamlico, Carolina Algonquian)." *Native American Language Net: Preserving and Promoting Indigenous American Indian Languages.* http://www.native-languages.org/lumbee.htm (accessed on June 4, 2011).

Stilling, Glenn Ellen Starr. "The Lumbee Indians: An Annotated Bibliography Supplement." January 15, 2010. *Appalachian State University Libraries.* http://linux.library.appstate.edu/lumbee/ (accessed on June 4, 2011).

Menominee

Name

Menominee (pronounced *muh-NOM-uh-nee*), sometimes spelled Meno-mini, means "Wild-Rice People." This name comes from their reliance on wild rice. The French also called them *Folle Avoines,* or "Crazy Oat Indians," but the tribe called themselves *Mamaceqtaw,* or "the people."

Location

The Menominee Indian Tribe of Wisconsin Reservation is located 45 miles (70 kilometers) northwest of Green Bay. The reservation contains about 235,000 acres, most of them thickly forested. It consists of several villages scattered across Menominee County. The Menominee also own land in Winnebago County.

Population

In 1634, from the Menominee population numbered between 2,000 to 4,000. In 1768, that number had dropped to 800, but it had increased to 1,930 by 1854, and to 2,917 in 1956. In the 1990 U.S. Census, 8,064 people identified themselves as Menominee. About 3,400 of them lived on the reservation. The 2000 U.S. Census showed 8,691 Menominee; by 2010, that count had fallen slightly to 8,374, with a total of 11,133 people claiming some Menominee heritage.

Language family

Algonquian.

Origins and group affiliations

The Menominee are believed to have occupied areas in Michigan and Wisconsin for five thousand years or more. Menominee oral history says they originated near Sault (pronounced *SOO*) Sainte Marie in Michigan's Upper Peninsula. Around the year 1400, they were forced westward by the Potawatomi and Ojibway (see entries). Together with the

111

Contemporary Menominee Communities

Wisconsin

❶ Menominee Indian Tribe of Wisconsin

Shaded area

☐ Traditional lands of the Menominee along the present-day Michigan-Wisconsin state line

A map of contemporary Menominee communities. MAP BY XNR PRODUCTIONS. CENGAGE LEARNING, GALE. REPRODUCED BY PERMISSION OF GALE, A PART OF CENGAGE LEARNING.

Winnebago and Ojibway, the Menominee are one of the original tribes of Wisconsin and parts of Michigan. All three tribes share characteristics with newer arrivals, such as the Sac and Fox (see entry) and the Potawatomi.

At one time, the Menominee controlled nearly ten million acres, lands that stretched from the Great Lakes to the Mississippi River. Mainly hunter-gatherers, they also did some hunting and fishing. The Menominee, a brave and generous people, managed to survive although surrounded by larger and more powerful tribes. American settlers and loggers, however, took more and more Menominee land until the Natives were finally confined to a reservation after 1856. By the early 2000s, the Menominee were a relatively prosperous people whose traditional culture remained vital.

HISTORY

French disrupt peaceful existence

The Menominee have inhabited their territory for at least five thousand years, the longest of any Wisconsin tribe. Their first encounter with Europeans happened when Frenchman Jean Nicolet (pronounced *Nik-o-LAY*; 1598–1642) passed through their territory in 1634, looking for a passage to China. Over the next thirty years, the Menominee had little interaction with French traders, but they suffered at the hands of other tribes who did, largely because of the fur trade.

The fur trade in Canada and around the Great Lakes resulted in intense rivalries among Native tribes. Eager to trade furs for French goods, some hunters began to expand their activities onto lands others regarded as theirs. Stronger tribes began forcing weaker ones westward. Refugees from the Ojibway and Potawatomi tribes crowded into Menominee lands. The invasion was disruptive for everyone. Wars broke out among tribes competing for food and land. Many people starved to death or became victims of warfare and diseases.

Menominee warrior Amiskquew wears a traditional feathered headdress and face paint. © LEBRECHT MUSIC AND ARTS PHOTO LIBRARY/ALAMY

AMISKQUEW,
A MENOMINIE WARRIOR

Trading post established

Contact between the Menominee and the French began when the French established a trading post at Green Bay, Wisconsin, in 1667. By then, there were fewer than four hundred Menominee left, and they became dependent on fur trading. French goods such as metal kettles, steel tools, cloth, needles, and scissors made life easier. Trade altered forever the Menominee's ancient way of life, turning a people who had once hunted only for what they needed into a people who hunted for profit. Trade may also have saved the tribe from dying out. The French maintained peace among rival tribes to protect trade, and the Menominee were spared more warfare. Eventually, overtrapping led to a surplus of furs, and the French abruptly ended trade in the area in 1696.

Important Dates

c. 3000 BCE: The Menominee inhabit territory in Michigan.

1400: The Menominee are pushed westward into their present homeland near Green Bay, Wisconsin.

1817–56: The Menominee make eight treaties with United States and move to a reservation.

1909–30: Tribal sawmill provides employment, but tribe must sue for managerial control.

1954: Menominee federal tribal status is terminated; it is restored in 1973.

1979: The Menominee form a tribal legislature.

Involvement in European and American wars

The Menominee resumed their hunting, fishing, and gathering lifestyle, but throughout the 1700s, they found themselves caught up in warfare between the French, British, and American colonists, who fought to dominate North America. When they could not avoid conflict, the Menominee sided with the French, who had never tried to take over their lands. After the French were defeated in the French and Indian War (1754–63; war fought in North America between England and France involving some Native people as allies of the French), the Menominee allied with the British. They fought against the colonists in the American Revolutionary War (1775–83; the American colonists' fight for independence from England) and in the War of 1812 (1812–15; a war in which the United States defeated Great Britain). By this time, at least ten Menominee villages existed. The Menominee at last befriended the victorious Americans, who built a fort at Green Bay in 1815. Soon a trading post operated at the Menominee village of Minikani.

Treaty period

Americans wanted land. Vastly outnumbered, the Menominee surrendered more and more land, not always peacefully. Between 1817 and 1856, the Menominee made eight treaties with the United States. A treaty signed in 1831 granted the tribe eight cents an acre for three million acres of wooded land. By 1850, nearly all tribal lands were in the hands of settlers. The Menominee tried to fight for their homeland, but the pressure was too much for them. The Wolf Treaty of 1854 established a reservation in northern Wisconsin. Later, a small group of Potawatomi joined them there.

Loggers come

The Menominee sent 125 volunteers to the Union army during the American Civil War (1861–65; a war between the Union [the North], which was opposed to slavery, and the Confederacy [the South], which was in favor of slavery). This was an amazing number considering that the tribe numbered only about 2,000. Menominee warriors fought at the battles of Vicksburg and Petersburg. Menominee also guarded the men charged in the conspiracy to assassinate President Abraham Lincoln (1809–1865; served 1861–65) while the conspirators awaited trial and execution.

After the Civil War, American timbermen came to Wisconsin to exploit the forests. They tried every means they could think of, legal and illegal, to deprive the Menominee of their timber, but they failed.

"Model" community fails

In the 1800s, reformers decided the friendly Menominee should be converted and "civilized," meaning they should adopt a culture more like the European Americans. In 1831, the reformers constructed a community called Winnebago Rapids. It was to serve as a model for future "civilizing" of other Native communities. Winnebago Rapids consisted of a dozen houses and a school, farm, blacksmith shop, and sawmill. This experiment in peaceful coexistence through education and good example was a total failure, however. The Menominee rejected the model homes; some even used them to stable their horses. They tore up the flooring for firewood and slept in their traditional shelters pitched nearby. They refused to listen to the lessons of the teachers and preachers.

By 1870, the Menominee had established three villages along the Menominee River and another eight or so to the south, as well as a Christian mission at Shawano. They resisted efforts to turn them into farmers and based their economy on logging. They were remarkably successful in this endeavor.

Logging success nearly destroys tribe

By 1890, with their logging profits, the Menominee built a hospital and school and set up their own police and court system. At a time when most other Native American tribes were adjusting to reservation life, the Menominee were seen as a model of prosperity and modern thinking. Oddly enough, this success nearly caused their destruction when the U.S. Congress adopted a termination policy in the 1950s.

Termination was part of the larger U.S. plan to assimilate Native Americans to make them more like white Americans. Termination of a tribe ended the special relationship between the tribe and the

U.S. government, thus stopping certain government funding and services and making the tribes subject to state taxes. Many Menominee could not pay their taxes and lost their land. The Menominee were soon among the poorest people in the state of Wisconsin.

Anger over termination grew. In 1970, the Menominee formed a protest movement called Determination of Rights and United for Menominee Shareholders (DRUMS). Through demonstrations and court actions, DRUMS slowed the sale of tribal lands. Finally, in 1973, President Richard Nixon (1913–1994; served 1969–74) signed the Menominee Restoration Act, restoring tribal status to the reservation.

Over the years, the Menominee have found themselves engaged in quarrels with sportsmen and conservationists regarding the use of their ancestral lands. In 1996, federal judge Barbara Crabb decided that the Menominee have no special rights to these lands because the federal government had never told them that they would retain the right to hunt, fish, and gather on their ceded lands. As with many tribes, laws about use of traditional lands remain an ongoing struggle. Even if these rights are granted, the tribes may find themselves in conflict with local law enforcement or non-Natives who resent their freedom to hunt and fish without regulations.

RELIGION

The Menominee believed in a Great Spirit who made the sun, the stars, the earth, and animal spirits. In their creation story, one of those spirits, Great Bear, asked the Great Spirit to transform him into a man. His wish was granted, but he soon felt lonely, so he asked a golden eagle, Thunderer, to become his brother. Great Bear then asked a beaver to join him, and she became Beaver Woman. This small family then "adopted" other spirits, who became the first Menominee. An All Animals' Dance was occasionally held to honor the characters of the creation story.

Like the Ojibway, the Menominee had a religious society called the Medicine Lodge Religion (Midewiwin), with the main purpose of prolonging life. The society taught morality, proper conduct, and a knowledge of plants and herbs for healing. Another religion, the Drum (or Dream) Dance Religion, holds that dreams can make a person sick if they are not acted out. Many Menominee retain elements of these two traditional religions, even those who belong to Christian churches.

Roman Catholicism, which was introduced by the French in the 1600s, is the most common religion among Menominee today. The Native American Church has been embraced by some Menominee in rural areas. This church combines Christian and Native beliefs and practices, and it features an all-night ceremony of chanting, prayer, and meditation.

LANGUAGE

The dialect, or variety, of the Algonquian language spoken by the Menominee is most closely related to Cree (see entry) and Fox (see Sac and Fox entry). The Menominee used the language of the Ojibway in the fur-trade days as a second language for speaking with outsiders.

By the 1920s, the Menominee language was rarely used, and by 1965, only a few hundred people spoke it. In the early 2000s, though, the language was being used and taught at four tribal schools on the reservation and at the College of the Menominee Nation in Keshena.

The Menominee language frequently borrows from Ojibway, Siouan, and French languages. Having no word of their own for "warrior," the Menominee, Plains Cree, and Western Chippewa use the Dakota (see entry) word for warrior: *akicita as okiccita.* *P⁻os⁻oh* is a Menominee greeting; it also means "good-bye."

GOVERNMENT

In the early days, the Menominee were loosely organized, with a tribal council that governed informally. After Native refugees from the fur-trade wars arrived and threatened the Menominee way of life, a more formal type of government became necessary. Members of the tribal council, usually elders from each clan (group of related families) appointed a chief to take command during wars with the refugees. Later, the job of the chief evolved to maintain order, approve tribal policies, direct ceremonies, and care for the welfare of his people.

When the Menominee reservation was established in 1854, the tribe became subject to U.S. laws. Programs were set up to assimilate the people by turning them into farmers so they would blend into the general population. The Menominee resisted and became successful loggers. They also established their own police and court systems. They enjoyed success and prosperity until the federal termination policy in the 1950s placed tribal government in the hands of the state of Wisconsin. As a sovereign nation independent of the United States, the Menominee had not paid taxes in the past. When their reservation became a county of Wisconsin, they were forced to sell valuable lake property to pay taxes. Struggling to keep their lumber operations going, they soon became impoverished.

In 1973, the Menominee Restoration Act was signed, reestablishing the former reservation. In 1977, the tribe adopted a constitution, and in 1979, it formed a tribal legislature. The nine-member tribal legislature elects a chairperson, a body of judges, and a general council. Although in the past, the chiefs, or *okenaws,* inherited their positions, they are now elected.

ECONOMY

Farming rejected

Before the arrival of Europeans, the Menominee supported themselves mainly by hunting and gathering the abundant wild rice of their territory. They believed that to plant crops other than rice would offend the Creator.

Reformers in the 1800s tried to turn the Menominee into farmers. The Menominee chose instead to sell white pine commercially. In 1909, the U.S. government supplied the Menominee at Neopit with a state-of-the-art sawmill, which provided full tribal employment, but it refused to turn over management of the mill to the tribe.

Economy based on forests

In 1930, the Menominee sued for greater tribal control of the mill. Thirteen lawsuits were filed, but the Menominee received no satisfaction from the courts. Meanwhile, more than 200 Menominee served in World War II (1939–45; a war in which Great Britain, France, the United States, and their allies defeated Germany, Italy, and Japan), and back home, fifty women kept the tribal sawmill going. In 1954, the federal government terminated Menominee tribal status, resulting in a loss of certain federal benefits. The 2,917 Menominee were plunged into poverty. They were forced to sell prime lakefront sites to white developers. Upset, Menominee united behind the organization called Determination of Rights and Unity for Menominee Shareholders (DRUMS). By 1973, they recovered their federal tribal status, and logging activities resumed in full.

The Menominee have become known for their successful forest-management techniques. For every tree harvested, the Menominee plant one in its place. They increased their wooded acreage by 10 percent in the twentieth century. Sometimes called "Timber Indians," they manage the maple, beech, birch, hemlock, oak, basswood, black spruce, tamarack, cedar, and red, white, and jack pine trees that forest 220,000 acres of their 234,000-acre homeland. Menominee Tribal Enterprises limits the annual cut to 29 million feet and uses a particular pattern for harvesting that allows for sustainability (keeping the forest filled with new trees).

The Menominee manage their land using three basic principles. Menominee president Lawrence Waukau described them when he spoke before the United Nations in 1995: "First, [forest land] must be sustainable for future generations. Second, the forest must be cared for properly to provide for the needs of the people. And third, we keep all the pieces of the forest to maintain diversity."

Ma'nabus Held by the Trees

Many Native American tribes told stories to their children to teach them lessons. In many Menominee tales, Ma'nabus often did wrong and ended up in trouble.

> Ma'nabus once killed some game. Two trees near him rubbed together by the wind squeaked loudly. Ma'nabus climbed up to see what the trouble was and the trees held him fast, despite his entreaties, while the animals stole his meat. When it was all gone the trees released him and he went away hungry.

SOURCE: Skinner, Alanson, and John V. Satterlee. "Ma'nabus Held by the Trees." *Anthropological Papers of the American Museum of Natural History, Vol. XIII, Part III: Folklore of the Menomini Indians.* New York: The American Museum of Natural History, 1915. Available online at: http://digitallibrary.amnh.org/dspace/bitstream/2246/152/1/A013a03.pdf (accessed on December 1, 2011).

Other economic pursuits

By the end of the twentieth century, the tribe had expanded its economic base to include a casino and a hotel, which provided much-needed jobs. The Menominee Nation became the largest employer in the area. In addition to tribal government and industrial employment, the casino and the school district provide the greatest number of jobs. Since the tribe joined the Northwoods Niijii Enterprise Community (NNEC) in 1998, it has been actively developing new businesses. In the early twenty-first century, the tribe's enterprises were once again thriving.

DAILY LIFE

Children played with dolls, bows and arrows, and hoops made of birchbark. In the winter, entire families gathered around the fire to listen to stories.

A reconstructed Menominee bark lodge in Green Bay, Wisconsin, was originally built as a chapel for French missionaries.
© NORTH WIND PICTURE ARCHIVES

Buildings

Traditional dwellings The Menominee traditionally lived in large villages in the summer. They built dome-shaped wigwams with frames made of sapling (young trees), covered with mats of cedar or birch bark. Inside, mats made of cattails provided insulation and protection from rain; they were sometimes colored with dyes made from fruits and berries. Animal skins or grass mats were placed on the ground or on raised sleeping platforms. The Menominee preferred to cook and eat outside, weather permitting.

In the winter, smaller groups of extended families retreated to their hunting grounds, where they built dome-shaped wigwams similar to their summer homes. Outlying buildings included sweat lodges for purification before ceremonies or for curing diseases, a lodge where women retreated during their menstrual periods, places for dreaming and fasting, and a lodge for the medicine man.

Contemporary dwellings As late as the 1950s, a few elderly Menominee still lived in bark houses. An exhibit on display at the tribally operated Logging Camp Museum in Keshena, Wisconsin, shows a restored Menominee camp typical in the early twentieth century. It features a bunkhouse, cook shanty, wood butcher's shop, blacksmith shop, saw filer's shack, horse barn, office, 100-foot (30-meter) cedar-roof shed, and loggers' locomotive.

In the early 2000s, most Menominee lived in homes no different from non-Natives, with one exception: some families posted small totem poles outside the front door.

Clothing and adornment

The early Menominee wore little clothing in warm weather. In cool weather, they wore buckskin breechcloths (garments with front and back flaps that hung from the waist), leggings, and moccasins, with cloaks for formal occasions, much like their Ojibway neighbors. Snowshoes made winter travel easier. They used oil and grease to soften their skin and long hair, and they sometimes painted their skin as well.

They adorned their clothing with satin ribbon and porcupine quills in geometric patterns such as diamonds, triangles, leaves, crosses, deer heads, and thunderbirds. European glass beads were woven into hair streamers and sashes.

In the nineteenth century, full gathered skirts similar to those worn by the settlers became popular. Fashionable men's wear at the turn of the twentieth century included cotton shirts, sometimes with ruffles, silk ribbons, and decorative pins made of a nickel alloy called German silver.

An early twentieth-century photograph shows Menominee men wearing checkered loggers' shirts and slouch hats intermingling with men in suits or feathered fur caps and elaborately embroidered robes. Women are dressed like their German-American neighbors, except for the addition of turquoise and silver or beaded jewelry.

Food

Menominee were called the "Wild-Rice People" because that was their principal crop. Wild rice is a cereal grass that grows in lakes and streams. Menominee women stood in a canoe and reached for the tall, hollow rice stalks. They held them over the boat and shook them so that the wild rice fell into the canoe. The Menominee considered harvesting wild rice to be both a spiritual and an economic activity. Wild rice was boiled and often flavored with maple syrup. Today, some Menominee gather and sell both wild rice and maple syrup.

Women also gathered nuts, fruits, and berries. Menominee men supplemented the diet by hunting ducks and geese. They caught fish with spears and nets made of animal sinew; their favorite catch was sturgeon. All this combined to make a very healthy, well-rounded diet. Early explorers commented on the good health of the Menominee people.

Nineteenth-century Menominee who were willing to take up farming grew rye, potatoes, oats, corn, melons, and fruit trees, in addition to beans, peas, turnips, wheat, and buckwheat. Some also raised hogs. Farmers and wild-rice gatherers often shared the fruits of their labors.

Healing practices

The Menominee believed that illness came from supernatural powers and evil witches, so they relied on a shaman (pronounced *SHAH-mun* or *SHAY-mun*), or medicine man. He brought a bag of remedies that he had received from his father or his teacher. His bag might contain healing roots and herbs, charms such as deer tails, carved wooden puppets, and a medicine stick for offerings to the spirits.

Herbal remedies were many and varied. Treatments for swellings, sores, loose mucus, and colds came from trees. The Menominee used mint for pneumonia. They had herbal medicines for poison ivy and boils, female disorders and childbirth, urinary and venereal diseases, stomach and intestinal disorders, diarrhea, sleeplessness, and lung trouble. Insecticides, enemas, eyewashes, and painkillers were important. The herb called "Seneca snakeroot" became so popular as a healing remedy that the Menominee traded, overcollected, and almost exterminated it. People used skunk cabbage and wild or chokecherries on wounds.

During the French and Indian War (1754–63), Menominee warriors brought smallpox back to their villages; more than one-quarter of their people died. U.S. soldiers carried smallpox and cholera into Wisconsin in the 1830s, where another 25 percent of the population died. The Natives had no effective defense against the diseases until inoculation (vaccination against disease) became widespread.

In 1977, the tribe built the first Native-owned and operated health facility in the country. They also ran a treatment center that offered outpatient services, drug and alcohol abuse programs, and family therapy.

A portrait of a Menominee family taken in Wisconsin in 1931 includes several generations. LIBRARY OF CONGRESS

Education

Menominee children traditionally learned by example. Soon after moving to the reservation in 1854, the Menominee built a school, but they lost it when a 1954 law terminated the reservation. Toward the end of the twentieth century, with profits acquired from timber, the Menominee built a college and four reservation schools attended by more than five hundred children. The College of the Menominee Nation, which opened in 1993, offers a variety of degree programs and has agreements with other colleges so students can complete work in fields such as human services and nursing.

CUSTOMS

Clan structure and rituals

The Menominee are divided into groups called Bear and Thunderer (see "Religion"). Each group consists of clans whose members consider one another brothers and sisters. Membership is passed down through the father. The Bear symbol was a female bear with a long tail, and Thunderer

A young boy dances at a Gathering of Warriors Powwow in Keshena, Wisconsin, an annual event put on by the Veterans of the Menominee Nation. © AP IMAGES/CORY DELLENBACH

was represented by an eagle, which the Menominee believed to be the most beautiful and powerful bird of the country, perched upon a cross.

Today, the Menominee retain some of their ancient rites. For example, they leave tobacco offerings at a stone called Spirit Rock to please the hero Manabozho, who turned a greedy warrior to stone for requesting eternal life. Menominee oral history states that when Spirit Rock crumbles away, the Menominee will perish.

Festivals

Menominee of old held a Beggars' Dance in the fall, which celebrated the maple syrup season. Modern Menominee hold two annual powwows: the Veterans Powwow over Memorial Day weekend and the Annual Menominee Nation Contest Powwow the first weekend in August. At these powwows, members of several different tribes participate in dance contests and tribal drumming performances.

Hunting and gathering rituals

Before gathering wild rice, the Menominee threw tobacco (considered a sacred substance) onto the water to please the spirits. When hunting, they took only what they needed for food, clothing, and sleeping mats. They hunted with bows lubricated with bear grease and arrows made of pine or cedar. Bear was a favorite prey, and when one was killed a special ceremony and feast was held, to which all a hunter's friends were invited.

Burial

The dead were buried and a spirit house marked the grave. Some Menominee still follow this burial custom.

Games

Because the Menominee had ample food to meet their needs, they also had leisure time. Lacrosse, a game of Native American origin, was a favorite pastime for Menominee men. It was played on a field by two teams of ten players each. Participants used a long-handled stick with a webbed pouch (a racket) to get a ball into the opposing team's goal. The Menominee played lacrosse with a deerskin ball stuffed with hair and rackets made of saplings.

CURRENT TRIBAL ISSUES

In 2010, the U.S. Department of the Interior denied the Menominee bid to build a casino in Kenosha, Wisconsin. The Potawatomi opposed the project as competition for their own casino in Milwaukee. One of the reasons given for the rejection is that the casino is about 200 miles from the reservation. Getting approval for off-reservation casinos is difficult, but the Menominee indicted that they would continue to lobby for the Kenosha facility.

The Menominee are being held up as an example of what can be accomplished with proper forest management. Over the past century, they have harvested approximately 2.25 billion board feet of timber. Yet they have more timber now than they did when they started. The tribe attributes it to careful management, and many groups come to study their methods.

The Menominee's strong commitment to the environment is obvious in other ways. They joined forces with other area tribes to protest an underground zinc and copper mine by the Wolf River that was expected to put out 44 million tons of toxic waste. To ensure that the land would remain sacred, the Menominee and Potawatomi purchased the land in 2003. That action allowed the tribes to use the water and the land around it as they always have—for rice gathering and religious purposes—and ensured that the water would remain pollutant free. In explaining the tribes' choice to reject the mining operation, the Sacred Land Film Project quoted Sokaogon pipe carrier Robert Van Zile: "Water is necessary for life, metals are needed for wealth—which is more important? I will not sit back and let corporate greed rob our future generations of their rights to have access to pure water."

NOTABLE PEOPLE

Ada Deer (1935–) is a lifelong advocate for social justice. She helped create Determination of Rights and Unity for Menominee Shareholders (DRUMS), which was instrumental in convincing Congress to reinstate the Menominee tribe after it was terminated in 1954. When Congress confirmed her nomination as the first woman to head the U.S. Bureau of Indian Affairs, she said: "I want to emphasize [that] my administration will be based on the Indian values of caring, sharing, and respect.... These values have been missing too long in the halls of government."

Tribal leader Oshkosh (1795–1858), also known as Claw, was known for his efforts to promote peaceful coexistence with white settlers. Despite his best efforts, Menominee lands were taken, and he was forced to oversee the removal of his people to a reservation that was only a tiny portion of their former homeland.

BOOKS

Bial, Raymond. *The Menominee*. New York: Marshall Cavendish Benchmark, 2006.

Peroff, Nicholas C. *Menominee Drums: Tribal Termination and Restoration, 1954–1974*. Norman: University of Oklahoma Press, 2006.

Riordan, Robert. *Medicine for Wildcat: A Story of the Friendship between a Menominee Indian and Frontier Priest Samuel Mazzuchelli*. Revised by Marilyn Bowers Gorun and the Sinsinawa Dominican Sisters. Sinsinawa, WI: Sinsinawa Dominican Sisters, 2006.

Shillinger, Sarah. *A Case Study of the American Indian Boarding School Movement: An Oral History of Saint Joseph's Indian Industrial School*. Lewiston, NY: Edwin Mellen Press, 2008.

WEB SITES

Corbin, Amy. "Sacred Land Film Project: Wolf River." *Christopher McLeod/ Earth Island Institute*. http://www.sacredland.org/wolf-river/ (accessed June 8, 2011).

"Menominee Culture." *Menominee Indian Tribe of Wisconsin*. http://www. mpm.edu/wirp/ICW-54.html (accessed on June 7, 2011).

"Menominee Indian Tribe of Wisconsin." *Great Lakes Inter-Tribal Council*. http://www.glitc.org/programs/pages/mtw.html (accessed on June 7, 2011).

Menominee Indian Tribe of Wisconsin. http://www.menominee-nsn.gov/ (accessed June 8, 2011).

"Menominee Oral Tradition." *Indian Country*. http://www.mpm.edu/wirp/ ICW-138.html (accessed on June 7, 2011).

Redish, Laura, and Orrin Lewis. "Native Languages of the Americas: Menominee." *Native Languages of the Americas: Preserving and Promoting American Indian Languages*. http://www.native-languages.org/menominee. htm (accessed on June 7, 2011).

Sultzman, Lee. "Menominee History." *First Nation Histories*. http://www. dickshovel.com/men.html (accessed on June 7, 2011).

Miami

Name

Miami (pronounced *my-AM-ee*), also called Maumee. The name may come from the Miami-Illinois word *Myaamia,* meaning "allies." The Chippewa called the Miami *Omaumeg* (also *Oumami* or *Oumamik*), meaning "people who live on the peninsula." The tribe is sometimes called *Twigh Twees* or *Twaatwaa* after the sound a crane makes.

Location

The Miami originally lived in the area around the Great Lakes in parts of present-day Indiana, Illinois, Michigan, Wisconsin, and Ohio. During the 1800s, the majority of them were forced to move first to Missouri, then Kansas, and finally to Oklahoma. Today, the main groups of Miami are concentrated in Indiana, Kansas, and Oklahoma.

Population

Prior to European contact, there may have been as many as 15,000 Miami. That total fell to about 4,500 soon after the European arrival in the late 1600s. It decreased again over the next few decades to approximately 2,000. Estimating the number of Miami during these early periods is difficult because only warriors were counted. According to the 1910 U.S. Census, 226 Miami lived in the United States; of those, 123 lived in Oklahoma and 90 lived in Indiana. The 2000 census showed that 3,784 people identified themselves as Miami only, whereas 6,420 claimed to have some Miami heritage. Of the people who claimed to be Miami only, 1,526 resided in Indiana, 352 in Oklahoma, and 334 in Kansas.

Language family

Algonquian.

Origins and group affiliations

In the 1600s, the Miami lived with the Mascoutens along the southern end of Lake Michigan. At times, they also lived with the Kickapoo. The Miami and the Illinois were often thought of as one tribe. Although both tribes spoke a

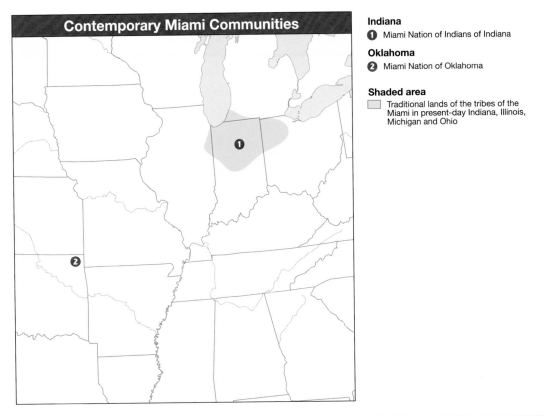

Contemporary Miami Communities

Indiana
1 Miami Nation of Indians of Indiana

Oklahoma
2 Miami Nation of Oklahoma

Shaded area
Traditional lands of the tribes of the Miami in present-day Indiana, Illinois, Michigan and Ohio

A map of contemporary Miami communities. MAP BY XNR PRODUCTIONS. CENGAGE LEARNING, GALE. REPRODUCED BY PERMISSION OF GALE, A PART OF CENGAGE LEARNING.

similar language and were sometimes allies, they considered themselves two distinct groups. Originally, the Miami consisted of six bands: Piankashaw, Wea, Atchatchakangouen, Kilatika, Mengakonkia, and Pepicokia. Some of these groups later merged, became separate tribes, or disappeared altogether. The Miami traded with all the tribes in the Great Lakes region except the Chickasaw and the Dakota (see entries), who were their enemies. In the late 1700s, the Miami led an alliance of other Great Lakes tribes that included the Ojibway, Potawatomi, and Shawnee (see entries).

Some researchers believe the Miami descended from the prehistoric Fisher and Huber tribes who lived in the southern Lake Michigan area. When the Europeans arrived, the Miami were living in the Great Lakes region and controlled most of the waterways. Though they had a reputation as fierce fighters and retaliated when attacked, they preferred peace, and as a result, they relocated many times. In the early twenty-first century, most Miami lived in two areas of the country—Indiana and Oklahoma—although some remained in Kansas during that migration.

HISTORY

Ancient ancestors

Some researchers believe the Miami are related to the Mississippian culture (see Mound Builders entry). Excavations revealed stone spear points dating to 8000 BCE in the territory the Miami once inhabited. Others believe the Miami arrived in this part of the country at a later date. By the time of the first European contact in the mid-1600s, the Miami were living in the area of present-day Green Bay, Wisconsin.

Trading troubles

During the 1500s and 1600s, French explorers set up trading posts in the Great Lakes region. European diseases had preceded their arrival, and many Native American tribes had become ill or died due to epidemics (uncontrolled outbreaks of disease). Those that survived were vying for the French trade by trapping beaver to exchange for guns, blankets, mirrors, tools, glass beads, and alcohol.

When the area became overtrapped, the Beaver Wars (1641–1701) broke out, and Native Americans fought with each other for control of the trade and for better hunting grounds. In the 1660s, the Miami and the Illinois settled on the western side of the Mississippi River to avoid Iroquois (see entry) raids. A year after the Seneca destroyed Miami villages in 1687, the Miami broke away from the Illinois tribe, with whom they had been fighting, and moved back to northern Indiana.

French-British conflicts

In the early 1700s, the French established forts to protect their soldiers and trappers. When the British sent trading parties to the area, the French warned them to stay out of the territory. The British ignored them and

Important Dates

mid-1600s: The Miami encounter Europeans and provide scouts to guide Father Jacques Marquette and Louis Joliet to the Mississippi River.

1641–1701: The Miami engage in the Beaver Wars.

1755–63: The Miami ally with France during the French and Indian War. When the British win, the king forbids American settlers to move west of the Appalachian Mountains.

1790: Led by Little Turtle, the Miami defeat General Harmar and his American army.

1791: In the greatest Native American defeat of the U.S. Army, the Miami win against General Arthur St. Clair.

1794: The Miami lose the Battle of Fallen Timbers and are forced to sign the Treaty of Greenville in 1795.

1846: The Miami divide. One band stays in Indiana; the other goes to Kansas.

1867: The Kansas tribe relocates to Oklahoma.

1897: The U.S. government terminates the tribal status of the Indiana Miami.

1996: The Miami Tribe of Oklahoma adopts a revised constitution.

threatened to attack any tribes who traded with France. In 1732, a group of three hundred Natives—Miami, Piankashaw, and Wea—died after drinking brandy. Some said the French had poisoned the alcohol, hoping the people would distrust the British and trade with them instead.

Increasing hostilities led to the French and Indian War (1754–63; a war fought in North America between England and France involving some Native Americans as allies of the French), and most Miami allied themselves with France. After the British defeated the French, the British turned French trading posts into forts. Many Miami moved to present-day Indiana to avoid further confrontation.

Most tribes viewed the British victory as positive because the king refused to allow American colonists to move west of the Appalachian Mountains. They believed their territory was now secure from white invasion.

Chief Little Turtle led the Miami to victory in battles against American troops in 1790 and 1791. © NORTH WIND PICTURE ARCHIVES

The American Revolution

The Americans colonists, however, had no intention of following the British king's orders. When the American Revolution (1775–83; the American colonists' fight for independence from England) began, the commander of the British army, Henry Hamilton (c. 1734–1796), offered the Native people rewards for attacking the Americans. Many tribes took Hamilton up on his offer. The Miami did not, even though they supported the British.

As the war dragged on, the Miami and several other tribes, under the leadership of Chief Little Turtle (1752–1812), aided the British, believing a British victory would prevent American colonists from taking over their land. After the Americans won the war in 1783, settlement expanded into the Great Lakes area. The U.S. government divided the land into parcels and gave it the colonists.

Harmar and St. Clair Defeats

The Miami formed a confederation with the Delaware, Shawnee, and Potawatomi (see entries) tribes headed by Little Turtle. Constant skirmishes over frontier land led President George Washington (1732–1799; served 1789–97) to send troops to the area in 1790. The first army of 1,500 soldiers commanded by Brigadier General Josiah Harmar (1753–1813) outnumbered Little Turtle's small band, but the Miami chief's tactics defeated the stronger American army.

In 1791, Washington sent a larger army of three thousand troops to the area, led by General Arthur St. Clair (1736–1818). The Miami again emerged triumphant. With more than six hundred dead and almost three hundred wounded, the Americans suffered their worst defeat ever in a battle against the Native Americans.

Leaders of several tribes sign the Treaty of Greenville in 1795, which ceded most of what is now Ohio and other lands to the U.S. government. © THREE LIONS/GETTY IMAGES

Battle of Fallen Timbers

After St. Clair's defeat, Washington appointed General Anthony Wayne (1745–1796) commander of the Northwest army in 1792. When tribes attacked a supply train in 1794, Wayne's army attacked their villages and destroyed crops. Little Turtle urged his people to try for peace, but few agreed, so he turned his command over to Shawnee leader Blue Jacket (c. 1745–c. 1810).

Wayne and Blue Jacket met at Fallen Timbers, Ohio. Knowing that the Natives always fasted before a battle, Wayne waited several days until the tribes were weak with hunger and some had left to find food. Then he attacked. Many Native Americans were killed, and Blue Jacket's men retreated to Fort Miami, where the British refused to help them. Without British support, the tribes had to agree to Wayne's terms. They signed the Treaty of Greenville in 1795, giving the U.S. government most of Ohio and parts of several adjoining states. Not all the tribes agreed with this decision, and bloodshed continued for several decades.

Sale of land

The Americans soon desired more land. In spite of the Greenville treaty, many settlers moved onto Miami land. William Henry Harrison (1773–1841), who later became president of the United States, used Native American debts and the lure of alcohol to acquire more land. Over the next decade, Native Americans gave up more than twenty-one million acres.

In 1805, Tenskwatawa (1775–c. 1836), a Shawnee prophet, convinced many tribes to return to Native traditions and stay away from alcohol. His brother, Tecumseh (1768–1813), also urged the people not to sell any more land to the whites. However, a group of peace chiefs from several tribes, including Little Turtle of the Miami, sold land in Indiana and Illinois under the Fort Wayne Treaty.

More relocations

Other treaties signed between 1818 and 1840 gave up the rest of Miami land. Only one small band had land left, that owned by Chief Meshingomesia. The rest of the Miami moved to Kansas in 1846. Between five hundred and fifteen hundred Miami stayed behind; many had intermarried with whites. By 1872, fewer than three hundred of this group remained, and the U.S. government divided the land among them.

During his lifetime, Chief Jean Baptiste Richardville (also called *Peshewa,* or "Wildcat"; c. 1761–1841) negotiated to prevent the Miami from being relocated. After he died, his son-in-law, Francis Lafontaine (*Topeah,* or "Frost on the Bushes"; 1810–1847), took his place. Although Topeah kept half of the tribe in Indiana, he oversaw the forced move to Kansas Territory. He died the following year on his return trip to Indiana.

About 550 Miami relocated to Kansas. Colonists soon followed, and when Kansas became a state in 1862, the settlers asked the government to remove the Natives. Five years later, the Miami agreed to a treaty giving up their Kansas land. They moved to Oklahoma and, along with several other tribes, purchased 6,000 acres. In 1893, the government divided that land into smaller individual properties and took the rest. By the 1930s, neither Miami tribe had any land left.

Through all those years, the Miami Tribe of Oklahoma kept its federal recognition status. In 1897, however, the U.S. government terminated the tribal status of the Indiana Miami, claiming that the Miami had lost their tribal heritage by marrying into and fully adapting to white society. Without federal recognition the Indiana Miami do not have the right to govern themselves as a separate nation or receive government funding and other benefits. As of 2011, the Indiana Miami continued to petition for the return of their tribal status.

Struggles in the early twentieth century

During the early 1900s, Miami farmers lived in poverty. Many purchased goods on credit, and whites often demanded repayment in land, so the majority ended up landless. Most Miami in Indiana lived like the Americans. They spoke English, dressed like Americans, and sent their children to public schools. Although some retained their culture, many intermarried with whites and adopted their ways.

In spite of their assimilation, or adaptation to mainstream culture, many Miami felt the effects of prejudice. They faced not only insults but also physical violence. To help the tribe, Chief Camillus Bundy (1854–1935) began holding a yearly Miami reunion (see "Festivals"). He also was instrumental in organizing the tribe as the Miami Nation of Indians of Indiana in 1923. The tribe went against federal policy of that time period and asked the government to honor past treaties. Bundy wrote to then-president Calvin Coolidge (1872–1933; served 1923–29):

> Once having been recognized by the Congress and government of this union, no one has the right to dissolve us and destroy us as a race, but they have been doing so, and are doing so, and through it all we have been reduced to a plight which is a reproach on this nation. America owes us an obligation. We appeal to you now as its head.

Although the Miami did not succeed in these requests, they kept trying, and they also worked for federal recognition. One of the difficulties they faced was that many of them had intermarried with whites and tried to live like the rest of society. The government used that as reason for denying their petition for federal recognition. This meant that they were not considered an independent nation, nor could they receive any federal benefits. They also were told that it was too late for them to receive the land they had been promised in treaties years before.

Two of the main Miami activists of the era were Bundy and Victoria Brady. In 1928 and 1929, when the legislation requiring the U.S. government to return land to the Miami tribe did not pass, Brady protested by occupying the offices of the Bureau of Indian Affairs (BIA). When papers related to the Miami claims were lost, she ransacked an office. Meanwhile, Bundy and his family, who had lost their farm, camped in tents in their family cemetery. They did not expect the government to take this land, but Bundy was jailed for refusing to leave the land when ordered.

World War II and after

In 1937, the Indiana Miami organized and adopted bylaws. Two years later, the Oklahoma Miami adopted a constitution. The two tribes began to work together for their land rights. When World War II (1939–45; a war in which Great Britain, France, the United States, and their allies defeated Germany, Italy, and Japan) began, the Miami put aside their land claims and supported the war effort. More than twenty-five thousand Native Americans joined the service to fight for the United States during the war.

Once the war ended, the Miami returned to fighting for their legal claims. This time both groups filed separately. In the 1960s, the government agreed to settle two of their many claims but postponed payment. With the death of the leader of the Indiana group, Ves Godfroy, infighting ensued among the Indiana Miami.

At the same time, the government funded construction of a dam in Indiana that flooded 14,000 acres of former tribal land, including several cemeteries. Removal and reburying the remains caused friction. By the time the claims were paid in 1969, each person received little more than $1,200. By 1982, all the factions had united as the Miami Indians of Indiana.

Even though the Oklahoma Miami were federally recognized, they did not fare much better. The tribe had no land, and money for legal battles came from donations. Settlements to the tribe were meager, and the terms of many treaties were never fulfilled.

RELIGION

The Miami's main gods were the Great Hare and the Sun. Lesser deities, called *manitous,* included inanimate (nonliving) objects as well as living beings. Some manitous included thunder, lightning, tornadoes, and the spirits of animals. The people offered prayers and tobacco to manitous for protection. The Underwater Panther was one of the most feared manitous because it caused wild waves with the flick of its tail. The people offered it tobacco so they could fish and travel safely.

Various religious societies formed in the tribe. Some revolved around clan war-bundles, packets that contained sacred objects to help warriors win battles. Other societies were composed of people who had received visions from the same manitou spirit. Warriors who had performed heroic acts in battle made up another society; their bravery indicated they had special powers.

During the late 1700s, some Miami accepted the teachings of Neolin the Delaware Prophet, who encouraged tribes to return to their Native ways and give up white men's goods, such as alcohol and guns. Other Miami, influenced by the Jesuit or Baptist missionaries, converted to Christianity. Adopting Christian beliefs altered Miami society in many ways. One major change occurred in women's roles. Previously they had been equal to men; now men were considered dominant. By the mid-1800s, most of the tribal leaders had become Baptists, so councils became predominately male.

Miami words

aamaawia	"bee"
alemwa	"dog"
aya	"hello"
mihko	"red"
miiciwa	"eat"
moohswa	"deer"
niihka	"friend"
shikaakwa	"skunk"
waapanswa	"rabbit"

LANGUAGE

The Miami and Illinois were close dialects (varieties) of the Central Algonquian language. The Miami language was considered dead in 1965, when the last of the Native speakers died. In 1988, however, a graduate student, David Costa, began to study the language. He interviewed a few elders who had heard the language as children and recalled some words. With their help and written documents, he reconstructed the basics of the language.

Since 1995, the Miami Nation has continued Costa's work by searching written records from past centuries to reclaim their language. They also developed programs to teach the language to their children.

GOVERNMENT

The main divisions of the Miami tribe were clans (groups of people related by a common ancestor), and each clan elected its own chief. In addition, the Miami had tribal chiefs, village chiefs, war chiefs, and peace chiefs. Men and women both held these positions. Women chiefs had the power to end feuds and wars. Because the society was matrilineal, mothers passed down the position of hereditary chief to their children.

Hereditary chiefs also handled religious duties. Once the Europeans arrived and disease killed many people, however, some of the tribe's belief in the chief's power dwindled. In spite of this, the Miami had great respect for their chiefs. Generally, the head chief did not go to war but acted as a diplomat. Sometimes women who had visions accompanied a war party.

In the early twenty-first century, the Miami Nation of Oklahoma had a chief and a second chief as well as a tribal council. Because they received federal recognition, they operated as an independent nation. Recognition also entitled them to federal funds and benefits. The Miami Tribe of Indiana has been waiting since 1995 for federal recognition. As of 2011, it did not qualify for federal help or for any additional payments for lost lands. The tribe still maintains traditional leadership and holds tribal meetings as it have done throughout its history.

ECONOMY

Early economy

The Miami were hunters and gatherers who lived near the water for most of the year and then migrated to the prairie during the winter to hunt buffalo. They also farmed, raising corn, fruit, and vegetables to supplement their diet.

After the arrival of the Europeans, the Miami entered the fur trade. They controlled most of the ports in the Great Lakes region, and shrewd business people like Tacumwah (c. 1720–c. 1790) and her son, Chief Richardville (c. 1761–1841), got rich from the fur trade and from dominating ports along the waterways.

Twentieth-century economy

After the Miami relocated to Kansas and later Oklahoma, they struggled to survive. By the 1900s, many men in Indiana worked on the railroads or at circuses. Three different circuses had headquarters near Peru, Indiana, and the Miami worked in the food stands, cared for and trained wild animals, and sometimes performed circus acts. Many men also served as cooks, firemen, and engineers on the four railroads in the area.

During the Great Depression (1929–41; the period, following the stock market crash in 1929, of struggling economies and few jobs), the circuses closed, putting many Miami out of work. The state welfare office denied them benefits because they were Native Americans. The Bureau of Indian Affairs did not acknowledge them as a tribe, so they were not eligible for federal funds either. To stay alive, many people reverted to hunting and fishing, but they were arrested for violating state hunting regulations. In 1933, Elijah Shapp wrote: "We the Miami Indians of Indiana want our land and money that is due us.… My people are starving."

Present-day economy

In 1990, the Miami Tribe of Indiana purchased a tribal complex in Peru, Indiana, and started Little Turtle Daycare Center. They opened a shelter, arts and crafts workshops, an archive, and a museum that they fund mainly through bingo proceeds. In the 2000s, the fluctuating U.S. economy affected members of the Miami Nation of Indiana, and unemployment continued to be a problem.

The Western Miami founded an organization, Miami Tribe of Oklahoma Business Development Authority (MTOBDA), whose mission was to develop and manage business enterprises so the tribe remained self-sufficient. In 1995, these Miami joined with the Modoc to operate the Stables Casino near the Modoc Tribal Complex. The Miami then opened another casino, Miami Tribe Entertainment Casino, located at their tribal complex. The tribe also owned the 1,000-acre Tahway Farms with its crops, pecan groves, and cattle; the Miami Trader Gift Shop to sell Native arts and crafts; Envira Tech Environmental Testing Lab; and several other businesses. According to 2000 U.S. Census statistics, this branch of the Miami Nation had an amazing zero percent unemployment. That meant everyone in the tribe who wanted to work had a job. In the early 2000s, Miami Nation Enterprises oversaw tribally owned companies and worked to improve the economy. Some of the tribe's largest enterprises are the casinos, a movie theater complex, and business and technology services.

DAILY LIFE

Families

In Miami families, both men and women hunted, fished, and tanned hides. The men typically prepared the fields, and women planted and tended the crops. Women also prepared meat, gathered wood, and sewed the bark canoes together. When the tribe migrated from place to place, it was usually the woman's job to carry the material for the wigwam on her back and to build the house. Men went to war, but sometimes women accompanied them (see "Government"). Both genders did storytelling, artwork, music, and healing.

The equal division of labor also extended to the children. Boys and girls both learned to work at the same jobs as their parents. An early European observer noted that both sexes were treated equally and that illegitimate children were treated the same way as legitimate children. It was acceptable, and not uncommon, for unmarried Miami women to have children.

Mothers carried their babies in cradleboards strapped to their backs. The Miami did not believe in physical punishment, so they only scolded their children. Many Indian tribes also used storytelling as a way to help children learn proper behavior.

The family line passed down through the mother's brother, but children belonged to their father's clan. People from the same clan could not marry each other.

BUILDINGS

The Miami had winter and summer villages. During the growing season, they lived near the water. Summer homes were 12 by 20 feet (3.5 by 6 meters) with high gabled roofs and bark-covered exteriors. People spent most of their time outdoors; they usually cooked and ate outside.

In the winter, they constructed lodges covered with bark or mats made of woven reeds placed over a framework of saplings. Their homes, called *wikiami,* were oval with a fire pit in the center. They stored their possessions at the back and placed sleeping platforms around the sides.

A Native American family uses a travois and dogs carrying packs to transport their possessions. © NORTH WIND PICTURE ARCHIVES

The Miami sometimes situated their towns on hills and surrounded them by palisades (fences made of logs). Villages had sweat lodges; they also had larger wooden longhouses for ceremonies and councils.

TRANSPORTATION

Because the Miami lived around lakes and rivers, they knew how to travel by water. Although the men hollowed out large trees to make dugout canoes or built birchbark canoes, they often traveled on land. Before the Spanish brought horses to America, the tribe used dogs as pack animals. Sometimes dogs were loaded down with goods. Other times, the Miami harnessed the dogs to frames made from wooden poles called *travois* (truh-VOY). They lashed their possessions to the travois or to wooden sleds attached to the poles, and the dogs dragged the goods as they moved from camp to camp. The sleds were important for traveling through snow during the winter.

CLOTHING AND ADORNMENT

Because the men wore so little clothing, Europeans nicknamed the Miami the "naked" or "tattooed men." Men wore breechcloths (fabric secured at the waist that passes between the legs) and tattooed most of their body. In the winter, they wore leather shirts and leggings.

Women dressed in deerskin skirts and leggings. They often painted the skirts and breechcloths with red dyes. Females tattooed their cheeks, arms, and chests. The people preferred going barefoot but wore moccasins in the winter.

Miami headdresses were simple, usually a beaded headband with a few red feathers. Women had long hair, which they braided or rolled into a bun. Men adopted the Mohawk hairdo and often added a porcupine roach for decoration. Roaches were made of porcupine hair dyed bright colors. Both men and women painted their faces.

After the Europeans arrived, some Miami dressed similarly to the newcomers. Women wore short calico (printed cotton) dresses with red leggings underneath and buckskin moccasins. They draped a long length of cotton over their shoulders as a shawl. Others wore full, ankle-length skirts with brightly colored blouses and draped decorated shawls or blankets around their shoulders. Leggings, skirts, shawls, and moccasins were often adorned with silk-ribbon appliqué and glass beads.

Men wore frock coats with ruffled shirts underneath but kept their breechcloths, leggings, and moccasins. They wrapped cloth around their heads like turbans.

FOOD

Although the people hunted and gathered, they also farmed. Crops included beans, melons, squash, pumpkins, tobacco, and corn. The tribe was known for its maize (corn), which had tender, white kernels. This variety of corn is called "Silver Queen" today. Corn was eaten in many ways and was dried and ground into flour. Women also collected roots, nuts, berries, and fruits.

In the late autumn, the men spent several weeks hunting buffalo. When they found a herd, they set a circular fire in the grass around the animals, leaving one opening. As the buffalo rushed away from the blaze, the men stationed themselves near the opening and shot them with bows and arrows. The women jerked the meat (cut it into long thin slices and dried it in the sun) or broiled it. They also spun thread of buffalo hair to make bags to carry the meat. The fur made robes and blankets for winter.

In addition to bison and deer, the tribe hunted other large game, such as elk, wildcat, lynx, and bear. The hunters divided the meat among all the people. As large game grew scarce, the men hunted muskrat, opossum, porcupine, raccoon, turtle, and woodchuck. They also ate a variety of small birds as well as ducks, geese, and turkey. Toward the end of the winter, the Miami tapped trees for sap and boiled it in birchbark containers to make maple syrup.

EDUCATION

Children learned by watching their elders. Older Miami were expected to serve as examples of proper behavior, and youngsters looked up to them.

By the early 1900s, most Miami in Indiana went to school with the settlers. Many boys preferred learning traditional skills like hunting and trapping to sitting indoors in a one-room schoolhouse. Once the Miami had lost most of their land, few children could attend high school. They had to find jobs to help support their families. Not until after 1945 did many Miami get a higher education.

In 2001, Miami University in Oxford, Ohio, developed the Myaamia Project to preserve Miami Nation history, culture, and language. The

Rabbit and Possum

Many tribes tell tales to explain how different animals acquired their physical features. This Miami story describes why the rabbit's upper lip is divided into two parts.

> The Possum and the Rabbit gambled together to see if it should be dark all the time or light all the time. Possum kept singing a song that it should be dark, and he sang this over and over. Rabbit kept singing his song that it should be daylight. Along toward morning, Rabbit began to get a little bit tired. Possum said, "You might as well give it up, Rabbit. It's going to be night all the time." Well, they argued about this. Then Possum said to Rabbit, "Suppose you did win and daylight came to stay. Why, children would abuse you. They would chase you into a hollow log and take a stick and twist the fur off of you." Rabbit said, "I don't care. They'll have lots of fun playing with me anyway." Now, while they were arguing, Rabbit kept singing, "Daylight, daylight, daylight!" And when Possum looked around, there he saw the daylight was coming. He grabbed Rabbit's mouth to make him shut up, and split his upper lip. That's why Rabbit has a split lip.

SOURCE: Stand, Nancy, as told to Truman Michelson, 1916. Available online at http://www.museum.state.il.us/muslink/nat_amer/post/htmls/popups/be_rabbit.html (accessed on June 7, 2011).

university has an art museum to showcase Miami arts and crafts. Students from the Miami tribe are offered scholarships to attend the university. In Indiana, the Saakaciweeyankwi Miami Tribal Youth Summer Educational Program teaches children about the traditional Miami culture through music, crafts, and workshops with elders.

HEALING PRACTICES

In the late summer, the tribe gathered bark, fruits, roots, leaves, and berries for medicine. They used wild ginger for colds, wahoo bark for fevers, wild cherry teas for hiccoughs, black willow for skin problems, prickly ash for toothaches, chestnuts for coughs, and milkweed for warts. For an earache, they blew tobacco smoke into the ear.

The Miami followed a practice called *Midewiwin* ("Spirit Doings"). *Mide* priests held rituals for illness and encouraged people to behave properly. Although these priests had a high rank, they were not as important as healers.

ARTS

The area where the Miami lived was rich in clay, which they used in making pottery. Rivers and lakes provided many reeds that the tribe used for matting and to construct the walls of their homes.

The Miami were known for their quillwork, beadwork, and embroidery. They decorated their clothing and moccasins with appliquéd designs. Silk ribbon work adorned leggings and moccasins. After they adopted European dress, women used traditional needlework on their shawls and skirts.

In the early and mid-1900s, many people believed the Miami and their traditions would die out. Few engaged in traditional crafts, and little was done to pass on these skills. During the 1960s, however, the Miami began holding classes to teach the skills to younger generations.

CUSTOMS

Birth and naming

A woman giving birth stayed in a hut opposite her husband's. If the delivery took too long, large groups of men would rush toward the hut firing guns, believing that frightening her would help.

Before the mother and baby returned to the family home, the mother bathed. Her husband cleaned the hut by shaking out all the skins and removing all the ashes from the fire. Then he lit a new fire and invited her into the hut.

Many children were given names that represented natural objects or a quality the parents hoped their child would acquire. Others were named for respected ancestors.

Puberty

Both boys and girls trained for vision quests when they were very young. To do this, they fasted (went without food and drink). At puberty, boys used black paint or charcoal on their faces; girls used dirt. The teens fasted for long periods of time until they saw an animal spirit.

Marriage and divorce

A man and woman might decide to marry, or their families could make the decision for them. The chief in a village would sometimes choose a wife for a man. Once the selection had been made, the man's father sent female relatives to the woman's house with cloth, kettles, guns, skins, and meat. If the woman took these presents, she sent gifts in return. This meant they were married. Then the groom gave his bride an expensive gift, such as a horse.

To mark the marriage, families exchanged gifts. The woman's eldest brother gave her the best meat from his hunting season. She in turn gave it to her husband's mother, who divided it among her family. Then the mother-in-law gave vegetables to the bride's family.

Both husbands and wives had the right to leave the marriage. To divorce a spouse, all a person had to do was walk away. If a husband abused his wife, she could kill him without being punished. Spouses who stayed married were expected to be faithful. If a Miami wife cheated on her husband, her nose was clipped. A man could marry more than one wife if he could afford it.

Festivals

The Miami marked several occasions with dances and ceremonies. When warriors returned victorious, the tribe held the bison dance. Harvesting corn called for the Green Corn Ceremony.

Every year since 1903, the Miami Indians of Indiana have held a reunion. Started by Camillus Bundy, the get-together originally occurred near former villages. After a council meeting, the men ate first, then the women and children. People dressed in ceremonial costumes and participated in games, dancing, and music. Today, families still gather in Wabash, Indiana, once a year to engage in these traditional activities.

War etiquette

Miami warriors used bows and arrows, tomahawks, spears, and buffalo-hide shields. They often ate their prisoners of war. One family was trained to roast the prisoner; then the body was eaten. The tribe had religious rituals that were part of the ceremony. In later years, Little Turtle tried to stop this practice.

Death rituals

When a person died, the Miami dressed the body in good clothes and laid it out in the lodge. After a short wake, four nonfamily members carried the corpse to the grave. They placed food and water in the grave, and an elder begged the dead not to take any of the living along on its journey. They exposed the body's chest, and relatives walked around the grave and laid a hand on it. Then they covered the body.

A body might be buried in different ways. The Miami sometimes laid it flat in a shallow grave lined with bark or planks. They also buried corpses in sitting positions. Other times, they split a tree and hollowed it out. They enclosed the body and fastened the tree to the ground with stakes. If they buried the body on the surface, they made a small log enclosure around it, tilting the logs in to meet on top. Some bodies were laid on a scaffold high in the air until only the bones were left.

After the burial, an elder of the same sex stayed at the grave four nights. The Miami believed it took four days before the spirit started on its journey. The Milky Way was the path it took, but it could be tempted back by evil spirits and never arrive in the spirit land.

Soon after the funeral, the tribe engaged in the dead person's favorite dance or activity. When the first corn (*mimjipi,* meaning "corn spirit") was harvested, it was fed to spirits of dead relatives. One year after the death, children of the deceased adopted a new parent. Then the dance or activity was performed again to mark the end of the mourning period.

CURRENT TRIBAL ISSUES

The Miami Tribe of Oklahoma is working with Miami University of Oxford, Ohio, on the Myaamia Project. This initiative has developed a variety of ways to teach children and adults to speak their language. A multimedia Web site immerses viewers in a whole language experience, and readers can pass smart technology pens over the pages of books to hear the correct pronunciation of words. The research project also collects information about traditional uses of plants for cooking and healing. Using this information and technology, the Miami will be able to pass their traditional culture on to future generations.

In April 2011, a series of storms in the Midwest devastated the area that is home to several tribes, including the Miami. Other area tribes have been assisting communities as they recover and rebuild.

The Miami Nation of Indiana is seeking state recognition, which extends them rights under the Native American Free Exercise of Religion Act of 1993 and the Indian Arts and Crafts Act of 1990. The first act allows them to practice their religion and hold ceremonies, which in the past have been challenged. The second gives craftspeople the ability to label their products as Indian-made. With state recognition, the Miami Nation would qualify for some federal services, but they need federal recognition to gain access to the Bureau of Indian Affairs and Indian Health Service programs. Until they receive federal recognition, they have no status as an independent nation.

NOTABLE PEOPLE

As the son of a Mahican mother and a Miami war chief, Little Turtle (Mishikinakwa; c. 1752–1812) could not inherit his father's position; still, he proved to be a mastermind of war strategies and earned the honor of leading the Miami. He was known for his routs of American forces at Harmar's Defeat (1790) and St. Clair's Defeat (1791). After the his people's defeat in 1794 by General Anthony Wayne (1745–1796), Little Turtle agreed to peace terms and signed the Greenville Treaty, ceding most of the state of Ohio and parts of Indiana to the Americans. When he signed the treaty, he said, "I am the last to sign it, and I will be the last to break it." Afterward, he promoted peace. He also helped his tribe by encouraging vaccinations and discouraging the use of alcohol.

Although most of the Miami supported the French, Memeskia (d. 1752), nicknamed "Old Briton," allied himself and his band of Piankashaw with the British during the early 1700s. He established the village of Pickawillany, which grew into a large trading center. Memeskia outwitted French attacks several times, but when he executed some French soldiers, the French along with several other tribes—Ottawa, Ojibwa, and Potawatomi—retaliated. Warriors cut out Old Briton's heart, then cooked and ate his body in front of the tribe.

Tacumwah (c. 1720–c. 1790; "Parakeet"), sister of Little Turtle, also called Marie-Louise Pacanne Richardville, served as chief. One European, Henry Hay, not realizing women could hold positions of power, wrote in 1789 that Richardville "is so very bashful that he never speaks in council, his mother who is very clever is obliged to do it for him." A successful businesswoman, Tacumwah controlled the fur trade in the Wabash Valley area of present-day Indiana. Her son, Chief Jean Baptiste de Richardville (c. 1761–1841), inherited his mother's wealth and became a millionaire. While he was alive, he kept the tribe together in their Indiana homelands. He served as chief from 1816 to 1841, and his skilled negotiations won important concessions for the tribe from the U.S. government.

BOOKS

Costa, David J. *Narratives and Winter Stories.* Oxford, OH: Myaamia Publications, 2010.

Hayward, Clarence E. *The Lost Years: Miami Indians in Kansas.* Newton, KS: Mennonite Press, 2010.

Meginness, John Franklin. *Frances Slocum the Lost Sister of Wyoming: The Story of a Quaker Girl's Abduction and Life among the Miami Indians.* East Yorkshire, UK: Leonaur, 2011.

Rafert, Stewart. *The Miami Indians of Indiana: A Persistent People, 1654–1994.* Indianapolis: Indiana Historical Society, 1999.

Strack, Andrew J. *How the Miami People Live.* Edited by Mary Tippman, Meghan Dorey and Daryl Baldwin. Oxford, OH: Myaamia Publications, 2010.

Wilson, Frazer Ells. *The Peace of Mad Anthony: An Account of the Subjugation of the Northwestern Indian Tribes and the Treaty of Greeneville.* Kila, MN: Kessinger Publishing, 2005.

WEB SITES

Glen Black Laboratory of Archaeology. "The Ohio Valley-Great Lakes Ethnohistory Archives: The Miami Collection." *Indiana University.* http://gbl.indiana.edu/ethnohistory/archives/menu.html (accessed on June 7, 2011).

"Miami Indian Tribe." *Native American Nations.* http://www.nanations.com/miami/index.htm (accessed on June 7, 2011).

"Miami Indians." *Ohio History Central.* http://www.ohiohistorycentral.org/entry.php?rec=606 (accessed on June 7, 2011).

Miami Nation of Oklahoma. http://www.miamination.com/ (accessed on June 7, 2011).

The Myaamia Project at Miami University. http://www.myaamiaproject.com/ (accessed on June 7, 2011).

"Official Site of the Miami Nation of Indians of the State of Indiana." *Miami Nation of Indians.* http://www.miamiindians.org/ (accessed on June 7, 2011).

Micmac (Mi'kmaq)

Name

Micmac (pronounced *MICK-mack*). Also called Mi'kmaq (preferred in Canada, with Mi'kmaw used for the singular or as an adjective), Mikmaque, Migmagi, Mickmakis, Mikmakiques. The meaning of the name is uncertain; some say it is a word for "allies," or possibly "family." Others believe it refers to the Maritime provinces of Canada. The Micmac call themselves *Lnu* or *Inu* (pronounced *EE-noo*), a term that also is applied to all indigenous peoples. In Canada, the name Mi'kmaq is most often used.

Location

The Micmac once thrived in the Maritime provinces of Canada, including the present-day regions of Cape Breton Island, Nova Scotia, Prince Edward Island, New Brunswick, and the Gaspé (pronounced *gas-PAY*) Peninsula. Until recent years in the United States, the Micmac moved often and formed a scattered, landless community. In the early twenty-first century, the Aroostook band of Micmac Indians lived in communities in northern Maine. The Micmac in Canada lived on various reserves or in rural communities.

Population

The Micmac numbered about 4,500 before the Europeans arrived in the 1500s. By 1700, disease had reduced the tribal population to about 2,000. In the 1990s, the population of Micmacs in Canada stood at about 15,000. According to the 1990 U.S. Census, 2,726 people identified themselves as Micmac in the United States. In 1996, registered Micmacs in Canada numbered 19,891, in addition to the 4,500 unregistered people of Micmac origin. In 2000, the U.S. Micmac population totaled 2,739.

Language family

Algonquian.

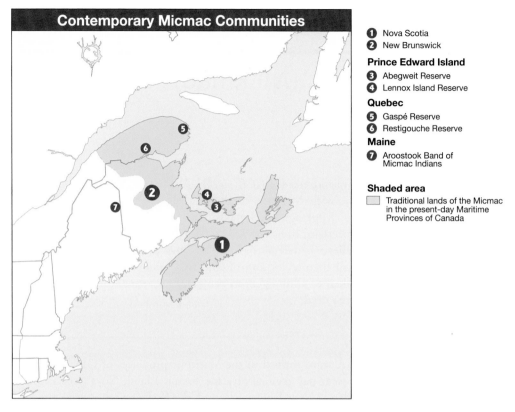

Contemporary Micmac Communities

1. Nova Scotia
2. New Brunswick

Prince Edward Island
3. Abegweit Reserve
4. Lennox Island Reserve

Quebec
5. Gaspé Reserve
6. Restigouche Reserve

Maine
7. Aroostook Band of Micmac Indians

Shaded area
Traditional lands of the Micmac in the present-day Maritime Provinces of Canada

A map of contemporary Micmac communities. MAP BY XNR PRODUCTIONS. CENGAGE LEARNING, GALE. REPRODUCED BY PERMISSION OF GALE, A PART OF CENGAGE LEARNING.

Origins and group affiliations

The Micmac are members of a larger group of tribes called the Wabanaki (pronounced *wah-buh-NOK-ee*). According to a oral history, the Micmac hero and creator Glooskap brought the Micmac out of the earth and taught them how to survive in Canada's lands by the Atlantic Ocean. Before the Europeans arrived around 1500, the eight groups that make up the Micmac lived in scattered bands across northeastern and eastern Canada. The early Micmac also visited Anticosti Island, off the coast of New Brunswick, and Labrador, where they battled with Inuit (see entry) tribes.

The Micmac may have been hunting, fishing, and gathering in their northern region since the time of the last ice age, some ten to twenty thousand years ago. The wandering Micmac were so well adapted to their environment that their culture changed very little before the Europeans arrived in the 1500s.

HISTORY

Early European visitors

Nearly one thousand years ago, the legendary Norwegian explorer Leif Erikson (c. 970– c. 1020), son of the discoverer of Greenland, may have landed on Canada's Atlantic coast and traveled west, setting up a camp in a land he called Vinland around 1001. A settlement believed to be his was discovered in the 1950s in Newfoundland, Canada, near traditional Micmac territory.

The history of the Micmac people from the early sixteenth century on was closely intertwined with that of the Europeans who arrived about that time. The Europeans came from France, Spain, Portugal, and other places, looking for the abundant fish and furs, especially beaver, found in Micmac territory.

The beginning of fur trade

In July 1534, the French explorer Jacques Cartier (pronounced *zhock kar-tee-AY*; 1491–1557) arrived at the mouth of Canada's St. Lawrence River. He was on an expedition to find gold and to locate a water passage to the Far East. He found neither, but he did find furs. The Micmac were eager to trade with him. Europeans fell in love with beaver hats, and the Micmac enjoyed the French goods, including guns, metal kettles, steel tools, cloth, needles, and scissors, that they received in exchange for beaver and other furs. The fur trade dominated French-American relations for the next 250 years.

Cartier tried and failed to establish settlements in Micmac lands, mostly because of the hostility of the neighboring Iroquois (see entry), who also wanted a trading relationship with the French. In time, however, the Micmac drove the Iroquois out of the area. Cartier eventually returned to France. Because of religious wars at home, the French did not return to the Gaspé Peninsula to resume trade with the Micmac for seventy-five years.

Important Dates

1534: French explorer Jacques Cartier meets the Micmac on the Gaspé Peninsula, beginning a long association between the French and the Micmac.

1590: The Micmac force Iroquoian-speaking Natives to leave the Gaspé Peninsula; as a result, the Micmac dominate the fur trade with the French.

1763: By the Treaty of Paris, France gives Great Britain the Canadian Maritime provinces, including Micmac territory.

1775–83: The Micmac support American colonists in the American Revolution.

1960s: The Micmac begin to recover some economic independence.

1982: The Aroostook Micmac Council is established at Presque Isle, Maine.

1991: The Micmac get federal recognition and $900,000 to buy land.

The Micmac in New France

In 1604, the king of France granted control over the fur trade in the St. Lawrence River area to a French nobleman. The French called the area New France. They founded the colony of Port Royal on the coast of present-day Nova Scotia in what was then Micmac territory. Around 1610, priests from the Society of Jesus (known as Jesuits) came from France to convert the Natives to the Roman Catholic religion. A local Micmac chief was baptized and took the French name Henri Membertou (d. 1611). He was the first Native American baptized in New France. Membertou helped the French make the colony a success. In turn, they offered his people trading opportunities and French grain to use during the difficult months of winter.

The same year Membertou was baptized, the Micmac chief Panounias (pronounced *pa-NOO-nee-us*) became the guide and protector of French soldier and explorer Samuel de Champlain (c. 1567–1635). In the spring of 1605, Panounias and Champlain traveled south into Abenaki (see entry) land, looking for places to set up a trading post and colony. Violence erupted between the Micmac and Abenaki, and over the next two years, several Micmac, including Panounias, were killed. In 1607, seeking revenge, Henri Membertou led a group of Micmac bands to raid an Abenaki village. With their superior French weapons, the Micmac killed ten Abenaki; the rest fled. The Micmac soon increased their power in the area and started more favorable trading relationships with local farmers.

Europeans bring war and disease

In addition to goods and technology, Europeans brought deadly diseases. Between the time of Cartier's initial contact and the return of the French some seventy-five years later, the Micmac population dropped from an estimated 4,500 to about 3,000. European fishermen brought smallpox, throat infections, and intestinal diseases. The Micmac had little or no resistance to these diseases. Some tribe members, introduced to alcohol by the Europeans, became alcoholics and died prematurely. Because of these problems and the large number of warriors who were killed in battle, the Micmac population continued to drop well into the eighteenth century.

The Micmac remained close allies of the French throughout more than a century of intermittent wars with Great Britain over lands in present-day Canada. Micmac soldiers fought alongside French and

Canadian soldiers in early wars during the seventeenth century until the French and Indian War (1754–63; war fought in North America between England and France involving some Native tribes as allies of the French).

The British take Canada

In 1760, the British, led by General James Wolfe (1727–1759), seized the city of Quebec, Canada. When Montreal fell the following year, the British took control of New France, including Micmac territories. In 1763, Great Britain received Canada and the Maritime provinces from the French as part of the Treaty of Paris that ended the French and Indian War. The Micmac lost a strong ally and trading partner when France withdrew from their territory.

At this time, British colonists looking for land to farm arrived in the Maritime provinces. During the American Revolution (1775–83; the American colonists' fight for independence from England), the Micmac favored the Americans, perhaps hoping that overthrowing the British would restore French rule. After 1781, the British government granted land in Micmac territory to colonists who had lost their own lands farther south as a result of their loyalty to Great Britain during the American Revolution. During the War of 1812 (1812–15; a conflict between the British and American armies), the Micmac remained neutral.

Micmac in Canada

Over time, the British government restricted the Micmac land and movements. Through a series of treaties, the Micmac were moved onto smaller reserves (the Canadian term for reservations) in their original territories. During the mid- to late nineteenth century, some Micmac who lived in the United States crossed the border into Canada to find work. By the early 1900s, many of these people had become permanent residents at Indian reserves or in small Canadian towns.

The economy of the Canadian Micmac declined during the nineteenth and early twentieth centuries as their traditional way of life broke down. Micmac men took jobs in shipyards and railroads or as lumbermen and loggers. The jobs were low paying and usually temporary. Commercial hunting of marine animals as a source of oil ended for the Micmac when petroleum products replaced porpoise and whale oil as a source of machine oil. Some Micmac joined the Canadian army during World War I (1914–18; a war in which Great Britain, France, the United

States, and their allies defeated Germany, Austria-Hungary, and their allies) and World War II (1939–45; a war in which Great Britain, France, the United States, and their allies defeated Germany, Italy, and Japan).

During the 1960s, the Micmac in Canada began to recover some economic independence. Many men discovered they liked construction work on high-rise buildings, work that paid well and satisfied their need for steady employment. Micmac women trained as nurses, teachers, secretaries, and social workers. Although many of the reserves in Canada still reflect the rural poverty of the early twentieth century, the Micmac have begun to adapt to the changes of a new era.

One struggle all Canadian tribes have is the issue of sovereignty. The Micmac view themselves as a separate nation; Canada insists they are subject to federal laws. In an effort to preserve their rights, the tribe formed the Mi'kmaq Rights Initiative. They continue to seek agreement on the best ways to maintain both tribal and treaty rights now and in the future.

The Aroostook Band of Micmac

In 1970, some Micmac in the United States joined with other off-reservation Native groups to form the Association of Aroostook Indians (AAI) in an effort to fight poverty and discrimination. The state of Maine recognized them as a tribe in 1973, and they became eligible for services through the Department of Indian Affairs, scholarships, and free hunting and fishing licenses. The AAI was later dissolved, but the group gained legal status as the Aroostook Micmac Council in 1982, with headquarters in Presque Isle, Maine. In the 2000s, without a reservation to live on, the Aroostook people are making efforts to retain their Native culture.

RELIGION

The Micmac share many beliefs with other Algonquian-speaking tribes, including the belief in the Algonquian creator-hero called Glooskap and in the Great Spirit Manitou. Glooskap, who did good deeds for the Micmac, was a giant who came from across the sea in a granite canoe. When he reached land, there were no people to greet him, so he split open an ash tree with his great bow, and the first humans stepped out from the tree.

The main focus of Micmac belief was the sun, to which they prayed twice a day in long ritual songs and identified with the Great Spirit Manitou. Another tribal god was Skatekamuc, a ghostlike spirit whose appearance in a dream indicated that death was near.

Another important belief is that all living being have souls. Humans are composed of three parts—the physical body, the life-soul (the living organs of the body including the breath, heart, brain, and muscles), and the free-soul, which was separate from the body. The free-soul had two parts, the living and the dead. When a person died, the free-soul of the dead could go to the land of the dead or stay on the earth to haunt the living.

The Micmac also believed in witches, who could cause disease by casting spells. The Micmac spiritual world was inhabited by "little people" who played tricks that helped or hurt the Micmac according to their whim. They could be cast out with holy water or palm fronds saved from Palm Sunday (a Roman Catholic holy day).

The conversion of tribal members to the Catholic faith was largely complete by the late seventeenth century. Many Micmac converted because they hoped that European Catholic rituals could save them from the diseases the Europeans brought. The power of shamans (spiritual healers; pronounced *SHAH-munz* or *SHAY-munz*) may have also increased at this time as the Micmac's terror of the European diseases grew stronger. By the 1900s, many Micmac had become Roman Catholics but still retained some of their traditional beliefs.

In the 1970s, Noel Knockwood (1932–), elder and spiritual leader of the Micmac, encouraged his people to return to their traditional religion. As a result of his efforts, Nova Scotia now recognizes Native Spirituality as an official religion. During the early 2000s, there was a renewed interest in the ceremonies, music, and language of the past. In some cases, traditional Micmac beliefs are blended with the Catholic faith.

LANGUAGE

The Micmac language is the most northerly of the Eastern Algonquian languages and is related to the languages of the Abenaki and Passamaquoddy tribes of New England.

In the seventeenth century, a Catholic missionary developed hieroglyphics (picture symbols) for the language, but in time the system fell out of use. In the eighteenth century the Micmac developed a writing system using the Latin alphabet. Catholic priests used the newer system to translate the Bible into Micmac and to publish a Native-language newspaper. Another system of writing the language was developed in the 1970s and is still used.

In the mid-2000s, most Micmac had French surnames (last names). Although some people spoke Micmac at home, most had French or English as their main language. The Micmac became concerned that their language was dying and that their children would not be able to speak it. When the Jesuits celebrated their 400th anniversary of landing in North America in 2011, the Canadian Mi'kmaq requested the religious group's help in preserving the Mi'kmaw language. Other efforts at language preservation can be found at Cape Breton University in Nova Scotia, which offers many courses in Mi'kmaw culture and language as part of its indigenous (native) studies program.

GOVERNMENT

The leader of the Micmac tribe was called the *sagamore.* His power was based on consensus (general agreement by the tribe) rather than force. He made peace between families, arranged for wars against common enemies, and helped settle disagreements. Some chiefs also resolved differences over trapping territories in the French fur trade. The chief's heirs could not inherit his power. Micmac chiefs earned their position, often through prestige and status.

In the twenty-first century, the Micmac Nation was composed of the Aroostook band of Micmac Indians in Maine and of bands residing in Canada. The Aroostook band is governed by a chief, a vice chief, and council members who are elected for two-year terms.

ECONOMY

Early lifestyle

For many centuries, the Micmac were hunter-gatherers. They wandered the land until they began trading furs with the French. As they were forced to give up additional land and the numbers of fur-bearing animals decreased in the mid-1600s, the Micmac had to find other means of survival. Some continued to hunt sea mammals in the Bay of Fundy. They processed and sold porpoise oil, a practice that stopped during the mid-1800s when petroleum came into use. Still reluctant to end their hunting traditions, the Micmac found jobs as guides for sportsmen, worked for commercial fisheries, or labored in logging camps. The Micmac strongly resisted becoming farmers. A few tried farming potatoes, but only for their own table.

By the early 1900s, many Micmac, after a long history of wandering in search of food and resources, settled on various reservations. Women and children stayed behind while the men alternated between working away from home and returning to live with their families.

Modern economy

During the twentieth century, some Micmac took jobs as seasonal laborers. Families supported themselves by selling crafts, especially splint baskets, and by government welfare. Some tribe members harvested ash trees to make the baskets. Micmac in the United States also worked in logging, river driving, blueberry agriculture, and potato picking. Many crossed into Canada to gain employment.

In 1991, the U.S. government passed the Aroostook Band of Micmacs Settlement Act. The act recognized the Micmac as a tribe, entitling members to various federal services and benefits. It also established a $900,000 fund to buy 5,000 acres of land for the tribe. In the mid-1990s, the Micmac Tribal Council in Maine began the Micmac Development Corporation to oversee tribal economic development and to look into the possibility of establishing a casino and resort business. The tribe also began pursuing ownership of a power station on the Penobscot River. By the early 2000s, Micmac people owned several retail businesses and trucking companies. They had obtained industrial and manufacturing contracts that became an important part of the tribe's economy.

DAILY LIFE

Buildings

The Micmac lived in small family groups instead of villages. Their homes were light and easy to move. The most typical residence was the cone-shaped wigwam, made of poles covered by bark, hides, woven grass mats, evergreen branches, or (in more recent times) tarpaper and cloth. The homes had a hearth at the center, and belongings were stored around the edges. For sleeping, the Micmac placed furs over boughs on the floor. In the summer, they may have lived in longhouses that could hold several families. Even in the mid-nineteenth century, the Micmac still lived in bark wigwams.

Clothing and adornment

In earlier times, the Micmac made clothes from moose or deer hides bound together with sinew (animal tendons). They also used animal hair to make clothing. Both men and women wore leather undergarments and had long hair. The men dressed in loincloths, and the women wore skirts. They covered their feet with moccasins and their legs with leggings of animal hide. In cold weather, men wore a traditional "eared" headdress that covered the scalp. It rose up in points like a bat's ears and draped over the top of their overcoats like a cape. When hunting seals they wore sealskin, with head and flippers attached, as a disguise that allowed them to get close enough to the seal herd to approach their prey. Men wore snowshoes in winter.

After the French came, the Micmac began to wear clothing of broadcloth. They mixed it with garments of traditional design. Micmac women wore caps that came to a peak, similar to hats worn by fifteenth-century Portuguese fishermen. They used threads and quills to decorate overcoats obtained by trading furs with the French.

Foods

Before contact with Europeans, the Micmac hunted and gathered their food. Their only crop was tobacco, raised for ceremonial purposes. Smelt, herring, Canada geese, goose eggs, sturgeon, partridge, salmon, eel, elk, bear, and caribou also formed important parts of their diet. The Micmac used specialized weapons and containers to hunt. They used barbed wooden spears for catching fish and fished mainly at night by torchlight. The Micmac fished from hump-shaped canoes. They collected fat, which they often ate as a snack or stored for later use in birchbark containers.

The Micmac sometimes also ate roots, nuts, and berries that they made into loaves. They boiled and ate yellow pond lily, marsh marigold, wild leeks, milkweed flowers, cattail, and berries. They exchanged leather pelts for metal tools, dried peas, beans, and prunes.

Healing practices

The Micmac believed that there were both good and evil spirits. A person with extraordinary powers, a *buoin* or shaman, had power to call on these spirits or to intercede on another's behalf. Many Micmac relied on the spiritual powers of a buoin to combat deadly diseases.

The tribe used herbs to promote healing. Gargling with wild black-berry root helped sore throats. A concoction of unripened cranberries was used to draw out venom from poisoned arrows. Teas made from the bark of white oaks and dogwood eased diarrhea and fevers. A salve related to ginseng root was used to heal wounds.

Today, the Aroostook band of Micmac receive health-care services through the Micmac Health Department, which includes a clinic and fitness center as well as departments for contract health, community health, environmental health, behavioral health, and youth services.

EDUCATION

Traditional education in the Micmac community consisted of elders passing on their knowledge in a one-to-one situation. During the early twentieth century, children were forced to attend boarding schools, where they had to learn American ways. As a result, the bond between the elders and youth no longer existed; younger generations did not learn the language or customs of their ancestors. In 2000, the Micmac in Maine opened Aroostook Band of Micmacs Cultural Community

A box made by a Micmac artist is an example of the intricate quillwork for which the tribe became known. © PEABODY ESSEX MUSEUM, SALEM, MASSACHUSETTS, USA/THE BRIDGEMAN ART LIBRARY

Education Center to educate people about both historical and contemporary Micmac culture.

ARTS

Crafts

The Micmac were known for their elaborate and colorful beadwork and quillwork (designs made with porcupine quills), which they used to decorate robes, moccasins, necklaces, armbands, and other items. Micmac quillwork reached its peak in the Victorian Era (1837–1901; the years when Queen Victoria ruled England), when the popularity of ornamental items like boxes, pincushions, and wall hangings was at its height among Americans. The Micmac also made attractive strings of beads called wampum from the shells they found on the shoreline.

Tools

The Micmac used a variety of weapons and tools such as spears, bows and arrows, snares, and leisters, or three-pronged fish spears. They harpooned seals, and hunters made birchbark "callers" shaped like megaphones to imitate moose calls. Their tools changed after Europeans arrived. Instead of using stone and bone for hooks or spear tips, they used iron.

Europeans adopted some of the Micmac tools and inventions, which were superior to their own. Snowshoes and toboggans became important to both cultures. The Micmac also made several types of canoes that were light and easy to repair. They had various styles for inland water travel and one for longer trips up the coast.

CUSTOMS

Festivals

Like other Algonquian tribes, the Micmac traditionally held ceremonies to thank the spirits for their generosity and to ask for continued blessings. Such ceremonies usually included dancing, feasting, sport, games, and gift-giving.

In August 1994, the Aroostook band of Micmacs hosted its first annual powwow, a three-day festival that featured Micmac crafts, food, and games.

Rabbit and the Moon Man

According to this Micmac tale, Rabbit, a great hunter, is determined to catch the thief who has been stealing from his traps. He is startled by a flash of light, but he pulls his rope snare tight to catch the robber.

When he came near his traps, Rabbit saw that the bright light was still there. It was so bright that it hurt his eyes. He bathed them in the icy water of a nearby brook, but still they smarted. He made big snowballs and threw them at the light, in the hope of putting it out. As they went close to the light, he heard them sizzle and saw them melt. Next, Rabbit scooped up great pawfuls of soft clay from the stream and made many big clay balls. He was a good shot and he threw the balls with all of his force at the dancing white light. He heard them strike hard and then his prisoner shouted.

Then a strange, quivering voice asked why he had been snared and demanded that he be set free at once, because he was the man in the moon and he must be home before dawn came. His face had been spotted with clay and, when Rabbit went closer, the moon man saw him and threatened to kill him and all of his tribe if he were not released at once.

Rabbit was so terrified that he raced back to tell his grandmother about his strange captive. She too was much afraid and told Rabbit to return and release the thief immediately. Rabbit went back, and his voice shook with fear as he told the man in the moon that he would be released if he promised never to rob the snares again. To make doubly sure, Rabbit asked him to promise that he would never return to earth, and the moon man swore that he would never do so. Rabbit could hardly see in the dazzling light, but at last he managed to gnaw through the bowstring with his teeth and the man in the moon soon disappeared in the sky, leaving a bright trail of light behind him....

The man in the moon has never returned to earth. When he lights the world, one can still see the marks of the clay, which Rabbit threw on his face. Sometimes he disappears for a few nights, when he is trying to rub the marks of the clay balls from his face. Then the world is dark; but when the man in the moon appears again, one can see that he has never been able to clean the clay marks from his shining face.

SOURCE: Macfarland, Allan A. *Fireside Book of North American Indian Folktales.* Harrisburg, PA: Stackpole Books, 1974.

Family life

Because of the often harsh conditions in which they lived, the Micmac became a very self-sufficient people, able to survive by their wits. In the winter, they scattered into small family groups to find what little food was available. In the summer, they reunited in larger groups. The Micmac considered all members of the tribe as equals, and individual initiative was highly prized. Males had to kill a large animal, such as a moose, to be recognized as adults. In addition, a Micmac man could not marry until he had spent two years with his fiancée's father and proved his abilities as a provider.

Hunting

For the Micmac, each month was associated with the pursuit of a different wild resource. They hunted seal and cod in January, smelt (a small fish) in March, geese in April, and young seals in May. They gathered eel or hunted for moose in September, sought elk and beaver for meat in October, and went ice fishing in December. While trying to capture seals, the Micmac sometimes disguised themselves in animal skins and stalked them, using clubs to kill their prey.

CURRENT TRIBAL ISSUES

Major concerns of the Micmac in the twenty-first century are justice and cultural preservation. In many cases, those two goals are intertwined. The Canadian and provincial governments signed an agreement in 2010 with the Mi'kmaq of Nova Scotia that promises to ask their input on all proposed activities or projects. The Mi'kmaq hailed it as a step in the right direction. They have been pushing for more say in many areas, including the legal arena.

A Canadian Mi'kmaw teenager, Donald Marshall Jr., was falsely convicted of murder in the 1980s and served an eleven-year jail term, an injustice that prompted a change in the legal system. A court was set up at the Eskasoni Mi'kmaq Community in Nova Scotia to handle Mi'kmaq cases. Mi'kmaq ideas of justice differ from those of the Canadian courts, however, and this can cause conflicts.

The Mi'kmaq believe in *apiqsigtoagen,* or "mutual forgiveness." The age-old procedure for handling a case calls for hearing both sides, then allowing for a calming-down period where people examine their behavior and then later reconnect through forgiveness and restitution. In the first decades of the 2000s, several groups formed to protect aboriginal rights in the legal system. Some of these initiatives were the Mi'kmaq Legal Support Network (MLSN), Mi'kmaq Justice Institute, Mi'kmaw Court Worker Program, and Mi'kmaw Customary Law.

On the other side of the border, the U.S. Micmac were busy with their own battles for legal justice. In 2006, a federal judge ruled that the state of Maine did not have civil or criminal jurisdiction (power to enforce laws) on tribal lands. This was a victory for the Micmac and reinforced their sovereignty (self-government).

Mi'kmaw women in Newfoundland began efforts to become more empowered. One organization that is helping with this effort is the Newfoundland Aboriginal Women's Network (NAWN). NAWN offers support, conferences, and other tools to develop leadership skills and reinforce cultural values.

In 2011, the Canadian government agreed to provide funding to save an ancient Mi'kmaw burial ground. Soil erosion is causing the Malagawatch cemetery on Cape Breton Island to sink into the lake. The Mi'kmaq are working to find ways to prevent destruction of the gravesites at this location, which has served as a traditional gathering place for centuries.

NOTABLE PEOPLE

Henri Membertou (d. 1611) was an important Micmac chief, a Catholic convert, and an ally of the French. He was known as a shaman who could predict the future, walk on water, and cure people of diseases.

Chief Panounias (d. 1607) guided the French explorer Samuel de Champlain (c. 1567–1635) into the interior of North America (see "History"). His death led to warfare between the Native Americans of Acadia and the Penobscot.

Anna Mae Aquash (born Anna Mae Pictou; 1945–1975) was an American Indian Movement (AIM) activist who struggled to promote the rights of Native people in North America. She was found murdered on the Pine Ridge Reservation in South Dakota at the height of civil rights protests in the 1970s. Aquash became a symbol of American Indian protest and activism.

BOOKS

Alger, Abby L. *In Indian Tents: Stories Told by Penobscot, Passamaquoddy and Micmac Indians.* Park Forest, IL: University Press of the Pacific, 2006.

Andersen, Raoul R., and John K. Crellin. *Miśel Joe: An Aboriginal Chief's Journey.* St. John's, Newfoundland: Flanker Press, 2009.

Lacey, Laurie. *Micmac Medicines: Remedies and Recollections.* Halifax, Nova Scotia: Nimbus, 1993.

McBride, Bunny. *Our Lives in Our Hands: Micmac Indian Basketmakers.* Gardiner, ME: Tilbury House Publishers, 1990.

Paul, Daniel. *We Were Not the Savages.* Winnipeg, Manitoba: Fernwood Publishing, 2006.

Paul, Elizabeth. *The Stone Canoe: Two Lost Mi'Kmaq Texts.* Kentville, Nova Scotia: Gaspereau Press, 2007.

Wallis, Wilson D. *The Micmac Indians of Eastern Canada.* Minneapolis: University of Minnesota Press, 2009.

Whitehead, Ruth Holmes. *The Micmac: How Their Ancestors Lived Five Hundred Years Ago.* Halifax, Nova Scotia: Nimbus, 1983.

Whitehead, Ruth Holmes. *Micmac Quillwork: Micmac Indian Techniques of Porcupine Quill Decoration: 1600-1950.* Halifax, Nova Scotia: Nova Scotia Museum, 1991.

WEB SITES

Aroostook Band of Micmacs. http://www.micmac-nsn.gov/ (accessed on June 1, 2011).

Augustine, Stephen. "Mi'kmaq." *Four Directions Teachings: Aboriginal Online Teachings and Resource Centre.* http://www.fourdirectionsteachings.com/transcripts/mikmaq.html (accessed on June 1, 2011).

Chisolm, D. "Mi'kmaq Resource Centre," *Cape Breton University.* http://mrc.uccb.ns.ca/mikmaq.html (accessed on May 15, 2011).

Mi'gmaqMi'kmaq Online Talking Dictionary. http://www.mikmaqonline.org/ (accessed on June 1, 2011).

"Mi'kmaq Portraits Collection." *Nova Scotia Museum.* http://museum.gov.ns.ca/mikmaq/default.asp (accessed on June 1, 2011).

"Mi'kmaqResources." *Halifax Public Libraries.* http://www.halifaxpubliclibraries.ca/research/topics/mikmaqresources.html (accessed on June 1, 2011).

Paul, Daniel N. "We Were Not the Savages."*First Nation History.* http://www.danielnpaul.com/index.html (accessed on June 1, 2011).

"Traditional Mi'kmaq Beliefs."*Indian Brook First Nation.* http://home.rushcomm.ca/˜hsack/spirit.html (accessed on June 1, 2011).

The Mound Builders: Poverty Point, Adena, Hopewell, and Mississippian Cultures

Name

The four known mound-building cultures of North America are the Poverty Point, Adena, Hopewell, and Mississippian cultures. Their names, usually taken from the place where relics of their societies were found, refer to a way of life and a cultural period, not a tribe. No Mississippian cultures survived into the eighteenth century.

Location

The Poverty Point culture is named after the northeastern Louisiana plantation where remnants of it were discovered. Other communities of the culture existed along the lower Mississippi River. Watson Brake is also located in northern Louisiana along the Ouachita River. The Adena culture inhabited present-day West Virginia, Ohio, Kentucky, and Indiana. The Hopewell culture probably began in the Illinois Valley and spread into Ohio and then across the Midwest region. The vast Mississippian culture's territory extended from the mouth of the Illinois River in the north to the mouth of the White River in Arkansas in the South, and eastward along the Ohio and Tennessee Rivers to what is now North Carolina.

Population

The populations of the mound-building cultures are unknown, but at times they probably reached well into the millions. Population estimates for Poverty Point are about 5,000 inhabitants; the Adena culture is estimated to have been from 8 to 17 million; the Mississippian city of Cahokia alone is estimated to have had between 40,000 and 75,000 inhabitants during the twelfth century.

Language family
Unknown.

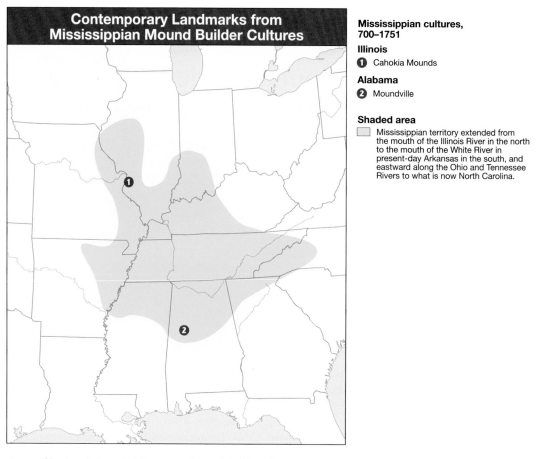

Contemporary Landmarks from Mississippian Mound Builder Cultures

Mississippian cultures, 700–1751

Illinois
❶ Cahokia Mounds

Alabama
❷ Moundville

Shaded area
☐ Mississippian territory extended from the mouth of the Illinois River in the north to the mouth of the White River in present-day Arkansas in the south, and eastward along the Ohio and Tennessee Rivers to what is now North Carolina.

A map of landmarks from the Mississippian Mound Builder cultures. MAP BY XNR PRODUCTIONS. CENGAGE LEARNING, GALE. REPRODUCED BY PERMISSION OF GALE, A PART OF CENGAGE LEARNING.

Origins and group affiliations

The relationship between the mound-building cultures is not clear. Scientists have not proved any direct descendancy from one culture to the next, although some have noted a connection between the Spiro and the Caddo (see entry), and between the Mississippian and the Natchez (see entry). With the exception of Watson Brake, which has been dated to about 3500 BCE, it is clear, however, that the cultures were in contact, particularly through trade networks, and that the influence from one to the next was profound. The sequence of these cultures is as follows: The Poverty Point culture spanned the period from about 1500 BCE to 700 BCE. The Adena culture appeared around 500 BCE and flourished until about 100 BCE, and the Hopewell culture followed from 100 BCE to 550–750 CE. The Mississippian culture was the last, existing from about 700 CE to 1751 CE.

Although there are many things still unknown about the mound-building cultures that thrived in vast territories of the Northeast and the Southeast for nearly three thousand years, the mounds and artifacts left behind give a fascinating glimpse into some highly complex societies. Evidence paints a portrait of people with complicated political systems, highly developed social customs and religious rites, and a thriving artistic community.

HISTORY

Types of mounds

The people of the mound-building cultures—the Poverty Point, Adena, Hopewell, and Mississippian cultures—left behind remnants of four types of mounds. Effigies (pronounced *EFF-a-geez*)—mounds shaped like animals such as snakes, birds, or bears—were built along the Great Lakes and in Wisconsin, Michigan, and Iowa. Cone-shaped mounds were built in the Ohio River valley. Flat-topped pyramids were built in the lower Mississippi region. Walls of earth, sometimes reinforced by stone, were constructed in the central Midwest.

Important Dates

1400 BCE: People of the Poverty Point culture are constructing large burial mounds and living in planned communities.

500 BCE: The Adena people build villages with burial mounds in the Midwest.

100 BCE: Hopewell societies construct massive earthen mounds for burying their dead and possibly other religious purposes.

700 CE: The Mississippian culture begins.

1200: The great city of Cahokia in the Mississippi River Valley flourishes.

1539–43: The Spanish treasure hunter Hernando de Soto becomes the first European to make contact with Mississippian cultures.

1731: The French destroy the Natchez, the last Mississippian culture. Most survivors are sold into slavery in the Caribbean.

Poverty Point culture (1500 BCE to 700 BCE)

Effigy mounds and dirt embankments that form six concentric circles extending about three-quarters of a mile in total length were found at the site of Poverty Point on the lower Mississippi River in Louisiana. Most can only be observed from the air. Other square, rectangular, and hexagonal mounds have also been found at the site. It is estimated that five thousand people lived at Poverty Point at its height.

People of the Poverty Point culture built large burial mounds and lived in planned communities. Important people in the tribe were buried in the mounds, which often had temples built on top of them. Archaeologists consider these communities the first chiefdoms (villages governed by one principal leader) north of Mexico. The reason for the decline of this civilization by 700 BCE is unknown.

Adena culture (500 BCE to 100 CE)

The Adena culture, named after the estate in Ohio where its remnants were first discovered in 1901, had a population estimated at between eight and seventeen million at its height. The Adena were the first people in the present-day United States known to construct earthen mounds in which they regularly buried their dead. The mounds were often shaped in animal or geometric designs.

When the early American settlers first saw the Adena mounds, some ignored them, but others were fascinated. Some nineteenth-century writers theorized that they were built by the Toltecs or Aztecs of Mexico, while others thought the "First Empire Builders," as some called the Adena, might have been Hebrews, Greeks, Persians, Romans, Vikings, Hindus, or any group who had ever built a mound in the Old World. The common belief was that Native Americans had not built the mounds, because colonists made the erroneous assumption that they were incapable of planning and developing such vast monuments. In 1894, Cyrus Thomas, an ethnologist (a person who studies the practices and beliefs of different cultures) working for the Smithsonian Institution, published a paper showing that the mounds were the work of a number of different cultures that were part of the family of American Indian tribes.

Scholars disagree on whether or not the Adena were descendants of the earlier Poverty Point culture, but most believe that there was some interaction between the two cultures.

Hopewell culture (100 BCE to 550–750 BCE)

The Hopewell culture may have grown out of the earlier Adena culture. Discoveries there have included copper effigies of fish, birds, and serpent heads, as well as beads, axes, ornaments, a ceremonial antler headdress of carved wood, and tens of thousands of freshwater pearls and shell beads.

The Hopewell culture was more highly developed than that of the Adena, with richer burial customs, more sophisticated art, grander ceremonies, a stricter system of social classes, and more advanced farming practices. Items found at Hopewell burial sites included ear spools (a type of earrings) and skulls. The skulls showed that devices had been used to fashion the heads of infants, as they grew, into unusual shapes. The shapes showed a person's status in the society and were considered attractive.

The Hopewell people specialized in stonework, and examples of it occur as far away as Florida. The Hopewell extended their influence from New England to the lower Mississippi region. The culture began to decline around 550 CE for unknown reasons. Some theories suggest climate changes, crop failure, epidemics, and civil war, among other reasons.

Hopewell mounds rose from 6 to 70 feet (2 to 20 meters) high. During the eighteenth and nineteenth centuries, there were fantastic theories about the origins of the Hopewell mounds. One of the most popular beliefs at that time was that a civilized society had made the mounds, but that the Native peoples had killed them. Some people even suggested that Europeans had built them. U.S. president Thomas Jefferson (1743–1826; served 1801–9) examined a mound near his home at Monticello, Virginia, and proclaimed that they were clearly built by American Indians.

Present-day Wisconsin is the site of a middle Mississippean mound. © NORTH WIND PICTURE ARCHIVES

Mississippian culture (700 CE to 1751 CE)

The Mississippian civilization of Temple Mound Builders began in the Mississippi River Valley around 700. It was at its height between 1000 and 1200, when the people built the great cities of Cahokia and Moundville.

Cahokia may have been the largest and most powerful city in eastern North America. Centrally located for both north-south and east-west trade exchanges, Cahokia flourished from about 900 to 1250. It was home to a gigantic 100-foot-high (30-meter-high) mound and more than one hundred other mounds in its 6 square miles (15 square kilometers). Estimates of the population of the city of Cahokia alone ranged between 40,000 thousand and 75,000 during the twelfth century. Nearby were many smaller towns and villages.

A replica of a thatched hut used by Mississipean people is part of the Cahokia site in Illinois. Between 900 and 1200, Cahokia was likely the largest city on the North American continent. © JOSEPH SOHM/THE IMAGE WORKS

The 300-acre (120-hectare) site of Moundville is located south of present-day Tuscaloosa, Alabama. Its 100-acre (40-hectare) public square was surrounded by twenty pairs of mounds and enclosed by wooden fences. Moundville was the capital of a large prehistoric nation with a number of smaller district capitals that sent many of their resources and finely crafted goods to be enjoyed by Moundville's rich rulers.

Decline of Mississippian culture

Temple Mound Builders still lived in the Mississippi River Valley in the sixteenth century when the Spanish first entered the region. Over the next two centuries, the population of the region began to perish. The decline may have been due to European diseases, to which the Native Americans had no resistance. Overpopulation and overcrowding, plus the problem of what to do about urban waste, might also have contributed. Massive crop failures possibly linked to changes in the climate may have played a part.

Some historians believe that when the Europeans first came to North America, a few of the tribes still living in the Mississippi and Tennessee river valleys were direct descendants of the Temple Mound Builders. Except for the Natchez tribe, however, one of the only remaining Mississippian societies known to the early European explorers and fur traders, few of the Native peoples had more than dim memories of the way of life of their ancestors. Very little was recorded about Mississippian tribes living at the time of European contact.

Sometime between 1539 and 1542, tribes who lived in the region where the Temple Mound Builders thrived forced the expedition of the Spanish treasure hunter Hernando de Soto (c. 1496–1542) to retreat down the Mississippi River. More than a century later, the French moved into the area and came into contact with the Natchez people, who lived on the Mississippi River in present-day western Mississippi. The French decided to impose taxes on the Natchez fur trade. From 1729 to 1731, the two cultures battled until the French, with the help of their Choctaw (see entry) allies, destroyed the Natchez nation and sold most of the survivors into slavery in the Caribbean. A few Natchez sought safety with neighboring tribes and continued their struggle against the Europeans. As the Natchez were absorbed into the other tribes, all that remained of the Mississippian culture was gone.

RELIGION

Not a great deal is known about the religion of the mound-building societies. While earlier societies generally built their mounds as burial memorials, the later Mississippian mounds became temples for an aristocratic priesthood. Priests in this advanced culture, as well as artists, could devote themselves fully to their professions, while their communities provided for them.

The Natchez, the last of the Mississippian people, may provide insight into the religion of the Mississippian culture. The Natchez credited their origin to the Sun God. According to their creation beliefs, a man and woman came to Earth to teach humans the proper way to live. The man was the younger brother of the sun. He told the people to build a temple and to place inside it a sacred fire that was to be kept always burning; he explained that the fire was a piece of the sun he had brought to Earth.

The sacred priest-leader of the Natchez was called the Great Sun, and he was regarded as part god. His primary duty was to maintain the sacred fire in the temple. The Great Sun dressed in rich clothes and was carried from place to place so he would never touch the ground. Only certain people were permitted into his presence, and they had to follow strict rules when approaching him. No one could watch him eat or even touch the dishes from which he ate. During the few times that he walked, servants spread mats on the path before him. He rarely even used his hands. One French Catholic priest reported that if he wanted to give the remains of his meal to relatives, "he pushed the dishes to them with his feet."

Spanish explorers who wrote about the Natchez tell of the Great Sun's practice of greeting his elder brother, the sun in the sky, with ritual song and prayer. Every month, the entire tribe went to the temple and paid tribute to the Great Sun. He generally appeared before them wearing a feathered crown and seated in an ornate chair carried by eight throne bearers. When the French destroyed the Natchez, they captured the Great Sun and sent him into slavery in the Caribbean.

LANGUAGE

It is not known what language was spoken by the Temple Mound Builders, or even if different groups of them spoke the same language.

DAILY LIFE

Buildings

Adena mounds were usually cone-shaped and contained many burial remains. They were used repeatedly for generations. The Adena mounds were probably also used for religious purposes other than burial. The most famous Adena earthwork is Serpent Mound in Adams County, Ohio, a 5-foot-high, 20-foot-wide (1.5-meter-high, 6-meter-wide) mound shaped like a snake that measures 800 feet long (250 meters) from the mouth to the tail. If it could be stretched out in a straight line, it would measure about 1,300 feet (400 meters). The snake has an egg-shaped object in its mouth. The mound cannot be fully viewed from ground level because it lies on top of a 100-foot (30-meter) ridge. It may have been built as a message to the gods that lived above in the air or the sky.

The Hopewell Grave Creek Mound in Moundville, West Virginia, is among the largest man-made earthworks ever created. It required three million basketloads of earth to build, and the people transported all of the earth without horses or carts. Fort Ancient, near Lebanon, Ohio, has walls that extend more than 3.5 miles (4 kilometers) and stand from 4 to 23 feet (1 to 7 meters) high. The continuity of the walls is broken by seventy openings. The Hopewell built it about three centuries before the arrival of Christopher Columbus (1451–1506).

The most impressive structures of the Mississippian culture were the temple mounds that loomed over their towns and villages. These mounds were built entirely of dirt carried to the site in baskets, a process that took a long time. Some mounds were massive. The one known as Monk's Mound at Cahokia was built in a series of fourteen stages between 900 and 1150. When finished, it stood 100 feet (30 meters) high and covered more than 16 acres at its base.

The mounds were rectangular in shape and flat on top. They were used both as temples and as burial sites. When the mounds were filled with bodies, more room was made by leveling the top, adding another layer of earth, and raising a fresh temple complex. The tops of other mounds became sites for trading, festivals, and other public functions.

Mississippian temples, like the society's houses, were built from wood and interwoven cane stalks or small branches covered with a plaster made from mud. Some farmers had two separate houses: an open home with good air circulation for warm weather, and an insulated home with a fireplace and areas dug beneath the floor to store food in cold weather.

Clothing

Members of the Adena, Hopewell, and Mississippian cultures wore decorated loincloths (flaps of material that covered the back and front and were suspended from the waist) and necklaces made from engraved stones. Mississippians often adorned their bodies with tattoos or painted their faces. Some very wealthy people wore headdresses decorated with feathers, animal fur, pearls, or even precious metals such as copper or galena, an ore of lead. The rulers of the Mississippian culture went to their graves in fancy dress.

Food

The Adena gathered native plants, many of which are now considered weeds. They ate goosefoot, giant ragweed, pigweed, hickory nuts, bottle gourds, squash, and sunflowers. They did not eat corn, like the later Mississippian people, because at that time the only corn that grew in North America was not well suited to the climate where the Adena lived. They used the little bit of corn they grew only for ceremonies.

Much of the early Mississippian diet was based on hunting and fishing. When the people learned to grow large supplies of corn and beans, they moved beyond what hunting and gathering alone allowed. A variety of corn that could withstand cold, wet weather was introduced to the Mississippi Valley between 800 and 1000 CE. About the same time, fast-growing beans—kidney, navy, pinto, snap, and pole—were brought from Mexico. The beans were allowed to climb up the stalks of growing corn.

Healing practices

The Mississippian, like the Adena and the Hopewell, suffered from a variety of diseases, including arthritis, infections by parasites, and tuberculosis, a lung disease. Pictures on ancient pots show people with bent spines, a deformity that often is associated with tuberculosis. The pots might have held herbal remedies to treat their ailments.

A group of Mound Build-ers harvest a crop of corn. © NORTH WIND/NORTH WIND PICTURE ARCHIVES. ALL RIGHTS RESERVED.

ARTS

Hopewell works of art showed a delicate, free-flowing style. Artists made shell drinking cups, gold silhouettes, and effigy pipes in the image of frogs, owls, and alligators. Artists used copper to fashion beads, collars, pendants, and effigies. At one grave site, a large head-dress was discovered with imitation deer antlers made of copper-covered wood.

An engraved ceramic cup created by the Mississippian or Hopewell is an example of how the ancient people expressed their culture through art. © MPI/STRINGER/ARCHIVE PHOTOS/GETTY IMAGES

Mississippian mound builders expressed their culture through their pottery, which was often of outstanding quality and even displayed a sense of humor. One existing example is a jar shaped in the form of a very fat human leg and foot, while another depicts a face with a comical expression. Small statues have been found that may have been intended for use in their temples or as burial goods to accompany a Great Sun or a Lesser Sun into the afterlife. Such ceramics also may have played a central role in the trade between the Mississippian and a large network that extended from the Gulf of Mexico in the South and the Great Lakes in the North, and from the Rocky Mountains in the West to the Appalachians in the East. Skilled artists made baskets, pottery, leather garments, shell beads, copper ornaments, and stone tools.

The shell, copper, and various types of stone must have been imported, because they do not naturally occur near the homeland of the Temple Mound Builders.

CUSTOMS

Social rank

The Natchez were the last of the Mississippian culture. Eighteenth-century French observers in the homeland of the Natchez described their social ranking system. The most important people were the Great Sun and his relatives, who made up the upper class. Below them were the nobles, followed by the honest men, and at the bottom were the despised commoners known as the "Stinkards."

The Great Sun could only marry partners from the lowest class of the society, the Stinkards. The Great Sun's brothers (the Lesser Suns) and his sisters (the Women Suns) also could only marry Stinkards. But the children of the Women Suns were permitted to keep their mother's social rank, and one of them would usually become the next Great Sun when his uncle died. The children of the Great Sun and the Lesser Suns did not retain their parents' high rank.

Stinkards who married into the top social class remained Stinkards all their lives. They could not eat with their spouses and had to stand in their presence. If they offended their high-ranking spouses in any way, they could be killed and replaced. The only way Stinkards could improve their own status was by showing extreme bravery during wartime.

Games

The Adena broke up their daily routine by playing games and holding athletic contests; the whole village probably participated. Children had toys like dolls, little canoes, and sleds, and adults had dice made from bones to use for gambling.

The Mississippian culture shared some customs with many modern tribes. Experts who study the remains of ancient cities say that Cahokia contained large ball courts and special stones that were probably used for playing a game called *chunkey*. In this game, stones were rolled across the ground while players threw spears at the spot where they believed the stones would stop. The winner was the player who landed his spear nearest the stone's stopping place. The Great Plains tribes played chunkey during the nineteenth century.

Death and burial

During the earliest Adena period, people wrapped bodies in bark. In later times, they sometimes left them outdoors until predators, weather, or other natural processes had removed the flesh from the bones; then they were buried. Sometimes they cremated the bodies or buried them, rather than leaving them outdoors. They set the bodies in their graves either stretched out full length or flexed, with the knees drawn up. Corpses of honored dead were coated with red dye or graphite (a type of soft lead) and covered with hundreds of delicate shell beads.

Adena mounds were designed to hold many bodies over a period of years. A mound might begin as a shallow pit grave, with a small pile of dirt heaped over it. As more corpses were added, more and more earth was also added to the mound, which sometimes reached a height of 70 feet (20 meters).

The Hopewell built huge burial houses. They performed cremations in clay-lined pits. They surrounded the dead with special grave goods, and they often covered individual graves with low earthen mounds. Top members of society received spectacular burials. Their corpses were surrounded with high-quality artistic goods made of wood and metal.

The remnants of Mississippian pottery and sculpture show that the people of this culture thought often about death and the afterlife. Upon the death of the Great Sun or his relatives—his mother White Woman, his brothers the Lesser Suns, and his sisters the Woman Suns—some of their spouses and servants believed that it was their duty and a great honor to accompany the deceased into the afterlife. They willingly went to their own deaths. Others were not quite so willing but were sent to their deaths anyway by Mississippian officials.

Some anthropologists (people who study cultures) believe Mississippian officials may have given drugs to people who were about to become human sacrifices. The drugs made the victims unconscious; they were then killed and buried with the ruler to accompany him or her into the next life. Unlike the people of the Adena and Hopewell cultures that came before, however, the Mississippian people apparently saw no need to bury their dead with fabulous treasures.

CURRENT TRIBAL ISSUES

Until about 1800, when they began venturing beyond the eastern area of the continent, most English-speaking colonists did not encounter Native American mounds. When they expanded their settlements beyond the Appalachian Mountains, they plowed over many mounds.

During the nineteenth century, scholars such as Frederic Ward Putnam, director of the Peabody Museum of Archaeology and Ethnology at Harvard University, saved quite a few Adena mounds from destruction. In 1887, Putnam raised more than $5,000, which enabled Harvard to buy an important mound in Ohio from its owner. In 1900, Harvard University gave Serpent Mound to the state of Ohio on the condition that it would be preserved and opened to the public.

Several of the Hopewell mounds have become part of the current American landscape, without regard to, or respect for, their historical meaning. For example, during World War II (1939–45; a war in which Great Britain, France, the United States, and their allies defeated Germany, Italy, and Japan), the U.S. Army built a training camp near the Hopewell Culture National Historical Park, formerly known as "Mound City," and badly damaged the site. Grave Creek Mound in West Virginia has a racetrack built around its base and a saloon erected at the top. In Belpre, Ohio, there is a mound in the parking lot of a fast-food restaurant. In Newark, Ohio, part of the Newark Earthworks makes up a country club golf course. Furthermore, in Huntington, West Virginia, visitors can observe a mound from a seat on a roller coaster ride.

During the twentieth century, farmers, vandals, and highway builders destroyed many more of the mounds. The preservation of the mound builders' earthworks and relics has become the responsibility of the states in which they are found, and some are operated as historical sites by those states.

Cahokia in Illinois is the site of the Cahokia Mounds State Historic Site, which preserves the remains of 68 of 120 of these ancient mounds, and the Cahokia Mounds State Park. Many of these sites are open to the public and feature museums and relics that celebrate and explain the region's mound-building heritage.

Many existing earthworks have been worn down to rough shapes in overgrown rural fields and riversides, while others are being preserved. Of more than 1,100 known sites in the state of Arkansas, only two remain relatively untouched. The still uncertain fate of the mounds remains in the hands of present and future generations.

Evidence uncovered in 2003 by researcher Lisa A. Mills at the Hopewell Mound Group in Ohio has tied these ancient people with the Ojibway (see entry) and Kickapoo. Although the study was too small to reach more than uncertain conclusions, Mills also found some DNA links with other present-day tribes: Apache (see entry), Iowa, Micmac (see entry), Pawnee (see entry), Pima (see entry), Seri, Southwest Sioux (see entry), and Yakima (see entry). To date, no tie to the Cherokee (see entry) tribe has been found, although many people believed these two groups were connected. The most startling information to emerge from this study is that DNA from the Hopewell samples is closely related to that of Asian people, especially those from China, Korea, Japan, and Mongolia.

BOOKS

Joseph, Frank. *Advanced Civilizations of Prehistoric America: The Lost Kingdoms of the Adena, Hopewell, Mississippians, and Anasazi.* Rochester, VT: Bear & Company, December 21, 2009.

McMillin, Laurie Hovell. *Buried Indians: Digging Up the Past in a Midwestern Town.* Madison: University of Wisconsin Press, 2006.

Milner, George R. *The Moundbuilders: Ancient Peoples of Eastern North America.* New York: Thames & Hudson, 2005.

PERIODICALS

Beck, Melinda. "The Lost Worlds of Ancient America." *Newsweek* 118 (Fall–Winter 1991): 24.

WEB SITES

"The Adena Mounds." *Grave Creek Mound State Park.* http://www.adena.com/adena/ad/ad01.htm (accessed June 7, 2011).

"Ancient Architects of the Mississippi." *National Park Service, Department of the Interior.* http://www.cr.nps.gov/archeology/feature/feature.htm (accessed on July 10, 2007).

"Ancient DNA from the Ohio Hopewell." *Ohio Archaeology Blog,* June 22, 2006. http://ohio-archaeology.blogspot.com/2006/06/ancient-dna-from-ohio-hopewell.html (accessed on July 10, 2007).

"Ancient Moundbuilders of Arkansas." *University of Arkansas.* http://cast.uark.edu/home/research/archaeology-and-historic-preservation/archaeological-interpretation/ancient-moundbuilders-of-arkansas.html (accessed on June 10, 2011).

Glenn Black Laboratory of Archaeology. "Burial Mounds." *Indiana University.* http://www.gbl.indiana.edu/abstracts/adena/mounds.html (accessed June 7, 2011).

Johnson, Russ. "The Mississippian Period (900 AD to 1550 AD)" *Memphis History.* http://www.memphishistory.org/Beginnings/PreMemphis/MississippianCulture/tabid/64/Default.aspx (accessed June 7, 2011).

"Moundville Archaelogical Park." *University of Alabama Museums.* http://moundville.ua.edu/ (accessed on June 10, 2011).

National Park Service. "Poverty Point." *U.S. Department of the Interior.* http://www.nps.gov/popo/index.htm (accessed June 7, 2011).

Ohio History Central. "Adena Mound." *Ohio Historical Society.* http://www.ohiohistorycentral.org/entry.php?rec=2411 (accessed June 7, 2011).

SEAC (Southeast Archeological Center). "The Mississippian and Late Prehistoric Period (A.D. 900–1700)." *U.S. Department of the Interior.* http://www.cr.nps.gov/seac/misslate.htm (accessed June 7, 2011).

Narragansett

Name

The name Narragansett (pronounced *nah-ruh-GAN-sit*) refers to both the people and the place where they lived. Some believe it means "people of the little points and bays." The name currently applies to living members of the Eastern Niantic and Narragansett tribes.

Location

At the height of their authority, the Narragansett occupied most of present-day Rhode Island. They lived mainly along the Atlantic Coast and in the valleys and forests west of Narragansett Bay. As of 2007, the Narragansett Indian Tribe owned a 1,940-acre (780 hectares) reservation 45 miles (72 kilometers) south of Providence, Rhode Island. No one had lived on the reservation since the mid-1990s; most Narragansett lived in Rhode Island and Massachusetts. By 2000, however, sixty people lived on the reservation, and the population continued to grow as more housing was built on tribal land.

Population

Population estimates in the year 1600 range from 4,000 to 30,000 Narragansett. In the 1990 U.S. Census, 2,564 people identified themselves as Narragansett. In 2000, that number dropped to 2,228.

Language family

Eastern Algonquian.

Origins and group affiliations

The Narragansett tribe is one of the oldest in North America, dating back about eleven thousand years. Powerful Narragansett chiefs controlled certain groups of Massachusett, Nipmuck, Pokanoket, Wampanoag (see entry), Coweset, Shawomet, Mashapaug, and Manissean Indians who lived in southern New England and New York State.

The Narragansett may have been the largest and strongest Native American tribe in New England when British colonists arrived in the New

A map of contemporary Narragansett communities. MAP BY XNR PRODUCTIONS. CENGAGE LEARNING, GALE. REPRODUCED BY PERMISSION OF GALE, A PART OF CENGAGE LEARNING.

World. The Narragansett were a generous and friendly people. When Puritan minister Roger Williams (c. 1603–1683) made his way to Rhode Island after being expelled from Massachusetts in 1636, he was warmly welcomed. The Narragansett gave him land that became the city of Providence, Rhode Island. When other settlers followed, however, wars broke out, and in less than forty years, the Narragansett nation had been nearly destroyed.

HISTORY

Early contact with Europeans

Prehistoric peoples inhabited the northeastern United States at the end of the last Ice Age, around 11,000 BCE. They were wandering hunters of large mammals, but they were forced to change their lifestyle when the great ice caps melted and the Arctic mammals died or moved farther north. Those who settled along the coast, rivers, streams, and bogs of New England between 10,000 and 700 BCE were the ancestors of the Narragansett.

The Italian explorer Giovanni da Verrazano (c. 1485–c. 1528) visited the area in 1524 and lived among the Narragansett for fifteen days. He wrote that the people "have the most civil customs that we have found on this voyage.… Their manner is sweet and gentle." Over the next century, European contact with the Narragansett increased gradually; relations were usually friendly.

Seafaring Europeans came to Rhode Island because the nearby waters provided one of the richest fishing grounds in the world. They brought trade goods made of iron to exchange with the tribe. They also brought foreign diseases such as smallpox and plague. The Narragansett managed to escape the worst epidemics (uncontrolled outbreaks of disease), which destroyed most of the Wampanoag and others. Survivors of other tribes joined the Narragansett, making the tribe even stronger than it had been.

Important Dates

1524: Italian explorer Giovanni da Verrazano visits the Narragansett, beginning European relations with the tribe.

1675: The Great Swamp Fight during King Philip's War nearly wipes out the tribe.

1880: The Rhode Island state legislature attempts to break up the tribe.

1934: The Narragansett Indian Tribe incorporates and creates a constitution and bylaws.

1983: The U.S. government officially recognizes the Narragansett tribe.

2007: The Northern Narragansett Indian Tribe of Rhode Island incorporates.

Settlers come, wars follow

In 1636, the Massachusetts Bay Colony banished Puritan minister Roger Williams and a few of his followers. Colonial officials forced Williams to leave the colony because he spoke out against taking Native land by force and against punishing people whose religious beliefs were different. Narragansett chief Miantonomi had heard of Williams. He welcomed Williams and his followers and gave them a place to build their homes.

Over the next forty years, the Narragansett were frequently involved in wars with other tribes as they tried to maintain their dominance over New England. They also had to contend with more and more British settlers. In 1675, the United Colonies of New England began King Philip's War (1675–76) against the Wampanoag. They also declared war on the Narragansett because the great Narragansett chief Canonchet, son of Miantonomi, refused to surrender Wampanoag refugees from the war.

On December 16, 1675, the colonial army laid siege to a Narragansett stronghold and destroyed it in what became known as the Great

Swamp Fight. One participant of the battle estimated that between 600 and 1,000 Narragansett warriors died. Their parents, widows, and children were hunted down and brutally treated. By the end of King Philip's War in the summer of 1676, possibly as few as two hundred Narragansett remained alive.

Survivors on the reservation

Of the surviving Narragansett, some were sold into slavery. Others merged with the Niantic, a related tribe; the combined group took the name Narragansett. They maintained themselves as a small independent unit on a 64-square-mile (165-square-kilometer) reservation in southern New England for more than two hundred years. In 1880, however, the Rhode Island legislature purchased the reservation, hoping to break up the tribe. Despite this, the Narragansett remained a community and, in the 1920s, began a long struggle to win back their ancestral lands.

In 1978, the Narragansett finally won a lawsuit against the state of Rhode Island for the return of some of their traditional territory. In 1983, the Narragansett won recognition from the U.S. government. Federally recognized tribes are those with which the U.S. government maintains official relations. Without federal recognition, the tribe does not exist as far as the government is concerned, so it is not entitled to financial or other government help.

Tribal division

Because federal recognition was based on tribal rolls from the 1800s, the Narragansett decided to confine its membership to direct descendants of those individuals. Many were told they no longer belonged to the tribe. These people incorporated as the Northern Narragansett Indian Tribe of Rhode Island. They then sought federal recognition. Rather than rely on casino income, the newly created tribe decided to develop partnerships with state and local governments to provide employment for its members.

RELIGION

The Narragansett believed in a creator god called *Cautantowwit*. He made the first people from stone, then smashed them to create the ancestors of all other people. Second in importance to Cautantowwit was a spirit called *Chepi,* who descended from the souls of the dead. Specially trained healers could call upon his power. Chepi was feared because he could punish people who behaved improperly by causing them to become sick or die. Chepi warned those who followed the English lifestyle that evil consequences would result if they did not return to their traditional way of life.

The Narragansett also believed in many lesser gods and powerful spirits, such as the crow who gave them their staple crops, corn and beans, after he stole them from Cautantowwit's garden.

Many Natives in southern New England believed that an unusual or outstanding event had to be the work of the god *Manittoo.* Because of this belief, the colonists, who knew metallurgy (the science of metals), sailing technology, printing, and writing, were often viewed as gods. The English colonists had an easier time among the Narragansett because of this belief.

LANGUAGE

All southern New England Indians, including the Narragansett, spoke related languages of the eastern Algonquian family. A study done in 1861 declared that nobody had spoken Narragansett regularly since before 1816. According to the Summer Institute of Linguistics, no Narragansett person knew or used their native language in 1997.

By the beginning of the twenty-first century, the Narragansett were working to revive their language. Using books written during colonial times and other research sources, several scholars pieced together the vocabulary and grammar of this extinct language. The Aquidneck Indian Council, with support from The Rhode Island Committee for the Humanities, published a book with basic language instruction. The council also developed classroom materials.

Roger Williams wrote a book published in 1643 called *A Key into the Language of America.* It remains the largest collection of Narragansett vocabulary. Later efforts, dating from 1769 to 1879, added eighty-two words, raising the total known to about two hundred. Isolated terms, such as *wigwam* and *powwow,* have become well known. Williams listed information about the tribal customs as well as the language and how it related to the Eastern Algonquian dialects (language varieties) of the Massachusett, Pequot (see entry), Mohegan, and Wampanoag tribes.

GOVERNMENT

The Narragansett lived under the authority of lesser chiefs called *sachems* (pronounced *SAY-chums*), under the command of a grand sachem, who lived in the largest village. The position was hereditary (handed down to relatives), and often a sachem shared power with another person. The favorite arrangement was to share power with a nephew. When there were no close male relatives, a female relative might become a sachem.

The sachems ensured that all members of the tribe had enough land to support themselves. People paid for their services in corn, deerskins, and food. Sachems were careful to treat their subjects well, because it was a matter of pride and wealth to have a large number of subjects. If a family disagreed with a sachem's decisions, it could join another tribe.

In the eighteenth century, Rhode Island abolished the position of sachem as the U.S. government began taking over tribal lands. The Narragansett ignored this action and continued to act under the authority of sachems and a tribal council.

In 1983, the Narragansett won recognition from the federal government. In the early twenty-first century, the tribal government was run by an elected tribal council and a chief sachem, a medicine man or woman, a secretary, an assistant secretary, a treasurer, and an assistant treasurer. The government also consisted of several departments, including housing, health, education, human services, natural resources, and finance. Vocational training, community planning, real estate rights protection, historic preservation, health care, and child care are other programs administered by the tribe.

ECONOMY

The Narragansett traditionally farmed, fished, hunted, and gathered to provide themselves with a varied diet. When they won recognition from the federal government in 1983, they became eligible for public education, health care, job training, and housing aid. They set about trying to make themselves self-sufficient.

In the early 2000s, the largest single employer of the Narragansett was the tribal government. Others affiliated with the reservation maintained a community garden, harvested trees, or worked in the building trades in nearby towns. Some worked in the tourist trade at the Dover Indian

Trading Post in Rockville and at the Narragansett Indian Longhouse, which offered lectures and tours. Most tribal members worked in the nearby communities as doctors, lawyers, teachers, artists, fishermen, lobsterman, cooks, and masons.

DAILY LIFE

Families

In the Narragansett tradition, men not only provided for their own families but helped others in need. This remains a common practice among the people today.

For recreation, Narragansett men in traditional times enjoyed smoking and gossiping, playing games such as an early version of football, throwing dice, and dancing. Women were often busy with food cultivation and preparation; they prided themselves on interesting recipes that combined several different foods.

Buildings

The Narragansett migrated in both winter and summer. In the summer, they took advantage of good lands for planting and gathering, and in the winter, they settled in a warmer place with good hunting. They sometimes had to move when fleas and other biting insects became troublesome or to avoid infection when illness struck their village. Their wigwams, or *wetus,* had to be portable and easy to take apart and reassemble. Roofs were made of chestnut or birch bark attached to the top of bent poles, which were stuck in the ground. In cold weather, they insulated the wigwams with mats or animal skins attached to the roof and spread on the floor. Smoke from the fire escaped through a hole in the roof.

Two or more families sometimes shared the same wigwam. The Narragansett also built shacks so family members could sleep near their crops to protect young plants from birds and other predators. In the winter, they stayed in longhouses for greater warmth. A longhouse is a long, narrow, single-room building used as a communal dwelling.

In the 1940s, the Narragansett built a traditional longhouse on the reservation to serve as a community center. In the 1990s, the tribe began constructing a community center and fifty homes on the reservation. The community center also housed a senior meal center and child-care facilities.

Succotash

The Narragansett introduced the earliest European settlers to their native dish, called *msickquatash* by the natives and succotash by the settlers. The original dish consisted of corn and lima beans, picked fresh from the garden. New England housewives enlivened the dish by adding green peppers and other vegetables shipped from the West Indies.

> 1 cup fresh or frozen baby lima beans
> salt to taste
> 1 cup fresh or frozen corn kernels
> 4 Tablespoons (1/2 stick) butter OR
> 1/4 cup heavy [whipping] cream
> freshly ground pepper to taste

In a large saucepan, boil the beans in salted water to cover until nearly done. Add the corn kernels and cook until tender, just a few minutes. Drain, stir in the butter, and check seasoning, adding salt and pepper to taste.

SOURCE: McCullough, Frances, and Barbara Witt. *Classic American Food without Fuss.* New York: Villard Books, 1996, p. 151–152.

Food

Before the Europeans destroyed the Narragansett culture, the tribe's food supply was plentiful and varied. Along the coast and in the swamps and streams, women caught spawning alewives, clams, oysters, lobster, and other shellfish. In the woods, they collected wild onions, chestnuts, strawberries, and other plants in season. Men prepared the fields for planting, and women planted and harvested the crops, including corn, beans, and squash. Some of the favorite dishes of the tribe included johnnycake, corn chowder, quahog (clam) chowder, and Indian pudding (made from boiled cornmeal sweetened with molasses).

Men hunted duck, pigeon, deer, rabbit, squirrel, bear, and beaver. In the winter, they fished through the ice. They also grew their own tobacco and molded or carved special pipes for smoking it. To smoke a peace pipe with another person signified the formation of a new friendship.

Clothing and adornment

Little is known about the traditional clothing worn by the Narragansett. In the summer, men most likely wore breechcloths, a type of garment secured at the waist that passes between the legs. Women wore leather or woven skirts. Beads were popular; wampum (beads carved from the shells of local clams) acted as both decoration and money.

Healing practices

Narragansett healing practices went hand in hand with their religion. People known as *pawwaws* (this is where the term "powwow" comes from) presided over religious and healing ceremonies. To gain their respected positions, pawwaws had to be able to communicate with the spirit world and to heal or injure others. They might demonstrate their power by creating magic arrows from the hair of an enemy or by causing a real arrowhead to injure someone. However, pawwaws more often relied on massage and the laying on of hands to cure the sick. They were usually men. Women skilled at making medicines from plants were called on to attend the birth of a child.

In the mid-2000s, medicine men, and sometimes women, still played an important role in tribal life. Their care was supplemented on the reservation by the tribally administered Narragansett Indian Health Center. The Center offered traditional care by spiritual leaders and medicine people along with other options for physical care, substance abuse, and mental health programs as well as a lab and pharmacy.

Education

Historically, the Narragansett considered elders the most important people in the tribe. The elders passed on culture and traditions, and they were treated with great respect. This continues to be the case.

To help everyone in the tribe become employable, productive, and self-sufficient, the Education Department of the tribal government provides financial assistance to college students. It also holds adult education programs and offers tutoring for children who need help with schoolwork.

CUSTOMS

Marriage

Historians believe that three generations of two different families lived together in one house. A woman may have moved in with her husband's family when she married. Sachems married only women of high rank, such as the daughter of another sachem. Sometimes sachems had two or three wives, if they could afford to support them.

Festivals

The Narragansett honored Cautantowwit, the creator, with a *nickommo*, a special ceremony in which they sacrificed their most precious possessions by burning or burying them. They also honored him with a feast of thanksgiving in autumn. Foods consumed at the feast included turkey, corn, beans, cranberries, and pumpkin pie.

Death and dying

Elderly men prepared the bodies of the dead for burial. They rubbed them with mud or soot. They placed objects in the grave to accompany the soul to Cautantowwit's house, where the dead lived much as they had on Earth. Sometimes a sick or dead person's home was burned to prevent infection or a visit from the evil spirit who had afflicted the person. A dead person's name was never mentioned again.

CURRENT TRIBAL ISSUES

The Narragansett continue to strive for economic self-sufficiency. The tribe hoped to build a casino on land they owned, but they needed state approval before construction could proceed. In Rhode Island, only the state can run lotteries. The state refused permission because a tribal casino might cause attendance at state gambling facilities to drop. The casino plan suffered a major setback in 2006 when Rhode Islanders voted against it. The tribe tried to have the land taken into federal trust, which would allow for a casino, but the state went to court and blocked the Narragansett request. This challenge led to a 2009 U.S. Supreme Court decision that stated that the government would only take land into trust for tribes that had been recognized before 1934. This decision is one that will have widespread effects. For many tribes, it could mean that they will not be able to build casinos, which are usually put on trust land.

In another ongoing difficulty with the government, the Narragansett people fought over their right to sell tax-free cigarettes. As a sovereign (self-governing) nation, the Narragansett believed they could sell duty-free products; the state disagreed. In 2003, state police raided a store on the reservation. The tribe took the case to court and won in 2005. The state appealed, however, and in 2006, the tribe lost because of an agreement it had signed in 1978 promising to abide by state laws. The Narragansett then sued for police brutality during the arrest. They did not win, and instead, in a 2008 trial, several members of the Narragansett tribe were charged with misdemeanors for resisting arrest. These incidents, along with others, have made many of the Narragansett people wary of dealing with the outside community.

NOTABLE PEOPLE

The Narragansett sachem Miantonomi (d. 1643), who originally befriended the English colonists, was one of the first to try to create a pan-Indian alliance (an alliance that included members of different tribes) against the English. In a famous speech, he said: "These English having gotten our land, they with scythes cut down the grass, and their hogs spoil our clam banks, and we shall all be starved." Miantonomi could not overcome rivalries among tribes, however. The Mohegan tribe executed him in 1643.

Other notable Narragansett include Canonchet, Miantonomi's son and successor, a leader during King Philip's War; Canonicus, Miantonomi's uncle, who governed internal matters in the tribe while Miantonomi dealt with external problems; and Quaiapen, a female sachem and Canonicus's daughter-in-law, who led part of the tribe in King Philip's War.

Narragansett Sachem Miantonomi, who tried to organize various tribes into an alliance against the English colonists, is taken into captivity. © NORTH WIND PICTURE ARCHIVES

BOOKS

Barron, Donna Gentle Spirit. *The Long Island Indians and their New England Ancestors: Narragansett, Mohegan, Pequot and Wampanoag Tribes.* Bloomington, IN: AuthorHouse, 2006.

Big Toe. *Walk Softly on the Earth: The Words and Wisdom of Narragansett Elder Big Toe.* Audio CD. Monterey, MA: BMA Studios, 2004.

Geake, Robert A. *A History of the Narragansett Tribe of Rhode Island: Keepers of the Bay.* Charleston, SC: History Press, 2011.

Gordon, Raymond G., Jr., ed. *Ethnologue: Languages of the World,* 15th ed. Dallas, TX: SIL International, 2005. Available online at http://www.ethnologue.com/ (accessed on June 1, 2011).

Moondancer and Strong Woman. *A Cultural History of the Native Peoples of Southern New England: Voices from Past and Present.* Newport, RI: Bauu Press, 2007.

Silverman, David J. *Red Brethren: The Brothertown and Stockbridge Indians and the Problem of Race in Early America.* Ithaca, NY: Cornell University Press, 2010.

PERIODICALS

Bakst, C. M. "Reflections on the Verdicts in the Narragansett Indian Smokeshop Trial." *The Providence Journal,* April 5, 2008. Available online at http://www.projo.com/extra/2003/smokeshop/content/projo_20080404_smokeshop_verdict.302f9f22.html (accessed on June 9, 2011).

WEB SITES

Ethnologue Report for Language. "Mohegan-Montauk-Narragansett." *SIL International.* http://www.ethnologue.com/show_language.asp?code=mof (accessed on June 1, 2011).

Redish, Laura, and Orrin Lewis. "Narragansett Culture and History Links." *Native Languages of the Americas.* http://www.native-languages.org/narragansett_culture (accessed on June 1, 2011).

Narragansett Indian Tribe. http://www.narragansett-tribe.org/ (accessed on June 1, 2011).

Waabu O'Brien, Frank. "Bringing Back Our Lost Language." *New England Algonquian Language Revival.* http://www.bigorrin.org/waabu1.htm (accessed on June 1, 2011).

Ojibway

Name

Ojibway (pronounced *oh-JIB-way*) means "puckered up," and it is thought to come from the way the tribes' moccasins were gathered at the top. Ojibway is also spelled Ojibwe, Ojibwayy, Ojibwa, and Otchipwe. The traditional name is *Anishinaabe* (Anishinabe, Anishinaubeg, Anishinabek, Neshnabek), which means "original people" or "first people." The Ojibway have sometimes been called the Chippewa, which most likely was a mispronunciation of their name. In all the United States treaties, the people were listed as Chippewa, but the Anishinaabe Nation's constitution lists Chippewa and Ojibway separately.

Location

The Ojibway flourished north of Lake Huron and northeast of Lake Superior at the time of European contact. Most now live on American reservations located in Michigan, Wisconsin, Minnesota, North Dakota, Montana, and Oklahoma. In Canada, they live mainly in Ontario, Manitoba, Alberta, and Saskatchewan.

Population

The French estimated that there were about 35,000 Ojibway in the 1600s, but other historians say there may have been two or three times that number spread out over a wide area. According to the 2000 Census, 110,857 Ojibway people resided in the United States. In 2001, 20,890 Ojibway lived in Canada. By 2010, the U.S. Census counted 112,757 Ojibway, with a total of 170,742 people claiming some Ojibway heritage.

Language family

Algonquian.

Origins and group affiliations

The Algonquian-speaking peoples, including ancestors of the Ojibway, migrated from an area north of the St. Lawrence River westward into the

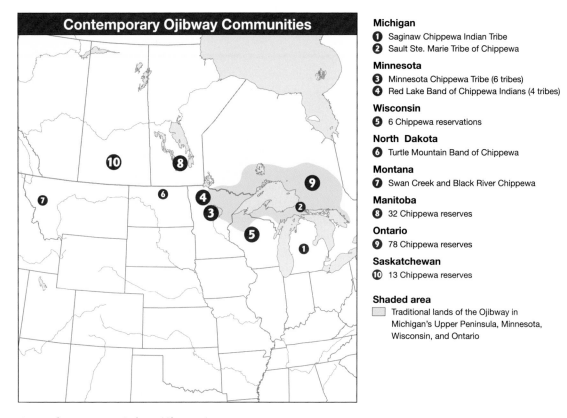

Contemporary Ojibway Communities

Michigan
1 Saginaw Chippewa Indian Tribe
2 Sault Ste. Marie Tribe of Chippewa

Minnesota
3 Minnesota Chippewa Tribe (6 tribes)
4 Red Lake Band of Chippewa Indians (4 tribes)

Wisconsin
5 6 Chippewa reservations

North Dakota
6 Turtle Mountain Band of Chippewa

Montana
7 Swan Creek and Black River Chippewa

Manitoba
8 32 Chippewa reserves

Ontario
9 78 Chippewa reserves

Saskatchewan
10 13 Chippewa reserves

Shaded area
　 Traditional lands of the Ojibway in Michigan's Upper Peninsula, Minnesota, Wisconsin, and Ontario

A map of contemporary Ojibway (Chippewa) communities. MAP BY XNR PRODUCTIONS. CENGAGE LEARNING, GALE. REPRODUCED BY PERMISSION OF GALE, A PART OF CENGAGE LEARNING.

Great Lakes region about 900 CE. After Europeans arrived, the Ojibway split into several groups. Some joined an alliance with the Potawatomi and Ottawa (see entries) in Michigan and Ontario, called the Council of Three Fires. The Salteaux Ojibway in Michigan's Upper Peninsula met and were influenced by the Cree (see entry). Around 1830, a group moved to the Great Plains, took up local customs, and became known as the Plains Ojibway or Bungees.

The Ojibway were a huge group who dominated the vast Great Lakes region for centuries. At one time, they may well have been the most powerful tribe in North America. In the early 2000s, the Ojibway formed the sixth-largest Native American group in the United States. Their attempts to adapt to a modern world while preserving elements of their ancient culture have been remarkably successful.

HISTORY

The Ojibway migrated with other Algonquin peoples from an area north of the St. Lawrence River in Canada westward into the Great Lakes region beginning around 900. No one knows exactly why the Ojibway left the region. They may have been trying to escape diseases brought by Norse explorers who came about 1000. Among the Ojibway, the story of the move has been handed down from generation to generation. It describes how the Algonquin nations moved to the Great Lakes from a salt sea in the east, possibly Hudson Bay. The people suffered great hardship during their migration, which lasted several hundred years.

Encounters with the French

At the time of the first contact with Europeans, the Ojibway were concentrated in the eastern part of Michigan's Upper Peninsula. Frenchman Étienne Brûlé (c. 1592–1633) arrived in 1622 looking for a water passage to Asia. He encountered the Ojibway at a place now known as Sault Sainte Marie (pronounced *SOO Saint Marie*). Because of the rapids at the site, the French gave the Ojibway the name *Salteurs,* or *Salteaux,* meaning "people of the rapids." (An extremely fast-moving part of a river is called the rapids.)

Fur traders and missionaries soon followed the French explorers. By the late seventeenth century, the Ojibway had become heavily engaged in the fur trade with the French. They traded animal skins for European items such as guns, alcohol, cloth, utensils, and beads. They became wealthy, powerful, and dependent on French goods.

Now in possession of weapons and wanting to take more furs, the Ojibway expanded their territory. Between 1687 and the late 1700s, they spread into lower Michigan, northern Minnesota, Wisconsin, and parts of Canada. The Ojibway displaced many other tribes as they moved. It has been said that no other tribe has come close to controlling such a huge area.

Important Dates

1622: Frenchman Étienne Brûlé encounters the Ojibway at present-day Sault Sainte Marie.

1755–63: To protect their trade interests, the Ojibway ally with the French against the British during the French and Indian War.

1830: Many Ojibway move to Canada to avoid being forced to live southwest of the Missouri River. Others remain behind and work out ways to keep plots of land.

1968: Three Ojibway—Dennis Banks, George Mitchell, and Clyde Bellecourt—found the American Indian Movement (AIM) in Minneapolis, Minnesota, to raise public awareness about treaties the federal and state governments violated.

1983: The U.S. Court of Appeals rules that past treaties protect Ojibway rights to hunt, fish, and gather on the lands of their ancestors.

1988: After the passage of the Indian Gaming Regulation Act, the Ojibway exercise their rights as a sovereign (self-governing) nation by establishing casinos on reservations.

2011: As part of the Anishinaabe Nation, the Ojibway write a joint constitution.

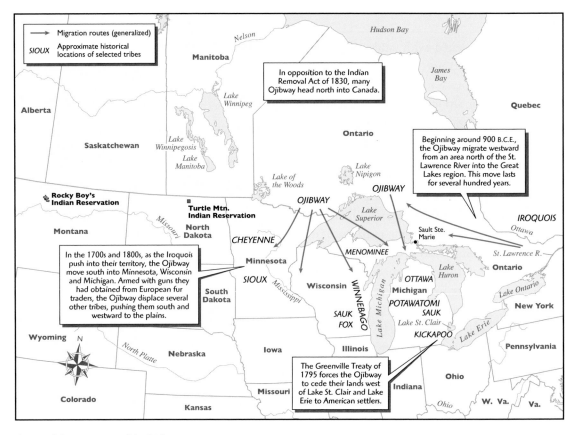

A map of the migrations of the Ojibway. MAP BY XNR PRODUCTIONS. CENGAGE LEARNING, GALE. REPRODUCED BY PERMISSION OF GALE, A PART OF CENGAGE LEARNING.

French displaced by British

In the mid-eighteenth century, France and England were engaged in the French and Indian War (1754–63; a war fought in North America involving some Native tribes as allies of the French). To protect their trade interests, the Ojibway sided with the French. Many Ojibway (mainly women) intermarried with the French. These Ojibway women and their families, as well as those of Ojibway warriors fighting with the French, often traveled from battle site to battle site because it was too dangerous to remain behind without protectors. This constant moving disrupted traditional family life.

French resistance to the British in Canada ended in 1760, leaving the British in control of Ojibway territory there. The British, who sought revenge for Ojibway support of their enemy, forbade trade with the

Ojibway. In turn, French influence in Michigan also came to and end. The Ojibway's long dependence on trade changed, as did their way of life.

American settlers arrive

The Ojibway took the British side in the American Revolution (1775–83; the American colonists' fight for independence from England) because of an even greater threat—American settlers encroaching (moving) on Ojibway lands. After the British lost the war, the Ojibway fought against American aggression, but they were forced by a series of treaties to give up much of their land in Michigan to American settlers. An era of treaty signings began, and each treaty further stripped the Ojibway and neighboring tribes of the best property, forcing them onto less desirable lands. Poverty and the spread of infectious diseases contributed to a hard life for the Ojibway.

More migrations

Around 1830, many Ojibway moved to the Great Plains and became known as the Plains Ojibway, or Bungees. Riding horses they acquired from the Spanish, they populated areas in what are now North Dakota, northeastern Montana, southern Manitoba, and southeastern Saskatchewan.

The Indian Removal Act was passed in 1830. It directed that all tribes should be moved to Indian Territory (present-day Oklahoma and Kansas). Many Ojibway moved north to Canada instead. Others remained behind and tried to keep individual plots of land that had been granted to them according to U.S. government policy of allotment. Allotment, which divided the land into individual plots, was adopted in the mid-nineteenth century, but it went against the Native custom of holding lands as a community. The Ojibway received small parcels of land; the rest was sold to settlers. Taxes were levied on these plots, and the Ojibway were often unable to pay. Because of this, they were forced to give up their land. During the 1860s, many Ojibway were removed to Indian Territory along with other tribes.

American Indian Movement founded

Battles raged during the twentieth century between the Native peoples and the U.S. government over issues such as forced removal, land use, and the freedom to practice ancient religions. The civil rights movement of the 1950s and 1960s, with its emphasis on the rights of minorities, led to a surge of activism. The Red Power Movement began as a series of public protests that focused the eyes of the world on American Indian issues. In 1968, three Ojibway—Dennis Banks (1937–), George Mitchell (1933–), and Clyde Bellecourt (1939–), founded the American Indian Movement (AIM) in Minneapolis, Minnesota.

AIM is a vocal and controversial organization. During its 1973 seizure of the village of Wounded Knee in South Dakota, AIM organized individuals from many tribes to hold off federal forces in an armed standoff. Two activists were killed, and many others were wounded. AIM's goals are civil rights for all Native peoples and the revival of tribal religion. The group also seeks to raise public awareness of treaty rights violations by federal and state governments.

RELIGION

Traditional beliefs

Ojibway oral tradition teaches that the Creator, Kitche Manitou, created the world in five stages. First, the rock, water, fire, and wind were formed. From these four elements the sun, earth, moon, and stars were made. During the third stage plants began to grow. Then animals, and later people, emerged.

According to traditional Ojibway belief, the sun is father and the earth is mother of all living things. The sun and the earth provide everything necessary to sustain all life. As the Anishinaabe or "first people," the Ojibway feel an obligation to care for and live in harmony with Mother Earth.

The Midewiwin ("good hearted") was the religious society of the Ojibway. It may have developed in response to diseases brought by the French. Members, who could be men or women, were called "Mides." They underwent a long training period before becoming members of the society. Their main purpose was to prolong life (see "Healing practices"). They acted as healers and taught morality and good conduct. Other names for the society are Grand Medicine Society, Medicine Lodge Society, and Mide Society.

European religious influences

French Catholic missionaries came in the 1600s and tried to convert the Ojibway, with little success. Two possible reasons for the lack of conversions are resistance on the part of the local Mides and the fact that the people lived in remote areas. The Midewiwin retained a stronghold over the Ojibway for a long time, but the society declined at the end of the nineteenth century, in part because of efforts to forcing the Ojibway and other tribes to conform to the larger American culture.

In the early 2000s, many Ojibway practiced a religion that combined elements of their traditional beliefs with Christianity. Some tribes had revived the Midewiwin traditions and held seasonal gatherings for healing and strengthening their communities.

LANGUAGE

The Ojibway language, called Ojibway, Ojibwemowin, or Anishinaabemowin, survived decades of educational policies that sought to replace it with English. The language once seemed to be heading for extinction, but it is now taught on the reservations and at colleges and universities. Approximately fifty thousand people in the northern United States and southern Canada use the Ojibway language. Speakers of the five main dialects (varieties), including the Ottawa (see entry), can understand each other.

The mastery of spoken language is important to the success of an Ojibway adult. Parents and grandparents encourage children to develop the art of oration. The ability to speak well requires skills in describing things or events elegantly and in great detail.

GOVERNMENT

In the early days, Ojibway groups were not highly organized because they were small and spread out over such a wide area. Each group had its own tribal leader and council. Election to the *ogimaa,* or "leaders," was based on merit rather than heredity. Leaders were usually men

Ojibway Language

The Ojibway did not have a system for writing language. They communicated special events to future generations by drawing pictographs on birch bark or buckskin. The following are samples from the Ojibway vocabulary:

wi'giwam	"dwelling"
nasa'ogan	"tepee"
nenan'dawi'iwed	"one who treats the sick by administering remedies"
dja'sakid	"one who treats the sick by non-material means" (commonly called a juggler)
a'dikina'gun	"cradleboard"
ina'bandumo'win	"vision or thing dreamed"
mide'	"a member of the Midewiwin"
mide'wayan	"bag carried by a *mide'*"
Boozhoo	"hello"
Miigwech	"thank you"
Aaniin ezhi'ayaayan	"How are you?"
Nimino'ayaa	"I'm fine."
Mino'ayaag	"All of you be well."

who had distinguished themselves in battle or who were wise and generous. Ogimaa candidates had to demonstrate outstanding speaking ability.

In the twenty-first century, most tribes operated under forms of government they adopted after the Indian Reorganization Act was passed in 1934. That act provided government loans and other services to reservations if the bands agreed to adopt new constitutions and reorganize their governments. Most did so, and developed elective governing bodies.

In the early 2000s, the Ojibway in Canada formed the Anishinaabe Nation with the Ottawa, Potawatomi, Algonquin, Chippewa, Lanaape, Mississauga, and Nbiising. These eight nations wrote a joint constitution in 2011.

ECONOMY

Early economy

Living surrounded by lakes and forests, the Ojibway were skilled at fishing, hunting large game, gathering nuts and berries, and growing foods that required a short growing season, such as squash and sunflowers. They gathered in summer villages to fish and plant gardens. They divided in winter and moved to their hunting grounds.

Ojibway men harvest wild rice in the Minnesota wetlands.
© NATHAN BENN/ALAMY

After contact with Europeans, the Ojibway became skilled traders. By the late seventeenth century, thousands of fur pelts were being shipped from Sault Sainte Marie and Detroit. Although it went against the Ojibway tradition of killing animals only to provide food and clothing, the tribe became so dependent on trade that they overtrapped beaver.

Economy under U.S. government

On the reservations, the Ojibway later earned money through the sale of their land and timber rights. They often received far less money than these were worth, and the money was barely enough to live on. Life on reservations, which were often located in remote areas where the soil was poor, led to reliance on government welfare.

After 1945, most Ojibway moved to urban areas to find work. They were employed in a wide range of occupations. Those who lived on reservations experienced high rates of unemployment (that is, those who wanted to work could not find work). They supported themselves through seasonal work, including forestry, farming, tourism, trapping, and harvesting wild rice.

Since the 1970s, lawsuits have affirmed Ojibway treaty rights and permitted them to support themselves on the land and lakes. In the 1983 Voight Decision, the U.S. Court of Appeals ruled that Ojibway rights to hunt, fish, and gather on the lands of their ancestors are protected by past treaties. Reservations also began to support small businesses: bait shops, campgrounds, clothing manufacturers, construction companies, fish hatcheries, hotels, lumber stores, marinas, restaurants, and service stations.

Income from casinos

Many tribes in the United States have turned to gaming as a way to create jobs and make money. Casinos generate millions of dollars and employ thousands of Ojibway people who previously could not find work. Tribes have invested gaming income in the purchase of ancestral lands, road and home construction, and social services, such as health and education. Some reservations have passed laws requiring employers on reservations to give preference to tribal members in hiring.

DAILY LIFE

Families

The Ojibway worked hard to care for each other and their families. Sharing is a highly valued virtue, and those who are fortunate enough to acquire a wealth of goods or food were expected to share with those who had less. In spite of the struggles to survive, families found time to embroider, carve, make and play with toys, tell stories, and play games.

Buildings

The traditional Ojibway dwelling, the wigwam, was made of birch bark or cattail mats covering an arched pole frame. Twine or strips of leather tied poles together. The wigwam could be in the shape of a cone or dome, and it was often built on a slope with ditches dug away from it to drain rainwater. The Ojibway sometimes lived in tepees made of birch bark, buckskin, or cloth stretched around a conical frame of poles tied together at the top.

Family members slept in the wigwam with their feet toward the fire. In cold weather, an older person remained awake to watch the fire. On warm nights, the family sometimes slept out in the open.

Other buildings in an Ojibway village included a sweat lodge for curing illness or for spiritual purification, a building used by members of the Midewiwin, and a wigwam for menstruating women.

Food

The Ojibway were mainly hunter-gatherers. Men used bows and arrows and snares for hunting deer, moose, bear, beaver, lynx, mink, marten, otter, rabbit, and caribou. Strips of meat were often smoked or dried to make a food called jerky. Dog meat was a popular menu item at feasts.

Women gathered berries and nuts and collected sap to make maple syrup and sugar in the spring. They harvested wild rice from rivers and lakes in Minnesota and Wisconsin. If the climate permitted, they planted gardens of corn, beans, squash, and pumpkins.

Clothing and adornment

The Ojibway made clothing from green leaves, cloth woven from nettle-stalk fiber, and tanned hides. They used the green leaves for head coverings in hot weather. Nettle-stalk cloth was used for women's underskirts.

Chippewa Wild Rice

Wild rice was a staple food for the Ojibway because it could be stored and eaten during the winter when fresh foods were scarce. Wild rice is actually the seed of a special grass, a different species from white rice. One Ojibway legend tells about Wenebojo, the trickster, who heard the grass in the lake calling to him. He made a canoe and paddled out into the lake with his grandmother, Nokomis. The grass told them it was good to eat, so Wenebojo and Nokomis tried it. The Ojibway have been eating wild rice ever since.

　　1 cup wild rice, washed well in cold water
　　21/2 cups water
　　11/2 teaspoons salt
　　4 strips bacon cut into julienne strips [thin
　　　　strips about 11/2–2 inches long]
　　6 eggs
　　1/4 teaspoon pepper
　　2 tablespoons minced chives
　　Bacon drippings plus melted butter or
　　　　margarine to measure 1/3 cup

Place the wild rice, water, and 1 teaspoon salt in a saucepan, and bring slowly to a boil. Reduce heat and simmer, covered, until all water is absorbed.

Fry the bacon in a large, heavy skillet. Drain bacon on paper toweling. Save drippings [the bacon grease left in the pan].

Beat the eggs with 1/2 teaspoon salt and the pepper until light. Pour into the skillet in which you browned the bacon, and brown the eggs lightly. Then turn gently, as you would a pancake, and brown on the other side. When eggs are firm, cut into julienne strips.

Lightly toss the bacon, julienne egg strips, chives, bacon drippings plus melted butter or margarine with the rice. Serve hot as a main dish.

Serves 4 to 6.

SOURCE: Kimball, Yeffe, and Jean Anderson. *The Art of American Indian Cooking.* Garden City, NY: Doubleday, 1965, p. 107.

The tribe made dresses, pants, breechcloths, shirts, and moccasins from hides. The Ojibway put muskrat or rabbit skins or cattail down over their chests and inside moccasins for extra warmth during the cold winter months. Small children wore fitted hoods made of deer hide with a flap that could be brought forward to shade the eyes. Women used rabbit skins to make children's shoes, hats, and blankets.

After the Ojibway acquired blankets from traders, they made them into capes, winter coats (with hoods), and skirts (wrapped and fastened with belts). Woolen cloth dyed black or dark blue was especially favored. The women decorated clothing made from this cloth with beads laid out in floral designs or with silk ribbons.

The Ojibway adorned themselves with natural materials and later with items acquired through trade. They made necklaces of berries, small bones, and animal claws, along with wooden or glass beads brought by Europeans. Earrings, which were worn mainly by elderly men, were made of fur, bone, or heavy coins. Long ago, men wore large nose rings and brass bracelets acquired from trade. Young men wore fur bands decorated with beading around their wrists and ankles. Dance costumes were embellished with tassels of horsehair dyed red and covered with tin at the top.

The Ojibway kept their hair long, and men usually wore braids. In times of war, the men sometimes shaved their heads Mohawk-style (see Mohawk entry). They might apply stripes of red and yellow paint to their hair or wear leather headbands with feathers standing up in back. Warriors often wore headdresses, dyed bright colors, clipped to their hair. They made these headpieces of porcupine or deer hair (or, on the southern plains, of black turkey beards) with a feather in them. Some men wore long feathered headdresses like the Sioux (see Dakota, Lakota, and Nakota entries). Women wound their hair in cloth or, on festive occasions, braided it in two braids with a long strip of otter fur over each braid.

In the nineteenth and twentieth centuries, clothing was adorned with sleigh bells, small mirrors, and pieces of tin. Beaded bands held the men's leggings in place. In the early twenty-first century, Ojibway often wore moccasins or beaded shirts, but they only dressed in traditional clothing for special occasions such as dances.

Healing practices

Ojibway believed illness resulted from displeasing supernatural spirits or from social failures, such as not hosting a feast after a successful hunting trip. They believed that the sick should be treated both spiritually and physically. Relatives carried a sick person to a healer's lodge and brought tobacco, considered sacred, for the healer to smoke. The rising smoke alerted the spirits that the healer was thinking of them. Cedar was sometimes burned to purify the air and to treat a contagious illness; sage was burned as a disinfectant.

The healer, usually a member of the Midewiwin society (see "Religion"), might frighten the patient to start the healing process, or he might sing. Ojibway healers had an extensive knowledge of plants and herbs used to treat illnesses. It is said that they introduced European sailors to rose hip tea, which prevented the illness called scurvy, caused by a lack of vitamin C.

Education

Children were considered a gift to all the people, and bringing them up properly was everyone's responsibility. Children learned by observing. Not listening to others, especially to elders, was considered extremely rude. Children were taught to choose words with care and to think before they spoke. Quarreling and bickering were not tolerated, and children learned not to argue or to criticize others.

When the reservation system was established in the mid-1800s, the U.S. government took control of Ojibway education. Children went to day schools or to boarding schools where they were taught manual labor and housekeeping skills. Often they were separated from their parents and were severely punished for disobeying the rules or for speaking their tribal language.

In the early 2000s, most Ojibway children attended public schools, but some reservations established Head Start programs, preschools, elementary schools, and special classes in Ojibway culture, history, and language. Several reservations also had tribal colleges.

ARTS

Music and dancing are important parts of Ojibway ceremonies. Their songs and dances look to nature for inspiration. As Fred Benjamin, an Ojibway elder, explained in *Circle of Life:*

> The Great Spirit [told them] to make songs out of what they saw. Like the leaves when the wind blows they're shaking; they make a little noise. That's how they got the idea to put bells on their legs. And sometimes you see a fowl, like an eagle, an owl, a chickenhawk. The Native American people looked at them, the way they'd swing their wings, how they'd go down and up. That's how they'd make the pitch of their songs.

Ojibway elders, especially women, were often expert storytellers, sometimes acting out a story while telling it. The tradition of Ojibway storytelling has been kept alive through the works of notable modern authors such as Ignatia Broker (1919–1987), Maude Kegg (1904–1996),

Grandmother at Indian School

Ojibway writer Linda LeGarde Grover, a professor of American-Indian studies at the University of Minnesota–Duluth, is an enrolled member of the Bois Forte band of the Minnesota Chippewa Tribe.

Left on scrubbed wooden steps to
   think
about disobedience and forgetfulness
she feels warm sun on the back of her
   neck
as she kneels on the pale spot worn
by other little girls' tender sore knees,
a hundred black wool stockings
grinding skin and stairs,
beneath one knee a hard white navy
   bean.
Unreal distant lightening flickers pale
flashes down her shins, felt by other
uniformed girls marching to sewing
   class
waiting for their own inevitable return
to the stair, to think and remember
   what happens
to girls who speak a pagan tongue.
try to forget this pagan tongue
Disobedient and forgetful she almost
   hears
beyond the school yard
beyond the train ride
beyond little girls crying in white iron
   beds

her mother far away
singing to herself as she cooks
and speaking to quietly with Grandma
   as they sew
the quilt for the new baby,
and laughing with the aunties
as they wash clothes
the little bean,
does it hurt?
Bizaan, gego mawi ken, don't cry
she thinks, moving her knee so the
   little bean
feels only the soft part, and not the
   bone
how long can I stay here?
And when Matron returns to ask if
   she's thought
she says yes,
I won't talk like a pagan again
and she stands and picks up the little
   bean
and carries it in her lonesome lying
   hand
until lights out,
when the baby bean
sleeps under her pillow.

SOURCE: Grover, Linda LeGarde. "Grandmother at Indian School." *The Indian at Indian School.* Native Writers Chapbook Series 2. Little Rock: Sequoyah Research Center/University of Arkansas at Little Rock, 2008.

and many others. Ojibway people in Michigan and Minnesota keep their culture alive in many ways. They sponsor storytelling events, arts and crafts exhibitions, and powwows (special ceremonies in which members of several different tribes gather for singing, dancing, and feasting).

CUSTOMS

Birth and naming

When a baby was born, guns were fired to alert the village. A riotous feast celebrated the occasion. Ojibway believed that being born into a rowdy environment would make the child brave. Children were given six names; some names were revealed in dreams. The child was usually known by a nickname.

Puberty

The Ojibway practiced special rituals for boys or girls entering puberty. They believed that during a woman's menstrual period, or "moon time," the manitou (spirits) were a strong presence in her life, and she could easily harm herself or others. Therefore, a menstruating woman was kept away from cooking and spiritual activities. When a girl had her first period, she was isolated for four days and nights in a little wigwam made for her by her mother. She was not to eat during this time and was instructed not to touch her body or face with her hands. She used a stick to scratch herself if necessary. Afterward, the tribe gave a feast in her honor.

An Ojibway woman carries a papoose on her back in an illustration from 1826. © MPI/ STRINGER/ARCHIVE PHOTOS/ GETTY IMAGES

Boys entering puberty were required to fast (not eat or drink) and pursue a vision quest. A boy's father took him into the woods and made a nest for him in a tree, leaving him there for several days but checking on him periodically. A boy sometimes had to perform the ritual several times before he had a vision of a spirit to guide him. A feast was held when a boy killed his first game.

Marriage

Ojibway people identify themselves by their clan (a group of related families). A man had to marry a woman from another clan, and their children belonged to the father's clan. When a man and woman and the woman's parents agreed to a marriage, there was no formal wedding ceremony. The couple lived with the woman's family for a trial period of one year. If the relationship was not satisfactory or if the wife failed to become pregnant, the man could return to his parents.

A couple who wished to remain together usually built their own lodge, or they might choose to live with the man's family. Marital separation was allowed, and after a time the parties could remarry. Men who could support another family might have more than one wife, each having her own section of the lodge. Some men designated a head wife, who was the only one to have children. Intermarriage (marriage to non-Ojibway, including non-Indians) was acceptable, and by 1900, many Ojibway were of mixed heritage, typically French and Ojibway.

War and hunting rituals

Ojibway warriors were famous and feared. Before a war party left for battle, the tribe often held a ceremony called the Chief Dance. During the Chief Dance, the people asked the spirits to protect the departing warriors. They offered tobacco and food and played a special drum.

When Ojibway hunters killed a bear, the tribe held a bear ceremony and feast. To show their respect for the bear, they laid out its body and carefully cut it up. They placed foods that bears liked, such as maple sugar and berries, next to the body of the "visitor," the bear. Everyone ate bear meat and promised the spirits that if another bear should come their way, it too would be treated with respect.

Death and mourning

The Ojibway dressed their dead in the finest clothing and wrapped the body in a blanket and birchbark. Sometimes they painted the face, the moccasins, and the blanket with special substances. Because the dancing ghosts (the northern lights) were also painted this way, they believed the painted dead would join these dancing ghosts.

They removed the body from the wigwam through the west side and put it into a grave, along with food and other necessities for the spirit's journey to the afterworld. A close family member danced around the open grave. Then it was filled, and a funeral ceremony was performed. They later built a bark house and put the symbol of the deceased's clan over the grave.

Family members were expected to mourn for about one year, and mourning rituals were complicated. They wore special clothing and made

Women as Okitcita

Any Ojibway man, woman, or child could become an *okitcita,* or strong-hearted warrior, by performing a brave deed. A person won the honor of wearing an eagle feather stripped in front (one half of the feather was pulled partway off so it drooped down) by counting coup (being one of the first four to touch an enemy, dead or alive, with a hand or a hand weapon) or scalping an enemy. For killing an enemy, a man received a white eagle feather; a woman earned a black one. The narrator of these true stories told of two *okitcitakwe,* or women *okitcita,* from the early 1900s.

One of these, Cinoskinige, obtained her title in this manner:

She always went out with the warriors, and on one occasion when a Sioux was shot from his horse, she ran to count coup upon him. Being a woman she was outstripped in the race by three men, but succeeded in striking the fourth coup, killing the Dakota with her turnip digging-stick. The men then scalped him, and she painted her face with his blood.

Another renowned old woman at Long Plains was out with a party who were digging turnips on the prairie. They were attacked and surrounded by Sioux who rode round and round them, firing. The men fought them off, while the women hastily dug a rifle pit to conceal the party. In the meantime the men were all wounded. The pit being finished, this woman crept out under fire and rescued each of the men, dragging them back to the pit. In this manner she became an okitcitakwe.

SOURCE: Skinner, Alanson. "Women as Okitcita." *Anthropological Papers of the American Museum of Natural History, Vol. XI, Part VI: Political Organization, Cults, and Ceremonies of the Plains-Ojibway and Plains-Cree Indians.* New York: The American Museum of Natural History, 1914. Available online at http://digitallibrary.amnh.org/dspace/bitstream/2246/147/1/A011a01.pdf (accessed on June 5, 2011).

a spirit bundle containing a lock of the deceased's hair. A widow placed food in front of her husband's spirit bundle and slept with the bundle. She could not be seen in public or wear cheerful clothing. When a baby died, the mother carried the child's clothing in a cradleboard (a board onto which babies are strapped) for a year. Once a year, the tribe held a mourner's ceremony, during which mourners were comforted and given gifts. Then loved ones were expected to stop grieving and join the community again.

CURRENT TRIBAL ISSUES

Casino gambling on reservations is a controversial issue. Those in favor point out that gambling boosts reservation economies. Those against argue that gambling proceeds end up in the pockets of a privileged few (even non-Natives) and do little to benefit the entire reservation community. Nevertheless, most U.S. reservations have built casinos.

Key issues facing the Ojibway include economic development to reduce the numbers of unemployed people, improved medical treatment to combat illnesses such as diabetes and alcoholism, better management of natural resources, protection of treaty rights, and an emphasis on higher education. Some Ojibway groups are still seeking federal recognition.

In Canada, a 2008 Water Declaration stated that First Nation peoples should be protected from water contamination and should have their water rights, treaties, and self-government respected. Yet the government has been slow to take action. In 2010, the Anishinaabe staged a peaceful protest to draw attention to the high levels of mercury in the English-Wabigoon River system. This contamination has affected the reserves (Canadian term for reservations) of Wabaseemoong and Grassy Narrows for forty years. Those communities are not the only ones that have felt the impact of industries, mining, and pollution on their water sources and land. Many projects were started on First Nations territory without the band's consent and are now causing health and/or environmental problems.

The Grassy Narrows band has also been fighting clear-cut logging on their traditional territories. They have used a blockade to peacefully stop the logging, and they want more say in the use of their land. They would be willing to allow sustainable logging if areas are left undisturbed so their medicinal plants and the native animals can flourish.

In the 2000s, the former Council of Three Fires nations—Ottawa, Ojibway, and Potawatomi—have reunited and combined with other First Nations—Algonquin, Chippewa, Lanaape, Mississauga, and Nbiising—to form the Anishinaabe Nation. They plan to use their newly formed alliance for the betterment of their member nations and other First Nations. These eight bands strengthened their connection by writing a joint constitution in 2011. With greater political clout, they should to be able to challenge unfair government practices and reestablish many of the rights that have been denied them over the years.

NOTABLE PEOPLE

Jane Johnston Schoolcraft (1800–c. 1842) was the daughter of a Scots-Irish fur trader and an Ojibway woman from Sault Sainte Marie. She was one of the first Native American women to publish poetry; in her poems she described Ojibway culture, her love of nature, and her respect for piety and faith. Her husband, a mid-nineteenth-century government Indian agent named Henry Rowe Schoolcraft (1793–1864), wrote about the Ojibway with his wife's assistance. The 1855 poem "Hiawatha," by American poet Henry Wadsworth Longfellow (1807–1882), is based on Mr. Schoolcraft's writings about the Ojibway.

Activist Clyde Bellecourt (1939–) was one of the founders of the American Indian Movement (AIM) and a powerful force in major activist struggles of the early 1970s. AIM was founded by Ojibway Dennis Banks (1937–), George Mitchell (1933–), and Bellecourt in 1968.

Leonard Peltier (1944–) also figured prominently in AIM. He has been in prison since 1976 after a conviction for killing two Federal Bureau of Investigation (FBI) agents. There has been widespread protest of his imprisonment, since many believe he did not receive a fair trial.

BOOKS

Bellfy, Phil. *Three Fires Unity: The Anishnaabeg of the Lake Huron Borderlands.* Lincoln: University of Nebraska Press, 2011.

Blackbird, Andrew J. *History of the Ottawa and Chippewa Indians of Michigan.* Charleston, SC: Nabu Press, 2010.

Broker, Ignatia, *Night Flying Woman: An Ojibway Narrative.* St. Paul: Minnesota Historical Society Press, 1983.

Circle of Life: Cultural Community in Ojibwe Crafts. Duluth: St. Louis Historical Society, Chisholm Museum and Duluth Art Institute, 1984.

Kegg, Maude. *Portage Lake: Memories of an Ojibwe Childhood.* Edmonton: University of Alberta Press, 1991.

Kurath, Gertrude, Jane Ettawageshik, and Michael D. McNally. *Art of Tradition: Sacred Music, Dance, and Myth of Michigan's Anishinaabe, 1946–1955.* East Lansing: Michigan State University Press, 2009.

Levine, Michelle. *The Ojibway.* Minneapolis, MN: Lerner Publications, 2006.

Morriseau, Norval. *Legends of My People.* Edited by Selwyn Dewdney. Toronto, Ontario: Ryerson Press, 1965.

Palazzo-Craig, Janet. *The Ojibwe of Michigan, Wisconsin, Minnesota, and North Dakota.* New York: PowerKids Press, 2005.

Peacock, Thomas, and Marlene Wisuri. *The Four Hills of Life: Ojibwe Wisdom.* Afton, MN: Afton Historical Society Press, 2006.

Peacock, Thomas, and Marlene Wisuri. *Ojibwe Waasa Inaabidaa: We Look in All Directions.* Afton, MN: Afton Historical Society Press, 2002.

Teichroeb, Ruth. *Flowers on My Grave: How an Ojibwa Boy's Death Helped Break the Silence on Child Abuse.* New York: HarperCollins Publishers, 1998.

Treuer, Anton. *The Assassination of Hole in the Day.* St. Paul: Minnesota Historical Society Press, 2011.

White, Bruce. *We Are at Home: Pictures of the Ojibwe People.* St. Paul, MN: Minnesota Historical Society Press, 2007.

WEB SITES

"Anishinaabe Chi-Naaknigewin/Anishinabek Nation Constitution." *Anishinabek Nation.* http://www.anishinabek.ca/uploads/ANConstitution.pdf (accessed on May 16, 2011).

Mille Lacs Band of Ojibwe. http://www.millelacsojibwe.org/ (accessed on June 5, 2011).

Pitawanakwat, Lillian. "Ojibwe/Potawatomi (Anishinabe) Teaching." *Four Directions Teachings.* http://www.fourdirectionsteachings.com/transcripts/ojibwe.html (accessed on June 5, 2011).

Redish, Laura, and Orrin Lewis. "Native Americans of the Americas: Chippewa (Ojibway, Anishinaabe, Ojibwa)." *Native Languages of the Americas.* http://www.native-languages.org/chippewa.htm (accessed on June 5, 2011).

Saginaw Chippewa Indian Tribe. http://www.sagchip.org/ (accessed on June 5, 2011).

The Sault Tribe of Chippewa Indians Official Web Site. http://www.saulttribe.com/ (accessed on June 5, 2011).

Turtle Mountain Chippewa Indian Heritage Center. http://chippewa.utma.com (accessed on June 5, 2011).

Ottawa

Name

Ottawa (pronounced *AH-tah-wah*) comes from the Algonquian word *adawe* meaning "to trade." The First Nations in Ontario are called *Odawa.* The Ottawa people refer to themselves as *Anishinaabe,* which means "original person." The name Ottawa has been written many different ways over the years, but some of the most common spellings are Adawe and *Outa-ouac,* the French name for the tribe. Other spellings sometimes used are Odaawaa, Odawe, and Odawu. At times, the name started with an *A* rather than an *O,* for example, Ahtawwah, Attawa, Atowa, Atawawa, and Autawa.

Location

The tribal history of the Anishinaabe (also called Anishinabek) Nation, of which the Ottawa were a part, indicates that they migrated from the Atlantic coast to the Great Lakes area. By the 1600s, the Ottawa had established villages in southeastern Ontario along the northern and eastern coasts of the Georgian Bay in Lake Huron, which included the Bruce Peninsula, and on Manitoulin Island in the bay. Their lands also included the upper and lower Michigan peninsulas by the Great Lakes. In the late 1600s, Iroquois attacks kept the Ottawa on the move. From Manitoulin Island and then Mackinac Island, some Ottawa settled around Detroit, Michigan, or along the Maumee River in Ohio. A few joined the Wyandot (Huron; see entry) on land along Lake Erie that extended east from Detroit to Beaver Creek in Pennsylvania. By 1830, some Ottawa had established villages in Indiana, Illinois, and Wisconsin; those who settled there were removed to Iowa in 1834. In 1837, several bands moved to Kansas; that land was later sold, and the people were removed to Indian Territory in Oklahoma in 1867. In the twenty-first century, most Ottawa bands were concentrated mainly in Ontario, Michigan, and Oklahoma.

Population

When the Europeans arrived in the 1600s, the Ottawa population was estimated to be around 5,000. Unlike many of the other tribes, the Ottawa were not as decimated by the epidemics (uncontrolled spread of diseases) that

Contemporary Ottawa Communities

Michigan
1. Detroit
2. Mackinac Island

Ontario
3. Manitoulin Island

Shaded area

The traditional lands of the Ottawa villages in southeastern Ontario along the northern and eastern coasts of the Georgian Bay in Lake Huron, which included the Bruce Peninsula, and on Manitoulin Island in the bay. Their lands also included the upper and lower Michigan peninsulas by the Great Lakes.

A map of contemporary Ottawa communities. MAP BY XNR PRODUCTIONS. CENGAGE LEARNING, GALE. REPRODUCED BY PERMISSION OF GALE, A PART OF CENGAGE LEARNING.

ran through many tribes, so their population stayed somewhat stable during that time. After the tribe scattered during the late 1600s, few records were kept to account for the total population. In 1867, only about 200 Ottawa moved to Oklahoma; the rest had died. In the early 1900s, an estimate of the groups living with other bands was about 4,700. At that time Manitoulin and Cockburn Islands had 1,497 Chippewa and Ottawa combined, so about half that number would have been Ottawa. The Seneca School in Oklahoma listed 197. The 1910 U.S. Census showed 2,717 Ottawa, with the majority being in Michigan, where they numbered 2,454. Oklahoma had 170. The rest were living in Wisconsin, Kansas, Nebraska, and Pennsylvania. By 2000, about 10,677 Ottawa made their homes in Canada and the United States. A decade later, the estimated population was 15,000. The 2010 census counted 7,272 Ottawa in the United States, with a total of 13,033 claiming some Ottawa heritage.

Language family

Algonquian.

Origins and group affiliations

According to Chief Outaouiboy in 1700, the Ottawa had four main divisions: Kishkakon (Bear), Sinago (Gray Squirrel), Sable (Sand), and Nassauaketon (Fork People). Another group, the Keinouché (Pike or Pickerel), also written Kenouche, is sometimes listed, but they may have been a division of the Sable. These bands were subdivided into many smaller bands. Some early sources mention several dependents of the Ottawa, including the Chisérhonon, Squierhonon, and Hoindarhonon. The Ottawa allied with the Wyandot (Huron; see entry) for defense and trade, but did not completely trust them. Both of these tribes maintained a good bartering relationship with the French, and later the British; they also fought alongside them in several wars. The Ottawa, Ojibway (see entry), and Potawatomi (see entry) formed an alliance, the Council of Three Fires, to defeat the Iroquois Confederacy (see entry) and the Sioux (see Dakota entry). The council later joined the Western Lakes Confederacy, or Great Lakes Confederacy, which united them with tribes such as the Algonquin, Meskwaki, Nipissing, Sac (see Sac and Fox entry), and Wyandot. Today, as part of the Anishinaabe Nation, the Canadian Odawa and their original Three Fire allies are closely tied to five other First Nations, including the Algonquin, Chippewa, Lanaape, Mississauga, and Nbiising. These eight bands strengthened their connection by writing a joint constitution in 2011.

As part of the Anishinaabe Nation, the Ottawa were one of a group of tribes that dominated the Great Lakes area before the European arrival. Although some sources called them nomadic, excavations have indicated that they planted corn, and they also established trade routes and control of the waterways. They were experienced businesspeople long before they became involved in the French fur trade in the 1600s. Along with the Wyandot (or Wendat; see entry), whom the French called *Huron,* they gathered beaver pelts to exchange for European goods. By the mid-1600s Iroquois attacks had dispersed most of the tribe, but some of the Ottawa and Wyandot continued their bartering relationship with the French and later the British. As the Ottawa refugees gradually lost their traditional homelands through war and removal, the tribe ended up in several different states as well as Canada. Yet they left their mark at stops along the way—a major river, the capital of Canada, and many counties and landmarks—as proof that they were once a dominant nation.

Important Dates

1615: Ottawa meet Samuel de Champlain at Georgian Bay.

1651: Ottawa and Wyandot settle at Green Bay, Wisconsin, after Iroquois attacks.

1763: Chief Pontiac leads the Great Lakes tribes in a rebellion against the British.

1836: Michigan Ottawa give up most of their land and are given a temporary reservation; Canadian Ottawa sign Bond Head agreement.

1862: Canadian Ottawa are forced to move to reserves.

2007: Michigan gives the Ottawa hunting and fishing rights.

2011: As part of the Anishinaabe Nation, the Ottawa write a joint constitution.

HISTORY

Pre-European culture

The Ottawa may be descendants of the Saugeen complex, a culture that lived around Lake Huron and the Bruce Peninsula during the Middle Woodland period (200–300 BCE to 700–900 CE). Although the people were hunter-gatherers, they may have grown plants such as squash or gourds. Remains indicate that gourds may have been used as food containers. The Saugeen, who lived in bands of about fifty people, buried their dead in mounds with grave goods similar to those of the Hopewell people.

By around 1400, the Ottawa lived on islands in Lake Huron, particularly Manitoulin Island, often called their traditional homeland. Some had also settled near the mouth of the French River. The Ottawa, who traveled great distances in their birchbark canoes, traded with other tribes throughout the Great Lakes region. Goods included cornmeal, sunflower oil, tobacco, pelts, mats, and herbs.

Relations with the French

In 1615, the French explorer Samuel de Champlain (c. 1567–1635) met a group of Ottawa at Georgian Bay. As skilled traders, the Ottawa were soon engaged in the European fur business. They traveled to other tribes in the Great Lakes area to bring pelts back to the Huron (see Wyandot entry) villages, located near the French settlements. Although the Ottawa and Huron had fought in early years, they collaborated to handle the trade. Within a few decades, the Ottawa were supplying two-thirds of the furs reaching Montreal. For more than a century, they remained key players in the fur trade.

Overtrapping led to a decline in beaver by the 1630s. The Winnebago stopped the Ottawa from moving farther west, and when the Ottawa sent negotiators, the Winnebago killed and ate them. The French intervened to prevent war and worked out a truce that allowed the fur trade to expand as far as Lake Michigan. Some Ottawa then moved from Manitoulin to Mackinac Island.

Rivalry with Assegun and Iroquois

In 1640, the Assegun fought with the Ottawa and Ojibway moving into their territory. The two allies forced the Assegun into lower Michigan, but the Assegun retaliated by raiding Ottawa villages and fighting with the Mascouten against the Ottawa.

The Iroquois League became a dominant force in the Beaver Wars (intertribal fighting for control the fur trade during the 1600s) because they had secured guns from the Dutch. When the Iroquois destroyed Huron villages in 1649, the Huron and Tionontati refugees (now called the Wyandot) fled north, where they joined the Ottawa. To escape the Iroquois, the Ottawa and Wyandot first moved in 1651 to Green Bay, Wisconsin, then to the Potawatomi (see entry) village of Mitchigami on Wisconsin's Door Peninsula the following year. In 1656, the Ottawa moved again so that they could continue to conduct the fur trade. Some moved to Lac Courte Oreilles, a large lake in northern Wisconsin. Others went to Keweenaw Bay or with the Wyandot to the Mississippi River, where they settled near Lake Pepin. After the Ottawa initiated an attack on the Iroquois, the counterattack drove the Ottawa north to Black River (Wisconsin), where the Wyandot built a fort. The Ottawa, though, headed east to Chaquamegon Bay in Lake Superior, where the Wyandot later joined them. The Jesuit priest Claude-Jean Allouez (1622–1689) established a mission there.

Movement of the Ottawa

Because the Iroquois now controlled the waterways, the Ottawa allied with the Ojibway and Wyandot and fought their way to Montreal to trade furs. As the beaver supply became depleted, the Ottawa and other Green Bay tribes moved farther west into Dakota (see entry) lands. Skirmishes broke out, and in 1669, the Dakota asked for a peace treaty. When the Dakota arrived to discuss terms, however, the Ottawa killed and ate them. The Dakota struck back by burning alive the Ottawa chief Sinago.

In 1670, the priests moved the mission to St. Ignace, which they thought would be safer for the Ottawa and Wyandot, but the Seneca burned it the following year. Some Ottawa and Wyandot stayed, and the mission was rebuilt. Other bands moved back to Manitoulin, where missionaries built St. Simon and promised to protect them.

Changes to the fur trade

Also in 1670, the British established the Hudson's Bay Company, which ended the French monopoly of the fur trade. Because other tribes could trade directly with the British, the Ottawa lost their role as middlemen. To continue to make money, the Ottawa and Ojibway expanded their territory and remained the main supplier of furs to the French.

In 1687, Canadian governor Jacques-René de Brisayde Denonville (1637–1710) created the Great Lakes Alliance, consisting of the Ottawa, Wyandot, Ojibway, Fox and Sac (see entry), Illinois, Miami (see entry), Mascouten, and Kickapoo. The Ottawa and the Wyandot held a place of honor in the group as the "eldest children of Onontio," the French governor. The French and their allies fought the Iroquois and managed to push them out of the Great Lakes area. Although the Iroquois offered the Ottawa a peace treaty, the Ottawa refused and stayed loyal to the alliance.

The Ottawa received a great blow in 1696 when King Louis XIV ended the French fur trade because of the missionaries' insistence that it was detrimental to the tribes' spiritual well-being. The Ottawa led a revolt against the French, and many traders were killed. Some of the tribes, including the Ottawa, traveled to New York to trade with British. In 1701, the French finally persuaded the alliance to sign a peace treaty.

Relocation of the Ottawa

By that time, most of the Ottawa had moved to Mackinac Island with the Wyandot. The two groups lived together until some of them moved to the Detroit area around 1701, at the invitation of Antoine de la Mothede Cadillac (1658–1730), who had opened a new trading post. About 1706, the Ottawa band that had been living on Michigan's Lower Peninsula joined them at Mackinac. As more tribes poured into Detroit, the area became overcrowded, and wars broke out among the allies, called the Fox Wars (1712–16 and 1728–37). The Ottawa eventually ended the war by saying they did not want to "eat" the Fox.

Over time various Ottawa bands had spread out. A large number of Ottawa lived at the lower end of Lake Michigan at Waganakisi (L'Arbre Croche) on Grand Traverse Bay. They extended their territory to encompass the eastern shore to St. Joseph River, but others moved to northeastern Illinois and southern Wisconsin. Those still on Manitoulin shared the island with Chippewa (see Ojibway entry). Some Ottawa, along with the Wyandot, occupied land along Lake Erie that stretched from Detroit to Beaver Creek, Pennsylvania.

Chief Pontiac confronts British colonel Henry Bouquet in 1764 for intentionally using infected blankets to spread smallpox among the Native American people. © MPI/GETTY IMAGES

Smallpox epidemic

In 1755, the Ottawa sided with the French against Great Britain in the French and Indian War (1754–63). As part of their war tactics, the British gave the Ottawa a small tin box, promising that it would do the tribe good but warning them not to open it until they reached their village.

All the people gathered around to watch as their warriors opened the smaller and smaller tin boxes inside. Finally, they opened the last box to find small particles inside. Many of them inspected the gift to see if

Native American warriors burn a ship in the Detroit River in an offensive led by Chief Pontiac against the British in 1763. © NORTH WIND PICTURE ARCHIVES/ ALAMY

they could figure out what it was. They did not discover the contents of the box until later, when smallpox broke out among them. Whole families became ill, and soon many lodges were filled with dead bodies. The Ottawa healers knew of no way to cure smallpox, and many of them died as well.

Pontiac's Rebellion

By the time the French and Indian War drew to a close, the British had defeated the French. The Ottawa, along with other tribes, wanted to prevent British settlers from moving into Ohio Country and taking over their lands. In 1763, Ottawa chief Pontiac (c. 1720–1769), led an attack on the British Fort Detroit. The tribes raided settlements and captured Fort Sandusky.

The English fought back under the leadership of two colonels, John Bradstreet (1714–1774) and Henry Bouquet (1719–1765). In September 1764, the Wyandot and Ottawa ran out of ammunition, and many of them surrendered, but Pontiac remained at large. The next month, Bouquet subdued the Delaware, Shawnee (see entries), and Seneca, and marched several hundred captives to Fort Pitt. The Ottawa who refused to submit moved to Walpole Island in Lake St. Clair, Canada, with the Potawatomi and Chippewa. Others still in Canada were on Cockburn and Manitoulin Islands and along the shore of Lake Huron.

Although Pontiac's rebellion had ended, he did not surrender until July 1766. To avoid further conflict, England passed a law that all colonists had to live east of the Appalachian Mountains; the western lands were given to the Native peoples. Within a short time, however, colonists began defying the order and settling on tribal lands, sparking new conflicts.

Conflict with the Americans

During the American Revolutionary War (1775–83), the Ottawa sided with England. Even after the British surrendered, the Ottawa did not give up. In January 1785, the United States made peace with the Ottawa and several of their allies in a treaty signed at Fort McIntosh. Another treaty was negotiated the following year, but, as settlers continued to violate the terms, the tribes called a council fire.

In 1788, the Americans requested another meeting at Fort Harmar. Some of the allies, including the Wyandot and Detroit Ottawa, agreed to attend, but many of the other tribes continued to ambush settlers. Some Ottawa and Ojibway even attacked the soldiers who were building the council house for the peace treaty negotiations. The Fort Harmar Treaty, signed in January 1789, set the new boundary at the Muskingum River. The tribes who had not agreed to the terms did not honor it. Neither did American settlers.

Treaties with the United States

President George Washington sent General Anthony Wayne to Ohio Country, and in 1794, he defeated the Ottawa and their allies at the Battle of Fallen Timbers. The tribes who signed the Treaty of Greeneville the following year gave up most of their Ohio territory, except for the northwest, which allowed the Detroit Ottawa to keep their lands.

That treaty was only the first in series of agreements that led to the loss of Ottawa land. An 1805 treaty ceded the northern Ohio land to the Connecticut Land Company for $16,000. Two years later, the Detroit Ottawa, along with the Ojibway, Potawatomi, and Wyandot, moved to an Ohio reservation after selling the seven million acres they owned in southeastern Michigan. The Brownstown treaty in 1808 took even more of their land. Some Ottawa moved to Walpole Island and nearby Ontario. Others tried to settle with the Arbre Croche, who refused to take them in.

By 1817, the Ohio bands had six small reservations along the Maumee and Auglaize Rivers. The Ottawa of Blanchard's Fork of Great Auglaize River were forced west to Oklahoma around 1832. The Ottawa also lost the land along shore of Lake Michigan in series of treaties, culminating in 1833 with the Chicago Treaty, which removed them to northeastern Kansas along the Missouri River.

Tribal status changes

As part of their agreement with the United States in 1836, the Ottawa in Michigan had given up most of their property in exchange for keeping some traditional land as a reservation. The United States amended the 1836 treaty to limit the Ottawa's time on this Manistee Reservation to five years. Many Ottawa, worried about their future on this temporary reservation, began buying property near their traditional summer villages. Those on the reservation lobbied for a new treaty, but the United States put the Manistee Reservation land up for sale in 1848, and it was bought by timber companies.

The Treaty of Detroit in 1855 turned the Ottawa land into allotments, small individual parcels of property, which went against the tribe's beliefs of holding all land in common. At that time, the government dissolved the Ottawa and Chippewa Nation (a group that did not even exist). Not all Ottawa bands signed the agreement, but the government insisted the tribe had been terminated. This led to more than a century of legal battles to restore the Ottawa's tribal rights.

Loss of land

Over the next few years, fraud deprived many Ottawa of their lands. After Kansas became a state, most of the Ottawa living there became citizens to get their land allotments, but those who wanted to retain their tribal status bought land and moved to Oklahoma with the Shawnee. By 1891, most had been forced to give up much of this land because of allotments.

At the same time the Ottawa in the United States were being moved, the Ottawa in Canada were also having land struggles. Although the government had recognized Anishinaabe rights to Manitoulin Island in the 1836 Bond Head agreement, by 1862, the Canadian government wanted the land for settlers. The Ottawa bands refused to sign the treaty, but two days later the government said the treaty had been signed. The Anishinaabe whose names appeared on the document had no authority to sign and the validity of the signatures has often been questioned, but most of the bands were moved to small reserves. Only Wikwemikong, on the eastern side of the island, remained unceded land.

Fight for rights

As the Ottawa in the United States turned over their lands and became citizens, the government ended federal services but often did not pay the treaty money the bands had been promised. In 1905, the Ottawa in Michigan won a lawsuit against the U.S. government and were paid for the fraud and treaty violations.

In 1934, the U.S. Indian Reorganization Act allowed tribes to reorganize their governments, so tribal councils were reinstated. The following year the Little River band made its first attempt at recognition and failed. A few years later, the Oklahoma Ottawa reorganized under the Oklahoma Indian Welfare Act, but Congress later terminated them.

In 1946, the U.S. Indian Claims Commission let tribes sue the federal government for outstanding treaty claims. In 1948, the Ottawa formed the Northern Michigan Ottawa Organization to take legal action. A successful suit resulted in payment for the Grand River band.

STRUGGLE FOR RECOGNITION

That same year, the Little River band tried again for federal recognition but was denied. In the mid-1950s, the U.S. government terminated the Ottawa Tribe. Not until 1978 was the tribe restored. Its tribal constitution was ratified the following year. It took until 1980 before the government recognized the Grand Traverse band of Ottawa and Chippewa; its constitution was ratified in 1988. The Little River band, who had applied for a third time in 1970, was finally granted recognition in 1994. Other groups continue to fight to regain their status with the federal government, although the state has recognized some of the tribes.

In 2007, the state of Michigan negotiated the Inland Hunting Consent Decree Agreement with five tribes, including the Grand Traverse band of Ottawa and Chippewa Indians, the Little Traverse Bay band of Odawa Indians, and the Little River band of Ottawa Indians. This agreement allows the tribes to hunt, fish, and gather on their own land as well as on any government properties where those practices are allowed.

RELIGION

Traditional beliefs

For centuries the Ottawa worshipped and offered sacrifices to a Supreme Being, or Great Spirit. By day the sun was the eye of the Great Spirit; at night it was the moon and stars, so the people were always under the watchful eye of this Great Spirit. The creator of the earth was Nanabozho, the Great Hare, and the Underwater Panther was the ruler of the waters, animals, and birds. The Ottawa also called on a variety of supernatural beings called *manitok,* which could be good or evil. For example, rivers, fire, and forests were beneficial, whereas storms, snakes, and cold were bad.

To appease the spirits, hunters offered tobacco, hides, or dogs before they set off to find food. One spring ceremony occurred during jubilees. The Ottawa put their winter clothing on a pole and held up the garments, so the Great Spirit would look down on them with compassion.

Religious stories

Even before the missionaries arrived, the Ottawa had stories and beliefs that were similar to those the Europeans brought with them. The Ottawa had a great flood story, which was reminiscent of Noah and the ark from the Christian Bible, although in the Ottawa story, a great canoe to rescue the animals.

A story told about Nanabozho is that maple trees once produced pure syrup, but to make it more difficult for people, Nanabozho added water. He also poked his staff into every other tree, changing the delicious fat that people ate from inside the trees to hard hearts.

Moral code

Prior to European arrival, the Ottawa lived by a moral code of twenty-one precepts that was similar to the Ten Commandments. Some of the rules they followed were to honor the Great Spirit, to respect parents and elders, and to refrain from lying, stealing, swearing, or being lazy. The people were also warned not to make fun of anyone who was physically challenged. No one was to mock the mountains, rivers, or particularly thunder, which produced the rain that kept the monsters under the earth from eating people.

Parents reminded their children of these precepts, and the rules were repeated at feasts and councils. Everyone believed that the Great Spirit could see them at all times, so even when they hid in their wigwams they were never out of the divine view. Those who kept the laws would go to the spirit land, where they would dance to the drum of the head spirit, Tchi-baw-yaw-booz. Breaking the rules meant an afterlife of hunger and traveling the earth, unable to find the road that the good spirits took.

Spiritual leaders

Traditionally, three religious societies existed. The Midewiwin and Wabeno were known for their powers of healing. The Jossakeed foretold the future and participated in the shaking-tent ritual. These shamans, or prophets, entered a special tent or lodge where spirits visited them. The tents were built with 10- to 12-foot (3- to 4-meter) poles set in a circle, covered with animal skin or canvas, leaving an opening at the top.

The people lit a fire nearby and smoked pipes as a shaman sang to call up the spirits. Then he either crawled into the tent or threw his blanket or robe into the tent. As he did so, the tent shook and filled with voices or noises. Not all of the voices were understandable, but if a person asked a question, someone could translate the answers.

European religious influences

Although Catholic priests worked among the Ottawa from the mid-1700s on, they had little success in converting the people to Catholicism. In the early 1820s, however, a convert named Andowishat Arbre Croche influenced many Ottawa to become Christians. The missionaries also tried to get the Ottawa and other bands to adopt European ways.

The Catholic Church gained members on Mackinac and Manitoulin Islands as converts shared their faith with relatives and friends there. A mission was built at Seven Mile Point. Meanwhile, Protestant missionaries worked with many of the other bands, including the Ottawa in Kansas and later Oklahoma.

LANGUAGE

The Ottawa, or Odawa, language is one of five dialects of Ojibwe, a division of the Algonquian language family. Speakers of the various Ojibwe dialects could easily understand each other. Ottawa, like the other dialects, is mainly composed of nouns and verbs. In fact, close to three-fourths of the words in the language are verbs. Nouns and verbs are divided into two kinds—animate and inanimate. Animate words have a life or spirit, while inanimate ones do not. Because Ojibwe speakers did not have an alphabet, they adopted the English alphabet.

When the Ottawa were sent to boarding school, where they were punished for speaking their own language, many of the younger generations lost their ability to converse in their native language. By the late 1900s, the Ottawa dialect was dying out. In 1991, the Native American Language Preservation Act provided funds to address this issue. In 1993, the first annual language and culture event was held in Alden, Michigan, and it still takes place in Manistee every year. Many gather to revive the Anishinaabe language and culture.

Ottawa Words

As with many other languages, Anishina-abemowin, the language the Ottawa speak, often uses phrases to express single words in English.

January	*Manido Giizis* (Spirit Moon)
February	*Makwa Giizis* (Bear Moon)
March	*Naabidin Giizis* (Snow Crust Moon)
clock	*dabagiiswaan* (an object that measures the sun)
telephone	*giigaadoobii' aapikonhs* (small speaking wire)
medicine	*mshkiki* (strength from the earth)
village	*odeno* (place of many hearts)

In 2000, Manistee students began learning their language, which they call Anishinaabe-mowin, in school. Little River band of Ottawa Indians started a family language and culture camp to reintroduce the language. Other Ottawa tribes have also added language programs for both children and adults. In Canada, a greater number of people retained their native language, particularly at Wikwemikong Unceded Indian Reserve, where more than two-thirds of the population still speaks Anishinaabemowin. Kenny Pheasant, who grew up speaking his native language on Wikwemikong Reserve, is one of the promoters of teaching Anishinaabe-mowin to children. A grant from the Administration for Native Americans (ANA) has allowed the Ottawa to create language materials including CDs, a Web site, and language camps. Since the turn of the century, Anishinaabemowin has become one of the healthiest North American languages.

GOVERNMENT

Early bands were autonomous and had war chiefs in addition to several chiefs per village. Most decisions, though, were made by a council composed of the adult men from the village or region. After pressure from the Europeans, chiefs were elected. Candidates generally came from the former chief's family, and they could be women. For the most part, chiefs had little authority. The Europeans tried to change that among tribes that allied with them.

Murderers were entitled to a jury trial, but the jurors were relatives of the defendant and the victim. After both sides had had their say, the victim's family received compensation. Then a pipe was passed. The victim's family could choose whether to accept it or kill the murderer. Prior to European arrival, murders were almost nonexistent.

In 2011, the Anishinaabe Nation, composed of the Odawa, Algonquin, Chippewa, Lanaape, Mississauga, Nbiising, Ojibway, and Potawatomi, wrote a joint constitution.

ECONOMY

Because most bands lived along the shores, fishing was of primary importance to the Ottawa. Northern bands did ice-hole fishing during the colder months. The Ottawa's traditional homelands had a temperate climate, which allowed them to plant a variety of crops in spring and harvest in the fall. Hunting supplemented their diets, but they were not known for their skill. Before the arrival of the Europeans, the Ottawa had already established themselves as excellent traders. They had taken control of important waterways and traveled extensively to exchange goods with many different bands. Therefore, the Ottawa easily moved into the French fur trade when the opportunity arose. Along with the Wyandot (Huron), they became middlemen and used their contacts with other tribes to supply the French with beaver pelts. After Iroquois attacks scattered them, some Ottawa, along with refugee Wyandot, reestablished their trade in a new location.

As missionaries introduced new techniques and tools to improve agriculture along with new crops, the Ottawa gradually abandoned their seasonal migration for hunting. By the 1800s, many Ottawa had turned solely to farming, either on their own farms or on those owned by others. Some became lumbermen. During the following century, Ottawa began working in nearby towns. In the 2000s, several tribes had turned to small businesses, restaurants, tourism, and casinos to improve their economy. Other bands, particularly those without federal recognition, struggled with high unemployment rates.

DAILY LIFE

Families

Parents taught their children to live by the twenty-one precepts. Children also learned their future responsibilities by imitating and helping their parents with daily chores. When darkness fell, all children were expected to be in their own lodges for the night.

Buildings

Most villages were situated on lakeshores or riverbanks. The people built dome-shaped birchbark houses called *waginogan,* or wigwams, with arched roofs. Most had four central fires, and each fire was shared by two or three families. The outer walls were covered with mats made of bulrushes. Women gathered the plants while they were green, steamed them,

A man wearing traditional Native dress dances at a powwow in Ottawa, Canada. © MICHELLOISELLE

and then laid them in sun to bleach. The bulrushes were dyed with natural dyes before being woven into mats about 6 to 8 feet (2 meters) long and 4 feet (1 meter) wide.

Villages were laid out with homes close together, and they always included sweat lodges. The Ottawa sometimes used palisades, or fences made of sharpened wooden stakes, to protect their villages. For hunting, they took portable cone-shaped tents that they covered with mats or bark. By the 1830s, log homes had become the norm. Roofs of the log homes were often made of birchbark.

Clothing and adornment

The French explorer Samuel de Champlain (c. 1567–1635) in 1615 recorded that the first time he saw the Ottawa, the men had no clothing except a fur cloak. Their bodies were entirely covered with tattoos, and their faces were painted. The French also noted that the Ottawa wore a variety of ornaments. Both men and women had nose rings and several piercings in each ear that were decorated with copper, shell, and bone ornaments. These materials were also used for necklaces, along with claws and teeth. Later visitors mentioned breechclouts with front and back flaps that were decorated with quillwork designs and full-body tattoos of snakes, lizards, and geometric designs in red, black, green, and brown. The Ottawa often added belts with quillwork, woven sashes, different colored armbands, and woven shoulder bags of nettle fiber with animal or bird designs.

Most men wore their hair short and greased upright in front. A popular style involved a center tuft standing straight up from front to back and shaved on sides with a porcupine roach (tuft of stiff animal hair) clipped to the hair. Sometimes men shaved their heads and left only a scalplock hanging at the crown. Another style included two to four braids hanging down the back. Many men used leather headbands with feathers standing up in the back, although by the 1800s, some had adopted the long headdresses of the Dakota (see entry).

Later, clothing made of deerskin became common. In cold weather, men wore fringed leggings that they gartered below the knee. They added robes of small animal pelts lined with woven strips of rabbit fur for warmth and used snowshoes to travel. Women also wore rabbit skin robes over long deerskin dresses with sleeves that detached. Most kept their hair in one long braid in the back.

By the 1800s, European fabric had replaced deerskin for daily wear. Women decorated their cloth skirts and blouses with fancy beadwork. The Ottawa of this time used Hudson's Bay blankets and silver in place of their traditional cloaks and ornaments. Those who converted to Christianity followed the missionaries' ban on jewelry and wore their hair in European styles.

Food

Their nearness to water meant most bands relied heavily on fish, which they smoked for winter use. Group hunts added deer, beaver, bear, fox, partridge, hare, raccoon, and other small animals to their diet. To show respect for the animals, the people sang or talked to a bear's spirit before they killed it. Women cooked meat by roasting, frying, or boiling it. They also made it into a soup with corn, one of the crops they tended along with beans, squash, and other vegetables. Corn was ground into meal to make bread that was baked in ashes or in hot sand. Ottawa women also picked berries, collected maple sap, and used lichen or tree bark for meals when food was scarce. In the spring, all the bands arrived at Waganaksing in canoes filled with venison, bear meat preserved in oil, maple sugar, deer tallow, and honey.

Beginning in the 1820s, many people planted crops introduced by the Europeans—fruit, wheat, potatoes, turnips, and various vegetables— and kept livestock. Most bands had cattle and pigs. Some kept poultry and sheep. Dogs were kept as pets or to eat.

Tools

Early tools included wooden digging tools with scraperlike ends, wooden clubs, bows, round leather shields, and mortars and pestles made of log. After French contact, the Ottawa traded for tomahawks and other iron implements.

Education

Traditional education consisted of children learning by working with and imitating their parents. Andrew Jackson Blackbird (c. 1815–1908), who later became a translator for the U.S. government, recalled his father inventing an Ottawa alphabet that he called *Paw-pa-pe-po*. His father, Chief Mack-e-te-be-nessy, taught others to read and write.

By the 1800s, the government or religious institutions had established schoolhouses, and children were sent there to board (to live there during the school year). Students did chores in addition their studies. Girls learned to cook and clean. Canadian Ottawa learned French manners, and all classes were taught in French. In the United States students learned English. Children were punished for speaking their native languages. Classes in Catholic or Protestant religious instruction were also part of the curriculum, so students lost their traditional culture, language, and religion.

In Canada, parents paid the school by sending huge birch bark boxes filled with sugar, which the priest who ran the school took to Detroit to trade. He often used some of the money to buy fabric to make European-style clothing for the pupils. Priests were also known to instruct Native families to live in a more "civilized" manner, which to them meant that women should only do household chores and not work outdoors and that everyone should adopt European customs and manners.

Abuses in Education In the late 1800s, the Kansas Ottawa gave 20,000 acres of their allotted land for a university. The agreement was that their children would be educated free of charge, but a few years later, they were moved from the area.

In some areas, federal agents from the Office of Indian Affairs, who were supposed to distribute money for students' education, did not do their duty. For example, a survey taken in 1856 indicated the Maitowaning schoolhouse was decayed. In spite of records stating that twenty children were enrolled, half had never showed up once, and most had attended less than two weeks of the previous quarter.

One of the most devastating forms of abuse occurred in some of the residential schools, where some of the priests or teachers physically or sexually abused students.

Healing practices

Religion and healing were intricately tied together. Two of the religious societies—the Midewinin, or Medicine Society, and the Wabeno society—used their connections with the spirit world to cure illness. The men and women in the Medicine Society had to be initiated during a medicine feast. In addition to healing with spiritual power, the Ottawa used a variety of herbal medicines.

ARTS

Ottawa crafts

The Ottawa were known for their skill in quillwork, which they used to decorate a variety of objects, including birchbark boxes. Matting and black ash basketry were also traditional art forms.

Over time some of the traditional crafts turned into commercial enterprises. Women had done leather appliqué and beadwork, porcupine quill, and moose hair embroidery for centuries. As the children went to residential schools, however, they no longer learned these crafts. Instead, students learned to spin, knit, and weave at the schools. Woodworking, such as carving wooden bowls and spoons, continued but was gradually replaced by building log homes, furniture, and plank boats rather than birchbark canoes.

Reviving the traditional arts

Today, many bands are trying to revive the traditional arts. The Grand Traverse band of Ottawa and Chippewa has opened the Eyaawing (pronounced a-yah-wing) Museum and Cultural Center to preserve and share their arts, culture, and history.

The Burt Lake band received funding for its Anishinaabe Bmaadiziwin Naagademing ("Taking Care of Our Way of Life") Traditional Arts Project. The program pairs learners with a skilled craftsperson. After the students master the craft, they go on to mentor someone. In this way, the band hopes to continue the legacy of their traditional arts.

Opened in 1975, the Odawa Native Friendship Centre in Ontario is committed to cultural development. The organization teaches skills to the youth through various programs and activities, including the Annual Summer Odawa Pow Wow, attended by more than 18,000 visitors.

CUSTOMS

Social organization

The four groups—Kishkakon, Sinago, Sable, and Nassauaketon—that comprised the Ottawa did not always live together. They were composed of subgroups with their own villages and chiefs who made their own decisions.

The Legend of the Two Who Escaped

Ottawa oral history says that when the band settled on the Island of Manitoulin, another group of people, the Mi-shi-ne-macki-naw-go, lived there. The area around the Straits of Mackinac was called Michilimackinac after this tribe. One night as the Ottawa were celebrating a victory over the We-ne-be-goes, the Seneca massacred all of the Mi-shi-ne-macki-naw-go except two young lovers. According to Andrew Jackson Blackbird (c. 1815–1908), a translator for the U.S. government who was the son of an Ottawa chief, this was the young couple's fate.

> After everything got quieted down, they [the lovers] fixed their snow-shoes inverted and crossed the lake on the ice, as snow was quite deep on the ice, and they went towards the north shore of Lake Huron. The object of inverting their snowshoes was that in case any person should happen to come across their track on the ice, their track would appear as if going towards the island. They became so disgusted with human nature, it is related, that they shunned every mortal being, and just lived by themselves, selecting the wildest part of the country. Therefore, the Ottawas and Chippewas called them 'Paw-gwa-tchaw-nish-naw-boy.' The last time they were seen by the Ottawas, they had ten children--all boys, and all living and well. And every Ottawa and Chippewa believes to this day that they are still in existence and roaming in the wildest part of the land, but as supernatural beings....

> And whoever would be so fortunate as to meet and see them and to talk with them, such person would always become a prophet [to] his people, either Ottawa or Chippewa. Therefore, Ottawas and Chippewas called these supernatural beings 'Paw-gwa-tchaw-nish-naw-boy,' which is, strictly, 'Wild roaming supernatural being.'

> Sometimes hearing unknown noises or feeling a presence let the Ottawa know these beings were nearby. The people would then leave tobacco or another gift for the them.

SOURCE: Blackbird, Andrew J. *History of the Ottawa and Chippewa Indians of Michigan,* Chapter 3. Ypsilanti, MI: Ypsilantian Job Printing House, 1887. Available online at Lockard, Vicki, and Paul Barry, "Canku Ota—A Newsletter Celebrating Native America" 87 (May 17, 2003). *Turtletrack.* http://www.turtletrack.org/CO_FirstPerson/Blackbird/CO_04052003_Blackbird_Ch03.htm (accessed June 5, 2011).

In the Arbre Croche and Grand River bands, inheritance passed down through the father's side. As many as fifty different clans were listed by the early 1900s. Totems included bear, wolf, panther (also panther's foot and panther's track), beaver, eagle, gull, henhawk, sparrow hawk, pike, and forked tree.

Birth and naming

Mothers-to-be stayed away from their husbands during pregnancy and for forty days after the baby was born. Most babies were given a family name when they were about six months old, but names were changed later in life on special occasions. At the naming ceremony, the shaman pierced the child's nose and ears. Children were strapped to cradleboards until they were around three years old and had been weaned.

Puberty

One of the Ottawa's twenty-one precepts stated that the youth up to the age of twenty should disfigure their faces with charcoal and fast for at least ten days every year until they dreamed about the future. Both boys and girls fasted to receive guardian spirits in their dreams. Once girls began their menses, they stayed in the women's hut monthly during their periods.

Marriage

Parents chose a spouse for their son. They would take presents to the girl's parents, and, if her family agreed, the man's parents brought the girl home with them. Then they cautioned their son to be kind to his wife and cherish her. Neither the young husband or wife had any say in whom they married.

In spite of that, most couples stayed married; unfaithfulness was the only reason for divorce. If a man divorced his wife for any other reason, she could take any of his possessions, tear out his hair, or disfigure his face. Wives could not leave their husbands; their husbands had the right to kill them if they did.

Wealthier husbands could have more than one wife. Some men married their wives' sisters, but no one was allowed to marry cousins or second cousins.

Death and burial

Customs for burial included cremation, burial, or placing the body on a scaffold. Most people were buried, and a post carved with pictographs marked the grave. A few days after the burial, people brought food to the grave. To show their sadness, the bereaved blackened their faces or scratched themselves with sharp stones. Each year everyone joined in a mourning ceremony that included decorating the graves, fasting, and feasting.

Every three years or so, the bones of all the dead were cleaned of flesh. Then the bones were tied into mats or put in bark coffins. Then, like the Wyandot, the Ottawa held a Feast of the Dead.

The Ottawa believed everyone had two souls, one that departed at death. The other soul went to the afterlife, a pleasant country. To reach the afterworld, these souls left the village and passed over a shaky bridge above a raging river.

War rituals

The Ottawa were known for scalping and torturing their prisoners. Sometimes they ate them. Other captives they adopted into the tribe. When they wanted to welcome an important visitor, they engaged in mock battles.

Games and festivities

Competitions, such as lacrosse and footraces, against teams from their own community or against other villages were popular. The boys often tried to best each other at shooting small game or wrestling. Adults enjoyed games of chance with dice or straws.

When all the tribes met to spend the summer together, they began by holding a feast for the dead. People greeted each other with the word *ne-baw-baw-tche-baw-yew,* which meant "we are going around as spirits." During the feast, they tossed food into the fire for the spirits of the dead. Other celebrations included medicine and fire dances. Dances were often held at night to the accompaniment of drums, gourd rattles, and singing. After all the festivities, people settled down to plant their crops.

CURRENT TRIBAL ISSUES

Although some of the tribes have succeeded in gaining federal recognition, others are still struggling with this issue. One of the groups facing this problem is the Burt Lake band. The 1836 treaty set aside land along Burt Lake, Michigan, called Indian Point, for the Ottawa who lived there. After waiting for years for the government to formally set aside the land, the band members pooled their money and purchased the land.

Records show the taxes were paid, yet in 1900, Sheriff Fred Ming sold the land for back taxes to John W. McGinn, a timber speculator. To gain possession of the property, they waited until the men had left for work, forced the women and children out of the houses, and burned the homes to the ground. The Burt Lake band scattered to find housing. Legal procedures did not regain their land, which McGinn had sold to developers. The U.S. government denied the Burt Lake band's petition for recognition, giving as one of the reasons that the band had not stayed together as a community.

In 2009, the band started legislative action to gain recognition. The Burt Lake band, like most other federally unrecognized Ottawa tribes, has been recognized by the state. Tribes are also working to establish their treaty rights, gain payments for land that was taken, and keep their freedom to hunt, fish, and gather on their traditional lands.

In 2011, the Catholic Church offered a settlement to the Ottawa and other tribes who, as children, had suffered sexual abuse in the residential schools.

In spite of the many strides the bands have made, a higher percentage of their people compared to the general population still suffer from health problems, high unemployment rates, substance abuse, and domestic violence. Communities have introduced programs to address many of these issues. Frequently, these problems stem from the loss of traditional culture and livelihoods, so tribes have been working to keep their traditions and language strong and to pass them on to the next generations.

One effort in Canada has been the founding of the Anishinaabe Nation to reestablish the bonds between the Algonquin, Chippewa, Lanaape, Mississauga, Nbiising, Ottawa, Ojibway, and Potawatomi. In the political arena, the group has worked together to benefit all the bands. In 2010 they successfully blocked the government's planned 13 percent harmonized sales tax. In 2011, these eight nations wrote a joint constitution.

NOTABLE PEOPLE

One of the greatest leaders of the Native people, Chief Pontiac (c. 1720–1769) formed an alliance of Great Lakes tribes in 1763 to fight the British who were encroaching on their homeland. Under his leadership, the group destroyed nine of eleven English forts. Surrounded by two British commanders, most of his warriors surrendered, but Pontiac did not give in until two years later.

Another famous Ottawa chief was Ningweegon (Negwagon or Little Wing; d. 1839), who supported the United States during the War of 1812. When the British ordered him to take down the American flag, he refused. Instead he wrapped it around his arm and said that, if they took the flag, they must also take his heart. The British allowed him to keep flying the flag. In the 1836 treaty, the United States awarded Ningweegon an annuity of $100.

The son of Ottawa chief Mack-e-te-be-nessy (Black Hawk), Andrew Jackson Blackbird (c. 1815–1908) became a tribal leader and historian. His book, *History of the Ottawa and Chippewa Indians of Michigan*, published in 1887, provided important information on nineteenth century life from a Native perspective. Blackbird also served as an interpreter for the United States. Relatives of Andrew Blackbird included Chiefs Ningweegon and Shaw-be-nee, who served for the United States in the War of 1812, and Chief Wa-ke-zoo, a prophet and magician.

Daphne Odjig (1919–), born in Wikwemikong Unceded Indian Reserve, is an artist who has received many awards for her Woodlands-style work, including the Order of Canada. She was influential in starting the Professional Native Indian Artists Incorporation, also called the Indian Group of Seven, artists who collaborated to promote their work and to make the Native arts accessible and understandable to the general public.

In 2010, Derek J. Bailey, the tribal chairman of the Grand Traverse band of Ottawa and Chippewa, was appointed to the National Advisory Council on Indian Education by President Barack Obama.

BOOKS

Bellfy, Phil. *Three Fires Unity: The Anishnaabeg of the Lake Huron Borderlands*. Lincoln: University of Nebraska Press, 2011.

Blackbird, Andrew J. *History of the Ottawa and Chippewa Indians of Michigan*. Charleston, SC: Nabu Press, 1887, 2010.

Brehm, Victoria. *Star Songs and Water Spirits: A Great Lakes Native Reader*. Tustin, MI: Ladyslipper Press, 2010.

Kurath, Gertrude, Jane Ettawageshik, and Michael D. McNally. *Art of Tradition: Sacred Music, Dance, and Myth of Michigan's Anishinaabe, 1946–1955*. East Lansing: Michigan State University Press, 2009.

McClurken, James M. *Our People, Our Journey: The Little River Band of Ottawa Indians*. East Lansing: Michigan State University Press, 2009.

Switzer, Maurice. *We Are a Treaty People*. North Bay, Ontario: Union of Ontario Indians, 2011.

WEB SITES

"A Tribal History of the Little Traverse Bay Bands of Odawa Indians." *Little Traverse Bay Bands of Odawa Indians,* 2011. http://www.ltbbodawa-nsn.gov/tribalhistory.html (accessed June 4, 2011).

"Ahnii." *WikwemikongUnceded Indian Reserve,* 2011. http://www.wikwemikong.ca/ (accessed May 17, 2011).

"Anishinaabe Chi-Naaknigewin/Anishinabek Nation Constitution." *Anishinabek Nation,* March 3, 2011. http://www.anishinabek.ca/uploads/ANConstitution.pdf (accessed May 16, 2011).

"History: We Are the Anishnaabek." *The Grand Traverse Band of Ottawa and Chippewa.* http://www.gtbindians.org/history.html (accessed May 13, 2011).

"Notre Collection: Chiefs." *National Film Board of Canada,* March 8, 2010. http://www.onf-nfb.gc.ca/eng/collection/film/?id=51393&lg=en&exp=&v=h (accessed June 5, 2011).

Ottawa Tribe of Oklahoma. http://www.ottawatribe.org/history.htm (accessed May 13, 2011).

Pheasant, Kenny. "Anishinaabemowin." *Little River Band of Ottawa Indians,* 2011. http://www.anishinaabemdaa.com/anishinaabemowin.htm (accessed May 13, 2011).

Redish, Laura, and Orrin Lewis. "Ottawa Indian Fact Sheet." *Native Languages of the Americas,* 2009. http://www.bigorrin.org/ottawa_kids.htm (accessed May 15, 2011).

Sultzman, Lee. "Ottawa History." *First Nations Histories,* October 11, 2006. http://www.tolatsga.org/otta.html (accessed May 16, 2011).

Surtees, Robert J. "Treaty Research Report: Manitoulin Island Treaties." *Treaties and Historical Research Center: Indian and Northern Affairs Canada,* 1986. http://www.blacksbay.com/aboriginals/Manitoulin%20Treaties.pdf (accessed June 3, 2011).

Twardowski, Lynda. "The Fire Not Forgotten," March 13, 2008. The Burt Lake (Cheboiganing) Band of Ottawa and Chippewa. http://www.burtlakeband.org/portal/?q=TCArticle/alias (accessed June 4, 2011).

"Tribal Government." *Little River Band of Ottawa Indians.* https://www.lrboi-nsn.gov/ (accessed May 13, 2011).

Weiser, Kathy. "The Ottawa Indians." *Legends of Kansas,* April 2010. http://www.legendsofkansas.com/ottowaindians.html (accessed May 16, 2011).

Wyrick, Lula. Interview by Nannie Lee Burns, July 20, 1937. "Indian-Pioneers Papers Collection." *University of Oklahoma, Western History Collections.* http://digital.libraries.ou.edu/whc/pioneer/papers/6790%20Wyrick.pdf (accessed May 20, 2011).

Pequot

Name

The name Pequot (pronounced *PEE-kwot*) comes from an Algonquin word meaning "destroyers," referring to the warlike nature of the group in early times. The Pequot call themselves "Fox People." In the early twenty-first century, there were two Pequot tribes: the Mashantucket (Western Pequot) and Paucatuck (Eastern Pequot).

Location

Before Europeans arrived, Pequot lands covered all of southeastern Connecticut from the Nehantic River to the Rhode Island border. Today, about one-half of U.S. Pequot live on or near two reservations in Connecticut: the Eastern Paucatuck Pequot Reservation in New London and the Mashantucket Pequot Reservation in Mashantucket. The other half live mainly in Rhode Island and Massachusetts.

Population

In 1620, there were about 6,000 Pequot, including those who later became the Mohegan. Before the Pequot War of 1637, the Pequot numbered about 3,000. After the Pequot War, fewer than 1,500 survived, and by 1762, the population was down to 140. In 1974 there were fewer than 55 Pequot, but according to the 1990 U.S. Census, 679 people identified themselves as Pequot. In 2000, that number had risen to 1,334; of those, 590 were Mashantucket Pequot.

Language family

Eastern Algonquian.

Origins and group affiliations

Historians have different opinions about Pequot origins. Some say they moved from upper New York to eastern Connecticut in about 1500, whereas others say they have lived in Connecticut for a much longer time. In 1633, a group of Pequot, later called Mohegan, split off from the original tribe and

Contemporary Pequot Communities

Connecticut
1. Eastern Paucatuck Pequot Reservation
2. Mashantucket Pequot Reservation

Shaded area
Traditional Pequot lands in present-day southeastern Connecticut

A map of contemporary Pequot communities. MAP BY XNR PRODUCTIONS. CENGAGE LEARNING, GALE. REPRODUCED BY PERMISSION OF GALE, A PART OF CENGAGE LEARNING.

became their enemies. Several years later, the Pequot lost the Pequot War of 1637. Many Pequot survivors were sold or given into slavery; others took refuge with the Algonquin, Narragansett (see entry), Eastern Niantic, and Metoac tribes. They were soon absorbed into those tribes, and the Pequot tribe was considered "perished." The British colonists forced the few Pequot survivors of the war to join the Mohegan. Those Pequot became the ancestors of the two current Pequot tribes: the Mashantucket and the Eastern Pequot Tribal Nation.

Before Europeans came, the Pequot controlled Connecticut, fiercely guarding their hunting grounds against other tribes. After Europeans started the fur trade, the Pequot tried to control it, which led to the bloody conflict and near-destruction of the tribe in the Pequot War of 1637. After that, the tribe was rarely heard from over the next three hundred years. The story of how they went from power to poverty and triumphed to become owners of one of the world's richest casinos is truly astonishing.

HISTORY

Pequot enlarge their territory

Until their land was invaded by British settlers in the early 1600s, the Pequot farmed, hunted, fished, waged war, and dominated Connecticut. Before they ever saw Europeans, the tribe benefited from the French and British presence. This is because these newcomers were diminishing the powers of many Pequot rivals. Tribes to the north, who liked the European goods they received in exchange for furs, waged wars for control of the fur trade in what is now Canada. British slave ships traveled along the Atlantic Coast, kidnapping Native Americans and leaving behind diseases such as smallpox that killed many Natives. While other tribes were occupied with trade wars and sickness, the Pequot and Narragansett (see entry) became the two most powerful tribes in the Connecticut–New York region.

Important Dates

1600: The first Dutch trading post opens in Pequot territory.

1637: Massacre at Mystic ends Pequot War and nearly destroys the tribe.

1972: Pequot land claim filed.

1983: Mashantucket Pequot Indian Land Claims Settlement Act provides federal recognition.

1992: Foxwoods Casino opens.

2005: Eastern Pequot Tribal Nation loses federal recognition status gained in 2002.

Relations with Dutch

The first Pequot encounter with Europeans was with the Dutch, who built a trading post in Connecticut in 1622. The Dutch planned to trade with all tribes in the region, but the Pequot had other plans—they wanted total control. Their attacks on other tribes to gain this control upset both the other tribes and the Dutch, who in 1622 took the Pequot sachem (chief) Tatobem prisoner. The Dutch threatened to kill Tatobem if the Pequot did not change their ways; they also demanded a ransom for his release.

The Dutch expected the Pequot to bring beaver skins as ransom, but the Pequot brought wampum instead. The Dutch had no idea the value the tribes placed on wampum, the small white or dark purple beads made from shells. The furious Dutch leader ordered Tatobem killed. When the Pequot heard of this outrage, they burned down the trading post.

The Dutch leader was replaced by a new one, who apologized to the Pequot and built a new trading post. Trade began again, with the Pequot firmly in charge. Soon, the Dutch were trading for both furs and wampum, and the Pequot resumed their attacks on neighboring tribes.

Uncas and the Mohegans

When the Pequot grand sachem died in 1631, the Pequot tribal council chose Sassacus as the new grand sachem. Uncas, who was married to the daughter of Sassacus, had expected to be chosen, and he was angry. The quarrel between the two men escalated until Uncas broke off relations completely.

Accompanied by fifty Pequot warriors and their families, Uncas established a new village on the Connecticut River. The group took the name Mohegan, which means "wolf," and set up a long and profitable trading relationship with British colonists. Uncas supported the British against his former Pequot kin in the Pequot War of 1637, and eventually, under his leadership, the Mohegan became one of the most powerful tribes on the Atlantic Coast.

The Mohegan proved to be as fierce as the Pequot had been, and many small tribes in Connecticut were swallowed up by them.

When Uncas died, his sons carried on his policies. Historians agree that the fighting among tribes hastened the settlers' takeover of Native American lands in New England. The Mohegan tribe eventually lost most of its land to the settlers.

In 1994, the Mohegan reached an agreement with the state of Connecticut in which the state allowed the tribe to buy 700 acres of its former homeland, which had once included most of the state. The Mohegan Indian Reservation was established.

Uncas is probably most famous as a character in the book *The Last of the Mohicans*, written by James Fenimore Cooper (1789–1851) and published in 1826. Cooper may have been writing about the Mahican (not Mohican) tribe of the Hudson River valley, but he took the name of the character Uncas from the Mohegan tribe of Connecticut.

They now fought not only for control of other tribes' hunting grounds but also for control of the seashell beds along Long Island Sound. These beds were the best source of wampum.

Massachusetts colonists want Connecticut

In 1620, the Puritans, a Protestant group who opposed the Church of England, established a colony in Plymouth, Massachusetts. The Puritans competed with the Dutch for control of trade in Connecticut. The colonists called Connecticut "paradise." They wanted Pequot territory, especially the Connecticut River valley, containing the only waterway in the area. The river ran from the Atlantic Ocean into the rich Canadian hunting grounds. The Pequot resisted British settlement; they were one of the first of the New England tribes to do so.

In 1633, with rivalry heating up in Connecticut between the Dutch and the Massachusetts colonists, a bitter fight broke out among the Pequot. Chief Sassacus (1560–1637) wished to maintain relations with the Dutch. His son-in-law, Uncas (c. 1588–1682), favored the British. Uncas and his followers broke away from the Pequot and formed a new tribe they called Mohegan.

Relations between the two groups were very bad. They often attacked one another, disrupting trade throughout the region. When a Boston, Massachusetts, trader was murdered, the British blamed the Pequot. They demanded that Sassacus hand over the persons responsible, but he refused. At about the same time, the Pequot were hit by a smallpox epidemic, and the British forced the Dutch to close their trading post and leave. Now very weak from disease, the Pequot had no Dutch allies. More Massachusetts colonists were welcomed into Connecticut by the

The attack on the Pequot fort in 1637 by the British in alliance with the Mohegan and Narragansett killed hundreds of Pequot women, children, and elderly people who were trapped inside. © NORTH WIND PICTURE ARCHIVES.

pro-British Mohegan. Hostilities grew, with the Pequot on one side and the Mohegans, the Massachusetts colonists, and all the rival tribes on the other side.

Pequot War of 1637

In 1636, a second Boston trader was killed, and again the British blamed the Pequot. Puritan preachers spoke out in church against the tribe, calling the Pequot an evil force that must be destroyed. In response, a vengeful army of colonial soldiers destroyed a Pequot village. Early in 1637, Sassacus retaliated by leading a raid against several Connecticut settlements, beginning the Pequot War.

Because the Pequot had made so many enemies fighting for control of the fur trade, no other tribe came to their aid. One day, while three hundred Pequot warriors from the village of Mystic were away on a raid, their former kinsmen, the Mohegan, joined the British and the Narragansett tribe in a surprise attack on the undefended Pequot fort. Between three hundred and seven hundred Pequot, mostly women, children, and the elderly, were trapped inside as the fort was set ablaze. Back in Plymouth, when the governor heard the news, he called the massacre a "sweet sacrifice."

When the Pequot warriors returned, they were heartsick to find their families dead and their village destroyed. Now broken in spirit and starving, they divided into small groups and fled. The colonists, not content with having won the war, were determined to destroy the Pequot tribe. They hunted down and killed many people, but Sassacus was their main target.

Aftermath of war

With nowhere to turn, Sassacus sought refuge with his tribe's enemies, the Mohawk (see entry). They cut off his head and sent it to the British colonists. The remaining Pequot surrendered, and they signed a peace treaty in 1638.

Under the terms of the peace treaty with the colonists, the Pequot tribe was dissolved. Pequot warriors were executed. Women and children were sold into slavery in the West Indies or given as slaves to the Mohegan, Narragansett, Metoac, and Niantic.

The Pequot who were given in slavery to their relatives, the Mohegan, had an especially hard time. They were forbidden to call themselves

Pequot, and they were treated so cruelly that in 1655 the colonists took them away from the Mohegan and moved them to eastern Connecticut. In 1666, 2,000 acres became the Mashantucket (Western) Pequot Reservation in Ledyard. About twenty years later, 200 acres called the Lantern Hill Reservation were set aside for the Paucatuck (Eastern) Pequot.

Most Pequot slowly drifted away from the reservations because they could not earn a living there. By 1910, there were only sixty-six Pequot living in Connecticut, and the state of Connecticut had illegally sold most of their land.

Revival

By the 1970s, only one tumbledown home remained on the Mashantucket Pequot Reservation. It housed the families of two half-sisters, Elizabeth George Plouffe and Martha Langevin Ellal. The two feisty old women struggled to hold on against white overseers who refused to let them use tribal money for repairs. Sometimes they were forced to chase off trespassers at gunpoint. When they died in the 1970s, their relatives realized they must take over their elders' dream—to hold onto their land—or watch it die. With that, a truly astounding American success story began.

A lawsuit was filed in 1976 to recover Pequot land that had been illegally sold by the state. The case was settled in 1983. The settlement, called the Mashantucket Pequot Indian Land Claims Settlement Act, gave the tribe more than $700,000 and granted federal recognition. Federally recognized tribes are those with which the U.S. government maintains official relations. With federal recognition came the right to open a gambling casino.

In 1992, the tribe opened a grand casino. By 1998, Foxwoods was one of the world's largest and most profitable casinos. The few hundred individuals who were able to prove that they had Pequot ancestry suddenly found themselves the richest Native Americans in the United States.

Eastern Pequot Tribal Nation

Matters have not gone as well for the Eastern Pequot. As of the mid-1990s, the state of Connecticut recognized the tribe, but they were not granted federal recognition. Without federal recognition, the tribe does not exist as far as the federal government is concerned, and it is not entitled to financial or other help.

In the early 1980s, the Eastern Pequot had broken into two separate groups, Paucatuck Eastern Pequot and Eastern Pequot. They rejoined to become the Eastern Pequot Tribal Nation and to seek federal recognition. In 2002, the government granted their petition, but in 2005, that decision was overturned. Powerful interest groups in Connecticut fought the petition for tribal recognition because they did not want a casino in their area. That year, another group, the Wiquapaug Eastern Pequot Tribe, originally part of the petition, claimed to be separate from the Eastern Pequot.

RELIGION

Little is known about the Pequot's traditional religious beliefs and practices because the tribe was nearly destroyed soon after contact with Europeans. It is known only that their religion was based on a deep attachment to the land.

One Pequot achieved fame for his Methodist religious beliefs—nineteenth-century writer William Apess (1798–1839), the first widely published Native author. His early books dealt with his own conversion to Christianity and the conversion of five Pequot women. Apess argued that American Indians might be one of the "lost tribes of the Israelites," Hebrews who fled after being conquered by the Assyrians in the eighth century. Apess skillfully made his case that, as lost tribes, they were the chosen people of God.

LANGUAGE

The version of the Algonquian language that the Pequot spoke was also spoken by the Mohegan, Narragansett (see entry), Niantic, Montauk, and Shinnecock tribes. For almost 350 years, no one spoke Pequot because the 1638 Treaty of Hartford forbade the tribe from using their language. In 2002, the tribe's Historical and Cultural Preservation Committee held a conference on the importance of language and began the difficult process of reviving the Pequot language, much of which no longer survived.

GOVERNMENT

Because they were so often at war with other tribes, the Pequot had to be well organized under a strong leader. Pequot chiefs called *sachems* (pronounced SAY-chums) ruled with the advice of tribal councils.

Pequot Words

Thirty-five Pequot words were recorded in 1762:

uhpuckackip	"gull"
neuyewgk	"my wife"
muckachux	"boy"
squas or *quausses*	"virgin girls"
pouppous	"infant newborn"
nehyashamag	"my husband"
m'ssugkheege	"bass"
podumbaug	"whale"
sucksawaug	"clam"
muschundaug	"lobster"
yewt	"fire"
nupp	"water"
souchpoun	"snow"
sokghean	"rain"
mattuck	"trees"
wewautchemins	"Indian corn"
mushquissedes	"beans"
tommonque	"beaver"
kuchyage	"nose"
skeezucks	"eyes"
cottoneege	"mouth"
nahteah	"dog"
muckasons	"shoes"
cuzseet	"foot"
wuttun	"wind"
meeun	"Sun"
weyhan	"Moon"
tohcommock	"beach"
wumbanute	"white"
suggyo	"dark" or "black"
keeguum	"arrow"
teatum	"I think"
moche	"I will"
gynchen	"I kill"
mundtu	"God"
cheeby	"evil spirit" or "devil"

SOURCE: *News from Indian Country* 8, no. 5 (March 1994): 10; 9, no. 15 (September 1995): 5B.

After the Pequot's removal to reservations in the 1600s, the tribe came under the control of the state of Connecticut, which often mismanaged reservation affairs. State officials allowed Pequot land to be leased and then lost to white colonists. By the 1940s, the Pequot had been forbidden to hold gatherings or spend the night on the reservation without state permission. By the 1970s, scarcely any Pequot were left on the reservation.

In the mid-1970s, members of the tribe returned to the Mashantucket Reservation to reestablish the community. They adopted a constitution

The Importance of Wampum

To the Native Americans of the Northeast, wampum was not simply "Indian money." Tribes used it for many different purposes. They believed that the exchange of wampum and other goods established a friendship, not just a profit-making relationship.

To make wampum, they ground and polished wampum shells into small, cylindrical shapes like beads. They used a stone drill to make a small hole in each bead. These were either strung on cords made from animal tendons or used loose.

Tribes used wampum as personal adornment. It often signified a person's rank in society; the more wampum one wore, the higher one's rank. Many people were buried with supplies of wampum; wealthier people were buried with more wampum than poor people.

Sometimes wampum was used to pay tribute to a more powerful tribe. After the Pequot War of 1637, because the British spared the lives of the Pequot who went to live with the Mohegan, the British forced the Mohegan tribe to pay an annual tribute in wampum. Tribal members also gave wampum to their sachems to support them and to show gratitude for their services.

Tribes used wampum to pass down their history from generation to generation. They wove designs into belts as a way of recalling important events. The colors of the wampum beads had meaning: white was a symbol of peace, while black (purple) meant war or mourning. They used wampum belts to communicate with other tribes. If the message communicated on a belt made the other tribe angry, members kicked the belt around to show their contempt for the contents.

Among many other uses, wampum served as ransom for captured prisoners, as prizes for winning at games or sports, as payments to healers for curing the sick, and as tokens of a young man's affection or his marriage proposal. Warriors often wore necklaces made from wampum to remind them that they were fighting not only for their wives and children, but also for material goods. A person accused of murder might offer a gift of wampum to the victim's family; if the family accepted, the murderer's life would be spared.

and set up a seven-member elected council to oversee tribal affairs. Council members are elected for three-year terms, and an Elders Council, made up of all tribe members over age fifty-five, provides advice, decides on tribal membership, hears cases referred by the tribal council, and proposes constitutional amendments. In the 1990s, the tribal council had to contend with huge numbers of non-Native visitors to their casino. To deal with the situation, the tribe wrote and enforced laws; they also established a court and a police force. Visitors to the casino become subject to reservation law.

The Mashantucket Pequot tribe became proficient at dealing with the U.S. government. They passed this skill along to young people by funding an internship program that paid college students a salary while they learned how to represent the interests of the Pequot and other tribes before the U.S. Congress in Washington, D.C.

ECONOMY

The traditional Pequot economy was based mainly on farming. Hunting and fishing were secondary. For the brief time between their first contact with the Dutch in 1600 and the near-destruction of the tribe in 1637, the Pequot carried on a lively trade in furs and wampum. At a time when metal money was rare even in the courts of European kings, the Pequot were largely responsible for making wampum a major trade item in the colonies.

By the early 1800s, two-thirds of the Pequot people lived on the reservation, earning money by crafts such as basketry. They continued at these occupations until early in the twentieth century, when most of those who knew the crafts had died. Other Pequot worked in the American economy, first as servants or on whaling ships, and later in a variety of fields.

Casino brings huge benefits

A dramatic turnaround in the Pequot economy occurred with the opening of the Foxwoods Casino in 1992. In 1995, Kevin Chappell described the effects of casino riches on tribal members in *Ebony* magazine: "The tribe's good investments have resulted in a grand lifestyle for its members. Each person who proves … that he or she is at least one-sixteenth Pequot is given a new house, a managerial job or training paying a minimum of $50,000 per year, free education from private elementary school through graduate school (with a $30,000 annual stipend while in college), free healthcare and free day-care. Pequot mothers are paid $30,000 annually with medical benefits for five years, even if they don't work and choose to stay home to raise their children."

The casino's success had a tremendous impact on the state of Connecticut as well. In the early 1990s, the state was suffering from an economic downturn because defense-related industries were shutting down, and defense workers were out of work. Thousands of those workers found jobs at Foxwoods, which by the late 1990s was the largest employer in

The Pequot tribe opened the very successful Foxwoods Resort Casino in Ledyard, Connecticut, in 1992. © AP IMAGES/BOB CHILD.

the state. The Pequot paid the state 25 percent, or at least $100 million, of the total money earned from slot machines each year.

The Mashantucket Pequot were generous with casino profits. They donated millions of dollars to the Special Olympics; other money went to finance playground equipment. A 1995 gift to the Smithsonian Institution's National Museum of the American Indian (NMAI)—$10 million—was the largest donation in Smithsonian history. "I guess you could call us wealthy people," tribal chairman Skip Hayward told a news conference following the donation. "We were wealthy before we had money, because we had a love of the land … our ancestors and our culture."

Although many people acknowledge the financial benefits the casino has brought to the state and the tribe, local citizens complain about the traffic and the changes to their lifestyle. Some worry that because the reservation is a sovereign nation, the tribe can continue to build and expand without consulting the surrounding communities. They also believe the casino has had a negative financial impact on businesses in the area, although others contend it caused economic growth. Reflecting the downswing in the economy at the end of the first decade of 2000, casino profits took a dip but still remained in the multimillions.

DAILY LIFE

Buildings

For winter use, the Pequot built longhouses like those of the Iroquois. In the summer, they lived in portable wigwams near their hunting and fishing grounds. Because they were so often at war, their villages were usually built on hilltops and were surrounded by palisades (fences of sharpened sticks) to keep out intruders.

By 1720, Pequot lived in fewer, larger, and more permanent communities. Most villages contained both frame structures and wigwams. Outbuildings included sweat lodges, animal pens, storage facilities, wells, stone walls, and small stone piles scattered over one or two acres.

Food

The Pequot grew beans and corn (the beans were allowed to twine up the cornstalks), squash, and tobacco. The land was stony and good soil was scarce, so women planted corn in scattered plots both near and away from their villages. The plots were heavily fertilized with dead fish. By 1732, the lands of the 250 or so Pequot who lived at Mashantucket Reservation had been reduced to only 14 acres. There they cultivated apple trees and raised sheep and pigs.

Clothing and adornment

The Pequot dressed in buckskin clothing suitable to the colder climate of Connecticut. Favorite decorations were wampum beads. Whereas in other northeastern tribes, only important people adorned themselves with wampum, nearly everyone in the Pequot tribe wore wampum ornaments. After trade began with Europeans, the Pequot added exotic feathers to their clothing.

Education

The Mashantucket Pequot Museum and Research Center, opened in 1998, presents the story of the Mashantucket Pequot Tribal Nation. It is the only Native-owned and operated institution of its kind. The complex promotes Native heritage, scholarship, and preservation of the culture through a public museum and a research facility.

ARTS

Ceramic vessels have been found dating to about three thousand years ago. The Pequot made their clay pots from coils of clay that they smoothed using plain or cord-wrapped paddles. Over time, these pots became more elaborate and included decorations pressed into the wet clay with different tools. To harden their pots, women laid them around the fire with the open side facing the heat. After the pots had dried, they were rolled into the embers and covered with a few inches of wood chips, dried bark, or corncobs. Once the fire died out, the pots were ready to use, and they were strong enough to withstand the heat of hearth cooking.

Women wove baskets from wood splints that had been pounded into thin strips and soaked to make them flexible. They also wove mats from bulrushes that they dyed or used in their natural red and brown colors to make designs. The Pequot hung these decorative mats on the walls or used them to cover the floors and sleeping platforms. Other mats were made of cattail and sewn together to be durable. These were used to cover the outsides of the houses.

CUSTOMS

Festivals

The Mashantucket Pequot tribe hosts an annual powwow. A powwow is a celebration at which the main activities are traditional singing and dancing. In modern times, the singers and dancers at powwows often come from many different tribes.

Burial

The Pequot buried their dead with bows and arrows and great quantities of wampum beads. After their defeat in the Pequot War of 1637, grave robbers often ransacked the burial sites of Pequot dead and stole the wampum. Learning of these crimes, many tribes gave up the custom of marking the graves of their dead.

Big Eater's Wife

According to this Pequot tale, Big Eater married a beautiful woman. Soon, she decided she wanted a different husband, so one day while Big Eater was fishing, she paddled off in a canoe with food and her mortar and pestle (a stone bowl and grinding tool). Big Eater saw her and chased her.

"Now I'll catch her," he thought. Then the woman threw her mortar out of the canoe over the stern. At once all the water around him turned into mortars, and Big Eater was stuck. He couldn't paddle until at last he lifted his canoe and carried it over the mortars. By the time he gained clear water again, his wife was a long way off.

Again he paddled furiously. Again he gained on her. Again he almost caught her. Then she threw her pestle over the stern, and at once the water turned into pestles. Again Big Eater was stuck, trying to paddle through this sea of pestles but unable to. He had to carry his canoe over them, and when he hit open water again, his wife was far distant. Again Big Eater drove through the water with all his strength. Again he gained on her; again he almost caught her. Then from the stern of her canoe the woman threw the eggs out. At once the water turned into eggs, and once more Big Eater was stuck. The eggs were worse than the mortar and pestle, because Big Eater couldn't carry his canoe over them. Then he hit the eggs, smashing them one by one and cleaving a path through the gooey mess. He hit clear water, and his wife's canoe was only a dot on the horizon. Again he paddled mightily.

Slowly he gained on her again. It took a long time, but finally he was almost even with her. "This time I'll catch you!" he shouted. "You have nothing left to throw out." But his wife just laughed. She pulled out a long hair from her head, and at once it was transformed into a lance. She stood up and hurled this magic lance at Big Eater. It hit him square in the chest, piercing him through and through. Big Eater screamed loudly and fell down dead. That's what can happen to a man if he marries a ghost-witch.

SOURCE: "Native American Legends: Big Eater's Wife." *First People.* http://www.firstpeople.us/FP-Html-Legends/Big_Eaters_Wife-Pequot.html (accessed on December 1, 2011).

CURRENT TRIBAL ISSUES

In the early twenty-first century, the Eastern Pequot still sought federal recognition and struggled over land ownership and other rights issues.

The Mashantucket Pequot have been honored for their environmental work, which includes creating wetlands, developing nonpoint-source pollution plans, monitoring air quality, and protecting the water supply. They believe it is their duty to care for the earth because people are only a small part of the whole cycle of life.

Meanwhile, the Mashantucket Pequot continue their efforts to add land to their reservation. Reservation lands are free from property taxes and other state and federal laws. This freedom causes hostility among non-Native residents of Connecticut, especially business owners, who say it is unfair. Many neighbors also object to the constant traffic and commotion at the casino.

For their part, the Pequot say much of the anger is due to racism, because about half of the members of the tribe are African Americans. Tribal council member Gary Carter, who is black, explained, "Most of it is racial. There are people who believe that dark-skinned people shouldn't be making money, and they'll do anything they can to try to stop us. But what they don't realize is, to protect ourselves, we know how to play their games." The Pequot believe that their present-day financial success offsets some of the losses they suffered after Europeans arrived on the continent.

NOTABLE PEOPLE

Chief Sassacus (c. 1560–1637) became the Pequot grand sachem in 1632. Under his leadership, Pequot territory grew to include most of present-day Connecticut and Long Island. He bravely led his people through the Pequot War (1637) but was killed trying to hide from the British.

Other notable Pequot include Sachem Robin Cassacinamon, who led the Mashantucket Reservation from its founding in 1667 until his death in 1693; minister and writer William Apess (1798–1839); and Elizabeth George Plouffe (1895–1973) and Martha Langevin Ellal (d. c. 1973), who fought to retain tribal land.

BOOKS

Barron, Donna Gentle Spirit. *The Long Island Indians and Their New England Ancestors: Narragansett, Mohegan, Pequot & Wampanoag Tribes.* Bloomington, IN: AuthorHouse, 2006.

Bodinger de Uriarte, John J. *Casino and Museum: Representing Mashantucket Pequot Identity.* Tucson: University of Arizona Press, 2007.

Gardiner, Lion. *A History of the Pequot War.* Cincinnati, OH: J. Harpel for W. Dodge, 1860.

Lassieur, Allison. *The Pequot Tribe.* Mankato, MN: Capstone Press, 2002.

Wheeler, Richard Anson. *The Pequot Indians: An Historical Sketch.* Charleston, SC: Nabu Press, 2010.

PERIODICALS

Chappell, Kevin. "Black Indians Hit Jackpot in Casino Bonanza." *Ebony* 50, no. 8 (June 1995): 46.

WEB SITES

"Eastern Pequot Archaeological Field School." *Archaeological Institute of America.* http://www.archaeological.org/fieldwork/afob/2226 (accessed June 8, 2011).

Mashantucket Museum and Research Center. http://www.pequotmuseum.org/ (accessed on June 1, 2011).

"Pequot Lives: Almost Vanished." *Pequot Museum and Research Center.* http://www.pequotmuseum.org/Home/MashantucketGallery/AlmostVanished.htm (accessed June 8, 2011).

Redish, Laura, and Orrin Lewis. "Pequot Culture and History." *Native Languages of the Americas.* http://www.native-languages.org/pequot_culture.htm (accessed June 8, 2011).

Potawatomi

Name

The name Potawatomi (pronounced *pot-uh-WOT-uh-mee*) comes from the Ojibway (see entry) word *potawatomink*, which means "people of the place of fire." The Potawatomi call themselves *Nishnabek*, meaning "true or original people."

Location

Ancestors of the Potawatomi originally lived on the East Coast of the United States. In the early 2000s, they lived on scattered reservations and communities in southern Michigan and the Upper Peninsula of Michigan, in northern Indiana, northeastern Wisconsin, northeastern Kansas, and central Oklahoma. They also resided on several reserves in Canada. (Reserve is the Canadian term for reservation.)

Population

In the early 1800s, the Potawatomi numbered between 9,000 to 10,000. In the 1990 U.S. Census, 16,719 people identified themselves as Potawatomi. About 2,000 more lived in Canada. Beginning with the 2001 census, Canada no longer provided separate population statistics for the Potawatomi. The tribe was grouped with the other two members of the Three Fires Confederacy, the Ottawa and Ojibway (see entries). In 2000, the U.S. Census showed that 16,164 Potawatomi lived in the United States; by 2010, the count had risen to 20,412, with a total of 33,771 people claiming some Potawatomi heritage.

Language family

Algonquian.

Origins and group affiliations

The ancestors of the Potawatomi lived on the East Coast of the United States, but according to their tradition, after receiving a message from the spirit world, they migrated westward. Sometime before the early 1600s, they split

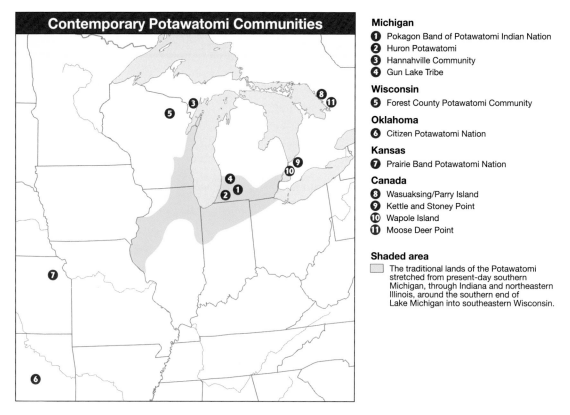

Contemporary Potawatomi Communities

Michigan
1. Pokagon Band of Potawatomi Indian Nation
2. Huron Potawatomi
3. Hannahville Community
4. Gun Lake Tribe

Wisconsin
5. Forest County Potawatomi Community

Oklahoma
6. Citizen Potawatomi Nation

Kansas
7. Prairie Band Potawatomi Nation

Canada
8. Wasuaksing/Parry Island
9. Kettle and Stoney Point
10. Wapole Island
11. Moose Deer Point

Shaded area

The traditional lands of the Potawatomi stretched from present-day southern Michigan, through Indiana and northeastern Illinois, around the southern end of Lake Michigan into southeastern Wisconsin.

A map of contemporary Potawatomi communities. MAP BY XNR PRODUCTIONS. CENGAGE LEARNING, GALE. REPRODUCED BY PERMISSION OF GALE, A PART OF CENGAGE LEARNING.

into three factions near the Michigan Straits of Mackinac. The three groups came to be known as the Potawatomi, the Ojibway, and the Ottawa. After separating, the Three Fires Confederacy, as they called themselves, retained a special relationship, often living in the same communities and supporting each other in battles against Europeans and Americans. In 2011, the former Three Fires allies reunited to write a constitution. Five other First Nations—the Algonquin, Chippewa, Lanaape, Mississauga, and Nbiising—joined them as part of the Anishinaabe Nation.

Potawatomi history is marked by tribal expansion and transformation from a hunter-gatherer culture to a farming culture and later to a buffalo-hunting culture. Before Europeans arrived, the tribe lived near the rivers and lakes of lower Michigan. After contact with the French, the Potawatomi replaced their canoes with horses and became fur traders and buffalo hunters. Due to a series of treaties and colonists settling on their land, many Potawatomi were relocated to the southern-central states. In the mid-2000s, the Potawatomi were scattered throughout the midwestern and prairie states; some lived on reservations, but many lived in cities and other rural areas.

HISTORY

Pre-European contact

Early Potawatomi were hunter-gatherers living on the western side of the Great Freshwater Sea (present-day Lake Huron). They clustered in what is now southern Michigan, residing in villages beside streams and lakes, which provided abundant fish and waterways for traveling. By the end of the 1500s, some Potawatomi had settled in northern Indiana.

In the 1600s, Europeans moved westward from the Atlantic coast. As the settlers increased their landholdings, they displaced the tribes who, in turn, migrated farther west themselves. Facing an influx of hostile tribes, the Potawatomi made their way to the western side of Lake Michigan into present-day Wisconsin. After a prolonged war with the invading Iroquois Confederacy (see entry), the Potawatomi yielded southern Michigan and moved farther into middle and northern Wisconsin and northern Michigan.

Alliance with the French

The move west brought the Potawatomi into contact with agricultural tribes, and they soon added farm crops to their diet. They also met Europeans for the first time. French fur traders and Catholic missionaries had arrived about 1640. The tribe began to hunt furs for the French, and, influenced by the missionaries, some Potawatomi converted to Roman Catholicism. A military alliance with the French made the Potawatomi stronger than their neighbors,

Important Dates

c. 1640: The Potawatomi meet their first Europeans, French traders in search of beaver and missionaries seeking converts to the Roman Catholic faith.

1656: The Iroquois win the war against the Algonquian confederation (which includes the Potawatomi). Potawatomi flee to northern Michigan and Wisconsin.

1690: The Iroquois' hold on Michigan weakens; Potawatomi resettle in lower Michigan and move into Illinois and southern Wisconsin.

1761: The Potawatomi switch allegiance from the French to the British; they later help the British by attacking American settlers during the American Revolution.

1795: Representatives of defeated Potawatomi sign the Treaty of Greenville with the United States, ending hostilities. U.S. government takes over Potawatomi lands for settlers.

1830: The Indian Removal Act is passed. United States forces Native tribes to leave their lands and resettle on reservations.

1953–54: Under the leadership of tribal chair Minnie Evans, the Prairie band successfully fights to avoid termination of its federal status.

1990: The Hannahville Potawatomi open the Chip-in Casino at Escanaba, Michigan.

1998: The Prairie Band Casino opens, employing 750 people, and the Citizen band adds a radio station to its other holdings.

2011: As part of the Anishinaabe Nation, the Potawatomi write a joint constitution.

and they soon controlled trade routes. By the 1670s, the Potawatomi were strong enough and had forged enough alliances with other tribes to push the Iroquois out of Michigan in the 1690s. After the Potawatomi returned, tribal expansion began in earnest. The Potawatomi evolved from farmers into traders and wide-ranging hunters.

Impact of horse and buffalo

Contact with European settlers brought two major changes to the Potawatomi economy. It introduced metal weapons and tools, such as hoes and rakes. It also encouraged the Potawatomi to replace their traditional means of travel, the birchbark canoe, with horses. The use of horses meant the tribe could participate in autumn buffalo hunts on the prairies. Horses also extended their traveling range, bringing the Potawatomi into contact with new tribes and new territory. This contact sometimes resulted in battles as the Potawatomi clashed with tribes already living in the area.

Buffalo brought about another change in Potawatomi life, encouraging them to become nomads who roamed widely. The tribe became less dependent on living near rivers or lakes because they now had an alternate food source. They built villages farther inland, used buffalo hides for shelter and clothing, and used other parts of the animal to make tools.

The Potawatomi used French-supplied weapons and horses to lay claim to an ever-expanding territory. At their height in the mid-1800s, the Potawatomi had a homeland that stretched from southern Michigan through northern Indiana and northeastern Illinois, and around the southern end of Lake Michigan in southeastern Wisconsin.

When the French lost control of the Great Lakes region around 1695, the Potawatomi allied themselves with the British, the new military force in the area. At British urging the Potawatomi harassed American settlers who were pushing their way into the Midwest. The tribe also fought as British allies during the American Revolution (1775–83; the American colonists' fight for independence from England). In 1795, battles between the Potawatomi and the Americans ended when the Potawatomi and other tribes signed the Treaty of Greenville.

Dealings with the U.S. government

The Treaty of Greenville began an era of decline for the Potawatomi as the U.S. government desired their land for American settlers. Their territory shrank, and food became scarce. Between 1795 and 1837, the

Potawatomi signed thirty-eight treaties with the United States, yielding more than half their land in exchange for cash, food, goods, services, and eventually, reservations.

Along with this loss of land came the U.S. government policy called "removal." Under this policy, Natives were relocated from their ancestral lands to places farther west. Relocation of the tribes left Indian lands open for settlers.

"Removal"

In the case of the Potawatomi, the Indian Removal Act of 1830 meant that the majority of the tribe left their homelands for reservations west of the Mississippi River. The Indiana Potawatomi were moved to Kansas during a forced march called the "Trail of Death." More than 150 Potawatomi died during this terrible journey, half of them children. The Potawatomi from Wisconsin and Illinois were removed to Iowa and then Kansas. In Kansas, the Mission band separated from the Prairie band, and in 1867, they moved to a reservation in Oklahoma, where they now live as the Citizen band.

Not all Potawatomi were willing to go to the reservation, and some fled into Canada. Others hid out in Michigan and eventually received permission to settle on a reservation there. The relocation process lasted from 1835 to 1867.

The Potawatomi today

In the late 1990s, six distinct bands of Potawatomi lived in the United States and a seventh band lived in Canada. The Canadian band numbered about two thousand people, descendants of the Potawatomi who fled from the United States during the "removal."

In 2007, seven bands resided in the United States. Canada also had several reserves with significant Potawatomi populations. Because different tribes live on the same reserves and because intermarriage is common, the Canadian government no longer keeps separate population statistics for the Potawatomi. The Potawatomi are generally grouped with the Ottawa and Ojibway, the other two members of the Three Fires Confederacy.

Of the seven U.S. bands, the Citizen band in Oklahoma is the largest. The Citizen Potawatomi are the most assimilated, meaning they have blended into white culture, and many are Christians. The federal

Pisehedwin, a member of the Potawatomi tribe, stands with others in front of his Kansas farm home in 1877. NATIONAL ARCHIVES AND RECORDS ADMINISTRATION.

government recognizes them as a tribe. This means that the U.S. government negotiates with the tribe as if it were a distinct nation, the same way it does with other nations. Federally recognized tribes are also entitled to financial and other assistance.

The Forest County band, by contrast, is the most traditional, using the Potawatomi language and keeping tribal religious rituals and customs alive. They live in northern Wisconsin and are a federally recognized tribe.

The Hannahville Potawatomi were recognized as a tribe by the federal government in 1936. They live in Upper Michigan, where they settled after fleeing the forced removals of the 1830s.

The Huron Potawatomi moved from southern Michigan to Kansas during the removal period. Although they were once federally recognized as a tribe, recognition was withdrawn in 1902. Without federal recognition, the tribe did not exist as far as the government was concerned, so it was not entitled to financial and other help. In 1995, the Huron Potawatomi regained their federal recognition.

Pokagon Potawatomi escaped removal because of a treaty. They remained in southwestern Michigan. Due to the influence of French missionaries, many members of this tribe became Roman Catholics. The Pokagon lost their tribal status with the federal government in 1934 but were re-recognized in 1994.

The Prairie band of Potawatomi, who now live in Kansas, were originally from the lands west of Lake Michigan. They were first removed to Iowa and later to Kansas as settlers pushed ever westward. The Prairie band is a federally recognized tribe.

In 1999, the Match-E-Be-Nash-She-Wish band, also called the Gun Lake Tribe, won federal recognition. Since that time the tribe has been working to create a 146-acre (60-hectare) reservation. They also have plans to open a casino in western Michigan.

RELIGION

Traditional Potawatomi religion is not a separate practice but runs through every aspect of tribal life. Religion connects the tribe members to their community, to nature, to their ancestors, and to the supernatural world. Potawatomi are connected to their ancestors through the Great Chain of Being (*Matchimadzhen*), which links past, present, and future generations.

Supernatural beings include the cultural hero, Wiske, and his more evil brother, Chipiyapos. Potawatomi people communicated with the spirit world and gained protection and guidance through visions. They achieved visions through fasting (not eating) and through the power of a personal medicine bundle, a collection of sacred objects.

A number of religious leaders, ranging from various types of shamans (pronounced *SHAH-munz* or *SHAY-munz*) to the priests of the Midéwiwin society, provided spiritual direction for Potawatomi communities. The Midéwiwin, or Medicine Society, was open to both men and women of any village who had special powers for foretelling and influencing the future. Each Potawatomi clan had its own sacred bundle, along with its own special dances, songs, and chants. The clan established its own rules of behavior for the members.

Contact with European settlers exposed the Potawatomi to Protestant and Catholic missionaries, and some converted to the new religions. Others reacted to this influence on their culture by joining movements they encountered in neighboring tribes that revived the old ways. One such movement originated with the Shawnee Prophet, a Kickapoo Indian who attracted many Potawatomi followers (see Shawnee entry).

One religious movement, the Dream Dance, began with the vision of a Santee Dakota (see Dakota entry) woman in 1876. In her vision, she saw the end of U.S. expansion and Native domination of the land. By the 1950s, the Dream Dance found expression among many tribes, who saw it as a message of hope and brotherhood. The Prairie Potawatomi, for instance, saw the message as a need to express their cultural identity and to preserve their traditional values.

In the early twenty-first century, religion in the Potawatomi communities encompassed Christianity, the Dream Dance, and the Native American Church. The tribe blended these beliefs with its traditional emphasis on a balanced relationship with nature, respect for elders, and humility before the powers of the spiritual world.

LANGUAGE

The Potawatomi spoke a version of the central Algonquian language that shared many sounds and words with the languages of the Sac and Fox (see entry) or Kickapoo tribes. The Potawatomi language in structure is similar to southern Ojibway and Ottawa.

GOVERNMENT

Historically, each Potawatomi village was ruled by a chief, called a *wkema*, or leader. The village selected a chief, who was a senior member of the clan and a man of good character. If he was strong and wealthy enough, he could rule over several villages, but this did not happen often.

The *wkema* was assisted by a council of adult males who approved the chief's decisions and by a society of warriors called the *wkec tak*. A man called the "pipelighter" carried announcements, arranged ceremonies, and called council meetings.

Relationships among the widely scattered Potawatomi villages (they had villages in four states) were kept strong through social ties such as marriage. As the Potawatomi nation expanded, new villages were founded, but the people retained close ties to their old villages and clans. The clans, such as the Bear Clan and the Wolf clan, were large extended family groups that were associated with different animals.

In the early 2000s, each Potawatomi community lived on its own reservation. Federally recognized tribes were sovereign (in charge of their land and affairs). They had their own governments, laws, police, and services, similar to any other independent country. Most Potawatomi groups are governed by elected tribal councils.

In Canada, the Anishinaabe Nation—composed of the Odawa (Ottawa), Algonquin, Chippewa, Lanaape, Mississauga, Nbiising, Ojibway, and Potawatomi—reunited. The tribes wrote a joint constitution in 2011 and were working together to reestablish a traditional government.

ECONOMY

Historic livelihood

In early times, the Potawatomi were hunter-gatherers, living according to the seasons. They settled near rivers, streams, or lakes and hunted the creatures that flourished there. After European contact, they traded small animal pelts with the French and later the British.

After the Potawatomi were forced to flee northward to escape the Iroquois in about 1640, they learned agricultural methods from their new neighbors, the Sac and Fox (see entry), Kickapoo, and Winnebago, and became farmers. The women of the tribe tended crops, while the men hunted. By this time, however, the men tracked the larger game abundant in the northern woods, such as elk, bear, deer, and beaver. The Potawatomi economy depended heavily on trading these animal hides for European weapons, tools, cooking utensils, and cloth.

Twentieth-century economy

In the late 1900s, the Potawatomi held a wide variety of jobs. Many of the Prairie band, who lived on a reservation in Kansas north of Topeka, had turned to the gaming industry and had opened a casino and bingo parlors. The Prairie Band Casino and hotel, a $37 million-dollar complex, opened in 1998 and provided jobs for many people both on and off the reservation.

In the first half of the twentieth century, the Hannahville Potawatomi in northern Michigan relied on agriculture and forestry. They farmed small plots whose crops included corn, squash, beans, pumpkins, and potatoes. Hunting and fishing rounded out their diet. Cash came from running sawmills, which turned the local timber into building materials. By the 1950s, the timber was exhausted, and the tribe sought a new source of income. In 1990, they opened the Chip-in Casino in Escanaba, which provided them with regular employment and money to invest in programs to help the tribe.

The Wisconsin Potawatomi, the Forest County band, relied on timber for jobs and income into the 1950s. When their forests were exhausted, they too turned to casinos and later owned two, one in Milwaukee and the other in Carter, Wisconsin. They also owned a gas station, leased a smoke shop, and had their own logging crew.

The Potawatomi in southern Michigan, the Huron and the Pokagon, traditionally farmed and fished. Many of the Huron Potawatomi still live on the 120-acre (50-hectare) Pine Creek Reservation. The Pokagon have no reservation, and many have assimilated, participating in the culture of the cities around them. In the mid-2000s, they developed the Four Winds Casino Resort, which has a casino, a hotel, retail businesses, and restaurants all under one roof to provide jobs for many tribal members and those in nearby communities.

The Citizen band Potawatomi in Oklahoma intermixed with the neighboring culture, and many are of mixed blood. They hold pow-wows (see "Festivals") each June to preserve their Native heritage. The tribe owned and operated a golf course, a restaurant, gaming parlors, convenience stores, a bank, a museum and gift shop, and a racetrack. In 1998, they purchased a radio station that broadcasts from Shawnee, Oklahoma.

Casinos benefit tribes

In the early 2000s, many Potawatomi continued to live in poverty because of high unemployment. One of the concerns was to create jobs that would allow the people to live and work on the reservations, so they could maintain their culture. With the opening of casinos, many tribes added more jobs, but on reservations where seasonal employment was the main livelihood, unemployment reached as high as seventy percent during the off-season. As more tribes opened casinos or gaming facilities, the profits from these made a difference in each band's economy and allowed tribes to fund initiatives to help the community.

DAILY LIFE

Education

As children, Potawatomi learned to bravely accept hardships such as hunger and danger. Both boys and girls played with toys that prepared them for traditional adult roles in the tribe. Boys used bows and arrows; girls played with cornhusk dolls.

As of the early 2000s, some tribes run their own schools on the reservations, whereas other children attend public schools. Potawatomi people in the late twentieth century turned their energies to the revival of Native language skills and cultural traditions. Many communities periodically hold powwows where they express their spiritual beliefs through dancing, singing, and drumming.

The Forest County group operates the Even Start program, which provides weekly language classes, as well as flash cards and videotapes for use in the home. It also runs the Fire Keeper Alternative Education Program to provide basic academic instruction for students who are having difficulty in school. The school also teaches cultural subjects such as language, singing, drumming, and crafts.

Buildings

Originally, Potawatomi summer homes were rectangular wigwams on the shores of lakes and rivers. The people used saplings that grew nearby as a skeleton for the wigwam, draping the structure with woven mats or sheets of bark. A smoke hole in the roof provided ventilation. Dome-shaped winter wigwams were smaller to conserve heat. Some Potawatomi later lived in log cabins like their American neighbors.

Food

Traditionally, fish was a staple in the Potawatomi diet. The people also hunted wild game, such as muskrat, squirrel, raccoon, porcupine, turtle, duck, goose, and turkey. Meat from wolves and dogs was featured at certain rituals. Later large game, such as buffalo and deer, became common. The Potawatomi also gathered local wild foods, such as wild rice, red oak acorns, sap for maple syrup, grapes, chokecherries, plant roots, and a large variety of berries.

Farm crops included corn, beans, squash, and tobacco. Modern Potawatomi crops vary according to the tribe's location and climate.

A traditional meal might include meat, gravy, corn soup, frybread, boiled potatoes, and hominy (a dish made from corn).

Clothing and adornment

The Potawatomi wore clothing made from the hides of the animals they ate. They also wore woven fabric garments. Originally, they used shells found alongside streams as beads to decorate their hair, body, and clothing. They later used metal decorations.

Both men and women wore their hair long. Women usually wore one long braid at the back. In times of war, warriors shaved their heads except for a scalp lock, a long lock of hair on the top of a shaven head. They put red and black paint on their faces.

ARTS

Oral literature

Before their contact with the settlers, the Potawatomi relied heavily on their oral (spoken) tradition to pass down stories and customs from one generation to the next. They also used a system of pictographs (picture symbols) to help people remember complicated rituals and story details. These pictographs were drawn on birchbark scrolls.

Potawatomi elders told stories to instruct Potawatomi children in how to live a respectful and spiritual life. In the twenty-first century, many Potawatomi communities continue to share knowledge and cultural traditions through storytelling.

Potawatomi culture continues to fascinate people today. In 1994, Potawatomi dances were the subject of a program performed by the Milwaukee Ballet. The ballet was danced to an original composition based on Potawatomi legends.

CUSTOMS

Children

Potawatomi children were called by different names as they grew up. During the first year, a child was simply called "infant." On the child's first birthday, the clan gave him or her a name. During their youth, children were called "young boy" or "young girl."

The Adventure of a Poor Man

The following story emphasizes the need to show respect for the dead by performing the proper rituals and reveals the importance of hospitality in Potawatomi society. The story begins with a poor man who had few friends leaving for a hunting expedition. He kills a deer and sets up camp to cook it. Suddenly two strange, silent men appear.

"Hau," said the man, "My friends, you frightened me…. I am poor. No one brought me up to know what to do under such circumstances. I should like to know who you are, but I do not know how to ask." The two smiled and nodded to him in a friendly manner, so he went on: "Well, I shall feed you, and do what I can for your comfort." They nodded again. "Are you ghosts?" the hunter inquired. Again they smiled and bowed, so he began to broil meat on the coals, as one does for the souls of the dead.

Now it happened that this man was camped right in the midst of an ancient and forgotten cemetery, and, guessing something of the sort, he offered prayers to the dead in his own behalf, and for his wife and child. He offered to make a feast of the dead, and always to mention the names of the two visitors, or at least to speak of them.

The very next day he killed four bucks right in the trail and luck went with him wherever he traveled. When he got home, he told his wife what had happened, and how he had been frightened when these two naked, soundless men stood there. He told her to help him prepare a feast for them, although he did not know their names, for he hoped that these ghosts would help them to become accepted by society. He made a scaffold and invited one of the honorable men of the tribe, and told him of the strange adventure which had befallen him. He explained that he did not know how to go about giving a feast of the dead, and he turned it over to the elder.

The old man said that the poor man had done the right thing, and that the appearance of these ghosts was a good omen. So the feast was held.

A long time passed, and the poor man became a very great hunter, but he never forgot to sacrifice holy tobacco to the two spirits. He could even find and kill bears in the wintertime, something that no one else even thought of doing, but he could locate their dens at will. At length he even became one of the leaders of the tribe, and held the office of the man who was supposed to apprise the people of the arrival of visitors. He was the first to give presents to visiting strangers, and his name was N'wä'k'to, or "Keeps-on-even-with-everything."

SOURCE: Skinner, Alanson. "The Adventure of a Poor Man." *Bulletin of the Public Museum of the City of Milwaukee* 6, no. 3: 1927.

John Maskwas, a member of the Potawatomi tribe, poses for a portrait in 1898. DENVER PUBLIC LIBRARY, WESTERN HISTORY COLLECTION, F.A. RINEHART, CALL NO X32134. REPRODUCED BY PERMISSION.

Childhood ended for the Potawatomi at puberty. A girl was considered a woman after she started her menstrual cycle, and girls typically married at a younger age than boys. Boys reached maturity through dream quests and hunting.

Festivals

The Citizen band in Oklahoma hosts one of the country's largest annual powwows, a several-day celebration of Native culture. Events include meals with traditional foods and storytelling. Also popular with Native and non-Native audiences are the highly competitive dance contests, with dances such as the Grass Dance (in which dancers wear bunches of grass at their belts) and the Northern Shawl Dance.

Death and burial

Traditionally Potawatomi funeral rituals were conducted by the clan of the deceased. They dressed a body of man in his best clothing and laid him out with prized and everyday belongings, such as his moccasins, rifle, knife, money, ornaments, food, and tobacco.

The dying person decided how to dispose of his body. Bodies could be buried in a variety of positions—standing, sitting, or lying down. The corpse could also be placed above ground in the fork of a tree. The burial site was marked with a post painted with pictograms to show the dead person's clan. After a death, the chief mourner adopted a replacement relative from the clan.

CURRENT TRIBAL ISSUES

As with many other tribes, a major issue for the Potawatomi has been to convince the U.S. government of the legality of Potawatomi claims to land, fishing and hunting rights, and self-rule.

The Potawatomi are concerned with protecting their natural resources. The Forest County community formed part of an action group that opposed the proposed establishment of a zinc-copper sulfide mine in northeastern Wisconsin. To prevent the mine and the environmental damage that would occur, the group partnered with the Sokaogon Chippewa Mole Lake Band to buy the mine site in 2003 with casino profits. In 2006, they purchased additional rights from the owners of the Crandon Mine site, so the site cannot be used for mining in the future. Air and water quality have been an ongoing concern for many groups, so reservations are monitoring these issues and working to restore environmental balance.

The casinos that have opened have greatly improved the economy and have provided employment and business development opportunities for the Potawatomi. In the early 2000s, the tribes' high-school dropout

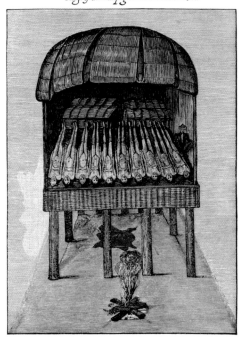

A tomb from North Carolina in the 1500s holds the bodies of embalmed Potawatomi chiefs. © NORTH WIND PICTURE ARCHIVES

rates were higher than in the rest of the U.S. population. With increased money flowing into the bands, they have been able to establish remedial and scholarship programs that assist students with educational needs. Many groups also worked to bring job-training programs to the reservations. Improved social services include alcohol treatment programs, day care, and legal assistance to deal with many of the problems the tribes face.

In Canada in the early twenty-first century, former members of the Three Fires Confederacy reestablished old bonds. They united as the Anishinaabe Nation along with five other bands—the Algonquin, Chippewa, Lanaape, Mississauga, and Nbiising. In the political arena, the group has worked together to benefit all the bands. For example, in 2010, the group successfully blocked the government's planned 13 percent harmonized sales tax. The Anishinaabe Nation in 2011 wrote a joint constitution.

NOTABLE PEOPLE

One of the most influential individuals in twentieth-century Potawatomi history was Minnie Evans (d. 1971), tribal chair of the Prairie band of Kansas in the 1950s. In 1953, the U.S. government decided to terminate the federally recognized status of this band of Potawatomi. Through the policy of termination, aimed at many tribes in the 1950s, the government sought to end its trust relationship with those deemed capable of assimilating (blending) most easily into mainstream society. As termination would have ended vital government-provided services and threatened protection of tribal resources, Minnie Evans led the Prairie band in fighting the process. Along with Prairie band tribal members James Wahbnosah and John Wahwassuck, she testified before Congress in 1954, leading an opposition movement that prevented the termination of her tribe.

Letourneau (Blackbird) was chief of the village of Milwaukee in the eighteenth century; he kept his people safe by convincing many of his warriors not to side with the British during the American Revolution. Main Poche (French for "withered hand") was a war chief and medicine man who led resistance to American colonization during the early 1800s.

BOOKS

Bellfy, Phil. *Three Fires Unity: The Anishnaabeg of the Lake Huron Borderlands*. Lincoln: University of Nebraska Press, 2011.

Landes, Ruth. *The Prairie Potawatomi: Tradition and Ritual in the Twentieth Century*. Madison: University of Wisconsin Press, 1970.

Levier, Frances, and Patricia Sulcer. *Grandfather, Tell Me a Story: An Oral History Project Conducted by the Citizen Band Potawatomi Tribe of Oklahoma.* OK: The Citizen Band Potawatomi Tribe, 1984.

Mcmullen, John William. *Ge Wisnemen! (Let's Eat!): A Potawatomi Family Dinner Manual.* Charleston, SC: CreateSpace, 2011.

———. *The Last Blackrobe of Indiana and the Potawatomi Trail of Death.* Evansville, IN: Bird Brain Publishing, 2011.

Sanna, Ellyn. *Potawatomi.* Philadelphia, PA: Mason Crest Publishers, 2004.

Skinner, Alanson. *Medicine Ceremony of the Menomini, Iowa, and Wahpeton Dakota, with Notes on the Ceremony among the Ponca, Bungi Ojibwa, and Potawatomi.* Memphis, TN: General Books, 2010.

WEB SITES

Chippewas of Kettle and Stony Point First Nation. http://www.kettlepoint.org/home.html (accessed on June 5, 2011).

Deer Lake First Nation. http://www.deerlake.firstnation.ca/ (accessed on June 5, 2011).

Forest County Potawatomi. http://www.fcpotawatomi.com/ (accessed on June 5, 2011).

Larry, Mitchell. *The Native Blog.* http://nativeblog.typepad.com/the_potawatomitracks_blog/potawatomi_news/index.html (accessed on June 5, 2011).

Match-e-be-nash-she-wish Band of Pottawatomi. http://www.mbpi.org/ (accessed on June 5, 2011).

Nottawaseppi Huron Band of Potawatomi Indians: Pine Creek Indian Reservation. http://www.nhbpi.com/ (accessed on June 5, 2011).

Pitawanakwat, Lillian. "Ojibwe/Potawatomi (Anishinabe) Teaching." *Four Directions Teachings.* http://www.fourdirectionsteachings.com/transcripts/ojibwe.html (accessed June 5, 2011).

Pokagon Band of Potawatomi Indians. http://www.pokagon.com/ (accessed on June 5, 2011).

Prairie Band Potawatomi Nation. http://www.pbpindiantribe.com/ (accessed on May 20, 2011).

Wasauksing First Nation (Georgian Bay, Ontario, Canada). http://www.wasauksing.ca/ (accessed on May 20, 2011).

Powhatan

Name

Powhatan (pronounced *pow-uh-TAN* or *pow-HAT-un*) meant "waterfall" in Virginia Algonquian. It was the name of an individual tribe and also the name of an alliance of thirty to forty tribes and groups united by their language, their location, and their political leader, Chief Wahunsonacock (also known as Powhatan; c. 1550–1618) and his family.

Location

The Powhatan lived in what is now the state of Virginia, in the area along the coastal plain known as the Tidewater. Their northern boundary was the Potomac River; the southern boundary was the Great Dismal Swamp on the border between Virginia and North Carolina. Some Powhatan fled north to Pennsylvania and New Jersey and lived with the Lenape (see Delaware entry). In the early twenty-first century, descendants of the Powhatan lived primarily in Virginia and New Jersey.

Population

In the early 1600s, the Powhatan tribe was estimated to number about 135 to 165 people, whereas the Powhatan Confederacy consisted of between 3,900 and 10,400 people. In the 1990 U.S. Census, 785 people identified themselves as members of the Powhatan tribe. In 2000, that number had declined to 568, but 2,055 were members of a tribe of the original Powhatan Confederacy. According to the National Park Service, the population in 2010 was about 3,400 for the eight Powhatan direct-descended tribes and 2,392 for the three Powhatan-related ones.

Language family

Algonquian.

Origins and group affiliations

The Powhatan Alliance lasted only from about 1570 to 1650. Today, reservations exist in the states of Virginia, New Jersey, and Rhode Island that are named for tribes who were part of the alliance. Along with the Powhatan tribe

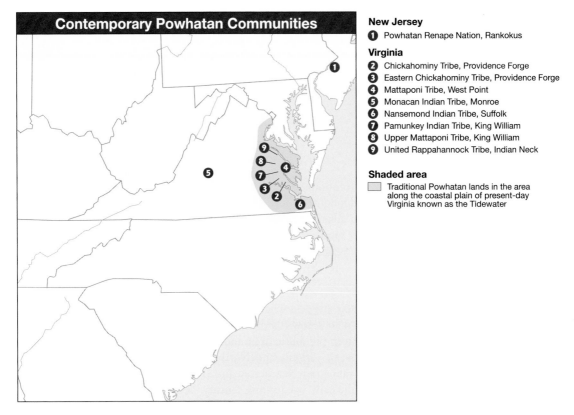

Contemporary Powhatan Communities

New Jersey
1. Powhatan Renape Nation, Rankokus

Virginia
2. Chickahominy Tribe, Providence Forge
3. Eastern Chickahominy Tribe, Providence Forge
4. Mattaponi Tribe, West Point
5. Monacan Indian Tribe, Monroe
6. Nansemond Indian Tribe, Suffolk
7. Pamunkey Indian Tribe, King William
8. Upper Mattaponi Tribe, King William
9. United Rappahannock Tribe, Indian Neck

Shaded area
Traditional Powhatan lands in the area along the coastal plain of present-day Virginia known as the Tidewater

A map of contemporary Powhatan communities. MAP BY XNR PRODUCTIONS. CENGAGE LEARNING, GALE. REPRODUCED BY PERMISSION OF GALE, A PART OF CENGAGE LEARNING.

itself, some of the tribes of the confederacy were the Arrohatek, Appamattuck, Pamunkey, Mattaponi, Chiskiack, Chickahominy, Nansemond, Rappahannock, and Kecoughtan tribes.

When the Europeans first arrived in the New World, several different, independent groups had formed a union with one another under the name of the Powhatan Alliance. In fact, the oldest treaty written in North America was enacted among the Powhatan nations in 1646. For thousands of years, the people had lived along coastal areas of the mid-Atlantic. After the Europeans came, the Powhatan struggled to survive war, illness, prejudice, and the disruption of their culture. Diseases brought by the Europeans wiped out half the tribe by the late 1600s. Stories of the Powhatan remain popular, especially those about the historical but often fictionalized figure Pocahontas.

HISTORY

Hostile contact with Europeans

The first contact between the Powhatan and Europeans took place around 1525, when Spanish explorers visited coastal Virginia. In 1560, the Spanish wanted to establish a Catholic mission in the area that was later called the Tidewater. They kidnapped the son of a local chief, took him to Cuba, taught him Spanish and the Christian religion, and renamed him Don Luis de Velasco after a Spanish viceroy of that name.

In 1570, he returned to his homeland with several missionaries. Finding his people starving, he left the Spaniards and returned to his home. He later returned to the mission with a war party and killed the missionaries. In 1571, a group of Spaniards launched a raid in retaliation and killed thirty Powhatan people.

In 1584, the British created a colony on Roanoke Island in Virginia. Six years later, a group of new British settlers arrived with supplies. They found that all the colonists had disappeared. There were rumors that the Powhatan had killed them. (For another theory on what happened to these colonists, see Lumbee entry.)

Important Dates

1570: The Spanish attempt to establish a mission in Powhatan territory but are driven away or killed by the Natives.

1590: Powhatan consolidates his power over Tidewater, Virginia.

1607: The British colonists of the Virginia Company arrive in Powhatan territory.

1618: Powhatan dies and his title passes to his brother, Opichapam.

1646: A treaty with the British ends the Powhatan Wars.

1651: Colonists establish first Indian reservation near Richmond, Virginia, for remaining Powhatans.

1980: The state of New Jersey recognizes the Powhatan Renape Nation. Other tribes of the Powhatan Alliance gain state recognition in Virginia during the 1980s.

1982: The Powhatan Renape Nation negotiates for 350 acres (141 hectares) of state-owned land for the Rankokus Indian Reservation.

2010: The state of Virginia has recognized a total of eleven Powhatan tribes.

Powhatan extends his rule

During the late 1500s, Chief Powhatan (c. 1550–1618) was creating an empire in what is now Virginia. He had inherited a confederacy of six tribes from his father, but the ambitious leader quickly expanded his domain. It is not known for sure how large the Powhatan Confederacy was, but estimates range from 128 to 200 villages, consisting of as many as 8,000 or 9,000 people and encompassing thirty tribes. Communities under Powhatan's rule received military protection and adhered to the confederacy's well-organized system of hunting and trading boundaries.

An illustration from John Smith's General History *depicts Pocahontas saving him from execution at Powhatan's command, an event that many historians doubt happened.* © KEAN COLLECTION/STAFF/ARCHIVE PHOTOS/GETTY IMAGES.

In return, subjects paid a tax to Powhatan in the form of food, pelts, copper, and pearls.

Jamestown founded

In 1607, a group of British colonists established a fort on the James River near Chesapeake Bay in Powhatan territory. They did not know they were trespassing on land ruled by a shrewd and powerful head of state. Powhatan remained highly suspicious of the newcomers, but at the same time, they maintained peaceful relations. In the first year of the new colony, the Powhatan captured John Smith (c. 1580–1631), one of the colonists. Smith later wrote his account of the event, creating the basis for the continuing American legend of Powhatan's daughter Pocahontas (c. 1595–1617). Smith said that the Powhatan threatened to execute him, but Pocahontas rescued him. He also claimed that Pocahontas later persuaded her father to send food to the starving colonists.

There are good reasons to doubt Smith's story, but by most accounts, the Jamestown settlers would have perished from starvation had it not been for the Powhatan's help.

A group of descendants of the original alliance, the Powhatan Renape in New Jersey, point out that Smith enjoyed making up stories that made him look good. He only told the story about his rescue by Pocahontas after she had become famous. Previously he never mentioned a near-execution or Pocahontas. Many historians believe that the event Smith experienced was not an execution, but a special ceremony to make Smith a subchief under Powhatan.

The British later kidnapped Pocahontas and held her hostage in Jamestown to ensure the good behavior of her father, Chief Powhatan. She married the British colonist John Rolfe (1585–1622) in 1614. Rolfe experimented with planting Brazilian tobacco in Virginia and is often credited with successfully establishing tobacco as a cash crop. This contributed to making the colony financially successful. In 1616, the Virginia Company, a major financial backer of the Jamestown colony, sponsored a trip to England for Pocahontas, John Rolfe, and their infant son, Thomas. On that trip, Pocahontas was introduced to Queen Anne (1574–1619), before whom she became a spokesperson for the Jamestown colony. While in England, Pocahontas caught an infectious disease (probably pneumonia) and died on March 21, 1617.

The First and Second Powhatan Wars

Powhatan died in 1618, and his title passed to his brother. Opichapam was a weak leader, but his reign was short. His power passed to another brother, Opechancanough, in 1622. The new chief, who had headed the Pamunkey tribe for many years, considered the British his enemies. He attacked the colonists on March 22, 1622, hoping to drive them out of his territory. About one-fourth of the colonists died in this First Powhatan War.

The struggle continued for about ten years, with lulls when the Powhatan ran out of food or the British ran out of gunpowder. The first war ended in 1632 when the Powhatan and the British colonists signed a truce, but warfare started up again not long after that and continued for many decades. The once mighty Powhatan began to lose their power, while the once vulnerable colonists grew in strength and numbers. By 1675, the

Powhatan Confederacy had been demolished, and the remaining Natives were forced to live under Virginia law.

The Powhatan people who survived began to speak English and adopt British ways. After 1646, the remaining Powhatan groups were sent to separate areas of their tribal lands.

RELIGION

Worshipping the creator

The main god the Powhatan worshipped was Okewas, sometimes called Okeus. Okewas, who appeared in the form of a young man, was a vengeful god who created the world. Anyone violating his strict moral code met with misfortune. Special priests told the people what Okewas wished from them. Those priests held ceremonies at his temples and made sacrifices to fend off his anger. The priests also healed the sick, identified criminals, and made sure Okewas's image was carried into battle. Priests could be identified by the way they wore their hair, shaved on the right side of the head except for a single lock of hair on the scalp.

The afterlife

The Powhatan believed the afterlife was a time of unending singing and dancing. In their traditions, upon dying, the soul traveled along a path lined with berries and fruit bushes eastward to the sun, the home of the Great Hare. Halfway to the sun, the soul entered the wigwam of a lovely female spirit who provided corn and other refreshments. After reaching the sun, the soul found its ancestors eating with the Great Hare. The soul eventually reentered the world of the living in a new form.

The Powhatan wars destroyed most of the group's traditional ways of life. By about 1800, Protestant missionaries had most likely converted most of the Powhatan people to Christianity. In 1865, Powhatan people founded the Pamunkey Indian Baptist Church.

LANGUAGE

Most scholars believe that the language spoken by the Powhatan, a dialect (variety) of the Eastern Algonquian family, has become extinct. Although many Powhatans spoke the language in 1750, by 1800, it had almost died out. Modern Powhatan speak English. Their identity as a tribe, which would entitle them to certain rights and benefits, has been challenged in the Virginia courts because they have not spoken a Native language during the past two centuries.

GOVERNMENT

The Powhatan tribe was traditionally ruled by a male or female leader. Leadership positions were passed down through the women of the tribe. The common people of the tribe paid tribute to the leader in the form of corn, skins, game, and copper. As a result, the leaders could afford to wear elaborate clothing, eat the highest-quality food, and live in larger-than-average houses. Leaders had almost absolute rule over their subjects. They could order the punishment or death of people who committed offenses. Priests ranked second in command.

Each village also had its individual leader. He or she paid tribute (tax) to superiors and received tribute from lower members of the tribe. Next came councilors, men who gained their position for accomplishing feats of strength or bravery. Along with priests and the tribal leader, these men made up the council that had power to declare war.

ECONOMY

In Powhatan families, duties were generally divided by gender. Women usually tended to the farming, gathering, and drying of food. They planted beans, corn, squash, and tobacco. Older children helped their mothers plant and weed gardens. Women wove mats and baskets, prepared animal hides, and made pottery.

Men hunted and fished, and sometimes engaged in trade. The Powhatan had paths interlinking their villages. They carried out long-distance trade by receiving and passing along items from far-off places along these trails. Women sometimes accompanied the men on trade journeys to paddle the canoes so the men could keep their hands free to handle weapons.

DAILY LIFE

Families

Families usually consisted of a married couple, their children, and the grandparents from one or both sides. These extended families of six to twenty people shared a house. Sometimes brothers and their families lived in the house, too. Most people married between ages thirteen and fifteen. Occasionally, a wealthy man had two or more wives and families. Chief Powhatan was said to have had a dozen wives.

Buildings

Powhatan houses, called *yehakins,* were generally long and narrow. They were made by bending saplings (young trees) and covering them with mats woven from marsh reeds, rushes, or bark. The bent saplings formed a semicircular roof. Poles buried in the ground helped support the roof. Houses usually had one room with a door at either end. In the summer, the mat walls were rolled up or taken off to provide fresh air. Low platforms lining the walls served as work areas during the day and as beds at night.

The other main structure in a Powhatan village was a temple for the worship of their gods. The Powhatan often built temples on hills or ridges that overlooked the village. Constructed in the same way as the houses, temples were 60 to 100 feet (20 to 30 meters) long and faced in an east–west direction. At the eastern part of the temple, near the entrance, the people kept fires burning. The dried bodies of dead tribal leaders were guarded by wooden images of Okewas and other spirits in a room that faced the west. The tribe sometimes used temples for storage of food, goods, and other valuables. Some villages were surrounded by palisades, logs or stakes driven into the ground to form a fence.

Clothing and adornment

Because the area where they lived was very warm, the Powhatan kept clothing to a minimum. In the summer, children generally went naked until they reached puberty. Adults wore breechcloths (material that went between the legs and fastened at the waist) made of deerskin or grasses. In the winter, they added deerskin or turkey feather cloaks, moccasins, and leggings. When it was very cold, they wore a layer of animal grease for insulation.

Hairstyles varied according to a person's social status and gender. Men shaved the right side of their scalps (to keep their hair from tangling in their bowstrings). Young women shaved the front and sides of their heads and braided the hair that remained; married women wore their hair in a long braid in back.

Women wore tattoos of animals and plants, made by rubbing soot into cuts made in the skin with copper knives. Men and women both painted their shoulders; they sometimes painted their faces or even their whole bodies with white, yellow, blue, red, or black paints made of natural materials. Designs could be enhanced with soft down from birds or shiny bits of dirt. Both sexes wore jewelry made of glass, copper, or bone beads.

Food

Most food came from hunting, fishing, farming, and gathering wild plants. The tribes moved upriver in the winter months to a place where deer, raccoons, and turkey were more plentiful. They fished with nets, hooks and lines, and bows and arrows. They also caught shellfish. When farming, they moved from one field to another as the soil became depleted. The Powhatan grew corn, beans, and squash. Women, children, and old men gathered walnuts, hickory nuts, acorns, and chestnuts. Hazelnut trees were common throughout the wooded areas of the Northeast. Natives ate hazelnuts raw or roasted, ground them into flour, or crushed them to make nut oil, which they used in cooking. To prepare for winter, they stored food in underground pits or elevated storage areas near the family home.

Powhatan Hazelnut Soup

2 1/4 cups ground, blanched
    hazelnuts
2 packages (4 1/2 gram) instant beef
    broth
2 scallions, washed and sliced
2 Tablespoons minced parsley
5 cups water
1 teaspoon salt
1/8 teaspoon fresh ground pepper

Place all ingredients in a large saucepan, and simmer together gently, stirring occasionally, for one hour. Serve hot. Make the servings small; the soup is rich.

SOURCE: Kimball, Yeffe, and Jean Anderson. *The Art of American Indian Cooking.* Garden City, NY: Doubleday, 1965, p. 175.

Education

Powhatan children trained for their roles in society beginning at a young age. Both mothers and fathers taught their sons to hunt. Every morning, the mother threw a piece of moss in the air. A boy had to hit it with his arrow before he could have breakfast. Boys also learned to make tools from stones and shells. They used these tools to carve bowls, make weapons, and hollow out logs to make canoes that could carry up to thirty people. Girls learned gardening and meal preparation. They also were taught to make pottery and prepare animal skins to be made into clothing and purses.

By the mid-1700s, Christian missionaries had taught many young men Christianity, English, and arithmetic. Much later, schools for Native children opened in Virginia, but they taught students little about their Native culture. For example, during the 1930s, the teacher of a pottery

A large clay jar is an example of the pottery made by the Pamunkey tribe. © MARILYN ANGEL WYNN/GETTY IMAGES

school on the Pamunkey reservation instructed students to use a pottery wheel instead of traditional Pamunkey pottery-making techniques. Until a high school opened in 1950, none of the Virginia Indian schools went beyond seventh grade. In the 1960s, Virginia schools ended their policy of segregation (separating the races in schools), marking the end of Native schools there.

Healing practices

Powhatan priests used their influence with the gods to diagnose diseases and prescribe cures. They used rituals and herbs to treat sore throats, infections, diarrhea, fevers, and poisoning.

ARTS

Pottery

For more than two hundred years, women of the Pamunkey tribe were famed for their pottery made of clay found on their reservation. They strengthened the raw clay with crushed and burned mussel shells and used their hands to shape the objects. Then they smoothed the surface with a mussel shell. They sometimes etched a pattern on the surface before placing the piece in a fire to harden.

Dancing

The Powhatan danced for both religious purposes and amusement. Music accompanied the dancing. The Powhatan made rattles from dried gourds filled with pebbles or seeds. They also stretched animal skins over wooden bowls to make drums. Flutes were made from pieces of cane.

Dramatic production

Around 1880, the Pamunkey staged a production of the popular story of Pocahontas, a story that is more legend than historical fact. Rather than wearing the scanty clothing that was traditional, they donned elaborately beaded costumes.

CUSTOMS

Festivals

The Powhatan's main harvest took place each year from August through October. With food plentiful and the workload lightened, the people chose this time of year to hold their major religious ceremonies. Unfortunately little is known about their rituals because the British did not record the details.

Today, thousands of people gather in King William, Virginia, every Memorial Day for the annual Spring Festival held at the Sharon Indian School on Upper Mattaponi tribal grounds. This tribe was once part of the Powhatan Coalition. Festivities include the sharing of Native foods, storytelling, arts and crafts, dancing, games and rides for children, and educational programs.

Naming

A person's name was very important in Powhatan tribes. A man who was known for his abilities in hunting and bringing food home to his family would obtain a name that reflected his skills. Throughout his life, a man's changing status was reflected in the way his name changed. At a celebration marking the birth of a new baby, the father would announce its name. Later, the mother gave the child a nickname. If a boy showed some special ability, such as skill with a bow and arrow, his father gave him another name relating to this ability. If he performed a brave deed, the chief might give him still another, a name-title that singled him out as special.

Puberty

Powhatan boys who wanted to be leaders underwent a dangerous rite called *Huskanow.* The ceremony began with feasting and dancing. Then the older men took the boys out of the village and pretended to sacrifice them. The boys were expected to lie still for many hours. They stayed in the forest for several months under the watchful eye of their elders. The boys were later beaten and had to drink hallucination-causing drugs; some became so agitated that they had to be kept in wooden cages. They were then "reborn" and allowed to return to their families. Any sign that a boy was reverting to the ways of boyhood required him to undergo a second Huskanaw. Few boys could endure the experience a second time, and many died in the process.

Courtship and marriage

Young women were considered ready for marriage as soon as they reached puberty. Before young men could marry, they had to prove they could hunt, fish, and take care of a family. Young people courted each other with gifts of food. Parents generally bargained for the bride price, the goods a young man gave a young woman's family to marry their daughter. He gathered the items, presented them to her family, and went home. The bride then traveled to his home, where his father performed the marriage ceremony by joining their hands and breaking a string of beads over their heads.

Funerals

The Powhatan wrapped the bodies of the dead in animal skins or rush mats before burying them. They also placed beads with the body for use in the afterlife. Women served as mourners; they blackened their faces and wept for the entire day following the death. The tribe sometimes placed bodies on high scaffolding to decompose. Every few years, they buried all the bones together in large pits.

CURRENT TRIBAL ISSUES

The biggest problem facing descendants of the Powhatan is gaining recognition from federal and state governments. This recognition is essential for receiving many government services and benefits and for becoming a self-governing nation. Before the 1960s, only two groups had regained their status in Virginia as independent tribes within the boundaries of their traditional lands. The other tribes that made up the Powhatan Alliance were presumed to be extinct. However, during the 1970s and 1980s, several other groups fought for and received recognition by the state of Virginia. In addition, the state of New Jersey recognized the Powhatan Renape Nation in 1980. By 2010, the state had recognized eleven Powhatan tribes; many others were still waiting for recognition.

In 2011, a bill was introduced to give federal recognition to the Chickahominy, Eastern Chickahominy, Monacan, Nansemond, Rappahannock, and Upper Mattaponi tribes. One of the difficulties Virginia tribes face is that in 1924, the state allowed only two classifications: white or colored. All official records, from birth certificates to driver's licenses, used one of these two categories. This action erased all traces of Native heritage. As a result, the tribes—even the ones who have been living on the same reservations since the 1600s—have no proof of their ancestry. In addition to this, the federal government is reluctant to recognize Virginia tribes, because recognition gives the bands the right to build casinos. Casinos are illegal in Virginia. To allay the legislators' fears, the tribes signed away their rights to operate casinos.

The Powhatan Renape Nation in New Jersey, which had received state-owned land for the Rankokus Indian Reservation in 1982, is in a struggle to maintain its site. It does not pay the Department of Environmental Protection (DEP) for the land, and the department planned to take back all but five acres. By agreement, the tribe would keep its museum and mock village used for educational groups but would lose the fields, wild animals, and other buildings, which the DEP says have fallen into disrepair.

At the same time, the Nansemond Indian Tribal Association (NITA) has been trying to acquire 99 acres at Lone Star Lakes Park in Suffolk, Virginia, It wants to set up a village, a cultural center, and a museum to be used to introduce schoolchildren to Powhatan history.

NOTABLE PEOPLE

Wahunsonacock (c. 1550–1618), better known as Powhatan, led the Powhatan Coalition between 1570 and his death in 1618. A clever politician, he united the tribes of Coastal Virginia under his rule. He once asked the British, "Why should you take by force from us that which you can have by love? Why should you destroy us, who have provided you with food?"

Probably the best-known Powhatan was his daughter, Pocahontas (1595–1617), whose real name was Metoaka. Many Powhatan tribe members today trace their ancestry to the Rolfes, her last name after she married an Englishman. She died when she was in her early twenties.

BOOKS

Brimner, Larry Dane. *Pocahontas: Bridging Two Worlds.* New York: Marshall Cavendish Benchmark, 2009.

Carbone, Elisa. *Blood on the River: James Town 1607.* New York: Viking, 2006.

Chenoweth, Avery, and Robert Llewellyn. *Empires in the Forest: Jamestown and the Making of America.* Earlysville, VA: Rivanna Foundation, 2010.

Mossiker, Frances. *Pocahontas: The Life and the Legend.* New York: Alfred A. Knopf, 1976.

Rice, James D. *Nature and History in the Potomac Country: From Hunter-Gatherers to the Age of Jefferson.* Baltimore, MD: The Johns Hopkins University Press, 2009.

Rountree, Helen C. *Pocahontas, Powhatan, Opechancanough: Three Indian Lives Changed by Jamestown.* Charlottesville: University of Virginia Press, 2006.

Sita, Lisa. *Pocahontas: The Powhatan Culture and the Jamestown Colony.* New York: PowerPlus Books, 2005.

Waselkov, Gregory A., Peter H. Wood, and Tom Hatley, eds. *Powhatan's Mantle: Indians in the Colonial Southeast.* Rev ed. Lincoln: University of Nebraska Press, 2006.

WEB SITES

Cotton, Lee. "Powhatan Indian Lifeways." *National Park Service.* http://www.nps.gov/jame/historyculture/powhatan-indian-lifeways.htm (accessed on June 1, 2011).

Pamunkey Indian Tribe. http://www.pamunkey.net/ (accessed on June 1, 2011).

Monacan Indian Nation. http://www.monacannation.com (accessed on June 1, 2011).

The Official Nansemond Indian Tribal Association Website. http://www.nansemond.org/joomla/ (accessed on June 1, 2011).

"Powhatan Indian Village." *Acton Public Schools: Acton-Boxborough Regional School District.* http://ab.mec.edu/jamestown/powhatan (accessed on June 1, 2011).

"Powhatan Language and the Powhatan Indian Tribe (Powatan, Powhatten, Powhattan)." *Native Languages of the Americas: Preserving and Promoting Indigenous American Indian Languages.* http://www.native-languages.org/powhatan.htm (accessed on on June 1, 2011).

Rankokus Indian Reservation. http://www.powhatan.org/ (accessed on June 1, 2011).

Stebbins, Sarah J. "Chronology of Powhatan Indian Activity." *National Park Service.* http://www.nps.gov/jame/historyculture/chronology-of-powhatan-indian-activity.htm (accessed on June 1, 2011).

The Upper Mattaponi Indian Tribe. http://www.uppermattaponi.org (accessed on June 1, 2011).

Sac and Fox

Name

Several different backgrounds have been given for the Sac and Fox name. One theory says that the name came from a federal government mistake during the signing of 1804 treaty. Another explanation is that the French called the Fox people "Foxes" after the name of one of the tribe's clans. In any case, the Fox called themselves *Meshkwakihug* or *Meskwâki (Mesquakie),* meaning "red earth people," for the type of earth from which they believed they were created. The Sac (pronounced *sack*) called themselves *Osakiwung,* meaning "yellow earth people." Before they united with the Fox, their tribe was also known as the *Sauk.* Another name for the Sauk was *Thâkîwaki,* which was translated as "people coming forth" (from the outlet or the water).

Location

The Sac and Fox tribes lived in Michigan, Wisconsin, Illinois, Iowa, Missouri, Kansas, and Nebraska. One of the largest villages in North America was Saukenuk, located between the Rock and Mississippi Rivers in Illinois. At one time, the town included approximately four thousand Sac and Fox people. When the Europeans arrived, the Sac and Fox inhabited southern Michigan and Wisconsin. The Sac and Fox people now live, for the most part, on reservations in Oklahoma, Iowa, and Kansas.

Population

The Sac and Fox were originally two closely related but separate tribes. There were 2,500 Fox and about 3,500 Sac in the early 1600s. In the 1990 U.S. Census, 3,168 people identified themselves as Sac and Fox. In 2000, that number had risen to 4,375.

Language family

Central Algonquian.

Origins and group affiliations

Current members of the tribe are descendants of the Sac and Fox peoples of the Great Lakes region. The Sauk (Sac) originally lived in the Lower Peninsula of Michigan with their neighbors, the Fox. Before they became one tribe, the

Contemporary Sac and Fox Communities

Kansas and Nebraska
❶ Sac and Fox Tribe of Missouri in Kansas and Nebraska

Iowa
❷ Sac and Fox of the Mississippi in Iowa (Mesquakie Indian Settlement)

Oklahoma
❸ Sac and Fox Reservation, Oklahoma

A map of contemporary Sac and Fox communities. MAP BY XNR PRODUCTIONS. CENGAGE LEARNING, GALE. REPRODUCED BY PERMISSION OF GALE, A PART OF CENGAGE LEARNING.

Sauk and Fox were allies with each other and with the Kickapoo. They traded with the Potawatomi (see entry) and Chippewa, but at times they fought with them. Along with many other groups, they allied with the Confederacy of Three Fires, which included the Ojibway, Ottawa (see entries), and Potawatomi, to defend themselves from common enemies. Some of these rival tribes were the Iroquois Confederacy and the Dakota (see entries).

The Sac and Fox people have shared a close association for centuries. They were outstanding hunters who were also known for their bravery. The Sac and Fox culture was based upon respect for life, which included not only their own lives and those of their families and communities, but also the earth and all living creatures. Although the people living on Sac and Fox reservations today participate in mainstream American life, they are doing their best to retain aspects of their traditional culture.

HISTORY

The Fox people probably originated in southern Michigan and may have been a part of the Sac tribe centuries ago and then split off. When the French encountered them some time during the early to mid-1600s, the Fox were divided into two groups. One group lived in central Wisconsin along the Fox River, and another lived in northern Illinois. The Sac people originated around Saginaw Bay in Michigan.

Trouble with the French

During the 1600s, the Fox grew hostile to French traders moving into their territory, perhaps because the French traded with the Dakota (see entry), an enemy tribe. The Fox charged a toll for French traders to cross their land along the Fox River, an important waterway between Lake Michigan and Dakota lands. The Fox placed a flaming torch on the riverbank, marking their territory as a signal to the traders to pay up or suffer the consequences—death. The Fox, like the Iroquois, also traded with the British. Conflicts with the French resulted in the Fox Wars (1712–37), conflicts that had disastrous consequences for the Fox.

The First Fox War (1712–16) began as the result of an incident in 1712. The Illinois Fox and several other tribes friendly to the French had been invited to join a French settlement near Fort Detroit in Michigan. Misunderstandings developed among these groups, and the French and their Native allies attacked the Fox, inflicting heavy losses on the tribe. The surviving Fox fled to join other tribe members in Wisconsin. There Fox harassment of French traders increased. The angry French sent two military expeditions against the Fox in the Second Fox War (1728–37). They succeeded in winning all of the Fox tribes' allies to the French side and then nearly destroyed the Fox tribe.

The Sac were driven out of their territory near Michigan's Saginaw Bay at the same time as the Fox. They, too, relocated to Wisconsin. With the help of the Fox and other tribes, the Sac then drove the Illinois tribe from Illinois Territory on the Mississippi River and occupied that region themselves.

Important Dates

Early 1600s: The Fox make first contact with French traders.

1712: Losses in the Fox War with the French drive the Fox to Wisconsin.

1733: The Sac and Fox tribes merge.

1833: The Sac and Fox are forced west of the Mississippi River.

1859: Members of the Fox tribe separate from the Sac and return to Iowa.

1993: The Sac and Fox Nation defines its reservation as a "Nuclear Free Zone."

1994: The Sac and Fox of Missouri organize as a federally recognized tribe.

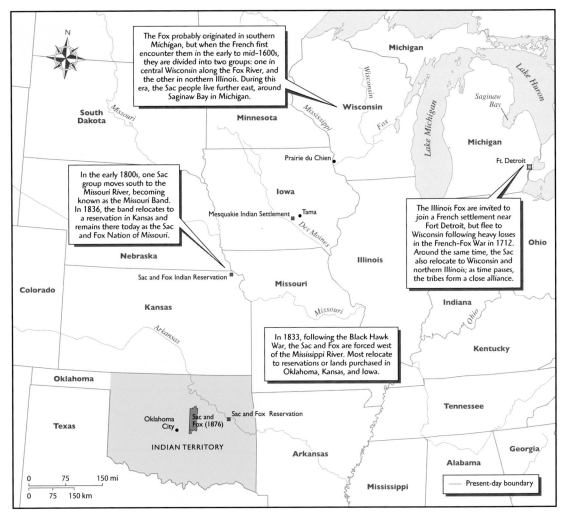

A map showing the migrations of the Sac and Fox through the mid-nineteenth century. MAP BY XNR PRODUCTIONS. CENGAGE LEARNING, GALE. REPRODUCED BY PERMISSION OF GALE, A PART OF CENGAGE LEARNING.

Fox join the Sac

As time passed, the Fox formed a close alliance with the Sac. Outsiders considered the two groups a single tribe, but between themselves they retained their individuality, as they still do. During the 1760s, with their numbers declining, the Sac and Fox moved south. By the early 1800s, they occupied the land along the Mississippi, primarily on the eastern bank. Their territory stretched from the mouth of the Des Moines (pronounced *duh-MOYNE*) River to the Prairie du Chien (pronounced *doo-SHEEN*) area in southern Wisconsin. They enjoyed abundant fishing and fertile farmland that produced plentiful harvests. They maintained a successful trading relationship with the French, Spanish, and British.

Division among the group

As the 1800s began, the Sac and Fox encountered increased pressure from settlers. Internal disagreements caused one Sac group to move south to the Missouri River. They became known as the Missouri band. In 1836, this group relocated to a reservation in Kansas on the Nebraska border. They remained there as the Sac and Fox Nation of Missouri.

In 1825, the Sac people who lived along the Mississippi divided into two groups. One relocated to southeast Iowa. The other, followers of the Sac warrior Black Hawk (1767–1838), stayed with him at Rock Island, Illinois. They tried to reclaim the land of their ancestors east of the Mississippi, but were stopped and defeated in the Black Hawk War (1832) by the U.S. Army and hostile Dakota Indians. The U.S. government then forced them to move farther west to a reservation in Kansas. Some refused to leave Iowa and hid from U.S. troops.

Disputes developed between the Sac and Fox who had gone to Kansas. By 1860, some of the Fox had left Kansas and gone back to Iowa where they bought land near the town of Tama. A smaller group moved in with the Kickapoo, then later moved to northern Mexico.

The remaining Sac and Fox sold their Kansas land and relocated to a 750,000-acre (303,500-hectare) reservation east of Oklahoma City. By 1891, the U.S. government had given most of this land to settlers. By the end of the next century, the Sac and Fox Reservation in Stroud, Oklahoma, had less than 1,000 acres.

Members of the Sac and Fox Reservation in Iowa used their own money to buy lands that now amount to more than 7,000 acres. Although their official name is the Sac and Fox of the Mississippi in Iowa, they prefer to be called the Mesquakie Indian Settlement.

RELIGION

Views on creation and the earth

The Sac and Fox believed that the universe was divided into two halves. The Great Manitou spirit ruled the Powers of the Sky, or Upper Region. Lesser spirits, such as the earth, sky, waters, forests, and intelligent animals, ruled the Powers of the Earth, or Lower Region. The Sac believed that the world was created by Gretci Munito, a powerful old man who lived forever.

Both the Sac and Fox visualized the earth on which they lived as a woman, who provided them with all their food. The Fox practiced a ceremony of apology for taking life when they killed animals, cut trees, gathered plants, or took minerals. A Fox speaker in William Jones's book, *Ethnography of the Fox Indians,* explains:

> We do not like to harm trees. Whenever we can, we always make an offering of tobacco to the trees before we cut them down. If we did not think of their feelings … before cutting them down, all the other trees in the forest would weep, and that would make our hearts sad, too.

Death, spirits, and Christianity

The Fox believed that when a person died, the soul traveled through a series of villages to a final resting place beyond the sunset. Only the souls of the good went farther than the first village. Evil people were sent to the home of Machi Manitou, the chief evil spirit. Shamans (medicine men; pronounced *SHAH-munz* or *SHAY-munz*) could talk to the spirit world.

The Sac believed that the soul followed the Milky Way and crossed a river before entering the land of the dead. A figure called the "Brain Taker" tried to smash the head of anyone attempting to cross the river. If the soul naviagated the river swiftly and safely, there would be feasting and rejoicing when it entered the land of the dead. If the soul was caught, its brains would be destroyed.

The Sac and Fox believed that human beings were both helped and hurt by spirits. During the ceremony called Vision Quest, the tribe sought the aid of spirits.

Present-day culture is still based on respect for life and for all creation. More recent religious practices include the Drum Dance, the Native American Church, and Christianity. Many Sac and Fox today are Christians or members of the Native American Church. Founded in the nineteenth century, the Native American Church combines Christian and Native beliefs and practices and features an all-night ceremony composed of chanting, prayer, and meditation.

LANGUAGE

The languages spoken by the Sac and the Fox were Central Algonquian dialects (varieties) closely related to each other and to the language of the Kickapoo. During the early part of the twentieth century, much effort went into preserving the early language and tales of the people. As a result a Sac-Fox dictionary, a Sac-Fox alphabet, and many books of Sac and Fox tales provide information about the language. Nevertheless, in the early twenty-first century, the language was considered endangered because many speakers were elderly, and the reservations were located so far from one another. The Sauk language, in particular, was only spoken by a few people. Efforts are being made to revive the language.

Influences from the Sauk language still linger in names given to some of the places they lived. The city of Chicago got its name from the Sauk word *shekâkôhaki,* meaning "land of onions." Wild onions once grew in that area. Saginaw Bay came from *Sâkînâwe,* which translates to "Sauk country."

GOVERNMENT

The early Sac and Fox were governed by a clan system. (Clans are groups of related families.) Some clan names were Fish, Ocean, Thunder, Bear, Fox, Indian Potato, Deer, Beaver, Snow, and Wolf. Separate societies were formed for games, ceremonies, and warfare. Members of those societies did not have to be of the same clan.

Three types of chiefs led the Sac and Fox tribes: a peace chief, a war chief, and a religious leader known as a shaman. Leadership roles were sometimes passed down from generation to generation. Other leaders were chosen based on their merits. The tribal council made the final decision as to who would serve as chief. The chief who gathered the most followers had the greatest influence.

Women were not permitted to be chiefs in the early days, but they participated in public meetings and gave advice on matters of importance. By the 1990s, many women held leadership positions, including the role of principal chief. A committee operates as the elected governing body for enrolled members of the tribe and transacts business on the tribe's behalf. The Sac and Fox Court, begun in 1885, tries cases involving members of the tribe.

ECONOMY

Pre-twentieth-century economy

The early Sac and Fox were village dwellers who followed an annual cycle of hunting, farming, and trading. Every year, they traded thousands of dollars' worth of beaver pelts to the Europeans in exchange for horses, animal traps, firearms, blankets, and cooking utensils.

In the nineteenth century, the Sac and Fox who lived on the reservation in present-day Oklahoma traditionally owned communal land. In 1887, the U.S. government adopted an allotment policy and insisted that the people follow the custom of individual land ownership. Most of the Natives could not raise sufficient food on their individual lots, particularly because they did not own the appropriate tools and had no money to buy them. Many ended up selling their property to settlers.

Modern times

The tribe suffered economic hardship well into the twentieth century. Homes often lacked heat and water, and medical and educational opportunities were limited. Many people ended up working as laborers on land they had once owned.

In the mid-1990s, unemployment on the Oklahoma reservation ran about 22.5 percent, meaning that more than one-fifth of people who wanted to work could not find a job. Per capita income was about $6,204, only one-third of that of most Americans. (Per capita income is the average income one person earns in one year.)

In the early 2000s, individual members of the Oklahoma Sac and Fox leased their land for farming and grazing purposes. An important business operation was the tribe's Indian Country Bingo facility located in Stroud. In the mid-1990s, members of the Sac and Fox Reservation in Oklahoma reacquired more than 4,000 acres of land that housed the Cushing Industrial Park. That complex included a 25,000-square-foot (2,300-square-meter) building and a warehouse facility. The tribe also operated an arts and crafts outlet, a grocery store, a tribal museum, and a modern campground. By the end of the first decade, casino income was helping the tribe.

By 2005, the tribe of the Meskwaki Nation in Iowa, which owned 80 acres in 1857, had increased its land holdings to more than 7,000 acres and had set aside an additional 700 acres off-reservation for farming and a wildlife refuge. Employment opportunities available on the reservation included the casino, the tribal government, a convenience store, and the settlement school. Many tribe members also worked in nearby communities.

As with the other two Sac and Fox Nations, casino income benefitted the Sac and Fox Nation of Missouri, which operates its gaming facility and restaurant businesses in Powhattan, Kansas. Money from casinos fund many programs to assist tribal members on the reservations.

DAILY LIFE

Families

Women played an important role in Sac families and in tribal life. The society was matrilineal (tracing kinship through the mother), so children took on the tribe and clan of their mothers. Mothers took charge of their homes and everything in them. They also owned the fields. Women of the tribe decided whether a son could inherit his father's role as chief.

The basic unit of the Fox tribe was the extended family, made up of parents, children, grandparents, and other relatives. It usually consisted of between five and thirty members. Children spent most of their time playing. Boys were taught hunting skills, whereas girls learned cooking and sewing.

Buildings

When the Europeans first encountered them, the Fox lived in summer camps consisting of several rectangular frame lodges surrounded by palisades, fences made of large pointed stakes. Their houses, called lodges, were very similar to those of the Sac. Lodges were up to 60 feet (18 meters) long and housed several families. They were covered with elm bark matting and had two entrances. The eastern door was called "where daylight appears," and the western door on the opposite side was called "where the sun goes down." Wide benches covered with bark lined the sides of the walls and were used for sitting and sleeping.

Personal possessions and objects belonging to the clan were either hung from the ceiling or stored under the benches. They stored food in bark-lined holes in the ground. Although the tribes sometimes made campfires in the lodge, they did most of their cooking in temporary brush shelters set near the lodge.

In the winter, as food became scarce, Sac and Fox families usually left their villages and settled in smaller encampments. Their winter homes were small wigwams, no more than 15 feet (4 meters) wide, built of poles and covered with reed mats. Round roofs allowed snow and rain to roll off easily. They covered the doors and floors with bearskins and buffalo robes and used a central fire pit to prepare food and provide warmth.

Although villages were usually small, a European visitor to a Sac village in 1766 described it as having ninety houses, many sheds for smoking meat, and regularly spaced streets.

Clothing and adornment

The Sac and Fox wore clothing decorated with buffalo hair or plant fibers woven in arrows or zigzags. Some garments were decorated with quills and ribbon work. In the summer, the men usually wore moccasins and a breechcloth (a piece of material that went between the legs) of tanned deerskin or elk skin. Women wore wraparound skirts of tanned deer or elk skin with thong belts and moccasins. In colder weather, the men usually added leggings and a shirt. Women wore ponchos and leggings. Both sexes wore garters and belts. Summer clothing included lightweight robes made of deerskin or elk skin. Painted buffalo robes were worn in winter.

Accessories such as hawk and eagle feathers, long sashes worn around the waist, and animal-skin pouches were very popular. Grizzly bear–claw necklaces were highly prized because they were so hard to win. Both sexes

An illustration from the 1850s depicts a group of Sac and Fox warriors. © NORTH WIND PICTURE ARCHIVES.

pierced their ears and wore rings, hoops, and feathers through them. The use of body paint was common. Although the two tribes dressed similarly, they used different designs and colors when they painted their bodies so they could be told apart.

Some Fox men dyed their hair blue. Warriors of the Sac and Fox often shaved their hair Mohawk-style (see Mohawk entry) or shaved off all their hair except for one long lock on the top of their heads. Some men wore porcupine roaches, which were headpieces made from porcupine or deer hair, often dyed bright colors. The women of both tribes wore their hair long, holding it in place with a decorated hair binder.

Food

The Sac and Fox hunted waterfowl, deer, and moose, following the animal herds during the winter months. Women farmed and gathered berries, nuts, honey, wild potatoes, fruits, and herbs to supplement their diet. Crops included corn, beans, squash, pumpkin, and melon. They collected sap and made maple syrup in winter to flavor their food. Food was wrapped in bark and stored in a hiding place near the lodge.

The Fox held two organized buffalo hunts each year. When they found a herd, the hunters surrounded it and started a grass fire. Meanwhile, a skilled archer killed the lead buffalo. With the herd leaderless and unable to escape because of the fire, the panicked buffalo were easy to kill. When the men returned with the carcasses, the women stripped, cleaned, dried, and packed the meat, and they prepared the hides for making clothing and for trading.

Education

Sac and Fox boys were taught to make bows and arrows and to hunt. Girls learned to cook, sew, and tend a garden.

In the late 1800s, the U.S. government built boarding schools on the reservations. They separated children from their parents and taught them to live like the settlers. Students learned to build fences, sew, and tend cattle. Many parents did not like the system or its emphasis on manual labor, so they would not permit their children to attend the schools. Christian missionaries who taught at the schools tried, with little success, to convert the children to Christianity.

In the early 2000s, children living on the Sac and Fox reservation in Oklahoma attended public schools in neighboring communities.

Students and teachers gather outside the day school at the Sac and Fox Agency in Indian Territory in the late 1800s. NATIONAL ARCHIVES AND RECORDS ADMINISTRATION.

The tribe sponsored a summer camp that taught the Sac and Fox language to children. The Mesquakie Indian Settlement in Iowa had its own elementary and secondary school, where children could learn about their culture. Many students benefited from college scholarships and other programs that encouraged higher education.

Healing practices

Tribal members learned religious prayers and dances from shamans, who led ceremonies to ensure success in war and farming or to cure illnesses. Medicine men and women were both respected and feared, because even "good" shamans had the power to put bad spells on people. Good shamans

A Fox Tale

The Sac and Fox enjoyed gathering around a fire during the winter months to hear short tales about tribal practices and morality. Many of their stories, including the following selection, have been preserved.

Once upon a time there was a youth who blackened (his face) and fasted. He had been blessed by the manitous. And when he was visited by his father, "Come, O father, do let me eat!" he said to his father. Four days had passed since he had eaten.

"My dear son, I want you to fast two days more, but no longer." Then the old man went back home. He was implored by his son to let him eat, (but) he could not be prevailed upon by him.

So in the morning when the old man went to take another look at his son, lo, the youth had disappeared from the place where he was staying! There was a spring at the brook near by. There the old man went. He went there to look over the bank, and behold! Lying there, on the flat of his belly, and drinking water, was his son. As he looked at him, lo, (his son) changed partly into a fish! He ran to his son to catch him, but he slipped hold of him and he lost his son.

Thereupon was the spring swollen with water, and the place where (the youth) escaped became a lake. For many a year it was common for the people, as they went canoeing about, to see catfishes down in the water. One catfish was white; it wore yellow ear-rings; that one was the youth who had fasted over-much. One catfish was black, and that was his wife. And there were also four other tiny little catfishes; they were (all) white, (and) they wore yellow ear-rings. These went swimming past side by side, abreast and in line, these the offspring of him that had fasted overlong.

SOURCE: Jones, William. "Fox Texts." *Publications of the American Ethnological Society*, Vol. 1. Leyden: E. J. Brill, 1907.

cured people by sucking out any illness-causing objects injected by bad shamans or witches. The Fox feared witches, who became active at night, passing through the forest disguised as balls of blue-green light. Shamans gave their patients advice, charms, and remedies to counteract bad spells cast by witches; they also dispensed herbal remedies for illnesses.

ARTS

The Sac and Fox were known for combining form and beauty in everyday objects. They used feathers, plant fibers, wood, and stone to adorn bags, boxes, and even weapons. The Fox made ribbonwork panels out of several layers of different colored ribbons and cut-out floral or geometric shapes. After encountering Europeans, the Sac and Fox added European goods to their designs, including colored beads, woven cloth, and metal.

Some members of the tribe sell traditional artwork either on their own or in conjunction with others. In the late 1900s, the Sac and Fox Nation of Oklahoma opened the Sac and Fox Gallery, a retail store that sold arts and crafts made by members of the tribe.

CUSTOMS

Festivals

The Fox celebrated a successful harvest at great festivals that involved horse races and an early version of the game known as lacrosse. Lacrosse is a game of Native origin played on a field by two teams of ten players each. Participants use a long-handled stick with a webbed pouch to put a ball into the opposing team's goal. The Fox also played a ball game between two teams in which one hid a ball or stone under a blanket, and the other had to find it.

The Sac and Fox Nation of Oklahoma host an annual powwow in mid-July that features Native American dancing and arts and crafts. They also host tribal feasts. The Sac and Fox Reservation in Tama County, Iowa, has hosted an annual powwow that celebrates their heritage and spirituality.

One unusual holiday the people hold is Victory Day. This came about as a result of a lawsuit that began in the 1980s. In 1983, the Sac and Fox Nation began issuing license plates to its members. The state of Oklahoma objected, but after a ten-year court battle, the Sac and Fox Nation won. The Supreme Court ruled that as a sovereign (self-governing) nation, the tribe could operate its own licensing bureau. To celebrate this decision that reinforced its rights to govern its own people, the tribe holds Victory Day every May 17, the day the case was decided.

Puberty

As part of the puberty ritual, Sac and Fox boys were sent out to begin their vision quest. A vision quest involved praying and fasting (going without food and water) alone, waiting for a special vision from a spirit, and collecting special objects, such as stones and feathers, to represent the newly gained power. Boys also had to accomplish a heroic deed. Males were considered full adults around age twenty. Female rituals began at first menstruation. The girl was sent to a lodge by herself and was allowed no visitors for ten days.

Courtship and marriage

Most young men married by age twenty; their wives were three to four years younger. To court his intended bride, the man offered services and gifts. If the bride-to-be and her parents accepted, the couple married and moved into the bride's family home. The young man then fulfilled his promises to the family. After two or three years, the couple usually moved to their own home and began having children. Marriage to more than one wife was allowed; generally, a man married a sister or cousin of his first wife.

Death and mourning

Sac and Fox who died were either buried or placed on a platform. Sometimes a warrior might be buried lying or sitting on top of an enemy. Occasionally the tribes sacrificed a dog and buried it with the dead person to be a companion in the afterlife. The mourning period for family members of the deceased lasted from six months to a year. During this time, the mourners blackened their faces and wore shabby clothing to show their grief.

War rituals

If an enemy tribe killed a Sac or Fox, the victim's family might organize a raid to get even. The man who led a raid fasted (stopped eating). He also built a special lodge and hung a strip of red cloth in front of it to signal that he planned a raid. Those who wanted to participate came in and smoked a pipe with him. Sometimes wives accompanied their husbands on raids. As they approached the enemy, the leader rode in front carrying his sacred pack (a container with items such as animal teeth and eagle feathers that gave him special powers). If the raid was not successful, the warriors returned to their village separately. If it was successful, they returned together, sending a messenger ahead to announce their victory.

Sac and Fox warriors wore special headdresses into battle. They were made of animal hair dyed red and tied to a strip of hair on their scalps. The warriors shaved the rest of their heads and painted them with colorful designs. Unless the weather was very cold, they left their upper bodies bare. They sometimes painted human hands on their backs or shoulders

Chief Keokuk was a prominent Sac leader in the early 1800s. © MCKENNEY & HALL.

with white clay. The hands showed how many enemies they had slain. After a successful raid, the Fox painted their tribal symbol on a tree near where the enemy had fallen.

CURRENT TRIBAL ISSUES

In 1992, seventy-five-year-old tribe member Grace Thorpe, the daughter of Olympic athlete Jim Thorpe (1888–1953), led a fight against the construction of a storage site for highly radioactive material on tribal land in Oklahoma. Using research that showed the harm that exposure to radiation could cause, Grace Thorpe began a movement opposing the facility. In February 1993, her tribe, the Sac and Fox Nation, voted against having the storage site built on its land. In so doing, the it turned down $2.8 million that the U.S. government would have paid them and became the first tribe in Oklahoma to declare a "Nuclear Free Zone" on their tribal lands. Although that money could have helped members in poverty, the Sac and Fox stayed true to their traditions of honoring the earth.

The Sac and Fox have always emphasized the importance of protecting the earth and using resources wisely. In keeping with this belief, the Meskwaki Nation began monitoring the wind in 2011 with the intent of setting up a wind farm on its Iowa land. The wind farm will not only generate renewable energy but also will provide much-needed employment.

Recent Sac and Fox tribal leaders have asserted certain rights as a sovereign nation. Those rights include taxing businesses, issuing license plates, maintaining control over lands and resources, and governing according to Sac and Fox modern law.

During the first decades of the 2000s, the various Sac and Fox groups have improved their economy through casino income. Money from gaming funds important educational and social services projects.

One project that has been developed recently is a training program. Native teens have much higher suicide rates than the rest of the country.

To lower these statistics, community members are being trained to spot warning signs, and they are taught how to assist potential victims.

NOTABLE PEOPLE

Sac leader Keokuk (1783–1848) rose to power because of his skills as a warrior, politician, and orator. He signed many treaties, giving Sac and Fox land to the American government, against the wishes of his rival, Black Hawk (1767–1838). He later skillfully defended Sac land interests against Dakota claims of ownership. Black Hawk led a party of warriors against the settlers in the1832 Black Hawk War to reclaim lands in Illinois and Wisconsin.

Jim Thorpe was born in 1888 on the Sac and Fox Reservation in Oklahoma. He played both professional baseball and football and made the hall of fame in both sports. In 1950, the Associated Press voted Jim Thorpe, an Olympic champion, the greatest athlete in the first half of the twentieth century. In 1954, a year after Thorpe died, a town in Pennsylvania was named in his honor.

In 1993, Jim Thorpe's daughter, Grace, known as Wind Woman, founded the National Environmental Coalition of Native Americans (NECONA) to fight the dumping of nuclear waste on Native American lands.

BOOKS

Drake, Benjamin. *The Great Indian Chief of the West; or, Life and Adventures of Black Hawk.* Charleston, SC: Bibliobazaar, 2006.

Jones, William. *Ethnography of the Fox Indians.* Washington, DC: Government Printing Office, 1939.

Hagan, William T. *The Sac and Fox Indians.* Norman: University of Oklahoma Press, 2008.

Hall, John W. *Uncommon Defense: Indian Allies in the Black Hawk War.* Cambridge, MA: Harvard University Press, 2009.

Kennedy, J. Gerald. *Life of Black Hawk, or Ma-ka-tai-me-she-kia-kiak. Dictated by Himself.* New York: Penguin Books, 2008.

McDaniel, Melissa. *The Sac and Fox Indians.* New York: Chelsea Juniors, 1995.

Smith, Henry. *The Expedition against the Sauk and Fox Indians, 1832.* Charleston, SC: Nabu Press, 2010.

Von Ahnen, Katherine. *Charlie Young Bear.* Minot, CO: Roberts Rinehart Publishers, 1994.

Wakefield, John *A. History of the War between the United States and the Sac and Fox Nations of Indians.* Cranbury, NJ: Scholar's Bookshelf, 2006.

WEB SITES

McCollum, Timothy James. "Sac and Fox." *Oklahoma Historical Society.* http://digital.library.okstate.edu/encyclopedia/entries/S/SA001.html (accessed on June 5, 2011).

Redish, Laura, and Orrin Lewis. "Sac and Fox Culture and History Links." *Native Languages of the Americas.* http://www.native-languages.org/sac-fox.htm (accessed on June 5, 2011).

Sac and Fox Nation. http://www.sacandfoxnation-nsn.gov/ (accessed on June 5, 2011).

"Sac and Fox Tribe." *Meskwaki Nation.* http://www.meskwaki.org/ (accessed on June 5, 2011).

Sultzman, Lee. "Sac and Fox History Links." *First Nations.* http://www.tolatsga.org/sf.html (accessed on June 5, 2011).

Wampanoag

Name

Wampanoag (pronounced *wam-puh-NO-ag*). The name is probably a variation of *Wapanacki,* meaning "eastern people." The Wampanoag have also been called Massasoit, Philip's Indians, and Pokanoket (from the name of their principal village).

Location

The Wampanoag occupied about forty villages in northern Rhode Island and southeastern coastal Massachusetts and its offshore islands (now known as Martha's Vineyard and Nantucket) at the time of European contact. Most still live in New England.

Population

There were an estimated 15,000 Wampanoag around 1600. In the 1990 U.S. Census, 2,145 people identified themselves as Wampanoag. In 2000, there were 2,488 Wampanoag, including the 430 members of the Wampanoag Tribe of Gay Head, who prefer to call themselves Aquinnah Wampanoag.

Language family

Eastern Algonquian.

Origins and group affiliations

Ancestors of the Wampanoag most likely occupied territory in northern Rhode Island and southeastern coastal Massachusetts for twelve thousand to fifteen thousand years. The Wampanoag traded with many New England tribes, particularly the Mohican, Mohegan, and Delaware (see entry). They were enemies of the Narragansett (see entry), Mohawk (see entry), and other Iroquois tribes (see Iroquois Confederacy entry) and allies of the British colonists.

The Wampanoag were a peaceful agricultural people before Europeans arrived. Diseases from Europe nearly destroyed the tribe, and the newcomers demanded increasing amounts of their land. The Wampanoag had originally welcomed the British colonists, called the Pilgrims (religious

Contemporary Wampanoag Communities

Massachusetts
❶ Aquinnah Wampanoag
❷ Mashpee Wampanoag

Shaded area
☐ Traditional Wampanoag lands in present-day northern Rhode Island and southeastern Massachusetts and its offshore islands

A map of contemporary Wampanoag communities. MAP BY XNR PRODUCTIONS. CENGAGE LEARNING, GALE. REPRODUCED BY PERMISSION OF GALE, A PART OF CENGAGE LEARNING.

separatists who sailed to North America in search of a home where they could freely practice their religion), at the beginning of the seventeenth century and helped them through their first rough winters. The Pilgrims, however, permanently disrupted Wampanoag life.

HISTORY

Peaceful life unravels

For thousands of years before Europeans came to the Americas, the Wampanoag occupied villages along the Atlantic coast in southern New England, living comfortably off the fruits of agriculture, hunting, and fishing. Because the region was heavily populated even before the British arrived, the Wampanoag decided among themselves who could hunt where. Their arrangement was different from tribes in other areas of the country, where the land was less populated and hunters could move over very wide areas.

In the 1500s and 1600s, Europeans established a presence along the Atlantic coast. Before the Wampanoag had much contact with Europeans, they experienced the effects of that presence. The French to the north, wanting more and more furs from their Native trading partners, encouraged the various tribes to expand their territory into Wampanoag lands. War with the Narragansett (see entry) and other tribes resulted. At the same time, fishing and trading vessels sailed along the New England coast, bringing new diseases to Native peoples who had no resistance to them. Some Wampanoag were taken captive by Europeans and sold as slaves in Europe.

Important Dates

1621: Chief Massasoit allies with Pilgrims.

1676: King Philip's War results in the destruction of life, loss of land, and the end of a way of life for New England tribes.

1928: The Wampanoag Nation is reunified after living on separate reservations for more than two hundred years.

1987: The Gay Head Wampanoag (Aquinnah) receive federal recognition.

2007: The Mashpee Wampanoag receive federal recognition.

The Pilgrims arrive

When the first Pilgrims arrived in 1620 at a place they called Plymouth (in present-day Massachusetts), the Wampanoag there had endured nearly a century of terrible experiences with Europeans. In the previous ten years, three disease epidemics, probably brought by Europeans, had killed as many as three-quarters of the Wampanoag population. Those who remained were forced to pay tribute to the Narragansett Indians, now the most powerful people in the region.

The Wampanoag, however, welcomed the British and gave them invaluable assistance, teaching them to hunt and fish and to grow native crops by "hilling," a system of planting corn kernels in rows of small hills. Without this help, the Pilgrims probably would not have survived the punishing New England winter.

In 1621, Chief Massasoit (c. 1580–1661) signed a treaty of friendship with the colonists in hopes of securing their help against the Narragansett and Micmac (see entry), who came into the possession of European weapons and were becoming troublesome. At some point, Massasoit granted the colonists permission to occupy Plymouth Colony; the colonists believed they now owned the land. After the first harvest that autumn, the Wampanoag and Pilgrims celebrated by having a feast together. People sometimes refer to this meal as the first Thanksgiving, but it was not an annual tradition, and the holiday as it is currently celebrated did not begin until many years later.

An illustration from the 1600s depicts members of the Wampanoag tribe succumbing to smallpox, a European disease to which Native Americans had no immunity. © NORTH WIND PICTURE ARCHIVES.

Fifty years of good relations followed during which the British assisted the Wampanoag in skirmishes against other tribes. The friendship was so strong that just before his death, Massasoit, who was called "King" by the British, was granted permission by the General Court of Plymouth to give British names to his sons. However, the friendship that Massasoit carefully nurtured was already turning on him toward the end of his life, as new colonists arrived who saw the Wampanoag as little more than obstacles to taking the land as their own.

Under Puritan influence

New settlers, called the Puritans, arrived in large numbers. (Puritans were Protestant reformers who followed strict religious standards.) The Puritans preached Christianity to the Wampanoag and tried to force observance of their laws. They arrested Natives for hunting on the Sabbath (the day of worship) or for observing ancient traditions they considered "savage." Natives who agreed to convert to Christianity were called "praying Indians." To keep them separate from their unconverted neighbors, the Puritans resettled them in new communities, called "praying towns." By 1675, the "praying Indians" in New England numbered about 2,500.

Puritan efforts to convert the Wampanoag did not cause nearly as much resentment as their expansion westward. They defeated different tribes and took over their lands. By the time Massasoit's son, Wamsutta (or Alexander), succeeded him as grand sachem (pronounced *SAY-shem*; chief) in 1661, Native resentment had reached a high pitch. The Puritans, who considered Wamsutta too arrogant, invited him to Plymouth for a conference. While there, he became ill and died suddenly; some historians believe he was probably poisoned. His brother, Metacomet (King Philip; c. 1639–1676) succeeded him. By this time, it was obvious that the settlers had plans for unlimited expansion into Native territory. They had come close to destroying the Pequot (see entry) and had established fourteen reservations in the northeast that restricted Native rights and forced them off their lands.

Chief Metacomet launched what was known as King Philip's War against the colonists in 1675. © HULTON ARCHIVE/STRINGER/HULTON ARCHIVE/GETTY IMAGES.

King Philip's War

Metacomet was a military genius. Before launching King Philip's War (1675–76; a general Native uprising to resist continued expansion of the British colonies in New England), he declared: "Soon after I became *sachem* they disarmed all my people.... Their land was taken.... I am determined not to live until I have no country." Of all the revolts carried out against the colonists by Algonquian-speaking peoples, this war came the closest to succeeding. Metacomet gathered an army made up of warriors from the Abenaki (see entry), Nipmuck, Narragansett, and Wampanoag tribes. The army attacked more than half of the British settlements in New England. For a time, it held its own in the war against the Puritans. However, the tribes were so weakened by epidemics that even their allied forces did not have the strength to win. By the time the war was over, the colonists had nearly exterminated the Wampanoag, Nipmuck, and Narragansett. Betrayed by his own people, including Wampanoag "praying Indians," and cut off from food, King Philip was forced to fall back into Rhode Island's cedar swamps. His defeat and death in July 1676 ended Native military action in southern New England.

After the war, colonial armies hunted and killed Natives, whether they were enemies, neutral, or friendly, and then divided their lands. Metacomet was beheaded, and his head was displayed on a post in Plymouth for twenty-five years as a warning to all who were inclined to resist colonial expansion. Widows and orphans were sold as slaves in the West Indies; "praying Indians" and enemy warriors alike were imprisoned, and many refugees fled. Only four hundred Wampanoag survived the war. Gradually, over the next two hundred years, the population climbed above two thousand.

In the twenty-first century, the Wampanoag people were concentrated mainly on the Aquinnah Reservation in Martha's Vineyard and on Cape Cod in Massachusetts, although some were scattered throughout the New England area. Four other groups are Herring Pond Wampanoag Tribe, Pocasset Wampanoag Tribe, Seaconke Wampanoag Tribe, and Chappquiddick Tribe of the Wampanog Indian Nation. The Chappaquiddick Wampanoag are mainly located in Rhode Island and Massachusetts, and the Seaconke Wampanoag live in Rhode Island. The other two tribes live in Massachusetts.

RELIGION

Helen Attaquin, an Aquinnah Wampanoag, described her people's worldview in her essay, "There Are Differences" (from the book, *Rooted Like the Ash Trees*). She said: "Indians do not believe in a 'universe' but in a 'multiverse.' Indians don't believe that there is ONE fixed and eternal truth; they think there are many different and equally *valid* truths." The appreciation that there exists "more than one way to view this earth of ours, and more than one way to share it" may have restrained the Wampanoag from simply ridding their shores of the Europeans with "their bristling armament [weapons] and the frightening aroma of death-causing diseases."

Wampanoag traditions center around the Great Spirit called *Kiehtan,* who made all things. *Manitou,* guardian spirits in the form of birds, fish, and animals, watch over the people. The Wampanoag believe the Great Spirit sent a spirit called Crow about one thousand years ago with gifts of corn and bean seeds in his ears. With these gifts, the people ceased being wanderers, settled down, and planted gardens.

Early European explorers along the Atlantic Coast saw and wrote about religious ceremonies conducted by shamans (medicine men; pronounced *SHAH-munz* or *SHAY-munz*) at powwows. Powwow means "brings together." Explorers used the word to refer to the shaman and the ceremonies he or she conducted. Shamans performed magical feats the explorers called "juggling," made possible by spiritual helpers.

The Pilgrims and Puritans brought Christianity to the Wampanoag. In the massacre of Indians that took place after King Philip's War, some Christian Wampanoag were allowed to survive. Afterward, more surviving Wampanoag turned to Christianity. Even as Wampanoag communities died out or consolidated over the years, efforts to practice ancient ceremonies continued, and they still do to this day. For example, the Aquinnah Wampanoag give thanks to the Great Spirit for the berries they harvest during their annual celebration of Cranberry Day.

Massachusett Place Names

The Massachusett language survives mainly as Massachusetts place names and personal titles, often a mispronunciation of the original Native version. Gay Head was called *Aquinnah* ("land under the hill"); Hyannis was *Anayanough* ("warrior's place"); *Sakonet* means "black-goose place" or "rocky outlet"; *Pautuxet* is "at the little falls"; *Cowasit* refers to "pine place"; and *Mashpee* is "great pond or cove."

The first syllables of both Massachusetts ("big hill") and Mississippi ("big river") derive from the Algonquian superlative "massa-." *Massasoit* (translated loosely as "big chief" or "great commander") was the title given to Grand Sachem Ousemequin (Yellow Feather).

LANGUAGE

The Wampanoag were speakers of an Eastern Algonquian dialect (variety) known as Massachusett. Most Eastern Algonquian speakers could understand other dialects, although some islanders had difficulty communicating with mainlanders.

Although the Wampanoag language, along with other Massachusett languages, had been considered extinct for more than one hundred years, two women began the Wampanoag Language Reclamation Project in 1993. Jessie Littledoe Baird, a member of the Mashpee Wampanoag Tribe, and Helen Manning, an Aquinnah Wampanoag, wanted to revive the language. Since then, scholars have studied old books to piece together the words and grammar. One of these was a Bible translated into Wampanoag by a British minister, John Eliot (1604–90), in 1631. In addition, several other old books and documents containing records of the language have been referenced to revive the Wampanoag language.

GOVERNMENT

Prior to European contact

At the time of contact with Europeans, the Wampanoag lived in about forty villages with a Grand Sachem (Great Chief) at their head. Under him were lesser chiefs called *sachems* and *sagamores*. These chiefs had little actual authority but were highly respected. The position was handed down from father to son; if there were no male heirs, a woman could become a queen sachem. Sachems advised on the best areas for planting, hunting, and fishing. They devised punishments for those who broke rules. The sachem and a council of warriors (distinguished by extreme physical strength and special powers given to them by the spirits) decided when to make war.

After King Philip's War

By the early 1700s, many Wampanoag had been placed on reservations called "plantations." In the early 2000s, the two largest groups were Gay Head (Aquinnah) on Martha's Vineyard and Mashpee on Cape Cod.

In 1928, two Wampanoag men, Eben Queppish and Nelson Simons, brought together the Mashpee, Gay Head (Aquinnah), and Herring Pond communities as the Wampanoag Nation. The Wampanoag reorganized in 1975, adding the Assonet and Nemasket people.

The Aquinnah Wampanoag gained federal recognition in 1987, which gives them certain legal rights and privileges in their relations with the U.S. government. For example, recognition brought them $3 million to build housing for the elderly and a hospital. Aquinnah Wampanoag own 485 acres of land and are governed by an elected tribal council; the council also has a traditional chief and a medicine man as members. All council meetings are open to the public, and the tribe can override council decisions by a majority vote.

The Mashpee Wampanoag Tribe owns 55 acres and is governed by an elected tribal council. The tribe maintains traditional governing roles by electing a sachem, a medicine man, clan matriarchs, and an elder council.

In 2007, the tribe received federal recognition, which entitled it to act as a sovereign (self-governing) nation. The action also brought other benefits, including an influx of federal funds.

ECONOMY

In early times

After the Wampanoag became an agricultural people, they lived on corn, beans, and pumpkins, supplementing their diet by hunting and fishing. People helped one another prepare fields for planting in the spring. Women then took care of planting everything except for tobacco, a male specialty.

In the winter, the people moved inland to hunting camps, where individual extended families "owned" specific hunting territories and passed them down from father to son. (Extended families include parents, children, grandparents, and other relatives.)

The Wampanoag also traded with neighboring tribes. The favorite trade items were soapstone pipes and bowls and wampum beads. (Wampum beads are cut from shells. Long strings of the beads were used as money and for other purposes.) Trade items obtained from the Narragansett were traded with the Abenaki, along with corn seeds, in exchange for birch bark to make canoes.

After King Philip's War nearly destroyed the tribe, the remaining Wampanoag worked as whalers, day laborers, domestic servants, farmers, soldiers, and basket makers. The Mashpee Manufacturing Company, which incorporated in 1867, made and marketed brooms, baskets, and other wooden wares.

Present day

The Aquinnah Wampanoag lands include the Cliffs of Gay Head, a popular tourist destination on Martha's Vineyard; cranberry bogs; and a herring run. The tribal government employs some members of the tribe; others are involved with tourism. The tribe also began an environmental laboratory and fish hatchery to increase the amount of shellfish in the waters along the coast. This initiative benefited the surrounding communities as well as the tribe.

The Mashpee Wampanoag acreage is neither populated nor developed. The people live in the town of Mashpee in the popular resort destination of Cape Cod. The town's economy depends on tourism and summer visits by people who own property there. Some tribe members support themselves in construction, agriculture, and fish farming. In 2000, the Mashpee Wampanoag opened an equestrian center to board, show, and train horses. They also run a museum that is listed in the National Register.

DAILY LIFE

Families

In the summer, Wampanoag families enjoyed a communal existence, with neighbor helping neighbor, and people enjoy a fair amount of leisure time. Men often engaged other tribes in games of chance and endurance. During the long, cold months of winter, the people withdrew into smaller groupings of extended families. Men gathered around the fire and fashioned arrowheads out of stone. Women wove baskets and mats. Elders told stories and children listened.

Buildings

Before European contact, the Wampanoag built dome-shaped wigwams, or *wetus,* from long sapling poles, which were stuck in the ground, then bent and tied together. Walls were made of bulrushes woven into mats; the people laid similar mats out on the floor or placed them atop special raised racks for sleeping. A smoke hole at the top of the dwelling did not always keep the structure from becoming too smoky for comfort. If this happened, the Wampanoag might sleep out under the stars.

Other buildings in a village were smokehouses, sweat lodges for purification, and dance houses for celebrating. When it was time for the seasonal move, the Wampanoag left the buildings' pole frames behind to be used again the following year.

After European colonization, fortified dwellings on hilltops provided safety. The Wampanoag eventually incorporated European hardware and furniture, and some moved to shingled homes similar to those of their European neighbors.

Food

Food in New England was plentiful and varied. The Wampanoag grew corn, squash, cucumbers, and beans and used herring as fertilizer for their crops. They gathered wild rice, nuts, and berries. They used hooks, lines, and spears to catch fish, crabs, lobsters, eels, and whale. They hunted fowl, beaver, and deer. Fish and meat were dried on racks or smoked, placed in cedar baskets, then stored in underground pits.

Clothing and adornment

Men generally wore breechcloths, garments with front and back flaps that hung from the waist that were often decorated with quillwork or embroidery. They donned animal-skin leggings and deerskin robes in cold weather. Women generally wore wraparound skirts with a belt. After European contact, they often wore dresses made from two skins sewn at the sides with straps at the shoulders.

Healing practices

Wampanoag religion and medicine went hand in hand. They believed angry spirits caused illness. Herbal treatments and sweat lodges (for ridding the body of poisons) were the remedies of choice. Various groups used different herbal treatments. Remedies were administered by shamans, those who had received visions in childhood telling them to become medicine people. The Aquinnah Wampanoag believed that snake oil would heal stiff joints, whereas other groups used ground wintergreen leaves mixed with animal grease for this purpose.

During King Philip's War, the Wampanoag and their allies used fire against Europeans because by then they knew them to be the disease-bearers. They had observed during the plague of 1617 that the Pequot and Narragansett came through with little damage. The Wampanoag believed the sickness stopped at Narragansett country because of a burning ceremony that destroyed all of the plague victims' belongings, a ceremony the Wampanoag did not then share.

Education

Wampanoag children learned mainly by observing. Girls watched women plant, prepare, and preserve food; prepare skins to make clothing; and weave baskets and mats. Boys learned endurance by running and by surviving cold, pain, and hunger.

Certain boys were chosen by the warrior council to undergo tests to determine their fitness as warriors. If they passed the first round of tests, they fasted (went without food and drink) and drank a special cleansing liquid that made them vomit. Warrior trainees learned to use war clubs and bows and arrows in close encounters with the enemy. They were

King Philip's Prophecy

The following is part of a speech given by King Philip to his counselors and warriors. A prophecy is an oral or written prediction of things to come.

> Brothers, you see this vast country before us, which the Great Spirit gave to our fathers and us; you see the buffalo and deer that now are our support. Brothers, you see these little ones, our wives and children, who are looking to us for food and raiment [clothing]; and you now see the foe before you, that they have grown insolent and bold; that all our ancient customs are disregarded; the treaties made by our fathers and us are broken, and all of us insulted; our council fires disregarded, and all the ancient customs of our fathers; our brothers murdered before our eyes, and their spirits cry to us for revenge. Brothers, these people from the unknown world will cut down our groves, spoil our hunting and planting grounds, and drive us and our children from the graves of our fathers, and our council fires, and enslave our women and children.

SOURCE: Apess, William. "Eulogy on King Philip, as Pronounced at the Odeon, in Federal Street, Boston." In *On Our Own Ground: The Complete Writings of William Apess, a Pequot.* Edited by Barry O'Connell. Amherst: University of Massachusetts Press, 1992.

taught the advantage of surprise and the techniques of silent ambush. If they passed this second more rigorous round of tests and were age sixteen or older, they became members of the warrior council, known and admired for their courage, strength, and wisdom.

During the assimilation movement, the U.S. government forced Natives to adopt white ways. Over the years the Wampanoag attempted to become like the neighboring whites and, as a result, gave up their language for English and changed their ways of life. In the early twenty-first century, Wampanoag children attended local public schools, but the tribe was working to revive the language and pass down traditional customs. To assist the Wampanoag in preserving their heritage, the Mashpee tribe opened a museum to educate the public as well as future generations of children about the tribe's history and culture.

ARTS

Through the years, the Wampanoag have retained their heritage by learning and practicing traditional crafts such as basketry, woodworking, and stone carving. The people made unusual pottery. They shaped the multicolored clays of Gay Head into pots, bowls, and jugs. They sometimes drew patterns into the clay with pieces of shell. The pottery was sunbaked because kiln firing dulled the colors.

CUSTOMS

Birth and naming

Children were prized by the Wampanoag. At birth, babies were given a "true" name and a nickname. True names were sacred and were known only to the immediate family and to village leaders.

Puberty

A boy who had not been chosen for warrior training (see "Education") underwent a ritual in which he was blindfolded, led into the forest, and left there alone. He had to survive for an entire winter using only his wits, a bow and arrow, a knife, and a hatchet. He sometimes had dreams; these were later explained by a medicine man or woman, who might decide from hearing about the dreams that the boy had the potential to become a medicine man himself.

Marriage

Men moved in with their wives' families after marriage. Wampanoag men sometimes chose wives from other tribes to make political alliances. Powerful chiefs sometimes married two or more wives.

War and hunting rituals

The Wampanoag went to war when wrongs were committed against them. If another tribe trespassed on their hunting or fishing territory or on an especially productive berry patch, they felt obligated to attack.

To prepare for battle, warriors painted their bodies black, red, green, or white. The colors came from charcoal or from berries and plants, so the choice of colors depended on what was in season. They held a war dance; sound effects included beating the ground with sticks and emitting piercing war cries. The tribe requested the help of the spirits to make the warriors quick and cunning. Warriors drank a tea made from juniper berries to help the blood clot in case they were wounded.

Once the Wampanoag engaged in battle, it was every man for himself. Warriors fought independently, seeking personal honor and glory. Those who distinguished themselves earned eagle feathers to wear in their hair. Sometimes the widow of a slain warrior took up his weapons and fought in his place.

Men sought the help of the spirits for a successful hunt. They set off with empty stomachs, because it gave them an incentive to find prey more quickly. The Wampanoag killed only what they needed, and they used every part of the catch. The bones of a slain beaver were returned to the stream from which it came, in the belief that the beaver would be reincarnated (come back to life) and able to be hunted again.

National Day of Mourning

Helen Attaquin (1923–1993), an Aquinnah Wampanoag, wrote that her people care most about preserving their culture, land base, and their right to make their own decisions as a separate nation. In recent years, the anniversaries of events such as the Pilgrim's landing and the first feast of thanksgiving have become opportunities for the Wampanoag and others to express their displeasure at the way their culture has been decimated. For example, in 1970, five hundred people responded to a protest call to "bury Plymouth Rock." The tribes called the event a National Day of Mourning, and Native American activist Frank Wamsutta James (1923–2001) gave a speech. In it he asked: "How can they expect us to sit and smile and eat turkey as they continue to dig up our graves and display our bones?"

Burial

The Wampanoag wrapped the dead in furs or grass mats and put their moccasins in their hands; food and other necessities were buried with the body for the journey through the afterworld. Mourners blackened their faces and held an evening burial ceremony. Afterward, the name of the deceased was never spoken again.

Festivals and Games

The tribe held a special weeklong celebration at harvest time to thank the spirits for the gift of food. Everyone gathered at the dance house for singing, dancing, feasting, and playing games. They placed a pot of corn on the fire, and its rising smoke joined the spirit powers where they dwelled.

The Aquinnah Wampanoag of Martha's Vineyard celebrate Cranberry Day on the second Tuesday in October. In earlier days, the medicine man or woman decided when the cranberries were ripe and informed the people. The harvest could take days or even weeks, depending on the size of the crop. The Aquinnah Wampanoag also hold a Spring Dance in April; the tribe's Noepe Cliff Singers and Dancers perform.

The Mashpee still play fireball, a traditional game that is played in the dark. A ball made of deerskin is set on fire, and players kick or throw the flaming ball past their opponents to score a goal.

CURRENT TRIBAL ISSUES

One of the Wampanoag's greatest difficulties results from living in a summer resort area. During warm weather, wealthy and famous tourists flock to the area, causing housing prices and other costs to soar. Many people struggle to pay for living quarters and often cannot afford the steep summer rental prices.

Because they are a federally recognized tribe, the Aquinnah Wampanoag qualify for government assistance to build subsidized housing for their people. This housing is affordable because payments are not fixed; they vary based on the owner's or renter's salary. People with low incomes pay less than those with more money. For more than a decade, the Aquinnah Wampanoag have also been trying to get government permission to build a casino that would bring in additional income to combat poverty.

After waiting almost twenty-five years, the Mashpee Wampanoag finally received federal recognition in 2007. This long process began in 1974, when they first filed their petition with the Bureau of Indian Affairs. Because they now have federal recognition, they are entitled to financial and other government help, including assistance that will allow them to build affordable housing. It also means that the U.S. government considers the Mashpee Wampanoag a sovereign (self-governing) nation.

Ever since the tribes received federal recognition, they have been trying to set up casinos. Initially, they were both competing for the same spot in Fall River, Massachusetts, but several potential deals fell through. A 2009 U.S. Supreme Court decision said that the government would only take land into trust for tribes that were recognized before 1934. That meant neither Wampanoag tribe qualified for trust land, which is usually needed to run a casino. In 2011, both tribes were looking for new options for opening gaming facilities.

Four other Wampanoag groups have received state recognition, but not federal recognition—Herring Pond Wampanoag Tribe, Pocasset Wampanoag Tribe, Seaconke Wampanoag Tribe, and Chappquiddick Tribe of the Wampanog Indian Nation. In 2010, the Pocasset Wampanoag Tribe expressed interest in putting a casino on their property at the Watuppa Reservation. They indicated that, because they own land in Fall River, the Mashpee should have consulted them about plans to build a casino in Fall River. The 2009 Supreme Court decision, however, raises the difficulty of any of these tribes getting their reservation land put in trust.

A one-dollar coin minted in 2011 shows the 1621 Treaty between the Wampanoag and the Pilgrims.

NOTABLE PEOPLE

Massasoit (c. 1580–1661) was a Wampanoag chief who encouraged friendship with British settlers in the early 1600s. Because of this, Massasoit was forced to wage frequent attacks against hostile Native groups not inclined to welcome the settlers. Massasoit eventually came to resent the Europeans' growing encroachment (taking over of land). His son, Metacomet (King Philip), turned resentment into war in 1675.

Weetamo (also spelled Weetamoo or Weetamoe; c. 1635–1676) led a group of warriors in battle in King Philip's War after the death of her first husband, Wamsutta. She was killed in a surprise attack on her village, and her naked body was found floating in a river. The Pilgrims beheaded her and posted her head on a pole alongside Metacomet's as a grisly warning to their enemies. Weetamo has become a romantic heroine in Native American lore.

Squanto (c. 1600–1622) was one of twenty Wampanoag from the village of Pautuxet who was kidnapped by British explorer Thomas Hunt in 1614 and sold as a slave in Spain. Rescued and set free, he made his way home, only to find that nearly his entire village had been wiped out in an epidemic. Squanto is remembered as the British-speaking guide and agricultural advisor to the Pilgrims at Plymouth colony.

BOOKS

Barron, Donna Gentle Spirit. *The Long Island Indians and Their New England Ancestors: Narragansett, Mohegan, Pequot & Wampanoag Tribes.* Bloomington, IN: AuthorHouse, 2006.

Breen, Betty, and Earl Mills, Sr. *Cape Cod Wampanoag Cookbook: Wampanoag Indian Recipes, Images & Lore.* Santa Fe, NM: Clear Light Books, 2001.

Carlson, Richard G., ed. *Rooted Like the Ash Trees: New England Indians and the Land.* Naugatuck, CT: Eagle Wing Press, 1987.

Cunningham, Kevin, and Peter Benoit. *The Wampanoag.* New York: Children's Press, 2011.

Cwiklik, Robert. *King Philip and the War with the Colonists.* Englewood Cliffs, NJ: Silver Burdette Press, 1989.

Dresser, Thomas. *The Wampanoag Tribe of Martha's Vineyard: Colonization to Recognition.* Charleston, SC: History Press, 2011.

Leibman, Laura Arnold. *Experience Mayhew's Indian Converts: A Cultural Edition.* Amherst: University of Massachusetts Press, 2008.

Levy, Janey. *The Wampanoag of Massachusetts and Rhode Island.* New York: PowerKids Press, 2005.

Moondancer and Strong Woman. *A Cultural History of the Native Peoples of Southern New England: Voices from Past and Present.* Newport, RI: Bauu Press, 2007.

Mwalim. *A Mixed Medicine Bag: Original Black Wampanoag Folklore.* Roxbury, MA: Talking Drum Press, 2007.

WEB SITES

Manning, June. "Wampanoag Living." *Martha's Vineyard Magazine.* May–June 2010. http://www.mvmagazine.com/article.php?25216 (accessed on June 9, 2011).

Mashpee Wampanoag Tribe. http://mashpeewampanoagtribe.com/ (accessed on June 1, 2011).

"Other Stories and Information." *Wampanoag Tribe of Gay Head.* http://www.wampanoagtribe.net/Pages/Wampanoag_Way/other (accessed on June 1, 2011).

Redish, Laura, and Orrin Lewis. "Native Languages of the Americas: Wampanoag (Massachusett, Natick, Massasoit, Nantucket, Mashpee)." *Native Languages of the Americas.* http://www.native-languages.org/wampanoag.htm (accessed on June 1, 2011).

Waabu O'Brien, Frank. "Bringing Back Our Lost Language." *New England Algonquian Language Revival.* http://www.bigorrin.org/waabu1.htm (accessed on June 1, 2011).

"The Wampanoag." *Boston Children's Museum.* http://www.bostonkids.org/educators/wampanoag/html/what.htm (accessed on June 1, 2011).

Wyandot (Huron)

Name

The people the French called the Huron (*HYUR-uhn*) went by the name Ouendat, or Wendat (*WHEN-duht* or *WHEN-dooht*), meaning "peninsula people." Ouendat has also been translated as "the one language" or "the one land apart." The Wendat were later called Wyandot (pronounced *WHY-an-dot*). Other variations of the tribal name include Guyandot and Guyandotte.

The name Huron most likely came from the French word *hure*, sometimes translated as "boar's head" or "shock of hair." The Europeans could have been comparing the Huron hairstyles to the bristles on a boar's head (see "Clothing and adornment"). Another possibility is that the name is from the French word *huron*, which meant either "rough" or "ruffian." In either case, many people now see the name *Huron* as derogatory, although the present-day Canadian First Nation is known as Huron-Wendat. Groups in Kansas and Michigan use the name Wyandot. Those who moved to Oklahoma adopted the spelling of Wyandotte.

Location

Wyandot tradition states that their original home was between the coast of Labrador and James Bay. As they moved south, their history indicates they took over the northern bank of the St. Lawrence River. Their next moves were to the south shore of Lake Ontario and to Niagara Falls. Under pressure from the Iroquois (see entry), they migrated north from present-day Toronto.

Archaeological evidence shows that prior to European contact, the people had established large villages along the north shore of Lake Ontario. Their trading empire stretched throughout Ontario and parts of Quebec, and some lived as far south as West Virginia. In the 1600s, the majority lived west of Lake Simcoe and east of Georgian Bay. Attacks by the Iroquois scattered the tribe to Quebec and the Great Lakes states. The Huron-Wendat relocated several times before settling outside Quebec City, Canada. Other Wyandot groups went west to Michigan, Wisconsin, Illinois, and Ohio. Most of the people were later forced into eastern Kansas and then Oklahoma, two states where many still live.

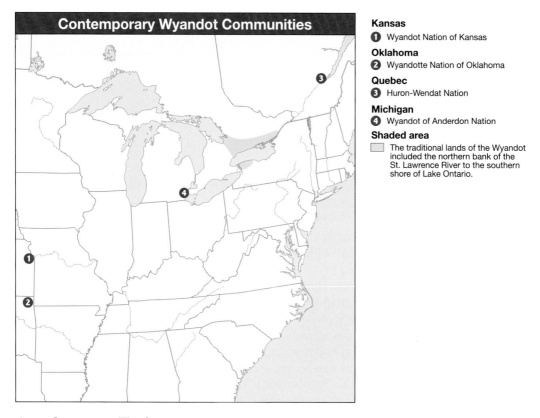

Contemporary Wyandot Communities

Kansas
1 Wyandot Nation of Kansas

Oklahoma
2 Wyandotte Nation of Oklahoma

Quebec
3 Huron-Wendat Nation

Michigan
4 Wyandot of Anderdon Nation

Shaded area
☐ The traditional lands of the Wyandot included the northern bank of the St. Lawrence River to the southern shore of Lake Ontario.

A map of contemporary Wyandot communities. MAP BY XNR PRODUCTIONS. CENGAGE LEARNING, GALE. REPRODUCED BY PERMISSION OF GALE, A PART OF CENGAGE LEARNING.

Population

In the early 1600s, the Wendat population numbered between 18,000 to 30,000. A census taken in 1639, following a smallpox epidemic, indicated that there were fewer than 12,000 people, but the census takers had also counted the nine villages of the Petun. Experts estimate that the Wendat accounted for about three-fourths of that number, or about 9,000. Disease, starvation, and war further decimated the population. Now called Wyandot, approximately 1,000 people fled to present-day Michigan and Wisconsin with the Neutrals and Tionontati; others were adopted into the Iroquois Confederacy. By the early 1800s, fewer than 200 Huron-Wendat people lived in Canada. In 1908, this count had risen to 466 people. By 1994, the population had reached 2,650, and in 2009, Canada recorded 3029 registered Huron-Wyandot. By 2010, the Wyandot and Wyandotte in the United States numbered about 5,500.

Language family

Iroquoian.

Origins and group affiliations

The Wendat (or Huron) Confederacy was composed of four or five closely allied groups. The Attignawantan (People of the Bear) and the Attigneenon-gnahac (People of the Cord or Barking Dogs) were the first to unite during the 1400s. They were later joined by the Arendarhonon (People of the Rock) and the Tahontaenrat (People of the Deer). Some sources indicate that the Ataronchronon (People of the Marshes or Bog) were also part of the confederacy.

Some experts suggest that the Wyandot are related to the Algonquin as well as to the Iroquois and that their language is linked to that of the Dakota (see entry). The Wyandot were closely connected to the Tionontati (called the *Petun*, or Tobacco People, by the French), the Erie, and the Neutral nations. All of these groups had a common enemy in the Iroquois, so they fought as allies and at times lived together when fleeing Iroquois attacks. The Wendat Confederacy also had close relations with the Nipissing, Ottawa (see entry), and Algonquin bands in the Ottawa Valley. The Wyandot were part of the Seven Nations of Canada, or the Seven Fires, a group of tribes who switched their allegiance from the French to the British in 1760. Prior to that, the Wyandot had served as intermediaries in trade between the French and other northeastern tribes.

Ancestors of the Wendat, as the people were called then, lived in present-day Ontario from about 500 CE on. In the 1400s, they formed a powerful confederacy that allowed them, following the European arrival in 1609, to dominate the French fur trade as middlemen for many of the northeastern tribes. In 1649, their main rivals, the Iroquois, armed with guns by the Dutch, exacted revenge and destroyed the confederacy. After losing their homeland Ouendake or Wendake (later called Huronia), remnants of the Huron-Wendat, now called Wyandot, along with several allies, scattered to Lorette, Canada, or to the northern and midwestern United States. In 1999, the groups reunited as the Wendat Confederacy.

HISTORY

Wendat (Huron) confederacy

For about five hundred years, the people lived by hunting and gathering, but by 1000, they had begun to farm. Their first crop, corn, was followed by sunflowers for oil and later by beans and squash over the next few centuries. By the early 1400s, two groups—Attignawantan

Important Dates

1400s: Two tribes unite to start the Wendat Confederacy.

1614: The Wendat sign a formal trade agreement with the French.

1649: Iroquois force the Wendat from their homeland. The Wendat flee with the Tionontati, and they take the name Wyandot.

1697: Huron-Wendat settle at Jeune Lorette.

1842: The Wyandot are the last tribe to give up their land in Ohio.

1867: U.S. government recognizes the Wyandotte Tribe of Oklahoma.

1985: U.S. government pays Wyandot $5.5 million for land claims.

1999: Wendat Confederacy is reestablished.

(People of the Bear) and the Attigneenongnahac (People of the Cord or Barking Dogs)—had united to form the Wendat (Huron) Confederacy, the first of the Iroquoian confederacies in the region.

Later, two groups who had been living along the St. Lawrence River between Montreal and Quebec became part of the confederacy. In the late 1500s, the first of these bands, the Arendarhonon (People of the Rock), joined them, followed by the Tahontaenrat (People of the Deer) a decade later. The Ataronchronon (People of the Marshes or Bog) are often listed as a fifth member of the confederacy, but they may have been a sub-tribe of the Attignawantan, the largest group in the confederacy, who also took a leadership role.

This political alliance, advantageous for both trade and defense, also allowed the member nations to resolve differences and make joint decisions. Because of the emphasis the tribes placed on autonomy, participation in confederacy decisions was voluntary. Each band sent representatives to the joint council at the village of Ossossane but maintained its own identity, traditions, and territory.

Arrival of the europeans

The early 1600s saw a flurry of European activity as newly arrived French missionaries and traders competed for Wendat loyalty. It was at this time that the Europeans began calling the Wendat "Huron." In 1610, the French explorer Samuel de Champlain (c. 1567–1635) sent young Étienne Brûlé (c. 1592–1633) to the area to train as an interpreter. The French wanted to enlist the powerful Wendat Confederacy as a partner in their fur-trading ventures. The Wendat formalized this alliance with the French at Quebec in 1614. As part of the trading agreements, the French promised to support the confederacy's ongoing battles with the Iroquois (see entry). In 1615, Champlain kept that promise by joining an attack on the Onondaga and Oneida to the south.

Earlier that same year, the first Catholic missionary, Joseph Le Caron (1586–1632), arrived. Over the next decades, several other missionaries followed, including Gabriel Sagard and Jean de Brébeuf (1593–1649), who supervised the first settlement in Ontario, Sainte-Marie. The priests met with much resistance at first, but after epidemics of smallpox and measles killed many people between 1635 and 1640, some families turned to Christianity. Others held Europeans responsible for the deaths and wanted to drive the missionaries out. This issue caused conflict among the Wendat Confederacy, but the members remained unified about trade.

Iroquois fight back

With French backing, the Wendat gained control of the fur trade along the St. Lawrence River. As the number of beaver decreased in their homeland, the Wendat established relationships with surrounding tribes, who traded furs in exchange for crops and European goods. The Iroquois Confederacy, who had no such advantage, supplied the Dutch with beaver pelts. By the 1640s, however, the Iroquois had obtained guns, which they used to gain the upper hand.

Skirmishes and surprise attacks between the two confederacies and their allies intensified throughout that decade and led to the Beaver Wars (1648–57). For the Wendat, these raids culminated in two deadly attacks in 1649. The Iroquois set the mission village of St. Ignace afire while the Wendat slept. They then proceeded to do the same to St. Louis, another mission village nearby. Those whom the Iroquois did not take prisoner, they massacred, including Fathers Gabriel Lalemant and Brébeuf. It is said that Brébeuf endured the torture so courageously that the Iroquois ate his heart and drank his blood in tribute.

The Confederacy scatters

The remaining Wendat fled, accompanied by the Jesuits and French. Some headed to Georgian Bay, while others sought refuge with other groups, including the Petun, Neutral, Erie, and Ottawa (see entry). More than six thousand Wendat and French spent the winter on Gahoendoe (Christian) Island in Georgian Bay, where thousands died of starvation and disease. That June, many of the survivors set out for Quebec. Some who wintered on different islands as well as refugees from other bands attacked by the Iroquois straggled to Quebec during the next year.

Some Wendat settled on Ile d'Orléans, but after a Mohawk (see entry) attack, they negotiated a peace treaty with the Iroquois Confederacy. As part of the terms, various Iroquois bands adopted some of the Wendat, although the Onondaga massacred the male captives who joined them. The remaining Quebec Wendat spent the next several decades moving from place to place until they reached Jeune Lorette. Because the soil there was too sandy for crops, they turned from farming to manufacturing. Now called the Huron-Wendat, they continue to produce goods on their Wendake Reserve.

Wyandots flee to United States

Meanwhile the Iroquois continued to stalk and attack the Attignawantan who had joined the Tionontati. After the Iroquois destroyed their village, the two bands fled to Mackinac Island in present-day Michigan. From that point on, this union of Attignawantan and Tionontati, who may have been kin, went by the name of Wyandot. Along with the Ottawa, the Wyandot retreated to Rock Island in Green Bay (present-day Wisconsin) on Lake Michigan. Under continuing pressure from the Iroquois, the Wyandot and Ottawa moved inland to the Mississippi River and then migrated north to Chequamegon (Wisconsin) on Lake Superior, which was Lakota (see entry) territory. There the Wyandot resumed the French fur trade.

A palisade fence, the type of which the Wyandot used to defend against invaders, stands on the grounds of the museum at the former settlement at Sainte-Marie Among the Hurons in Midland, Ontario, Canada. © DEREK GALE/ALAMY.

After an attack led by Alexandre de Prouville, the Marquis de Tracy (c. 1603–1670), the Iroquois signed a peace treaty in 1667 that lasted for twenty years. The Wyandot conflicts had not ended, however. Difficulties with the Lakota meant a move to Michilimackinac (present-day Michigan) a few years later. To protect themselves, they built their town on a promontory, or a high point of land jutting out into the water, and surrounded it with twenty-five-foot-high palisades. Palisades are fences made of wooden stakes. These defenses could not protect them from a traitor. In 1686, a Wyandot betrayed a hunting party of his people to the Iroquois, ending the peace. Hostilities began anew, and the Wyandot and Ottawa moved south to Detroit in 1701. Some Wyandot settled in Ohio on the south shore of Lake Erie or on the Sandusky plains in 1730.

The war years

Divisions among tribal members around the time of King George's War (1744–48) almost led to a Wyandot civil war. The clan mothers intervened to stop it, but hostilities led some members to break off and set up another village. This group later moved to the White River in Indiana.

After 1740, the Wyandot switched allegiance several times as Ohio Country became caught up in various wars between the French, British, and Americans. Land claims in the area were also hotly contested, with the Europeans and Americans all laying claim to Ohio. The many tribes in the area, although they allied themselves with the British or French for trading or during war, believed the land belonged to them.

Loss of territory

Battles ensued, and treaties were made and broken. Following several treaties that moved the Wyandot ever farther west, the Americans, who wanted the land to pay debts incurred during the Revolutionary War, attacked the Ohio tribes. Although the allied tribes achieved some major victories, General Anthony Wayne (1745–1796) defeated them at the Battle of Fallen Timbers in 1794. The Wyandot ceded all of their land except Sandusky and Detroit in the Treaty of Greenville in 1795. A series of treaties in the early 1800s resulted in the loss of even more property.

After the bitter defeat, whiskey and tribal disharmony caused major problems for the people. During the War of 1812 (1812–15), some sided with the United States, others with the British. When the war ended, the British supporters stayed at Anderdon in Ontario. The pro-American Wyandot signed additional treaties, including one in 1817 giving up their land along Lake Erie for the Grand Reserve, twelve square miles at Upper Sandusky, and the Cranberry Reserve, a one-mile-square tract on a cranberry swamp.

In 1818, two additional treaties granted the Wyandot a few extra miles for the Grand Reserve and added a reserve at Big Springs. In return the Michigan Wyandot had to give up their capital at Brownstown. A Congress passed the Indian Removal Act in 1930, and by 1842, the Wyandot had sold their lands in Ohio and Michigan. The last tribe to leave Ohio, the Wyandot ended up in Kansas, where they purchased part of a reservation from the Delaware.

"Citizen" vs. "Indian" tribes

Although 664 Wyandot left Ohio in 1845, government approval for the land purchase did not come until 1848. Two years later, a delegation went to Washington, D.C., to negotiate a new treaty, giving up their claim to the 148,000 acres that they had been promised. Instead, they had decided to become citizens and accept individual land allotments. Although some Wyandot opposed it, the treaty went through, and the people no longer had their tribal status. Many Wyandot lost their property during the financial hardships of the American Civil War (1861–65). The issue of slavery also divided the group at this time, as some were slaveholders while others were abolitionists.

In 1867, the government gave the Wyandot a reservation in present-day Oklahoma. The traditional part of the tribe went to Oklahoma and petitioned to regain their tribal status as the Wyandotte Tribe of Oklahoma. They received recognition that year, and the government gave them permission to purchase 20,000 acres between the Neosho River and the Missouri state line for their reserve. The Wyandotte no longer considered the "absentee" or "citizen" Wyandot in Kansas as members of the tribe. The absentees could rejoin the tribe only if someone adopted them or if they received special permission. For more than a century, relationships were strained between the two groups, sometimes called the "Citizen" and "Indian" parties, referring to the choices they made to become citizens (Kansas Wyandot) or to remain part of the traditional tribe (Oklahoma Wyandotte).

Recognition and reconciliation

In 1950, the U.S. government terminated the Wyandotte Tribe of Oklahoma, which had been created in 1937, but the tribe was later recognized in 1978. In 1985, the U.S. government paid Wyandot descendants the sum of $5.5 million. The money was compensation for tribal land the government took in 1842. At that time, the property had been worth $1.50 per acre, but the government had only paid the Wyandot seventy-five cents per acre. In the early 1990s, the Wyandot Nation of Kansas, incorporated in 1959, began petitioning for federal recognition.

In 1999, the Wyandot Nation of Kansas, Wyandotte Nation of Oklahoma, Wyandot Nation of Anderdon (Trenton, Michigan), and the Huron-Wendat of Wendake (Quebec, Canada) met in Midland, Ontario. The four nations came together in their historic homeland to celebrate the 350th anniversary of their dispersion from Ontario and Quebec. They participated in a ceremony of reconciliation on June 4 and 5, the first step in reforming the Wendat Confederacy, which was reaffirmed on August 27, 1999.

RELIGION

Traditional beliefs

The Wendat believed that everything in nature, both animate or inanimate, had a spirit. They called the most powerful of these spirits *oki*. This name also applied to their shamans (pronounced *SHAH-munz* or *SHAY-munz*), or healers, as well as to mighty warriors and even people they considered mad, or crazy. The sky, with its ability to control the weather, was the dominant *oki*, followed by the moon and sun. Water, too, held a position of importance. To win favor with these spirits, the people held dances and feasts, offered tobacco, and at times sacrificed enemy prisoners.

Animals also had spirits, and the people believed that each clan had descended from the animal for which it was named. The Wendat creation myth stated that Big Turtle had made Great Island (North America) and carried it on his back. Little Turtle created the sun, moon, and most stars. Mud Turtle made the happy hunting grounds, or afterlife, and the hole in the earth that the sun rises through after it has set at night. To show respect for animals, the people treated animal bones with care. They never burned them or fed them to dogs.

Huron-Wendat Words

Kweh (pronounced kway) is used to greet people. *Tizameh* (pronounced tih-zhuh-may) is "thank you." Some other Huron-Wendat words are:

anue	"bear"
yeentso	"fish"
yunyenoh	"dog"
oughscanoto	"deer"
skat	"one"
tindee	"two"
shenk	"three"

Conversion to Christianity

French missionaries, who arrived in the early 1600s, wrote that the people respected the Catholic religion, but most did not convert. Following deadly epidemics that killed many of their people, more of them became Christians, believing it might keep them safe. In letters to their superiors, though, the missionaries despaired because the converts still practiced their traditional religion along with Christianity. Many traditional Wendat rejected Catholicism and wanted to expel the missionaries because they blamed them for the epidemics.

By the twentieth century, most Huron-Wendat in Canada had become Catholics. Methodists, who began the first transcontinental mission in America in the 1930s, converted many Wyandot in the United States.

LANGUAGE

The members of the Wendat Confederacy spoke related dialects of the Iroquoian language. Because the Wendat served as intermediaries in the fur trade, the French and any tribes who supplied the confederacy with furs used the Wendat language to communicate with each other. Although the last native speakers died in the 1960s, the language was recorded in many dictionaries during the 1600s and 1700s. Words can be written with the regular twenty-six-letter alphabet and two additional letters, but sometimes a special font is used. Anthropologist John Steckley, a non-Native, used his collection of centuries-old dictionaries to teach himself the language. The Huron-Wendat now speak French, whereas the Wyandot/Wyandotte speak English. Both the Wyandotte in Oklahoma and the Huron-Wendat in Quebec have developed programs to keep their native language alive.

GOVERNMENT

Early government

The Wendat government operated on several levels. The first was the clan level. Each of the twelve clans had a council with a chief. These five-person councils had at least four women on them. This group decided any issues that were clan-related and selected the clan chief, an office that could be hereditary but was also subject to group approval. The next level, the tribal council, consisted of clan chiefs, the sachem (elders), and any men who had been invited to the council fire.

Each clan had both a civil chief and a war chief, and the people could replace any chief who did not do his duty. The new chief took over the titles, regalia, and name of his predecessor. A civil chief was known for his wisdom, generosity, and speaking ability. The civil council met in the longhouse, and any man of over thirty years old could attend. War chiefs met privately outside the village and kept their plans secret. The leadership of the Wendat Confederacy council was composed of chiefs from each village.

At all councils, votes were taken by clan, and before a decision was adopted, all members had to agree. A French writer once commented that the decision-making process was lengthy because everyone at a council could have a say. Before each person expressed an opinion, he had to summarize all the arguments others had made to that point. The discussion continued until all present could agree. Although the process was democratic, the suggestions of sachems or other influential leaders could carry more weight, and eloquent speakers could sway the crowd. Because the Wendat believed in autonomy, no one was bound by the council decisions. If individuals, clans, or villages disagreed with a ruling, they were free to disregard it.

Ancient Clans

The twelve original clans are listed below. The ones with asterisks are still in existence.

Big Turtle*
Little Turtle*
Mud Turtle
Wolf*
Bear*
Beaver
Deer*
Porcupine*
Striped Turtle
Highland Turtle, or Prairie Turtle
Snake*
Hawk

When the warriors marched, the Wolf clan took charge and positioned themselves wherever they felt they were most needed. The rest of the clans marched in order of the list, with the Big Turtle clan in the lead.

Encampments formed a pattern that resembled a turtle. The Wolf clan again had their choice of positions, either in the center of the shell or at the turtle's head. The Big Turtle clan occupied the right foreleg spot, with the others ranged around in order. This pattern was followed in building ancient villages and in council seating. The sachem sat either in the center or by the door.

Crime and punishment

Only two crimes were punishable by death—treason and stinginess. People believed these two offenses harmed the whole tribe, so they dealt with them harshly. Anyone in the tribe was free to murder a person convicted of either crime without penalty. Other punishments required the criminal to make restitution to the victim. In the case of murder, a criminal might be tied to the victim's corpse as it rotted if the criminal's family did not pay enough in restitution.

Wyandot constitution

When the Wyandot of Kansas wrote their constitution in 1873, they used a similar structure for setting up their government. Each group of three clans selects one of their chiefs as principal chief to represent all three clans. The person receiving the next highest number of votes is secondary chief. The Wolf clan elects a mediator.

ECONOMY

Agriculture

Once hunter-gatherers, the Wendat settled into farming around 1100. Their major crop was corn, followed over the next few centuries by beans, squash, and tobacco. Every ten to twenty years, they relocated their villages as the quality of the soil declined.

Trade

After the arrival of the Europeans, the tribes switched to a trading economy, and they soon became the middlemen between the French and other northeastern tribes. Pelts were not their only goods; they also traded corn, tobacco, dried berries, fish, wampum beads, mats, and hemp.

Their extensive trade routes ran throughout the St. Lawrence and Great Lakes region. The person who constructed each route and his descendants held the right to control passage through it. People of his own tribe paid a fee to use the path, whereas outsiders from other tribes were forbidden to travel on it.

Goods were also transported along the extensive river systems in the area. The Wendat's birchbark canoes gave them an advantage over their major rivals in the fur trade, the Iroquois, who had heavier elmwood canoes. Even after the Iroquois destroyed Ouendake, the Wendat managed to continue their trading relationships, first with the French and then later with the British.

Manufacturing

The Huron-Wendat who settled in Jeune Lorette lost their hunting and fishing territory in 1701. The land there was not suitable for farming, so they turned to manufacturing to make their livings. They continue to produce traditional goods, such as canoes, moccasins, and snowshoes, on their reserve into the twenty-first century.

DAILY LIFE

Families

Clan members were like cousins and could not marry each other. In the early history of the tribes, only certain clans could intermarry. Property and clan identity passed down through the mother's side, which meant children were always of a different clan from their fathers. With many extended families living together in a longhouse, adults were expected to provide role models for the children. Children were never scolded or punished, because the Wyandot believed it was wrong to humiliate anyone, especially the young. Parents were very affectionate to their children, and aunts often became like second mothers.

Buildings

Most villages were built on higher ground for defense, and palisades, or rows of pointed stakes up to five deep, surrounded the larger villages. The Wendat built their homes near water and trees, which were necessary for firewood and building material. Good soil for farming was also important. Once the soil and resources were gone in an area, the people moved to a new location. This usually happened every ten to twenty years.

Most villages had about eight hundred people. Larger settlements might have up to one hundred longhouses with two thousand or more inhabitants. Between six to twenty-four families lived in each longhouse. Most families had about six members. Women oversaw the longhouses,

Indian Trade Whiskey

When the Europeans arrived, they introduced alcohol to the tribes. Alcohol was used as a bribe or as trade goods. Other times the Europeans tried to get the Natives drunk to incite them to violence against an enemy or to get them to sign a treaty. The ingredients in this recipe might explain why the Indians often called it "*fire* water."

>   1 Handfull red peppers
>   1 Qt. Black molasses
>   Missouri River Water (as required)
>   1 Qt. Alcohol
>   1 lb. Rank Black Chewing Tobacco
>   1 Bottle Jamaica Ginger

The pepper and tobacco were boiled together. When cool other ingredients were added and stirred. As the Indian became drunk, more water was added.

SOURCE: "Indian Trade Whiskey." *Kansas City Museum*. http://www.wyandot.org/whiskey.htm (accessed June 10, 2011).

A Wyandot Cradle Song

Born in 1870, Hen-Toh was the great-nephew of William Walker, a Wyandot chief who later became Nebraska Territory's provisional (temporary) governor. When B.N.O. Walker, or Hen-Toh, was four years old, his family was removed from Kansas. He was raised in northeastern Missouri's Indian Territory. During his lifetime, he made it his mission to preserve Wyandot culture and oral traditions in writing. Hen-Toh recorded the stories and songs that he had heard as he was growing up so that they would not be forgotten by future generations.

Wyandot mothers sang this lullaby to their babies, who slept in cradleboards. *Tsa-du-meh* means "mother." In this lullaby, the word for "father" is *Hi-a-stah*.

> Hush thee and sleep, little one,
> The feathers on thy board sway to and fro;
> The shadows reach far downward in
>   the water
> The great old owl is waking, day will go.

Rest thee and fear not, little one,
Flitting fireflies come to light you on
  your way
To the fair land of dreams, while in the
  grasses
The happy cricket chirps his merry lay.

Tsa-du-meh watches always o'er her
  little one,
The great owl cannot harm you, slumber on
'Till the pale light comes shooting from
  the eastward,
And the twitter of the birds says night
  has gone.

SOURCE: Hen-Toh (Bertrand Nicholas Oliver Walker). "A Wyandot Cradle Song." *Yon-Doo-Shah-Weah (Nubbins)*. Oklahoma City: Harlow Publishing Company, 1924. Available online from *American Native Press Archives and Sequoyah Research Center*. http://anpa.ualr.edu/digital_library/henyond/henyond.htm (accessed May 10, 2011).

and all the families worked together. Usually the senior matron of the clan was in charge.

Longhouses ranged from 25 to 30 feet wide (8 to 9 meters) and could be 100 to 240 feet (30 to 75 meters) long. Some even reached 295 feet (90 meters). Longhouses were made of sheets of cedar, ash, or elm bark woven onto arched pole frames. Houses had vaulted roofs with holes in them to let out smoke from the fires in the center of the longhouse. Bark or skins closed off door and roof openings when needed.

Each end of the house usually had storage for corn and firewood, and pits were dug in the floor for additional storage. Food and clothing hung from poles. In the summer everyone used the long sleeping platforms on either side of the house, but in the winter, they slept close to the fire. Life inside a longhouse was smoky, and fleas and mice were common.

Clothing and adornment

Because they were plentiful, deer and beaver hides were used for clothing. Both men and women wore sleeveless fringed tunics of deerskin. When the weather turned cold, they added sleeves, held in place by straps across the back. A belt under the tunic held leg coverings in place. Women also wore skirts. Robes, often worn fur-side in, kept them warm, with black fox being the most popular fur. Men carried decorated shoulder purses. Moccasins, which had flaps and gathered toes, were covered with cornhusks when it was muddy or snowy. Snowshoes were a necessity for winter travel.

In the summer, warriors wore fringed kilts or breechclouts that hung down almost to their knees. They sported one upright feather and a hanging feather, with a cluster of small feathers. Chiefs might have a feathered cap.

For special occasions, the Wyandot wore finger-woven sashes and clothing of blackened buckskin. Outfits were painted with red designs and often had red borders, more so after cloth replaced the skins. Decorative designs of porcupine quillwork or dyed moose hair embroidery were popular. The Huron-Wendat in Canada still make moose hair decorations and rosettes.

Women often had one braid and decorated their hair with bone combs, wampum, or glass beads. Because the Wyandot valued individuality, men wore different hairstyles. Some men had Mohawks with porcupine roaches, or tufts of stiff animal hair, attached. Only men painted and tattooed their bodies.

Food

The growing season was short, about three and a half months, so the Wyandot planted corn that ripened in 90 to 120 days. Villages were often clustered inside a surrounding cornfield. By the early 1600s, the people had about seven thousand acres of corn. It was the main ingredient in soups and sagamite, a corn porridge. Women also pounded corn into flour to make bread. Other staple foods included beans, squash, pumpkins, and sunflowers for oil. In addition to tending these crops, women gathered bulrush roots, maple sap, nuts, berries, and other fruits. During famines, the people ate acorns.

Men hunted for game, such as deer and birds. Beaver were valuable for their pelts and for their meat. Sometimes the men trapped and fattened bears for special feasts. The people also ate domesticated dogs. Fish was part of their diet along with other shore creatures, such as turtles, crabs, and clams. Men caught whitefish, pike, sturgeon, catfish, and trout with nets, bonehead spears, or weirs (traps under the water). To preserve them, the fish were smoked and dried.

Education

Children received little formal training, but they were taught to be patient and endure hardship, to control their emotions, and to be kind to others. Girls helped their mothers with chores, whereas boys learned to hunt and fish. Boys were trained to be brave and to save their anger for war. They developed their courage by burning or cutting themselves.

Beginning in the 1600s, the French pressured parents to send their boys to the religious orders. In 1867, the Canadian government took control of Indian education under the British North America Act and sent the children to boarding schools run by religious institutions. Abuse, both physical and sexual, was a problem at many schools. Many children died from diseases that spread rapidly through the schools.

During the 1960s, as the government became less involved in native schooling, welfare agencies took many children from their families and sent them to adoption organizations. Many children never saw their parents again.

Healing practices

Three causes of illnesses The Wyandot claimed illness had three main sources: natural causes, witchcraft, and desires of the soul. A medicine man cured problems stemming from natural causes, such as arrow wounds, with herbs, poultices, sweating, and good advice. More than 275 plants were used as medicines, including wild sarsaparilla for open sores and turnip roots for colds. The French were surprised to discover that the Native people's knowledge of medicine and surgery was superior to their own. If the patient did not respond to the prescribed treatment, an *ontetsan*, or religious healer, was called in, because the people believed witchcraft had caused any lingering illness.

The third cause of illness was unfulfilled personal desires. The Wyandot believed suppressing these longings led to illness or madness. To resolve these cases, the healer first discovered what the patient needed through dream interpretation. Then the healer found someone who owned that object and gave it to the patient.

Duties of a healer *Ontetsan* had several different functions: foretelling the future, controlling the weather, healing the sick, and finding lost items. They interpreted the dreams of others and used their own visions and dreams to find solutions to problems. In addition to prescribing feasts, dances, and games, they told people how to conduct their lives. Most often men were healers, and women took charge of spiritual problems.

The *ontetsan* used magic, spells, feasts, and dances to combat witchcraft and also had the power to identify the witch who had cast the spell. Because witchcraft was punishable by death, some chiefs used this to get rid of those they considered undesirable.

Healing rituals The tribe had a three-day feast called *Ononharoia* that centered on healing unfulfilled desires. Often this feast was held when a well-known person became ill. People pretended to be crazy and demanded things they said they had dreamed about, but they did it in riddles. The owner of the object gave them whatever they asked for. On the last day, everyone went into the woods to get rid of their craziness. The feast benefited people by sharing the tribe's wealth. It also helped the participants get rid of negative emotions.

Curing societies were also of major importance in helping the sick. Members of the societies either inherited their powers or received them in dreams. One society used the Dance of Fire to heal illness. As they danced, these healers stuck their hands into boiling water or put burning coals in their mouths. Other societies had different rituals for ridding people of illness.

ARTS

Traditional arts included beadwork, pottery, basket making, weaving, and woodworking. Wampum belts were created from beads made of shell. The designs had special meanings and were often used to commemorate a special event, such as the signing of a peace treaty.

Women wove baskets, nets, and mats out of the hemp they gathered. Reeds, bark, and cornhusks were also used to create crafts. Baskets and leather bags were painted or decorated with porcupine quillwork.

Men carved wooden bowls, utensils, and shields. They also made stone tools and stone or clay pipes. The Huron-Wendat in Canada still make many traditional crafts, such as pottery, birchbark canoes, snowshoes, and moccasins.

CUSTOMS

Birth and naming

Children did not belong first to their parents, but to the clan, so the clan named each baby. Each clan had a list of appropriate names that represented characteristics of the animal from which its members had descended. When someone died, the next child of that gender born into the clan received that name. If, however, a child had an unusual mark or feature or strange occurrences were connected with the birth, the women of the council came up with a name that fit. These special names were not passed on to another child when the person died. Names were given at the Green Corn Feast each year, and babies had their ears pierced when they were named.

Puberty

Young men fasted for up to thirty days in a special shelter. Sometimes a section of the longhouse was partitioned off for that purpose. During that time, they hoped to receive special powers or abilities in a vision. The dream spirit that came to them would teach them how to access this gift through songs or rituals.

Marriage

Teens could have premarital sexual relations as long as they had them at night or in a private place. They could not have relationships with anyone from their mothers' clan or any close relatives on their father's side, including first cousins. Some young couples later married. Others lived together and were free to have other relationships. Couples did not have to marry, but if they did, they stayed monogamous.

Before a couple could marry, the man and the woman as well as both sets of parents had to agree to the union. Most parents wanted prestigious marriages for their children. The girl's parents usually evaluated the prospective husband to be sure he would be a powerful warrior and good hunter.

Divorce

Either person could initiate a divorce. If a wife asked her husband to leave, he took only his clothes with him. If a man wanted a divorce, he told his wife. He also informed her parents, because the couple usually lived with them. Because inheritance passed down through the mother's side, property belonged to the women. Many young couples got divorced, but divorce was rare after the couple had children. When children were involved, relatives tried to help the couple resolve differences.

Death and afterlife

Funeral rituals When someone died, the Wyandot wrapped the body in a fur robe and placed it on a mat in a flexed position. For several days, another clan watched over the body while people gave speeches about the dead person's virtues. On the third day, a feast was held with the departed's spirit in attendance. People heaped expensive gifts on the dead person. Most of these gifts went to the bereaved or to those who helped with the funeral. Some bodies were placed on a scaffold high above the ground with some of the grave goods, but warriors were buried and a shrine was placed over the grave.

Feast of the Dead Every eight to twelve years, all the bodies were dug up for the Feast of the Dead. Women cleaned the flesh off the bones and burned it, unless the person had died recently. They wrapped the bones or bodies in beaver robes to carry them to the village where the feast was held. All the villages celebrated together and used a common grave, which was a large pit lined with beaver robes.

At the site young men and women competed in funeral games, such as archery, and mourners offered prizes in honor of their dead relatives. After a display of grave goods and other rituals, the whole bodies went in first, and then villages took turns putting in bones and grave goods. Some of the items were broken to release the souls of the objects, so they could accompany the dead on their journey to the afterlife. Not all gifts went into the grave. Some were given to the relatives of deceased. Then the pit was covered with mats, bark, and sand, which were then weighted down with logs.

Beliefs about the afterlife The Wyandot believed that a person had two spirits. One departed for the village of the dead after the feast. Each tribe had a village of the dead in the direction of the setting sun. The people believed the souls gathered there in beaver robes, carrying their grave goods, and traveled on a path to the Milky Way. Souls of dogs went there, too. The trip took them past a head-piercer who took out their brains. They walked across a log over raging river that was guarded by a fierce dog. If the dog scared them, they fell off the log and drowned. After many months, the dead arrived in a new village and lived life as they had in their previous village.

The second soul stayed near the corpse until the Feast of the Dead and then was released so it could be reborn. These souls were resurrected in the name-giving ceremonies for babies or for people adopted from other tribes.

War and warriors

Young boys were trained to use weapons. They proved their endurance by burning their flesh with flaming sticks or cutting themselves. To show their courage, young men had to sneak into an enemy village and capture a prisoner or take a scalp. The scalps were hung from poles to confirm a warrior's skill.

The Wyandot preferred to make surprise attacks on the Iroquois, their sworn enemy. At times the tribe laid siege to a village to force the enemy to come out and fight. After a battle, the Wyandot bound the wounds of the injured, who were then carried in baskets on the backs of young warriors. Heavily guarded until everyone returned to the village, prisoners were either tortured or adopted into the tribe.

Games and Ceremonies

Favorite pastimes Games were held for pleasure, as a response to a dream, or to cure illness. Some of the most popular were gambling games. Both the players and the spectators bet, often wagering everything they owned or even their families. Baggattaway, a game like lacrosse, was another sport the people enjoyed. Village teams played against each other or against teams from other villages. Some of the many other sports that the tribe enjoyed were spear-throwing, wrestling, archery, and racing. Both foot races and canoe races were held. Other games included birchbark cards, dice, cat's cradle, and snowsnake, in which participants competed to slide a carved stick the farthest across the crusted snow.

A young man wearing traditional Huron-Wendat dress and face paint participates in a dance contest at the Wendake Powwow.
© FRANCIS VACHON/ALAMY.

Feasts and dances The Wyandot celebrated four main kinds of feasts: healing, gratitude, prewar singing, and farewell feasts, which the dying gave for their friends. Men held singing feasts to gain status. A crier announced the feasts. The most elderly crier heralded events of greatest importance. During a feast the giver circulated to entertain the guests with song and talk. Most feasts included contests, games, rituals, and dances. Formal dances were held to welcome important guests, celebrate a victory, cure an illness, or appease the spirits.

The Green Corn Feast was a major yearly event. At this feast the clans named the babies who had been born that year. Adoptees were also formally accepted into the tribe and given their clan names.

CURRENT TRIBAL ISSUES

For more than a century, the Wyandotte Nation of Oklahoma and the Wyandot Nation of Kansas were embroiled in a legal battle over the

Huron Cemetery in Kansas City, Kansas. The Wyandotte, who had legal control of it, wanted to develop it as a gambling center, which upset the Wyandot, because they did not want their ancestors' remains moved. In 1999, the two tribes settled their differences, and the Wyandotte set their sights on a building nearby. In 2004, the Wyandotte opened a casino in trailers nearby, which the state raided and closed. The gambling facility reopened in 2008, housed in a former Scottish Rite temple in Kansas City. The state challenged the legality of the casino but lost a ten-year legal battle.

The state and the tribe were again at odds in 2010 over Wyandotte plans to build a casino in Park City, Kansas. Two of the state's objections were that the local residents had voted against gambling and that the property did not qualify to be taken into trust. The major concern, though, was that the Wyandot casino would be in direct competition with a proposed state-owned gambling facility in an adjacent county. This could reduce the amount of income the state would get from its casino.

In 2008, the Huron-Wendat filed a claim against Quebec to be reimbursed for lands that had once been theirs. The 14,913-square-mile (24,000-square-kilometer) area includes Quebec City and Trois-Rivieres. The Huron-Wendat's successful claim in the year 2000 for a 1.6-square-mile (2.5-square-kilometer) piece of land outside of Quebec City netted the band $12 million.

All of the groups are working on environmental clean-up issues. The Wyandotte Nation of Oklahoma is dealing with heavy-metals contamination. The Wyandot in Quebec have been instrumental in the reclamation of a formerly contaminated industrial site, which is being turned into a natural habitat of marsh and wet prairie. This area, together with other land along Lake Erie and the Detroit River, is part of the U.S. Fish and Wildlife Service's Detroit River International Wildlife Refuge.

NOTABLE PEOPLE

Chief Tarhe fought to prevent settlers from taking over the Ohio Country both in Lord Dunmore's War (1774) and in the Battle of Fallen Timbers (1794). After the defeats, he advocated peace and signed the Treaty of Greenville (1795). In his seventies, Chief Tarhe fought for the Americans in the Revolutionary War (1775–83). He died in 1818 at age seventy-six.

Born in 1874, Eliza Burton "Lyda" Conley was the first Native American woman lawyer to argue before the Supreme Court. When she and her sisters, Helena and Ida, discovered that Congress had authorized the sale of the Huron Cemetery in Kansas City, Kansas, they became determined to save it and put up a fortified shed on the grounds. Conley also defended the cemetery in court, even though she had not yet passed the bar. Although she lost, a bill was introduced in Congress to make the land a historic monument, and in 1971, the cemetery was placed on the National Historic Register, long after Conley's death in 1946.

BOOKS

Barbeau, Marius. *Huron and Wyandot Mythology*. Ottawa, Ontario: Government Printing Bureau, 1915.

Seeman, Erik R. *The Huron-Wendat Feast of the Dead: Indian-European Encounters in Early North America*. Baltimore: The Johns Hopkins University Press, 2011.

Steckley, John L. *Words of the Huron*. Waterloo, Ontario: Wilfrid Laurier University Press, 2007.

Trigger, Bruce G. *The Children of Aataentsic: A History of the Huron People to 1660*. Montreal, Quebec: McGill-Queen University Press, 2000.

WEB SITES

"Address of Tarhe, Grand Sachem of the Wyandot Nation, to the Assemblage at the Treaty of Greeneville, July 22, 1795." *Wyandotte Nation of Oklahoma*. http://www.wyandotte-nation.org/history/tarhe_greenville_address.html (accessed May 12, 2011).

Huron-Wendat Nation. http://www.wendake.com/ (accessed May 12, 2011).

Kopris, Craig, and the Wyandotte Nation of Oklahoma Language Committee. "Wyandotte Language Lessons." *Southern Oregon University*. http://cs.sou.edu/~harveyd/acorns/wyandotte/ (accessed May 12, 2011).

Redish, Laura, and Orrin Lewis. "Wyandot/Huron Indian Language." *Native Languages of the Americas*, 2009. http://www.native-languages.org/wyandot.htm (accessed May 11, 2011).

Snook, Debbie. "Ohio's Trail of Tears." *Wyandotte Nation of Oklahoma*, 2003. http://www.wyandotte-nation.org/culture/history/published/trail-of-tears/ (accessed May 11, 2011).

Wyandot Nation of Anderdon. http://www.wyandotofanderdon.com/ (accessed May 13, 2011).

Wyandot Nation of Kansas. http://www.wyandot.org/ (accessed May 13, 2011).

Wyandotte Nation of Oklahoma. http://www.wyandotte-nation.org/ (accessed May 13, 2011).

Subarctic

Subarctic

The Subarctic region covers the vast interior of what is now Alaska and Canada, stretching some 3,000 miles (4,800 kilometers) from the Yukon River to the coast of Labrador. To the north, it borders the Arctic tundra, a stretch of treeless plains around the Arctic Circle that remains frozen most of the year, with subsoil that never thaws. To the south, it runs along the temperate rainforests of the coastal Northwest, the mountain forests of the Plateau, the grasslands of the Plains, and the woodlands of the Northeast. Although there is tundra in the northern parts and at higher elevations of the Subarctic area, it consists mainly of *taiga*—a Russian word meaning "land of little sticks"—a good description of the scraggly spruce trees that often characterize the region.

Two broad cultural groups are usually included as part of the Subarctic region: the Athabaskan (also known as the Dene) in Alaska and western Canada and the Algonquin-speakers in central and eastern Canada (Cree, Anishinaubeg, Métis, and Innu). It should be noted that *Athabaskan,* a Cree term, is still in use in Alaska but is frowned upon in Canada. *Anishinaubeg* (the plural of *Anishinaabe*) is how the Ojibway often refer to themselves, whereas *Innu* is the preferred term for those formerly known as Montagnais and Naskapi. Although the Athabaskan and Algonquin communities are separated by different languages both within and between themselves, the fairly consistent nature of the forest across the Subarctic leads to certain similarities in lifestyle among them, especially their reliance on caribou and moose as primary subsistence animals.

Living inland in a challenging climate, the relatively scattered, nomadic (wandering) peoples of the Subarctic region tended to experience the arrival of non-Natives later than did other tribal nations. The early non-Natives arriving in the region were mostly fur trappers, followed by missionaries and miners. Although the Subarctic groups were left somewhat more alone than other groups, in the latter half of the twentieth century, their mineral, timber, and hydroelectric (producing electricity from water) wealth caught the attention of the industrial world. In response,

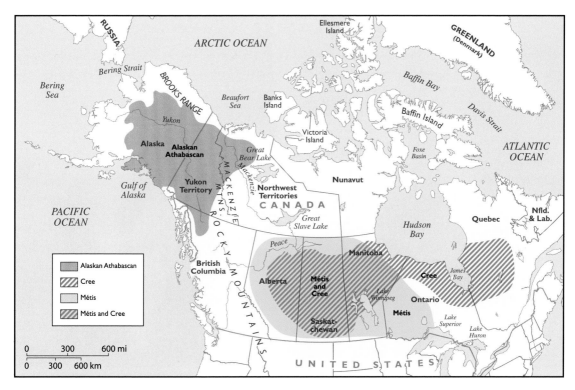

A map showing some contemporary Native communities in the Subarctic region. MAP BY XNR PRODUCTIONS. CENGAGE LEARNING, GALE. REPRODUCED BY PERMISSION OF GALE, A PART OF CENGAGE LEARNING.

they have asserted their sovereignty (self-rule) in an effort to have a say in shaping their future.

Origins

The Dene Nation (Athabaskan) in the Dehcho (Mackenzie River) delta of Canada dates its existence to at least thirty thousand years ago. Subarctic oral literature is full of creation stories set in a mythic time when people and animals could talk to each other, an era in which tricksters like Raven and Wolverine (Dene), Nanabush (Anishinaubeg), and Wesucechak (Cree) had many adventures that helped shape the world. These characters, however, are not always confined to particular areas or groups. The stories are told to entertain and to convey fundamental attitudes about the earth and its creatures. The Koyukon in Alaska have a lovely story in which Dotson'Sa (The Great Raven) creates the world. As retold by John Smelcer, it tells of a place full of giant animals, many that no longer exist, and of a great flood that drowns the earth. Dotson'Sa tells Raven to save

Missionaries camp in Alaska Territory on their way to the Klondike gold fields in Canada's Yukon Territory in 1897. © CORBIS.

animals aboard a big boat. One of the rescued animals, Muskrat, swims below and brings up mud to rebuild the earth. Dotson'Sa populates the new land with people made from clay. Versions of this story are widespread in Athabaskan (Dene) country.

Archaeologists (people who study the artifacts left behind by ancient civilizations) have only sketchy information on how or when human beings came to inhabit the Subarctic. Most believe that ice-age migrations over the Bering Land Bridge were involved. (Many scientists believe that sometime about twenty-five thousand to fifteen thousand years ago, a land bridge formed from lands that are now under the waters of the Bering Strait. They believe that over a period of years, small groups of hunters crossed the land bridge from Asia to Alaska. Eventually, these people and their descendants spread throughout North and South America.) The archaeologists' uncertainty about when human beings inhabited the

Subarctic region is due to scarce digging sites, acidic soils, erosion, and the nomadic lifestyles of inhabitants who traveled lightly and left few artifacts of metal, bone, or stone.

To summarize John W. Ives, this is how scientists think the Na-Dene people (whose language covers the largest territory in the Subarctic) came to be. As early as ten thousand years ago, following an original migration over the Bering Strait, proto-Dene (the earliest to be identified as a group) people began to develop their own identity. The locale of this genetic (relating to biological hereditary traits) and cultural birth seems to have been in the northwestern section of the Subarctic. Later periods saw a movement of Dene-speakers westward into the Dehcho (Mackenzie River) delta; another movement southward into the Northwest Coast and northern California (the Tlingit, Haida, Eyak, and Hupa tribes); and a relatively recent split, perhaps just prior to European contact, that took the Dine (Navajo) and Apache peoples into the Southwest. As Kerry Abel has pointed out, oral history and scientific evidence suggest that a natural disaster (maybe a volcanic eruption) motivated the dispersal (the group's breaking up and spreading out). To the dispersal, we can add the Tsuu T'ina (Sarsi), a group of Dene-speakers who joined the Blackfoot Confederacy on the northern Plains.

Meanwhile, Algonquian speakers came to inhabit the central and eastern parts of the boreal (northern) forest: the Innu in Labrador, the Cree around Hudson Bay, the Anishinaubeg (Ojibway) just south of the Cree, and finally, the recent mixed Indian-white population known as Métis. Two linguists, Richard A. Rhodes and Evelyn M. Todd, reported that proto-Algonquin people may have originated in southern Ontario and spread out into Cree and Anishinaubeg lands from there. Archaeologist James V. Wright has asserted that the caribou-hunting way of life remained more or less unchanged in Algonquin country for over seven thousand years.

Relations between scientists and Native people have not always been happy. Many local people are skeptical of the Bering Strait Land Bridge theory. Writer Vine Deloria Jr. in his spirited critique has pointed out the scarcity of physical evidence, the daunting mountain ranges on either side of the land bridge, and the lack of oral history about crossing a land bridge. He also points out the political motivations involved in suggesting that if Native Americans are merely immigrants then perhaps their claims to the land are not so deep after all. Nevertheless, cooperative ventures between archaeologists and Native elders began in the 1980s in several places in both Alaska and Canada. These studies have incorporated such elements as oral history and traditional place names, thus giving elders a new sense of purpose and younger people employment and a chance to learn about their past. In some cases commissioned by tribes themselves, such work draws upon the depth, richness, and complexity of traditional knowledge about the land.

Living from the land

Generally speaking, life in the Subarctic follows the rhythm of the seasons. Although there are significant differences within and between groups, the boreal forest and nearby tundra have produced a subsistence lifestyle (a way of life in which people hunt or gather the things they need to survive) that transcends many boundaries.

During the Subarctic's long winter, when temperatures can drop to negative 50 degrees Fahrenheit or below, snow blankets the ground and ice locks up rivers and lakes. In the summer, when temperatures can top 90 degrees Fahrenheit, animals and people move around more freely, but forest fires become a threat, and in boggy areas, clouds of mosquitoes harass anything that moves. The sun ebbs and flows throughout the year, barely rising at the winter solstice but virtually not setting at high summer. In between, there are two short but vivid seasons, autumn and spring, which usher in the ice and break it up, respectively. Autumn and spring also set the stage for annual migrations of caribou, geese, ducks, and salmon.

The two most important animals across the Subarctic are caribou and moose, whose meat, hide, bone, and sinew traditionally went into clothing, tents, tools, and, in some places, moose skin-covered boats. Caribou tend to migrate in herds between summer calving grounds and winter ranges, while moose tend to be solitary and migrate within smaller areas. In pre-contact times, bands that stressed moose hunting had to remain small, perhaps the size of an extended family, at least until summer fish camps could support larger populations. Caribou-hunting groups could be somewhat larger and had to travel farther. The extra hunters probably were needed to deal with herds. Some peoples hunted (and still hunt) both animals, though now with rifles instead of spears.

The Gwich'in (Kutchin) in northern Alaska and the adjacent Yukon Territory depend on the Porcupine caribou herd, some 160,000 animals that each spring migrate north from the boreal forests, across the Porcupine River, and onto the Arctic plains, where calves are born. In the fall, they return inland. Until the turn of the twentieth century, Gwich'in hunters were known to build fences to corral some of the animals. Slobodin has documented that, because the Gwich'in and the caribou were closely related in early times as described by Gwich'in mythology, the human heart still has a piece of caribou heart in it, and vice versa; they can share each other's thoughts.

When caribou and moose are not available, smaller game such as snowshoe hare, beaver, muskrat, otter, porcupine, squirrel, migratory geese, and grouse are hunted. Animals that are taken rarely, or only in limited places, include bear, musk-ox, elk, Dall sheep on some mountains, bison in lands bordering the Great Plains, and sea mammals in coastal areas. Many rivers provide salmon in the summer, while other waterways offer pike, whitefish, and grayling. Dried fish sustains both people and sled dogs during colder months. Forests and tundra yield bark for baskets, firewood, and wood for snowshoes and spears, as well as Labrador tea, medicines, berries, roots, greens, and, in pre-contact times, seeds that were used for beadwork. The trapping of animals for the fur trade, a development of the past two hundred years, has also become an essential part of the economy throughout the Subarctic; pelts are most valuable when trapped in fall and winter.

The annual migrations between summer fish camps and winter hunting and trapping ranges still occur throughout most of the boreal forest, though many people now have permanent homes. Old-time housing might vary from semi-subterranean (partly underground) structures and temporary double lean-tos in Alaska to oval or conical tents in Canada; most were home to multiple families. In traditional times, government generally operated by consensus (general agreement amongst the group), with headmen of extended families making decisions based on discussions with elders and other members of the family. At summer camps, or among larger caribou-hunting communities, more people had to agree. Relations with other groups could alternate between warfare and trading, or even intermarriage, depending on circumstances. This complexity continued when non-Native people started coming into the north country.

Tribal distribution

Although the various Subarctic peoples have many similarities in their lifestyles, they do see themselves as belonging to bands and nations. Rivers are a typical focal point for organizing the landscape and distinguishing people's homelands. One of the biggest rivers, the Yukon, flows almost 1,900 miles (3,100 kilometers) from the upper Yukon Territory in Canada, through interior Alaska, to Norton Sound; its major tributaries include the Porcupine (which also begins in Canada), the Koyokuk, and the Tanana. The Yukon, along with the Kuskokwim River, is a defining feature of interior Alaska, the westernmost geographical and cultural region in the Subarctic. The Athabaskan (Dene) peoples here include the Koyukon around the Koyokuk and Yukon rivers; the Tanana around the Tanana River; the Deg Hit'an (formerly known as Ingalik) in west-central Alaska around the lower Yukon and Kuskokwim Rivers; the Dena'ina in south-central Alaska around Tikahtnu (Cook Inlet) and Yaghanen (the Kenai Peninsula); the Ahtna around Ts'itu (the Copper River) just east of the Dena'ina; and the Eyak in the Copper River delta, an Athabaskan (Dene)-derived people who developed close ties with the coastal Tlingit.

The section immediately to the east of interior and south central Alaska is known as the Cordillera, a series of roughly connected mountain ranges between the Yukon River to the west and Dehcho (the Mackenzie River) to the east. Its northern part includes much of the Brooks Range around the Alaska/Yukon Territory border, home to the Gwich'in people and the Han just below them, whereas farther south it reaches into the Rocky Mountains in interior British Columbia and northwest Alberta, making homelands for the Kaska, Tahltan, Sekani, Carrier, and Chilcotin. The cultures and subsistence practices of those closer to the Northwest Coast and the Plateau reflect ties with those tribes.

The Dehcho (Mackenzie River) delta to the east of the Rocky Mountains, unlike the Yukon, drains into the Beaufort Sea instead of the Pacific. This area is Denedeh, homeland of the Dene Nation of Canada, which is situated between the Cordillera and Hudson Bay. Although its formal membership has been evolving, in the mid-1980s the Nation listed the following constituents: the Dinjii Zhuh (Gwich'in or Locheux) in the north; the K'ashot'ine (Hareskin) northwest of Sahtú (Great Bear Lake); the Tlicho (Dogrib) between Sahtú and Tucho (Great Slave Lake); the Deh Gàh Got'ine (Slavey or Dene Dhá) along Dehcho and south of Tucho; the Shihts Got'ine (Mountain People), who live a little farther downriver; the Denesoliné (Chipewyan), the largest group, whose area extends between the big lakes, Hudson Bay, and as far north as the Arctic coast; and some Cree and Métis immigrants.

Geographically, the Dehcho area overlaps the western side of the Canadian Shield, a massive plate of bedrock that was scraped by glaciers and erosion during the last ice age, leaving lowlands around both Dehcho and Hudson Bay, along with great mineral wealth underground. The relatively low elevations make for some enormous lakes, which aside from Sahtú (Great Bear Lake) and Tucho (Great Slave Lake), include Lake Athabasca, Reindeer Lake, and Lake Winnipeg. Because the Shield wraps around Hudson and James Bays all the way into Labrador, it makes up about half of Canada.

To the south of Denedeh, around the Peace River, live the Dene-speaking Beaver people; they are not members of the Nation but are related culturally. Their immediate neighbors to the east are the Cree, Algonquin-speakers whose language comes from an entirely separate family. (Some Cree fled into Northern Alberta in the late 1780s during a smallpox epidemic; their descendants became members of Denedeh.) Bands of Cree extend from the western forests all the way around Hudson and James Bays well into Labrador. The easternmost of these bands, the Innu, call their homeland in eastern Quebec and Labrador *Nitassinan.*

Other speakers of Algonquian dialects live in the southern reaches of the Subarctic. Some Anishinaubeg live in Manitoba and Ontario, along rivers that drain into the Hudson and James Bays. (Most live in the Great Lakes area, not in the Subarctic.) In the area around lower Lake Winnipeg live a people known as Saulteaux, cousins of the Anishinaubeg. Also south of Dehcho, in parts of Alberta, Saskatchewan, and Manitoba, live the Métis, descendants of unions between European fur trappers and Cree, Anishinaubeg, and Saulteaux women. In their two hundred years of existence, the Métis have maintained the subsistence lifestyle of their Native ancestors, hunting, trapping, and fishing in the boreal forest, although their proximity to the Great Plains introduced an element of the bison-hunting lifestyle as well.

Historical changes

European goods and diseases worked their way through Native trading networks in the Subarctic region well before actual explorers and fur traders started building forts there in the late eighteenth century. Russian trade goods came into interior Alaska via annual Inuit trade fairs in the mid- to late eighteenth century. The French and British came into the Subarctic from the East and Southeast, allowing Algonquin middlemen to trade

A gold prospector pans for gold in the Klondike, Yukon Territory, Canada, circa 1898. © HULTON ARCHIVE/ GETTY IMAGES.

firearms and other items for furs. Coastal Tlingit traders used Russian goods to bolster their business dealings with the Athabaskan (Dene) in the southern Cordillera.

Relations with non-Natives involved less warfare than in other regions because fur traders generally were more interested in gaining a supply of pelts than in stealing land. However, increasing dependence on outside goods did affect subsistence practices and occasionally resulted in violence. For example, the people on what is now Newfoundland, Canada, the Beothuk, misunderstood the private property concepts of French and English fishermen. Branded as thieves, they were hunted down for a scalp bounty and died out by the early nineteenth century.

In Alaska, where Russians brutally enslaved coastal tribes for the fur trade, the Ahtna, who lived in upper Ts'itu (the Copper River), repelled more than one party of Russians in the early colonial period. In one harrowing account told by Katie and Fred John, in the winter of 1794 to 1795, a party of Russians drove the men out of a village to freeze to death and conscripted the women to tan hides. The Russians' Dena'ina guide purposely mistranslated certain dialogue to give the Ahtna men time to retaliate, which they did, killing the entire party. No white people lived among the Upper Ahtna until after the Klondike gold rush of 1898, in part because the coastal Tlingit discouraged outsiders from disrupting their own trade relations with the interior.

In most parts of the Subarctic, where violent confrontations with outsiders did not occur, fur traders established posts that by degrees greatly affected the lives of Native people. The introduction of sled dogs enabled the people to do more trapping but also increased pressure on summer fish camps to produce food. The need to tend to trap lines affected the location and duration of winter camps, lessening mobility. Intermarriage was not uncommon and had far-ranging effects. The Métis nation, which grew out of mixed-race marriages, included both fur-trapping people in the north and buffalo-hunting people on the plains.

The dominant trading company, the Hudson's Bay Company, controlled forts and land from Hudson Bay to the Yukon until 1869, when it sold its huge territory to Canada. Conflicts between the Métis and Canada led to the only armed conflicts on the western Canadian frontier. These ended with the Second Riel Rebellion in 1885 near the Saskatchewan River, when Métis patriot Louis Riel (1844–1885) and Cree compatriots were finally defeated. Tensions between the Métis and the Canadian government over land and sovereignty continue to this day.

Other contacts between Natives and fur traders demonstrated the creativity and adaptability of Subarctic peoples. The introduction of trade beads, the fur trade, and missionary instruction led to the blossoming of Athabaskan (Dene) beadwork, which formerly had been done with quills and seeds. Floral embroidery was introduced in the eastern Athabaskan (Dene) region in the nineteenth century and spread as far as Alaska. Kate C. Duncan has documented the long history of ornamented Athabaskan (Dene) art on such items as clothing, mittens, moccasins, baby-carrying straps, and dog blankets. Similarly, early contacts with Europeans led the Algonquin-speaking Innu to develop a tradition of painted caribou-skin coats that echoed the garments worn by Europeans. As documented by Dorothy K. Burnham, the coats were in use for well over two centuries, ending in the early twentieth century. These Athabaskan (Dene) and Innu developments show how outside materials and ideas breathed new life into old traditions.

As with clothing and embroidery, Native people responded enthusiastically to new songs and dances. The Hudson's Bay Company established a post at Fort Yukon in 1847, where men from Scotland, France, Canada, and the Orkney Islands introduced fiddle music to the Gwich'in and Han peoples. The locals loved fiddling so much that, even after the fort closed twenty years later, they continued to play at social gatherings. Tribes farther south, such as the Tanana, learned of fiddling from Americans, and they incorporated it into ceremonial potlatches (feasts celebrating major life events, such as birth, death, or marriage, in which goods are given away to show the host's wealth and generosity) and a big celebration known as Nuchalawoya in late spring. Native people were often excluded from dance halls where non-Natives enjoyed such music, so the Native people incorporated fiddling into their own events. Starting in 1983, the Athabaskan Old-Time Fiddling Festival became an annual attraction in Fairbanks, Alaska. There audiences experience nineteenth-century Orkney Island fiddling, jigs, and reels, and Athabaskan (Dene) people, some who cannot understand each other's dialects, have an art form that all can appreciate.

While these gradual adaptations were taking place, the superpowers of Canada and the United States were preparing to exert their authority over the Subarctic. The United States bought Alaska from Russia in 1867, but it was not until Alaska approached statehood in the late 1950s that the Native people realized the enormity of their potential land loss. Neither treaties nor reservations had been established in the American Subarctic, as had been done in the lower forty-eight states. Desire to build the Trans-Alaska Oil Pipeline led the government in 1971 to enact the Alaska Native Claims Settlement Act (ANCSA), which assigned to the Natives some 40 million acres of land and almost $1 billion in exchange for relinquishing their aboriginal claims in the rest of Alaska. The land was divided among thirteen regional corporations, the largest of which is Doyon, Ltd., representing most of the Athabaskan (Dene) peoples of interior Alaska.

Meanwhile, tribal councils still exist, which leads to some confusion about who truly represents the future of the people. In the 1990s, the village of Venetie sued the state, insisting that despite the ANCSA, their village fits the definition of "Indian Country" as exhibited in the rest of the states. (Indian Country is a term used in federal law that includes reservations, scattered Native American home sites, and sometimes areas near reservations as well. By law, tribal governments in Indian Country have the authority to make and enforce their own laws and negotiate government-to-government with the United States.) Although Venetie won the case in the lower courts, the Supreme Court overturned that verdict in 1998, ruling that Venetie did not meet the definition of Indian Country. In any case, the challenge for Doyon, as well as for the other corporations and tribal councils, is to navigate the modern capitalist economy without losing sight of basic cultural values.

Ancient subsistence practices and modern industries often do conflict. The Gwich'in, who number more than seven thousand people in both Alaska and Canada, have been resisting the efforts of the U.S. Congress and the coastal Inuit to develop an oil field in the Arctic National Wildlife Refuge. Although they live inland, the Gwich'in depend on the Porcupine Caribou herd whose calving ground is in the refuge. They fear that oil development in the delicate tundra environment will threaten the survival of the herd. The presence of Inuit people on the other side of the question prevents a simplistic Native-versus-non-Native interpretation of this conflict.

Canadian peoples face similar dilemmas, as the industrial world has taken a great interest in their oil, mineral, timber, and hydroelectric resources. Like the United States, Canada never bothered to make treaties in most of its northern reaches, so the late twentieth century witnessed a flurry of efforts to settle the land claims of the various nations, an agonizing process for the aboriginal people. The Innu, for example, have resisted efforts to develop resources in Nitassinan until their land rights are settled, knowing full well that such development is already happening. They have been negotiating directly with mining and timber companies in an effort to provide economic benefit for the people while protecting their subsistence base in the ecosystem (the way that a community and the environment work together). In 2001, the Innu Nation and the government of Newfoundland and Labrador signed a Forest Process Agreement, which gives the people a voice in resource management.

Since few people, if any, in the Subarctic live totally outside the cash economy, villages and towns across Alaska and Canada are attempting to balance the creation of jobs with the well-being of the land and people. This is a daunting challenge, but the various Athabaskan (Dene) and Algonquin nations have long traditions of survival in their favor.

BOOKS

Abel, Kerry. *Drum Songs: Glimpses of Dene History.* Montreal, Quebec: McGill–Queen's University Press, 1993.

Bastedo, Jamie. *Reaching North: A Celebration of the Subarctic.* Markham, Ontario: Red Deer Press, 2002.

Carlos, Ann M. *Commerce by a Frozen Sea: Native Americans and the European Fur Trade.* Philadelphia: University of Pennsylvania Press, 2010.

Corwin, Judith Hoffman. *Native American Crafts of the Northwest Coast, the Arctic, and the Subarctic.* New York: Franklin Watts, 2002.

Cruikshank, Julie, with Angela Sidney, Kitty Smith, and Annie Ned. *Life Lived Like a Story: Life Stories of Three Yukon Native Elders.* Lincoln: University of Nebraska Press, 1990.

Cruikshank, Moses. *The Life I've Been Living.* Fairbanks: University of Alaska Press, 1986.

Deloria, Vine, Jr. *Red Earth, White Lies: Native Americans and the Myth of Scientific Fact.* New York: Scribner, 1995.

Doak, Robin. *Subarctic Peoples.* Mankato, MN: Heinemann-Raintree, 2011.

Duncan, Kate C. *Northern Athapaskan Art: A Beadwork Tradition.* Seattle: University of Washington Press, 1989.

Ember, Melvin, and Peter N. Peregrine, eds. *Encyclopedia of Prehistory,* Vol. 2: *Arctic and Subarctic.* New York: Kluwer Academic/Plenum Publishers, 2001.

Handbook of North American Indians, Vol. 6: *Subarctic.* Ed. June Helm. Washington, DC: Smithsonian Institution, 1981.

Ives, John W. "Sketch of Athapaskan Prehistory." *A Theory of Northern Athapaskan Prehistory.* Boulder, CO: Westview Press, 1990.

Krear, H. Robert. *Four Season North: Exploration and Research in the Arctic and Subarctic.* New York: Vantage Press, 2006.

Mishler, Craig. *The Crooked Stovepipe: Athapaskan Fiddle Music and Square Dancing in Northeast Alaska and Northwest Canada.* Urbana: University of Illinois Press, 1993.

Peoples of the Arctic and Subarctic. Chicago: World Book, 2009.

Piper, Liza. *The Industrial Transformation of Subarctic Canada.* Vancouver, British Columbia: UBC Press, 2009.

Sassaman, Kenneth E., and Donald H. Holly, Jr., eds. *Hunter-Gatherer Archaeology as Historical Process.* Tucson: University of Arizona Press, 2011.

VanStone, James W. *Athapaskan Adaptations: Hunters and Fishermen of the Subarctic Forests.* Chicago: Aldine Publishing, 1974.

Vaudrin, Bill. *Tanaina Tales from Alaska.* Norman: University of Oklahoma Press, 1969.

Watkins, Mel, ed. *Dene Nation: The Colony Within.* Toronto, Ontario: University of Toronto Press, 1977.

Wiggins, Linda E., ed. *Dena—The People: The Way of Life of the Alaskan Athabaskans Described in Nonfiction Stories, Biographies, and Impressions from All Over the Interior of Alaska.* Fairbanks: Theata Magazine, University of Alaska, 1978.

Wunder, John R., and Kurt E. Kinbacher, eds. *Reconfigurations of Native North America: An Anthology of New Perspectives.* Lubbock: Texas Tech University Press, 2009.

WEB SITES

Arctic Athabaskan Council. http://www.arcticathabaskancouncil.com/ (accessed on June 10, 2011).

Arctic Circle. http://arcticcircle.uconn.edu/Museum/ (accessed on June 10, 2011).

Dene Cultural Institute. http://www.deneculture.org/ (accessed on June 10, 2011).

"First Peoples of Canada: Communal Hunters." *Canadian Museum of Civilization.* http://www.civilization.ca/cmc/home (accessed on June 10, 2011).

Inuit Circumpolar Council (Canada). http://www.inuitcircumpolar.com/flash_player_icc_select.php (accessed on June 10, 2011).

Alaskan Athabascan

Name

Alaskan Athabascan (pronounced *uh-LAS-ken ath-uh-PAS-ken;* also spelled "Athabascan" or "Athapascan"). The name came from a Canadian lake the Cree called *Athabasca,* which means "grass here and there." The Cree also applied the name to the people who lived on the opposite side of the lake. Today the term also refers to the language spoken by eleven groups of Alaska Natives. The Alaskan Athabascan call themselves *Dene* (or *Dinnie*), meaning "the People."

Location

The Alaskan Athabascan are a Subarctic people who live in an area directly south of the true Arctic regions. Their land stretches from the border of the Canadian Yukon Territory to just beyond the Arctic Circle. They once wandered throughout a vast region, but after the Europeans came they built villages of fifty to five hundred people along the Yukon, Koyuckuk, Tanana, and Copper Rivers. Most of them still live in those areas in the early twenty-first century. Few villages have roads leading into them and must be reached by boat, snowmobile, or plane.

Population

In the 1850s, there were more than 10,000 Alaskan Athabascan. In the 1990 U.S. Census, 14,198 people identified themselves as Alaskan Athabascan. In 2000, the census showed 14,520 Alaska Athabascan, as well as 18,838 people who claimed some Alaska Athabascan heritage; by 2010, the census counted 15,623 Alaska Athabascan in the United States, with a total of 22,484 people noting an ancestral connection to the tribe.

Language family

Athabascan.

Origins and group affiliations

The Athabascan were among the first people to arrive in North America. According to scientists, they crossed a land bridge that linked Siberia and Alaska as many as forty thousand years ago. The Southern Athabascan

Traditional Alaskan Athabaskan Communities

Alaskan Athabaskans today live in communities along the Yukon, Koyukuk, Tanana, and Copper Rivers in the region from the Canadian Yukon Territory into Alaska.

Shaded area

Traditional lands of the Alaskan Athabaskans in present-day Alaska and Canada

A map of traditional Alaskan Athabaskan communities. MAP BY XNR PRODUCTIONS. CENGAGE LEARNING, GALE. REPRODUCED BY PERMISSION OF GALE, A PART OF CENGAGE LEARNING.

are the Apache and Navajo, and the Northern Athabascan remained in Alaska. Eleven groups of Athabascan-language speakers now live in the interior of Alaska. They are the Ahtna (also called Ahtena), Han, Holikachuk, Deg Xinag, Koyukon, Kutchin (Gwich'in), Tanacross, Tanaina (Dena'ina), Tanana, Upper Tanana, and Upper Kuskokwim peoples.

The Alaskan Athabascan people have lived for centuries in the vast, awe-inspiring, and sometimes forbidding wilderness of rolling, ice-covered hills and evergreen forests of the Subarctic region. Short summers of twenty-four-hour sunlit days are followed by long, often brutal winters with heavy snowfalls. The people share a feeling of kinship with the animals on which they once depended for existence. Their relations with the U.S. government have been unusual compared to those of many other tribes because they were not torn from their homelands and forced onto reservations. Living in remote locations where roads are few, these hardy people retained many of their old ways while adopting useful elements of modern culture.

HISTORY

Explorers unwelcome

Shortly after 500 CE, Athabascan speakers split into three major divisions: the Alaskan, who remained in the cold northwest, and the Plains and Southwestern branches, which moved east and south. Athabascan became the most widespread language family in North America. The Alaskan Athabascan settled in an area to the east of their current territory, but the Tlingit (see entry) pushed them out in prehistoric times. In their new territory they battled neighboring Inuit (see entry) and won, laying claim to the subarctic interior of Alaska.

The Alaskan Athabascan pursued a nomadic (wandering) existence based mostly on hunting until the arrival of the Russians in the late 1700s. Because of the vast area in which they lived, the various groups met the Russians at different times. Some had already heard how fur traders were enslaving the Eyak people of Prince William Sound, Alaska, forcing them to hunt and trap for Russian gain. Even though some groups did not see their first white men until well into the 1800s, they spoke of a new race who would come, kill their people, and take away their hunting grounds.

The Russians, British, and Americans appreciated the high-quality furs available throughout Alaska and hastened to establish trading posts. Conflicts arose. On four separate occasions, Russian explorers were massacred during expeditions within Alaskan Athabascan territory. In 1796 and 1818, the Ahtna and neighboring tribes killed three different Russian exploring teams as they attempted to locate the source of the Copper River. In 1847, another group met the same fate. One early explorer wrote about the Tanana, "They are always opposed to any exploration of their country."

Those whites who established relations among the Alaskan Athabascan fell victim to their wars with other tribes—wars in which the Athabascan sought revenge for trespassing or wars that occurred because a group was suspicious of and hostile to strangers. In 1851, a group of Koyukon descended upon the town of Nulato, killing the inhabitants as well as the Russian traders in residence. The unfriendly reputation of the Alaskan Athabascan, combined with the unwelcoming nature of their territory, kept immigration to a minimum during this period.

Important Dates

1769–83: Samuel Hearne and Alexander Mackenzie are the first European explorers to penetrate Alaskan Athabascan territory, looking for furs and a route to the Pacific Ocean. Russian fur traders are not far behind.

1818–19: While exploring the Copper River, two separate Russian expeditions are massacred by the Ahtna.

1896: Discovery of gold brings hordes of miners and settlers to Alaska.

1962: The Tanana Chiefs Conference is formed to pursue land claims for the Alaskan Athabascan people.

1971: Alaska Native Claims Settlement Act is passed, awarding 40 million acres of land and more than $960 million to Alaskan Natives.

2011: The Council of Athabascan Tribal Governments (CATG) received $1.1 million to cover unpaid Indian Health Service contract claims.

Missionaries and miners

The discovery of gold in 1896 in Yukon Territory in northwest Canada, just above the Alaska border, began the ten-year Klondike Gold Rush, changing the Native way of life in Alaska forever. For the first time since the United States bought Alaska from the Russians in 1867, Americans saw Alaska as a valuable addition to American territory. The stampede for gold between 1898 and 1900 brought thousands of people into Alaskan Athabascan territory. The Athabascan had little interest in gold, however. Meanwhile, their lands were taken over by settlers who introduced alcohol and harmful hunting practices, such as hunting for trophy heads rather than food. This created a feeling of mistrust between Native Alaskans and whites that persists today.

Christian missionaries coming into Alaska at the same time also changed traditional life. Settlers and priests demanded conformity to their culture, so Native languages, ceremonies, and healing rites were often abandoned. Still, some Alaskan Athabascan were protected from efforts to change their culture by the size of Alaska and their remote locations. Some did not come into any regular contact with whites until World War II (1939–45; a war in which Great Britain, France, the United States, and their allies defeated Germany, Italy, and Japan), when the U.S. military built the Alaska Highway (which opened up the territory for later settlement), established air strips for landing planes, and stationed military troops there.

Alaska Natives organize against oppression

Throughout the early 1900s, major projects were planned on or near Native Alaskan lands, often without consulting the people. Natives protested by forming of the Alaskan Native Brotherhood in 1912. It was not until 1962, however, that the Alaskan Athabascan established their own organization, called the Tanana Chiefs Conference, to address land issues. Land rights had become increasingly important for the Alaskan Athabascan as whites fished, hunted, and trapped wherever they wished throughout Native territory. The issue came to a head when an oil pipeline was proposed across traditional lands. The Tanana Chiefs Conference and other Alaska Native organizations won a victory when the Alaska Native Claims Settlement Act (ANCSA) passed in 1971.

The ANSCA awarded Alaska Natives 40 million acres of land and more than $960 million in return for their rights to the rest of Alaska. The ANCSA also resulted in the formation of twelve regional corporations in Alaska to oversee economic development and land use. A path was cleared for the construction of the pipeline, and millions of acres were set aside for parks and wilderness areas. Still, hunting rights remain a problem. Alaska Natives object to white trophy hunters who kill moose for the antlers and allow the meat to rot. Furthermore, as sports hunters use modern technology to track their game, Alaskan Athabascan hunters using ancient hunting techniques cannot compete.

RELIGION

The Alaskan Athabascan live a life in close harmony with nature. Their traditional beliefs are based on their relationship with the supernatural spirits in plants, animals, and natural phenomena. The spirit world includes both well-meaning and evil characters that have to be kept happy with songs, dances, and charms. One of the most feared spirits among the Alaskan Athabascan was *Nakhani,* or the "Bush Indian." In the summer, people said Nakhani loitered around the camps at night, waiting to steal children and attack hunters.

Probably the most important aspect of their religion is the connection they have with the animals on which they depended for their very existence. The Athabascan considered animals equal to them and believed people would be reborn after death as animals.

In the 1800s Russian Orthodox missionaries reached the Alaskan Athabascan, but their numbers were few and the territory they had to cover was vast. Sometimes their only contact was brief; they came to a village and baptized everyone in it at the same time, then moved on. The Alaskan Natives did not object, and may even have thought the ritual was part of the trading process

Alaskan Athabascan Words

Each of the groups has their own language, so the words are quite different. The numbers from one to five are shown below in three of the ten languages.

Ahtna Numbers

Ts'ełk'ey	"one"
Nadaeggi	"two"
Taaggi	"three"
Dunghi	"four"
Kwulai'	"five"

Gwich'in Numbers

Ihłak	"one"
Neekaii	"two"
Tik	"three"
Dàang	"four"
Ihłokwinlì'	"five"

Koyukon Numbers

K'eeł	"one"
Neteekk'ee	"two"
Tokk'ee	"three"
Denk'ee	"four"
K'eełts'ednaale	"five"

Some Russian missionaries remained after the sale of Alaska. Their influence increased and can still be seen in Alaska. Protestant, Episcopalian, and Catholic missionaries followed the Russians. These religious groups helped the Athabascan and other groups in their fight to keep their land, but they discouraged many traditional rituals. The missionaries disapproved of the gift-giving ceremonies called potlatches, and during the 1880s the government banned them. Anyone who participated in a potlatch could be imprisoned. The Athabascan had to hold their ceremonies secretly until the law was changed in 1951. Because the ritual was hidden for so long, most potlatches today are not the lengthy and involved affairs of the past, but instead they have been shortened to a single day or an evening. (See "Ceremonies, potlatches, and games.") By the mid-2000s, nearly all Alaskan Athabascan professed to be Christians.

LANGUAGE

The term "Athabascan" refers to a language family spoken by the Southern Athabascan—Apache and Navajo (see entries)—and the Northern Athabascan in Alaska. Generally the term is used to refer to the Athabascan speakers of Alaska.

In the early twenty-first century, the Athabascan languages, which are a subdivision of Athabascan-Eyak-Tlingit, were broken down into the following subgroups: Ahtna, Tanaina, Deg Hit'an, Holikachuck, Upper Kuskokwim, Koyukon, Tanana, Tanacross, Han, and Gwich'in. Although figures vary from group to group, it is estimated that about 21 percent of Alaskan Athabascan peoples still speak their language. Borrowing from other languages has occurred throughout Alaska, where a mix of Inuit, Russian, and Athabascan people continue to live side by side.

GOVERNMENT

Before Europeans came to their lands, Athabascan leaders were only needed when several families came together and formed bands, usually to hunt and gather. Then they chose the person with the qualities best suited for a particular task to be their leader, or "boss." When the band broke up, the leadership position ended.

A man who wished to be a leader held frequent potlatches (gift-giving ceremonies). This was the major way for the man to gain the respect of his own and neighboring groups. After increased contact with whites, the leader's role expanded. He became the middleman between his people and white traders.

By 1906, Americans had introduced the concept of elected chiefs and village councils to the Athabascan. This system of government—elected chiefs and tribal councils—remains in place, but the villages were made "corporations" with the 1971 passage of the Alaska Native Claims Settlement Act (ANCSA). The act placed twelve large regional corporations in charge of the economic development and land use of the villages, which also incorporated. Americans assumed that profit-making corporations would improve the lives of Alaskan Natives, but this manner of governing conflicted strongly with Native traditions. Disagreement arose among the corporations, the traditional village leaders, and the state of Alaska. The state wanted the land developed in the usual way of American cities, but the Alaska Athabascan want to use it in ways more in keeping with their traditions. Some Alaska Natives worked to get land ownership transferred from the corporations to the traditional tribal governments.

An Alaskan Athabascan family displays furs from its winter trapping catch. © JOEL BENNETT/ CORBIS.

ECONOMY

Since prehistoric times, the Athabascan economy has been based on hunting. During the period of fur trading with the Russians, a money-based economy developed, and it became firmly established during the

Klondike Gold Rush. Great profits were made by supplying meat, furs, and labor to the Russians. The Athabascan people developed a liking for the tobacco, tea, and other luxuries they bought from the Russians, and they soon looked upon these as necessities. Guns made their hunting much easier. As they came to depend on manufactured goods, they gave up migrating in small groups and settled down in villages near trading posts. Some continued old practices in a new way: they left for fish camps each summer but used the villages as a winter base while they trapped animals. As they killed more and more caribou with rifles, caribou herds decreased. Overhunting reduced the fur supply, and hunting became an occupation only for the most skilled and efficient.

Twentieth-century economy

With American troops stationed in Alaska during World War II, Athabascan wages increased as they helped supply military installations with food. A decline set in after the war when the posts closed down and the soldiers left.

In the twentieth century, Alaskan Athabascan economy depended on working for wages, although some people still trapped, hunted, and fished for part of the year. Some men left their villages to work as laborers at fish canneries and mines. Since the 1960s, many have been employed as summer forest firefighters for the U.S. Department of the Interior. The major employers in the region became the mining, fishing, lumbering, and oil industries, but the best jobs went to educated workers from outside the state. The majority of jobs available to the Athabascan were at the lower-paying levels.

The Alaskan Athabascan continue to strive for economic independence. With the award money they received under the Alaska Native Claims Settlement Act of 1971, they established businesses that are prospering. For example, Ahtna, Inc., a regional corporation, engages in construction work, oil pipeline maintenance, and other profitable ventures. Still, in some Athabascan communities many people are unemployed or underemployed, and many families depend on wage labor supplemented by government welfare and food stamps to survive. Others, such as the Telida (Upper Kuskowim) and Takotna (Ingalik), who live in the traditional manner and depend mainly on subsistence activities for survival, have an unemployment rate of zero percent.

DAILY LIFE

Families

Athabascan families were made up of a mother, father, their children, and grandparents. Some households contained two families who shared tasks, and winter villages might consist of five households. The Athabascan spent almost all their time preparing to hunt, hunting, and then drying and processing the products of a successful hunt. Famine was a constant threat, and the only way to survive was to be prepared. The people were generous in good times and bad, sharing what they had with others.

Education

For the Athabascan, childhood was short, and parents believed it should be filled with freedom and joy because adult life would be hard. Children were rarely spanked and heard few harsh words. They learned by observing and through storytelling.

Childhood ended at puberty, during which boys and girls were kept apart from one another in special huts for at least a year and learned from their elders all the skills they needed to know to survive. Afterward, they were ready to marry.

Christian missionaries first introduced formal, Western-style schooling in the 1800s. They established boarding schools, which allowed them more control over childrens' lives. They discouraged children from speaking the Athabascan language, causing tension when the children returned to their families. Some families kept their children at home, but in the 1930s, the government declared that all children had to attend schools. This split up families because mothers lived with their children near the schools, while the fathers went hunting. Some young men dropped out of school during hunting season.

In spite of the difficulties, literacy (the ability to read and write) increased, along with an awareness of and involvement in the outside world. By the early twenty-first century, more and more Alaska Natives were attending college. The Alaska Native Corporations (ANCs) assist students who need scholarships for university and trade school educations.

Buildings

Summer dwellings were rectangular bark houses that were easy to set up and offered protection from the rain. During the spring and fall hunting seasons, the Alaskan Athabascan constructed skin-covered tepees or brush lean-tos set up face to face, a structure known as the double lean-to. After the Europeans came, the people began to use canvas instead of skins for tepees.

Winter houses varied from log cabins to round buildings covered with hide and sunk partly underground. Smoke houses and underground bark-and earth-covered sheds that served as freezers were also typical. Common to all Alaskan Athabascan was a specially built house for the potlatch ceremony. As their lifestyles changed and more Athabascan lived year-round near trading posts, permanent log cabins became the preferred architectural style.

Food

The harsh climate and widely scattered food resources required almost constant migration. Fruits and vegetables were scarce or nonexistent, and the coming of cranberry, blueberry, and salmonberry seasons caused much rejoicing. The main staple in the Alaskan Athabascan diet was caribou, supplemented by moose and mountain goat when they were available.

A delicacy among the Alaskan Athabascan was roasted young caribou antler. The antler was cooked over the fire and the charred velvet peeled back to reveal a tender, tasty inside. Small game, including rabbit, ground squirrel, and porcupine, provided additional variety.

Fishing, especially for salmon and whitefish, was of secondary importance. It became more essential when sled dogs were introduced, as they were fed fish. Traders introduced the Alaskan Athabascan to tea, alcohol, and tobacco, three products now in widespread use.

Travel

In the warmer months, the Alaskan Athabascan traveled by boat or raft because the spring thaw left large amounts of standing water over the landscape. Winter travel was by snowshoe, with sleds and toboggans to carry heavy loads.

In the early 2000s, four-fifths of Alaska could not be reached by roads and was seldom visited. Yet Alaska Natives still lived there. In addition to the old ways of getting around, they also used snowmobiles, airplanes, and boats.

Clothing and adornment

Any differences in clothing among the Alaskan Athabascan groups were in the decorative details. Caribou was the skin of choice for clothing. In the winter, tanned hides with the hair left on were worn as capes. Summer capes were similar, but the hair was removed. Winter clothing was bulky to protect against the elements: rabbit, sheep, and deerskin robes were worn over fringed, hooded shirts and pants with moccasins attached. Mittens were attached to a string that hung around the neck.

The Alaskan Athabascan were accomplished embroiderers and used quills, beads, and colored threads to brighten their wardrobes. Face painting, tattooing, ear and nose piercing, and feather adornments were popular, as were necklaces and hair ornaments made of teeth, claws, stones, ivory, and bone.

Healing practices

The Athabascan believed that supernatural spirits bestowed power upon men and women who became healers, or shamans (pronounced *SHAH-munz* or *SHAY-munz*). Healing power came to shamans in dreams and visions, when the spirit taught the dreamer the songs and dances that would help cure sicknesses. Shamans sang the songs and performed the dances over a patient while sucking, massaging, or blowing on the afflicted area.

Experts who were not shamans also used plants for curing. These included potions of cottonwood for curing colds, juniper berries for internal ailments, and spruce needles for stomachaches. Bloodletting—the removing of blood from a vein—and daily baths in a sweathouse were also common practices.

Christian missionaries discouraged belief in shamans, and by the 1930s, few shamans would admit to their skills. Settlers brought new diseases and alcoholic beverages to Alaska Natives. By the 1950s, tuberculosis, an infectious lung disease, had become widespread. The U.S. government responded to the problem by building modern hospitals in the villages and by introducing better health- and dental-care practices. Contemporary health problems that plague the Alaskan Athabascan people include extremely high rates of teen suicide and alcoholism.

ARTS

The Athabascan have been working to pass on their traditional crafts through the Recovering Voices—Alaska's Living Cultural Treasures program. Some of the men who are skilled in snowshoe building held a master artists' workshop in 2011 with the intent of teaching this dying art to younger people. Only a handful of men still practice the art. Another attempt at reviving culture is the Athabascan Ceremonial House. This traditional-style log building with a sod roof was first used to hold a potlatch in January 2011. The celebration was the first large-scale potlatch to be held in the Anchorage area since 1939.

CUSTOMS

Marriage

A girl was considered ready to marry soon after she reached puberty, and her parents chose a slightly older husband. Preference was given to young men who had demonstrated excellent hunting skills. The couple usually moved into the home of the bride's family. For a year or two, the young man worked for his in-laws before setting up his own home. By then, he had mastered two hunting territories—those of his family and of his wife's family; this was useful knowledge during lean times.

The partner system

Men chose male partners to be their close friends for life. The two agreed to help each other when help was needed, to offer hospitality to one another, and to always respect one another.

Hunting rituals

In keeping with their belief that animals had souls, Alaskan Athabascan hunters observed many prohibitions, such as never killing a dog, wolf, or raven. Ravens were spared because they might be the spirits of dead people; killing them would bring bad luck in hunting. Hunters carried medicine bags that contained lucky objects such as animals' teeth and claws. If a woman touched his medicine bag, a hunter would lose his power.

Tom Kizzia, a newspaper reporter who spent two years visiting remote areas of Alaska and interviewing the people he encountered,

Alaskan Athabaskan hunters were prohibited from killing a raven, which they considered to be the spirits of dead people; to kill a raven was said to bring bad luck in hunting. © JOE MCDONALD/PHOTOSHOT.

wrote a book in which he described how early Native Alaskans killed a bear using only a spear. They believed you should "walk right up to the bear, stare him in the eye, let him know you're going to kill him. Then show a sudden flash of fear, to make the bear drop his guard, and that's when you make your thrust. Hunters wrapped leather around the spear handle at a bear's arm's length from the point, so they would know not to let their hand slip too close."

Ceremonies, potlatches, and games

Winter was the time for celebrating, and the Athabascan enjoyed feasting, dancing, singing, reciting myths, and making speeches; all of this activity helped groups maintain contact with other groups. Since the coming of Christian missionaries, these winter festivities have been joined to the Christmas celebration.

Two major festivities still held by Alaskan Athabascan are the pot-latch and the stick dance. Both are weeklong gift-giving ceremonies that honor the dead. In the past, a potlatch might also be held to celebrate a girl's reaching puberty or to call attention to a man's wealth. During the ceremony, tribal members perform their spirit songs and dances, feast, and receive the plentiful gifts distributed by the hosts.

The stick dance is held in March and is hosted by a widow to honor her dead husband. Men carry a fifteen-foot-long pole into the village hall on the fifth evening of the ceremony, and women decorate it with ribbons and furs. Thirteen dances are held with the stick as a focal point. This ritual also includes feasting and distributing gifts. Sometimes the event takes years of planning and saving.

The Athabascan people were extremely fond of games, especially a ball game using animal bladders that were either inflated or stuffed with grass. In modern times, softball is popular, and organized teams often travel by boat to compete with rival teams.

Death and burial

Russian Orthodox missionaries introduced the concept of burying the dead, instead of cremating or exposing dead bodies to the elements as the Athabascan had done before. Funerals were usually arranged by old men of another family group, who prepared the body while younger men dug the grave. They were thanked for their services at a potlatch and were given gifts of guns, blankets, eagle feathers, and digging tools. The Athabascan believed that the life spirit left the dead body during the potlatch feast.

CURRENT TRIBAL ISSUES

In modern times, the tribe has problems with alcoholism, dependence on government welfare payments for survival, and hunting rights issues. The effort to solve their common problems has unified the people, and they continue to work on community improvements.

Other issues of concern for the Athabascan are the sale, by the state of Alaska, of surrounding lands for development and hunting rights. Various Athabascan and other Native Alaskan organizations are protest-ing government deals with mining, oil, hydroelectric power, and other non-Native companies that have established or plan to locate businesses on traditional lands. The people are concerned about the environmental, economic, and social impacts of these industries. Several communities have pointed to health issues stemming from some of these industries. For example, studies showed higher-than-usual rates of cancer in Fort Chipewyan, which is downstream from the oilsands; deformed fish have been found in Lake Athbasca and other areas near the oilsands.

In 2011, the charred bones of a three-year-old Ice Age child were found in a semi-subterranean home on top of animal bones and plant remains. This find, which is about 11,500 years old, indicates that Athabascan peoples may have lived in the Tanana Valley from ancient times.

NOTABLE PEOPLE

Velma Wallis (1960–) is an Athabascan writer who has written several stories about her people's struggle to survive in a harsh environment. Among her works are *Bird Girl and the Man Who Followed the Sun: An Athabascan Indian Legend from Alaska* (1996) and *Two Old Women: An Alaskan Legend of Betrayal, Courage and Survival* (1994), which tells the shocking, but uplifting, story of two elderly women abandoned by their starving tribe.

Moses Cruikshank (1906–2006) was an Athabascan storyteller whose stories conveyed moral messages and shared personal experiences of his life and family. His book *The Life I've Been Living* was published in 1986.

David Salmon (1921–2007) served as an Episcopalian priest and an elder of the Gwich'in people. Salmon was instrumental in founding the Tanana Chiefs Conference, an organization to promote the welfare of Alaska Natives. He became Alaska's First Traditional Chief of the Interior three years before his death from cancer in 2007.

BOOKS

Brown, Tricia. *Children of the Midnight Sun*. Portland OR: Alaska Northwest Books, 2006.

Crowell, Aron L., ed. *Living Our Cultures, Sharing Our Heritage: The First Peoples of Alaska*. Washington, DC: Smithsonian Books, 2010.

Hoshino, Michio. *Hoshino's Alaska*. San Francisco: Chronicle Books, 2007.

Kizzia, Tom. *The Wake of the Unseen Object: Among the Native Cultures of Bush Alaska*. New York: Holt, 1991.

Meek, Barbra A. *We Are Our Language: An Ethnography of Language Revitalization in a Northern Athabascan Community*. Tucson: University of Arizona Press, 2010.

O'Brien, Thomas A. *Gwich'in Athabascan Implements: History, Manufacture, and Usage according to Reverend David Salmon.* Fairbanks: University of Alaska Press, 2011.

Solomon, Madeline. *Koyukon Athabaskan Songs.* Homer, AK: Wizard Works, 2003.

Tenenbaum, Joan M., and Mary Jane McGary, eds. *Denaina Sukdua: Traditional Stories of the Tanaina Athabaskans.* Fairbanks: Alaska Native Language Center, 2006.

Thomas, Kenny, Sr. *Crow Is My Boss: The Oral Life History of a Tanacross Athabaskan Elder.* Craig Mishler, ed. Norman: University of Oklahoma Press, 2005.

WEB SITES

Akimoff, Tim. "Snowshoe Builders Display Their Craft at the Anchorage Museum." *KTUU.* May 5, 2011. http://www.ktuu.com/news/ktuu-snowshoe-builders-display-their-craft-at-the-anchorage-museum-20110505,0,7760220.story (accessed on June 6, 2011).

"Alaska Native Language Center." *University of Alaska Fairbanks.* http://www.uaf.edu/anlc//anlc/languages/ (accessed on June 4, 2011).

"Athabascan." *Alaska Native Heritage Center Museum.* http://www.alaskanative.net/en/main_nav/education/culture_alaska/athabascan/ (accessed on June 6, 2011).

"Athabascan Music and Gwich'in Fiddling." *Fiddle Chicks.* http://www.fiddlechicks.com/athabascan/index.htm (accessed on June 2, 2011).

"Athabascan Winter Studies: The Dene' Indigenous People of Interior." *Alaska Native Knowledge Network.* http://ankn.uaf.edu/curriculum/Athabascan/Fairbanks_School_District/ANE_Program/appendixa.html (accessed on June 6, 2011).

"FAQ Alaska." *Statewide Library Electronic Doorway.* http://sled.alaska.edu/akfaq/akancsa.html (accessed on June 5, 2011).

Gwich'in Tribal Council. http://www.gwichin.nt.ca/ (accessed on June 5, 2011).

Media Action. "A Portrait of Nikolai." *Vimeo.* 2010. http://vimeo.com/14854233 (accessed on June 6, 2011).

———. "Excerpt from Youth-led Interview with Phillip Esai." *Vimeo.* http://vimeo.com/15465119 (accessed on June 6, 2011).

Nay'dini'aa Na' (Chickaloon Village) Traditional Council. "Re: Visit to the United States: Chickaloon Native Village Communication Regarding Indigenous Peoples Water and Sanitation Rights in Alaska." *Chickaloon Village.* February 22, 2011. http://www.treatycouncil.org/PDF/Independent%20Expert%20Communication%20CVTC%20Alaska.pdf (accessed on June 3, 2011).

Old Crow Yukon: Home of the Vunut Gwitchin First Nation. http://www.oldcrow.ca/ (accessed on June 5, 2011).

Redish, Laura, and Orrin Lewis. "Athabaskan (Na-Dene) Language Family." *Native Languages of the Americas: Preserving and Promoting Indigenous American Indian Languages.* http://www.native-languages.org/famath.htm (accessed on June 4, 2011).

Assiniboin

Name

Assiniboin (pronounced *uh-SIN-uh-boin*; sometimes spelled Assiniboine). The name comes from the Ojibway word *Asiniibwaan* meaning "those who cook with stones." Europeans called them *Stoney* because they heated stones and then dropped them in cooking pots to make the water boil. In Canada, they are sometimes still called by that name, although the tribe that officially bears the name Stoney is not part of the Assiniboin. The tribe refers to itself as the *Hohe Nakota* or *Nakoda Oyadebi. Nakota* means "generous ones."

Location

The Assiniboin originally lived in the area around Lake Superior in present-day northern Minnesota and southwestern Ontario. They migrated to the northern plains in Manitoba and to Saskatchewan. Some moved to North Dakota and Montana in the United States. In the early twenty-first century, the Assiniboin lived on two reservations in Montana and on six Canadian reserves (the Canadian name for reservations) in Saskatchewan and Alberta. Others lived off reserve in those provinces as well as in Manitoba. Some Assiniboin Sioux lived on the Yankton Reservation in South Dakota.

Population

In the early 1800s, the tribe numbered between 8,000 and 10,000. After the smallpox epidemics of the 1830s, that total dropped to approximately 6,000 in 1836. The U.S. Indian Report of 1890 placed the population at 3,008; in 1904, it was 2,600. In 2000, the U.S. Bureau of the Census reported a count of 4,109 people who said they were Assiniboin, whereas 5,120 indicated they had some Assiniboin heritage. In Canada in 2007, the number of people both on and off the jointly shared Assiniboin reserves totaled 9,460.

Language family

Siouan.

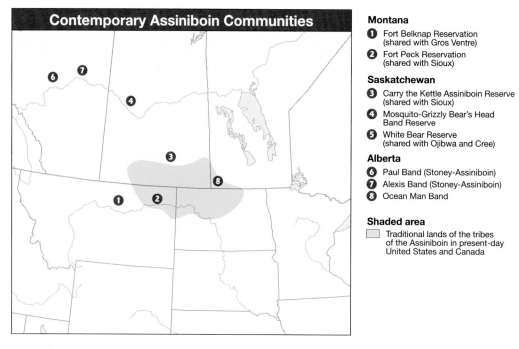

Contemporary Assiniboin Communities

Montana
1. Fort Belknap Reservation
   (shared with Gros Ventre)
2. Fort Peck Reservation
   (shared with Sioux)

Saskatchewan
3. Carry the Kettle Assiniboin Reserve
   (shared with Sioux)
4. Mosquito-Grizzly Bear's Head
   Band Reserve
5. White Bear Reserve
   (shared with Ojibwa and Cree)

Alberta
6. Paul Band (Stoney-Assiniboin)
7. Alexis Band (Stoney-Assiniboin)
8. Ocean Man Band

Shaded area
Traditional lands of the tribes
of the Assiniboin in present-day
United States and Canada

A map of contemporary Assiniboin communities. MAP BY XNR PRODUCTIONS. CENGAGE LEARNING, GALE. REPRODUCED BY PERMISSION OF GALE, A PART OF CENGAGE LEARNING.

Origins and group affiliations

Many historians believe the Assiniboin were part of the Lakota, Dakota, and Nakota tribes (see entries) when they lived in the Great Lakes region. During the 1600s, the Assiniboin split from the Yanktonai (see Nakota entry). According to Assiniboin oral history, however, the people say they are Algonquin. In either case, as they moved from the woodlands to the prairies, they allied with the Cree (see entry), Chippewa (see Ojibway entry), and Monsoni against the Sioux, Cheyenne, Blackfoot, Arikara, and Gros Ventre (see entries). They later traded with the Europeans and the Mandan, Hidatsa, and Arikara (see entry).

In 2007, the Assiniboin in Montana shared reservations with the Gros Ventre and Sioux. Canadian Assiniboin shared reserves with the Sioux, Cree, and Ojibway. The Assiniboin of Canada are closely linked to the Stoney First Nations people of Alberta, but are not the same.

Assiniboin oral history indicates that the tribe originated in the Lake of the Woods (Ontario) and the Lake Winnipeg (Manitoba) areas of Canada and that the people were descendants of the Algonquin. Historians, though, believe the tribe began as part of the Yanktonai band of Nakota. In the 1600s, the Assiniboin allied with the Cree, and the two tribes occupied the area around Lake Nipigon in present-day Minnesota. At one time, Assiniboin territory covered the area from the Saskatchewan and Assiniboin river valleys in Canada to the region north of the Missouri and Milk Rivers in the United States. Nomadic (wandering) hunter-gatherers, the Assiniboin traded with other tribes as well as with the Europeans. Settlers gradually pushed them west toward the Great Plains. By the early to mid-1800s, most of the bands, decimated by diseases like smallpox, had been moved to reservations.

HISTORY

Early migrations

Recent archaeological evidence suggests that Assiniboin oral history may have some basis in truth. In examining pottery from Sandy Lake, Minnesota, and Duck Bay, Ontario, scientists established a connection between these cultures, the Ojibway, an Algonquian culture, and the Wanikan and Psinomani, both Siouan cultures. One theory suggests the Algonquian and Siouan may have been united at one point and later separated into two distinct cultures. Both the pottery and the languages are similar. The Assiniboin, also a Siouan culture, may have been part of these earlier cultures from 1250 to 1500. The Assiniboin emerged as a distinct tribe, however, by 1550.

The first written mention of the tribe comes from the *Jesuit Relations* of 1640. According to one early historian, Edward S. Curtis, the Assiniboin split with the Yanktonai over a wrong done to their chief's wife. The Assiniboin moved north of Lake Superior, where they joined the Cree. Together, the two tribes moved west toward Lake Winnepeg (Manitoba) and defeated the Blackfoot, who lived in the area. They settled along the Saskatchewan and Assiniboin Rivers. There they became known for their canoeing skills and earned the nickname the "Paddlers."

Because their main livelihood was hunting buffalo, the Assiniboin migrated in search of the herds. Before horses were introduced, they

Important Dates

1640: First mention of the Assiniboin as separate from the Dakota tribe.

1744: The tribe splits into Stoneys and Assiniboin.

1804: The Assiniboin meet Lewis and Clark expedition at Mandan village and warn Mandan not to trade with Americans.

1830–37: The Assiniboin are decimated by smallpox.

1883–84: More than three hundred Assiniboin die of starvation at Wolf Point.

1927: Fort Peck tribes adopt their constitution.

1937: Fort Belknap organizes a tribal government under the Indian Reorganization Act and ratifies a constitution.

1960: Fort Peck Constitution is amended.

1979: Assiniboin Claims Council is reformed.

traveled on foot and used dogs to pull their supplies on a sort of sled called a travois (pronounced truh-VOI; see "Transportation").

European contact

In 1690, Henry Kelsey (c. 1667–1724) of the Hudson's Bay Company, the largest fur-trading business in the New World, traveled with Assiniboin traders from James Bay to Saskatchewan. In exchange for the hides and furs the tribe provided the company, they received guns, kettles, beads, cloth, and liquor. The Assiniboin earned a reputation as great buffalo hunters and as traders who dealt not only with the Europeans but also with many of the other tribes in the area, such as the Mandan, Hidatsa, and Arikara. In addition, many people traveled the trails the Assiniboin established, and their camps became important points of contact for European-Indian trade.

The Assiniboin territory extended from the Yellowstone River Valley to the Saskatchewan River in both the United States and Canada. The people hunted beaver, bear, antelope, and buffalo, and they raided along the upper Missouri River villages. With the many guns they had obtained through trade, the Assiniboin were formidable opponents, and many tribes feared them. They traded widely and also provided canoe fleets and protection for the British traders.

As more fur traders and settlers moved into the area, the Europeans pushed the Assiniboin farther west and south. Soon the tribe roamed the Great Plains of North Dakota and Montana. With the acquisition of horses, they easily enlarged their territory.

Tribal division

In 1744, the Assiniboin divided, and some bands moved south to the Missouri Valley and roamed the area between the Hudson Bay and Rocky Mountain regions. Others went west and settled the valleys of the Assiniboin and Saskatchewan Rivers in Canada.

Because many Native bands lived autonomously (independently) rather than organizing under a central authority, it was sometimes difficult to tell which tribes were related. In addition, the people were divided into both northern and southern as well as forest and prairie bands. Bands considered part of the Assiniboin in the 1800s included the Itscheabine, Jatonabine (People of the Rocks), Otopachgnato (The Broad Ones), Otaopabine (Canoe Paddlers), Tschantoga (People of the

Woods), Watopachnato (Big Devils), Tanintauei, and Chabin (People of the Mountains).

Lewis and Clark expedition

Every year, the Assiniboin headed to the Mandan villages in North Dakota for a trading festival. This area was a central location for many tribes, such as the Crow (see entry), Cheyenne, Cree, and Teton Sioux, who came to barter with the Mandan farmers. The buffalo hunters traded pelts, guns, and horses for corn.

When the Assiniboin arrived in 1804, the Corps of Discovery, headed by Meriwether Lewis (1774–1809) and William Clark (1770–1838), was at the Mandan village. President Thomas Jefferson (1743–1826; served 1801–09) had sent these men to find waterways to the Pacific Ocean. Lewis and Clark also hoped to persuade the Native Americans to trade with the Americans rather than the British.

Black Cat, the Mandan chief, set up a meeting between the Assiniboin and the Americans. Clark gave the Assiniboin chief some ribbons, and the Americans believed the meeting went well. The Assiniboin, though, feared that trade with the Americans would interfere with British relations. At first they threatened to attack the Mandans if they bartered with Americans, but by 1827, when the American Fur Company built Fort Union, the Assiniboin traded with them as well as the British.

Smallpox epidemics

In addition to trade goods, the Europeans brought strange new diseases with them to Indian territory. Because the tribes had no immunity to these illnesses, the diseases often swept through the whole tribe, killing many people. In 1830, almost two-thirds of the tribe died from small-pox. The next outbreak in 1832 was so great that the people could not even bury their dead. By 1837, the once-powerful Assiniboin, who had numbered between 20,000 and 33,000, had been reduced to 6,000.

Loss of territory

The treaty of 1851 assigned the Assiniboin land south of the Missouri River. Following the 1862 wars in Minnesota, fleeing Sioux (see Dakota, Lakota, and Nakota entries) moved onto this territory. Additional tribes arrived as buffalo became scarce in other areas. In 1871, the Fort Peck Indian Agency opened in an old stockade to aid the Sioux and Assiniboin.

By 1876, conflict over the 1851 treaty and the discovery of gold in the Black Hills resulted in the Battle of Little Bighorn (1876; see Lakota entry).

After the war, the Sioux and Assiniboin gave 20 million acres of land to the United States. The tribes at the Fort Peck Agency in Poplar and in Wolf Point, Montana, agreed to the creation of Fort Peck Indian Reservation. The tribes retained 2 million acres. Fort Belknap was also created at this time, and Montana opened former Native American lands to settlers.

American "wolfers" in Canada

In Canada in the 1870s, a band of Americans crossed the border to engage in illegal whiskey sales. More and more furs were exchanged for liquor, and the Hudson's Bay Company lost some of its trading power in the area because it did not pay in alcohol. Drunkenness became an increasing problem as the possession of alcohol denoted a man's status as a successful trapper. Fights broke out frequently; many resulted in death.

One gang of thirty to one hundred "wolfers" had stolen U.S. cannons and set up a base at an abandoned trading fort across the border from Montana. They smuggled in whisky to trade for buffalo hides. They earned the name "wolfers" because they poisoned the buffalo carcasses after the Native Americans had skinned them. Wolves and coyotes that came to eat the meat would die; the Americans also sold those furs. Native American dogs and even some people died, too, from eating the poisoned meat.

In 1873, the wolfers lost some horses. They took their revenge on an Assiniboin camp. Twenty-three Native Americans died, including women and children. Only one wolfer was killed. Although the murderers were later tried, not one was convicted. Because of incidents like these, Canadian authorities formed the North West Mounted Police, or Mounties, to establish law and order, control illegal whiskey trade, and move the Native Americans to reserves.

Struggle to survive

By the late 1800s, many tribes faced starvation. The buffalo population had declined due to overharvesting for trade, the large quantities shot by white hunters, and the diseases passed to the herds by horses. In the United States, an influx of settlers claimed tribal land. In Canada, many tribes were relocated onto reserves. With states (in the United States) and provinces (in Canada) now officially recognized by the federal governments, an increasing number of Assiniboin were forced to give up their land.

As the buffalo disappeared from the area, the Assiniboin had to rely on federal agencies for food. Many of these agencies had insufficient rations to meet the growing needs, and several severe winters added to the problem. In addition, frequent changes in agents, dishonest or cruel agents, and too little medical attention left many people starving and dying. During 1883–84, more than three hundred Assiniboin died of starvation at the Wolf Point sub-agency.

Adding to the tribes' suffering, Congress passed the General Allotment Act (also known as the Dawes Act) in 1887 and the Fort Peck Allotment Act in 1908. Native peoples, who had always held land in common and worked together to farm it, had to accept small individual plots of land. Even tribes who had never farmed, such as the Assiniboin, had their reservation land divided up and parceled out to them. The government gave some of the reservation land to the Great Northern (Burlington Northern) Railroad and the remaining 1.35 million acres to white settlers.

When gold was discovered in the Klondike in the 1890s, Canadian treaties took more Native land to create routes for goldseekers. The districts of Assinboia, Saskatchewan, and Athabaska became the province of Saskatchewan, and soon the whole area was under treaty to the Canadian government. The Assiniboin were moved to reserves, where each family of five was entitled to one square acre of land.

Early twentieth century

By the early twentieth century, the Assiniboin had all been relocated to reservations or reserves. Once again their total population had declined from the 6,000 reported in 1837 to 2,600 in 1904. In Montana, Assiniboin Canoe Paddler and Red Bottom bands shared the Fort Peck Reservation with the Dakota, Nakota, and Lakota. The Fort Belknap Reservation in Montana was home to both Assiniboin and Gros Ventre tribes. Together these two reservations had an Assiniboin population of a little over 1,200. The other half of the Assiniboin lived in Canada.

The Assiniboin had difficulty adjusting to life on their small land allotments. The change from hunting to farming was difficult; adjusting to living in confined spaces after roaming the prairies left many struggling to survive. Most became dependent on government support. In addition, government policies designed to assimilate them (make them more like whites) took away their religious freedom and made it difficult for them to retain their culture. Many children were sent to boarding schools, where they were forbidden to speak their language and were forced to adopt white ways.

In 1934, the U.S. government passed the Indian Reorganization Act. In addition to stopping land allotments, it also provided for tribes to organize their governments with federal assistance. Assiniboin at Fort Belknap accepted the new law and began their tribal government under it, but those at Fort Peck, who had written a constitution in 1927, refused to comply.

Twenty-first-century Assiniboin

At the beginning of the twenty-first century, the Assiniboin lived on two reservations in Montana and several reserves in Canada. Most of these were shared with other tribes. Many people faced the difficulties of poor housing, high unemployment, limited education, and alcoholism. To reduce crime, violence, and substance abuse, Fort Peck was one of seven tribes selected to participate in the U.S. Bureau of Justice Assistance program, Tribal Strategies Against Violence (TSAV). Working with government agencies, the tribe identified problems and developed partnerships to address them.

Environmental issues also concerned many Assiniboin. At Fort Belknap, the tribe struggled with water contamination and the reclamation of a landfill and gold mining area. It also began working to preserve area wetlands.

Water contamination also plagued Fort Peck. The tribe initiated a Municipal and Industrial Rural Drinking Water Program and began an irrigation system along the Missouri River in 2003. The tribe also met with nearby towns and began a $180 million water project to serve all the communities as well as the reservation.

In 2006, the Alexis band identified more than two thousand oil wells on tribal ground. The groups are all dealing with a variety of environmental concerns as industrial developments change the areas where they live.

RELIGION

The Assiniboin believed in a Great Creator, and they prayed, fasted, and made sacrifices to this power, which made all things. They also revered Thunder, Sun, and *Anú k-ite.* or "Double Face," who often appeared during the Sun Dance. To appease him, an Assiniboin might cut off his fingertip or some flesh from his arm. Double Face had two faces that looked the same, but he had two different voices. If he spoke to a war party, they could tell whether or not they would win the battle by the voice he used. The Sun Dance was held after the spring buffalo hunt. The people prayed, sang, drummed, danced, and fasted (went without food and water) to honor the Great Spirit. A feast concluded the ritual.

Vision quests were important to the tribe. Each person had his own spirit, obtained by fasting. Spirits could be animals or inanimate (nonliving) objects. Individuals performed rites alone or in groups. They sang, prayed, made offerings, and had a special pack of sacred objects (see "Puberty").

Prior to important ceremonies, the Assiniboin purified the body and soul by sweating in a sweat lodge. This is a special building with a floor made of broadleaf sage. A hot rock is placed in each of the four directions; two more rocks represent the earth and heaven. One man touches the pipe to each rock before lighting the pipe to pass it around. Each man sings, prays, and pours water on the hot rocks to create steam.

One ceremony called *Watíchaghe*, or "Make a Home," included building a nest for the Thunderbird. Similar to a Sun Dance, the rite lasted four days, but the people called on thunder rather than the sun. To begin this ritual, a man who had a vision begged other warriors to accompany him into the woods the next day. They brought back a 30-foot (9-meter) tree to use as the center pole for a lodge covered with skins. They made a Thunderbird nest in the tree fork from a bundle of sticks and carved symbols of a Thunderbird, lightning, and Double Face. At sunset, they began the dance, which lasted two more days. Women could dance, but only in the western part of the lodge, and they did not join in the piercing ceremony. Men's chests were pierced and tied to ropes. They danced until they had a vision, then tore themselves free of the ropes.

Dancing was an important part of many religious rituals. When the missionaries arrived in the 1800s, they tried to convert the tribes and pressured the government to pass laws to prohibit the dancing, especially the Sun Dance. After dancing was banned, most tribes practiced their religion in secret. They also planned their celebrations to coincide with the missionaries' religious holidays, so their dancing would not be interrupted. The Assiniboin gave up the Sun Dance in 1935 after two men at Fort Peck were hit by lightning.

In spite of that, other cultural traditions remain strong, and all generations take part in ceremonies. In the United States, many Assiniboin participate in the Medicine Lodge religion. In Canada, they call it the Rain Dance.

Assiniboin Words

wiⁿyaⁿ	"woman"
wiⁿcha	"man"
čhaŋté	"heart"
čhuŋwíⁿtku	"daughters"
hokšína	"boy"
haŋyákhena	"early morning"
khuwápi	"They chased it"
wi	"sun"
haⁿhepiwi	"moon"
mini	"water"
šúŋga-šana	"red fox"
waŋgáŋgaŋna	"old woman"
witháŋga	"large tepee"
yá!	"go!"

LANGUAGE

Assiniboin, often called *Nakota* or *Nakoda* by its own speakers, is a Siouan language, related to Dakota. The Stoney, who split from the original tribe, speak another dialect (variety) of the Nakoda language. Although the languages are similar, the two tribes do not understand each other well. About two hundred people in Montana, Alberta, and Saskatchewan spoke Assiniboin in the mid-2000s. In studies conducted in the early 2000s, the majority of Canadian and American Assiniboin speakers were over age sixty.

GOVERNMENT

The Assiniboin lived in nomadic camps that contained anywhere from several hundred members to as many as three thousand, most of them members of an extended family. Because their society was patrilineal, men took charge of leadership and decision making. The bands selected a headman or chief to handle relations with other tribes. They chose a good man who had superior hunting skills, outstanding achievement in battle, and a kind and generous heart. In certain situations, special leaders were selected—a war chief for battles, a hunting chief for buffalo hunts, or a chief for the soldiers's lodge.

A council guided the chief's actions. Elders, medicine men, pipe carriers, women, and heads of households were all part of the council. When the council met, the people listened to anyone who was wise. Decisions were made by consensus, which meant everyone had to agree.

Under the Indian Reorganization Act in 1934, the U.S. government gave tribes the opportunity to write their own constitutions. The Fort Belknap Indian Community Council adopted a constitution in 1937. It created a governing body composed of eight elected council members, four each from the Assiniboin and the Gros Ventre, elected every two years. The council also has three officers. The president and vice president appoint a secretary-treasurer who serves a four-year term.

The tribes at Fort Peck Reservation, however, rejected the Reorganization Act because they had already written a constitution in 1927.

The tribe amended this constitution in 1952 and adopted another in 1960. The Fort Peck constitution is one of the only modern Native American constitutions that still includes provisions for traditional tribal government. A Tribal Executive Board governs the reservation; it is made up of twelve members and four officers—a chairperson, vice chairperson, secretary-accountant, and sergeant-at-arms. With the exception of the secretary-accountant, the members serve two-year terms. Council members handle nine business committees and deal with tribal policy and business management.

In Canada, the Assiniboin formed Band Councils that are governed by a chief and councilors. They must obey the laws established by the Indian Act and the Canadian Constitution and be guided by the minister of Indian Affairs.

ECONOMY

Early economy

When the Europeans arrived, the Assiniboin were nomadic, migrating with their tepees wherever they found game. Once they had horses, they could cover even greater distances. After the Europeans arrived, the Assiniboin engaged in trade, exchanging pemmican (a nutritious and well-preserved mixture of meat and berries) and buffalo skins for guns, liquor, and other goods that they traded with various tribes in the area.

After the buffalo grew scarce and the bands were relocated to reservations, they struggled to support themselves. Losing their lands and being forced to become farmers left many Assiniboin poverty-stricken and starving. Most ended up dependent on governments rations.

Modern U.S. economy

In the mid-2000s, agriculture was the main industry on the Fort Peck Reservation. The tribe also had one of the first jointly owned oil wells in the United States. Manufacturing, mining, and tourism, along with an industrial park, provided employment opportunities.

Fort Belknap also has agriculture and ranching, tourism, a meat-packing plant, stone mining, and industrial space. The tribe's unemployment rate, however, was about 70 percent in 2005, meaning that almost three-fourths of the population could not find jobs. Taxes on tobacco products brought in about $150,000 each year; those funds were a necessity with so many people unemployed. In spite of that and other economic growth projects on the reservation, 80 percent of the students on the reservation qualified for the assisted school lunch program in 2010.

Present-day Canadian economy

The Alexis band operates several businesses as well as a casino. It has more than 148 oil and gas companies operating on tribal land. Mosquito-Grizzly Bear's Head Reserve joined six other First Nations to form Battlefields Tribal Council, a business-development enterprise. Carry the Kettle Assiniboine Reserve has agricultural land and operates a plastics plant, a potato plant, a service station, and a store that sells tobacco products.

The Assiniboin were nomadic, moving with the buffalo herds that they hunted. They lived in easily transported tepees. © THE STAPLETON COLLECTION/THE BRIDGEMAN ART LIBRARY.

Paul band's main income comes from farming operations and harvesting equipment. The Whitebear Reserve depends on recreational lands and tourism along with natural resources—oil and gas.

DAILY LIFE

Buildings

Like other Plains Indians, the Assiniboin lived in tepees, which allowed them to easily assemble and take down their homes as they followed the buffalo herds. Women were responsible for erecting the tepees, and dogs carried the poles and hides on travois (pronounced truh-VOI; see "Transportation"). Some villages contained as many as two hundred tepees. Larger tepees housed extended families or more than one family.

Tepees were supported by poles placed in the ground that met in the center. Women tied three main poles together and hoisted them up to brace the tepee. Then the other poles were set in place and covered with as many as fifteen to fifty buffalo hides sewn together. Men decorated their tepees with dream visions or scenes from their hunts or battles.

Tepees were not evenly shaped cones as they are sometimes depicted. They were shorter on one side and tilted away from the wind to make them secure even during storms. The Assiniboin angled the smoke hole to prevent cold winds from entering the tent. Angling also pulled the smoke from inside the tent, making it less smoky inside. By changing the direction the tepee faced in summer, the smoke hole drew cool air inside. Although the smoke hole usually remained open, a rope attached to it wound around the outside of the tent. Those inside the tepee could pull the flap closed to protect themselves from rain or snow.

Transportation

Because they moved often and needed to transport the large tepee poles, the Assiniboin used dogs to pull their home-building materials. They hitched a pole on either side of a dog and lashed a webbed frame (or poles) to the ends on the ground, so the dog dragged this triangular-shaped carrier behind it like a sled. The Assiniboin piled these carriers, called travois (pronounced truh-VOI), with their possessions. Each dog could pull up to 77 pounds (35 kilograms) on a travois, and families often owned several animals. After horses were introduced, the larger animals took over the job of transporting the tepees.

Tanning Hides

Preparing animal skins so they were soft enough to wear took time and talent. The hide had to stay in one large piece, so skinning an animal required skill. To make clothing, women first removed the hair and meat from the skin. Some tribes preferred dry scraping (using an animal bone or a stone tool to rub the meat from one side of the skin and the hair from the other). Other tribes mixed ashes into water and soaked the skins for a few days. They then pegged the hide to the ground or laced it to a wooden frame to keep it taut while they scraped.

After scraping the hides, women washed them and then stretched them on frames until they were almost as thin as paper. Once the hides dried, some tribes hung them over the fire for several hours to smoke. This gave them a brown color; many Plains tribes left the hides white. To finish and soften the hides, women mashed animal brains and rubbed them into the hides. More scraping and stretching followed until the hides were supple enough for clothing.

In early eras, women mixed minerals or clays with buffalo fat in turtle-shell bowls. They soaked the hip bone of a buffalo in water until it became like a sponge, then they painted designs on the clothing. In addition to painting scenes of battles or hunts, women also adorned their clothing with dyed porcupine quills, animal teeth, bones, or claws. Many women covered the yokes of their dresses with animal teeth. Later, most tribes used beads obtained through trade to decorate clothing and moccasins.

Because the Assiniboin originally lived near the lakes, they were known for their canoeing skills. They often transported traders along the rivers with their loads of furs. This earned them the nickname "Paddlers." During the 1800s, some of the Assiniboin called themselves *Otaopabine*. meaning "Canoe Paddlers." In modern times, a band by that name still lives on the Fort Peck Reservation.

Clothing and adornment

The Assiniboin made most of their clothing from the skins of elk, deer, and mountain sheep. Women painted dresses and shirts with scenes of wars or hunts. The clothing they made often told of their father's or husband's skill in battle or during a hunt.

Clothing designs indicated the wearer's status. If her husband was an outstanding hunter or trader, a wife's dress might be covered in elk teeth or animal claws. Sometimes men collected elk teeth to give to their brides. During the winter, the people wore buffalo robes for warmth, and men wore white wolfskin caps and used snowshoes for hunting.

Men rarely cut their hair. They twisted it into long, thin locks or tails and often added horsehair or other hair to make it even longer. Some men's hair touched the ground. Most of the time, they wound it on top of their heads in a coil. Women's hair was usually shorter.

In the early twenty-first century, regalia (traditional costumes) may be worn for weddings, naming ceremonies, powwows, or other special celebrations. Girls and women wear beaded elk hide, deer hide, or cloth dresses covered with shells, elk teeth, or jingles (cone-shaped pieces of tin that make sounds when they walk). The designs on their dresses often tell family stories or honor family members. Men may wear beaded outfits or beaded accessories, such as moccasins, belts, headbands, or vests.

Food

The Assiniboin depended on buffalo for most of their food, clothing, shelter, and tools. They often trapped the herds by driving them into compounds or over cliffs. They sometimes roasted the meat on spits, but most of the time they boiled it. They made containers from hide, put meat and water into them, and then added hot stones to make the liquid boil. The tribe's name, which means "those who cook with stones," came from this practice.

Northern bands of Assiniboin also hunted moose, bear, elk, porcupine, and beaver. In addition, most bands ate deer, antelope, mountain sheep, rabbit, gopher, chipmunk, fish, duck, partridge, and other birds. They traded furs for crops, especially Mandan corn. European traders often bartered for their pemmican, which they made from pounded, dried buffalo meat mixed with fat and dried berries.

Some Assiniboin gathered wild rice, and most ate plants, seeds, and roots that grew wild, such as turnips, chokecherries, raspberries, and bulrushes. Some sources indicate that they may have sacrificed and eaten dogs as part of religious rituals.

Education

Learning to hunt was an important part of a young boy's education. Children learned by playing games and modeling the behavior of their elders. In 1877, the government opened a boarding school to assimilate Native Americans (make them like whites). Assiniboin children who were sent there were not allowed to speak their native language or practice their customs.

In the early twentieth century, Mormons and Presbyterians ran missionary schools, but they had little success. In the early 2000s, students on the Fort Peck Reservation attended five public school districts for elementary through high school. Fort Peck Community College, a tribally controlled college, is located on the reservation, and Native American Education Service College, with one of strongest tribal studies programs in the United States, offers scholarships for its four-year programs, so students can attend college on or off reservation.

The Fort Belknap Education Department was established in 1977. Students have several different educational options on the reservation, including religious and public schools. Some children attend off-reservation boarding schools. Fort Belknap Community College opened in 1984.

Healing practices

Medicine men received their power from the spirits through visions. They healed people using songs, herbs, and sucking objects out of the patient's body. Some medicine men put the object in a wooden bowl, covered it with a cloth, and made it disappear. If herbs and sucking did not work, the medicine man played a bone flute.

One healing ritual was done by both men and women. They set up a long tepee, and the members of the healing society each carried the skin of an animal that contained *wakan* (sacred) power. Healers sat in two rows on each side and sang while they made throwing motions with the skins. When the patient fainted, they piled the skins on his body to draw out the evil and illness.

Some medicine people had the power to cause disease or death. People paid them for their services, and these medicine men worked their spells on birchbark or rawhide, punched four holes in important parts, and then buried it on a hilltop. Those who made deals with these men kept them secret for fear of retribution.

As of the first decade of 2000, Fort Belknap had a hospital and health center in Hays operated by the Indian Health Service. The tribe also offered health education programs. At Fort Peck, people have access to both the Verne E. Gibbs Health Center in Poplar and the Chief Redstone Clinic in Wolf Point. They, too, have community health programs in addition to mental health, dental, and eye care services.

ARTS

Quillwork

In modern times, Assiniboin women are known for their decorative clothing. In the past, elk teeth and porcupine quills adorned dresses, shirts, and moccasins. Women also painted decorations onto the fabric. Later, beading also became popular. Although beading is easier, many people still use porcupine quills. The quills must be pulled from the porcupine hide, washed, dyed, dried, and sorted by size before they can be used. Artists then soften the quills in their mouths to make them pliable and flatten them before creating decorations on hide or cloth.

An Assiniboin hand drum is representative of the type frequently used in the tribe's ceremonies and songs. © WERNER FORMAN/ART RESOURCE, NY.

Music

The Assiniboin believe the Thunder Beings gave their people the first song and drum, so music is very important to their culture. Singing involves all ages. Each person receives a special song during a vision quest (see "Puberty"); it is sacred and only used at appropriate times. Other ceremonial songs include the Sun Dance and Sweat Lodge songs, Ghost Dance Songs, and Death Songs accompanied by the hand drum. Social Songs accompany the Tea Dance or Round Dance (see "Festivals"); they signify friendship and may also be used at weddings or memorials. These are usually sung to both the hand drum and the big drum. Community members engage in singing with the big drum during powwows, celebrations that also include tribal dances.

To invite people to a powwow, a singer would sing outside some homes to get friends to accompany him. Then the group went from house to house and sang Doorway Songs (sometimes called "Begging Songs" or "Counting Buckets"). People would emerge from their houses and tell the singers what they would bring to the powwow. Although it is rarely done anymore, it was a way to invite people and solicit donations of food for the celebration.

CUSTOMS

Puberty

Each young man went on a vision quest to receive a guardian spirit and sacred song to help him throughout his life. He traveled to sacred grounds and fasted (went without food and water) for a period of one to four days. During that time, a vision of the young man's guardian spirit appeared to him. He might also be given a special song. Those who were pipe carriers received a bundle containing a pipe, wrapped in red cloth and tied with sage. To prepare themselves, they learned to use the sweat lodge, tobacco for offerings, and sacred songs. They received a song from the spiritual grandfathers that was only used at this special time.

Festivals

Originally, the Round Dance was a healing ceremony that became a social dance. Held in winter, it is a time for those who have died to dance with the living. People join hands and circle in a clockwise direction, moving up and down like the Northern Lights, which the people say are their ancestors dancing.

Annual celebrations at Fort Belknap Reservation include Milk River Indian Days, Hays Powwow, and Chief Joseph Memorial Days, which feature traditional dancing and cultural activities. Throughout the year they have rodeos, county fairs, and sporting events for residents.

Fort Peck holds Poplar Indian Days on Labor Day weekend with a powwow, dancing competition, and honoring ceremonies. Wolf Point Wild Horse Stampede in July attracts cowboys from all over the country.

The Assiniboin put the bodies of the deceased on a scaffold to keep them away from animals until the bodies were ready for burial. © OMAHA, NEBRASKA, USA/ALECTO HISTORICAL EDITIONS/THE BRIDGEMAN ART LIBRARY.

Death rituals

If a person died in winter, the tribe took the body with them and placed it on a scaffold, out of reach of animals, at each stop until they arrived at the burial grounds. They then placed the body in a sitting position in a 5-foot (1.5-meter) deep circular grave, which was lined with bark or skins. They covered the opening with logs, then heaped dirt on top.

The Assiniboin believed everyone had four souls. Three died with the body and the fourth lived inside a "spirit bundle." Friends of the deceased offered gifts until that spirit was released to follow the others.

CURRENT TRIBAL ISSUES

In 2009, a new requirement that people must show passports when they cross the United States–Canada border caused problems for many people. The Jay Treaty of 1795 granted North American tribes the freedom to trade and travel between the two countries. In spite of this, many are stopped and questioned at the border, and some have been denied entry. This is particularly difficult for tribes that have reservations or families on both sides of the border.

To increase energy in an environmentally safe manner, the Fort Peck reservation received government funds to monitor wind velocity for generating wind power. When the study showed that the area had sufficient wind, the tribe had two turbines installed. Once the equipment was running, the tribe realized it needed a way to control the turbines when winds got too strong or temperatures dropped well below zero. Local companies came to their aid and installed wireless networks that provide the needed feedback.

Founded in 2009, the Fort Peck Energy Company is owned half by the tribes and half by Native American Resource Partners. Together they have been doing exploratory drilling for more oil and gas opportunities. They hope to bring additonal jobs to the reservation along with greater income.

NOTABLE PEOPLE

A age eleven, Jumping Bull (1846–1890) fought bravely with his small bow when his tribe was attacked by the Sioux, who were under the command of Chief Sitting Bull (c. 1831–1890). When the Sioux tried to kill the boy, Sitting Bull stopped them. He said, "This boy is too brave to die! I take him as my brother." Later in life, Jumping Bull died defending Sitting Bull.

Two writers known for furthering tribal culture are Susan Braine, who served as chief operating officer of Koahnic Broadcast Corporation and helped launch Native Voice 1, a Native radio station, in 2006. She also writes for children. Bernelda Wheeler (1937–2005), an Assiniboin/Cree/Saulteaux storyteller and journalist, served as an advisor to the Aboriginal Film and Video Art Alliance. Monica Braine produced *If the Name Has to Go....* an award-winning documentary.

BOOKS

Miller, David, et al. *The History of the Fort Peck Assiniboine and Sioux Tribes, 1800–2000.* Helena: Fort Peck Community College, Montana Historical Society Press, 2008.

Morgan, Mindy J. *The Bearer of This Letter: Language Ideologies, Literacy Practices, and the Fort Belknap Indian Community.* Lincoln: University of Nebraska Press, 2009.

Reilly, John. *Bad Medicine: A Judge's Struggle for Justice in a First Nations Community.* Surrey, British Columbia: Rocky Mountain Books, 2010.

WEB SITES

Alexis Nakota Sioux Nation. http://www.alexisnakotasioux.com/ (accessed on June 7, 2011).

"Assiniboine History." *Fort Belknap Indian Community.* http://www.ftbelknap-nsn.gov/assiniboineHistory.php (accessed on June 6, 2011).

"Assiniboin Indian History." *Access Genealogy.* http://www.accessgenealogy.com/native/tribes/assiniboin/assiniboinhist.htm (accessed on June 7, 2011).

"Assinboin Indians." *PBS.* http://www.pbs.org/lewisandclark/native/idx_ass.html (accessed on June 7, 2011).

Fort Peck Tribes. http://www.fortpecktribes.org/ (accessed on June 4, 2011).

"Introduction to Carry the Kettle." *Carry the Kettle Band.* http://www.carrythekettle.ca/ (accessed on June 7, 2011).

"Native American Tribes Manage Wind Power Generation Turbines in Brutal Sub-Zero Conditions with D-Link Wireless Solution." *D-Link.* ftp://ftp10.dlink.com/pdfs/caseStudies/cs_FortPeckReservation.pdf (accessed on June 6, 2011).

Cree

Name

Cree (*kree*). Cree groups in different regions refer to themselves by various names, and they only use the term "Cree" when speaking or writing in English. The French called the people *Kristineaux,* most likely the French pronunciation for the tribe's name for themselves, *Kenistenoag.* The name became shortened to "Kri," spelled "Cree" in English.

Location

Canada's Cree live in areas spanning the nation's provinces from Quebec in the east to Alberta in the west. The group called Plains Cree lives in the parklands and plains of Alberta and Saskatchewan, and the Woodland Cree live in the forests of Saskatchewan and Manitoba. The Swampy Cree live in Manitoba, Ontario, and Quebec. American Cree are scattered throughout many states; some share the Rocky Boy's Reservation in Montana with the Ojibway (see entry).

Population

In the 1600s, there were an estimated 30,000 Cree. In Canada in 1995, there were at least 76,000 Cree. In the United States in 1990, 8,467 people identified themselves as Cree. A count of the population done by the U.S. Bureau of the Census in 2000 showed 2,445 Cree and 8,837 people who had some Cree heritage. Canadian Cree numbered 72,680 in 2001. In 2010, the census counted 2,211 Cree in the United States, with a total of 7,983 people claiming some Cree heritage.

Language family

Algonquian.

Origins and group affiliations

For more than six thousand years, the ancestors of the Cree lived near the Arctic Circle. Some Plains Cree intermarried with the French, creating the unique Métis culture (see next entry) of the Red River Valley. At various times, enemies of the Cree were the Blackfoot, the Nakota, the Ojibway,

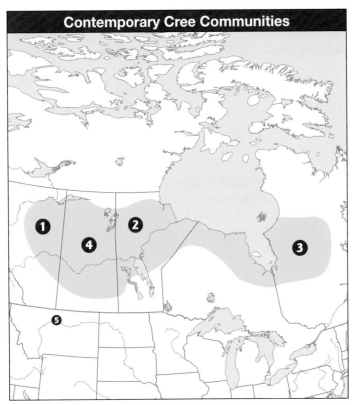

Contemporary Cree Communities

Canada
1. Alberta (more than 25 Cree reserves)
2. Manitoba (more than 20 Cree reserves)
3. Quebec (more than 9 Cree reserves)
4. Saskatchewan (more than 40 Cree reserves)

Montana
5. Rocky Boy's Reservation

Shaded area
Traditional lands of the Cree in present-day northern Manitoba, Saskatchewan, Alberta, northern Ontario, and northern Quebec

A map of contemporary Cree communities. MAP BY XNR PRODUCTIONS. CENGAGE LEARNING, GALE. REPRODUCED BY PERMISSION OF GALE, A PART OF CENGAGE LEARNING.

and the Athabascan (see entries). The Assiniboin (*uh-SIN-uh-boin*; see entry) were their major ally.

The early Cree lived among the lakes, rivers, and spruce forests of eastern Canada, where the winters were long, the summers were short, and their lives were regulated by the seasons. They respected the animals and land that supplied their needs, and many of their customs ensured the success of tribal hunters. Their gradual movement over an immense area made the Cree perhaps the most widespread of the Native American peoples.

HISTORY

Changes come

The Cree, who occupied lands in eastern Canada for thousands of years, have a complicated history. Before they had contact with Europeans, the Cree lived south and southwest of the Hudson Bay in northern Quebec, where they made all the tools, weapons, and warm clothing they needed to survive from the stones, trees, and animals around them. From these natural resources, they fashioned tents, spears, bows and arrows, cooking equipment, boats, sleds, and snowshoes.

When British explorer Henry Hudson (c. 1654–1611) arrived at Hudson Bay during the winter of 1610–11, trade began between the Cree people and Europeans. During the mid- to late 1600s, the Cree carried on a thriving trade in animal pelts, primarily beaver. They had an advantage in the new trade because they had experience in hunting and gathering over vast areas, and other tribes feared and respected them.

Middlemen in the fur trade

Between 1668 and 1688, Hudson's Bay Company, the powerful British trading company, set up posts at the mouths of rivers in Cree territory. Soon the Cree became middlemen in the fur trade, bringing European goods to remote inland tribes and returning with furs for European traders. The Cree were well adapted to the demands of a trapper's life. They used canoes, which allowed them to take advantage of the waterways, and they quickly became familiar with European ways. They used guns to hunt, to control access to the trading posts, and to ward off enemies and rivals.

Over time, the Cree gave up traditional tools for those of the Europeans and replaced their clothing of fur and animal skins for wool and cloth garments. They swapped furs for knives, axes, metal scrapers for preparing animal skins, fishhooks, brass kettles, rifles, blankets, and steel animal traps.

The Cree traded at British posts to the north and French posts to the south. For a while, their part in the fur trade made them the wealthiest and most powerful tribe in the region, but they soon paid a terrible price. They were exposed to new diseases, to which they had no immunity, and to liquor. About two-thirds of the Cree were wiped out

Important Dates

1668–88: The Cree become middlemen in the fur trade and the chief consumers of European trade goods.

1885: Along with the Métis, the Cree in the Saskatchewan River area fight Canadian forces in the Northwest Rebellion.

1905: Treaty No. 9 is signed at the Hudson's Bay Company's Moose Factory. For $8 upon signing and $4 a year thereafter, each Cree gives up all rights to his or her land.

1971: Quebec government unveils plans for the James Bay I hydroelectric project. Cree and Inuit protest the action in Quebec courts.

1994: James Bay II project is cancelled, largely due to the Quebec Cree's successful legal efforts.

2002: The Cree sign an agreement with Quebec ceding (signing over) property for a $3.5 billion settlement and a say in the management of their land.

2004: The tribe signs an agreement allowing two new electrical plants to be built.

by disease. Unlike other Native groups, however, the tribe's population ultimately increased, perhaps because people moved out of the disease-infested areas when necessary.

Moving west

By the 1730s, many Woodland Cree had relocated to the Great Plains of western Canada to escape epidemics and explore new fur-hunting areas. Some settled as far west as the Canadian Rocky Mountains. This made them less dependent on trading posts and allowed them to live in larger tribal groups. When the beaver were depleted from overhunting, the Cree substituted buffalo hides. They made most of the items they needed to survive from various parts of the buffalo.

Alliance with Blackfoot

For a time, the Woodland Cree used the resources of both the woodlands and Canada's Great Plains farther west. They formed an alliance with the Blackfoot (see entry) in what would soon become the United States. The Cree visited the Blackfoot in the spring and obtained furs from them, trapped their own, and returned east to trade them. Afterward, they hunted in the province of Saskatchewan before visiting the Blackfoot again. The Cree also supplied the Blackfoot with weapons to drive back their enemies.

Between 1790 and 1810, the Cree-Blackfoot alliance fell apart, and the trading system disappeared. By then, the Cree were using horses, which the Spanish had introduced to North America. Horses became so important to Cree society that they measured a person's status by the type and number of horses he owned.

Life on the Great Plains

By the mid-1800s, the Plains Cree were battling for control of land and resources. They often trailed the buffalo onto the territory of their enemies, which included their former partners the Blackfoot, as well as the Nakota, Crow, Cheyenne, Nez Perce, and Flathead tribes (see entries).

In 1870, buffalo were plentiful on the Great Plains, but within ten years, after widespread slaughter by settlers, only a small number remained. With the buffalo gone, the tribe faced constant starvation. Epidemics weakened or killed many Cree, and most people believed that their god, the Great Manito, had delivered them over to the Evil Spirit for their wickedness.

Attempts at farming

In the 1870s, while negotiating treaties with the Canadian government, the Plains Cree sought help to change to a farming-based economy. The government promised them tools and livestock but was slow to provide them. The Cree were given poor-quality grain, plows and wagons barely fit for use, and wild cattle that could not be hitched to the plow. The wheat the Cree received was useless, as there were no facilities for grinding the grain near their reserve (the Canadian term for reservation). In spite of this, the Cree made a success of farming, and area settlers soon argued that government assistance gave the Native Americans an unfair advantage.

The Métis rebellions

In 1885, the Plains Cree joined their relatives the Métis (see entry) in the Second Riel Rebellion to protect their land from the whites. The

The Rocky Boy's Reservation in northern Montana, seen here in 1936, was granted to the Ojibway and Cree tribes in 1915.
© HULTON ARCHIVE/GETTY IMAGES.

Riel Rebellions (1869 and 1885) were among the few wars that took place between First Nations (Canadian Natives) and the Canadian government. During the second rebellion, Cree chiefs Poundmaker (1842–1886) and Big Bear (c. 1825–1888) led warriors against the Northwest Mounted Police (Mounties), who patrolled Canada's western wilderness, and an army was sent from eastern Canada to put down the uprising. After two major battles, the Métis gave up the fight; Cree leaders eventually turned themselves in and served prison terms.

Following the conflict, a group of Cree left Canada and settled in the United States in northern Montana. They later joined a group of landless Ojibway (see entry), and in 1915, the homeless Native Americans were granted the Rocky Boy's Reservation, 50 miles (80 kilometers) south of the Canadian border. Cree people still live on this reservation with the Chippewa (Ojibway) in the early twenty-first century.

Loss of livelihood

In 1889, the Commission of Indian Affairs in Saskatchewan began a new farming system. It reduced each person's farming area to one acre of wheat and a garden of roots and vegetables. They also insisted the people use only simple tools and manufacture their own farm tools, such as hay forks or carts.

In part because of these new restrictions, many Plains Cree gave up farming. They soon fell behind in technology and struggled to catch up. Many ended up on Indian reserves, scratching out a meager living through farming, ranching, or manual labor.

Ontario Cree

In 1905, faced with increasing numbers of settlements, mining activities, and railway construction that threatened their way of life, the Woodland Cree signed Treaty No. 9 at the Hudson's Bay Company's Moose Factory. Those who did so received $8 upon signing and a payment every year after of $4 in treaty money. In return, they gave up all rights to their land. It remains unclear whether the Cree understood the treaty, which many of them signed by using picture symbols.

Between 1920 and 1940, hundreds of Cree in Ontario died from tuberculosis, flu, measles, whooping cough, and bronchitis, diseases that were new to their people and for which they had no resistance. During the 1940s, immunization and medicines were made available to the Ontario Cree. Still, their health-care and educational services remained poor.

Starvation was widespread due to a dramatic decline in the beaver and caribou they hunted for food. In addition, the provincial government strictly enforced its wild game laws, limiting when people could hunt and how much game they could take.

Twentieth-century challenges

In 1971, the Cree in the Province of Quebec were faced with a new threat. The Canadian government planned to dam the La Grande River and build electrical plants along the rapids. Electricity would be transmitted south to Montreal and to cities in the United States. At that time, fifty Cree and Inuit (see entry) hunters protested this James Bay Project in Quebec courts, arguing that it would threaten their way of life. They won their case, but the decision was overturned (see "Current tribal issues").

In 1975, the Cree signed the James Bay and Northern Quebec Agreement. This document recognized that the Cree had the same rights to health care and education as other Canadians, and that the Cree should decide how their lands will be managed.

Life for the Cree on most reserves remained difficult into the 1990s, and many residents lived on government welfare payments. They sent their children to schools on the reserve and received health care from a government nursing station. This way of living resulted in what has been called a "forced and numbing idleness," in the words of Rupert Ross in *Dancing with a Ghost: Exploring Indian Reality.* On top of a harsh economic situation, the Cree also face racial discrimination from many of their neighbors.

After receiving a large monetary settlement for the loss of their lands (see "Current tribal issues"), the Quebec Cree had capital to invest in economic growth. The guaranteed income for fifty years gave the tribe the opportunity for a brighter future.

RELIGION

Traditional beliefs

For the Cree, the life force, similar to the Christian idea of the soul, resided in all living beings. They also believed in spirits, ghosts, and demons, which sometimes revealed themselves in dreams.

The Plains Cree honored one powerful creator, the Great Manito, who controlled all things in the universe. Manito was too powerful to be approached directly for blessings. Instead, spirit powers called *atayo-hkanak* served as go-betweens. All unpleasantness, disease, and wickedness in life came from the Evil Manito.

The Cree repeated long prayers asking for help from the kind and caring gods. They used objects such as eagle feathers and eagle wings during these rituals, and many wore amulets (small objects encased in a beaded envelope) to keep evil away.

During times of near starvation, the Cree occasionally were forced to resort to cannibalism (eating the bodies of other humans). They viewed cannibalism with horror, however, and greatly feared the *windigos,* human beings who had eaten human flesh and been transformed into supernatural, man-eating giants.

Christianity

In the late 1880s, missionaries converted a number of Cree to Christian religions. The missionaries burned the drums of Cree people, hoping to end traditional Cree beliefs and practices, but many people retained their original beliefs.

Abishabis In the mid-1800s, a man named Abishabis ("Small Eyes"; d. 1843) called himself "Jesus" and with a friend, Wasiteck ("Light"), claimed to draw "The Track to Heaven" on paper or wood. These two prophets began a religious movement that spread from Manitoba to Ontario. Their followers sang psalms and painted books. An elder priestess helped spread the movement. They combined Christian teachings with Cree beliefs. People supported them with gifts of clothing and food, but they later turned against Abishabis when he wanted more goods for his followers. Some suspected him of robbing and murdering a family, so they seized and killed him. Many Cree believed he had become a windigo (see "Traditional beliefs").

LANGUAGE

Cree is an Algonquian language spoken by more than forty-five thousand people. The five dialects are Western/Plains Cree, Northern/Woodlands Cree, Central/Swampy Cree, Moose Cree, and Eastern Cree. Most speakers of the different dialects, especially those who live near each other, can understand each other.

The Cree language is written using a series of symbols called syllabics. These symbols are unique because the Cree use shapes for consonants and rotate them in the Four Directions to represent vowels. In the mid-2000s, children on most Cree reserves spoke their native language for the first years of elementary school, adding English a few years later.

GOVERNMENT

The Cree government was based on a system in which chiefs, councils, leaders, elders, women, and youth all participated in group decision making, and all voices were heard.

In the early twenty-first century, Canadian Cree villages were still headed by chiefs, and a grand chief presided over the Grand Council of the Cree, founded in 1974. The Cree hold a general assembly in a different community each year. Leaders report on events of the past year, and all the people discuss the course of Cree affairs for the year ahead.

The Chippewa-Cree on Rocky Boy's Reservation adopted a constitution in 1935, which they later amended in 1973. They are governed by a nine-member business committee elected by the people from the reservation's five districts.

ECONOMY

The Woodland Cree were hunters and fishermen who trapped in the winter, hunted goose in spring, and fished in the summer. They used bows and arrows, clubs, spears, and snares to capture large and small game. They later served as middlemen in the prosperous fur trade, trading first with the French and then the British.

The buffalo supplied more than just food for the Cree. Bones were carved into arrowheads; the skull served as a lamp in wet weather. The tail worked as a fly swatter. The Cree twisted the hair into rope and used tendons for bowstrings and sewing thread. Boiled bones made glue, and teeth were fashioned into ornaments and necklaces. They turned

The Seasons of a Cree Trapper's Life

Some Cree still rely on hunting, trapping, and fishing to survive, and their lives are regulated by the seasons. While many Cree live in villages in the winter, they go into the woods to bring back game to share with their people.

The trapping season runs from September through March, when the men snare beaver, lynx, otter, muskrat, mink, weasel, marten, red fox, arctic fox, wolf, and red squirrel. April through March is hunting season, when they pursue birds, such as geese, ducks, and loons. Men who live near the coast hunt beluga whales in June and July and seals in October. Fall is the time for hunting large game, such as bear and caribou. In the winter and spring, their prey is porcupine, rabbit, and grouse. Fishing takes place throughout the year, and in the summer, whole families use nets to catch whitefish, trout, arctic char, pike, sturgeon, and longnose sucker.

"A Cree Woman," photograph by Edward S. Curtis, 1926.
THE LIBRARY OF CONGRESS.

buffalo hooves into ladles and spoons, and they even burned the waste material, dried dung, for fuel.

DAILY LIFE

Families

The Woodland Cree shared the work, and both sexes knew how to perform the duties of the other. Men usually hunted, conducted raids and warfare, and protected their families. Women prepared meat, tanned, netted fish, killed beaver, watched over children, and tended the fires.

Buildings

Woodland Cree lived in both cone-shaped and dome-shaped wigwams covered with birchbark, pine bark, or caribou skins. For the Plains Cree, a large, hide-covered tepee that held ten or twelve people was the main dwelling. It had a three-pole foundation, a covering of twelve to twenty buffalo hides, and a central fireplace with a smoke hole.

Women made the tepees, assembled them, and owned them. Inside each tepee were beds made of bundles of dried grass or rushes, with buffalo robes placed over them for warmth. Pillows consisted of rawhide sacks filled with duck feathers.

Most Cree now live in homes with modern conveniences, but at winter camps, hunters live in *muhtukan,* rectangular-shaped houses made of logs and sod. They also build tepee-shaped structures called *michwaup* of logs and spruce boughs.

Clothing

Until about the age of five, most children wore little or no clothing. Babies were carried in sacks lined with soft moss that cushioned them and served as a diaper material.

During the summer, men wore leather breechcloths (flaps that hung from the waist and covered the front and back). In the winter, they wore leggings decorated with quill and beadwork. Except when the men wore buffalo robes, they usually left their upper bodies uncovered. They sometimes wore ponchos, often heavily quilled or beaded, but only for ceremonial occasions such as dances.

Women wore buffalo robes in all seasons. They also wore dresses made of two oblong pieces of cloth or hide, placed one on top of the other, sewed or laced together lengthwise, and worn with a fancy belt. They decorated the dresses with elk tusks and bear claws, as well as quill-work, beadwork, and painting. The Plains Cree beaded their clothes and other goods with elaborate floral designs. Painting on garments usually appeared in geometric designs of red and blue.

Cree made summer moccasins of one piece of hide sewn around the outside. They made winter moccasins of buffalo skin with hair turned to the inside for warmth, and often stuffed them with dried grass for more insulation. The Plains Cree wore snowshoes to gain an advantage over other tribes during winter warfare.

Adornments, hairstyles, and body painting

Cree headgear included a ring of buffalo hide with the hair on the out-side, rectangular summer visors made of hide, and ceremonial headdresses such as eagle feather bonnets and buffalo horn caps. People sometimes made ceremonial head coverings from entire skins of birds, especially the raven.

Popular jewelry included disc earrings made of mussel shells that hung from the ears by short thongs; necklaces made of buffalo teeth, elk tusks, or bear claws hung on tendons; and mussel shell necklaces fastened about the throat by a leather thong. Over time, beads and spangles pur-chased through the Hudson's Bay Company replaced these items.

Men plucked their facial hair. Both men and women parted their hair in the center and formed two braids. Women tied the two plaits together in back, whereas men tied them together in front. Some people length-ened their hair by weaving in additional horsehair. Warriors cut bangs into the front of their hair, stiffened them with grease, and combed them up into an erect wave. They brushed their hair with the rough side of a buffalo tongue and smeared red paint along the center part of their scalp.

Both genders created tattoos by working charcoal paste into punc-tures in their skin made by needles. Whereas men painted their arms and chests, women generally painted only their chins, cheeks, and foreheads. Face painting was accomplished by first greasing the face, then applying pigment. To make the paint, they colored clays, mixed them with water, and baked them into small cakes. They scraped the pigment off the cake and combined it with hot grease. Before entering battle, warriors often covered themselves with white clay over which they laid wet charcoal. When they returned from war, they blackened their faces.

Food

The Plains Cree regarded fishing as undignified for a hunter and only ate fish when hunting was poor. Buffalo was their main staple, but they also hunted moose, caribou, musk ox, elk, deer, and other game.

Their most important root food was the turnip, which they ate raw, roasted, boiled, or dried into a powder for soup. They also added berries to dried meat, especially in August, when buffalo meat had a poor taste. They ate the first berries of the season only after each family held its own ritual feast. Women cooked the berries, and an elderly man blessed them. In the spring, the people collected sap to make maple sugar and built fish traps.

When food was in short supply, the people gathered algae, fungus, and caribou dung, which they boiled and ate. Although the Woodland bands ate dog meat, the practice was less common among the Plains tribes.

Education

Cree children were allowed a great deal of freedom. They were never punished physically and were rarely scolded. They usually spent more time with their grandparents than they did with their parents, so grandparent-grandchild ties were very close. Elders helped them learn to make important decisions regarding personal, family, community, and tribal matters.

During the early twentieth century, the Anglican Church in Canada ran elementary schools (supported by the federal government) at various Cree communities. At Canadian boarding schools, children were expected to adopt white ways and never speak their native language.

The Cree School Board was created in the late 1970s to help reclaim an education based on Cree values and needs. As of the early 2000s, each Cree community in Quebec ran its own school under the management of the Cree School Board, in cooperation with the Quebec provincial department of education. Many children study the Cree language at school.

Healing practices

Healers called shamans (pronounced *SHAH-munz* or *SHAY-munz*) had much authority within the tribe. People considered shamans, who could cure illnesses and perform magic, links between the human and animal worlds. Shamans cured by singing, blowing on the patient, and sucking out the disease. They made use of tobacco and small charms for healing.

A tribe often had several shamans. Some Woodland Cree shamans practiced sorcery, but the Plains Cree rarely did. Shamans used dreams and rituals to make contact with the spirit world. The Cree believed that evil shamans could bring disease or misfortune upon victims if they chose.

The Cree practiced bloodletting (opening a vein to drain blood) to cure the sick, and they could set broken bones. Knowledge of medicinal plants was passed down through families or purchased from other informed bands. Entire plants, or just the root, stem, or bark, were used to cure ailments ranging from headaches to sexually transmitted diseases. Raw buffalo liver treated tuberculosis, and various teas relieved coughs or cleaned out the system. Cree treated frostbitten hands or feet by pricking them with a sharp bone and rubbing salt or snow around or into the frozen part.

Oral literature

The Cree god of campfire tales was called *Wisagatcak,* the Trickster. The people told a favorite story about a great flood that had taken place in the past. When the flood came, the Trickster constructed a raft to save the animals. He then used his magic to call upon the wolf to run about the raft with a ball of moss in his mouth, forming a new world where the Cree could once again hunt in peace.

CUSTOMS

Birth and Naming

Because they were often traveling, the Cree had no ceremonies connected with the birth of a child. Two or three older women attended the birth as midwives. Babies were strapped into a cradleboard and kept clean and dry with moss. If a woman had twins, one was killed because mothers could not nurse and care for two children in the harsh climate. If the twins were a boy and a girl, the boy was kept.

The High Cranberry Bush

The Cree tell of the Man-Who-Wanders, a magician who is sometimes wise and sometimes foolish. In this tale he saw cranberries floating on the water. He dove in after them but came up with nothing, so he dove deeper but still found none. Then he realized it was only a reflection and the real cranberries hung overhead.

Finally the thought of his stupidity began to annoy him, so he stood up and threw a few big stones into the water where the reflection of the berries seemed to mock him.

"So!" he cried. "That will teach you to trick me."

The river chuckled on its way as each splash the stones made leapt up into the face of the Man-Who-Wanders and made him splutter again.

As the old man was throwing the stones into the river, the cranberry bush decided to play a trick on him. The bush remembered how many tricks the magician had played on the birds, beasts, trees, and plants. Now, thought the bush, is my chance to get even.

"Well," he [the old man] told himself, "I will forget my troubles after I have eaten some of this good fruit." He reached up above his head to gather a handful of the tempting berries, then gasped. When his fingers almost touched the cranberries, the branches seemed to rise a little, just enough to keep the fruit beyond his reach.

"You must not try to match your magic against mine," he shouted in anger at the bush.

Once more he tried to pick some of the berries, but they were always just beyond the tips of his eager fingers. Now he became really angry and jumped up and down under the bush, shouting and clutching at the lowest branches. They still avoided his grasp, so he became angrier and angrier. He threw some big stones as hard as he could at the elusive berries. He managed to knock down only a few, but they were so squashed and juiceless that they were not fit to eat. As he scowled up at the brilliant berries, he did get some juice—in his eye.

"Hear me!" he shouted. "From now on you will remain tall. I will not eat your berries and nobody else will ever like their taste. You will always be scraggy. You will be known from now on as high-bush cranberry, so that you will never be mistaken for your sweet little sister. Sour berries, I have spoken!"

SOURCE: Macfarlan, Allan. *Fireside Book of North American Indian Folktales.* Harrisburg, PA: Stackpole Books, 1974.

Children were named at around age one by a shaman, who chose a name based on an incident or a character in one of his visions. During the child-naming ceremony, the baby was passed around the tepee from person to person; each one addressed the child by its new name and wished it future happiness. Children often received nicknames for special incidents in their lives. For example, a mother once left her baby girl unattended for a few minutes and returned to find the cradle surrounded by dozens of birds. From that point onward, she called her baby "Many-birds."

Vision quests

During puberty, a Cree boy took part in the most important rite of initiation into the tribe, the vision quest. This rite put him in touch with the spirit who would guide him through life, and during the ritual, he was taught a special song. The boy traveled with his father to a secluded spot—a bear's den, out on a raft in water, or on an unsaddled horse—for the duration of the quest. Wearing nothing but his breechcloth, the boy covered himself with white clay and built a brush shelter with his father. The father then made a pipe offering to the spirits and left the boy alone to pray and fast. The boy often undertook various feats of endurance in hopes of encouraging a vision. Sometime after returning to camp, he described his vision to others.

Female coming-of-age ceremony

At the time of a Cree girl's first menstruation, she was secluded for four nights in a small tepee at a distance from the village. An old woman stayed with her, telling her stories and teaching her the duties of an adult woman. During this time, the girl chopped wood, sewed, and prepared hides. It was then that a girl was most likely to receive a vision from a spirit. After the fourth and final night in seclusion, a feast was held in her honor in her father's tepee.

Festivals

The Sun Dance The most important Plains Indian ceremony, the Sun Dance, was called the All-Night-Thirst Dance by the Plains Cree. During the entire four-day ceremony, participants drank nothing. They tied cloth to poles as offerings to the gods.

Long ago, Sun Dancers engaged in a bloody rite in which they pierced their skin with a sharp buffalo horn threaded with a leather thong. They tied the thong to a pole or the rafters of a building. As they danced, they tore themselves free from the poles, and offered pieces of their flesh to the god Manito. They hoped to be blessed with a vision, to gain the gods' acceptance, or to give thanks for help they received in battle or in sickness.

Some groups did not practice the self-torture ritual but danced without food or water for four days, gazing at the sun and swaying back and forth until they fainted from exhaustion. In a modern form of the ritual, dancers stand behind green foliage and bend their knees while blowing on a whistle. As the sun's rays beat down on them, they fasten their gaze on one spot on the center pole, and they refrain from eating or drinking.

Shaking Tent Ceremony Another important ceremony was the Shaking Tent Ceremony (also called the Divining Booth), in which a shaman summoned spirits to a tent. After praying, fasting, and purifying himself in a sweat lodge, the shaman stripped to his breechcloth, then was bound with leather thongs and suspended inside the tent (the spirits were supposed to free him). Outside were onlookers and drummers.

When the spirits arrived, the tent began to shake. Voices and animal sounds could be heard coming from inside. Listeners could hear a conversation between the spirits and the shaman, with the shaman asking questions. Then the leather thongs binding the shaman would shoot out of the top of the tent. The last Shaking Tent Ceremony took place in 1962.

Walking Out Ceremony Young Cree children were not allowed to cross the threshold of their home by themselves until they had taken part in a Walking Out ceremony. At dawn on the day of the ritual, family and friends gathered with the village toddlers in a large tent, forming a circle around the children. Then, each child crossed the threshold with its parents or grandparents, went outside, and followed a path littered with fir branches to a tree about twenty feet away that symbolized nature. The child made a circle around the tree and returned to the tent to be congratulated by the village elders on becoming an official member of the tribe. A feast followed. This ceremony is still practiced.

The Grass Dance The most common ceremonial activity on the Cree reservations in modern times is the Grass Dance, also called the Warriors

Dance. Bundles of braided grass are tied to the dancers' belts; the bundles symbolize scalps. In the 1940s, when many Cree men were away fighting in World War II (1939–45; a war in which Great Britain, France, the United States, and their allies defeated Germany, Italy, and Japan), women kept the dance alive. After the war, the women continued to participate by dancing with the men who had returned home from battle.

Sweat baths and passing pipes Baths in a sweat lodge were used for ceremonial cleansing and for pleasure. Inside the lodge, men burned sweetgrass, shared a pipe, and poured water on hot stones to produce a refreshing steam.

All Cree rituals and social occasions began by sharing a pipe. Men passed the pipe in a clockwise direction. They believed the gods smoked along with them and listened to any requests they made during the ceremony. They braided grasses together in long strands, and during the ritual, they broke pieces off the strands and threw them onto live coals. The fragrant smoke that resulted was considered a purifying agent.

Hunting rituals

For the Cree, the hunt was not simply a source of food but also a great mystery. In their view, the gods had given them animals, and each animal had its own way of thinking and living. Animals made their own decisions to participate in the hunt, and in return, hunters made sure animals could grow and survive on the earth.

The Cree hunted buffalo by driving them into places where they would stumble—snowdrifts in the winter, marshes in the summer. Hunters then made the herd stampede into a corral-like structure called a pound, where they shot them with arrows. Before they butchered the animals, shamans climbed the wall of the pound and sang power songs. During the butchering, young boys undressed, climbed inside the pound, and threw buffalo intestines over the branches of a tree.

War rituals and raids

A Cree man gained respect in one of three ways: through warfare and raiding, by accumulating wealth, or by being generous. There was much social pressure on young men to participate in warfare, and those who did not were publicly shamed. When he took to the warpath, a man gave up his rights to material possessions. He took with him a sacred bundle containing a single article of war equipment; the bundles were believed to have magical properties. Often, a warrior was stripped of his belongings when he returned to the village; even the horses he took in raids were given to relatives and friends.

For the Plains Cree, war was a tournament. The objective was not to kill or to conquer other tribes, but to gain honors by "counting coup" (pronounced *COO*). Counting coup involved riding up to a live, armed enemy and touching him with a lance or coup stick. Four coups were enough to make someone a chief.

Raiding horses from another tribe was a warlike undertaking. The object of the raids was to steal as many horses as possible. Raiders did not wish to engage the enemy in battle, but if battles took place, a warrior rose in the ranks depending on the degree of danger involved. For example, a man who shot an enemy while he himself was under fire outranked one who killed an enemy during an ambush.

The more danger the warrior exposed himself to, the higher his merit. If a Cree male performed an act of bravery during his first raid, he was named a "worthy young man." His next step was to join a warrior society, and from there he might be made a chief. The position of chief was often hereditary (passed down from father to son), but if the chief's

Women from the Cree tribe gather in their camp along the Abitibi River in Ontario, Canada, circa 1900. © NORTH WIND PICTURE ARCHIVES.

son was deemed incompetent, another man could be given the position of chief. Ranking among chiefs depended upon their war exploits.

Courtship and marriage

The Cree did not place a high value on virginity, and it was common for unmarried couples to have sexual relations. Women usually married three or four years after their first menstruation. Men married around age twenty-five. High-ranking men often had two or more wives, and wives often had sexual relations with men other than their husbands.

Parents usually selected their children's mates. The father of a marriageable daughter would present a gift to the young man he considered a good match. If the young man's parents approved, they set up a new tepee for the couple. The bride sat inside, and then the groom entered the tent and sat down beside her. The bride offered him a new pair of moccasins, and if he accepted them, the marriage was sealed.

Funerals

Among the Cree, mourning was very dramatic. Close relatives dressed only in robes, left their hair loose, and cut gashes in their forearms and legs as a sign of their grief. They gave away the property of the deceased, but usually not to family members. The Cree believed that giving possessions to relatives would only lengthen the mourning period. They usually placed their dead in a grave dug about five feet deep and lined with a robe. Tepee poles were fitted over the body, a robe was placed over the poles, and a partially tanned cattle hide was fastened down over the area that had been dug; earth was placed over the rawhide to keep animals from disturbing the body.

CURRENT TRIBAL ISSUES

Modern Cree face many problems. Through schooling, religious efforts, and government intervention over the centuries, the people lost many of their traditional beliefs and customs as well as their livelihoods. As a result, the incidence of alcoholism, suicide, vandalism, and family violence increased. Most communities have instituted social programs to help their people cope.

The Cree have long been known for their political activism. For many years, they fought Quebec's plan for a $6 million hydroelectric project (a plant that generates electricity from water power). Although they received $300 million and hunting and fishing rights on 29,000 square miles

(75,110 square kilometers) of land, the first phase of the construction flooded one-third of their lands. The Cree managed to stop the project for eight years, but in 2002, they signed an agreement with Quebec that gave them $3.5 billion, payable over a fifty-year period, as well as part of the revenue and shared management of mining, forestry, and hydroelectric resources on their traditional lands. Many Cree saw this agreement as proof that the government recognized the tribe as a sovereign (self-governing) nation, something they had been trying to accomplish for decades.

The Paix de Braves Agreement the Cree signed with Quebec in 2002 became important when gold and diamonds were found on their land, and it also allowed the Cree to oppose plans for large-scale hydroelectric development in 2006. In 2007, they began negotiations on the nonfulfillment of the original James Bay Agreement. In another effort to maintain their land, the Cree became partners in the Cree-Quebec Forestry Board. This membership gives them the opportunity to manage their hunting grounds and assure that areas of mature forest will remain intact.

Resource development is a continuing concern for most bands. Many are located in areas where the government or private corporations want access to mining, hydroelectric power, timber, or other natural resources. The Cree must balance economic opportunities with their belief in environmental stewardship. This can be a difficult task, and not all members of the band agree on final settlements.

For example, in 2011, a group of members of the Moose Cree First Nation initiated a lawsuit against their own band over the Amisk-oo-skow Agreement that had been made with Ontario Power Generation to install hydroelectric plants on the Lower Mattagami River. The disgruntled group wanted to break away from the tribe and requested its own reserve. Also in 2011, the Moose Cree signed an agreement with Detour Gold Corporation, giving them a $1 million educational fund and employment opportunities as they proceed with developing the Detour Lake site. As with the many other Cree bands, the leaders of the Moose Cree are hoping to secure income that will help their people in the future, while keeping in mind the impact on the environment and community health.

NOTABLE PEOPLE

Buffy Sainte-Marie (c. 1942–) is a folk singer and Academy Award–winning songwriter as well as an advocate for tribal rights. She has written about North American Indian music and Indian affairs and is the author of *Nokosis and the Magic Hat* (1986), a children's adventure book set on a reservation.

Chief Poundmaker (1842–1886) was adopted as a boy by Blackfoot Chief Crowfoot (1830–1890) and named *Makoyi-koh-kin* (Wolf Thin Legs). In 1876, he sought better conditions for his people in treaty talks with the Canadian government. With his followers, he participated in the Métis rebellion, also called the Second Riel Rebellion, against the Canadian government in 1885. As a result, he was convicted of treason and imprisoned, and he died shortly after his release.

Other notable Cree include the head chief and resistance leader Big Bear (c. 1825–1888); Payepot (or Piapot; 1816–1908), a nineteenth-century leader of the Western Canadian Plains Cree; the painter and illustrator Jackson Beardy (1944–1984); the tribal leader Harold Cardinal (1945–2005); Jean Cuthand Goodwill (1928–1997), editor of *Tawow,* the first Canadian Indian cultural magazine; the playwright and novelist Tomson Highway (1951–); Plains Cree artist George Littlechild (1958–); recording artist Morley Loon; and the twentieth-century teacher and missionary Ahab Spence (1911–2001).

BOOKS

Bial, Raymond. *The Cree.* New York: Benchmark Books, 2006.

Bjorklund, Ruth. *The Cree.* Tarrytown, NY: Marshall Cavendish, 2009.

Erdoes, Richard. *The Sun Dance People: The Plains Indians, Their Past and Present.* New York: Random House, 1972.

Flannery, Regina. *Ellen Smallboy: Glimpses of a Cree Woman's Life.* Montreal: McGill-Queen's University Press, 1995.

Hansen, John George. *Cree Restorative Justice: From the Ancient to the Present.* Kanata, Ontario: J Charlton, 2009.

Niezen, Ronald. *Defending the Land: Sovereignty and Forest Life in James Bay Cree.* 2nd ed. Upper Saddle River, NJ: Pearson Prentice Hall, 2009.

Smith, Nicholas N. *Three Hundred Years in Thirty: Memoir of Transition with the Cree Indians of Lake Mistassini.* Solon, ME: Polar Bear & Co., 2011.

St. Germain, Jill. *Broken Treaties: United States and Canadian Relations with the Lakotas and the Plains Cree, 1868–1885.* Lincoln: University of Nebraska Press, 2009.

Pacheco, Bernadine. *My Mother's Memoirs: Crossroads.* San Diego, CA: Cree Publishing House, 2010.

WEB SITES

"Chippewa Cree Tribe (Neiyahwahk)." *Montana Office of Indian Affairs.* http://www.tribalnations.mt.gov/chippewacree.asp (accessed on June 3, 2011).

"Family Search: Chippewa-Cree Indians." *Church of Jesus Christ of Latter-Day Saints.* https://wiki.familysearch.org/en/Chippewa-Cree_Indians (accessed on June 3, 2011).

"Four Directions Teachings: Cree." *FourDirectionsTeachings.com.* http://www.fourdirectionsteachings.com/transcripts/cree.html (accessed on June 3, 2011).

Moose Cree Resource Protection. "Understanding and Knowledge." *Moose Cree First Nation.* 2009. http://www.moosecreeresourceprotection.org/mcfn.html (accessed on June 3, 2011).

"Native Languages of the Americas: Cree." *Native Languages of the Americas: Preserving and Promoting Indigenous American Indian Languages.* http://www.native-languages.org/cree.htm (accessed on June 9, 2011).

"Our Languages: Dene History & Background." *Saskatchewan Indian Cultural Centre.* http://www.sicc.sk.ca/heritage/sils/ourlanguages/dene/history/index.html (accessed on June 9, 2011).

"Quebec's Northern Crees." *Arctic Circle.* http://arcticcircle.uconn.edu/HistoryCulture/Cree/ (accessed on June 9, 2011).

"Rocky Boys." *Montana Office of Tourism.* http://www.visitmt.com/places_to_go/indian_nations/annishinabe-ne-i-yah-wahk-rocky-boys/ (accessed on June 3, 2011).

Rocky Boy's Indian Reservation. http://www.rockyboy.org/Site%20Map/Info%20Page.htm (accessed on June 3, 2011).

Swampy Cree Tribal Council. http://www.swampycree.com/ (accessed on June 9, 2011).

Innu

Name

Innu (pronounced IN-oo) means "people" in the tribe's own language, but for centuries after the European arrival, the Innu who visited French settlements along the St. Lawrence River were called *Montagnais,* or "mountain people." Those who lived in the northern tundra went by the name *Naskapi.* This has been translated as "people beyond the horizon." Other meanings sometimes given are "crude dressers," "uncivilized people," or "those with no religion." During the 1900s, archaeologists used the term *Montagnais-Naskapi* for the Innu. In the 1980s, the Innu reclaimed their original name. Although their name is similar to Inuit, the two words and groups are not connected.

Location

Because the people migrated as hunters and trappers, they had no specific boundaries to their traditional land. In the summer, they gathered along the St. Lawrence River or Gulf, at the Davis or Hamilton Inlets, or by the James or Hudson Bays in present-day Canada. Their territory may have extended north to Richmond Gulf. At times, they crossed the St. Lawrence to hunt south of the river after the fur trade had been established.

The Innu called their homeland *Ntisinan* (Nitassinan), meaning "our land." Ntisinan covers much of the Labrador Peninsula in eastern Canada. The land is divided between the provinces of Newfoundland and Labrador and Quebec. Most Innu live in one of the thirteen communities of Pessamit (Betsiamites), Ekuanitshit (Mingan), Kawawachikamach, Unamanshipu (La Romaine), Essipit (Les Escoumins), Mani-utenam (Maliotenam), Mashteuiatsh (Lac Saint-Jean), Matimekush (Matimekosh or Schefferville), Natashquan, Natuashish (formerly Utshimassit and Davis Inlet; Happy Valley–Goose Bay), Pakut-shipu (St. Augustine), Tshishe-shastshit (Sheshatshiu), and Uashat (Sept-Iles).

Population

No accurate counts have been made for the population in the early years, but experts believe that more than 4,000 Innu lived in an area of 300,000 square miles (482,800 square kilometers). Some estimates say the count

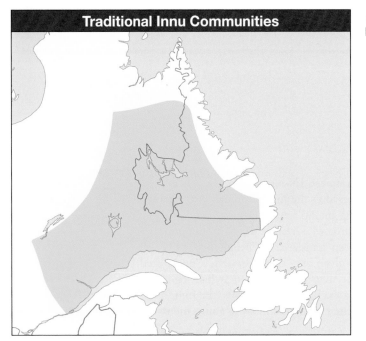

Traditional Innu Communities

Shaded area

◻ Traditional lands of the Innu, in present-day Quebec and Newfoundland & Labrador

A map of traditional Innu lands. MAP BY XNR PRODUCTIONS. CENGAGE LEARNING, GALE. REPRODUCED BY PERMISSION OF GALE, A PART OF CENGAGE LEARNING.

may have been much higher. Following the European arrival, death by starvation, diseases such as smallpox and tuberculosis, and occasional warfare reduced the population greatly. By 1857, estimates showed 3,910 Innu living in twenty-two locations. The decrease in numbers was reversed by the mid-1900s. A count in 1971 indicated 11,697 people lived in sixteen of the eighteen settlements. By the early 2000s, the population had grown to about17,000. According to the 2006 Canadian census, that number had reached 24,116.

Language family

Algonquian.

Origins and group affiliations

Because their languages and cultures are similar, the Innu are often linked with the Cree (see entry), particularly the Eastern Cree. Some older sources even suggested that the Innu were divided into three groups: the Naskapi, Montagnais, and East Cree. The Montagnais traded with the Algonquin, Iroquois (see entry), and Abenaki (see entry). Oral tradition indicates that the Innu and Inuit (see entry) were enemies who fought constantly.

The Innu, who have occupied the Quebec-Labrador Peninsula for two thousand years or more, may have been one of the first North American groups to encounter European explorers around 1000 CE. Prior to the arrival of French traders and missionaries, the Innu had already established extensive trade routes for products such as pottery and Ramah chert, a brittle stone used for making tools such as spears. They also migrated seasonally to make their living by hunting caribou. Beginning in the 1600s, Europeans pressured the Innu to give up their land, religion, and culture, with devastating results for their society. Since the late 1900s, the Innu have been working to regain their rights, reclaim their traditions, and rectify social problems.

Important Dates

1609: Montagnais join other bands and Samuel de Champlain to fight the Mohawk.

1800s: Trading-post bands develop.

1948: Canadian government moves Davis Inlet Innu to Nutak Island.

1961: Pakut-shipu band is moved to Unaman-shipu.

1969: Churchill Falls dam floods Innu land.

1990: Innu Nation is formed.

2009: Innu take control of their children's education.

HISTORY

Quebec-Labrador Peninsula prehistory

Archaeologists estimate that people first inhabited the Quebec-Labrador peninsula after the glaciers melted, about 8,000 to 9,000 years ago. These early inhabitants, called Maritime Archaic people, lived along the coast, which allowed them to take advantage of the abundant seafood and waterfowl. The Maritime Archaic people also hunted caribou for food, clothing, and tools until they disappeared about 3,500 years ago. Some experts believe the Maritime Archaic people may have been ancestors of the Innu, but no direct connections have been found between the two groups.

Over the next centuries, many different cultures made their home on the peninsula, but the ones that may have been the Innu's ancestors were the Point Revenge people, who lived in the area beginning about 1000 CE. As hunter-gathers, they moved from place to place seasonally and used their knowledge of the natural world to survive. They, too, depended on caribou for meat and hides, which they used for clothing and tents. They turned caribou bones, teeth, and antlers into tools and weapons.

Another group living along the coast, the Thule, were the ancestors of the Inuit. Competition with the Thule led the Point Revenge people to move farther inland, where they hunted and fished near the bays and rivers. Like their descendants, the Innu, the Point Revenge people migrated in a seasonal pattern. They caught marine animals in warmer weather and hunted for game during the colder months. They made efficient use of every part of the animals they captured as well as their environmental resources of stone and wood.

European arrival

Many explorers landed in the area, but the first were the Vikings, who established permanent settlements on the nearby island of Newfoundland around 1000 CE. Later European groups included the Portuguese, Dutch, French, and British. During the 1500s, the southern Innu had contact with Basque fishermen from the Pyrenees Mountains region of France and Spain. As they established trading posts along the St. Lawrence, Lake Melville, and Ungava Bay, French traders and missionaries tried to persuade the Innu to settle along the coast.

The Innu resisted European pressure and continued in the nomadic lifestyle they had used for generations. At the same time, many began establishing trading relationships, particularly with the French, who encouraged them to trap in exchange for European goods. Trips to the trading post became part of the seasonal cycle for many Innu. Because the Innu did not believe in owning property, they traveled to whatever trading post was nearby. This frustrated the Europeans, who did not understand the Innu way of life and wanted groups to commit to one trading post. Missionaries also tried to force the Innu to stay in one place.

Trading-post bands

By the mid-1800s, the Hudson's Bay Company had taken control of most of the fur trading. As overhunting decreased the number of animals, the Innu became more dependent on store-bought goods. Trading-post bands developed. These groups hunted near a post where they could trade for supplies. Because the Innu preferred to gather near coastal areas, most interior posts closed. By 1931, about twenty-seven local bands were associated with the various trading posts. Some of these sites later became permanent Innu settlements.

Traditional hunting practices changed as people developed closer ties with the trading posts. Rather than traveling in family groups, men usually left their families for months at a time to trap and hunt. The availability of guns also altered long-established methods of hunting. Prior to this, bands worked together to trap game and then shared their kill with others. However, at this point, the Innu were being encouraged to work for themselves rather than for the good of the group.

Competition for land

To deal with these conflicting expectations, the men shared their hunting grounds as they had in the past as long as the hunt was for themselves and their families. They set boundaries on the land when it was used for trading-post trapping.

In the early 1900s, settlers moved into the area to take advantage of the rising fur prices. Many of these settlers were the Métis (see entry). Of part European and part Inuit heritage, the Métis owned their own trap lines and claimed land that belonged to the Innu. Soon, they had taken over most of the Innu's best hunting grounds.

At the same time, some of the forests on Innu land were being cleared. Mines opened in their territory, and laws restricted Innu hunting. All of this, combined with the overhunting and overtrapping for the fur trade, left many Innu starving. To survive, the people often had to depend on assistance from missionaries, traders, or the government.

Changes to traditional lifestyles

As the Innu became more dependent on social assistance, they had to stay close to the permanent villages. This not only changed their migratory patterns, but it also meant assimilating into the society around them. Soon, many had given up their traditional way of life.

In 1948, the government closed the Davis Inlet trading post and moved the Innu from there to the island of Nutak, hoping to get them involved in the fishing industry. However, the Innu, who were used to forests, could not adjust to the barren and treeless island, which was Inuit land. Two years later, they walked back to Davis Inlet. The government later relocated them to Utshimassit on Iluikoyak Island, where most people lived in poorly built, leaky houses without running water, toilets, or electricity for more than three decades.

Confederation of Newfoundland and Canada

More changes were in store for the Innu in 1949 when Newfoundland and Labrador joined Canada as a province then called Newfoundland. For centuries, Newfoundland and Labrador had remained independent British colonies. During that time, the Newfoundland and Labrador government had not set up reserves (as reservations are called in Canada) or made treaties with any of the indigenous people, so Canada had to decide whether to extend its Indian Act of 1876 to the Innu and other First Nations people living there. Under the Indian Act, the government provided health, education, and other social services to the First Nations, Métis, and Inuit in the rest of Canada. The Canadian government, however, chose not to provide these services to the new province. Instead, it paid money to the province to take care of those needs.

Newfoundland and Labrador used part of the payment to build houses and schools in the 1960s. Unless children attended these schools, parents could not receive government assistance. The government's goal was to assimilate the younger generations and turn them from hunters to industry wage earners. In these schools, mainly run by religious groups, students were punished for speaking their native language and were taught that their religion and values were wrong. Even worse was the physical and sexual abuse many children experienced in the schools.

Forced relocations

In 1954, in an effort to alter traditional lifestyles, the government offered assistance to Innu who moved from their villages to larger cities. At the same time, industry began encroaching on Innu territory. The Innu were not consulted as mining, roads, railways, and commercial forestry interests cut through their land. In 1969, a dam built at Churchill Falls flooded thousands of square kilometers of forest, Innu ancestral lands, hunting grounds, birth sites, and burial sites. Many people lost their traps, canoes, fishing equipment, and other possessions.

To induce the Pakut-shipu band in St. Augustine to give up their nomadic ways, Indian Affairs forced them onto a ship and moved them to Unaman-shipu in 1961. The houses the people had been promised were never built, so the Innu returned to their former land in 1963. More than a decade later, they were forced to move to the opposite side of the river. This time the government built them houses but no school. To attend classes, children had to cross the river by canoe in warm weather or by snowmobile in the winter when the river was frozen.

Innu activism

Political activism for minority rights began to swell during the 1960s and 1970s. Civil rights protesters in America and Canada were demanding changes. The Innu joined the Mi'kmaq (see Micmac entry) and Inuit to

An Innu woman holds a sign protesting Canada's claim to Innu lands in Newfoundland in 1997. © CARLO ALLEGRI/AFP/GETTY IMAGES

form the Native Association of Newfoundland and Labrador (NANL) in 1973. In 1976, the Innu of Labrador broke away to create the Naskapi Montagnais Innu Association (NMIA), which later became the Innu Nation. In November 1977, NMIA filed its first land claim for territory in central Labrador.

In the 1980s, Canada signed a contract permitting military training exercises at Goose Bay in Labrador that allowed low-level flights over Innu land. The government ignored Innu complaints about the impact on the environment and on their people, so in 1988, Innu women and children started using nonviolent civil disobedience to draw attention to their plight. They blocked runways, camped by the air base, and occupied the bombing ranges. Although many Innu were arrested and environmental impact assessments were done, it took more than a decade for their protests to make an impact.

The Innu again spoke up for their rights after the discovery of a mine at Emish (Voisey's Bay) containing billions of dollars' worth of nickel. Within days of the 1993 find, 250,000 claims had been registered, and the Canadian government had given away about 62 square miles (100 square kilometers) of Innu and Inuit traditional land. In 1995, the Innu handed the mining company an eviction notice and protested at the site. After a two-week standoff, all parties came to an agreement. The Innu were granted royalties from the mine, but an even more important concession was the Innu relocation from the poverty of Utshimassit to a new home at Little Sango Pond.

Relocation to Natuashish

When the Innu had been moved to Utshimassit in 1967, the government had promised them homes, but for decades, most people lived in houses with leaky roofs, no plumbing or electricity, and little or no insulation in an area with below-freezing temperatures. They had been subjected to poverty, hardship, and abuse. The loss of their land, culture, livelihoods, self-esteem, and family ties led to the breakdown of Innu society. Social problems, such as alcohol abuse and domestic violence, resulted.

The severity of the situation first received major media attention in 1992 when six children died in house fire. The parents had been drinking at a party, and a lack of an adequate water supply and fire equipment added to the tragedy. The following year, a video that was released worldwide showed a group of Innu children trying to commit suicide by sniffing gas. In 1994, the government agreed to move the people to a better location, but even after final approval came in 1996, the move to Natuashish did not occur until 2003. This transfer, which cost about $280 million, ended up being one of the most expensive relocations in Canadian history.

Innu in the twenty-first century

In 2001, the province was renamed Newfoundland and Labrador. The following year, the federal government registered the Labrador Innu as Status Indians. This meant that the Innu now qualified for federal programs and services that Canada provides for other First Nations people.

The government also recognized Natuashish in 2003 and Sheshatshiu in 2006 as reserve lands.

Although the Inuit in Labrador signed the Labrador Inuit Land Claims Agreement with the federal government and the province of Newfoundland and Labrador in 2005, the Innu still had not completed their agreement by mid-2011.

RELIGION

Animal masters

Although variations existed in the different communities, the Innu share some basic beliefs. Each animal kingdom and some individual species, such as porcupine, bear, beaver, and caribou, has a spirit master. Some of the Innu, for example, recognize *Papakashtshihku* (*Papakassik*), the caribou master, as one of the most important and powerful spirits, as it has control over all the species.

Because the animal masters are responsible for providing game, the Innu have always respected them and treated animal bones with care. They never fed them to the dogs; instead, they put them on scaffolds or in trees, lakes, or rivers. They also put animal grease and leftovers in the fire and held a special feast, *makushan,* with the caribou long bones (see "Celebrations").

Hunters also followed a ritual to capture a bear. They laid fir branches in front of the den and called "grandfather" or "grandmother" to come out. After they killed the bear, they cleaned the cave and left an offering of tobacco or tea leaves on the floor or put it in the bear's mouth. Only men and mothers could eat bear meat. Children and childless women had to stay out of the house while the bear was cooked and eaten.

Communication with animal masters

The Innu communicated with the animal masters through scapulimancy, drumming, the shaking tent, and dreams. In scapulimancy, an animal bone is charred in the fire, usually a beaver pelvis or tibia, a porcupine or caribou scapula, or a fish jaw. The cracks and burns on the bones showed the Innu where to hunt.

Drumming, which was only done by older men who had dreamed about it, also told the Innu where to find caribou. The drummer watched for sparks on the drum as he played. These sparks revealed where to look and how many animals could be killed.

Shaking tent

The shaking tent ritual was performed in a small, cone-shaped tent located inside a larger tent. Caribou skin covered the tent and was held up by either four, six, or eight poles, depending on the shaman's spiritual power. The shaman, or *kakushapatak,* went into the tent to speak to the animal masters or to Innu who lived far away.

Mishtapeuat, huge beings that were not animals or humans, might join the shaman in the tent to interpret for the animal masters. Mishtapeuat could be good or evil; they had the power to heal, kill, or predict the future. At times, the shaman fought with spirits, such as *Atshen,* cannibal spirits who had hair on their hearts and no lips. As soon as the shaman put his head into the tent, it began shaking as a sign that a spirit had entered. The people who waited outside heard only sounds (knocks, water, thunder, or hooting owls) or Mishtapeuat's song.

Other spirits

In addition to Mishtapeuat, some other spirit beings were *Meminiteuat,* or cannibal monsters; *Tshiuetinush,* the north wind; and *Katshimetsheshuat,* spirits of the fog or dark. These latter beings were known for robbing people, tossing stones at tents, and kidnapping women. Children were warned not to wander away or they might get taken by Katshimetsheshuat.

One of the more unusual spirits was *Matshishkapeu,* the "Fart Man." He was humorous but powerful enough to control people and animal masters. The Innu believed that when someone passed gas, it was Matshishkapeu making the sounds. An older man and woman in the group translated the message.

Conversion to Christianity

When the Catholic missionaries arrived, they tried to stop the shaking tent and drumming traditions because they believed those were tools of the devil. Missionaries had a great influence over the people, and they took over naming the children, distributing food and sometimes government benefits, and working as schoolteachers. Most Innu had no way to communicate with the outside world except through the missionaries, who served as translators. Some missionaries used this power to force Innu to convert and assimilate (become more like other Canadians). And in several cases, it meant that physical and sexual abuse went unreported until decades later.

By the 1860s, many Innu had become Christians. In spite of pressure from the church, however, some continued to practice their traditional religion at the same time. They saw no contradiction in combining both beliefs.

LANGUAGE

The Innu speak Innu-aimun, one of the Cree-Montagnais-Naskapi dialects, which is a Central Algonquian language. Montagnais-Naskapi dialects are spoken in much of the southeastern coastal area of mainland Canada. These dialects are sometimes broken down into Sheshatshiu Innu-aimun, used in Labrador, and the Mushuau dialect of Natuashish, sometimes called Eastern Naskapi.

In spite of the many pressures to assimilate (change their culture to be like the rest of society), the Innu kept their native language. Children in Innu communities were mainly taught at school in English or French, but they learned their mother tongue at home. Almost all the Innu of Sheshatshiuare bilingual. By the end of the twentieth century, many native languages were considered to be dying, but statistics counted 9,335 Innu-aimun speakers in 1996. By 2001, that number had increased to 10,285. A decade later, the large majority of the Innu could speak their traditional language.

One project aimed at increasing the strength of the language is CURA (Community University Research Alliance). This group, funded by many organizations, is documenting the language and has developed Internet resources to make this information available to the communities through a Web site, a dictionary, lesson plans, and literacy training.

The Waswanipi Cree Reserve in Quebec, Canada, has street signs in both English and Cree, reflecting the efforts of Native people who speak variations of Cree, including the Innu, to preserve their language.
© FRANCIS VACHON/ALAMY

GOVERNMENT

Prior to the fur trade era, the Innu did not believe in owning land, and all resources were held in common. They had no chiefs until the Jesuit missionaries pressured them to elect leaders. Even then, however, they did not always comply. When the Innu had to negotiate with the French or with other bands, they selected their best orator, or speaker, to represent

Innu Words

Translation from Innu to English is sometimes difficult because concepts are between the two cultures are very different. One example of this is the months of the year. *August* in Innu-aimun is "the month when young ducks take flight for the first time." And *September* is "the month when male caribou rub their antlers to remove their velvet." Below are a few Innu words for animals.

minush	"cat"
atikuat	"caribou"
atimuss	"puppy"
namesh	"fish"
kukush	"pig"
maikan	"wolf"

them. The speaker did not make decisions for the group, however. The band made decisions by consensus. Everyone voiced an opinion, and the discussion continued until the group came to a decision that they all could agree on.

By the twentieth century, each Innu band had a chief and a tribal council. In 1973, the people began to organize politically to fight for their rights. Initially, the Labrador Innu joined the Mi'kmaq and Inuit in the Native Association of Newfoundland and Labrador (NANL). By 1976, the Innu had formed their own group, the Naskapi Montagnais Innu Association, which in 1990 became the Innu Nation. The people elect a president and board of directors for this organization, which negotiates land claims and protects Innu interests. The Innu Nation also oversees health care, education, and other social services.

Most of the Quebec Innu bands belong to one of two tribal councils: Mamuitun or Mamit Innuat. Mamuitun is composed of Essipit, Mani-utenam, Mashteuiatsh, Matimekush, Natashquan, and Uashat. The three groups who are part of Mamit Innuat include Ekuanitshit, Pakut-shipu, and Unaman-shipu. The tribal councils usually take charge of negotiations for the bands.

ECONOMY

For centuries, the Innu lived by fishing, trapping with deadfalls and snares, hunting, and gathering during the warmer months. They moved with the seasons and availability of game. That lifestyle changed with the introduction of the European fur trade. The Innu along the St. Lawrence had traded furs for cornmeal and tobacco, but interest in the iron tools and copper kettles of the Europeans led many Innu to form what were called "trading-post bands." Many Innu limited their territory to areas around a trading post so they could readily obtain goods as overhunting lowered the animal population. Originally, trading-post bands rarely contained more than 250 people, but as interior posts closed, the groups became larger. Some of these areas eventually turned into permanent settlements.

At one time, the Innu shared land. They continued to do so for their own personal needs, but they set up boundaries for any trapping done for Europeans. In 1945, after dogs were introduced, trappers could go farther afield. When fur-bearing animals became scarce, some Innu took work as laborers in nearby towns, but they continued to supplement their income with trapping.

By the 1970s, most people lived in villages all year. They built frame houses or lived in prefab houses put up by the government and did less hunting and trapping. With limited natural resources and few job opportunities, most Innu were no longer able to be self-sufficient. Many came to depend on government support to survive. Unemployment was as high as 80 percent by the end of the 1990s. In the early 2000s, some Innu bands had received compensation for the loss of their land and had negotiated royalties for mining done in their territory.

DAILY LIFE

Families

At one time, no clans or formal kinship groups existed for the Innu. Early sources indicate that parents handed down their inheritance to their sister's children rather than to their own. Most people had few possessions, however, so there was little to pass on.

A traditional family home for the Innu people is cone-shaped and covered with birchbark or animal hides. © MARTIN PAQUIN/ALAMY

A member of the Innu tribe wears traditional hunting garb. © HEMIS/ALAMY

Men and women each had their duties, but they could help with the other's jobs. Poor hunters might have trouble keeping a wife, and men were sometimes teased if they did women's work. One European writer, though, expressed surprise at how competent an Innu father was in caring for and comforting a baby, which European men did not do at that time. Older children, too, helped with child care.

Women made the decisions for their families and for anything related to their responsibilities, such as processing skins, distributing supplies, and gathering firewood. Their opinions could also influence the men's decisions.

Buildings

Most Innu lived in cone-shaped lodges, although sometimes they built rectangular, dome-shaped, or oval homes. To build their houses, the women chopped down trees to make twenty or thirty poles, while the men shoveled snow with wooden shovels or snowshoes. After the hole was 2 to 4 feet (about 1 meter) deep, the poles were pushed into the ground or the snow so that they met at the top. Large sheets of birchbark or caribou hides stitched together formed the outer walls. Openings were left for the door and for a smoke hole in the roof. Inside the Innu covered the ground or snow with fir branches. Sometimes they laid sealskin or mats on top.

About fifteen or twenty people slept in the lodge, with their heads near the fire. They used their packs to cushion their heads. Later, some made canvas mattresses filled with moose or caribou hair and used duck feathers to stuff small pillows.

On the western part of the Labrador Peninsula, moss-covered lodges were used in warmer weather. People covered poles with moss and turf, leaving an opening in the roof. Men sometimes dug out snow caves to sleep in when they were on the trail overnight. Hunting camps also had a rack made of poles where they placed antlers, bones, and animal skulls.

Clothing and adornment

Most clothing was made of smoked caribou hide held together by sinew. Coats had the most intricate decorations, but other clothing, including moccasins, had painted designs. The Innu wore leggings that fastened to a belt and had fringed and beaded sides. Fur coats of bear or beaver had detachable sleeves. People tied their coats shut with cord or dried animal intestines. Both men and women hooked a flap over their belts to make a pocket. Little clothing was worn indoors.

Farther north, the Innu wore parkas made of caribou hide, but they left the hair attached to the skin to keep them warmer. Rabbit skin was cut into strips and sewn into blankets and jackets. Moccasins or boots were often made of sealskin because sealskin was more water resistant than hide, and people layered several pairs of boots on top of each other. Snowshoes were usually laced with babiche, thongs of rawhide or sinew, but some were made of a long strip of wood with curved tips, almost like a short ski.

Women wound the hair on each side of their head around wooden rectangles and wrapped them with fabric or beads, so they had a clothlike pouch near each ear. They wore wool caps that had six triangles that met at the top. Red and navy triangles alternated. Rather than pulling these hats, or tuques, down over their ears, they set them on top of their heads and let the fabric fall forward so it almost lay flat.

Babies had diapers made of moss; they were wrapped in soft skins. They were often carried in leather bags that had been lined with moss.

Food

The Innu who lived along the St. Lawrence depended on eel for food, and they smoked it for year-round use. They also hunted beaver, porcupine, fox, squirrel, caribou, moose, bear, groundhog, and birds, especially waterfowl. Seals and turtles were found near the coast. Innu who lived in the interior fished in the lakes, where they caught sturgeon, trout, catfish, whitefish, pike, salmon, and smelt, among others. Women dug up russet potatoes and red martagon bulbs, a plant that had a licorice flavor.

Caribou Buckskin

Traditionally, caribou buckskin was the most important material used for clothing, boots, moccasins, house covers, and storage. Women prepared the hides and many of the products made from the hide. First they scraped the hides to remove all fur and then left them outside to freeze. The next step was to stretch the hide on a frame. After it was well-stretched, the women rubbed the hide with a mixture of animal brains and pine-needle tea to soften it. The dampened hide was formed into a ball and left overnight. In the morning, the women would stretch it again. Then they placed it over a smoker all night to smoke and tan it. The finished hide was made into clothing and decorated with painted patterns (see "Arts").

Innu Doughnuts

In telling how she learned to make this recipe, the author says, "I originally wrote out the recipe for Innu doughnuts sitting on an upturned bucket in an Innu tent redolent of [filled with] spruce boughs, wood smoke and frying fat as I watched Tshaukuesh make them. It was −30° outside and extraordinarily cozy in the tent."

> 2 cups of flour
> 1/3 cup of sugar
> 1 Tablespoon of baking powder
> 1 cup of water with 2 tablespoons of oil mixed in
> a handful of raisins or berries

Mix dry ingredients, add liquid and mix lightly, then stir in the berries or raisins. Drop by large spoonfuls onto a hot greased cast iron frying pan (Tshaukuesh used a lot more grease than I did so for authenticity…). Fry until golden brown on both sides, then drain on paper towels and sprinkle with sugar. Best eaten hot from the pan.

SOURCE: Yeoman, Elizabeth. "Innu Doughnuts." *Dinner in Strange Places.* July 14, 2010. http://dinnerinstrangeplaces.blogspot. com/2010/07/innu-doughnuts-recipe.html (accessed on June 10, 2011).

They also gathered maple sap and caught rabbits. Wild berries, grapes, apples, cherries, dandelion leaves, and hazelnuts rounded out their diet. Pine-needle tea kept them healthy.

Meats were eaten raw, frozen, or cooked by roasting or stone-boiling. Once the Innu had traded for European iron pots, they used those for most cooking. In addition to smoked fish and eel, the Innu smoke-dried moose. To do this, they cut the meat from the bones, then they stomped on the meat and pounded it until all the juices drained out. Slits were cut into thick slabs to let smoke penetrate it as it hung over the fire on poles. When it was dried, the Innu folded the meat up. This preserved it for use during the long winters.

The French introduced the Innu to bannock, a flat bread made of oats, which became a staple food. The Innu usually made bannock from flour and fried it. A dough similar to bannock was used to make doughnuts.

Tools

In addition to the axe and bow and arrow, the crooked knife was one of the most important tools for the Innu. The blade of the crooked knife was drawn toward the body rather than away, so care had to be taken when using it. Men carved snowshoe frames, canoe ribs, wooden shovels, and planks for canoes with it. Before the French arrived, the Innu made the knife from a beaver's incisor tooth tied to a wooden handle. Later, they used metal for the blade.

Ice picks, a trade item from the Europeans, helped the Innu get drinking water when the lakes were frozen. They also used the picks to set net traps in winter. The Innu made nets out of babiche, strips of cord or lacing made of caribou hide or sinew.

Even after they had trade goods, most Innu still used antlers, bones, wood, animal muscles and organs, fish skin, and stones to make traditional tools. Women used a knife made of caribou antler to scrape pelts.

The bone of a moose worked as a beamer, a tool for scraping pelts. Sewing needles were made of wood. Caribou leg skin was turned into storage containers. Whole skins of a muskrats with a hole in the head were made into tobacco pouches. Swimming paddles, semicircles of wood with a hole cut out for the hand, kept children and adult nonswimmers afloat.

Transportation

Women sat in the back of the canoes and paddled while men sat in front. Birchbark and cedar were used for canoes, but at times the Innu had to trade for the wood. Later, they used canvas rather than wood. Some also used French boats called *shallops*. When the ground was slushy, the Innu made a canoe-sled by adding runners onto crossbars that supported a canoe.

People wore snowshoes and dragged toboggans behind them by hooking a cord around their chests. Even children pulled small toboggans. The ill and elderly were often pulled on sleds. Goods were protected from ice and snow with a caribou hide or canvas sheet lashed over the sled.

In the mid-1900s, sled dogs pulled toboggans, or *komatik*. Later, snowmobiles became the most common form of transportation.

Education

Traditional education consisted of developing skills by working side by side with adults. Some of the most important lessons Innu children learned were survival skills. They began by playing with slingshots and small bows and arrows to learn to hunt for small animals. As they grew more proficient, they moved on to adult weapons, such as spears and, in later years, guns.

Children were taught to be cooperative, patient, and generous. Good humor was another virtue. Even young children were expected to do their share of the chores, but they were never punished. This led the French to believe that Innu children needed to be sent away to school where they would be properly disciplined.

Public school education In the 1900s, many children were sent to boarding schools, where they had little contact with their families. No longer could they go to the country, or *nutshimit,* to learn the traditional ways of their people.

At schools, most of which were run by religious groups, teachers punished students for speaking their language or following their religions. Many children suffered physical and even sexual abuse in addition to the loss of their culture. These educational practices and the marginalization of the Innu have been blamed for many of the social problems found in Innu communities in the later twentieth century. Even after changes were made, schooling was still not meeting the needs of the Innu community.

Culturally sensitive education Results of a major three-year study on Innu education were released in 2004 and 2005. The data showed that although the children had the ability and desire to learn, the schooling failed to take their culture into account, resulting in truancy, poor grades, and high dropout rates. Less than 30 percent of the students went on to high school, and among those who did, most were several years behind grade level in reading and math.

The study indicated that the educational system needed to be culturally relevant. The researchers suggested that a new curriculum be implemented. They believed that the education should be bicultural, be taught by the Innu themselves, be supervised by the elders, and use the Innu-aimun language exclusively at the elementary level. After that, students would learn English. Traditional skills were also to be part of the studies at all grade levels. By 2009, the Innu were given complete control of their children's education. A follow-up study showed dramatic improvements in reading, writing, and attendance.

Healing practices

Early medical arts The Innu did not have as many healing recipes from herbs as many other bands did, because plants were fewer in their territory. The early Point Revenge people may have used crushed buttercups for headaches and boiled cherry-tree bark for coughs, and the Innu also practiced bloodletting, making a cut to remove blood, for pain or swelling. Most Innu relied on spiritual healing rather than herbal remedies. They believed in living balanced lives and used positive psychology, such as not getting angry or holding grudges, to keep themselves healthy. They also used charms and beadwork to ward off illness and bad luck in addition to avoiding taboo activities. Life in the country, or *nutshimit,* was also considered vital to health. Healers called shamans cured the ill through rituals.

When people became ill, the members of the band pulled them on sleds as they traveled from place to place. During times of hardship, the sick were sometimes left behind. When sick people no longer wanted to eat, the Innu often killed them to prevent further suffering. After the missionaries arrived, the Innu left their sick at the missions.

Modern medicine The Quebec Innu had access to government health care under the Indian Act, but the federal government did not extend those benefits to the First Nations when Newfoundland and Labrador became a part of Canada in 1949. In 2001, the Labrador Innu met with the federal and provincial governments to work out the Labrador Innu Comprehensive Healing Strategy. One of the goals was to move beyond treating symptoms to taking care of the causes. This initiative received funding for creating on-reserve programs and services.

ARTS

Crafts

The Innu are known for their decorative caribou-skin coats, which are found in museums around the world. Innu women painted designs on the smoked hide using a variety of bone or wooden tools. They mixed tallow or oil with water and fish roe (eggs) as a base for natural dyes made of red or yellow ochre. Later, they obtained indigo (blue) and vermillion (red-orange) through trade. Intricate designs, sometimes inspired by dreams, were also painted on moccasins, boots, and other items of clothing.

Both women and men made *innikueuat* (dolls) for the children. Some were made of wood, or wood and caribou hide. Cloth later replaced the hide. One kind of doll that the Innu still produce is the "tea doll." Instead of stuffing the dolls with rags, they filled the body with tea. The supply of tea could be used when they ran out.

Oral literature

The Innu told two types of stories. *Tipatshimuna* are true stories about things people actually experienced. *Atanukana* tell about the creation of the world and times when animals and people could communicate. Many of these storied tell about *Kuekuatsheu*, the wolverine, who is often a trickster. Kuekuatsheu plays an important part in the Innu creation story.

According to the Innu, long ago when the land flooded, Kuekuatsheu put the animal species on a boat to save them. He asked the mink to bring up rocks and mud from underwater, and he used these to make an island for the people and animals.

CUSTOMS

Social organization

Usually three or four families lived together in a lodge. Several lodges were built close together in the winter, making a group of about fifty people. The Innu also gathered with other communities along the coast in summer or when fish spawned or waterfowl flocked. They used these times to celebrate, trade, and marry.

Childrearing

The Innu loved their children and took good care of orphans. Women usually cared for new babies, but older children and all adults, including men, cared for young children.

Children were never punished. A French missionary recorded a story about a French boy who had hit an Innu man with a drumstick. The Innu asked for a gift, which is how they compensated victims. The French refused, but instead promised to whip the boy. When the Innu man saw them preparing to hit the boy, he wrapped the boy in his coat and told the French to whip him in the boy's place.

Marriage

Men usually married in their early twenties, whereas women were in their late teens. Most people married a spouse from a nearby territory. Cross-cousin marriage was common. People looked for partners who were good at their responsibilities. After marriage, men usually stayed with their parents for three years, but they had to spend one winter with the wife's parents. Divorce was easy, and either partner could initiate it

Men could marry more than one wife. The practice of polygamy was most likely adopted because there were a greater number of women than men. After the Jesuit missionaries arrived and insisted that each man should only take one wife, the women were upset because it meant that some of them would never marry.

War and hunting

Oral tradition says that the Innu and Inuit warred with each other constantly long ago, but neither of these groups was known for being warlike. They did torture Iroquois (see entry) prisoners, though, and even women and children participated.

Hunting, which was critical to the tribe's survival, had many rituals attached to it. Shamans foretold of hunting success and located game, as did the practices of drumming and scalpimancy (see "Religion"). Individuals could also gain this knowledge through dreams. This ability was enhanced by following the right rituals and feasts.

The Innu believed that animals had power and could never be caught unless they chose to allow people to kill them. For this reason, the Innu never killed more than they needed or wasted any part of the animal. They always shared the meat with others. The people had great respect for animals and believed that only those who honored the animal spirits and treated the carcasses properly would have success in future hunts.

Feasts and Games

Celebrations One of the most important feasts, *makusas'n*, celebrated hunting and the caribou. During hunting trips, the caribou long bones were set aside. The day of the feast, hunters scraped the meat off the bones, and then the ends of the bones were crushed and boiled to extract the fat. The men cracked open the long bones and ate the raw marrow before sharing it with the women and children.

Some feasts were for men only. Sometimes, when food was abundant, women had their own feasts. At every feast, the Innu saved food for those who were not able to attend. The only time food was not set aside was at special feasts called "eatalls."

Ceremonial drumming always followed feasts. One man drummed at a time and sang the hunting songs he had received from his spirit. The music started with a leader, who then passed the drum to the senior member, who took a turn and passed it on. The music could go on for several hours or all night.

Games *Tapaikan* is a traditional Innu game. Players hold out a long carved bone pin and try to catch rings made of hollowed-out caribou hoofs or foot bones on the end of their pin or stick. Spruce branches are sometimes substituted for the rings. Other popular games are card games, cat's cradle, checkers, and *matsheshuatinakan* or *atshinakan* (fox game board), which was a wooden board with pegs. Balls, about the size of baseballs, were made of hide and stuffed with white moss or lichen, or old rags. Bingo became a favorite game later on.

CURRENT TRIBAL ISSUES

One of the major issues facing the Innu is the breakdown of their traditional culture, which has resulted in poverty, depression, and social crises, including drug and alcohol abuse, domestic abuse, and suicide. In 1999, Survival International reported that the Innu of northeastern Canada had the highest suicide rates in the world: 178 per 100,000 persons each year. The average rate in Canada was about 14 per 100,000 at that time. Many of the suicides were among the youth. The high suicide rate was believed to be related to several factors, including the loss of traditional culture. One initiative aimed at helping young Innu connect to their traditions is the Tshikapisk Foundation, which operates the Kamestastin Center. Kamestastin provides experiential, cultural, and spiritual learning programs for at-risk Innu youth, teaching them to live in harmony with the land and to preserve their Innu history, identity, and way of life. The foundation offers ecotourism and archaeological opportunities to help fund the programs.

Many of the problems the Innu face today stem from the changes to their culture and lifestyle after the arrival of the Europeans. Recognition for the Innu and respect for their rights has been an ongoing struggle. Since the turn of the century, the Innu have been involved in many lawsuits aimed at recovering their rights or being reimbursed for losses. In addition to gaining compensation for lands the Canadian government took from them, some Innu received damages for sexual abuse that occurred while they were attending residential schools.

The Innu have challenged the right of outside companies to exploit natural resources, such as through mining and building hydroelectric plants, on their traditional lands. They have demanded a say in what is done on their land and have requested a share of profits as well as employment opportunities in the industries conducted in their territory.

In spite of the many devastating problems the Innu are facing, they have made some strides in getting the world and the government to recognize their problems. To gain a greater voice, they are moving into the political arena. In 2011, Peter Penashue, head of the Innu Nation of Labrador, was the first Innu person ever appointed to the Cabinet of Canada. The Innu people hope that having representatives in government will ensure that their concerns are addressed in the future.

NOTABLE PEOPLE

Two twenty-first-century Innu who have often made the news are Daniel Ashini (1959–2009) and Peter Penashue (1964–). Both men participated in land claims talks and negotiations about the Emish (Voisey's Bay) nickel mine. Ashini played a key role in stopping the Dutch Royal Air Force's low-flying exercises over Innu territory and later served as president of Labrador's Innu Nation.

Penashue is the son of political and environmental activist Elizabeth "Tshaukuesh" Penashue (1944–), who was jailed several times for camping on airport runways to protest low-flying military flights. Tshaukuesh, an Innu elder, remained strongly opposed to the building of hydroelectric plants on Innu land, although her son was negotiating for them. Noted for his courage in speaking out about the sexual abuse he suffered at school and for overcoming alcoholism, Peter Penashue moved into politics by winning a seat in Parliament in 2011 and was appointed minister of intergovernmental affairs and president of the Queen's Privy Council. In the same election, Jonathan Genest-Jourdain (1980–) was also elected to the House of Commons. Penashue and Genest-Jourdain are following in the footsteps of Innu author Bernard Cleary (1937–), who in 2004 became the first Innu to serve in that capacity.

Other notable Innu people include Noel Negabamet (1600–1666), who served as an intermediary between the French and his people and worked for peace between the tribes in the fifteenth century; Matthew Rich, a land claims anthropologist and translator of Innu traditional stories; and the folk rock band Kashtin, popular during the 1980s and 1990s, started by Claude McKenzie (1967–) and Florent Vollant (1959–), who in 2001 won the Juno Award for Aboriginal Recording of the Year.

BOOKS

Anderson, Emma. *The Betrayal of Faith: The Tragic Journey of a Colonial Native Convert.* Cambridge, MA: Harvard University Press, 2007.

Henriksen, Georg, and Robert Paine. *Hunters in the Barrens: The Naskapi on the Edge of the White Man's World.* New York: Berghahn Books, 2010.

Kaneuketat. *I Dreamed the Animals: Kaneuketat: the Life of an Innu Hunter.* New York: Berghahn Books, 2008.

Samson, Colin. *A Way of Life That Does Not Exist: Canada and the Extinguishment of the Innu.* New York: Verso, 2003.

PERIODICALS

Dalsbø, E.T., "'We Were Told We Were Going to Live in Houses': Relocation and Housing of the Mushuau Innu of Natuashish from 1948 to 2003." *University of Tromsø,* May 28, 2010. Available from http://www.ub.uit.no/munin/bitstream/handle/10037/2739/thesis.pdf?sequence=3 (accessed on May 26, 2011).

WEB SITES

Armitage, Peter. "Religious Ideology among the Innu of Eastern Quebec and Labrador." *Université du Québec à Montréal.* http://www.unites.uqam.ca/religiologiques/no6/armit.pdf (accessed on May 24, 2011).

Canadian Heritage Information Network. "Communities & Institutions: Talented Youth." *Tipatshimuna.* http://www.tipatshimuna.ca/1420_e.php (accessed on May 19, 2011).

"Culture and History." *Innu Nation.* http://www.innu.ca/index.php?option=com_content&view=article&id=8&Itemid=3&lang=en (accessed on May 19, 2011).

Gangnier, Gary. "The History of the Innu Nation." *Central Quebec School Board.* http://www.cqsb.qc.ca/svs/434/fninnu.htm (accessed on May 24, 2011).

Jenny Higgins. "Innu Organizations and Land Claims." *Newfoundland and Labrador Heritage: Memorial University of Newfoundland,* 2008. http://www.heritage.nf.ca/aboriginal/innu_claims.html (accessed on May 19, 2011).

"Innu-aimun Traditional Stories." *Memorial University of Newfoundland.* May 31, 2010. http://www.innu-aimun.ca/modules.php?name=stories (accessed on May 19, 2011).

"Innu Youth Film Project." *Kamestastin.* http://www.kamestastin.com/ (accessed on May 24, 2011).

"Innu Experiential Education." *Tshikapisk Foundation.* http://www.tshikapisk.ca/home/11 (accessed on May 24, 2011).

Nametau Innu. "Your First Steps in the Innu Culture." *Musée Régional de la Côte-Nord.* http://www.nametauinnu.ca/en/tour (accessed on May 26, 2011).

"Newfoundland Labrador Threatens Innu Evictions." *Indian Law Resource Center.* 2008. http://www.indianlaw.org/node/301 (accessed on May 24, 2011).

Powers, Tim. "Peter Penashue: A Northern Light in Labrador." *The Globe and Mail.* May 3, 2011. http://m.theglobeandmail.com/news/politics/second-reading/silver-powers/peter-penashue-a-northern-light-in-labrador/article2009078/?service=mobile (accessed on May 24, 2011).

The Rooms, Provincial Museum Division. "Innu Objects." *Virtual Museum Canada.* 2008. http://www.museevirtuel-virtualmuseum.ca/edu/ViewLoit-Collection.do;jsessionid=3083D5EEB47F3ECDE9DA040AD0D4C956?method=preview⟨=EN&id=3210 (accessed on May 24, 2011).

Métis

Name

The word Métis (pronounced *may-TEE* or *meh-TIS*) comes from the Latin verb *miscere,* which means "to mix." The French used this name to refer to a group of Canadian mixed-race people. The Métis were also sometimes called half-breeds, mixed-bloods, or *Bois Brules,* a French term meaning "burnt wood," referring to skin color.

Location

The Métis originally wandered throughout modern-day Alberta and Saskatchewan in Canada and along the North Dakota border in the present-day United States. After 1885, the Métis could be found from Lake Superior to Alberta. In the twenty-first century, they are mostly located in western Canada along the Manitoba and North Dakota border, in southeastern Alberta, and in Saskatchewan. Two groups of about five thousand people each live in Ontario and Labrador.

Population

In 1821, there were about 500 Métis. Ten years later, in 1831, there were 1,300; in 1843, there were 2,600; in 1870, there were 12,000. No one identified themselves as Métis to U.S. census takers in 1990. In 1991, 135,285 people identified themselves to Canadian census takers as Métis. Canada's 2001 population count showed 292,305 Métis. Because the term *Métis* is used in two ways, the population counts differ widely. Some define it more narrowly as only the direct descendants of the original Métis; others use it to refer to all of mixed-blood heritage. Using the broader definition, a 2008 estimate suggested there were about 375,000 Métis.

Language family

The Métis speak a unique combination of Native languages and French *patois* (pronounced *pat-WAH,* a version of French the English sometimes call "Country French"), with occasional Scottish and Gaelic expressions. Gaelic is a language of Scotland and Ireland.

Traditional Métis Communities

Métis today live in communities scattered throughout Alberta, Saskatchewan, Manitoba, and the Northwest Territories. Some live in British Columbia, Labrador, Ontario, and Newfoundland.

Shaded area

Traditional lands of the Métis in Canada, in the prairie provinces of Alberta, Saskatchewan, and Manitoba

A map of traditional Métis lands. MAP BY XNR PRODUCTIONS. CENGAGE LEARNING, GALE. REPRODUCED BY PERMISSION OF GALE, A PART OF CENGAGE LEARNING.

Origins and group affiliations

The Métis are a group whose origins date back only a few hundred years. They are biracial descendants of First Nations women and European settlers. The majority share French and either Cree, Ojibway, or Assiniboin (pronounced *uh-SIN-uh-boin*) blood, but some trace their European origins to British, Scottish, Irish, or Scandinavian settlers and their Native origins to Inuit (see entry) women. There were many such offspring during the early years of the fur trade in Canada and the Great Lakes region.

The history of the Métis began with French fur traders who ventured into the woods and prairies of western Canada during the 1600s. Finding conditions there harsh and wild, the Frenchmen turned to the Native population for help. Far from home and lonely, they chose First Nations women as wives. The descendants of these couples, caught between two worlds, formed their own communities and developed their own culture.

Once united as the Métis, these people played an important role in the settlement of western Canada and in the formation of the new nation. Nonetheless, they have had many struggles to assert their rights to land and respect.

HISTORY

Birth of a nation

French fur traders known as *voyageurs* came to Canada in the 1600s and were welcomed by the Cree, Ojibwa, and Assiniboin (see entries). The Natives served as guides and provided the voyageurs with buffalo tongue, clothing, and pemmican, a long-lasting food that kept trappers fed through the winter months (see "Food"). The Frenchmen learned much about survival from them. The demand for furs among fashionable Europeans continued throughout the late seventeenth and early eighteenth centuries, bringing more French fur traders, who spent long days and nights in the wilderness trapping fur-bearing animals.

Most of the early traders supplied the Hudson's Bay Company, a British trading company located on the shores of the Hudson Bay. The Métis people were born of the unions between the French fur-trading men and the Native women who became their wives. Some of their sons grew up to become employees of trading companies, serving as trappers, hunters, guides, paddlers, and interpreters. Other boys became skilled buffalo hunters, who continued to keep the trading posts supplied with pemmican.

By the mid-1700s, a large mixed-blood population had settled around the Great Lakes. Communities of log cabins emerged at Sault Sainte Marie, Michigan, and other locations. As fur-bearing animals became scarce and settlers moved in from the East, many of these mixed-blood people moved westward to the Great Plains, where the distinctive Métis culture emerged.

Battle of Seven Oaks

Until 1780, the Hudson's Bay Company enjoyed complete control of trade in Canada. The company depended on the food supplies and know-how of the Métis for its survival. The rival North West Company then established a trading post of its own west of Lake Superior. The North West Company saw in the Métis people an excellent source of supplies

Important Dates

1816: Violence erupts during a Métis protest over the Pemmican Proclamation of 1814, and twenty-one Hudson's Bay Company employees are killed.

1821: The Hudson's Bay Company and the North West Company merge, putting many Métis out of work. The people scatter.

1869: The First Riel Rebellion takes place.

1870: The Manitoba Act allots 1.4 million acres of land to the Métis. Much of it is lost through trickery and misunderstanding.

1885: The Northwest Rebellion (Second Riel Rebellion) takes place.

1983: The Métis National Council is founded.

1989: Alberta passes the Métis Settlement Act, setting aside $310 million over a period of seventeen years to support the governing and operation of settlements.

and labor and lured them into their employ. With this new competition, the Hudson's Bay Company suffered heavy losses of money and supplies.

In 1811, the Hudson's Bay traders established a post at the point where the Red and Assiniboin Rivers join (near present-day Winnipeg, Manitoba, Canada), called the Red River Settlement. It lay directly on the preferred trading route of the North West Company. The Hudson's Bay Company encouraged the Métis population to move to this settlement. The nomadic (wandering) Métis obliged by forming a community there, but to the dismay of the Hudson's Bay Company, they continued to work for both trading companies.

Because they wanted sole rights to the pemmican supplied by the Métis, the Hudson's Bay Company passed the Pemmican Proclamation of 1814. Under this law, the Métis were prohibited from trading pemmican with anyone but the Hudson's Bay Company. Since their economy depended heavily on the sale of pemmican and two good customers were better than one, the Métis chose to ignore the law.

The situation erupted in violence in 1816, and twenty-one traders at the Hudson's Bay Company headquarters at Red River Settlement were killed, including the author of the Pemmican Proclamation. This episode was called the Battle of Seven Oaks.

Years of changes and rebellion

Five years later, the Hudson's Bay Company and the North West Company merged, and life changed forever for the Métis. Many were forced to find other ways of supporting themselves as excess trading posts were abandoned. Some Métis retained their strips of land along the Red River and farmed, forming the nucleus of what would later become the city of Winnipeg, Manitoba. Others moved to the plains and became wandering, year-round buffalo hunters. Still others adopted a combined lifestyle—during the winter months they established temporary settlements in the plains, and for the rest of the year they lived in their more permanent Red River community.

In 1867, the Canadian colonies united and formed the newly independent Dominion of Canada. Two years later, the Hudson's Bay Company sold its land holdings to the new government. The Canadian government encouraged people to settle the new territory and sent surveyors to the Red River Settlement to map out square plots of land to sell to pioneering colonists. They did not consult with or notify the Métis, who discovered their land was being sold by reading the newspaper. The surveyors completely disregarded the French-style settlement patterns of the Métis, whereby farms were built on long strips of land along the riverbanks. As Protestant settlers poured into their territory, the Métis saw clearly what the new English-speaking government had in store for them. More settlers would come to take over Métis lands and drive away the buffalo, and Catholicism and the French language would be scorned.

Furious, the Métis formed a resistance movement and asked the young and well-educated Louis Riel (1844–1885) to head it up. Riel and his supporters—who included a gang of rough-and-tumble buffalo hunters and several sympathetic Catholic priests—created an independent government at the Red River Settlement. They then bloodlessly took over a government fort near Winnipeg and sent a list of demands to Canada's prime minister. The stipulations included land rights, freedom of language and religion, representation in the Canadian government, and assurance that the Métis would be consulted on decisions about the Red River country. These actions became known as the First Riel Rebellion.

While Riel and his provisional (temporary) government negotiated with the central government, a local militia formed to oppose his rule in Red River. Learning of the plans to overthrow the new government, the Métis fought the militia and forced them to surrender. One member of the militia, however, planned another attack, and

E. RONJAT.

Louis Riel rebelled against the Canadian government in defense of the rights of the Métis people.
©MARY EVANS PICTURE LIBRARY/THE IMAGE WORKS.

the Métis arrested him, tried him, and sentenced him to death. His execution turned public opinion in Canada against Riel and his new government.

Although the National Committee of the Métis of the Red River only lasted a year, it had one success—or so they thought at the time. They negotiated the Manitoba Act of 1870 with the Canadian government. The Manitoba Act set aside 1.4 million acres of land for the Métis. The government promised to control the flood of settlers and to protect the French language and Catholic faith. The Red River Settlement became the center of what would now be called Manitoba. The Canadian government did not keep its end of the agreement, however. It did not pardon Riel for his part in the execution of the militia member, and it sent in troops to control the Métis. Louis Riel fled Manitoba for the United States.

The Northwest Rebellion of 1885

As the Métis expected, their lands were taken over, and the government refused to recognize their land claims. In 1885, Riel returned to lead the Northwest Rebellion, also known as the Second Riel Rebellion. Fired up by pride and a desire to form a new French Catholic nation in western Canada, a Métis army began to fight on March 26, 1885. The government sent thousands of troops to subdue the Métis and defeated them in the Battle of Batoche on May 12, 1885. Riel voluntarily surrendered to the authorities three days later.

Riel's trial for treason (betraying his country) became a political issue between French-speaking people in Quebec, who favored him, and the English-speaking people of Ontario, the seat of the government, who opposed him. Historians say that if Riel would have pleaded insanity, he probably would have gone free. He had spent some time in a mental institution, believed he was on a mission from God, and was known to behave and speak oddly at times. Riel refused to plead, declaring, "What belongs to us ought to be ours." He was found guilty of treason and hanged on November 16, 1885. The hanging caused something of a sensation worldwide. A Philadelphia newspaper predicted, "The ghost of Louis Riel will haunt Canadian statesmen for many a day." (More than a century later, in 1992, the Canadian House of Commons approved a motion recognizing Louis Riel's "unique and historic role as a founder of Manitoba.")

The scrip program

The constant battling over the land along the Red River finally forced the Canadian government to step in. In 1885, it appointed a commission to oversee land distribution to the Métis. This was to be accomplished through a system known as the scrip program. A scrip was a government certificate that could be exchanged for money or land. Some who did purchase land with scrip found the land was far from their existing community, no good for farming, and too small to hunt game. Some Métis took money instead of land. While some spent it and became poverty-stricken and landless, others used the money to move to the United States, Saskatchewan, or Alberta to start a new life.

The scrip program caused long-term problems between the Métis and other indigenous groups in Canada. Whereas the Métis received only land or money, some full-blooded Natives were offered treaties that granted them land and brought them under the protection of the government. They were able to remain united and receive benefits such as health care. The scrip program proved nearly fatal to Métis society, and the mistrust created between people who got scrips and people who got treaty settlements still exists today.

Modern times

Ever since the scrip program was enacted, Métis history has been marked by bleakness and filled with tales of land grabs and the government's complete disregard for the band's unique society. In the 1930s, several Métis leaders emerged, and the Métis Association of Alberta was formed. Political pressure on the Alberta government led to the passage of the Métis Betterment Act in 1938, which set aside lands for Métis settlements. Restoration of land has been slow in coming, however, and the only Canadian lands held in common by Métis people in the early twenty-first century are eight settlements in Alberta.

In the 1960s, when the rights of minorities became a worldwide issue, the Métis people forcibly reasserted the claims made by Métis leader Louis Riel in the 1880s and they continue to do so today. In an effort to rekindle cultural pride, the Métis uphold Riel as a hero. To them, Riel is a symbol of the independent minds of indigenous peoples who seek control over their own communities.

Métis Words

Because many Métis are part French, some of their words, especially the nouns, sound similar to French words when they are pronounced, but they are usually spelled differently. Most verbs reflect the people's Cree heritage. The language they speak is called Michif.

lawm	"man"
lo	"water"
meechishouw	"eat"
nakamouw	"sing"
portipik	"porcupine"
salay	"sun"
sh'yaen	"dog"
shipwaytay	"leave"
wawpouw	"see"
yeeboo	"owl"
zhwal	"horse"

RELIGION

The first Catholic missionaries arrived in Métis lands in 1818 and were quickly followed by Anglicans and Presbyterians. Catholic missionaries enjoyed success among French speakers, while the Anglicans were more successful among English-speaking Métis. Part of the Métis heritage was European, so the Christian religions were in many cases brought to the Americas by the original trappers and traders. The large population of French trappers brought Catholicism to many Métis settlements in the early days. As Europeans married Native women, Christian religions gained some Native elements. Organized religion served as a source of support and unity for the Métis and strengthened their sense of community.

LANGUAGE

Language has been a dividing factor throughout the history of the Métis. Some Métis speak Cree, others Assiniboin, and still others Ojibway (see entries) or any of several other languages, which have blended with French to create new local languages. The languages spoken by the Métis are a combination of Native tongues and French *patois,* with occasional Scotch and Gaelic expressions thrown in.

Because of the unusual nature of the languages, the Cree of the area created a new name for the Métis: *O-tee-paym-soo-wuk,* meaning "their-own-boss." Métis scholar Marcel Giraud wrote in his 1945 book *The Métis in the Canadian West* that "the language … normally alternated between the Native American dialects [varieties of languages] habitually used in the families, and the French of Quebec, modified by expressions from the Native American tongues … and modulated by singsong intonations that recalled the accents of the Natives and even today remain very characteristic." Currently, Métis language classes are offered, and books and dictionaries on the different dialects are available.

GOVERNMENT

From 1670 to 1857, the Hudson's Bay Company had complete authority over western and northern Canada, and its only interest was in trading furs and making money. Nearly all Métis people were employees of the Hudson's Bay Company, which appointed a governor and a council to oversee the Red River settlement (population 10,000 in 1867). Although this was not a democratic way of doing things, the Red River community generally supported it. The exception to this style of government were buffalo hunters, who had their own leaders.

In 1868, the territory was handed over to the Canadian government. The Métis worried that their entire way of life might soon vanish under the influence of an indifferent, faraway, English-speaking governing body. Because of this, Louis Riel organized the resistance movement. For one year, Riel oversaw the only legal government the Métis Nation has ever had.

The Métis still have no legal rights as a nation and no legal form of self-government except in Alberta. In the 1960s, the Métis organized themselves into groups such as the Manitoba Métis Federation, the Métis Association of Saskatchewan, and the Canadian Métis Society. However, the Métis still had difficulty getting the Canadian government to hear their issues, so many Métis organizations allied themselves with the broader Native American organization known as the Native Council, which speaks to the government on behalf of the Métis and other Native American groups.

Dissatisfied with efforts of the Native Council on their behalf, the Métis formed an organization that would address their claims on their terms in 1983. The Métis National Council petitions the government for land claims under the Manitoba Act of 1870, for inclusion of Métis texts and courses in Canadian schools, and for self-government. In 1985, the Canadian government set aside all discussion on Métis claims, deciding that a definition of Métis must be agreed upon first. After four centuries, that definition is still under debate, and this debate hinders Métis unification and their attempts to negotiate with the government as a sovereign people.

By the early twenty-first century, Alberta was the only Canadian province to heed Métis claims. In 1989, the Alberta-Métis Settlement Accord was signed, providing a framework for establishing a land base and self-government for the Métis people. The following year, Alberta amended its constitution and passed several additional acts that promised the Métis $10 million a year. The acts received royal approval in 1998,

Métis men hunt buffalo, which were key to sustaining the tribe's lifestyle and economy in the 1800s. WITH PERMISSION OF THE ROYAL ONTARIO MUSEUM. © ROM.

and in 2003, the Métis received $5.2 million to fund the General Council and individual settlements. These acts were the first efforts to give Métis the land and autonomy (self-government) they had been seeking for more than a century.

ECONOMY

Early livelihoods

The Métis began as either suppliers or employees for the Hudson's Bay Company. Suppliers hunted buffalo, which provided food, shelter, and clothing for the Métis people and was the source of pemmican they sold to the company. Historians say that without a dependable supply of meat for pemmican, there would have been no food to keep the trappers alive in the winter, and the fur trade would have failed. The Métis conducted communal buffalo hunts. Large parties set out on the hunt in their two-wheeled Red River carts pulled by horses or oxen (See "Transportation").

Employees worked as fur trappers, supervisors at the trading posts, pilots or crew members of the boats that carried furs up and down the Canadian waterways, interpreters, or guides.

When the Hudson's Bay Company left in 1868, Europeans attempted to convert the Métis at Red River Settlement to farming, but this did not suit the nomadic lifestyle of many. The work was not as reliable as the buffalo hunt. Soon the buffalo disappeared, so some people turned to farming. Others continued to trap, but that industry declined after 1945.

Living conditions for the Métis after the buffalo were gone became miserable. In an effort to escape poverty and discrimination, many enlisted in the armed forces during World War I (1914–18), World War II (1939–45), and the Korean War (1950–53).

Modern Economy

The great central plains area of Canada, where many Métis live, is a vast place of farmlands and ranches with a widely scattered population. Beginning in the 1950s, Métis families tended to settle in the prairie towns that sprang up, places where jobs in construction and low-paying service industries were available. In the early twenty-first century, many depended on such wage labor and government welfare payments to survive. There are still people, however, who live in isolated areas and maintain a version of the hunting-gathering lifestyle.

In 2010, the Canadian government established a $10 million Métis Economic Development Fund. In January 2011, the federal government agreed to use $3 million of that allotment to start an investment fund for the Manitoba Métis to develop natural resources and energy projects. The provincial government will contribute an additional $1 million. This fund will be used to invest in Métis-owned businesses to create jobs and drive economic growth.

DAILY LIFE

Families

The Métis usually lived in nuclear families, with parents and children forming a household. Many families spent their days on the move, especially during buffalo hunts. Because of this, a married couple often did not live near other family members.

Education

When the missionaries settled among the Métis in the early 1800s, many people had their first chance for a formal education. Mission schools for both boys and girls emphasized religious instruction and taught them European culture and ideas. For example, young Métis girls learned to bead and embroider in the European style, causing an evolution in Métis clothing and decorative style that still exists. By the mid-1800s, the Red River settlement where many Métis lived was a sophisticated and wealthy community. Some parents sent their boys off to be educated in Montreal, Quebec, but an advanced education for girls was not considered important by the Métis or most other societies of the time.

In the early twenty-first century, children attend public schools in the communities that have sprung up since the 1950s. The Manitoba Metis Federation Education Minister oversees schooling at all levels. The schools collaborate with the Louis Riel Institute, which provides cultural activities, and they have designed the Standing Tall program to decrease absenteeism and dropouts, and increase the quality of education. Community volunteers go into the schools to encourage and support student learning and make it culturally relevant.

Buildings

The Métis often built homesteads on long strips of land, preferably near a water source. The breadth of their land was measured by sight, with a plot "extending back from the river as far as one might distinguish a horse from a man … this was taken to be about four miles," explained Fraser Symington in *The Canadian Indian*. They made simple log structures and stretched buffalo hide taut over them. This covering offered protection from the elements while allowing sunlight to stream through. Descriptions of typical Métis home interiors illustrate the people's preference for simplicity.

Furnishings often served more than one use. Fewer pieces of furniture made it easier to host large gatherings—an important advantage, because Métis homes were the usual setting for fiddling and dancing parties.

Large groups of buffalo hunters established temporary winter encampments so that families could more easily follow the roaming beasts. These people were known as *hiverants* and lived in houses similar to those described above but simpler. As settlers streamed into their lands in the nineteenth century, some Métis chose to live permanently at their winter homes, and those structures became more sophisticated. By this time, Catholicism had become firmly rooted in Métis society, and the people often erected a large structure to house the local church and priest.

Transportation

The supply and demand of pemmican in the western Canadian fur trade was so crucial that the Métis created a new vehicle to transport large loads more easily. The ox-driven Red River carts enabled the Métis to travel thousands of miles over land and through marsh; they floated on logs across rivers and functioned as sleighs in the winter. Most important, they carried tons of pemmican to the trading posts. As a matter of family pride, the Métis lavishly decorated their Red River carts (see "Economy.").

Food

Twice a year, once in the spring and again on a smaller scale in the winter, entire Métis communities would set off to hunt buffalo. The great buffalo hunt was a cornerstone of Métis existence.

When the men came back from a successful hunt, Métis women prepared pemmican. They began by skinning and cutting the meat into thin strips, which they hung out to dry. Once the meat dried, the women pounded it, mixed it with berries and fat, and stored it in a huge sack made of buffalo hide, thus producing a highly nutritious, nonperishable food that was edible for years.

In modern times many Métis meals include fish and game they have caught themselves, just as they have always done.

Clothing and adornment

The Métis are so famous for their embroidery and beading skills that the Sioux and Cree (see entries) called them "the flower beadwork people." They created elaborate decorations for their homes, Red River carts, moccasins, and leggings. Young girls learned European decorative styles in the mission schools, resulting in fashions that combined European tailoring with Native fringe and decoration. The Métis also liked European hats. Whereas women favored a scarf or shawl draped about the head, men wore top hats adorned with ribbons, fur caps made from a variety of pelts, broad-brimmed felt hats, or round, flat hats called tams.

The most distinctive accessory was a sash called *l'Assomption,* borrowed from the French voyageurs of the sixteenth century. Made of brightly colored wool, this 10-foot (3-meter) length of fabric wrapped around the waist. It served to keep a man's coat closed, but it had many other uses. In addition to functioning as a washcloth, towel, saddle blanket, rope, or tourniquet to bind up wounds, it often held a hunting knife, a moneybag, and a fire bag, which was used to carry a pipe, tobacco, flint, and steel. The fringes on the sash could even be pulled off and used as sewing thread while traveling. Even now, some Métis wear this sash to display pride in their heritage.

Healing practices

Métis healing practices used elements of both European and Native traditions. This generally meant the people were healthier than the Native or European peoples in western Canada at the time. Still, they suffered diseases along with the rest of the population. Despite the Hudson's Bay Company's vaccination efforts, tuberculosis, measles, smallpox, and influenza had a terrible effect on the Métis in the nineteenth century.

CUSTOMS

Courtship, love, and marriage

In the early days, marriages were arranged by the family, and a person usually wed someone outside the community. Married life could be very lonely for wives, who were often left behind when their husbands were off working for long periods. Couples maintained a far-flung social network, though, connected by letter writing, message and gift exchanges, and gossip.

The Métis tended to be a romantic people, believing in passionate love and sometimes engaging in stormy, ardent affairs that led to violence or the abandonment of a spouse.

Celebrating the great buffalo hunt

The majority of Métis customs related to the great buffalo hunt, although the people often celebrated in a European rather than Native style. Their social gatherings tended to be casual and spontaneous instead of formal. The Métis were famous for their parties. Upon returning from the spring hunt, they hosted a homecoming gala consisting of a feast and dancing. They danced a unique pattern of up to thirty different steps called a Red River jig. This was performed to the accompaniment of a fiddle, another custom adopted from their European ancestors.

Along with eating and dancing, the Métis enjoyed card playing, drinking, and smoking. In fact, tobacco smoking was so popular among the Métis that when they canoed long distances, they measured the journey by the number of pipes they smoked along the way. In the early twenty-first century, the descendants of many of these Métis travelers are trappers in the northern regions of Canada, and they still measure their traplines in "pipes."

The boatman culture

Métis rivermen, while carrying furs up and down Canadian waterways, developed a culture of their own with singing as its core. They composed work songs, drinking songs, and love songs. When a fleet of boats approached a settlement, the boatmen put on their most festive clothing, including the *l'Assomption* sash (see "Clothing and adornment"), colorful leggings, and feather-trimmed hats.

Sundays and feast days

Reflecting the influence of the Catholic church on Métis society, the people were strict observers of the Sabbath (the holy day). Although they did worship, they also spent most Sundays socializing, gambling, and dancing. The Métis observed French religious holidays, such as St. Jean Baptiste Day on June 24, featuring organized sporting events and a feast. This observance is still held today, although it is primarily a day dedicated to celebrating French-Canadian pride.

CURRENT TRIBAL ISSUES

Because they have roots in two continents and because the exact mix of nationalities or ethnicities that makes up the Métis race has never been agreed upon, the people have always had a difficult time getting recognition as a Native group in Canada. They had some success in 1982, when the Constitution Act divided Canada's Native peoples into three groups: the Indian, the Inuit, and the Métis, with rights accorded to all three groups. However, the government does not treat the Métis as it does other aboriginal (native) peoples. The Métis continue to struggle with issues of group identity. These questions are often asked: Who is a Métis? Would anyone with mixed blood qualify as Métis, or do only the descendants of the particular groups of people qualify?

The uncertain status of the Métis has led to problems with the government over land use and development. For example, government-sponsored water projects have resulted in the flooding and destruction of Métis trapping territories. The Métis have complained that they are not consulted about such projects, nor are they compensated for their losses. These problems have led to mayhem and arrests.

In 1996, the Labrador Métis staged a peaceful demonstration to protest the government issuing a sports-fishing-lodge license on the sacred Eagle River. They claimed the river and its salmon would be damaged. Forty-seven Métis were arrested in the demonstration. One Labrador Métis stated, "My family can't even fish for some food for the table [because of government regulations] while foreigners and rich political types fly in to the Eagle River for their leisurely weekend fly fishing."

In 2011, the Métis of Alberta were still fighting for their rights. Alberta had been the first province to recognize the Métis and grant them rights. A court case in 2004 led to the passage of the Interim Métis Harvesting Agreement. This legislation, establishing Métis harvesting rights, was agreed on by both the Alberta government and the Métis National Council. A change in Alberta government, however, led to the termination of this policy, reversing years of forward-thinking policies affecting the Métis.

Although the Métis were promised 1.4 million acres after Louis Riel's provisional government was dissolved, that land was not distributed until a decade or more afterward. Even then, some people were never given their land. By the time the Métis received the property they had been promised, settlers had already claimed the best land. In 2011, the Manitoba Métis Federation (MMF) appealed to the Supreme Court of Canada, hoping for justice in this matter. The MMF is the governing body and political representative of the Métis Nation's Manitoba community. The MMF is also working with several different mining companies to develop high-grade minerals and precious metals, particularly nickel, on Métis land.

NOTABLE PEOPLE

Gabriel Dumont (c. 1837–1906) was a Métis buffalo hunter and military leader, the son of a Frenchman and a woman of the Sarcee tribe. He fired his first shot in a battle against the Sioux when he was twelve, and by the time he was twenty-five, he had been elected chief of the buffalo hunt, in charge of about three hundred Métis followers. Buffalo hunts were highly organized affairs and required firm, intelligent leadership. Dumont excelled at the task. He traveled to Montana to ask Louis Riel to head the Northwest Rebellion of 1885, and he served as Riel's second-in-command. He survived the battle, fled to Montana, and later traveled with William "Buffalo Bill" Cody's Wild West Show, billed as the "Hero of the Halfbreed Rebellion."

Tantoo Cardinal (1950–) is an actress who has appeared in plays, television programs, and films, including the American movies *Dances with Wolves* and *Legends of the Fall,* and the Canadian picture *Black Robe.* She was born in Anzac, Alberta, to a Cree mother and a white father. Her feelings of responsibility to the Native American world, coupled with her realization that through acting she could best reach people, induced Cardinal to become a professional actress. Cardinal was awarded the Eagle Spirit Award from the Native Indian Film Festival in 1990.

BOOKS

Barkwell, Lawrence J. *Women of the Metis Nation.* Winnipeg, Manitoba: Louis Riel Institute, 2009.

Foster, Martha Harroun. *We Know Who We Are: Métis Identity in a Montana Community.* Norman: University of Oklahoma Press, 2006.

Gordon, Irene Ternier. *A People on the Move: The Métis of the Western Plains.* Surry, British Columbia: Heritage House, 2009.

Lischke, Ute, and David T. McNab. *The Long Journey of a Forgotten People: Métis Identities and Family Histories.* Waterloo, Ontario: Wilfrid Laurier University Press, 2007.

Macdougall, Brenda. *One of the Family: Metis Culture in Nineteenth-Century Northwestern Saskatchewan.* Vancouver, British Columbia: UBC Press, 2010.

Penny, Josie. *So Few on Earth: A Labrador Métis Woman Remembers.* Toronto, Ontario: Dundurn Press, 2010.

Ponton, Lynn. *Métis: Mixed Blood Stories.* Santa Fe, NM: Sunstone Press, 2010.

Quan, Holly. *Native Chiefs and Famous Metis: Leadership and Bravery in the Canadian West.* Custer, WA: Heritage House, 2009.

WEB SITES

"Aboriginal Peoples: The Métis." *Newfoundland and Labrador Heritage.* http://www.heritage.nf.ca/aboriginal/metis.html (accessed on August 4, 2011).

Brown, Brian M. "Riel, Dumont, and the 1885 Rebellion." *A Little History.* 1997. http://www.alittlehistory.com/Mtfullst.htm (accessed on June 3, 2011).

"Louis Riel Institute." *Manitoba Metis Federation.* http://www.mmf.mb.ca/index.php?option=com_content&view=article&id=132&Itemid=128 (accessed on June 4, 2011).

"Metis Communities." *Labrador Métis Nation.* http://www.labradormetis.ca/home/10 (accessed on June 4, 2011).

"Métis: History & Culture." *Turtle Island Productions.* http://www.turtle-island.com/native/the-ojibway-story/metis.html (accessed on June 4, 2011).

Métis Nation of Ontario. http://www.metisnation.org/ (accessed on June 4, 2011).

"Michif Language." *Michif & Métis Cultural Site.* http://www.saskschools.ca/curr_content/creelang/index.html (accessed on June 4, 2011).

Redish, Laura, and Orrin Lewis. "Native Languages of the Americas: Michif (Mitchif, Metis Creole, French Cree)." *Native Languages of the Americas: Preserving and Promoting Indigenous American Indian Languages.* http://www.native-languages.org/michif.htm (accessed on June 4, 2011).

Where to Learn More

Books

Abel, Kerry. *Drum Songs: Glimpses of Dene History.* Montreal, Quebec: McGill–Queen's University Press, 1993.

Adams, Richard C. *A Delaware Indian Legend and the Story of Their Troubles.* Whitefish, MT: Kessinger Publishing, LLC, 2006.

Adamson, Thelma, ed. *Folk-tales of the Coast Salish.* Lincoln: Bison Books, 2009.

Aderkas, Elizabeth, and Christa Hook. *American Indians of the Pacific Northwest.* Oxford: Osprey Publishing, 2005.

Adil, Janeen R. *The Northeast Indians: Daily Life in the 1500s.* Mankato, MN: Capstone Press, 2006.

Agonito, Joseph. *Lakota Portraits: Lives of the Legendary Plains People.* Guilford, CT: TwoDot, 2011.

Agoyo, Herman, and Joe S. Sando, eds. *Po'pay: Leader of the First American Revolution.* Santa Fe, NM: Clear Light Publishing, 2005.

Akers, Donna L. *Culture and Customs of the Choctaw Indians.* Santa Barbara, CA: Greenwood, 2012.

The Aleut Relocation and Internment during World War II: A Preliminary Examination. Anchorage, AK: Aleutian/Pribilof Islands Association, 1981.

Alexander, Annie Lou. *Blood Is Red…So Am I.* New York: Vantage Press, 2007.

Alexie, Sherman. *The Absolutely True Diary of a Part-Time Indian.* Waterville, ME: Thorndike Press, 2008.

Alfred, Agnes. *Paddling to Where I Stand: Agnes Alfred, Kwakwaka'wakw Noblewoman.* Seattle: University of Washington Press, 2005.

Alger, Abby L. *In Indian Tents: Stories Told by Penobscot, Passamaquoddy and Micmac Indians.* Park Forest, IL: University Press of the Pacific, 2006.

Allen, John W. *Legends and Lore of Southern Illinois.* Carbondale: Southern Illinois University Press, 2010.

Andersen, Raoul R., and John K. Crellin. *Misel Joe: An Aboriginal Chief's Journey.* St. John's, Newfoundland: Flanker Press, 2009.

Anderson, Jeffrey D. *One Hundred Years of Old Man Sage: An Arapaho Life.* Lincoln: University of Nebraska Press, 2003.

Andersson, Rani-Henrik. *The Lakota Ghost Dance of 1890.* Lincoln: University of Nebraska Press, 2008.

Angell, Tony, and John M. Marzluff. *In the Company of Crows and Ravens.* New Haven, CT: Yale University Press, 2007.

Anthony, Alexander E., Jr., David Neil Sr., and J. Brent Ricks. *Kachinas: Spirit Beings of the Hopi.* Albuquerque, NM: Avanyu Publishing, 2006.

Archer, Jane. *The First Fire: Stories of the Cherokee, Kickapoo, Kiowa, and Tigua.* Dallas, TX: Taylor Trade, 2005.

Arnold, Caroline, and Richard R. Hewett. *The Ancient Cliff Dwellers of Mesa Verde.* New York: Clarion Books, 2000.

Aron Crowell, ed. *Living Our Cultures, Sharing Our Heritage: The First Peoples of Alaska.* Washington, DC: Smithsonian Institution, 2010.

Augaitis, Daina, Lucille Bell, and Nika Collison. *Raven Travelling: Two Centuries of Haida Art.* Seattle: University of Washington Press, 2008.

Ayagalria, Moses K. *Yupik Eskimo Fairy Tales and More.* New York: Vantage Press, 2006.

Bahti, Mark. *Pueblo Stories and Storytellers.* 3rd ed. Tucson, AZ: Rio Nuevo Publishers, 2010.

Bahti, Mark, and Eugene Baatsoslanii Joe. *Navajo Sandpaintings.* 3rd ed. Tucson, AZ: Rio Nuevo Publishers, 2009.

Bailey, Garrick, ed. *Traditions of the Osage: Stories Collected and Translated by Francis la Flesche.* Albuquerque: University of New Mexico Press, 2010.

Baker, Wendy Beth. *Healing Power of Horses: Lessons from the Lakota Indians.* Irvine, CA: BowTie Press, 2004.

Ball, Eve, Nora Henn, and Lynda A. Sánchez. *Indeh: An Apache Odyssey.* Reprint. Norman: University of Oklahoma Press, 1988.

Ballantine, Betty, and Ian Ballantine, eds. *The Native Americans: An Illustrated History.* Atlanta: Turner Publishing, 1993.

Bancroft-Hunt, Norman. *People of the Totem: The Indians of the Pacific Northwest.* Photographs by Werner Forman. New York: Putnam, 1979.

Barbeau, Marius. *Huron and Wyandot Mythology.* Ottawa, Ontario: Government Printing Bureau, 1915.

Barbour, Jeannie, Amanda J. Cobb, and Linda Hogan. *Chickasaw: Unconquered and Unconquerable.* Ada, OK: Chickasaw Press, 2006.

Barker, James H., and Ann Fienup-Riordan. *Yupiit Yuraryarait = Yup'ik Ways of Dancing.* Fairbanks: University of Alaska Press, 2010.

Barkwell, Lawrence J. *Women of the Metis Nation.* Winnipeg, Manitoba: Louis Riel Institute, 2009.

Barnett, James F., Jr. *The Natchez Indians: A History to 1735.* Jackson: University Press of Mississippi, 2007.

Barrett, Samuel Alfred. *Ceremonies of the Pomo Indians and Pomo Bear Doctors.* University of California Publications in American Archeology and Ethnology. 1917. Reprint. Whitefish, MT: Kessinger Publishing, 2010.

— — —. *The Washo Indians.* 1917. Reprint. Charleston, SC: Kessinger Publishing, 2010.

Barron, Donna Gentle Spirit. *The Long Island Indians and their New England Ancestors: Narragansett, Mohegan, Pequot and Wampanoag Tribes.* Bloomington, IN: AuthorHouse, 2006.

Bartram, William, and Gregory A. Waselkov. *William Bartram on the Southeastern Indians.* Lincoln: University of Nebraska Press, 2002.

Basel, Roberta. *Sequoyah: Inventor of Written Cherokee.* Minneapolis, MN: Compass Point Books, 2007.

Bastedo, Jamie. *Reaching North: A Celebration of the Subarctic.* Markham, Ontario: Red Deer Press, 2002.

Bauerle, Phenocia, ed. *The Way of the Warrior: Stories of the Crow People.* Lincoln: University of Nebraska Press, 2003.

Bean, Lowell John, ed. "Introduction." In *The Ohlone Past and Present: Native Americans of the San Francisco Bay Region.* Menlo Park, CA: Ballena Press, 1994.

Bean, Lowell John, and Florence C. Shipek. "Luiseño." In *Handbook of North American Indians.* Vol. 8: *California,* edited by Robert F. Heizer. Washington, DC: Smithsonian Institution, 1978.

Bean, Lowell, Frank Porter, and Lisa Bourgeault. *The Cahuilla.* New York: Chelsea House, 1989.

Beasley, Richard A. *How to Carve a Tlingit Mask.* Juneau: Sealaska Heritage Institute, 2009.

Becenti, Karyth. *One Nation, One Year: A Navajo Photographer's 365-Day Journey into a World of Discovery, Life and Hope.* Los Ranchos, NM: Rio Grande Books, 2010.

Beck, Mary G. *Heroes and Heroines: Tlingit-Haida Legend.* Anchorage: Alaska Northwest Books, 2003.

Beckwourth, James. *The Life and Adventures of James P. Beckwourth, Mountaineer, Scout, and Pioneer, and Chief of the Crow Nation of Indians.* Paris, France: Adamant Media Corporation, 2005.

Behnke, Alison. *The Apaches.* Minneapolis, MN: Lerner Publications, 2006.

Behrman, Carol H. *The Indian Wars.* Minneapolis, MN: Lerner Publications, 2005.

Belting, Natalia. *Whirlwind Is a Spirit Dancing: Poems Based on Traditional American Indian Songs and Stories.* New York: Milk and Cookies Press, 2006.

Bergon, Frank. *Shoshone Mike.* New York: Viking Penguin, 1987.

Berleth, Richard. *Bloody Mohawk: The French and Indian War and American Revolution on New York's Frontier.* Hensonville, NY: Black Dome, 2009.

Betty, Gerald. *Comanche Society: Before the Reservation.* College Station: Texas A&M University Press, 2005.

Bial, Raymond. *The Chumash.* New York: Benchmark Books, 2004.

— — —. *The Cree.* New York: Benchmark Books, 2006.

— — —. *The Delaware.* New York: Benchmark Books, 2006.

— — —. *The Menominee.* New York: Marshall Cavendish Benchmark, 2006.

— — —. *The Tlingit.* New York: Benchmark Books, 2003.

Bibby, Brian. *Deeper than Gold: A Guide to Indian Life in the Sierra Foothills.* Berkeley: Heyday Books, 2004.

Bielawski, Ellen. *In Search of Ancient Alaska: Solving the Mysteries of the Past.* Anchorage: Alaska Northwest Books, 2007.

Birchfield, D.L., and Helen Dwyer. *Apache History and Culture.* New York: Gareth Stevens, 2012.

Biskup, Agnieszka. *Thunder Rolling Down the Mountain: The Story of Chief Joseph and the Nez Percé.* Mankato, MN: Capstone Press, 2011.

Bjorklund, Ruth. *The Cree.* Tarrytown, NY: Marshall Cavendish, 2009.

— — —. *The Hopi.* Tarrytown, NY: Marshall Cavendish Benchmark, c. 2009.

Blackbird, Andrew J. *History of the Ottawa and Chippewa Indians of Michigan.* Charleston, SC: Nabu Press, 2010.

Bodine, John. "Taos Pueblo." *Handbook of North American Indians,* Vol. 9: *Southwest.* Ed. Alfonso Ortiz. Washington DC: Smithsonian Institution, 1979.

— — —. *Taos Pueblo: A Walk Through Time.* Tucson, AZ: Rio Nuevo, 2006.

Bodinger de Uriarte, John J. *Casino and Museum: Representing Mashantucket Pequot Identity.* Tucson: University of Arizona Press, 2007.

Bogan, Phebe M. *Yaqui Indian Dances of Tucson Arizona: An Account of the Ceremonial Dances of the Yaqui Indians at Pascua.* Whitefish, MT: Kessinger Publishing, 2011.

Bonvillain, Nancy, and Ada Deer. *The Hopi.* Minneapolis, MN: Chelsea House Publications, 2005.

— — —. *The Nez Percé.* New York: Chelsea House, 2011.

— — —. *The Zuñi.* New York: Chelsea House Publishers, 2011.

Boule, Mary Null. *Mohave Tribe.* Vashon, WV: Merryant Publishers Inc., 2000.

Bourque, Bruce J., and Laureen A. LaBar. *Uncommon Threads: Wabanaki Textiles, Clothing, and Costume.* Augusta: Maine State Museum in association with University of Washington Press, 2009.

Bowes, John P. *The Choctaw.* New York: Chelsea House, 2010.

Bradley, Donna. *Native Americans of San Diego County, CA.* Mt. Pleasant, SC: Arcadia, 2009.

Bragdon, Kathleen J. *The Columbia Guide to American Indians of the Northeast.* New York: Columbia University Press, 2005.

Braje, Todd J., and Torben C. Rick, eds.*Human Impacts on Seals, Sea Lions, and Sea Otters: Integrating Archaeology and Ecology in the Northeast Pacific.* Berkeley: University of California Press, 2011.

Bray, Kingsley M. *Crazy Horse: A Lakota Life.* Norman: University of Oklahoma Press, 2006.

Breen, Betty, and Earl Mills, Sr. *Cape Cod Wampanoag Cookbook: Wampanoag Indian Recipes, Images & Lore.* Santa Fe, NM: Clear Light Books, 2001.

Brehm, Victoria. *Star Songs and Water Spirits: A Great Lakes Native Reader.* Tustin, MI: Ladyslipper Press, 2010.

Brimner, Larry Dane. *Pocahontas: Bridging Two Worlds.* New York: Marshall Cavendish Benchmark, 2009.

Bringhurst, Robert. *A Story as Sharp as a Knife: The Classical Haida Mythtellers and Their World.* 2nd ed. Vancouver, BC: Douglas & McIntyre, 2011.

Bringing the Story of the Cheyenne People to the Children of Today. Northern Cheyenne Curriculum Committee. Helena, MT: Office of Public Instruction, 2009.

Broker, Ignatia, *Night Flying Woman: An Ojibway Narrative.* St. Paul: Minnesota Historical Society Press, 1983.

Brown, Dee. *Bury My Heart at Wounded Knee: An Indian History of the American West.* New York: Holt, Rinehart, and Winston, 1970.

Brown, James W., and Rita T. Kohn, ed. *Long Journey Home: Oral Histories of Contemporary Delaware Indians.* Bloomington: Indiana University Press, 2008.

Brown, John A., and Robert H. Ruby. *The Chinook Indians: Traders of the Lower Columbia River.* Norman: University of Oklahoma Press, 1988.

Brown, Joseph. *The Spiritual Legacy of the American Indian: Commemorative Edition with Letters while Living with Black Elk.* Bloomington, IN: World Wisdom, 2007.

Brown, Tricia, and Roy Corral. *Children of the Midnight Sun: Young Native Voices of Alaska.* Anchorage: Alaska Northwest Books, 2006.

— — —. *Silent Storytellers of Totem Bight State Historical Park.* Anchorage: Alaska Geographic Association, 2009.

Brown, Virginia Pounds, Laurella Owens and Nathan Glick. *The World of the Southern Indians: Tribes, Leaders, and Customs from Prehistoric Times to the Present.* Montgomery, AL: NewSouth Books, 2011.

Browner, Tara, ed. *Music of the First Nations: Tradition and Innovation in Native North America.* Urbana: University of Illinois Press, 2009.

Bruchac, Joseph. *Flying with the Eagle, Racing the Great Bear: Tales from Native North America*. Golden, CO: Fulcrum, 2011.

Bruemmer, Fred. *Arctic Visions: Pictures from a Vanished World*. Toronto, Ontario: Key Porter Books, 2008.

Brugge, Doug, Timothy Benally, and Esther Yazzie-Lewis. *The Navajo People and Uranium Mining*. Albuquerque: University of New Mexico Press, 2006.

Bullchild, Percy. *The Sun Came Down: The History of the World as My Blackfeet Elders Told It*. Lincoln: University of Nebraska Press, 2005.

Burgan, Michael. *The Arapaho*. Tarrytown, NY: Marshall Cavendish Benchmark, 2009.

— — —. *Inuit History and Culture*. New York: Gareth Stevens, 2011.

Burke, Heather, et al, eds. *Kennewick Man: Perspectives on the Ancient One*. Walnut Creek, CA: Left Coast Press, 2008.

Burns, Louis F. *A History of the Osage People*. Tuscaloosa: University of Alabama Press, 2004.

— — —. *Osage Indian Customs and Myths*. Tuscaloosa: University of Alabama Press, 2005.

Button, Bertha P. *Friendly People: The Zuñi Indians*. Santa Fe, NM: Museum of New Mexico Press, 1963.

Calloway, Colin G. *The Shawnees and the War for America*. New York: Viking, 2007.

Carbone, Elisa. *Blood on the River: James Town 1607*. New York: Viking, 2006.

Carlos, Ann M. *Commerce by a Frozen Sea: Native Americans and the European Fur Trade*. Philadelphia: University of Pennsylvania Press, 2010.

Carlson, Paul H., and Tom Crum. *Myth, Memory, and Massacre: The Pease River Capture of Cynthia Ann Parker*. Lubbock: Texas Tech University Press, 2010.

Carlson, Richard G., ed. *Rooted Like the Ash Trees: New England Indians and the Land*. Naugatuck, CT: Eagle Wing Press, 1987.

Carpenter, Cecelia Svinth, Maria Victoria Pascualy, and Trisha Hunter. *Nisqually Indian Tribe*. Charleston, SC: Arcadia, 2008.

Carter, John G. *The Northern Arapaho Flat Pipe and the Ceremony of Covering the Pipe*. Whitefish, MT: Kessinger Publishing, 2007.

Cashin, Edward J. *Guardians of the Valley: Chickasaws in Colonial South Carolina and Georgia*. Columbia, SC: University of South Carolina Press, 2009.

Cassidy, James J., Jr., ed. *Through Indian Eyes: The Untold Story of Native American Peoples*. Pleasantville, NY: Reader's Digest Association, 1995.

Cassinelli, Dennis. *Preserving Traces of the Great Basin Indians*. Reno, NV: Jack Bacon & Company, 2006.

Castillo, Edward D. *The Pomo*. Austin: RaintreeSteck-Vaughn, 1999.

Chalcraft, Edwin L. *Assimilation's Agent: My Life as a Superintendent in the Indian Boarding School System.* Lincoln: University of Nebraska Press, 2007.

Champagne, Duane, ed. *The Native North American Almanac.* Detroit: Gale, 1994.

Charles, Nicholas and Maria. *Messenger Spirits: Yup'ik Masks and Stories.* Anchorage, AK: N & M, 2009.

Chatters, James C. *Ancient Encounters: Kennewick Man and the First Americans.* New York: Simon and Schuster, 2001.

Chaussonnet, Valerie, ed. *Crossroads Alaska: Native Cultures of Alaska and Siberia.* Washington, DC: Arctic Studies Center, National Museum of Natural History, Smithsonian Institution, 1995.

Chehak, Gail, and Jan Halliday. *Native Peoples of the Northwest: A Traveler's Guide to Land, Art, and Culture.* Seattle: Sasquatch Books, 2002.

Chenoweth, Avery, and Robert Llewellyn. *Empires in the Forest: Jamestown and the Making of America.* Earlysville, VA: Rivanna Foundation, 2010.

Childs, Craig. *House of Rain: Tracking a Vanished Civilization across the American Southwest.* 2nd ed. New York: Back Bay Books, 2008.

Clark, Cora, and Texa Bowen Williams. *Pomo Indians: Myths and Some of Their Sacred Meanings.* Reprint. Charleston, SC: Literary Licensing, 2011.

Clark, Ella E. *Indian Legends of the Pacific Northwest.* Berkeley: University of California Press, 2003.

Clark, Jerry E. *The Shawnee.* Lexington: University Press of Kentucky, 2007.

Clow, Richmond L., ed. *The Sioux in South Dakota History: A Twentieth-Century Reader.* Pierre, SD: South Dakota State Historical Society Press, 2007.

Cobb, Amanda J. *Listening to Our Grandmothers' Stories: The Bloomfield Academy for Chickasaw Females, 1852–1949.* Lincoln: University of Nebraska Press, 2007.

— — —. *Massacre at Camp Grant: Forgetting and Remembering Apache History.* Tucson: University of Arizona Press, 2007.

Cone, Marla. *Silent Snow: The Slow Poisoning of the Arctic.* New York: Grove Press, 2005.

Confederated Salish and Kootenai Tribes. *Bull Trout's Gift: A Salish Story about the Value of Reciprocity.* Lincoln: University of Nebraska Press, 2011.

Cook, Franklin A. "Nunapitchuk, Alaska: A Yup'ik Eskimo Village in Western Alaska." *Anna Tobeluk Memorial School, Nunapitchuk, Alaska.* Lincoln: University of Nebraska Press, 2005.

Cook, R. Michael, Eli Gifford, and Warren Jefferson, eds. *How Can One Sell the Air?: Chief Seattle's Vision.* Summertown, TN: Native Voices, 2005.

Corwin, Judith Hoffman. *Native American Crafts of the Northwest Coast, the Arctic, and the Subarctic.* New York: Franklin Watts, 2002.

Costa, David J. *Narratives and Winter Stories.* Oxford, OH: Myaamia Publications, 2010.

Coté, Charlotte. *Spirits of Our Whaling Ancestors: Revitalizing Makah, and Nuu-chah-nulth Traditions.* Seattle: University of Washington Press, 2010.

Coyote, Bertha Little, and Virginia Giglio. *Leaving Everything Behind: The Songs and Memories of a Cheyenne Woman.* Norman: University of Oklahoma Press, 1997.

Cozzens, Peter. *The Army and the Indian.* Mechanicsburg, PA: Stackpole Books, 2005.

Crediford, Gene J. *Those Who Remain.* Tuscaloosa: University of Alabama Press, 2009.

Crompton, Samuel Willard. *The Mohawk.* Edited by Paul C. Rosier. New York: Chelsea House Publishers, 2010.

Medicine Crow, Joseph. *Counting Coup: Becoming a Crow Chief on the Reservation and Beyond.* Washingon, DC: National Geographic, 2006.

— — —. *From the Heart of the Crow Country: The Crow Indians' Own Stories.* Lincoln: University of Nebraska Press, 2000.

Crowell, Aron L. *Living Our Cultures, Sharing Our Heritage: The First Peoples of Alaska.* Washington, DC: Smithsonian Books, 2010.

Croy, Anita. *Ancient Pueblo: Archaeology Unlocks the Secrets of America's Past.* Washington, DC: National Geographic, 2007.

Cunningham, Kevin, and Peter Benoit. *The Wampanoag.* New York: Children's Press, 2011.

Curtin, Jeremiah. *Myths of the Modocs.* Whitefish, MT: Kessinger Publishing, 2006.

— — —. "The Yanas." In *Creation Myths of Primitive America.* Boston, MA: Little, Brown, and Company, 1903.

Curtain, Jeremiah, and Roland B. Dixon, eds. *Achomawi and Atsugewi Myths and Tales.* Reprint.Sandhurst, UK: Abela Publishing, 2009.

— — —. *The Plains Indian Photographs of Edward S. Curtis.* Lincoln: University of Nebraska Press, 2001.

— — —. "Salishan Tribes." In *The North American Indian.* Vol. 7. Edited by Frederick Webb Hodge. Norwood, MA: The Plimpton Press, 1911. Available online from http://curtis.library.northwestern.edu/curtis/viewPage.cgi?showp=1&size=2&id=nai.07.book.00000075&volume=7 (accessed on August 11, 2011).

— — — "Taos." In *The North American Indian (1907–1930).* Vol. 26. Reprint. New York: Johnson Reprint Corporation, 1970.

— — —. "Umatilla." In *The North American Indian,* edited by Fredrick Webb Hodge. Vol. 8. 1911. Available online from http://curtis.library.northwestern.edu/curtis/viewPage.cgi?showp=1&size=2&id=nai.08.book.00000129.p&volume=8#nav (accessed on August 11, 2011).

— — —. "The Washoe." In *The North American Indian*. Vol. 15. Edited by Frederick Webb Hodge. Norwood, MA: The Plimpton Press, 1926: 89–98. Available online from Northwestern University. http://curtis. library.northwestern.edu/curtis/viewPage.cgi?showp=1&size=2&id=nai.15. book.00000141&volume=15 (accessed on August 15, 2011).

Cushing, Frank H. *Zuñi Folk Tales*. Charleston, SC: Kessinger Publishing, 2011)

Cwiklik, Robert. *King Philip and the War with the Colonists*. Englewood Cliffs, NJ: Silver Burdette Press, 1989.

Dahlin, Curtis A., and Alan R. Woolworth. *The Dakota Uprising: A Pictorial History*. Edina, MN: Beaver's Pond Press, 2009.

Damas, David, ed. *Handbook of North American Indians,* Vol. 5: *Arctic*. Washington, DC: Smithsonian Institution, 1984.

Dangberg, Grace, translator. *Washo Tales*. Reprint. Carson City: Nevada State Museum, 1968.

De Angulo, Jaime. *Indian Tales*. Santa Clara, CA: Heyday Books, 2003.

De Capua, Sarah. *The Shawnee*. New York: Marshall Cavendish Benchmark, 2008.

De Laguna, Fredericæ. "Tlingit." In *Handbook of North American Indians: Northwest Coast*. Vol. 7, edited by Wayne Suttles. Washington, DC: Smithsonian Institution, 1990, pp. 203–28.

Decker, Carol Paradise. *Pecos Pueblo People through the Ages: "—And We're Still Here": Stories of Time and Place*. Santa Fe, NM: Sunstone Press, 2011.

Decker, Peter R. *"The Utes Must Go!": American Expansion and the Removal of a People*. Golden, CO: Fulcrum Publishing, 2004.

DeJong, David H. *Forced to Abandon Our Fields: The 1914 Clay Southworth Gila River Pima Interviews*. Salt Lake City: University of Utah Press, 2011.

Deloria, Vine, Jr. *Red Earth, White Lies: Native Americans and the Myth of Scientific Fact*. New York: Scribner, 1995.

Dempsey, L. James. *Blackfoot War Art: Pictographs of the Reservation Period, 1880–2000*. Norman: University of Oklahoma Press, 2007.

Denetdale, Jennifer. *The Long Walk: The Forced Navajo Exile*. New York: Chelsea House, 2008.

— — —. *The Navajo*. New York: Chelsea House, 2011.

Densmore, Frances. *American Indians and Their Music*. Kila, MN: Kessinger Publishing, 2010.

DeRose, Cat. *Little Raven: Chief of the Southern Arapaho*. Palmer Lake, CO: Filter Press, 2010.

Dial, Adolph L., and David K. Eliades. *The Only Land I Know: A History of the Lumbee Indians*. Syracuse: Syracuse University Press, 1996.

Dickey, Michael E. *The People of the River's Mouth: In Search of the Missouria Indians*. Columbia: University of Missouri, 2011.

Ditchfield, Christin. *Northeast Indians.* Chicago: Heinemann Library, 2012.

— — —. *Plateau Indians.* Chicago: Heinemann Library, 2012.

Doak, Robin S. *Arctic Peoples.* Chicago: Heinemann Library, 2012.

— — —. *Subarctic Peoples.* Mankato, MN: Heinemann-Raintree, 2011.

Doherty, Craig A. *California Indians.* New York: Chelsea House Publications, 2007.

— — —. *Northeast Indians.* Broomall, PA: Chelsea House Publications, March 2008.

— — —. *Southeast Indians.* Minneapolis, MN: Chelsea House, 2007.

Doherty, Craig A., and Katherine M. Doherty. *Arctic Peoples.* New York: Chelsea House, 2008.

— — —. *Great Basin Indians.* Minneapolis, MN: Chelsea House, 2010.

— — —. *Plains Indians.* New York: Chelsea House, 2008.

— — —. *Plateau Indians.* New York: Chelsea House, 2008.

— — —. *Southwest Indians.* Minneapolis, MN: Chelsea House, 2007.

Dolan, Edward F. *The American Indian Wars.* Brookfield, CT: Millbrook Press, 2003.

Donlan, Leni. *Cherokee Rose: The Trail of Tears.* Chicago, IL: Raintree, 2007.

Downum, Christian E. *Hisatsinom: Ancient Peoples in a Land without Water.* Santa Fe: School for Advanced Research Press, 2011.

Dresser, Thomas. *The Wampanoag Tribe of Martha's Vineyard: Colonization to Recognition.* Charleston, SC: History Press, 2011.

Driver, Harold E., and Walter R. Goldschmidt. *The Hupa White Deerskin Dance.* Whitefish, MT: Kessinger Publishing, 2007.

Drury, Clifford M., ed. *Nine Years with the Spokane Indians: The Diary, 1838–1848, of Elkanah Walker.* Glendale, CA: Arthur H. Clark Company, 1976.

DuBois, Cora. *The 1870 Ghost Dance.* Reprint. Lincoln: University of Nebraska, 2007.

Duncan, Kate C. *Northern Athapaskan Art: A Beadwork Tradition.* Seattle: University of Washington Press, 1989.

Dunn, Jacob Piatt. *Massacres of the Mountains: A History of the Indian Wars of the Far West 1815–1875.* Whitefish, MT: Kessinger Publishing, 2006.

Dutton, Bertha P. *Indians of the American Southwest.* Englewood Cliffs, NJ: Prentice-Hall, 1975.

Duval, Kathleen. *The Native Ground: Indians and Colonists in the Heart of the Continent.* Philadelphia: University of Pennsylvania Press, 2006.

Dwyer, Helen, ed. *Peoples of the Southwest, West, and North.* Redding, CT: Brown Bear Books, 2009.

Dwyer, Helen, and D. L. Birchfield. *Cheyenne History and Culture.* New York: Gareth Stevens, 2012.

Dwyer, Helen, and Mary A. Stout. *Nez Percé History and Culture.* New York: Gareth Stevens, 2012.

Eastman, Charles A. *The Essential Charles Eastman (Ohiyesa), Revised and Updated Edition: Light on the Indian World.* Michael Oren Fitzgerald, ed. Bloomington, IN: World Wisdom, 2007.

— — —. *From the Deep Woods to Civilization.* Whitefish, MT: Kessinger Publishing, 2006.

— — —. *The Soul of the Indian.* New York: Dodo Press, 2007.

Eaton, William M. *Odyssey of the Pueblo Indians: An Introduction to Pueblo Indian Petroglyphs, Pictographs and Kiva Art Murals in the Southwest.* Paducah, KY: Turner Publishing Company, 2001.

Ember, Melvin, and Peter N. Peregrine, eds. *Encyclopedia of Prehistory,* Vol. 2: *Arctic and Subarctic.* New York: Kluwer Academic/Plenum Publishers, 2001.

Englar, Mary. *The Iroquois: The Six Nations Confederacy.* Mankato, MN: Capstone Press, 2006.

Erb, Gene, and Ann DeWolf Erb. *Voices in Our Souls: The DeWolfs, Dakota Sioux and the Little Bighorn.* Santa Fe: Sunstone Press, 2010.

Erdoes, Richard. *The Sun Dance People: The Plains Indians, Their Past and Present.* New York: Random House, 1972.

Erickson, Kirstin C. *Yaqui Homeland and Homeplace.* Tucson: University of Arizona Press, 2008.

Erickson, Winston P. *Sharing the Desert: The Tohono O'Odham in History.* Tucson: University of Arizona Press, 2003.

Erikson, Patricia Pierce. *Voices of a Thousand People: The Makah Cultural and Research Center.* Lincoln: University of Nebraska Press, 2005.

Ezell, Paul H. "History of the Pima." In *Handbook of North American Indians,* Volume 10: *Southwest,* edited by Alfonso Ortiz. Washington, DC: Smithsonian Institution Press, 1983.

Falconer, Shelley, and Shawna White. *Stones, Bones, and Stitches: Storytelling through Inuit Art.* Toronto, Ontario: Tundra Books, 2007.

Fariello, Anna. *Cherokee Basketry: From the Hands of Our Elders.* Charleston, SC: History Press, 2009.

Field, Ron. *The Seminole Wars, 1818–58.* New York: Osprey, 2009.

Fitzgerald, Judith, and Michael Oren Fitzgerald, eds. *The Spirit of Indian Women.* Bloomington, IN: World Wisdom, 2005.

Forczyk, Robert. *Nez Percé 1877: The Last Fight.* Long Island City, NY: Osprey, 2011.

Foreman, Grant. *Indian Removal.* Norman: University of Oklahoma Press, 1972.

Foster, Martha Harroun. *We Know Who We Are: Métis Identity in a Montana Community.* Norman: University of Oklahoma Press, 2006.

Foster, Sharon Ewell. *Abraham's Well: A Novel.* Minneapolis, MN: Bethany House, 2006.

Fowler, Loretta. *The Columbia Guide to American Indians of the Great Plains.* New York: Columbia University Press, 2005.

Fradin, Dennis B. *The Pawnee.* Chicago: Childrens Press, 1988.

Frank, Andrew. *The Seminole.* New York: Chelsea House, 2011.

Freedman, Russell. *The Life and Death of Crazy Horse.* New York: Holiday House, 1996.

Gagnon, Gregory O. *Culture and Customs of the Sioux Indians.* Westport, CT: Greenwood, 2011.

Garfinkel, Alan P., and Harold Williams. *Handbook of the Kawaiisu.* Kern Valley, CA: Wa-hi Sina'avi, 2011.

Geake, Robert A. *A History of the Narragansett Tribe of Rhode Island: Keepers of the Bay.* Charleston, SC: History Press, 2011.

Geronimo. *The Autobiography of Geronimo.* St. Petersburg, FL: Red and Black Publishers, 2011.

Giago, Tim A. *Children Left Behind: Dark Legacy of Indian Mission Boarding Schools.* Santa Fe, NM: Clear Light Publishing, 2006.

Gibson, Karen Bush. *The Chumash: Seafarers of the Pacific Coast.* Mankato, MN: Bridgestone Books, 2004.

———. *The Great Basin Indians: Daily Life in the 1700s.* Mankato, MN: Capstone Press, 2006.

———. *New Netherland: The Dutch Settle the Hudson Valley.* Elkton, IN: Mitchell Lane Publishers, 2006.

Giddings, Ruth Warner. *Yaqui Myths and Legends.* Charleston, SC: BiblioBazaar, 2009.

Gipson, Lawrence Henry. *The Moravian Indian Mission on White River: Diaries and Letters, May 5, 1799, to November 12, 1806.* Indianapolis: Indiana Historical Bureau, 1938.

Girdner, Alwin J. *Diné Tah: My Reservation Days 1923–1938.* Tucson: Rio Nuevo Publishers, c2011.

Glancy, Diane. *Pushing the Bear: After the Trail of Tears.* Norman: University of Oklahoma Press, 2009.

Goddard, Pliny Earle. *Hupa Texts.* Reprint. Charleston, SC: BiblioBazaar, 2009.

———. *Life and Culture of the Hupa.* Reprint. Charleston, SC: Nabu Press, 2011.

———. *Myths and Tales from the San Carlos Apache.* Whitefish, MT: Kessinger Publishing, 2006.

———. *Myths and Tales of the White Mountain Apache*. Whitefish, MT: Kessinger Publishing, 2011.

Goodman, Linda J. *Singing the Songs of My Ancestors: The Life and Music of Helma Swan, Makah Elder*. Norman: University of Oklahoma Press, 2003.

Goodwin, Grenville. *Myths and Tales of the White Mountain Apache*. Whitefish, MT: Kessinger Publishing, 2011.

Gordon, Irene Ternier. *A People on the Move: The Métis of the Western Plains*. Surry, British Columbia: Heritage House, 2009.

Grafe, Steven L. ed. *Lanterns on the Prairie: The Blackfeet Photographs of Walter McClintock*. Norman: University of Oklahoma Press, 2009.

Grant, Blanche Chloe. *Taos Indians*. 1925 ed. Santa Fe: Sunstone Press, 2007.

Grant, Campbell. *Rock Paintings of the Chumash: A Study of a California Indian Culture*. Reprint. Santa Barbara, CA: Santa Barbara Museum of Natural History/EZ Nature Books, 1993.

Gray-Kanatiiosh, Barbara A. *Cahuilla*. Edina, MN: ABDO, 2007.

———. *Modoc*. Edina, MN: ABDO, 2007.

———. *Paiute*. Edina, MN: ABDO Publishing, 2007.

———. *Yurok*. Edina, MN: ABDO, 2007.

Graymont, Barbara. *The Iroquois*. New York: Chelsea House, 1988.

Green, Michael D., and Theda Perdue. *The Cherokee Nation and the Trail of Tears*. New York: Viking, 2007.

———. *The Columbia Guide to American Indians of the Southeast*. New York: Columbia University Press, 2001.

Grinnell, George Bird. *Blackfeet Indians Stories*. Whitefish, MT: Kessinger Publishing, 2006.

———. *The Cheyenne Indians: Their History and Lifeways*. Bloomington, IN: World Wisdom, 2008.

Guigon, Catherine, Francis Latreille, and Fredric Malenfer. *The Arctic*. New York: Abrams Books for Young Readers, 2007.

Gunther, Vanessa. *Chief Joseph*. Greenwood, 2010.

Guthridge, George. *The Kids from Nowhere: The Story behind the Arctic Education Miracle*. Anchorage: Alaska Northwest Books, 2006.

Hagan, William T. *The Sac and Fox Indians*. Norman: University of Oklahoma Press, 2008.

Hahn, Elizabeth. *The Pawnee*. Vero Beach, FL: Rourke Publications, Inc., 1992.

Haig-Brown, Roderick. *The Whale People*. Madeira Park, BC: Harbour Publishing, 2003.

Hancock, David A. *Tlingit: Their Art and Culture*. Blaine, WA: Hancock House Publishers, 2003.

Handbook of North American Indians, Vol. 6: *Subarctic.* Ed. June Helm. Washington, DC: Smithsonian Institution, 1981.

Harpster, Jack, and Ken Stalter. *Captive!: The Story of David Ogden and the Iroquois.* Santa Barbara, CA: Praeger, 2010.

Harrington, Mark Raymond. *Certain Caddo Sites in Arkansas.* Charleston, SC: Johnson Press, 2011.

Hayes, Allan, and Carol Hayes. *The Desert Southwest: Four Thousand Years of Life And Art.* Berkeley, CA: Ten Speed Press, 2006.

Hearth, Amy Hill. *"Strong Medicine Speaks": A Native American Elder Has Her Say: An Oral History.* New York: Atria Books, 2008.

Hebner, William Logan. *Southern Paiute: A Portrait.* Logan: Utah State University Press, 2010.

Heinämäki, Leena. *The Right to Be a Part of Nature: Indigenous Peoples and the Environment.* Rovaniemi, Finland: Lapland University Press, 2010.

Heizer, R. F., ed. *Handbook of North American Indians.* Vol. 8: *California.* Washington, DC: Smithsonian Institution, 1978.

Hessel, Ingo. *Inuit Art: An Introduction.* Vancouver, British Columbia: Douglas & McIntyre, 2002.

Hicks, Terry Allan. *The Chumash.* New York: Marshall Cavendish Benchmark, 2008.

— — —. *The Zuñi.* New York: Marshall Cavendish Benchmark, 2010.

Hill, George, Robert H. Ruby, and John A. Brown. *The Spokane Indians: Children of the Sun.* Norman: University of Oklahoma Press, 2006.

Himsl, Sharon M. *The Shoshone.* San Diego, CA: Lucent Books, 2005.

Hirst, Stephen. *I Am the Grand Canyon: The Story of the Havasupai People.* Grand Canyon, AZ: Grand Canyon Association, 2006.

Hobson, Geary. *Plain of Jars and Other Stories.* East Lansing: Michigan State University Press, 2011.

Hodge, Frederick Webb. "Dwamish." *Handbook of American Indians North of Mexico.* New York: Pageant Books, 1959.

Hogeland, Kim, and L. Frank Hogeland. *First Families: Photographic History of California Indians.* Berkeley: Heyday Books, 2007.

Holm, Bill. *Spirit and Ancestor: A Century of Northwest Coast Indian Art in the Burke Museum.* Seattle: Burke Museum; University of Washington Press, 1987.

Hooper, Lucile. *The Cahuilla Indians.* Kila, MN: Kessinger Publishing, 2011.

Hoover, Alan L. *Nuu-chah-nulth Voices, Histories, Objects, and Journeys.* Victoria: Royal British Columbia Museum, 2000.

Hopping, Lorraine Jean. *Chief Joseph: The Voice for Peace.* New York: Sterling, 2010.

Houston, James A. *James Houston's Treasury of Inuit Legends.* Orlando, FL: Harcourt, 2006.

Hungrywolf, Adolf. *Tribal Childhood: Growing Up in Traditional Native America.* Summertown, TN:Native Voices, 2008.

Hyde, Dayton O. *The Last Free Man: The True Story behind the Massacre of Shoshone Mike and His Band of Indians in 1911.* New York: Dial Press, 1973.

Hyde, George E. *Indians of the Woodlands: From Prehistoric Times to 1725.* Norman: University of Oklahoma Press, 1962.

Indians of the Northwest Coast and Plateau. Chicago: World Book, 2009.

Indians of the Southwest. Chicago: World Book, 2009.

Inupiaq and Yupik People of Alaska. Anchorage: Alaska Geographic Society, 2004.

Jacknis, Ira. *The Storage Box of Tradition: Kwakiutl Art, Anthropologists, and Museums, 1881–1981.* Washington, DC: Smithsonian Institution Press, 2002.

Jackson, Helen Hunt. *The Indian Reform Letters of Helen Hunt Jackson, 1879–1885.*Edited by Valerie ShererMathes. Norman: University of Oklahoma Press, 1998.

— — —. *Ramona.* New York: Signet, 1988.

James, Cheewa. *Modoc: The Tribe That Wouldn't Die.* Happy Camp, CA: Naturegraph, 2008.

Jastrzembski, Joseph C. *The Apache.* Minneapolis: Chelsea House, 2011.

— — —. *The Apache Wars: The Final Resistance.* Minneapolis: Chelsea House, 2007.

Jenness, Aylette, and Alice Rivers. *In Two Worlds: A Yu'pik Eskimo Family.* New York: Houghton Mifflin, 1989.

Jennys, Susan. *19th Century Plains Indian Dresses.* Pottsboro, TX: Crazy Crow, 2004.

Jensen, Richard E., ed. *The Pawnee Mission Letters, 1834-1851.* Lincoln: University of Nebraska Press, 2010.

Jeter, Marvin D. *Edward Palmer's Arkansaw Mounds.* Tuscaloosa: University of Alabama Press, 2010.

Johansen, Bruce E. *The Iroquois.* New York, NY: Chelsea House, 2010.

Johnsgard, Paul A. *Wind through the Buffalo Grass: A Lakota Story Cycle.* Lincoln, NE: Plains Chronicles Press, 2008.

Johnson, Jerald Jay. "Yana." In *Handbook of North American Indians.* Vol. 10: *Southwest,* edited by Alfonso Ortiz. Washington, DC: Smithsonian Institution, 1983.

Johnson, Michael. *American Indians of the Southeast.* Oxford: Osprey Publishing, 1995.

— — —. "Duwamish." *The Native Tribes of North America.* New York: Macmillan, 1992.

— — —. *Native Tribes of the Northeast.* Milwaukee, WI: World Almanac Library, 2004.

Johnson, Michael, and Jonathan Smith. *Indian Tribes of the New England Frontier.* Oxford: Osprey Publishing, 2006.

Johnson, Thomas H., and Helen S. Johnson. *Also Called Sacajawea: Chief Woman's Stolen Identity.* Long Grove, IL: Waveland Press, 2008.

— — —. *Two Toms: Lessons from a Shoshone Doctor.* Salt Lake City: University of Utah Press, 2010.

Jonaitis, Aldona. *Art of the Northwest Coast.* Seattle: University of Washington Press, 2006.

Joseph, Frank. *Advanced Civilizations of Prehistoric America: The Lost Kingdoms of the Adena, Hopewell, Mississippians, and Anasazi.* Rochester, VT: Bear & Company, December 21, 2009.

Josephson, Judith Pinkerton. *Why Did Cherokees Move West? And Other Questions about the Trail of Tears.* Minneapolis: Lerner Publications, 2011.

Josephy, Alvin M., Jr. *500 Nations: An Illustrated History of North American Indians.* New York: Knopf, 1994.

— — —. *Nez Percé Country.* Lincoln: University of Nebraska Press, 2007.

Kallen, Stuart A. *The Pawnee.* San Diego: Lucent Books, 2001.

Kaneuketat. *I Dreamed the Animals: Kaneuketat: the Life of an Innu Hunter.* New York: Berghahn Books, 2008.

Kavasch, E. Barrie. *Enduring Harvests: Native American Foods and Festivals for Every Season.* Old Saybrook, CT: The Globe Pequot Press, 1995.

Keegan, Marcia. *Pueblo People: Ancient Tradition, Modern Lives.* Santa Fe, NM: Clear Light Publishers, 1999.

— — —. *Taos Pueblo and Its Sacred Blue Lake.* Santa Fe: Clear Light Publishers, 2010.

Keegan, Marcia, and Regis Pecos. *Pueblo People: Ancient Traditions, Modern Lives.* Santa Fe, NM: Clear Light Publishers, 1999.

Kegg, Maude. *Portage Lake: Memories of an Ojibwe Childhood.* Edmonton: University of Alberta Press, 1991.

Kennedy, J. Gerald. *Life of Black Hawk, or Ma-ka-tai-me-she-kia-kiak. Dictated by Himself.* New York: Penguin Books, 2008.

King, David C. *The Blackfeet.* New York: Marshall Cavendish Benchmark, 2010.

— — —. *First People.* New York: DK Children, 2008.

— — —. *The Inuit.* New York: Marshall Cavendish Benchmark, 2008.

— — —. *The Nez Percé.* New York: Benchmark Books, 2008.

— — —. *Seminole.* New York: Benchmark Books, 2007.

Kiowa and Pueblo Art: Watercolor Paintings by Native American Artists. Mineola, NY: Dover Publications, 2009.

Kirkpatrick, Katherine. *Mysterious Bones: The Story of Kennewick Man.* New York: Holiday House, 2011.

Kissock,Heather, and Jordan McGill. *Apache: American Indian Art and Culture.* New York: Weigl Publishers, 2011.

Kissock, Heather, and Rachel Small. *Caddo: American Indian Art and Culture.* New York: Weigl Publishers, 2011.

Koyiyumptewa, Stewart B., Carolyn O'Bagy Davis, and the Hopi Cultural Preservation Office. *The Hopi People.* Charleston, SC: Arcadia Publishing, 2009.

Kristofic, Jim. *Navajos Wear Nikes: A Reservation Life.* Albuquerque: University of New Mexico Press, 2011.

Kroeber, Theodora. *Ishi in Two Worlds: A Biography of the Last Wild Indian in North America.* Berkeley: University of California Press, 2004.

Krupnik, Igor, and Dyanna Jolly, eds. *The Earth Is Faster Now: Indigenous Observations of Arctic Environmental Change.* Fairbanks, Alaska: Arctic Research Consortium of the United States, 2002.

Kuiper, Kathleen, ed. *American Indians of California, the Great Basin, and the Southwest.* New York: Rosen Educational Services, 2012.

— — —. *American Indians of the Northeast and Southeast.* New York: Rosen Educational Services, 2012.

— — —. *American Indians of the Plateau and Plains.* New York: Rosen Educational Services, 2012.

— — —. *Indigenous Peoples of the Arctic, Subarctic, and Northwest Coast.* New York: Rosen Educational Services, 2012.

Lacey, T. Jensen. *The Blackfeet.* New York: Chelsea House, 2011.

— — —. *The Comanche.* New York: Chelsea House, 2011.

Lankford, George E., ed. *Native American Legends of the Southeast: Tales from the Natchez, Caddo, Biloxi, Chickasaw, and Other Nations.* 5th ed. Tuscaloosa: University of Alabama Press, 2011.

Lanmon, Dwight P. and Francis H. Harlow. *The Pottery of Zuñi Pueblo.* Santa Fe: Museum of New Mexico Press, 2008.

Larsen, Mike, Martha Larsen, and Jeannie Barbour. *Proud to Be Chickasaw.* Ada, OK: Chickasaw Press, 2010.

Lenik, Edward J. *Making Pictures in Stone: American Indian Rock Art of the Northeast.* Tuscaloosa: University of Alabama Press, 2009.

Levine, Michelle. *The Delaware.* Minneapolis, MN: Lerner Publications, 2006.

— — —. *The Ojibway.* Minneapolis, MN: Lerner Publications, 2006.

Levy, Janey. *The Wampanoag of Massachusetts and Rhode Island.* New York: PowerKids Press, 2005.

Liebert, Robert. *Osage Life and Legends: Earth People/Sky People.* Happy Camp, California: Naturegraph Publishers, 1987.

Life Stories of Our Native People: Shoshone, Paiute, Washo. Reno, NV: Intertribal Council of Nevada, 1974.

Liptak, Karen. *North American Indian Ceremonies.* New York: Franklin Watts, 1992.

Little, Kimberley Griffiths. *The Last Snake Runner.* New York: Alfred A. Knopf, 2002.

Lloyd, J. William. *Aw-aw-tam Indian Nights: The Myths and Legends of the Pimas.* Westfield, NJ: The Lloyd Group, 1911. Available online from http://www.sacred-texts.com/nam/sw/ain/index.htm (accessed on July 20, 2011).

Lobo, Susan, Steve Talbot, and Traci L. Morris, compilers. *Native American Voices: A Reader.* 3rd ed. Upper Saddle River, NJ: Prentice Hall, 2010.

Lourie, Peter. *The Lost World of the Anasazi: Exploring the Mysteries of Chaco Canyon.* Honesdale, PA: Boyds Mills Press, 2007.

Macdougall, Brenda. *One of the Family: Metis Culture in Nineteenth-Century Northwestern Saskatchewan.* Vancouver, British Columbia: UBC Press, 2010.

Mann, John W.W. *Sacajawea's People: The Lemhi Shoshones and the Salmon River Country.* Lincoln, NE: Bison Books, 2011.

Margolin, Malcolm. *The Ohlone Way.* Berkeley, CA: Heyday Books, 1981.

― ― ―. *The Way We Lived: California Indian Stories, Songs, and Reminiscences.* Reprint. Heyday Books, Berkeley, California, 2001.

Marriott, Alice, and Carol K. Rachlin. *Plains Indian Mythology.* New York, NY: Thomas Y. Crowell, 1975.

Marshall, Ann, ed. *Home: Native People in the Southwest.* Phoenix, AZ: Heard Museum, 2005.

Marshall, Bonnie. *Far North Tales: Stories from the Peoples of the Arctic Circle.* Edited by Kira Van Deusen. Santa Barbara, CA: Libraries Unlimited, 2011.

Marsi, Katie. *The Trail of Tears: The Tragedy of the American Indians.* New York: Marshall Cavendish Benchmark, 2010.

McDaniel, Melissa. *Great Basin Indians.* Des Plaines, IL: Heinemann, 2011.

― ― ―. *The Sac and Fox Indians.* New York: Chelsea Juniors, 1995.

― ― ―. *Southwest Indians.* Chicago: Heinemann Library, 2012.

Mcmullen, John William. *Ge Wisnemen! (Let's Eat!): A Potawatomi Family Dinner Manual.* Charleston, SC: CreateSpace, 2011.

Melody, Michael E., and Paul Rosier. *The Apache.* Minneapolis: Chelsea House, 2005.

Merriam, C. Hart. *The Dawn of the World: Myths and Tales of the Miwok Indians of California.* Kila, MN: Kessinger Publishing, 2010.

Michael, Hauser. *Traditional Inuit Songs from the Thule Area.* Copenhagen: Museum Tusculanum Press, 2010.

Miles, Ray. "Wichita." *Native America in the Twentieth Century, An Encyclopedia.* Ed. Mary B. Davis. New York: Garland Publishing, 1994.

Miller, Debbie S., and Jon Van Dyle. *Arctic Lights, Arctic Nights.* New York: Walker Books for Young Readers, 2007.

Miller, Frederic P., Agnes F. Vandome, and John McBrewster, eds. *Nuu-chah-nulth People.* Beau Bassin, Mauritius: Alphascript Publishing, 2011.

Miller, Raymond H. *North American Indians: The Apache.* San Diego: KidHaven Press, 2005.

Milner, George R. *The Moundbuilders: Ancient Peoples of Eastern North America.* New York: Thames & Hudson, 2005.

Mooney, James. *Calendar History of the Kiowa Indians.* Whitefish, MT: Kessinger Publishing, 2006.

— — —. *Myths of the Cherokee.* New York: Dover Publications, 1996.

Mosqueda, Frank, and Vickie Leigh Krudwig. *The Hinono'ei Way of Life: An Introduction to the Arapaho People.* Edited by Susan Scott Hill. Concho, OK: Cheyenne and Arapaho Tribes of Oklahoma, 2008.

— — —. *The Prairie Thunder People: A Brief History of the Arapaho People.* Edited by Susan Scott Hill. Concho, OK: Cheyenne and Arapaho Tribes of Oklahoma, 2008.

Mossiker, Frances. *Pocahontas: The Life and the Legend.* New York: Alfred A. Knopf, 1976.

Mundell, Kathleen. *North by Northeast: Wabanaki, Akwesasne Mohawk, and Tuscarora Traditional Arts.* Gardiner, ME: Tilbury House, Publishers, 2008.

Myers, Albert Cook, ed. *William Penn's Own Account of the Lenni Lenape or Delaware Indians.* Somerset, NJ: Middle Atlantic Press, 1970.

Myers, Arthur. *The Pawnee.* New York: Franklin Watts, 1993.

Myers, James E. "Cahto." In *Handbook of North American Indians.* Vol. 8: *California,* edited by R. F. Heizer. Washington, D.C.: Smithsonian Institution, 1978: 244–48.

Neeley, Bill. *The Last Comanche Chief: The Life and Times of Quanah Parker.* New York: Wiley, 1996.

Nelson, Sharlene, and Ted W. Nelson. *The Makah.* New York: Franklin Watts, 2003.

Nez, Chester, and Judith Schiess Avila. *Code Talker.* New York: Berkley Caliber, 2011.

Nichols, Richard. *A Story to Tell: Traditions of a Tlingit Community.* Minneapolis: Lerner Publications Company, 1998.

Nowell, Charles James. *Smoke from their Fires: The Life of a Kwakiutl Chief.* Hamdon, CT: Archon Books, 1968.

O'Neale, Lila M. *Yurok-Karok Basket Weavers.* Berkeley, CA: Phoebe A. Hearst Museum of Anthropology, 2007.

Opler, Morris Edward. *Myths and Tales of the Chiricahua Apache Indians.* Charleston, SC: Kessinger Publishing, 2011.

Ortega, Simon, ed. *Handbook of North American Indians.* Vol. 12: *The Plateau.* Washington, DC: Smithsonian Institution, 1978.

Ortiz, Alfonso, ed. *Handbook of American Indians.* Vols. 9–10. *The Southwest.* Washington, DC: Smithsonian Institution, 1978–83.

Owings, Alison. *Indian Voices: Listening to Native Americans.* New Brunswick, N.J.: Rutgers University Press, 2011.

Page, Jake, and Susanne Page. *Indian Arts of the Southwest.* Tucson, AZ: Rio Nuevo Publishers, 2008.

Page, Susanne and Jake. *Navajo.* Tucson, AZ: Rio Nuevo Publishers, 2010.

Paige, Amanda L., Fuller L. Bumpers, and Daniel F. Littlefield, Jr. *Chickasaw Removal.* Ada, OK: Chickasaw Press, 2010.

Palazzo-Craig, Janet. *The Ojibwe of Michigan, Wisconsin, Minnesota, and North Dakota.* New York: PowerKids Press, 2005.

Peltier, Leonard. *Prison Writings: My Life Is My Sun Dance.* New York: St. Martin's, 2000.

Penny, Josie. *So Few on Earth: A Labrador Métis Woman Remembers.* Toronto, Ontario: Dundurn Press, 2010.

Peoples of the Arctic and Subarctic. Chicago: World Book, 2009.

Perritano, John. *Spanish Missions.* New York: Children's Press, 2010.

Philip, Neil, ed. *A Braid of Lives: Native American Childhood.* New York: Clarion Books, 2000.

Pierson, George. *The Kansa, or Kaw Indians, and Their History, and the Story of Padilla.* Charleston, SC: Nabu Press, 2010.

Pijoan, Teresa. *Pueblo Indian Wisdom: Native American Legends and Mythology.* Santa Fe: Sunstone Press, 2000.

Pritzker, Barry, and Paul C. Rosier. *The Hopi.* New York: Chelsea House, c. 2011.

Riddell, Francis A. "Maidu and Concow." *Handbook of North American Indians.* Vol. 8: *California.* Edited by Robert F. Heizer. Washington DC: Smithsonian Institution, 1978.

Rielly, Edward J. *Legends of American Indian Resistance.* Westport, CT: Greenwood, 2011.

Riordan, Robert. *Medicine for Wildcat: A Story of the Friendship between a Menominee Indian and Frontier Priest Samuel Mazzuchelli.* Revised by

Marilyn Bowers Gorun and the Sinsinawa Dominican Sisters. Sinsinawa, WI: Sinsinawa Dominican Sisters, 2006.

Rollings, Willard H. *The Comanche.* New York: Chelsea House Publications, 2004.

Rosoff, Nancy B., and Susan Kennedy Zeller. *Tipi: Heritage of the Great Plains.* Seattle: Brooklyn Museum in association with University of Washington Press, 2011.

Ruby, Robert H., John A. Brown, and Cary C. Collins. *A Guide to the Indian Tribes of the Pacific Northwest.* Norman: University of Oklahoma Press, 2010.

Russell, Frank. *The Pima Indians.* Whitefish, MT: Kessinger Publishing, 2010.

Ryan, Marla Felkins, and Linda Schmittroth. *Tribes of Native America: Zuñi Pueblo.* San Diego: Blackbirch Press, 2002.

— — —. *Ute.* San Diego: Blackbirch Press, 2003.

Rzeczkowski, Frank. *The Lakota Sioux.* New York: Chelsea House, 2011.

Seton, Ernest Thompson. *Sign Talk of the Cheyenne Indians.* Mineola, NY: Dover Publications, 2000.

Sherrow, Victoria. *The Iroquois Indians.* New York: Chelsea House, 1992.

Shipek, Florence Connolly. "Luiseño." In *Native America in the Twentieth Century: An Encyclopedia,* edited by Mary B. Davis. New York: Garland Publishing, 1994.

Shipley, William. *The Maidu Indian Myths and Stories of Hanc'Ibyjim.* Berkeley: Heyday Books, 1991.

Shull, Jodie A. *Voice of the Paiutes: A Story About Sarah Winnemucca.* Minneapolis, MN: Millbrook Press, 2007.

Simermeyer, Genevieve. *Meet Christopher: An Osage Indian Boy from Oklahoma.* Tulsa, OK: National Museum of the American Indian, Smithsonian Institution, in association with Council Oak Books, 2008.

Simmons, Marc. *Friday, the Arapaho Boy: A Story from History.* Albuquerque: University of New Mexico Press, 2004.

Sita, Lisa. *Indians of the Northeast: Traditions, History, Legends, and Life.* Milwaukee, WI: Gareth Stevens, 2000.

— — —. *Pocahontas: The Powhatan Culture and the Jamestown Colony.* New York: PowerPlus Books, 2005.

Slater, Eva. *Panamint Shoeshone Basketry: An American Art Form.* Berkeley: Heyday Books, 2004.

Smith, White Mountain. *Indian Tribes of the Southwest.* Kila, MN: Kessinger Publishing, 2005.

Snell, Alma Hogan. *A Taste of Heritage: Crow Indian Recipes & Herbal Medicines.* Lincoln: University of Nebraska Press, 2006.

Sneve, Virginia Driving Hawk. *The Cherokee*. New York: Holiday House, 1996.

— — —. *The Cheyenne*. New York: Holiday House, 1996.

— — —. *The Iroquois*. New York: Holiday House, 1995.

— — —. *The Nez Percé*. New York: Holiday House, 1994.

— — —. *The Seminoles*. New York: Holiday House, 1994.

Snyder, Clifford Gene. *Ghost Trails: Mythology and Folklore of the Chickasaw, Choctaw, Creeks and Other Muskoghean Indian Tribes*. North Hollywood, CA: JES, 2009.

— — —. *The Muskogee Chronicles: Accounts of the Early Muskogee/Creek Indians*. N. Hollywood, CA: JES, 2008.

Solomon, Madeline. *Koyukon Athabaskan Songs*. Homer, AK: Wizard Works, 2003.

Sonneborn, Liz. *The Choctaws*. Minneapolis, MN: Lerner Publications, 2007.

— — —. *The Creek*. Minneapolis: Lerner Publications, 2007.

— — —. *The Chumash*. Minneapolis, MN: Lerner Publications, 2007.

— — —. *The Navajos*. Minneapolis, MN: Lerner Publications, 2007.

— — —. *Northwest Coast Indians*. Chicago: Heinemann Library, 2012.

— — —. *The Shoshones*. Minneapolis, MN: Lerner Publications, 2006.

— — —. *Wilma Mankiller*. New York: Marshall Cavendish Benchmark, 2010.

Spalding, Andrea. *Secret of the Dance*. Orca, WA: Orca Book Publishers, 2006.

Spence, Lewis. *Myths and Legends of the North American Indians*. Whitefish, MT: Kessinger Publishing, 1997.

Spragg-Braude, Stacia. *To Walk in Beauty: A Navajo Family's Journey Home*. Santa Fe: Museum of New Mexico Press, 2009.

Sprague, DonovinArleigh. *American Indian Stories*. West Stockbridge, CT: Hard Press, 2006.

— — —. *Choctaw Nation of Oklahoma*. Chicago, IL: Arcadia, 2007.

— — —. *Old Indian Legends: Retold by Zitkala--Sa*. Paris: Adamant Media Corporation, 2006.

— — —. *Standing Rock Sioux*. Charleston, SC: Arcadia, 2004.

St. Lawrence, Genevieve. *The Pueblo And Their History*. Minneapolis, MN: Compass Point Books, 2006.

Stanley, George E. *Sitting Bull: Great Sioux Hero*. New York: Sterling, 2010.

Stern, Pamela R. *Daily Life of the Inuit*. Santa Barbara, CA: Greenwood, 2010.

Sterngass, Jon. *Geronimo*. New York: Chelsea House, 2010.

Stevenson, Matilda Coxe. *The Zuñi Indians and Their Uses of Plants.* Charleston, SC: Kessinger Publishing, 2011.

Stevenson, Tilly E. *The Religious Life of the Zuñi Child.* Charleston, SC: Kessinger Publishing, 2011.

Stewart, Philip. *Osage.* Philadelphia, PA: Mason Crest Publishers, 2004.

Stirling, M.W. *Snake Bites and the Hopi Snake Dance.* Whitefish, MT: Kessinger Publishing, 2011.

Stone, Amy M. *Creek History and Culture.* Milwaukee: Gareth Stevens Publishing, 2011.

Stout, Mary. *Blackfoot History and Culture.* New York: Gareth Stevens, 2012.

———. *Hopi History and Culture.* New York: Gareth Stevens, 2011.

———. *Shoshone History and Culture.* New York: Gareth Stevens, 2011.

Strack, Andrew J. *How the Miami People Live.* Edited by Mary Tippman, Meghan Dorey and Daryl Baldwin. Oxford, OH: Myaamia Publications, 2010.

Straub, Patrick. *It Happened in South Dakota: Remarkable Events That Shaped History.* New York: Globe Pequot, 2009.

Sullivan, Cathie, and Gordon Sullivan. *Roadside Guide to Indian Ruins & Rock Art of the Southwest.* Englewood, CO: Westcliffe Publishers, 2006.

Sullivan, George. *Geronimo: Apache Renegade.* New York: Sterling, 2010.

Suttles, Wayne, and Barbara Lane. "Southern Coast Salish." *Handbook of North American Indians.* Vol. 7: *Northwest Coast.* Edited by Wayne Suttles. Washington, DC: Smithsonian Institution, 1990.

Swanton, John R., and Franz Boas. *Haida Songs; Tsimshian Texts (1912).* Vol. 3. Whitefish, MT: Kessinger Publishing, 2010.

Sweet, Jill Drayson, and Nancy Hunter Warren. *Pueblo Dancing.* Atglen, PA: Schiffer Publishing, 2011.

Tenenbaum, Joan M., and Mary Jane McGary, eds. *Denaina Sukdua: Traditional Stories of the Tanaina Athabaskans.* Fairbanks: Alaska Native Language Center, 2006.

Tiller, Veronica E. Velarde. *Culture and Customs of the Apache Indians.* Santa Barbara, CA: ABC-CLIO, 2011.

Underhill, Ruth. *The Papago Indians of Arizona and their Relatives the Pima.* Whitefish, MT: Kessinger Publishing, 2010.

Van Deusen, Kira. *Kiviuq: An Inuit Hero and His Siberian Cousins.* Montreal: McGill-Queen's University Press, 2009.

Vanderwerth, W. C. *Indian Oratory: Famous Speeches by Noted Indian Chieftains.* Norman: University of Oklahoma Press, 1979.

Vaudrin, Bill. *Tanaina Tales from Alaska.* Norman: University of Oklahoma Press, 1969.

Viola, Herman J. *Trail to Wounded Knee: The Last Stand of the Plains Indians 1860–1890.* Washington, DC: National Geographic, 2004.

Von Ahnen, Katherine. *Charlie Young Bear.* Minot, CO: Roberts Rinehart Publishers, 1994.

Wade, Mary Dodson. *Amazing Cherokee Writer Sequoyah.* Berkeley Heights, NJ: Enslow, 2009.

Wagner, Frederic C. III. *Participants in the Battle of the Little Big Horn: A Biographical Dictionary of Sioux, Cheyenne and United States Military Personnel.* Jefferson, NC: McFarland, 2011.

Waldman, Carl. "Colville Reservation." In *Encyclopedia of Native American Tribes.* New York: Facts on File, 2006.

— — —. *Encyclopedia of Native American Tribes.* New York: Facts on File, 2006.

Wallace, Mary. *The Inuksuk Book.* Toronto, Ontario: Maple Tree Press, 2004.

— — —. *Make Your Own Inuksuk.* Toronto, Ontario: Maple Tree Press, 2004.

Wallace, Susan E. *The Land of the Pueblos.* Santa Fe, NM: Sunstone Press, 2006.

Ward, Jill. *The Cherokees.* Hamilton, GA: State Standards, 2010.

— — —. *Creeks and Cherokees Today.* Hamilton, GA: State Standards, 2010.

Warm Day, Jonathan. *Taos Pueblo: Painted Stories.* Santa Fe, NM: Clear Light Publishing, 2004.

Waters, Frank. *Book of the Hopi.* New York: Viking Press, 1963.

White, Bruce. *We Are at Home: Pictures of the Ojibwe People.* St. Paul, MN: Minnesota Historical Society Press, 2007.

White, Tekla N. *San Francisco Bay Area Missions.* Minneapolis, MN: Lerner, 2007.

Whitehead, Ruth Holmes. *The Micmac: How Their Ancestors Lived Five Hundred Years Ago.* Halifax, Nova Scotia: Nimbus, 1983.

Whiteman, Funston, Michael Bell, and Vickie Leigh Krudwig. *The Cheyenne Journey: An Introduction to the Cheyenne People.* Edited by Susan Scott-Hill. Concho, OK: Cheyenne and Arapaho Tribes of Oklahoma, 2008.

— — —. *The Tsististas: People of the Plains.* Edited by Susan Scott-Hill. Concho, OK: Cheyenne and Arapaho Tribes of Oklahoma, 2008.

Wiggins, Linda E., ed. *Dena—The People: The Way of Life of the Alaskan Athabaskans Described in Nonfiction Stories, Biographies, and Impressions from All Over the Interior of Alaska.* Fairbanks: Theata Magazine, University of Alaska, 1978.

Wilcox, Charlotte. *The Iroquois.* Minneapolis, MN: Lerner Publishing Company, 2007.

— — —. *The Seminoles.* Minneapolis: Lerner Publications, 2007.

Wilds, Mary C. *The Creek*. San Diego, CA: Lucent Books, 2005.

Wiles, Sara. *Arapaho Journeys: Photographs and Stories from the Wind River Reservation*. Norman: University of Oklahoma Press, 2011.

Williams, Jack S. *The Luiseno of California*. New York: PowerKids Press, 2003.

———. *The Modoc of California and Oregon*. New York: PowerKids Press, 2004.

———. *The Mojave of California and Arizona*. New York: PowerKids Press, 2004.

Wilson, Darryl J. *The Morning the Sun Went Down*. Berkeley, CA: Heyday, 1998.

Wilson, Elijah Nicholas. *The White Indian Boy: The Story of Uncle Nick among the Shoshones*. Kila, MN: Kessinger Publishing, 2004.

Wilson, Frazer Ells. *The Peace of Mad Anthony: An Account of the Subjugation of the Northwestern Indian Tribes and the Treaty of Greeneville*. Kila, MN: Kessinger Publishing, 2005.

Wilson, Norman L., and Arlean H. Towne. "Nisenan." In *Handbook of North American Indians*. Vol. 8: *California*. Edited by Robert F. Heizer. Washington DC: Smithsonian Institution, 1978.

Winnemucca, Sarah. *Life among the Paiutes: Their Wrongs and Claims.* Privately printed, 1883. Reprint. Reno: University of Nevada Press, 1994.

Wolcott, Harry F. *A Kwakiutl Village and School*. Walnut Creek, CA: AltaMira Press, 2003.

Wolfson, Evelyn. *The Iroquois: People of the Northeast*. Brookfield, CT: The Millbrook Press, 1992.

Woolworth, Alan R. *Santee Dakota Indian Tales*. Saint Paul, MN: Prairie Smoke Press, 2003.

Worl, Rosita. *Celebration: Tlingit, Haida, Tsimshian Dancing on the Land*. Edited by Kathy Dye. Seattle: University of Washington Press, 2008.

Wright, Muriel H. *A Guide to the Indian Tribes of Oklahoma*. Norman: University of Oklahoma Press, 1951.

Wyborny, Sheila. *North American Indians: Native Americans of the Southwest*. San Diego: KidHaven Press, 2004.

Wynecoop, David C. *Children of the Sun: A History of the Spokane Indians*. Wellpinit, WA, 1969. Available online from http://www.wellpinit.wednet.edu/shorthistory (accessed on August 11, 2011).

Wyss, Thelma Hatch. *Bear Dancer: The Story of a Ute Girl*. Chicago: Margaret K. McElderry Books, 2010.

Zepeda, Ofelia. *Where Clouds Are Formed: Poems*. Tucson: University of Arizona Press, 2008.

Zigmond, Maurice L. *Kawaiisu Mythology: An Oral Tradition of South-Central California*. Banning, CA: Malki-Ballena Press, 1980.

———. "Kawaiisu." In *Handbook of North American Indians, Great Basin.* Vol. 11. Edited by Warren L. D'Azavedo. Washington, DC: Smithsonian Institution, 1981, pp. 398–411.

Zimmerman, Dwight Jon. *Tecumseh: Shooting Star of the Shawnee.* New York: Sterling, 2010.

Zitkala-Sa, Cathy N. Davidson, and Ada Norris. *American Indian Stories, Legends, and Other Writings.* New York: Penguin, 2003.

Periodicals

Barrett, Samuel Alfred, and Edward Winslow Gifford. "Miwok Material Culture: Indian Life of the Yosemite Region" *Bulletin of Milwaukee Public Museum* 2, no. 4 (March 1933).

Barringer, Felicity. "Indians Join Fight for an Oklahoma Lake's Flow." *New York Times.* April 12, 2011, A1. Available online from http://www.nytimes.com/2011/04/12/science/earth/12water.html (accessed on June 18, 2011).

Beck, Melinda. "The Lost Worlds of Ancient America." *Newsweek* 118 (Fall–Winter 1991): 24.

Bourke, John Gregory. "General Crook in the Indian Country." *The Century Magazine,* March 1891. Available online from http://www.discoverseaz.com/History/General_Crook.html (accessed on July 20, 2011).

Bruchac, Joseph. "Otstango: A Mohawk Village in 1491," *National Geographic* 180, no. 4 (October 1991): 68–83.

Carroll, Susan. "Tribe Fights Kitt Peak Project." *The Arizona Republic.* March 24, 2005. Available online at http://www.nathpo.org/News/Sacred_Sites/News-Sacred_Sites109.htm (accessed on July 20, 2011).

Chief Joseph. "An Indian's View of Indian Affairs." *North American Review* 128, no. 269 (April 1879): 412–33.

Collins, Cary C., ed. "Henry Sicade's History of Puyallup Indian School, 1860 to 1920." *Columbia* 14, no. 4 (Winter 2001–02).

Dalsbø, E.T., "'We Were Told We Were Going to Live in Houses': Relocation and Housing of the Mushuau Innu of Natuashish from 1948 to 2003." *University of Tromsø,* May 28, 2010. Available from http://www.ub.uit.no/munin/bitstream/handle/10037/2739/thesis.pdf?sequence=3 (accessed on May 26, 2011).

Dixon, Roland B. "Achomawi and Atsugewi Tales." *Journal of American Folklore* 21. (1908): 159–77.

Dold, Catherine. "American Cannibal." *Discover* 19, no. 2 (February 1998): 64.

Duara, Nigel. "Descendants Make Amends to Chinook for Lewis and Clark Canoe Theft." *Missourian.* (September 23, 2011). Available online from http://www.columbiamissourian.com/stories/2011/09/23/descendants-make-amends-chinook-lewis-clark-canoe-theft/ (accessed on November 2, 2011).

Elliott, Jack. "Dawn, Nov. 28, 1729: Gunfire Heralds Natchez Massacre." *Concordia Sentinel.* November 5, 2009. Available from http://www. concordiasentinel.com/news.php?id=4321 (accessed on June 27, 2011).

Eskin, Leah. "Teens Take Charge. (Suicide Epidemic at Wind River Reservation)." *Scholastic Update,* May 26, 1989: 26.

Et-twaii-lish, Marjorie Waheneka. "Indian Perspectives on Food and Culture." *Oregon Historical Quarterly,* Fall 2005.

Griswold, Eliza. "A Teen's Third-World America." *Newsweek.* December 26, 2010. Available online from http://www.thedailybeast.com/articles/2010/12/26/ a-boys-third-world-america.html (accessed on July 20, 2011).

ICTMN Staff. "Washoe Tribe's Cave Rock a No-go for Bike Path" *Indian Country Today Media Network,* February 10, 2011. Available online at http://indiancountrytodaymedianetwork.com/2011/02/washoe-tribes-cave- rock-a-no-go-for-bike-path/ (accessed on August 15, 2011).

Johnston, Moira. "Canada's Queen Charlotte Islands: Homeland of the Haida." *National Geographic,* July 1987: 102–27.

Jones, Malcolm Jr., with Ray Sawhill. "Just Too Good to Be True: Another Reason to Beware False Eco-Prophets." *Newsweek.* (May 4, 1992). Available online at http://www.synaptic.bc.ca/ejournal/newsweek.htm (accessed on November 2, 2011).

June-Friesen, Katy. "An Ancestry of African-Native Americans." *Smithsonian.* February 17, 2010. Available online from http://www.smithsonianmag. com/history-archaeology/An-Ancestry-of-African-Native-Americans. html#ixzz1RN1pyiD1 (accessed on June 21, 2011).

Kowinski, William Severini. "Giving New Life to Haida Art and the Culture It Expresses." *Smithsonian,* January 1995: 38.

Kroeber, A. L. "Two Myths of the Mission Indians." *Journal of the American Folk-Lore Society* 19, no. 75 (1906): 309–21. Available online at http:// www.sacred-texts.com/nam/ca/tmmi/index.htm (accessed on August 11, 2011).

Lake, Robert, Jr. "The Chilula Indians of California." *Indian Historian* 12, no. 3 (1979): 14–26. Available online fromhttp://www.eric.ed.gov/ ERICWebPortal/search/detailmini.jsp?_nfpb=true&_&ERICExtSearch_Searc hValue_0=EJ214907&ERICExtSearch_SearchType_0=no&accno=EJ214907

Parks, Ron. "Selecting a Suitable Country for the Kanza." *The Kansas Free Press.* June 1, 2011. Available online from http://www.kansasfreepress. com/2011/06/selecting-a-suitable-country-for-the-kanza.html (accessed on June 17, 2011).

Rezendes, Michael. "Few Tribes Share Casino Windfall." *Globe.* December 11, 2000. Available online from http://indianfiles.serveftp.com/TribalIssues/ Few%20tribes%20share%20casino%20windfall.pdf(accessed on July 4, 2011).

Roy, Prodipto, and Della M. Walker. "Assimilation of the Spokane Indians." *Washington Agricultural Experiment Station Bulletin.* No. 628.

Pullman: Washington State University, Institute of Agricultural Science, 1961.

Shaffrey, Mary M. "Lumbee Get a Win, But Not without Stipulation." *Winston-Salem Journal* (April 26, 2007).

Shapley, Thomas. "Historical Revision Rights a Wrong." *Seattle Post-Intelligencer.* (December 18, 2004). Available online from http://www.seattlepi.com/local/opinion/article/Historical-revision-rights-a-wrong-1162234.php#ixzz1WBFxoNiw (accessed on August 15, 2011).

"Q: Should Scientists Be Allowed to 'Study' the Skeletons of Ancient American Indians?" (Symposium: U.S. Representative Doc Hastings; Confederated Tribes of the Umatilla Indian Reservation Spokesman Donald Sampson). *Insight on the News* 13, no. 47 (December 22, 1997): 24.

Siegel, Lee. "Mummies Might Have Been Made by Anasazi." *Salt Lake Tribune,* April 2, 1998.

Stewart, Kenneth M. "Mohave Warfare." *Southwestern Journal of Anthropology* 3, no. 3 (Autumn 1947): 257–78.

Trivedi, Bijal P. "Ancient Timbers Reveal Secrets of Anasazi Builders." *National Geographic Today,* September 28, 2001. Available online at http://news.nationalgeographic.com/news/2001/09/0928_TVchaco.html (accessed on June 29, 2007).

Trumbauer, Sophie. "Northwest Tribes Canoe to Lummi Island." *The Daily.* (August 1, 2007). Available online at http://thedaily.washington.edu/article/2007/8/1/northwestTribesCanoeToLumm (accessed on November 2, 2011).

Van Meter, David. "Energy Efficient." *University of Texas at Arlington,* Fall 2006.

Wagner, Dennis. "Stolen Artifacts Shatter Ancient Culture." *The Arizona Republic,* November 12, 2006.

Warshall, Peter. "The Heart of Genuine Sadness: Astronomers, Politicians, and Federal Employees Desecrate the Holiest Mountain of the San Carlos Apache." *Whole Earth* 91 (Winter 1997): 30.

Win, WambliSina. "The Ultimate Expression of Faith, the Lakota Sun Dance." *Native American Times.* July 4, 2011. Available online from http://www.nativetimes.com/index.php?option=com_content&view=article&id=5657:the-ultimate-expression-of-faith-the-lakota-sun-dance&catid=46&Itemid=22 (accessed on July 4, 2011).

Web Sites

"Aboriginal Fisheries Strategy." *Fisheries and Oceans Canada.* http://www.dfo-mpo.gc.ca/fm-gp/aboriginal-autochtones/afs-srapa-eng.htm (accessed on August 15, 2011).

"Aboriginal Peoples: The Métis." *Newfoundland and Labrador Heritage.* http://www.heritage.nf.ca/aboriginal/metis.html (accessed on August 4, 2011).

"About the Hopi." Restoration. http://hopi.org/about-the-hopi/ (accessed on July 20, 2011).

"Acoma Pueblo." *ClayHound Web.* http://www.clayhound.us/sites/acoma.htm (accessed on July 20, 2011).

"Acoma Pueblo." *New Mexico Magazine.*http://www.nmmagazine.com/native_american/acoma.php (accessed on July 20, 2011).

"Acoma'Sky City'" *National Trust for Historic Preservation.*http://www.acomaskycity.org/ (accessed on July 20, 2011).

"Address of Tarhe, Grand Sachem of the Wyandot Nation, to the Assemblage at the Treaty of Greeneville, July 22, 1795." *Wyandotte Nation of Oklahoma.* http://www.wyandotte-nation.org/history/tarhe_greenville_address.html (accessed May 12, 2011).

"The Adena Mounds." *Grave Creek Mound State Park.* http://www.adena.com/adena/ad/ad01.htm (accessed June 7, 2011).

Adley-SantaMaria, Bernadette. "White Mountain Apache Language Issues." *Northern Arizona University.* http://www2.nau.edu/jar/TIL_12.html (accessed on July 20, 2011).

Akimoff, Tim. "Snowshoe Builders Display Their Craft at the Anchorage Museum." *KTUU.* May 5, 2011. http://www.ktuu.com/news/ktuu-snowshoe-builders-display-their-craft-at-the-anchorage-museum-20110505,0,7760220.story (accessed on June 6, 2011).

Alamo Chapter. http://alamo.nndes.org/ (accessed on July 20, 2011).

Alaska Native Collections. *Smithsonian Institution.* http://alaska.si.edu/cultures.asp (accessed on August 15, 2011).

— — —. "Unangan."*Smithsonian Institution.* http://alaska.si.edu/culture_unangan.asp(accessed on August 15, 2011).

"Alaska Native Language Center." *University of Alaska Fairbanks.* http://www.uaf.edu/anlc//anlc/languages/ (accessed on June 4, 2011).

Alaska Yup'ik Eskimo. http://www.yupik.com (accessed on August 15, 2011).

All Indian Pueblo Council. http://www.20pueblos.org/ (accessed on July 20, 2011).

Allen, Cain. "The Oregon History Project: Toby Winema Riddle."*Oregon Historical Society.* http://www.ohs.org/education/oregonhistory/historical_records/dspDocument.cfm?doc_ID=000A9FE3-B226-1EE8-827980B05272FE9F (accessed on August 11, 2011).

"Alutiiq and Aleut/Unangan History and Culture."*Anchorage Museum.* http://www.anchoragemuseum.org/galleries/alaska_gallery/aleut.aspx (accessed on August 15, 2011).

Aluttiq Museum. http://alutiiqmuseum.org/ (accessed on August 15, 2011).

"Anasazi: The Ancient Ones." *Manitou Cliff Dwellings Museum.* http://www. cliffdwellingsmuseum.com/anasazi.htm (accessed on July 20, 2011).

"Anasazi Heritage Center: Ancestral Pueblos." *Bureau of Land Management Colorado.* http://www.co.blm.gov/ahc/anasazi.htm (accessed on July 13, 2011).

"The Anasazi or 'Ancient Pueblo.'" *Northern Arizona University.* http://www. cpluhna.nau.edu/People/anasazi.htm (accessed on July 20, 2011).

"Ancient Architects of the Mississippi." *National Park Service, Department of the Interior.* http://www.cr.nps.gov/archeology/feature/feature.htm (accessed on July 10, 2007).

"Ancient DNA from the Ohio Hopewell." *Ohio Archaeology Blog,* June 22, 2006. http://ohio-archaeology.blogspot.com/2006/06/ancient-dna-from-ohio-hopewell.html (accessed on July 10, 2007).

"Ancient Moundbuilders of Arkansas." *University of Arkansas.* http://cast.uark.edu/ home/research/archaeology-and-historic-preservation/archaeological-interpretation/ ancient-moundbuilders-of-arkansas.html (accessed on June 10, 2011).

"Ancient One: Kennewick Man." *Confederated Tribes of the Umatilla Reservation.* http://www.umatilla.nsn.us/ancient.html (accessed on August 11, 2011).

Anderson, Jeff. "Arapaho Online Research Resources." *Colby College.* http:// www.colby.edu/personal/j/jdanders/arapahoresearch.htm (accessed on July 2, 2011).

"Anishinaabe Chi-Naaknigewin/Anishinabek Nation Constitution." *Anishinabek Nation.* http://www.anishinabek.ca/uploads/ANConstitution.pdf (accessed on May 16, 2011).

"Antelope Valley Indian Peoples: The Late Prehistoric Period: Kawaiisu." *Antelope Valley Indian Museum.* http://www.avim.parks.ca.gov/people/ ph_kawaiisu.shtml (accessed on August 15, 2011).

"Apache Indian History." *Access Genealogy.* http://www.accessgenealogy.com/ native/tribes/apache/apachehist.htm (accessed on July 15, 2011).

"Apache Indians." *AAA Native Arts.* http://www.aaanativearts.com/apache (accessed on July 15, 2011).

"Apache Nation: Nde Nation." *San Carlos Apache Nation.* http://www. sancarlosapache.com/home.htm (accessed on July 15, 2011).

"Apache Tribal Nation." *Dreams of the Great Earth Changes.* http://www. greatdreams.com/apache/apache-tribe.htm (accessed on July 15, 2011).

"The Apsáalooke (Crow Indians) of Montana Tribal Histories." *Little Big Horn College.* http://lib.lbhc.edu/history/ (accessed on July 5, 2011).

Aquino, Pauline. "Ohkay Owingeh: Village of the Strong People" (video). *New Mexico State Record Center and Archives.* http://www.newmexicohistory.org/ filedetails.php?fileID=22530 (accessed on July 20, 2011).

"The Arapaho Tribe." *Omaha Public Library.* http://www.omahapubliclibrary. org/transmiss/congress/arapaho.html (accessed on July 2, 2011).

Arctic Circle. http://arcticcircle.uconn.edu/Museum/ (accessed on June 10, 2011).

"Arctic Circle." *University of Connecticut.* http://arcticcircle.uconn.edu/ VirtualClassroom/ (accessed on August 15, 2011).

"The Arctic Is…." *Stefansson Arctic Institute.* http://www.thearctic.is/ (accessed on August 15, 2011).

Arctic Library."Inuit" *Athropolis.*http://www.athropolis.com/library-cat. htm#inuit (accessed on August 15, 2011).

"Arikira Indians." *PBS.* http://www.pbs.org/lewisandclark/native/ari.html (accessed on June 19, 2011).

"Arkansas Indians: Arkansas Archeological Survey." *University of Arkansas.* http://www.uark.edu/campus-resources/archinfo/ArkansasIndianTribes.pdf (accessed on June 12, 2011).

Arlee, Johnny. *Over a Century of Moving to the Drum: Salish Indian Celebra-tions on the Flathead Reservation.* Helena: Montana Historical Society Press, 1998. Available online from http://www.archive.org/stream/his-toricalsketch00ronarich/historicalsketch00ronarich_djvu.txt (accessed on August 11, 2011).

Armstrong, Kerry M. "Chickasaw Historical Research Page." *Chickasaw History.* http://www.chickasawhistory.com/ (accessed on June 16, 2011.

"Art on the Prairies: Otoe-Missouria." *The Bata Shoe Museum.* http://www. allaboutshoes.ca/en/paths_across/art_on_prairies/index_7.php (accessed on June 20, 2011).

"Assiniboin Indian History." *Access Genealogy.* http://www.accessgenealogy.com/ native/tribes/assiniboin/assiniboinhist.htm (accessed on June 7, 2011).

"Assinboin Indians." *PBS.* http://www.pbs.org/lewisandclark/native/idx_ass. html (accessed on June 7, 2011).

"Assiniboine History." *Fort Belknap Indian Community.* http://www.ftbelknap-nsn. gov/assiniboineHistory.php (accessed on June 6, 2011).

"Athabascan." Alaska Native Heritage Center Museum. http://www.alaskanative. net/en/main_nav/education/culture_alaska/athabascan/ (accessed on June 6, 2011).

Banyacya, Thomas. "Message to the World." *Hopi Traditional Elder.* http:// banyacya.indigenousnative.org/ (accessed on July 20, 2011).

Barnett, Jim. "The Natchez Indians." *History Now.* http://mshistory.k12.ms.us/ index.php?id=4 (accessed on June 27, 2011).

Barry, Paul C. "Native America Nations and Languages: Haudenosaunee." *The Canku Ota—A Newsletter Celebrating Native America.* http://www. turtletrack.org/Links/NANations/CO_NANationLinks_HJ.htm (accessed on June 5, 2011).

"Before the White Man Came to Nisqually Country." *Washington History Online.* January 12, 2006. http://washingtonhistoryonline.org/treatytrail/ teaching/before-white-man.pdf (accessed on August 15, 2011).

Big Valley Band of Pomo Indians. http://www.big-valley.net/index.htm (accessed on August 11, 2011).

Bishop Paiute Tribe. http://www.bishoppaiutetribe.com/ (accessed on August 15, 2011).

"Black Kettle." *PBS.* http://www.pbs.org/weta/thewest/people/a_c/blackkettle.htm (accessed on July 4, 2011).

"Blackfeet." *Wisdom of the Elders.* http://www.wisdomoftheelders.org/program208.html (accessed on July 2, 2011).

"Blackfoot History." *Head-Smashed-In Buffalo Jump Interpretive Centre.* http://www.head-smashed-in.com/black.html (accessed on July 2, 2011).

Blackfeet Nation. http://www.blackfeetnation.com/ (accessed on July 2, 2011).

Boyer, Ruth McDonald, and Narcissus Duffy Gayton. "Apache Mothers and Daughters: Four Generations of a Family. Remembrances of an Apache Elder Woman." *Southwest Crossroads.* http://southwestcrossroads.org/record.php?num=825&hl=Apache (accessed on July 20, 2011).

British Columbia Archives. "First Nations Research Guide." *Royal BC Museum Corporation.* http://www.royalbcmuseum.bc.ca/BC_Research_Guide/BC_First_Nations.aspx (accessed on August 15, 2011).

Bruchac, Joe. "Storytelling." *Abenaki Nation.* http://www.abenakination.org/stories.html (accessed on June 5, 2011).

Brush, Rebecca. "The Wichita Indians." *Texas Indians.* http://www.texasindians.com/wichita.htm (accessed on June 9, 2011).

"Caddo Indian History." *Access Genealogy.* http://www.accessgenealogy.com/native/tribes/caddo/caddohist.htm (accessed on June 12, 2011).

"Cahto (Kato)." *Four Directions Institute.* http://www.fourdir.com/cahto.htm (accessed on August 11, 2011).

"Cahto Tribe Information Network." *Cahto Tribe.* http://www.cahto.org/ (accessed on August 11, 2011).

"Cahuilla." *Four Directions Institute.* http://www.fourdir.com/cahuilla.htm (accessed on August 11, 2011).

Cahuilla Band of Mission Indians. http://cahuillabandofindians.com/ (accessed on August 11, 2011).

"California Indians." *Visalia Unified School District.* http://visalia.k12.ca.us/teachers/tlieberman/indians/ (accessed on August 15, 2011).

California Valley Miwok Tribe, California. http://www.californiavalleymiwoktribe-nsn.gov/ (accessed on August 11, 2011).

Cambra, Rosemary, et al. "The Muwekma Ohlone Tribe of the San Francisco Bay Area." http://www.islaiscreek.org/ohlonehistcultfedrecog.html (accessed on August 11, 2011).

"Camp Grant Massacre—April 30, 1871." *Council of Indian Nations.* http://www.nrcprograms.org/site/PageServer?pagename=cin_hist_campgrantmassacre (accessed on July 20, 2011).

Campbell, Grant. "The Rock Paintings of the Chumash." *Association for Humanistic Psychology.* http://www.ahpweb.org/articles/chumash.html (accessed on August 11, 2011).

Canadian Heritage Information Network. "Communities& Institutions: Talented Youth." *Tipatshimuna.* http://www.tipatshimuna.ca/1420_e.php (accessed on May 19, 2011).

Carleton, Kenneth H. "A Brief History of the Mississippi Band of Choctaw Indians." *Mississippi Band of Choctaw.* http://mdah.state.ms.us/hpres/A%20Brief%20History%20of%20the%20Choctaw.pdf (accessed on June 12, 2011).

Central Council: Tlingit and Haida Indian Tribes of Alaska. http://www.ccthita.org/ (accessed on November 2, 2011).

Cherokee Nation. http://www.cherokee.org/ (accessed on June 12, 2011).

"Cheyenne Indian." *American Indian Tribes.* http://www.cheyenneindian.com/cheyenne_links.htm (accessed on July 4, 2011).

"Cheyenne Indian History." *Access Genealogy.* http://www.accessgenealogy.com/native/tribes/cheyenne/cheyennehist.htm (accessed on July 4, 2011).

"Chickasaw Indian History." *Access Genealogy.* http://www.accessgenealogy.com/native/tribes/chickasaw/chickasawhist.htm (accessed on June 16, 2011).

The Chickasaw Nation. http://www.chickasaw.net (accessed on June 12, 2011).

"Chief Joseph." *PBS.* http://www.pbs.org/weta/thewest/people/a_c/chiefjoseph.htm (accessed on August 11, 2011).

"Chief Joseph Surrenders." *The History Place.* http://www.historyplace.com/speeches/joseph.htm (accessed on August 11,2011).

Chief Leschi School. http://www.leschischools.org/ (accessed on November 2, 2011).

"Chief Seattle Speech." *Washington State Library.* http://www.synaptic.bc.ca/ejournal/wslibrry.htm (accessed on November 2, 2011).

"The Children of Changing Woman." *Peabody Museum of Archaeology and Ethnology.* http://www.peabody.harvard.edu/maria/Cwoman.html (accessed on July 15, 2011).

"The Chilula." *The Indians of the Redwoods.* http://www.cr.nps.gov/history/online_books/redw/history1c.htm (accessed on August 11, 2011).

Chinook Indian Tribe/Chinook Nation. http://www.chinooknation.org/ (accessed on November 2, 2011).

"Chinookan Family History." *Access Genealogy.* http://www.accessgenealogy.com/native/tribes/chinook/chinookanfamilyhist.htm (accessed on November 2, 2011).

"Chippewa Cree Tribe (Neiyahwahk)." *Montana Office of Indian Affairs.* http://www.tribalnations.mt.gov/chippewacree.asp (accessed on June 3, 2011).

"Chiricahua Indian History." *Access Genealogy.* http://www.accessgenealogy. com/native/tribes/apache/chiricahua.htm (accessed on July 20, 2011).

Chisolm, D. "Mi'kmaq Resource Centre," *Cape Breton University.*http://mrc. uccb.ns.ca/mikmaq.html (accessed on May 15, 2011).

"Choctaw Indian History." *Access Genealogy.* http://www.accessgenealogy.com/ native/tribes/choctaw/chostawhist.htm (accessed on June 21, 2011).

"Choctaw Indian Tribe." *Native American Nations.* http://www.nanations.com/ choctaw/index.htm (accessed on June 21, 2011).

Choctaw Nation of Oklahoma. http://www.choctawnation.com (accessed on June 12, 2011).

"Chumash." *Four Directions Institute.* http://www.fourdir.com/chumash.htm (accessed on December 1, 2011).

The Chumash Indians. http://www.chumashindian.com/ (accessed on August 11, 2011).

Clark, William. "Lewis and Clark: Expedition Journals." *National Geographic.* http://www.nationalgeographic.com/lewisandclark/record_tribes_020_5_1. html (accessed on June 19, 2011).

— — —. "Lewis and Clark: Missouri Indians." *National Geographic.* http:// www.nationalgeographic.com/lewisandclark/record_tribes_012_1_9.html (accessed on June 20, 2011).

"Coast Miwok at Point Reyes." *U.S. National Park Service.* http://www.nps. gov/pore/historyculture/people_coastmiwok.htm (accessed on August 11, 2011).

"Coastal Miwok Indians." *Reed Union School District.* http://rusd.marin. k12.ca.us/belaire/ba_3rd_miwoks/coastalmiwoks/webpages/home. html(accessed on August 11, 2011).

"Comanche." *Edward S. Curtis's The North American Indian.* http://curtis. library.northwestern.edu/curtis/toc.cgi (accessed on July 4, 2011).

"Comanche Indian History." *Access Genealogy.* http://www.accessgenealogy. com/native/tribes/comanche/comanchehist.htm (accessed on July 4, 2011).

"Comanche Language." *Omniglot.* http://www.omniglot.com/writing/coman- che.htm (accessed on July 4, 2011).

Comanche Nation of Oklahoma http://www.comanchenation.com/ (accessed on July 4, 2011).

"Community News." *Mississippi Band of Choctaw Indians.* http://www.choctaw. org/ (accessed on June 12, 2011).

Compton, W. J. "The Story of Ishi, the Yana Indian." *Ye Slyvan Archer.* July 1936. http://tmuss.tripod.com/shotfrompast/chief.htm (accessed on August 11, 2011).

The Confederated Salish and Kootenai Tribes. http://www.cskt.org/ (accessed on August 11, 2011).

Confederated Tribes and Bands of the Yakama Nation. http://www.yakamana-tion-nsn.gov/ (accessed on August 11, 2011).

Confederated Tribes of the Colville Reservation. http://www.colvilletribes.com/ (accessed on August 11, 2011).

Confederated Tribes of Siletz. http://ctsi.nsn.us/ (accessed on November 2, 2011).

Confederated Tribes of the Umatilla Indian Reservation. http://www.umatilla.nsn.us/ (accessed on August 11, 2011).

"Confederated Tribes of the Umatilla Indians." *Wisdom of the Elders.* http://www.wisdomoftheelders.org/program305.html (accessed on August 11, 2011).

"Confederated Tribes of the Yakama Nation." *Wisdom of the Elders.* http://www.wisdomoftheelders.org/program304.html (accessed on August 11, 2011).

"Connecting the World with Seattle's First People." *Duwamish Tribe.* http://www.duwamishtribe.org/ (accessed on November 2, 2011).

Conrad, Jim. "The Natchez Indians." *The Loess Hills of the Lower Missisipi Valley.* http://www.backyardnature.net/loess/ind_natz.htm (accessed on June 27, 2011).

Cordell, Linda. "Anasazi." *Scholastic.* http://www2.scholastic.com/browse/article.jsp?id=5042 (accessed on July 20, 2011).

"Costanoan Indian Tribe." *Access Genealogy.* http://www.accessgenealogy.com/native/tribes/costanoan/costanoanindiantribe.htm (accessed on August 11, 2011).

Costanoan Rumsen Carmel Tribe. http://costanoanrumsen.org/ (accessed on August 11, 2011).

"Costanoan Rumsen Carmel Tribe: History." *Native Web.* http://crc.nativeweb.org/history.html (accessed on August 11, 2011).

Cotton, Lee. "Powhatan Indian Lifeways." *National Park Service.* http://www.nps.gov/jame/historyculture/powhatan-indian-lifeways.htm (accessed on June 1, 2011).

Council of the Haida Nation (CHN). http://www.haidanation.ca/ (accessed on November 2, 2011).

"A Coyote's Tales—Tohono O'odham." *First People: American Indian Legends.* http://www.firstpeople.us/FP-Html-Legends/A_Coyotes_Tales-TohonoOodham.html (accessed on July 20, 2011).

"Creek Indian." *American Indian Tribe.* http://www.creekindian.com/ (accessed on June 12, 2011).

"Creek Indians." *GeorgiaInfo.* http://georgiainfo.galileo.usg.edu/creek.htm (accessed on June 12, 2011).

"Crow/Cheyenne." *Wisdom of the Elders.* http://www.wisdomoftheelders.org/program206.html (accessed on July 5, 2011).

"Crow Indian Tribe." *Access Genealogy.* http://www.accessgenealogy.com/native/tribes/crow/crowhist.htm (accessed on July 5, 2011).

Crow Tribe, Apsáalooke Nation Official Website. http://www.crowtribe.com/ (accessed on July 5, 2011).

"Culture and History." *Innu Nation.* http://www.innu.ca/index.php?option=com_content&view=article&id=8&Itemid=3&lang=en (accessed on May 19, 2011).

"Culture& History." *Aleut Corporation.* http://www.aleutcorp.com/index.php?option=com_content&view=section&layout=blog&id=6&Itemid=24 (accessed on August 15, 2011).

"Culture and History of the Skokomish Tribe." *Skokomish Tribal Nation.* http://www.skokomish.org/historyculture.htm (accessed on November 2, 2011).

Curtis, Edward S. *The North American Indian.* Vol.13. 1924. Reprint. New York: Johnson Reprint Corporation, 1970. Available online from *Northwestern University Digital Library Collections.* http://curtis.library.northwestern.edu/curtis/viewPage.cgi?showp=1&size=2&id=nai.13.book.00000192&volume=13#nav-Edward (accessed on August 11, 2011).

"Dakota Indian Tribe History." *Access Genealogy.* http://www.accessgenealogy.com/native/tribes/siouan/dakotahist.htm (accessed on July 5, 2011).

"Dakota Spirituality." *Blue Cloud Abbey.* http://www.bluecloud.org/dakotaspirituality.html (accessed on July 5, 2011).

"Dams of the Columbia Basin and Their Effects on the Native Fishery." *Center for Columbia River History.* http://www.ccrh.org/comm/river/dams6.htm (accessed on August 11, 2011).

Deans, James. "Tales from the Totems of the Hidery." *Early Canadiana Online.* http://www.canadiana.org/ECO/PageView/06053/0003?id=986858ca5fbdc633 (accessed on November 2, 2011).

Deer Lake First Nation. http://www.deerlake.firstnation.ca/ (accessed on June 5, 2011).

"Delaware Indian Chiefs." *Access Genealogy.* http://www.accessgenealogy.com/native/tribes/delaware/delawarechiefs.htm (accessed on June 8, 2011).

"Delaware Indian/Lenni Lenape." *Delaware Indians of Pennsylvania.* http://www.delawareindians.com/ (accessed on June 8, 2011).

"Delaware Indians." *Ohio Historical Society.* http://www.ohiohistorycentral.org/entry.php?rec=584 (accessed on June 2, 2011).

The Delaware Nation. http://www.delawarenation.com/ (accessed on June 2, 2011).

Delaware Tribe of Indians. http://www.delawaretribeofindians.nsn.us/ (accessed on June 2, 2011).

DelawareIndian.com. http://www.delawareindian.com/ (accessed on June 2, 2011).

Dene Cultural Institute. http://www.deneculture.org/ (accessed on June 10, 2011).

Deschenes, Bruno. "Inuit Throat-Singing." *Musical Traditions.* http://www.mustrad.org.uk/articles/inuit.htm (accessed on August 15, 2011).

"Desert Native Americans: Mohave Indians." *Mojave Desert.* http://mojavedesert.net/mojave-indians/ (accessed on July 20, 2011).

Dodds, Lissa Guimarães. "'The Washoe People': Past and Present." *Washoe Tribe of Nevada and California.* http://www.Washoetribe.us/images/Washoe_tribe_history_v2.pdf (accessed on August 15, 2011).

"Duwamish Indian Tribe History." *Access Genealogy.* http://www.accessgenealogy.com/native/tribes/salish/duwamishhist.htm (accessed on November 2, 2011).

"The Early History and Names of the Arapaho." *Native American Nations.* http://www.nanations.com/early_arapaho.htm (accessed on July 2, 2011).

Eastern Shawnee Tribe of Oklahoma. http://estoo-nsn.gov/ (accessed on June 12, 2011).

Eck, Pam. "Hopi Indians." *Indiana University.* http://inkido.indiana.edu/w310work/romac/hopi.htm (accessed on July 20, 2011).

Edward S. Curtis's The North American Indian. http://curtis.library.northwestern.edu/curtis/toc.cgi (accessed on August 11, 2011).

Elam, Earl H. "Wichita Indians." *Texas State Historical Association.* http://www.tshaonline.org/handbook/online/articles/bmw03 (accessed on June 9, 2011).

Ely Shoshone Tribe. http://elyshoshonetribe-nsn.gov/departments.html (accessed on August 15, 2011).

Etienne-Gray, Tracé. "Black Seminole Indians." *Texas State Historical Association.* http://www.tshaonline.org/handbook/online/articles/bmb18 (accessed on June 12, 2011).

Everett, Diana. "Apache Tribe of Oklahoma." *Oklahoma Historical Society.* http://digital.library.okstate.edu/encyclopedia/entries/A/AP002.html(accessed on July 15, 2011).

"Eyak, Tlingit, Haida, and Tsimshian." *Alaska Native Heritage Center Museum.* http://www.alaskanative.net/en/main_nav/education/culture_alaska/eyak/ (accessed on August 15, 2011).

Fausz, J. Frederick. "The Louisiana Expansion: The Arikara." *University of Missouri–St. Louis.* http://www.umsl.edu/continuinged/louisiana/Am_Indians/8-Arikara/8-arikara.html (accessed on June 19, 2011).

———. "The Louisiana Expansion: The Kansa/Kaw." *University of Missouri–St. Louis.* http://www.umsl.edu/continuinged/louisiana/Am_Indians/3-Kansa_Kaw/3-kansa_kaw.html (accessed on June 17, 2011).

———. "The Louisiana Expansion: The Missouri/Missouria." *University of Missouri–St. Louis.* http://www.umsl.edu/continuinged/louisiana/Am_Indians/2-Missouria/2-missouria.html (accessed on June 20, 2011).

— — —. "The Louisiana Expansion: The Oto(e)." *University of Missouri-St. Louis.* http://www.umsl.edu/continuinged/louisiana/Am_Indians/4-Oto/4-oto.html (accessed on June 20, 2011).

Feller, Walter. "California Indian History." *Digital Desert.* http://mojavedesert.net/california-indian-history/ (accessed on August 11, 2011).

— — —. "Mojave Desert Indians: Cahuilla Indians." *Digital-Desert.* http://mojavedesert.net/cahuilla-indians/ (accessed on August 11, 2011).

"First Nations: People of the Interior." *British Columbia Archives.* http://www.bcarchives.gov.bc.ca/exhibits/timemach/galler07/frames/int_peop.htm (accessed on August 11, 2011).

"First Peoples of Canada: Communal Hunters." *Canadian Museum of Civilization.* http://www.civilization.ca/cmc/home (accessed on June 10, 2011).

"Flathead Indians (Salish)." *National Geographic.* http://www.nationalgeographic.com/lewisandclark/record_tribes_022_12_16.html (accessed on August 11, 2011).

"Flathead Reservation." http://www.montanatribes.org/links_&_resources/tribes/Flathead_Reservation.pdf (accessed on August 11, 2011).

Flora, Stephenie. "Northwest Indians: 'The First People.'" *Oregon Pioneers.* http://www.oregonpioneers.com/indian.htm (accessed on August 15, 2011).

Forest County Potawatomi. http://www.fcpotawatomi.com/ (accessed on June 5, 2011).

Fort McDowell Yavapai Nation. http://www.ftmcdowell.org/ (accessed on July 20, 2011).

"Fort Mojave Indian Tribe." *Inter Tribal Council of Arizona, Inc.* http://www.itcaonline.com/tribes_mojave.html (accessed on July 20, 2011).

Fort Peck Tribes. http://www.fortpecktribes.org/ (accessed on June 4, 2011).

Fort Sill Apache Tribe. http://www.fortsillapache.com (accessed on July 20, 2011).

"Fort Yuma-Quechan Tribe." *Inter-Tribal Council of Arizona, Inc.* http://www.itcaonline.com/tribes_quechan.html (accessed on July 20, 2011).

Gangnier, Gary. "The History of the Innu Nation." *Central Quebec School Board.* http://www.cqsb.qc.ca/svs/434/fninnu.htm (accessed on May 24, 2011).

Gerke, Sarah Bohl. "White Mountain Apache." *Arizona State University.* http://grandcanyonhistory.clas.asu.edu/history_nativecultures_whitemountainapache.html (accessed on July 20, 2011).

"Geronimo, His Own Story: A Prisoner of War." *From Revolution to Reconstruction.* http://www.let.rug.nl/usa/B/geronimo/geroni17.htm (accessed on July 20, 2011).

"Gifting and Feasting in the Northwest Coast Potlatch." *Peabody Museum of Archaeology and Ethnology.* http://www.peabody.harvard.edu/potlatch/ (accessed on November 2, 2011).

Glenn Black Laboratory of Archaeology. "Burial Mounds." *Indiana University.* http://www.gbl.indiana.edu/abstracts/adena/mounds.html (accessed June 7, 2011).

— — —. "The Ohio Valley-Great Lakes Ethnohistory Archives: The Miami Collection." *Indiana University.* http://gbl.indiana.edu/ethnohistory/archives/menu.html (accessed on June 7, 2011).

Glover, William B. "A History of the Caddo Indians." Formatted for the World Wide Web by Jay Salsburg. Reprinted from *The Louisiana Historical Quarterly*, 18, no. 4 (October 1935). http://ops.tamu.edu/x075bb/caddo/Indians.html (accessed on June 12, 2011).

GoodTracks, Jimm. "These Native Ways." *Turtle Island Storytellers Network.* http://www.turtleislandstorytellers.net/tis_kansas/transcript01_jg_tracks.htm (accessed on June 20, 2011).

"Grand Village of the Natchez Indians." *Mississippi Department of Archives and History.* http://mdah.state.ms.us/hprop/gvni.html (accessed on June 27, 2011).

Great Basin Indian Archives. http://www.gbcnv.edu/gbia/index.htm (accessed on August 15, 2011).

Great Basin National Park. "Historic Tribes of the Great Basin." *National Park Service: U.S. Department of the Interior.* http://www.nps.gov/grba/historyculture/historic-tribes-of-the-great-basin.htm (accessed on August 15, 2011).

Greene, Candace S. "Kiowa Drawings." *National Anthropological Archives, National Museum of Natural History.* http://www.nmnh.si.edu/naa/kiowa/kiowa.htm (accessed on July 4, 2011).

"Haida." *The Kids' Site of Canadian Settlement, Library and Archives Canada.* http://www.collectionscanada.ca/settlement/kids/021013-2061-e.html (accessed on November 2, 2011).

"Haida Heritage Center at Qay'llnagaay." *Haida Heritage Centre.* http://www.haidaheritagecentre.com/ (accessed on November 2, 2011).

"Haida Language Program." *Sealaska Heritage Institute.* http://www.sealaska-heritage.org/programs/haida_language_program.htm (accessed on November 2, 2011).

"Haida Spirits of the Sea." *Virtual Museum of Canada.* http://www.virtualmuseum.ca/Exhibitions/Haida/nojava/english/home/index.html (accessed on November 2, 2011).

Handbook of American Indians. "Arikara Indian Tribe History." *Access Genealogy.* http://www.accessgenealogy.com/native/tribes/nations/arikara.htm (accessed on June 19, 2011).

Handbook of American Indians.. "Quapaw Indian Tribe History." *Access Genealogy.* http://www.accessgenealogy.com/native/tribes/quapaw/quapawhist.htm (accessed on June 20, 2011).

"History—Incident at Wounded Knee." *U.S. Marshals Service.* http://www.usmarshals.gov/history/wounded-knee/index.html (accessed on July 4, 2011).

"History: We Are the Anishnaabek." *The Grand Traverse Band of Ottawa and Chippewa.* http://www.gtbindians.org/history.html (accessed May 13, 2011).

"History and Culture." *Cherokee North Carolina.* http://www.cherokee-nc.com/history_intro.php (accessed on June 12, 2011).

"A History of American Indians in California." *National Park Service.* http://www.nps.gov/history/history/online_books/5views/5views1.htm (accessed on August 15, 2011).

"History of Northern Ute Indian, Utah." *Online Utah.* http://www.onlineutah.com/utehistorynorthern.shtml (accessed on August 15, 2011).

"History of the Confederated Tribes of the Siletz Indians." *HeeHeeIllahee RV Resort.* http://www.heeheeillahee.com/html/about_tribe_history.htm (accessed on November 2, 2011).

Hollabaugh, Mark. "Brief History of the Lakota People." *Normandale Community College.* http://faculty.normandale.edu/-physics/Hollabaugh/Lakota/BriefHistory.htm (accessed on July 4, 2011).

Holt, Ronald L. "Paiute Indians." *State of Utah.* http://historytogo.utah.gov/utah_chapters/american_indians/paiuteindians.html (accessed on August 15, 2011).

Holzman, Allan. "Beyond the Mesas [video]." *University of Illinois.* http://www.vimeo.com/16872541 (accessed on July 20, 2011).

— — —. "The Indian Boarding School Experience [video]." *University of Illinois.* http://www.vimeo.com/17410552 (accessed on July 20, 2011).

Hoopa Tribal Museum and San Francisco State University. http://bss.sfsu.edu/calstudies/hupa/Hoopa.HTM (accessed on August 11, 2011).

Hoopa Valley Tribe. http://www.hoopa-nsn.gov/ (accessed on August 11, 2011).

"Hopi." *Four Directions Institute.* http://www.fourdir.com/hopi.htm (accessed on July 20, 2011).

"Hopi." *Southwest Crossroads.* http://southwestcrossroads.org/search.php?query=hopi&tab=document&doc_view=10 (accessed on July 20, 2011).

"Hopi Indian Tribal History." *Access Genealogy.* www.accessgenealogy.com/native/tribes/hopi/hopeindianhist.htm (accessed on July 20, 2011).

"Hopi Tribe." *Inter Tribal Council of Arizona, Inc.* http://www.itcaonline.com/tribes_hopi.html (accessed on July 20, 2011).

"Hupa." *Four Directions Institute.* http://www.fourdir.com/hupa.htm (accessed on August 11, 2011).

"Hupa Indian Tribe." *Access Genealogy.* http://www.accessgenealogy.com/native/tribes/athapascan/hupaindiantribe.htm (accessed on August 11, 2011).

Huron-Wendat Nation. http://www.wendake.com/ (accessed May 12, 2011).

Hurst, Winston. "Anasazi." *Utah History to Go: State of Utah.* http://historytogo.utah.gov/utah_chapters/american_indians/anasazi.html (accessed on July 20, 2011).

Indian Country Diaries. "Trail of Tears." *PBS.* http://www.pbs.org/indiancountry/history/trail.html (accessed on June 12, 2011).

"Indian Peoples of the Northern Great Plains." *MSU Libraries.* http://www.lib.montana.edu/epubs/nadb/ (accessed on July 1, 2011).

Indian Pueblo Cultural Center. http://www.indianpueblo.org/ (accessed on July 20, 2011).

"Indian Tribes of California." *Access Genealogy.* http://www.accessgenealogy.com/native/california/ (accessed on August 11, 2011).

"Indians of the Northwest—Plateau and Coastal." *St. Joseph School Library.* http://library.stjosephsea.org/plateau.htm (accessed on August 11, 2011).

"Innu Youth Film Project."*Kamestastin.* http://www.kamestastin.com/ (accessed on May 24, 2011).

"The Inuit." *Newfoundland and Labrador Heritage.* http://www.heritage.nf.ca/aboriginal/inuit.html (accessed on August 15, 2011).

"Jemez Pueblos." *Four Directions Institute.* http://www.fourdir.com/jemez.htm (accessed on July 20, 2011).

"Jemez Pueblo." *New Mexico Magazine.*http://www.nmmagazine.com/native_american/jemez.php (accessed on July 20, 2011).

Jicarilla Apache Nation. http://www.jicarillaonline.com/ (accessed on July 15, 2011).

Johnson, Russ. "The Mississippian Period (900 AD to 1550 AD)" *Memphis History.* http://www.memphishistory.org/Beginnings/PreMemphis/MississippianCulture/tabid/64/Default.aspx (accessed June 7, 2011).

"The Journals of the Lewis and Clark Expedition: Nez Percé." *University of Nebraska.* http://www.nationalgeographic.com/lewisandclark/record_tribes_013_12_17.html (accessed on August 11, 2011).

Jozhe, Benedict. "A Brief History of the Fort Sill Apache Tribe." *Oklahoma Historical Society.* http://digital.library.okstate.edu/Chronicles/v039/v039p427.pdf (accessed on July 20, 2011).

"Kansa (Kaw)." *Four Directions Institute.* http://www.fourdir.com/kaw.htm (accessed on June 17, 2011).

"Kanza Cultural History." *The Kaw Nation.* http://kawnation.com/?page_id=216 (accessed on June 17, 2011).

"Kansa Indian Tribe History." *Access Geneology*. http://www.accessgenealogy.com/native/tribes/siouan/kansahist.htm (accessed on June 17, 2011).

Kavanagh, Thomas W. "Comanche." *Oklahoma Historical Society*. http://digital.library.okstate.edu/encyclopedia/entries/C/CO033.html (accessed on July 4, 2011).

— — —. "Reading Historic Photographs: Photographers of the Pawnee." *Indiana University*. http://php.indiana.edu/~tkavanag/phothana.html (accessed on July 6, 2011).

"Kawaiisu." *Four Directions Institute*. http://www.fourdir.com/Kawaiisu.htm (accessed on August 15, 2011).

"The Kawaiisu Culture." *Digital Desert: Mojave Desert*. http://mojavedesert.net/kawaiisu-indians/related-pages.html (accessed on August 15, 2011).

Kawaiisu Language and Cultural Center. http://www.kawaiisu.org/KLCC_home.html (accessed on August 15, 2011).

Kawno, Kenji. "Warriors: Navajo Code Talkers." *Southwest Crossroads*. http://southwestcrossroads.org/record.php?num=387 (accessed on July 20, 2011).

Kidwell, Clara Sue. "Choctaw." *Oklahoma Historical Society*. http://digital.library.okstate.edu/encyclopedia/entries/C/CH047.html (accessed on June 21, 2011).

"Kiowa Indian Tribe History." *Access Genealogy*. http://www.accessgenealogy.com/native/tribes/kiowa/kiowahist.htm (accessed on July 4, 2011).

"Kiowa Indian Tribe." *Kansas Genealogy*. http://www.kansasgenealogy.com/indians/kiowa_indian_tribe.htm(accessed on July 4, 2011).

Kiowa Tribe.http://www.kiowatribe.org/(accessed on July 4, 2011).

Kitt Peak National Observatory. "Tohono O'odham." *Association of Universities for Research in Astronomy*. http://www.noao.edu/outreach/kptour/kpno_tohono.html (accessed on July 20, 2011).

"Kwakiutl." *Four Directions Institute*. http://www.fourdir.com/kwakiutl.htm (accessed on November 2, 2011).

Kwakiutl Indian Band. http://www.kwakiutl.bc.ca/ (accessed on November 2, 2011).

"Lakota, Dakota, Nakota—The Great Sioux Nation." *Legends of America*. http://www.legendsofamerica.com/na-sioux.html (accessed on July 4, 2011).

"Lakota Page: The Great Sioux Nation." *Ancestry.com*. http://freepages.genealogy.rootsweb.ancestry.com/~nativeamericangen/page6.html (accessed on July 4, 2011).

"Lakota-Teton Sioux." *Wisdom of the Elders*. http://www.wisdomoftheelders.org/program203.html (accessed on July 4, 2011).

Larry, Mitchell. *The Native Blog*. http://nativeblog.typepad.com/the_potawatomitracks_blog/potawatomi_news/index.html (accessed on June 5, 2011).

"Leschi: Last Chief of the Nisquallies." *WashingtonHistoryOnline.* http://washingtonhistoryonline.org/leschi/leschi.htm (accessed on August 15, 2011).

"Lewis & Clark: Chinook Indians." *National Geographic.* http://www.nationalgeographic.com/lewisandclark/record_tribes_083_14_3.html (accessed on November 2, 2011).

"Lewis and Clark: Crow Indians (Absaroka)." *National Geographic Society.* http://www.nationalgeographic.com/lewisandclark/record_tribes_002_19_21.html (accessed on July 5, 2011).

"Lewis and Clark: Native Americans: Chinook Indians." *PBS.* http://www.pbs.org/lewisandclark/native/chi.html (accessed on November 2, 2011).

"Lewis & Clark: Tribes: Siletz Indians." *National Geographic.* http://www.nationalgeographic.com/lewisandclark/record_tribes_090_14_8.html (accessed on November 2, 2011).

"Lewis & Clark: Yankton Sioux Indians (Nakota)." *National Geographic.* http://www.nationalgeographic.com/lewisandclark/record_tribes_019_2_8.html (accessed on June 12, 2011).

Lewis, J.D. "The Natchez Indians." *Carolina—The Native Americans.* http://www.carolana.com/Carolina/Native_Americans/native_americans_natchez.html (accessed on June 27, 2011).

Lipscomb, Carol A. "Handbook of Texas Online: Comanche Indians." *Texas State Historical Association.* http://www.tshaonline.org/handbook/online/articles/bmc72 (accessed on July 4, 2011).

"The Long Walk." *Council of Indian Nations.* http://www.nrcprograms.org/site/PageServer?pagename=cin_hist_thelongwalk (accessed on July 20, 2011).

"Luiseño." *Four Directions Institute.* http://www.fourdir.com/luiseno.htm (accessed on August 11, 2011).

"Luiseno/Cahuilla Group." *San Francisco State University.* http://bss.sfsu.edu/calstudies/nativewebpages/luiseno.html (accessed on August 11, 2011).

"Lumbee History & Culture." *Lumbee Tribe of North Carolina.* http://www.lumbeetribe.com/History_Culture/History_Culture%20Index.html (accessed on June 4, 2011).

"Métis: History & Culture." *Turtle Island Productions.* http://www.turtle-island.com/native/the-ojibway-story/metis.html (accessed on June 4, 2011).

Métis Nation of Ontario. http://www.metisnation.org/ (accessed on June 4, 2011).

MacDonald, George F. "The Haida: Children of Eagle and Raven." *Canadian Museum of Civilization.* http://www.civilization.ca/cmc/exhibitions/aborig/haida/haindexe.shtml (accessed on November 2, 2011).

"Maidu." *Four Directions Institute.* http://www.fourdir.com/maidu.htm (accessed on August 11, 2011).

"The Maidu." *The First Americans.* http://thefirstamericans.homestead.com/Maidu.html (accessed on August 11, 2011).

"Maidu People." *City of Roseville.* http://www.roseville.ca.us/parks/parks_n_facilities/facilities/maidu_indian_museum/maidu_people.asp (accessed on August 11, 2011).

Makah Cultural and Research Center. http://www.makah.com/mcrchome.html (accessed on November 2, 2011).

The Makah Nation on Washington's Olympic Peninsula. http://www.northolympic.com/makah/ (accessed on November 2, 2011).

Manning, June. "Wampanoag Living." *Martha's Vineyard Magazine.* May–June 2010. http://www.mvmagazine.com/article.php?25216 (accessed on June 9, 2011).

Mashantucket Museum and Research Center. http://www.pequotmuseum.org/ (accessed on June 1, 2011).

Mashpee Wampanoag Tribe. http://mashpeewampanoagtribe.com/ (accessed on June 1, 2011).

"Massacre at Wounded Knee, 1890." *EyeWitness to History.* http://www.eyewitnesstohistory.com/knee.htm (accessed on July 4, 2011).

"Massai, Chiricahua Apache." *Discover Southeast Arizona.* http://www.discoverseaz.com/History/Massai.html (accessed on July 20, 2011).

May, John D. "Otoe-Missouria." *Oklahoma Historical Society.* http://digital.library.okstate.edu/encyclopedia/entries/O/OT001.html (accessed on June 20, 2011).

McCollum, Timothy James. "Quapaw." *Oklahoma Historical Society.* http://digital.library.okstate.edu/encyclopedia/entries/Q/QU003.html (accessed on June 20, 2011).

———. "Sac and Fox." *Oklahoma Historical Society.* http://digital.library.okstate.edu/encyclopedia/entries/S/SA001.html (accessed on June 5, 2011).

McCoy, Ron. "Neosho Valley: Osage Nation." *KTWU/Channel 11.* http://ktwu.washburn.edu/journeys/scripts/1111a.html (accessed on June 12, 2011).

McManamon, F. P. "Kennewick Man." *Archaeology Program, National Park Service, U.S. Department of the Interior.* http://www.nps.gov/archeology/kennewick/index.htm (accessed on August 11, 2011).

Media Action. "Excerpt from Youth-led Interview with Phillip Esai." *Vimeo.* http://vimeo.com/15465119 (accessed on June 6, 2011).

———. "A Portrait of Nikolai." *Vimeo.* 2010. http://vimeo.com/14854233 (accessed on June 6, 2011).

"Menominee Culture." *Menominee Indian Tribe of Wisconsin.* http://www.mpm.edu/wirp/ICW-54.html (accessed on June 7, 2011).

"Menominee Indian Tribe of Wisconsin." *Great Lakes Inter-Tribal Council.* http://www.glitc.org/programs/pages/mtw.html (accessed on June 7, 2011).

Menominee Indian Tribe of Wisconsin. http://www.menominee-nsn.gov/ (accessed June 8, 2011).

"Menominee Oral Tradition." *Indian Country.* http://www.mpm.edu/wirp/ICW-138.html (accessed on June 7, 2011).

Mescalero Apache Reservation. www.mescaleroapache.com/ (accessed on July 15, 2011).

"Metis Communities." *Labrador Métis Nation.* http://www.labradormetis.ca/home/10 (accessed on June 4, 2011).

"Miami Indian Tribe." *Native American Nations.* http://www.nanations.com/miami/index.htm (accessed on June 7, 2011).

"Miami Indians." *Ohio History Central.* http://www.ohiohistorycentral.org/entry.php?rec=606 (accessed on June 7, 2011).

Miami Nation of Oklahoma. http://www.miamination.com/ (accessed on June 7, 2011).

Miccosukee Seminole Nation. http://www.miccosukeeseminolenation.com/ (accessed on June 12, 2011).

"Mi'kmaq Resources" *Halifax Public Libraries.* http://www.halifaxpublicli-braries.ca/research/topics/mikmaqresources.html (accessed on June 1, 2011).

Mississippi Valley Archaeology Center at the University of Wisconsin–La Crosse, "Early Cultures: Pre-European Peoples of Wisconsin: Mississippian and Oneota Traditions." *Educational Web Adventures.* http://www.uwlax.edu/mvac/preeuropeanpeople/earlycultures/mississippi_tradition.html (accessed on June 20, 2011).

"Missouri Indian Tribe History." *Access Genealogy.* http://www.accessgenealogy.com/native/tribes/siouan/missourihist.htm (accessed on June 20, 2011).

"Missouri Indians." *PBS.* http://www.pbs.org/lewisandclark/native/mis.html (accessed on June 20, 2011).

"Miwok." *Four Directions Institute.* http://www.fourdir.com/miwok.htm (accessed on August 11, 2011).

Miwok Archeological Preserve of Marin. "The Miwok People." *California State Parks.* http://www.parks.ca.gov/default.asp?page_id=22538 (accessed on August 11, 2011).

"Miwok Indian Tribe History." *Access Genealogy.* http://www.accessgeneal-ogy.com/native/california/miwokindianhist.htm (accessed on August 11, 2011).

"Modoc." *College of the Siskiyous.* http://www.siskiyous.edu/shasta/nat/mod.htm (accessed on August 11, 2011).

"Modoc." *Four Directions Institute.* http://www.fourdir.com/modoc.htm (accessed on August 11, 2011).

"Modoc Indian Chiefs and Leaders." *Access Genealogy.* (accessed on August 11, 2011). http://www.accessgenealogy.com/native/tribes/modoc/modocindianchiefs.htm

Modoc Tribe of Oklahoma. http://www.modoctribe.net/ (accessed on August 11, 2011).

"Mohave Indian Tribe History." *Access Genealogy.* http://www.accessgenealogy.com/native/tribes/mohave/mohaveindianhist.htm (accessed on July 20, 2011).

"Mohave National Preserve: Mohave Tribe: Culture." *National Park Service.* http://www.nps.gov/moja/historyculture/mojave-culture.htm (accessed on July 20, 2011).

"The Mohawk Tribe." *Mohawk Nation.* http://www.mohawktribe.com/ (accessed on June 7, 2011).

Montana Arts Council. "From the Heart and Hand: Salish Songs and Dances: Johnny Arlee, Arlee/John T., Big Crane, Pablo."*Montana Official State Website.* http://art.mt.gov/folklife/hearthand/songs.asp (accessed on August 11, 2011).

Morris, Allen. "Seminole History." *Florida Division of Historical Resources.* http://www.flheritage.com/facts/history/seminole/ (accessed on June 12, 2011).

Muscogee (Creek) Nation of Oklahoma. http://www.muscogeenation-nsn.gov/ (accessed on June 12, 2011).

Museum of the Aleutians.. http://www.aleutians.org/index.html (accessed on August 15, 2011).

Mussulman, Joseph. "Osage Indians." *The Lewis and Clark Fort Mandan Foundation.* http://lewis-clark.org/content/content-article.asp?ArticleID=2535 (accessed on June 12, 2011).

Muwekma Ohlone Tribe. http://www.muwekma.org/ (accessed on August 11, 2011).

The Myaamia Project at Miami University. http://www.myaamiaproject.com/ (accessed on June 7, 2011).

Myers, Tom. "Navajo Reservation" (video). *University of Illinois.* http://www.vimeo.com/8828354 (accessed on July 20, 2011).

Nametau Innu. "Your First Steps in the Innu Culture." *Musée Régional de la Côte-Nord.* http://www.nametauinnu.ca/en/tour (accessed on May 26, 2011).

Narragansett Indian Tribe. http://www.narragansett-tribe.org/ (accessed on June 1, 2011).

"Natchez Indian Tribe History." *Access Geneology.* http://www.accessgenealogy.com/native/tribes/natchez/natchezhist.htm (accessed on June 27, 2011).

Natchez Nation. http://www.natchez-nation.com/ (accessed on June 27, 2011).

"Natchez Stories." *Sacred Texts.* http://www.sacred-texts.com/nam/se/mtsi/#section_004 (accessed on June 27, 2011).

National Library for the Environment. "Native Americans and the Environment: Great Basin." *National Council for Science and the Environment.* http://www.cnie.org/nae/basin.html (accessed on August 15, 2011).

National Museum of American History—Smithsonian Institution. "Pueblo Resistance: We Are Here." *Mexico State Record Center and Archives.* http://www.newmexicohistory.org/filedetails.php?fileID=23042 (accessed on July 20, 2011).

National Museum of the American Indian. "Central Plains." *Smithsonian.* http://americanindian.si.edu/searchcollections/results.aspx?regid=58 (accessed on July 4, 2011).

———. "Prairie." *Smithsonian.* http://americanindian.si.edu/searchcollections/results.aspx?regid=60 (accessed on June 12, 2011).

———. "Southern Plains." *Smithsonian.* http://americanindian.si.edu/searchcollections/results.aspx?regid=61 (accessed on June 20, 2011).

"Native Americans: Osage Tribe." *University of Missouri.* http://ethemes.missouri.edu/themes/1608?locale=en (accessed on June 12, 2011).

"Navajo (Diné)." *Northern Arizona University.* http://www.cpluhna.nau.edu/People/navajo.htm (accessed on July 20, 2011).

Navajo Indian Tribes History. *Access Genealogy.* http://www.accessgenealogy.com/native/tribes/navajo/navahoindianhist.htm (accessed on July 20, 2011).

The Navajo Nation. http://www.navajo-nsn.gov/history.htm (accessed on July 31, 2007).

"Nde Nation." *Chiricahua: Apache Nation.* http://www.chiricahuaapache.org/ (accessed on July 20, 2011).

"New Hampshire's Native American Heritage." *New Hampshire State Council on the Arts.* http://www.nh.gov/folklife/learning/traditions_native_americans.htm (accessed on June 5, 2011).

"Nez Percé." *Countries and Their Culture.* http://www.everyculture.com/multi/Le-Pa/Nez-Perc.html (accessed on August 11, 2011).

"Nez Percé (Nimiipuu) Tribe." *Wisdom of the Elders.* http://www.wisdomoftheelders.org/program303.html (accessed on August 11, 2011).

"Nez Percé National Historical Park." *National Park Service.* http://www.nps.gov/nepe/ (accessed on August 11, 2011).

Nez Percé Tribe. http://www.nezperce.org/ (accessed on August 11, 2011).

"Nisqually Indian Tribe, Washington." *United States History.* http://www.u-s-history.com/pages/h1561.html (accessed on August 15, 2011).

Nisqually Land Trust. http://www.nisquallylandtrust.org (accessed on August 15, 2011).

"NOAA Arctic Theme Page." *National Oceanic and Atmospheric Administration.* http://www.arctic.noaa.gov/ (accessed on August 15, 2011).

"Nohwike Bagowa: House of Our Footprints" *White Mountain Apache Tribe Culture Center and Museum.* http://www.wmat.us/wmaculture.shtml (accessed on July 20, 2011).

"Nootka Indian Music of the Pacific North West Coast." *Smithsonian Folkways.* http://www.folkways.si.edu/albumdetails.aspx?itemid=912 (accessed on August 15, 2011).

Northern Arapaho Tribe. http://www.northernarapaho.com/ (accessed on July 2, 2011).

Northern Cheyenne Nation. www.cheyennenation.com/ (accessed on July 4, 2011).

"Northwest Coastal People." *Canada's First Peoples.* http://firstpeoplesofcanada.com/fp_groups/fp_nwc5.html (accessed on August 15, 2011).

"Nuu-chah-nulth." *Royal British Columbia Museum.* http://www.royalbcmuseum.bc.ca/Content_Files/Files/SchoolsAndKids/nuu2.pdf (accessed on August 15, 2011).

"Nuu-chah-nulth (Barkley) Community Portal." *FirstVoices.* http://www.firstvoices.ca/en/Nuu-chah-nulth (accessed on August 15, 2011).

Nuu-chah-nulth Tribal Council. http://www.nuuchahnulth.org/tribal-council/welcome.html(accessed on August 15, 2011).

"Official Site of the Miami Nation of Indians of the State of Indiana." *Miami Nation of Indians.* http://www.miamiindians.org/ (accessed on June 7, 2011).

Official Site of the Wichita and Affiliated Tribes. http://www.wichitatribe.com/ (accessed on June 9, 2011).

Official Website of the Caddo Nation. http://www.caddonation-nsn.gov/ (accessed on June 12, 2011).

Ohio History Central. "Adena Mound." *Ohio Historical Society.* http://www.ohiohistorycentral.org/entry.php?rec=2411 (accessed June 7, 2011).

"Ohkay Owingeh." *Indian Pueblo Cultural Center.* http://www.indianpueblo.org/19pueblos/ohkayowingeh.html (accessed on July 20, 2011).

*Ohlone/Costanoan Esselen Nation.*http://www.ohlonecostanoanesselennation.org/(accessed on August 11, 2011).

Oklahoma Humanities Council. "Otoe-Missouria Tribe." *Cherokee Strip Museum.* http://www.cherokee-strip-museum.org/Otoe/OM_Who.htm (accessed on June 20, 2011).

Oklahoma Indian Affairs Commission. "2011 Oklahoma Indian Nations." *Pocket Pictorial Directory.* Oklahoma City: Oklahoma Indian Affairs Commission, 2011. Available from http://www.ok.gov/oiac/documents/2011.FINAL.WEB.pdf (accessed on June 12, 2011).

The Oregon History Project. "Modoc." *Oregon Historical Society.* http://www.ohs.org/education/oregonhistory/search/dspResults.cfm?keyword=Modoc&type=&theme=&timePeriod=&region= (accessed on August 11, 2011).

"The Osage." *Fort Scott National Historic Site, National Park Service.*http:// www.nps.gov/fosc/historyculture/osage.htm (accessed on June 12, 2011).

Osage Nation. http://www.osagetribe.com/ (accessed on June 12, 2011).

"Osage Indian Tribe History." *Access Genealogy.* http://www.accessgenealogy. com/native/tribes/osage/osagehist.htm (accessed on June 12, 2011).

The Otoe-Missouria Tribe. http://www.omtribe.org/ (accessed on June 20, 2011).

Ottawa Inuit Children's Centre. http://www.ottawainuitchildrens.com/eng/ (accessed on August 15, 2011).

Ottawa Tribe of Oklahoma. http://www.ottawatribe.org/history.htm (accessed May 13, 2011).

"Our History." *Makah Cultural and Research Center.* http://www.makah.com/ history.html (accessed on November 2, 2011).

"Pacific Northwest Native Americans." *Social Studies School Service.* http:// nativeamericans.mrdonn.org/northwest.html (accessed on August 15, 2011).

Paiute Indian Tribe of Utah. http://www.utahpaiutes.org/ (accessed on August 15, 2011).

The Pascua Yaqui Tribe. http://www.pascuayaqui-nsn.gov/ (accessed on July 20, 2011).

"The Pasqu Yaqui Connection." *Through Our Parents' Eyes: History and Culture of Southern Arizona.* http://parentseyes.arizona.edu/pascuayaquiaz/ (accessed on July 20, 2011).

"Past and Future Meet in San Juan Pueblo Solar Project." *Solar Cookers International.* http://solarcooking.org/sanjuan1.htm (accessed on July 20, 2011).

Pastore, Ralph T. "Aboriginal Peoples: Newfoundland and Labrador Heritage." *Memorial University of Newfoundland.* http://www.heritage.nf.ca/aboriginal/ (accessed on August 15, 2011).

Paul, Daniel N. "We Were Not the Savages."*First Nation History.* http://www. danielnpaul.com/index.html (accessed on June 1, 2011).

"Pawnee." *Four Directions Institute.* http://www.fourdir.com/pawnee.htm (accessed on July 6, 2011).

"Pawnee Indian Museum." *Kansas State Historical Society.* http://www.kshs.org/ places/pawneeindian/history.htm (accessed on July 6, 2011).

"Pawnee Indian Tribe History." *Access Genealogy.* http://www.accessgenealogy. com/native/tribes/pawnee/pawneehist.htm (accessed on July 6, 2011).

Pawnee Nation of Oklahoma. http://www.pawneenation.org/ (accessed on July 6, 2011).

"Pecos Indian Tribe History." *Access Genealogy.* http://www.accessgenealogy. com/native/tribes/pecos/pecoshist.htm(accessed on July 20, 2011).

"Pecos National Historical Park." *Desert USA.* http://www.desertusa.com/ pecos/pnpark.html (accessed on July 20, 2011).

"Pecos Pueblos." *Four Directions Institute.* http://www.fourdir.com/pecos.htm (accessed on July 20, 2011).

"People of Pecos." *National Park Service.* http://www.nps.gov/peco/historyculture/peple-of-pecos.htm (accessed on July 20, 2011).

"People of the Colorado Plateau: The Hopi." *Northern Arizona University.* http://www.cpluhna.nau.edu/People/hopi.htm (accessed on July 20, 2011).

"People of the Colorado Plateau: The Ute Indian." *Northern Arizona University.* http://cpluhna.nau.edu/People/ute_indians.htm(accessed on August 15, 2011).

"The People of the Flathead Nation."*Lake County Directory.* http://www.lakecodirect.com/archives/The_Flathead_Nation.html (accessed on August 11, 2011).

"Peoples of Alaska and Northeast Siberia." *Alaska Native Collections.* http://alaska.si.edu/cultures.asp (accessed on August 15, 2011).

"Pequot Lives: Almost Vanished." *Pequot Museum and Research Center.* http://www.pequotmuseum.org/Home/MashantucketGallery/AlmostVanished.htm (accessed June 8, 2011).

Peterson, Keith C. "Dams of the Columbia Basin and Their Effects of the Native Fishery." *Center for Columbia River History.* http://www.ccrh.org/comm/river/dams7.htm (accessed on August 11, 2011).

Peterson, Leighton C. "Tuning in to Navajo: The Role of Radio in Native Language Maintenance." *Northern Arizona University.* http://jan.ucc.nau.edu/-jar/TIL_17.html (accessed on July 20, 2011).

"Pima (AkimelO'odham)." *Four Directions Institute.* http://www.fourdir.com/pima.htm (accessed on July 20, 2011).

"Pima Indian Tribe History." *Access Genealogy.* www.accessgenealogy.com/native/tribes/pima/pimaindianhist.htm (accessed on July 20, 2011).

Pit River Indian Tribe. http://www.pitrivertribe.org/home.php (accessed on August 11, 2011).

"Pomo People: Brief History." *Native American Art.* http://www.kstrom.net/isk/art/basket/pomohist.html (accessed on August 11, 2011).

Porter, Tom. "Mohawk (Haudenosaunee) Teaching." *FourDirectionsTeachings.com.* http://www.fourdirectionsteachings.com/transcripts/mohawk.html (accessed June 7, 2011).

"Powhatan Indian Village." *Acton Public Schools: Acton-Boxborough Regional School District.* http://ab.mec.edu/jamestown/powhatan (accessed on June 1, 2011).

"Powhatan Language and the Powhatan Indian Tribe (Powatan, Powhatten, Powhattan)." *Native Languages of the Americas: Preserving and Promoting Indigenous American Indian Languages.* http://www.native-languages.org/powhatan.htm (accessed on on June 1, 2011).

"Preserving Sacred Wisdom." *Native Spirit and the Sun Dance Way.* http://www.nativespiritinfo.com/ (accessed on July 5, 2011).

"Pueblo Indian History and Resources." *Pueblo Indian.* http://www.puebloindian.com/ (accessed on July 20, 2011).

Pueblo of Acoma. http://www.puebloofacoma.org/ (accessed on July 20, 2011).

Pueblo of Jemez. http://www.jemezpueblo.org/ (accessed on July 20, 2011).

Pueblo of Zuñi. http://www.ashiwi.org/(accessed on July 20, 2011).

Puyallup Tribe of Indians. http://www.puyallup-tribe.com/ (accessed on November 2, 2011).

Quapaw Tribe of Oklahoma. http://www.quapawtribe.com/ (accessed on June 20, 2011).

"The Quapaw Tribe of Oklahoma and the Tar Creek Project." *Environmental Protection Agency.* http://www.epa.gov/oar/tribal/tribetotribe/tarcreek.html (accessed on June 20, 2011).

"Questions and Answers about the Plateau Indians." *Wellpinit School District 49 (WA).* http://www.wellpinit.wednet.edu/sal-qa/qa.php (accessed on August 11, 2011).

"Questions and Answers about the Spokane Indians." *Wellpinit School District.* http://wellpinit.org/q%2526a (accessed on August 11, 2011).

Redish, Laura, and Orrin Lewis. *Native Languages of the Americas.* http://www.native-languages.org (accessed on August 11, 2011).

"Research Starters: Anasazi and Pueblo Indians." *Scholastic.com.* http://teacher.scholastic.com/researchtools/researchstarters/native_am/ (accessed on July 20, 2011).

"The Rez We Live On"(videos). *The Confederated Salish and Kootenai Tribes.* http://therezweliveon.com/13/video.html (accessed on August 11, 2011).

The Rooms, Provincial Museum Division. "Innu Objects."*Virtual Museum Canada.* 2008. http://www.museevirtuel-virtualmuseum.ca/edu/ViewLoit Collection.do;jsessionid=3083D5EEB47F3ECDE9DA040AD0D4C956? method=preview⟨=EN&id=3210 (accessed on May 24, 2011).

Sac and Fox Nation. http://www.sacandfoxnation-nsn.gov/ (accessed on June 5, 2011).

"Sac and Fox Tribe." *Meskwaki Nation.* http://www.meskwaki.org/ (accessed on June 5, 2011).

San Carlos Apache Cultural Center. http://www.sancarlosapache.com/home.htm (accessed on July 20, 2011).

"San Carlos Apache Sunrise Dance." *World News Network.* http://wn.com/San_Carlos_Apache_Sunrise_Dance (accessed on July 20, 2011).

"San Juan Pueblo." *New Mexico Magazine.* http://www.nmmagazine.com/native_american/san_juan.php (accessed on July 20, 2011).

"San Juan Pueblo O'Kang." *Indian Pueblo Cultural Center.* http://www.indianpueblo. org/19pueblos/ohkayowingeh.html (accessed on July 20, 2011).

"The Sand Creek Massacre." *Last of the Independents.* http://www.lastoftheinde- pendents.com/sandcreek.htm (accessed on July 2, 2011).

"Seminole Indian Tribe History." *Access Genealogy.* http://www.accessgenealogy. com/native/tribes/seminole/seminolehist.htm (accessed on June 12, 2011).

Seminole Nation of Oklahoma. http://www.seminolenation.com/ (accessed on June 12, 2011).

Seminole Tribe of Florida. http://www.seminoletribe.com/ (accessed on June 12, 2011).

"Sharp Nose." *Native American Nations.* http://www.nanations.com/arrap/ page4.htm (accessed on July 2, 2011).

"The Shawnee in History." *The Shawnee Tribe.* http://www.shawnee-tribe.com/ history.htm (accessed on June 12, 2011).

"Shawnee Indian Tribe History." *Access Genealogy.* http://www.accessgenealogy. com/native/tennessee/shawneeindianhist.htm (accessed on June 12, 2011).

"Shawnee Indians." *Ohio Historical Society.* http://www.ohiohistorycentral.org/ entry.php?rec=631&nm=Shawnee-Indians (accessed on June 12, 2011).

Shawnee Nation, United Remnant Band. http://www.zaneshawneecaverns.net/ shawnee.shtml (accessed on June 12, 2011).

"A Short History of the Spokane Indians." *Wellpinit School District.* http://www.wellpinit.wednet.edu/shorthistory (accessed on August 11, 2011).

"Short Overview of California Indian History." *California Native American Heritage Commission.* http://www.nahc.ca.gov/califindian.html (accessed on August 15, 2011).

Sicade, Henry. "Education." *Puyallup Tribe of Indians.* http://www.puyallup-tribe. com/history/education/ (accessed on November 2, 2011).

"Simon Ortiz: Native American Poet." *The University of Texas at Arlington.* http://www.uta.edu/english/tim/poetry/so/ortizmain.htm (accessed on July 20, 2011).

Simpson, Linda. "The Kansas/Kanza/Kaw Nation." *Oklahoma Territory.* http:// www.okgenweb.org/-itkaw/Kanza2.html (accessed on June 17, 2011).

The Skokomish Tribal Nation. http://www.skokomish.org/ (accessed on Novem- ber 2, 2011).

Skopec, Eric. "What Mystery?" *Anasazi Adventure.* http://www.anasaziadventure. com/what_mystery.pdf (accessed on July 20, 2011).

Smithsonian Folkways. "Rain Dance (Zuñi)." *Smithsonian Institution.* http:// www.folkways.si.edu/TrackDetails.aspx?itemid=16680 (music track) and http://media.smithsonianfolkways.org/liner_notes/folkways/FW06510.pdf (instructions for dance). (accessed on July 20, 2011).

Snook, Debbie. "Ohio's Trail of Tears." *Wyandotte Nation of Oklahoma*, 2003. http://www.wyandotte-nation.org/culture/history/published/trail-of-tears/ (accessed May 11, 2011).

The Southern Arapaho. http://southernarapaho.org/ (accessed on July 2, 2011).

Southern Ute Indian Tribe. http://www.southern-ute.nsn.us/ (accessed on August 15, 2011).

Splawn, A. J. *Ka-mi-akin, the Last Hero of the Yakimas.* Portland, OR: Kilham Stationary and Printing, 1917. Reproduced by Washington Secretary of State. http://www.secstate.wa.gov/history/publications_detail.aspx?p=24 (accessed on August 11, 2011).

"Spokane Indian Tribe." *Access Genealogy.* http://www.accessgenealogy.com/ native/tribes/salish/spokanhist.htm (accessed on August 11, 2011).

"Spokane Indian Tribe." *United States History.* http://www.u-s-history.com/ pages/h1570.html (accessed on August 11, 2011).

Spokane Tribe of Indians. http://www.spokanetribe.com/ (accessed on August 11, 2011).

Sreenivasan, Hari. "'Apache 8' Follows All-Women Firefighters On and Off the Reservation." *PBS NewsHour.* http://video.pbs.org/video/2006599346/ (accessed on July 20, 2011).

Stands In Timber, John. "Cheyenne Memories." *Northern Cheyenne Nation.* http://www.cheyennenation.com/memories.html (accessed on July 4, 2011).

Stewart, Kenneth. "Kivas." *Scholastic.* http://www2.scholastic.com/browse/ article.jsp?id=5052 (accessed on July 20, 2011).

"The Story of the Ute Tribe: Past, Present, and Future." *Ute Mountain Ute Tribe.* http://www.utemountainute.com/story.htm (accessed on August 15, 2011).

Sultzman, Lee. *First Nations.* http://www.tolatsga.org/sf.html (accessed on June 5, 2011).

Swan, Daniel C. "Native American Church." *Oklahoma Historical Society.* http://digital.library.okstate.edu/encyclopedia/entries/N/NA015.html (accessed on August 11, 2011).

"Taos Pueblo." *Bluffton University.* http://www.bluffton.edu/~sullivanm/taos/ taos.html (accessed on July 20, 2011).

"Taos Pueblo." *New Mexico Magazine.* http://www.nmmagazine.com/native_ american/taos.php (accessed on July 20, 2011).

Taos Pueblo. http://www.taospueblo.com/ (accessed on July 20, 2011).

"Taos Pueblo: A Thousand Years of Tradition." *Taos Pueblo.* http://taospueblo. com/ (accessed on July 20, 2011).

"Territorial Kansas: Kansa Indians." *University of Kansas.* http://www. territorialkansasonline.org/~imlskto/cgi-bin/index.php?SCREEN=

keyword&selected_keyword=Kansa%20Indians (accessed on June 17, 2011).

"Throat Singing." *Inuit Cultural Online Resource.* http://icor.ottawainuitchildrens.com/node/30 (accessed on August 15, 2011).

"Tlingit Tribes, Clans, and Clan Houses: Traditional Tlingit Country." *Alaska Native Knowledge Network.* http://www.ankn.uaf.edu/ANCR/Southeast/TlingitMap/ (accessed on November 2, 2011).

"Tohono O'odham (Papago)." *Four Directions Institute.* http://www.fourdir.com/tohono_o'odham.htm (accessed on July 20, 2011).

"Totem Pole Websites." *Cathedral Grove.* http://www.cathedralgrove.eu/text/07-Totem-Websites-3.htm (accessed on November 2, 2011).

"Trading Posts in the American Southwest." *Southwest Crossroads.* http://southwestcrossroads.org/record.php?num=742&hl=chiricahua:: apache (accessed on July 20, 2011).

"Traditional Mi'kmaq Beliefs." *Indian Brook First Nation.* http://home.rushcomm.ca/-hsack/spirit.html (accessed on June1,2011).

"Tsmshian Songs We Love to Sing!" *Dum Baaldum.* http://www.dumbaaldum.org/html/songs.htm (accessed on August 15, 2011).

"Umatilla Indian Agency and Reservation, Oregon." *Access Genealogy.* http://www.accessgenealogy.com/native/census/condition/umatilla_indian_agency_reservation_oregon.htm (accessed on August 11, 2011).

"Umatilla, Walla Walla, and Cayuse." *TrailTribes.org: Traditional and Contemporary Native Culture.* http://www.trailtribes.org/umatilla/home.htm (accessed on August 11, 2011).

"Unangax & Alutiiq (Sugpiaq)." *Alaska Native Heritage Center.* http://www.alaskanative.net/en/main_nav/education/culture_alaska/unangax/ (accessed on August 15, 2011).

Unrau, William E. "Kaw (Kansa)." *Oklahoma Historical Society.* http://digital.library.okstate.edu/encyclopedia/entries/K/KA001.html (accessed on June 17, 2011).

Urban Indian Experience. "The Duwamish: Seattle's Landless Tribe." *KUOW: PRX.* http://www.prx.org/pieces/1145-urban-indian-experience-episode-1-the-duwamish(accessed on November 2, 2011).

The Ute Indian Tribe. http://www.utetribe.com/ (accessed on August 15, 2011).

"Ute Nation." *Utah Travel Industry.* http://www.utah.com/tribes/ute_main.htm (accessed on August 15, 2011).

Virtual Archaeologist. "The Like-a-Fishhook Story." *NDSU Archaeology Technologies Laboratory.* http://fishhook.ndsu.edu/home/lfstory.php (accessed on June 19, 2011).

"A Virtual Tour of California Missions." *Mission Tour.* http://missiontour.org/index.htm (accessed on August 11, 2011).

"Visiting a Maidu Bark House." *You Tube.* http://www.youtube.com/watch?v=fw5i83519mQ (accessed on August 11, 2011).

"The Wampanoag." *Boston Children's Museum.* http://www.bostonkids.org/educators/wampanoag/html/what.htm (accessed on June 1, 2011).

"Washoe." *Four Directions Institute.* http://www.fourdir.com/washoe.htm (accessed on August 15, 2011).

"Washoe Hot Springs." *National Cultural Preservation Council.* http://www.ncpc.info/projects_washoe.html (accessed on August 15, 2011).

"Washoe Indian Tribe History." *Access Genealogy.* http://www.accessgenealogy.com/native/tribes/washo/washohist.htm (accessed on August 15, 2011).

"We Shall Remain." *PBS.* http://www.pbs.org/wgbh/amex/weshallremain/ (accessed on July 20, 2011).

Weiser, Kathy. *Legends of America.* http://www.legendsofamerica.com (accessed on July 20, 2011).

"White Mountain Apache Indian Reservation." *Arizona Handbook.* http://www.arizonahandbook.com/white_mtn_apache.htm (accessed on July 20, 2011).

"White Mountain Apache Tribe." *InterTribal Council of Arizona.* http://www.itcaonline.com/tribes_whitemtn.html (accessed on July 20, 2011).

"White Mountain Apache Tribe: Restoring Wolves, Owls, Trout and Ecosystems" *Cooperative Conservation America.* http://www.cooperativeconservation.org/viewproject.asp?pid=136 (accessed on July 20, 2011).

"Who Were the Lipan and the Kiowa-Apaches?" *Southwest Crossroads.* http://southwestcrossroads.org/record.php?num=522&hl=chiricahua:: apache (accessed on July 20, 2011).

"Wichita." *Four Directions Institute.* http://www.fourdir.com/wichita.htm (accessed on June 9, 2011).

Wind River Indian Reservation. http://www.wind-river.org/info/communities/reservation.php (accessed on July 2, 2011).

Wind River Indian Reservation: Eastern Shoshone Tribe. http://www.easternshoshone.net/ (accessed on August 15, 2011).

WMAT: White Mountain Apache Tribe. http://wmat.us/ (accessed on July 20, 2011).

"Wounded Knee." *Last of the Independent.* http://www.lastoftheindependents.com/wounded.htm (accessed on July 4, 2011).

The Wounded Knee Museum. http://www.woundedkneemuseum.org/ (accessed on July 4, 2011).

Wyandot Nation of Anderdon. http://www.wyandotofanderdon.com/ (accessed May 13, 2011).

Wyandot Nation of Kansas. http://www.wyandot.org/ (accessed May 13, 2011).

Wyandotte Nation of Oklahoma. http://www.wyandotte-nation.org/ (accessed May 13, 2011).

"Yakima Indian Tribe History." *Access Genealogy.* http://www.accessgenealogy. com/native/tribes/yakimaindianhist.htm (accessed on August 11, 2011).

Yakama Nation Cultural Heritage Center. http://www.yakamamuseum.com/ (accessed on August 11, 2011).

"Yaqui." *Four Directions Institute.* http://www.fourdir.com/yaqui.htm (accessed on July 20, 2011).

"Yaqui and Mayo Indian Easter Ceremonies." *RimJournal.* http://www.rimjournal. com/arizyson/easter.htm (accessed on July 20, 2011).

"Yaqui Sacred Traditions." *Wisdom Traditions Institute.* http://www.wisdomtraditions. com/yaqui2.html (accessed on July 20, 2011).

"Yuma (Quechan)." *Four Directions Institute.* http://www.fourdir.com/yuma. htm (accessed on July 20, 2011).

Yuman Indian Tribe History." *Access Genealogy.* http://www.accessgenealogy. com/native/tribes/yuman/yumanfamilyhist.htm (accessed on July 20, 2011).

"The Yup'ik and Cup'ik People—Who We Are." *The Alaska Native Heritage Center Museum.* http://www.alaskanative.net/en/main_nav/education/ culture_alaska/yupik/ (accessed on August 15, 2011).

"Yup'ik Tundra Navigation." *Center for Cultural Design.* http://www.ccd.rpi. edu/Eglash/csdt/na/tunturyu/index.html (accessed on August 15, 2011).

"The Yurok." *California History Online.* http://www.californiahistoricalsociety. org/timeline/chapter2/002d.html# (accessed on August 11, 2011).

"Yurok." *Four Directions Institute.* http://www.fourdir.com/yurok.htm (accessed on August 11, 2011).

The Yurok Tribe. http://www.yuroktribe.org/ (accessed on August 11, 2011).

Zeig, Sande. *Apache 8* (film). http://www.apache8.com/ (accessed on July 20, 2011).

"Zuñi." *Northern Arizona University.* http://www.cpluhna.nau.edu/People/zuni. htm (accessed on July 20, 2011).

"Zuñi." *Southwest Crossroads.* http://southwestcrossroads.org/record. php?num=2&hl=zuni (accessed on July 20, 2011).

"Zuñi Pueblo." *New Mexico Magazine.* http://www.nmmagazine.com/native_ american/zuni.php (accessed on July 20, 2011).

"Zuñi Pueblos (Ashiwi)." *Four Directions Institute.* http://www.fourdir.com/ zuni.htm (accessed on July 20, 2011).

Index

Italics indicates volume numbers; **boldface** indicates entries and their page numbers. Chart indicates a chart; ill. indicates an illustration, and map indicates a map.

F

Fort Wayne Treaty, *1:* 132
Fort Yukon, *1:* 361
Fort Yuma, *3:* 1315, 1317
Foster-Parent Chant, *2:* 940
Four Corners, *3:* 970, 979, 980, 1069, 1130, 1157
Four Lakes, Battle of, *4:* 1659, 1695
Four Mothers, *2:* 584
Fourth of July Powwow, *4:* 1593
Fox. *See* Sac and Fox
Fox, Robert L., *2:* 688
Fox people. *See* Pequot
A Fox Tale (Sac and Fox), *1:* 303
Fox Wars (1712–16 and 1728–37),
    1: 220, 293
Franciscans in California, *4:* 1337–1340
Frank, Billy, Jr., *5:* 1921, 1939, 1940
Freedmen. *See also* African Americans; Slaves
    Cherokee, *2:* 522
    communities of, in Southeast, *2:* 474
    Seminole, *2:* 617
Frémont, John, *4:* 1533, 1575, 1621; *5:* 1806
French. *See also* Europeans
    Abenaki and, *1:* 15
    Arikara and, *2:* 671
    British and, *1:* 6, 129–130, 198–199
    Caddo and, *2:* 485–486
    ceding of Louisiana to Spain, *2:* 486
    Colville and, *4:* 1581
    Comanche and, *2:* 741
    Dakota and, *2:* 891, 893
    destruction of, *1:* 172
    exploration and settlement by, *2:* 472, 476
    Haida and, *5:* 1869
    Innu and, *1:* 427, 428, 440
    Iroquois and, *1:* 58–59
    Kansa and, *2:* 772–773
    Kiowa and, *2:* 794
    Menominee and, *1:* 113, 117
    Métis and, *1:* 452, 453, 458
    Miami and, *1:* 129–130
    Micmac and, *1:* 151–152, 158
    Missouri and, *2:* 813, 814–825
    Mound Builders and, *1:* 171
    Nakota and, *2:* 935, 937
    Natchez and, *2:* 547, 577–578, 578, 580–582

and the Northeast Nations, *1:* 56
    Ojibway and, *1:* 197–199, 200–201
    Osage and, *2:* 835–836, 844
    Ottawa and, *1:* 217, 218–219
    Potawatomi and, *1:* 261–262
    Quapaw and, *2:* 871, 872–873, 874, 875, 883, 886
    Sac and Fox and, *1:* 293
    search of Northwest Passage to China, *5:* 2057
    settlements of, *5:* 2057
    Spanish and, *2:* 486
    trade with, *1:* 129
    Wendat Confederacy and, *1:* 330
    Wichita and, *2:* 954–955, 962
French and Indian War (1754–63), *1:* 7, 18, 114
    Abenaki in, *1:* 16–18
    Cherokee in, *2:* 504
    Iroquois in, *1:* 59
    Menominee in, *1:* 114, 122
    Miami in, *1:* 129, 130
    Micmac in, *1:* 153
    Ojibway in, *1:* 197, 198
    Ottawa in, *1:* 221
    Shawnee in, *2:* 624
Frobisher, Martin, *5:* 2093, 2094
From the Deep Woods to Civilization (Eastern), *2:* 907
Fruit leather, *4:* 1647
Funerals. *See* Death, burials, funerals, and mourning
Fur Seal Act Amendments (1983), *5:* 2136
Fur trade, *1:* 5
    Abenaki and, *1:* 15, 25
    Alaskan Athabascan and, *1:* 367
    Arikara and, *2:* 671
    Assiniboin and, *1:* 384
    Chinook and, *5:* 1835
    Colville and, *4:* 1583–1584
    Cree and, *1:* 405–406
    Delaware and, *1:* 37
    explorers and, *5:* 1835
    Haida and, *5:* 1871
    Innu and, *1:* 428–429
    Lakota and, *2:* 914–915
    Makah and, *5:* 1909

Indian Recognition Act (1934), *2:* 694

Indian Removal Act (1830), *1:* 8, 60, 199, 261, 263, 334; *2:* 477–479, 506, 510, 549, 563, 621, 648

Indian Reorganization Act (1934), *1:* 202, 225, 383, 388, 390–391; *2:* 480, 676, 699, 753, 756, 857, 923, 939, 942; *3:* 1003, 1059, 1099, 1118, 1301, 1319; *4:* 1355, 1357, 1373, 1392, 1466, 1503, 1517, 1599, 1604, 1606, 1700; *5:* 1809, 1969, 2003, 2019, 2077

Indian Reorganization Act amendments (1936), *5:* 1874

Indian Shaker Church
  Chinook and, *5:* 1837
  Duwamish and, *5:* 1857
  Nisqually and, *5:* 1930
  in the Pacific Northwest, *5:* 1827–1828
  Siletz and, *5:* 1986–1987, 1991
  Skokomish and, *5:* 2002
  of the Yakama, *4:* 1699, 1706
  of the Yurok, *4:* 1556, 1565

Indian Territory, *1:* 8, 60. *See also* Indian Removal Act (1830)
  Caddo in, *2:* 487
  Chickasaw in, *2:* 528, 529–530
  Choctaw in, *2:* 549
  Creek in, *2:* 563–564
  Indian Removal Act (1830) and, *2:* 477–479
  Kiowa in, *2:* 795
  Osage and, *2:* 838
  Quapaw and, *2:* 875
  Seminole in, *2:* 602–603

The Indian Today (Eastman), *2:* 907

Indian War (1855–58), *5:* 1854

Indians of All Tribes, occupation of Alcatraz Island, *4:* 1538

The Indians of California, *4:* 1484

Indigenous Peoples Day, *4:* 1472

Individual Indian Money (IIM) accounts, *2:* 874, 888

Infant death in the San Carlos Apache, *3:* 1049

Influenza
  effect on Native people, *5:* 1822
  in the Inuit, *5:* 2095
  in the Iroquois Confederacy, *1:* 59
  in the Tlingit, *5:* 2016

Inland Hunting Consent Decree Agreement (2007), *1:* 225

Innikueuat (dolls), *1:* 443

Innu, *1:* 352, 361, **425–449**
  arts of, *1:* 443–444
  current tribal issues of, *1:* 446–447
  customs of, *1:* 444–446
  daily life of, *1:* 431 (ill.), 437–443, 438 (ill.)
  economy of, *1:* 436–437
  government of, *1:* 435–436
  history of, *1:* 427–433, 431 (ill.)
  language/language family of, *1:* 426, 435, 435 (ill.)
  location of, *1:* 355, 425, 426 (map)
  name of, *1:* 425
  notable people of, *1:* 447
  origins and group affiliations of, *1:* 426–427
  population of, *1:* 425–426
  religion of, *1:* 433–435
  resistance to resource development, *1:* 363

Innu Doughnuts (Innu recipe), *1:* 440

Intermarriage, Missouri and, *2:* 814

Internment camps in World War II, *5:* 2117, 2122–2123, 2124

Inuit, *1:* 362; *5:* 2056–2057, **2091–2114**
  arts of, *5:* 2107–2109
  Canadian government and, *5:* 2060–2061
  Central, *5:* 2092
  current tribal issues of, *5:* 2112 (ill.), 2112–2113
  customs of, *5:* 2109–2111
  daily life of, *5:* 2099 (ill.), 2100 (ill.), 2100–2107, 2102 (ill.)
  economy of, *5:* 2099–2100
  government of, *5:* 2099
  history of, *5:* 2093–2097, 2096 (ill.)
  language/language family of, *5:* 2091, 2098–2099
  location of, *5:* 2091, 2092 (map)
  name of, *5:* 2091
  notable people of, *5:* 2113
  origins and group affiliations of, *5:* 2091–2092
  population of, *5:* 2091
  relations with other groups, *1:* 150, 430–431, 436
  religion of, *5:* 2097–2098

N

O

U•X•L Encyclopedia of Native American Tribes, 3rd Edition

T

U•X•L Encyclopedia of Native American Tribes, 3rd Edition

U

X

Y